# BOURGEOIS LIBERTY AND
THE POLITICS OF FEAR

# Bourgeois Liberty and the Politics of Fear

*From Absolutism to Neo-Conservatism*

MARC MULHOLLAND

UNIVERSITY PRESS

Great Clarendon Street, Oxford, OX2 6DP,
United Kingdom

Oxford University Press is a department of the University of Oxford.
It furthers the University's objective of excellence in research, scholarship,
and education by publishing worldwide. Oxford is a registered trade mark of
Oxford University Press in the UK and in certain other countries

© Marc Mulholland 2012

The moral rights of the author have been asserted

First Edition published in 2012

Impression: 1

All rights reserved. No part of this publication may be reproduced, stored in
a retrieval system, or transmitted, in any form or by any means, without the
prior permission in writing of Oxford University Press, or as expressly permitted
by law, by licence or under terms agreed with the appropriate reprographics
rights organization. Enquiries concerning reproduction outside the scope of the
above should be sent to the Rights Department, Oxford University Press, at the
address above

You must not circulate this work in any other form
and you must impose this same condition on any acquirer

British Library Cataloguing in Publication Data

Data available

Library of Congress Cataloging in Publication Data

Data available

ISBN 978–0–19–965357–7

Printed in Great Britain by
MPG Books Group, Bodmin and King's Lynn

Links to third party websites are provided by Oxford in good faith and
for information only. Oxford disclaims any responsibility for the materials
contained in any third party website referenced in this work.

*To Victoria Lill*

# *Preface*

In 1842 a German poet living in Paris, Heinrich Heine, wrote that the politics of the bourgeoisie were 'motivated by fear'. When terrified of an unleashed working class, he argued, the middle classes abandoned their historical commitment to constitutional liberty. This was an early statement of an argument that went on to have a long, contested life. 'Bourgeois liberty' has a dual meaning: it is freedom for a particular class constituency to pursue its lifestyle and seek prosperity in a commercial environment. It is also an ideal: rights of speech, association, and petition required by the bourgeoisie but extending to all within society. But was the universal ideal of 'bourgeois liberty' undermined by the threat of 'proletarian democracy'? Bourgeois fear of the working class has been held responsible for betrayal of the pan-European revolutions of 1848, for the illiberal forms of unification in Italy and Germany, for liberal failure of nerve before Bolshevism in Russia in 1917, for the turn to interwar fascism, and for Western maintenance of military dictatorships during the Cold War. And then, as the traditional working class declined, did the middle classes recover their nerve? At stake in these debates were fundamental questions of liberty and social order, revolution, and counter-revolution. The argument at core gravitated around that most emotive of concepts: betrayal. Either the comfortable middle class betrayed workers, peasants, the poor, and liberty by siding with authoritarian repression; or ideological fanatics betrayed the people's trust and desire for civil and political liberties by instituting totalitarian collectivism. Decisions were forced by agitation, conspiracy, war, and repression. The following chapters examine this narrative.

Historical works emphasizing constitutionalism, class, and political meta-narrative are hardly fashionable these days. Defence for my approach inheres, I hope, in the account I give. It is worth saying something about terminology, however, for those who may find my usage quaint. 'Bourgeois' and 'bourgeoisie' are roughly equivalent to the historical sense of 'middle class' as used in Britain. But, of late, 'middle class' has come to designate that 25 per cent of the population on either side of median income, which has quite different connotations. In the United States, for example, 'middle class' includes most unionized workers. So although I use the terms interchangeably, I prefer 'bourgeois' as more precise. 'Proletarian' is roughly equivalent to 'worker'—but peasants, artisans, and professionals work too. By my designation, I wish to indicate a particular class condition, that of the unskilled or semi-skilled wage earner, or the worker possessed of skills so widely available on the labour market as to attract no marked salary premium from employers. In my usage, the proletarian need not work in a smoke-belching factory. Both terms, bourgeois and proletarian, have been the default common usage for much of my period across most of the countries I survey. They are therefore my default terms. I often refer to 'bourgeois liberalism' rather than simply 'liberalism' to avoid confusion that might arise from current American usage that folds the term 'liberal' into the socially egalitarian 'left'.

This is an avowedly 'constructed' history, in that it pursues a theme within an analytical narrative. Though I deal with a long period and wide geographical span, my coverage of events is selective, and chosen on the basis of relevance to the overall argument. Nor do I attempt a synthesis or critique of scholarly interpretations. Authorities are employed as 'expert witnesses' for the case I present. They would no doubt demur from much they might find herein. I have not written this book as a history of political thought, though that features, nor as an exercise in comparative or thematic political science. Still less have I written this book as an exercise in polemic or political advocacy. I have employed my particular models because I find them useful and interesting; they do not imply moral judgements one way or another. I am taking an argument and using it to make one kind of sense of a stretch of modern history. I certainly do not mean to imply that this approach is more valid than ones which, say, might take as their focus gender, nationality, or religion. The model of 'bourgeois liberty', in its various forms, has had a profound impact, both materially and intellectually, during the period under review. It is enough, I hope, to demonstrate and illustrate this.

\* \* \*

I first considered themes relevant to this book many years ago in the meeting rooms of Ballymena and Belfast. Few who were present at these gatherings, perhaps, would entirely agree with the answers here offered, but I am grateful that the questions were posed. A first presentation of my organizing argument was given to the John Simopolous dinner, for tutors and students, at my college of St Catherine's. John's generous response to this squib set me on the road to writing a full volume, which took place between full teaching terms. It would not have been the same without the stimulus of amazing students; I'm hugely grateful to them all. My thanks to Gervase Rosser, who showed me the intellectual advantage that comes with the privilege of teaching, marking, and examining. All my other college colleagues have been unfailingly supportive; Tom Pickles, J. C. Smith, Bart van Es, and Jon Healey went beyond the call of collegiality in talking through my ruminations.

Usually, I am a historian of Ireland. My colleagues in the field responded to the project here presented with generous enthusiasm. Discussions with Richard Bourke, Roy Foster, Matt Kelly, Ian McBride, Alan O'Day, and Senia Pašeta amongst others have contributed materially to the final product. Of scholars outside the field of Ireland, the knowledge and historical sense of Chris Brooke, Adrian Gregory, and Barbara Warnock have been reliable inspirations.

Michael Fisher, Ultán Gillen, and Richard Michaelis all very generously consented to read parts of the manuscript. Special mention must go to Tim Wilson who heroically read a draft of the entire book in double-quick time. Comments by all have been eminently wise, and saved me from many howlers. I should also like to record my gratitude to my editors at Oxford University Press, Christopher Wheeler and Stephanie Ireland, who adroitly guided me through the process of submission, and to Richard Mason, my copy-editor, and Nicola Sangster, my proof reader, who with speed and efficiency rescued me from many obscurities and solecisms. OUP's three anonymous readers made excellent suggestions that I have been very happy to act upon. Naturally only I am responsible for any errors of fact and judgement remaining.

Friends have proven remarkably tolerant of my moiderings on 'the book': they were always rocks of support. Particular thanks to Rachel Buxton, David Fowler, Gerald Lang, Catrin Lowe, Rónán McDonald, Julian McGale, Icarus Panchaud, Jessica Thomas, James Thompson, and Laura Warnock. As ever, my siblings—Kathleen, Ciarán, Pádraig, Deidre, Niall, Ita, Áine, and Breandan—provided unstinting familial solidarity. Eilís and Oisín Mulholland, and their mother Lois, keep me grounded with family on this island. My parents, Ita and Dominic, have been ever loving, inspirational, and wise. I owe everything to them.

My partner, Victoria Lill, has lived with this project as much as I have. Her ready interest, support, and perceptiveness consistently raised my game, and she has made a vital contribution to the finished work. Even more importantly, Victoria has been my best friend and true love for over a decade. I dedicate this book to her.

# Contents

Introduction ... 1

1. Absolutism and Transformation in England ... 13
   Capitalism and the State ... 13
   Taxation and Absolutism ... 15
   Britain and Constitutionalism ... 18
   The Agency of Constitutional Modernization ... 24
   'The People' and Law ... 27
   The Commercial-Fiscal State ... 29
   Conclusion ... 31

2. Revolution, Restoration, and Reform ... 33
   The French Revolution: Bourgeois? ... 33
   Restoration Europe ... 38
   The British Model ... 44
   The Model of the United States ... 46
   Conclusion ... 48

3. Holding Back the Tide ... 49
   Holy Alliance Europe ... 49
   International Relations ... 52
   Bourgeois Monarchy in France, Carlism in Spain ... 54
   Conclusion ... 58

4. The Turning Point ... 60
   Chartism ... 62
   Prelude to Revolution ... 65
   1848: Revolutionary High Tide ... 68
   Neo-Absolutism ... 73
   Revolution Betrayed? ... 75
   Conclusion ... 79

5. Liberalism and the State ... 80
   The Strengthened State ... 80
   British Equipoise, American Crisis ... 82
   Austria-Hungary and the Second French Empire ... 86
   Wars of Italian Unification ... 91
   Conclusion ... 95

## 6. Bismarck, Liberalism, and Socialism — 97
- The Constitutional Struggle in Prussia — 98
- German Unification — 101
- Socialists and Germany — 104
- The Paris Commune — 109
- Conclusion — 111

## 7. Capitalism and Socialism — 113
- 'Statised capitalism' — 115
- The Crisis of Liberalism — 120
- The Rise of Socialism — 123
- Taking on the State — 129
- Conclusion — 133

## 8. Democracy and State Power — 135
- Mass Suffrage and Party Politics — 135
- Socialists and Liberals — 139
- The 1905 Revolution — 144
- The Question of War — 149
- Conclusion — 152

## 9. Revolution and the 'Dictatorship of the Proletariat' — 153
- Socialists and the War — 155
- The Russian Revolution — 158
- Red Challenge — 164
- Conclusion — 172

## 10. Communism and Fascism — 173
- Revolution Derailed — 174
- Fascism in Italy — 178
- Fragile Equilibrium — 181
- Stalinism — 182
- The Impact of the Great Depression — 184
- Corporatism in Italy — 186
- The Nazi 'Revolution' — 187
- Conclusion — 192

## 11. Popular Front and War — 195
- Soviet Industrialization — 195
- A Progressive Bourgeoisie? The Popular Front — 197
- United Front in China — 203
- No Popular Front—Britain and the USA — 206
- The Second World War — 209
- Conclusion — 214

| | |
|---|---|
| 12. Cold War and the Fear of Subversion | 216 |
|     Consumerist Society | 218 |
|     Communized Eastern-Central Europe | 221 |
|     'Reds Under the Bed' | 224 |
|     The 'Third World' | 228 |
|     The Military-Industrial Complex | 234 |
|     Conclusion | 236 |
| 13. The Pivot of '68: New Left and New Right | 237 |
|     The Vietnam War | 237 |
|     Neo-Militarism | 239 |
|     The New Left | 241 |
|     The New Right | 246 |
|     Eurocommunism and Revolution | 250 |
|     The Crisis of Social Democracy | 253 |
|     Bourgeois Backlash | 254 |
|     Conclusion | 258 |
| 14. The Demise of the 'Red Menace' | 260 |
|     Workers and the Intelligentsia | 260 |
|     Communist China | 263 |
|     The Collapse of Communism | 266 |
|     The Washington Consensus | 272 |
|     Conclusion | 275 |
| 15. Bright Bourgeois Morning | 277 |
|     Neo-Conservatism | 277 |
|     To the Baghdad Station | 280 |
|     Nemesis | 289 |
|     Capitalist Crisis and Opportunity | 291 |
|     Conclusion | 295 |
| **Conclusions** | 297 |
| *Endnotes* | 309 |
| *Bibliographical Essay* | 351 |
| *Index* | 355 |

# Introduction

> I saw society split in two: those who possessed nothing united in a common greed; those who possessed something in a common fear. No bonds, no sympathies existed between these two great classes.
>
> *Alexis de Tocqueville, French liberal, 1848*[1]

> It is the involuntary work of the bourgeoisie to arouse in the proletariat that class consciousness which is necessarily directed against the bourgeoisie itself. History is full of such ironies. It is the tragical destiny of the bourgeoisie to be instructor of the class which from the economic and social point of view is its own deadly enemy.
>
> *Robert Michels, German sociologist, 1911*[2]

> These are the times that try men's souls.... The rich always betray the poor.
>
> *Henry Joy McCracken, Irish republican revolutionary, 1798*[3]

The following chapters survey a fundamental debate structuring politics in numerous societies since the early nineteenth century. At its centre is a single proposition: that the middle classes, while abstractly attached to civic and political liberty, tend to become more illiberal in reaction to the rise of the working class. A 'left-wing' framing of this problematic would go something like this:

> The modern, capitalist middle class, the bourgeoisie, has a historic interest in constitutional government, liberalism, and civic and religious freedom. At least since the revolutions of 1848, the wage-earning working class has also been to the forefront in supporting constitutional and democratic liberties. In any bout of revolutionary struggle to secure liberties, the middle class becomes afraid that the working class will go beyond demands for political equality, and will seek social equality. For the bourgeoisie, this represents a threat to their social and economic interests. Rather than risk social equality, the bourgeoisie allies with counter-revolutionary reaction against upstart workers. In effect, the bourgeoisie is willing to surrender political equality in order to defend social inequality. There is therefore a structural tendency for the middle class to betray liberal revolution. As the working class are left as the only reliable fighters for political liberty, any revolutionary struggle is likely either to outstrip the bourgeoisie and move towards a socialist recasting of society, or to be defeated.

Of course, in boiled-down form this summary fails to do justice to any particular iteration of the theme amongst left-wing thinkers. We may take as a pithy version, however, Leon Trotsky's definition of the 'fundamental object-lesson' of political history since 1848: 'wherever the proletariat appeared as an independent force, the bourgeoisie shifted to the camp of the counter-revolution. The bolder the struggle of the masses, the quicker the reactionary transformation of liberalism.'[4] Trotsky did not originate the idea, however. Middle-class conservatism arising from their fear of a 'Red Republic' was anticipated by the left-wing poet Heinrich Heine as early as 1842:

> The Parisian bourgeoisie are obsessed by a nightmare apprehension of disaster. It is not fear of a republic but an instinctive dread of communism, of those sinister fellows who would swarm like rats from the ruin of the present regime.... For what the bourgeoisie want above all is order and protection—protection of their existing property rights... [They] sense instinctively that today a republic... might become the instrument through which a new unacknowledged power would seize control, a proletarian party preaching community of goods. The bourgeoisie are therefore conservative by external necessity, not by inward conviction. Their politics are motivated by fear.[5]

This intuition was elaborated in 1962 by the British Marxist historian, Eric Hobsbawm, who divined in the flow and ebb of the French Revolution a pattern for the future:

> The main shape of French and all subsequent bourgeois revolutionary politics were by now clearly visible. This dramatic dialectical dance was to dominate the future generations. Time and again we shall see moderate middle-class reformers mobilizing the masses against die-hard resistance or counter-revolution. We shall see the masses pushing beyond the moderates' aims to their own social revolutions, and the moderates in turn splitting into a conservative group henceforth making common cause with the reactionaries, and a left wing group determined to pursue the rest of the as yet unachieved moderate aims with the help of the masses, even at the risk of losing control over them. And so on through repetitions and variations of the pattern of resistance—mass mobilization—shift to the left—split-among-moderates-and-shift-to-the-right—until either the bulk of the middle class passed into the henceforth conservative camp, or was defeated by social revolution. In most subsequent bourgeois revolutions the moderate liberals were to pull back, or transfer into the conservative camp, at a very early stage. Indeed in the nineteenth century we increasingly find... that they became unwilling to begin revolution at all, for fear of its incalculable consequences, preferring a compromise with king and aristocracy.[6]

In this view, the bourgeoisie are predisposed to betray liberty for all. This explains the persistence and recrudescence of reaction over the past two hundred years or so. It also explains why left-wing, working-class parties have had a tendency to take over liberal revolutionary movements, and why governments might emerge committed to pushing through socialistic programmes. The paradoxical outcome is that socialist revolutions are more likely in 'backward' illiberal countries, where the bourgeoisie is weak and vacillating. Socialist revolutions are less likely in the 'advanced' capitalist countries, where liberty has already been firmly established. The left-wing theorization of this process, whereby the bourgeoisie betrays its working-class allies in the struggle against authoritarianism, and so loses initiative to the socialist left wing, we may conveniently call, following Karl Marx (1818–1883) and then Leon Trotsky (1879–1940), 'revolution in permanence'. One stage follows the next until either the revolution is defeated or all independent bases for revolutionary class agency have been exhausted.

A right-wing framing of the same problematic would go something like this:

> Civil and political liberty is natural for a modern, market society. As a country struggles to modernize, however, the structures of traditional society disintegrate and there emerges a rootless, impoverished proletariat, understandably jealous and resentful of the rich and successful. These desperate masses are easy prey for demagogues, who will turn their rage against the entrepreneurial bourgeoisie. Class resentments can easily be exploited by fanatics or opportunists. Movements for liberal political reform can and likely will escalate out of control, leading to class warfare. Any attempt by fanatical idealists to level society will tend to destroy the long-term prospects for prosperity and, by destroying the countervailing power of widely distributed property, raise up untrammelled state power. At least until a country has sufficiently modernized to build up a prosperous middle class and give the working class a stake in capitalist society, sufficient order must be valued above generalized liberty.

Again, there are many variations on this argument. Common to all, however, is a recognition that bourgeois liberty may be turned against itself. The late nineteenth-century Polish liberal, Walerian Kalinka, was clear that the working-class and socialist movement posed 'the greatest threat to the contemporary order', but it was precisely the liberal 'right to free association' that exacerbated the threat: socialist triumph issued 'directly and inevitably from liberal principles'.[7] It was commonly held that decisive revolutionary action against dictatorship and liberal ideals of a free-enterprise society were incompatible. As Ludwig von Mises put it, 'the violence of war and revolutions is always an evil to liberal eyes…when revolution seems almost inevitable liberalism tries to save the people from violence, hoping that philosophy may so enlighten tyrants that they will voluntarily renounce rights which are opposed to social development'.[8] In this view, liberals must prefer authoritarianism to precipitous overthrow of oppression, so long as revolution poses a threat to the private ownership of productive property. Revolutions by their nature are prone to cumulative radicalization and hijack by extremists; they are unlikely to result in stable democracy. We may, following the language of Cold Warriors, refer to right-wing theorization of this process as 'subversion of liberty', whereby well-meaning individualist democrats are exploited by collectivist radicals, and then at best shunted to one side.

*  *  *

It would be as well at this point to attempt a definition of the social dramatis personae.

A noble writing early in the French Revolution defined the bourgeoisie as 'that entire class of men who live on wealth acquired from the profits of a skill or productive trade which they have accumulated themselves or inherited from their parents;…those…who have an income which is not dependent upon the work of their own hands'.[9] This definition has not really been bettered since. It makes the key point that bourgeois wealth comes from skill applied to production. It is not, therefore, in the same category as the traditional ruling class that used its juridical and legal status to extract rents, tithes, or taxes as of right. Nor are the bourgeoisie a class of direct producers. Instead they rely upon peasants, wage labourers, and craftsmen to provide them with the material goods by which they live. The bourgeoisie organize production, as capitalists, or they provide services certified by educational qualification, such as doctors, lawyers, and other professionals.

Beyond this, the bourgeoisie are always divided by economic interests, social identities, occupations, politics, and—above all—by income. They are not ever exclusively, or even primarily, an industrial class. They are entrepreneurs, landowners, professionals, state servants, military officers. For Pamela Pilbeam, the bourgeoisie was never 'a single class' for its 'different components had separate and distinct identities, interests and concerns'.[10] There is substantial diversity in the social origins of the middle class, and an enormous diversity of ranks within it. 'What the various segments of the bourgeoisie had in common was not a shared class position in a Marxian sense', argues Jürgen Kocka, 'but two other factors':

> First, they shared common opponents. In the eighteenth and nineteenth centuries, they set themselves apart from the world of aristocratic privilege, unrestricted absolutism, and religious orthodoxy; and in the nineteenth and twentieth centuries, from those below them, the lower strata, the people, the working class. Second, the different sections of the bourgeoisie shared a common culture, defined by a specific type of family life and unequal gender relations, respect for work and education, and emphasis on personal autonomy, achievement, and success; and by a specific view of the world and a typical style of life in which clubs, associations, and urban communication played an important role.[11]

Indeed, important to bourgeois culture is the notion of a civil society based upon voluntary associations. These have included organizations such as the Freemasons, literary societies, chambers of commerce, drama groups, prayer groups, missionary societies, temperance societies, philanthropic societies, civil-improvement committees and anti-crime watches, and political parties.

While Marx was straightforward in his definition of the proletariat, 'economically speaking', as 'nothing other than the "wage-labourer"', his definition of even the 'capitalist producer' was notably more capacious, being the 'owner of the entire surplus value, or perhaps better, as the representative of all who will share the booty with him'.[12] Still, Marx did argue that the bourgeoisie is a coherent class with a particular class *imaginaire*, because its belief in free-market competition arises out of common economic interests. The individual bourgeois favours the competitive market, as it allows him to buy and sell as necessary without 'artificial' impediment. This, Marx argued, generates a political consciousness:

> The bourgeoisie had to claim its share of political power, if only by reason of its material interests. Only the bourgeoisie itself could legally assert its commercial and industrial requirements. It had to wrest the administration of these, its 'most sacred interests' from the hands of an antiquated bureaucracy which was both ignorant and arrogant. It had to demand control over the national wealth, whose creator it considered itself. Having deprived the bureaucracy of the monopoly of so-called education and conscious of the fact that it possesses a far superior knowledge of the real requirements of bourgeois society, the bourgeoisie had also the ambition to secure for itself a political

status in keeping with its social status. To attain this aim it had to be able freely to debate its own interests and views and the actions of the government. It called this 'freedom of the press'. The bourgeoisie had to be able to enter freely into associations. It called this the 'right of free association'. As the necessary consequence of free competition, it had likewise to demand religious liberty and so on.[13]

The problem with Marx's analysis here, however, is twofold. On the one hand, it is hard to identify a common economic interest because only a minority of the bourgeoisie are actually entrepreneurs organizing production for the market, or living off the dividends of capitalist production. Most bourgeois are professionals, officers, salaried managers, civil servants, and so on, whose income is not derived, at least directly, through commerce. Moreover, there is not, in fact, a consistent bourgeois support for the economic free market. Outside Britain, passionate middle-class commitment to international free trade, for example, was a fleeting episode of the third quarter of the nineteenth century, at least until the 1970s. The middle classes are as likely to conspire against competitive markets as to promote them, the professions, notoriously, being a 'conspiracy against the laity'. The upper ranks of the middle class, in particular, have often adopted aristocratic tradition and elitism in a form of social closure calculated to pull the ladder up and away after they have climbed it.

For Max Weber (1864–1920), social groups are defined not simply by 'class' (quantitatively defined by him as arising from differential access to goods in the market), but also by 'status' (the amount of respect one could demand in any particular society or subset of society) and by 'party' (the capacity to influence policy formation).[14] Given this complex of determinants, one may wonder whether there is a basis for cohesive bourgeois politics at all. Weber's contemporary, Werner Sombart, thought not. Writing in 1909 he complained that, while 'aristocratic' agriculture in Germany only existed 'by the Grace of capital', the bourgeoisie had nonetheless entirely failed to 'develop a class consciousness of its own', its highest ideal being to marry into the titled nobility.[15] The bourgeoisie may have had a 'class' identity, but this is so vitiated by its 'status' anxiety that no solid 'party' orientation emerged from it. Indeed, a later famous account of the rise and fall of economic liberalism came close to denying the causal role of class interests in political history altogether. Karl Polanyi argued that a 'double movement' from the eighteenth century first saw the rise of a messianic free-market order, established by the state, only to be rolled back by counter-movement of politically mandated regulation. Polanyi denied that either movement was driven by class interests: the first was a utopian political experiment arising from ideology; the second was a spontaneous reaction in self-defence by society as a whole.[16]

Nonetheless, in this book I *shall* posit a complex but real commonality of class interests, reflected in political preferences, across the bourgeoisie as a whole. If most bourgeois are not capitalists employing wage labour to produce commodities for profitable sale, there is still a fundamental unity of economic interests underlying the variegated middle class of entrepreneurs, bureaucrats, rentiers, and professionals. At its core is a belief in the free market *in employment*. This evidently makes sense for the capitalist, who wishes to hire and fire as market conditions dictate, and who needs to set wages in light of their marginal market value rather than by social expectations (as representatives of the actual Parisian capitalists put it in 1791, 'liberty ought to exist for everyone, even the masters').[17] It is to the benefit also of passive rentiers holding stocks and shares in enterprises they hope to be securely profitable. This much is obvious, even allowing for the fact that employers usually strive to hold on to a 'permanent, non-mobile pool of white- and blue-collar workers' as a core workforce familiar with the techniques and implicit knowledge of the enterprise, so that 'flexibility' was always preferred to completely fluid, volatile labour markets.[18]

A flexible market in employment, however, benefits the wider professional and managerial bourgeoisie as it does the capitalist. Bilateral 'freedom of contract' tends to tightly cap the wages of unskilled and semi-skilled workers, for individual workers can be replaced without a serious impact on profitability, and so they have weak market leverage. Freedom of contract, however, has quite the opposite effect on those with relatively scarce skills, talents, or social attributes. It has often seemed that the professional is able to 'persuade society to set an agreed value on his service', as Harold Perkin puts it.[19] But this is by no mere sleight of hand. Professionals, specialists, and managers—even latterly celebrities—command substantial salaries because their skills, prestige, and talent multiply productivity or substantially increase market share for their employers. The most able individuals are amply rewarded because their retention is so much more important to the bottom line of enterprises than any unskilled or semi-skilled worker could hope to be. They offer enterprises a 'marginal productivity' above the base of interchangeable labour and skills. Generally, while blue-collar and lower level white-collar workers in a job might expect moderate advancement by seniority, managerial and professional employees are promoted much more steeply, and by performance.[20] They benefit from a free market in employment and promotion. So long as a goodly proportion of the market is private, and there exists the opportunity to transfer into analogous employment in the private sector, such upward pressure applies also to the salaries of the most valuable state employees.

Individuals of the bourgeoisie are able to offer 'positional goods'. Whilst standards of education, skills, and qualification might rise amongst the general population, it is only ever a minority with relatively advanced skills and talents that can supply an edge over competitors in the market. The more the employment market is competitive, the greater are the rewards for those 'near the top': 'Reward by relative performance', argue Robert Frank and Philip Cook, 'is the single most important distinguishing characteristic of winner-take-all markets.'[21] Even leaving aside the extremes of remuneration, more labour-market flexibility means more income dispersion.[22] The bourgeoisie, therefore, may be defined as that section of the population that deviates upwards from the median income level in direct proportion to the flexibility of the labour market. The bourgeoisie's 'natural' fraction in a free-market economy is probably about one fifth; this following from the logic of the 'Pareto principle' (or the 'Law of the Vital Few'), whereby even a graduated distribution of relevant aptitudes results in 20 per cent of a population engrossing 80 per cent of wealth. Sidney Webb calculated that the 'fortunate few' in late nineteenth-century Britain comprised one-fifth of the population. They were a few owners of capital, and that 'larger body of persons...able, from their education or cultivated ability, to choose occupations for which the competition wage is still high, owing to the relatively small number of possible competitors'. These 'fortunate few' more or less accord with the bourgeoisie as I define them.[23]

In the mid-twentieth century the American economist, Simon Kuznets, hypothesized that industrialization leads to an increase of income equality, with the richest 20 per cent or so benefiting disproportionately from economic growth. Once industrial society matures, however, inequality tends to reduce. This 'Kuznets Curve' remains controversial, but does seem to describe a real phenomenon. In Britain, for example, inequality certainly widened until about 1860; in the United States, inequality peaked around 1900.[24] With early industrialization, the premium for 'skill' grows fairly consistently, and the income gap between interchangeable labourers and the skilled middle classes widens. Stabilizing patterns of work, however, progressively de-commodified wage labour, so that it is buffered from the vagaries of the market.

If 'mature' industrialization arrested the surge towards inequality, the period between the onset of the Second World War and the breakdown of the Keynesian settlement in the 1970s saw an actual move towards greater equality. During the 'Great Compression' the differential between wage labour and bourgeois incomes was significantly squeezed. This, however, was contingent on a relatively rigid labour market, which in turn owed possibly to the strength of organized labour and certainly to the structures of large-scale Fordist production. (Even then, it did not efface differentials between workers and bourgeoisie, both entrepreneurial and professional). Before and after the 'Great Compression', flexible labour markets reigned, and these are the 'Gilded Ages' of bourgeois wealth, ostentatious in its upper reaches. For such eras, most wage earners (including the 'middle class', as the term is used in the United States) can expect a stagnating or falling share of national wealth. In the 1980s and early 1990s, for example, the average per annum salary rise for managers and supervisors in the US was nearly double that of wage workers.[25] In the quarter century to 2011, American men with only high-school degrees saw their incomes fall 12 per cent, while the income of the top 1 per cent in wealth saw their income soar by 18 per cent in just the last decade.[26]

Clearly, benefiting from labour-market flexibility is not simply a matter of individual genius or even luck. Socialization into 'bourgeois civil society' is crucial. Civil Society is a terrain structured by commercialism but not reducible to sheer economic calculation.[27] It is demarcated from the exercise of state power on the one hand, and from direct production by workers and peasants on the other. The point about bourgeois civil society, with its foundation of association, family, education, and assets of inherited property and wealth, is that it prepares its members to actualize their market potential not just through formal education, but also childhood socialization into habits of self-confidence, communication skills, and attunement with the dominant culture of success. Bourgeois 'habitus', as Pierre Bourdieu put it, generates valuable 'social capital' and 'cultural capital', which in turn leverages 'real' capital.[28] Marx himself remarked of bourgeois civil society that 'money and education are [its] prevalent criteria'.[29]

Marx, indeed, described the principle of remuneration on the basis of 'unequal individual endowment, and thus productive capacity' as 'bourgeois right'.[30] An almost universal middle-class commitment is to the idea of rising by dint of one's own merits, rather than by inherited privilege or institutional advantage. 'Career open to talents' is the political, indeed ideological glue that holds together the multifarious bourgeoisie. 'The contradiction between the *arrière ouverte aux talents* and inherited property' is, according to J. L. Talmon, 'the fundamental dichotomy of the bourgeois order'.[31] But there is no contradiction in bourgeois eyes: they feel justified in demanding that the time, money, and effort required to cultivate marketable 'talent' in their progeny should be guaranteed a return. Bourgeois opinion essentially supports the commercialization of life chances, natural talent certainly being rewarded, but rarely trumping the advantages of wealth. 'Career open to talents' functions, in effect, as a kind of alibi for those favoured by fortune.

\* \* \*

The modern working class, or proletariat, may be dealt with more briefly.[32] The wage earner is similar to all producers in that she wishes to secure the means by which she makes a living. However, while peasants could hope to own their own farm, or the artisan to become a master of a workshop in the long run, the wage earner can only enjoy secure possession of the means by which she makes a living—the ability to work for wages—by being guaranteed paid employment at a socially adequate level. This inclines the working class towards support for common regulation of the means of production, for a wage earner is simply unable to use her productive property on an individual basis. It does the worker little good to own one section of a conveyer belt, so for ownership to be meaningful it must be collectively owned, or at least subject to social regulation. Workers, therefore, are inclined to form socialistic preferences.

For Marx, it is particularly industrial wage earners (who comprised between 30 and 40 per cent of 'mature' industrial societies) who have political clout, being urban, close to the strategic nodes of power in modern states, concentrated geographically, and well positioned to bring pressure to bear by strike, demonstration, electoral organization, and even, in extremis, insurrection. Marx also trusted that workers would be strongly attached to such collectively guaranteed civil liberties as freedom of speech and freedom of association as being essential to their characteristic form of collective organization.

Marx assumed that because, under the ideal labour-market conditions of capitalism, 'the rate of [capital] accumulation is the independent, not the dependent, variable; the rate of wages, the dependent, not the independent, variable',[33] then wages can never be secure in quantity and regularity for workers. In practice, of course, wage labour is rarely quite so exposed to the vicissitudes of the market. 'Working life has been made tolerable in practice', observes E. H. Phelps Brown, 'only because there have been few labour markets in which competition has been really free.'[34] But as this implies, in so far as wages actually can be made tolerably regular and adequate under capitalism, there is no particular reason for workers to prefer collective ownership of the means of production over individual ownership of the attributes required for participating in the labour market (skills, contacts, and so on). While it is reasonable to conclude that most workers resent market fluctuation as destabilizing wage labour, there are many ways short of 'socialist transformation' by which wage security can be achieved. Most obviously, at least when labour has some bargaining power, workers share in common with the bourgeoisie an interest in a buoyant economy. More specifically, there are all manner of strategies for securing the value of wage labour. Examples include collective bargaining through trade unions, voting for welfarist political parties, investing in acquisition of marketable skills, opposing immigrant or migrant labour as likely to undercut wages, insisting upon nationalist pan-class solidarity, and so on.

'Proletarian democracy'—a term I borrow from Carl Schmitt[35]—as a phenomenon of the last two hundred years or so, is both a class constituency and an ethical goal. It designates a wage-earning class that relies upon its weight in numbers to assert its interests. But as these wage earners desire security and fair dealing in the labour market as a defence of their situation, this gives rise to an ideal of solidarity and rough egalitarianism more widely. The preference of the 'proletarian democracy' is certainly at odds with the hyper-flexible labour market and 'meritocracy' preferred by the bourgeoisie. Whether this preference actually takes a classically left-wing form, however, is highly contingent. Given that modern neo-liberal states pay out, if anything, even more in social spending to moderate the gyrations of the wage-labour life cycle than did the post-war Keynesian regimes, it is hardly right to say, as is so often assumed, that the political salience of wage labour is a thing of the past. Its usual mode of political articulation, however, mediated as it is through pan-class democratic parties, is quite distinct from any expectations canvased by Marx.

There are, in all, substantial grounds for 'proletarian democracy' and 'bourgeois civil society' to cooperate in establishing democratic liberties. But a tension remains between the bourgeois preference for flexible labour markets and the working-class interest in secure wage labour. As we shall see, these tensions were vitally important in the unfolding political history of modern states.

Peasants, generally speaking, were doughty defenders of individual private property, if not usually of the unfettered market. Stepniak, an observer of the nineteenth-century Russian peasant, wrote:

> The land is the object of the peasant's daydreams and longings...a *moujik*, even though he be poor,—provided he lives by the labour of his hands, on his own bit of land, without applying to anyone for assistance,—is an independent, self-confident man, enjoying his ample share of human dignity and self-respect.[36]

Peasants could be violently insurgent when struggling against landlord power. Indeed, they were generally more revolutionary—if we measure this by willingness to riot, arm, and physically take on ruling elites—than the more sedate proletariat. The peasant *jacquerie*, of elemental force and passion, was a more terrifying phenomenon than the working-class strike, demonstration, or even barricade set piece. However, once granted their own land, free of humiliating burdens of labour service and taxes linked to inferior status, yesterday's peasants become today's counter-revolutionaries, and bulwarks of conservative order. This was strikingly revealed by their dizzyingly rapid pacification in central Europe in 1848: from being the terror of monarchical order the peasantry became its greatest, if mostly passive, support. Where land hunger and rural oppression persisted, however, peasant agitation remained endemic, as in Italy into the 1920s and in Spain until the 1930s. The peasantry also played a major role in the Russian Revolutions of 1905 and 1917. Where agricultural labourers felt oppressed by employing farmers, or where landholdings were so fragmented that farmers were unable to conceive of self-sufficient proprietorship without substantial collective solidarity, peasants might rally to socialistic political movements. So, in the 1890s, the German socialists did win support in parts of that country's southwest. In Italy's Bologna, sharecroppers and labourers on the big landed estates espoused socialism. In Spain, anarchism appealed to peasants on the barely viable landholdings. In some French wine-growing areas particularly exposed to market fluctuations, socialists organized amongst small farmers.

Still, the default position of peasants was to resent the exactions of all the urban classes (parasitic, as they saw it, on rural labour), and generally the working classes were included in the hostile 'other'. Suspicious conservatism was perhaps the typical posture of small farmers. Defence of family-scale property was a constant, but the means varied. Peasants variously allied with landlords; carefully engaged with the commercial sector (reinforcing the family farm with wage labour and production for the market, in a complex but coherent 'pluriactivity'); solidarized around religion; persecuted ethnic groups stigmatized as usurers (notably the Jews); or cooperated with leftist revolutionaries. Their steady aim was to preserve from disruption a valued way of life around their small properties. Underneath all such expressions was an underlying peasant contempt for urban ways and attachment to self-sufficient productive property in land.

Constancy of ends and variety of means applied also to the petite bourgeoisie of workshop owners, shopkeepers, and petty traders. There was nothing 'inherently reactionary' about this class, as Geoffrey Crossick and Heinz-Gerhard Haupt explain.[37] They could be liberal, left-radical, reactionary, or fascist, depending on how they calculated their peculiar mode of property might best be protected under given circumstances. Indeed, as a rule, while a tangible link between class *imaginaire* and political expression applies to any class interest, its working out is always highly contingent. Men and women find ways of defending the means by which they make a living, but the political articulations by which they do so, for good or ill, depend upon potential allies, available opportunities, and inherited traditions.

\* \* \*

Niccolò Machiavelli, writing in the early sixteenth century, was disparaging in his characterization of the landed elites: 'by "gentry" are meant those who live idly on the abundant incomes yielded by their estates, without playing any role in cultivation or performing any other tasks necessary to life'.[38] It is true that gentry and aristocracy did not primarily make a living by organizing production (though they did often lend a hand). Rather they were a pre-eminently military, administrative, and political class. Large landowners were vital as administrators in the localities, assessing and collecting taxation, and administering justice, well into the nineteenth century. They swarmed at court, harassing the princely sovereign, but equally providing the personnel and contacts that made executive sovereign power able to function at all. They officered armies and navies, and before the nineteenth century were principally responsible for raising armed levies. In the absence of a professional civil service in the modern sense, gentry and aristocracy were indispensable to the integrity of any territorial state larger than a city and its hinterland. As we shall see, in the modern era the juridical and political power of classes constituted by honour rather than by proven 'merit' was to be called into question. Gentry, aristocracy, and nobility increasingly faced accusations that they were feudal relics, parasitic upon the productive economy and irredeemably wedded to faction, politicking, and warmongering.

Finally, the 'executive state' requires brief definition. Whether monarchical or republican, rooted in 'feudal' or bourgeois civil society, staffed by courtiers or professional politicians, legitimized by aristocracy or democracy, the executive state had to operate by rules defined by the realities of interstate competition. The continuity, stability, and flexibility of government were ends in themselves, because on freedom of governmental manoeuvre hung success or even simple survival in the unremitting contest with other states. The executive state could never passively 'reflect' the social interests of those they governed. It had, and has, an identity and interest, rooted in its social milieu to be sure, but nonetheless distinct and imperative.

* * *

Having established the organizing themes and subjects of this study, I will now fleetingly sketch some of its content. Before the continental revolutions of 1848, the European 'Springtime of Peoples', there was much confidence that commercial, middle-class, and bourgeois society was so dynamic that in time it must succeed in reorganizing society as a whole, not just economically but politically. A coherent liberal programme resting upon the interests of commercial civil society was widely acknowledged. As Derek Beales and Eugenio Biagini put it, 'economic liberalism meant business, and a parliamentary constitution meant power and security against the crown'.[39] Freedom to employ labour, take remunerative jobs, and accumulate wealth without vexatious taxation was widely appealing. In Britain, Richard Cobden (1804–1865), a British manufacturer and radical liberal, described the basis of reform movements, from anti-slavery to anti-Corn Law, as comprising 'the middle classes, backed by the more intelligent of the working classes, and led by the more honest sections of the aristocracy'.[40] The middle class seemed to be harbingers of a free and prosperous society. To the surprise of almost everyone, the 1848 liberal revolutions in Europe, though initially volcanic and all-conquering, collapsed with dizzying rapidity. Nonetheless, from the mid-nineteenth century, capitalism developed with unprecedented power and speed, but it was no longer so easy automatically to associate commercialism, a liberal middle class, and constitutional government. Bourgeois liberalism was mostly anaemic outside those countries—Britain, the United States, France, Belgium, Switzerland—where it had stormed the ramparts of absolutism before 1848. Still, with the spread of constitutionalism, few doubted that a new liberty was dawning, even if bourgeois civil society had to jostle with the lively legatees of aristocratic absolutism and the upstarts of 'proletarian democracy'.

With the Russian Revolution of 1917, a Red Menace loomed, and fear for the values of civil society recruited many an anxious bourgeois to authoritarian movements promising to combine modernization with security for middle-class property and prospects. By the 1930s it was painfully evident, outside of the old countries of 'bourgeois revolution', that the middle classes were prey to the appeals of 'new Caesars' of a terrible kind. Émile Vandervelde, the Belgian-born leader of international Social Democracy, in the mid-1930s wondered what had happened to that boundless middle-class energy and confidence that had once animated liberalism; such élan, he remarked ruefully, could now only be found 'among the reactionary bourgeoisie, when the task of the day is the strangulation of democracy'.[41] To be sure, the old liberal core countries of Britain and the United States, though only in alliance with Stalinist Russia, succeeded in re-conquering most of western Europe for liberal constitutionalism. But no wave of emancipatory bourgeois liberalism followed immediately worldwide. During the Cold War, the USA again and again preferred for its client states solidly anti-communist dictatorships to the perils of democratic self-determination. It supported authoritarian regimes and opposed revolutionary movements if so doing apparently served the greater security of the 'Free World' in the global Cold War.

But the story took a new turn sometime in the 1970s. The rollback of popular socialism and the collapse of Communism restored many of the conditions of the pre-1848 era. Communism's fall was the culmination of a historic eclipse of the idea of anti-capitalist socialism. As the veteran Trotskyist, Ernest Mandel, admitted sadly in 1990, 'Five generations of socialists and three generations of workers were convinced that socialism is possible and necessary. Today's generation is not convinced that it is possible.'[42] US neo-conservatives, in particular, concluded that democratic revolution could now be positively encouraged in the sure knowledge that socialist revolutionary movements would not thereby be sparked amongst the mobilized working class. From the Philippines to Ukraine, it was the Statue of Liberty rather than the Red Flag that inspired the masses.[43] History never comes to a full stop, however, and the debacle of the invasion of Iraq in 2003 and the Great Recession from 2008 suggested that the destiny of bourgeois civil society remained uncertain.

It is this bald summary that I hope to develop, deepen, and critique in the following chapters. In the conclusion, I shall restate the overview in, I hope, a more worked-out and nuanced form.

# 1
# Absolutism and Transformation in England

The idea that the bourgeoisie had a particular (if contested) destiny emerged from the historical experiences of the early modern period of European history. The span of years from medieval guilds to the French Revolution was looked back upon wonderingly, even by the 1840s, as the 'heroic age' of bourgeois revolution. Whilst dismissing glamorization, it is worth our while to revisit these historical assemblages, and to piece together again in bare outline the ascending line of bourgeois liberty which, from 1848, appeared to turn down.

## CAPITALISM AND THE STATE

It seems clear that acquisitive possessive individualism can be traced far back, centuries before the triumph of putative 'bourgeois society'. Examples of such 'bourgeois traits' as entrepreneurship can be found amongst aristocrats, landlords, and the peasantry.[1] For most of history, however, the merchant-capitalist existed in the interstices. They served a 'naturalistic' economy. Peasants, who amounted to at least 60 per cent of any pre-industrial population, apportioned their time between labour dedicated to family subsistence and labour to produce goods for sale to raise money for rents, taxes, and church tithes. Buying and selling consumer goods and labour entirely through the market was barely even conceived of as a possible basis for the organization of society.

Medieval and early-modern economy in Europe was not stagnant. The windmill, waterwheel, armament specialism, marine transport and navigation, optics, and precision engineering all increased productivity. The base for expanded commercialism was certainly present. As the land could support more people, there was a structural tendency towards population growth, which could either culminate in overshoot, Malthusian crisis, and famine, or the release of labour from agricultural production for secondary manufacturing and the carrying trade. With the European rounding of the African cape in 1488 and the 'discovery' of the Americas in 1492, the development of international trade took off. As specie and exotic imports such as spices and tobacco flooded European markets, even peasants looked for a piece of the action. They increasingly produced for the market specifically to exchange for consumer goods. It was opportunity rather than the stern whip of abject poverty that encouraged this 'industriousness'.[2] Slowly, entrepreneurs broke out from the limitations imposed by regulation of estate status, sumptuary laws, and the claims of the politically constituted elites.

By the eighteenth century, the bourgeoisie in western Europe made up perhaps 20 per cent of the urban population and 1 to 2 per cent of the rural population; roughly 3 to 4 per cent of the entire population. Only a small minority were capitalist organizers of production. Most were merchants, manufacturers, civil servants, and professionals in medicine and law. About 40 per cent of urban populations were artisans, mostly employed in workshops as owners ('masters') or apprentices. They were stalwart defenders of private property but suspicious of market forces, particularly free labour markets, and where they were able they arranged themselves into guilds to prevent easy entry into trades. A further 20 per cent of town-dwellers were domestic servants. Only another 20 per cent could be defined even as proto-proletarian. They were 'proletarians' without expectations of owning productive property, but as unskilled and often transient labourers they were confined to the fringes of core economic activity (usually they hauled loads). Proletarians were anomalous in a pre-industrial society that was overwhelmingly property-possessing.

It is clear that the economy was *revolutionized* in Europe and its offshoots in the later eighteenth and nineteenth centuries. So what changed? Many writers have emphasized the importance of institutions in allowing for industrialization. In the 1950s, social scientists pressed the case that strong property rights—including the right of the owner to use assets, to benefit and profit from them, and to sell or give them away—generated optimum conditions for capitalism.[3] This argument in due course had its impact on the historical study of the emergence of capitalism. Douglass North, for example, stressed that it was 'better specified property rights' rather than 'laissez faire' (the state leaving the economy to its own) which laid the basis for the industrial revolution.[4] Capitalism, in this view, was inherent in the collective action of economically rational individuals, but was inhibited by rent-seeking agents. Commercial economy had to be protected from the arbitrary demands of rent-seekers, whether 'feudal' lords or the tax-state. On this logic, the emergence of capitalism as the dynamo of the economy inescapably involved political transformations, not mere economic evolution.

There were institutional foundations to build upon. The system of law in Europe was long amenable to putative bourgeois civil society. European societies evolved a legalism based upon *passive* citizenship. Whereas the ancient world had defined citizenship as the *active* right to participate directly in government and/or state policymaking (a form of citizenship ever afterwards claimed by European aristocracies), the early modern state increasingly defined citizenship instead as the right of the individual to hold property, rights, and interests under the rule of law, which no ruler, or aristocrat could capriciously violate.[5] This notion of *passive* citizenship under the rule of law was particularly appropriate for bourgeois civil society. In such legalism, as Mike Macnair puts it, interests have to be '*analogised to* private property' to become 'justiciable', that is, capable of being arbitrated in court.[6] To extend legalism, thus, it was necessary to redefine all interests as private property rights. This was an important driver towards high capitalism, with law acting as an independent force. While lawyers, not coincidentally, were often political representatives of bourgeois civil society, they promoted the hegemony not of a class, but of law. This was to be important in the emergence of liberalism, which on principle (if less in practice) repudiated any one class turning the state to its own ends. A 'passive' citizenry secure in its property rights was virtually the definition of bourgeois civil society, and an ideal base for the state.

Capitalism only becomes the dominant economic organizing force when most goods, in particular labour, are traded on markets. This requires a political framework wherein private property rights are respected. A political transformation of the state, thus, was necessary for the triumph of capitalism. This transformation swept the West in the nineteenth century, but its preliminaries were established in leading countries by the eighteenth century.

## TAXATION AND ABSOLUTISM

Debates over the levying of taxation, at what level and for what purposes, have been historically endemic. Executive governments have required fiscal resources flexible enough to surge at time of war. Property owners have wanted predictable levels of tax agreed consensually. In the medieval and early modern era, it was generally expected that the monarch would 'live on his own', that is, pay for day-to-day operations out of a defined and discrete source of royal income. Additional expenditures were 'public', drawing upon taxation, and as such required the consent of the 'political nation'. The conceptual division between the private purse of the ruler and the public purse had existed in Roman law, and medieval legalists similarly drew a distinction, calling the public purse the *fisc*. Parliaments of nobles had to be convened by monarchs, usually in times of war, to seek consent for extraordinary taxes.

The executive state long relied upon the commercial sector for credit. Merchants were likely to have built up expertise in handling finance and a reputation for reliability as lenders and borrowers. 'Neither Kings nor Princes nor any [other] rank of men enjoy as much reputation or credit as a good merchant,' observed a Neapolitan merchant in 1458.[7] There were plenty of business opportunities for private individuals arising from state finance. John Calvin (1509–1564) noted mordantly that 'we see merchants getting rich in the midst of wars...for those who wage war are forced to borrow cash, as also the peasants and artisans, so they can pay their taxes'.[8] Governments, however, were often poor credit risks, frequently defaulting. In France, for example, there were repeated tacit state bankruptcies from the fourteenth century, allowing the Crown to refuse full repayment of loans and interest. If financiers got too snippy, there would be the prospect of show trials for excess profit-making. A famous case was that of the seventeenth-century financier and official, Nicolas Fouquet, who in 1661 narrowly avoided execution, instead being imprisoned in an isolated fortress for life, after he pressed his sovereign too importunately for repayment of debt. The wise moneylender or merchant, therefore, chose to play easy with aristocrats and officials.[9]

While the early modern state had a close relationship with the capitalist financier, it was a distinctly unequal relationship, with the capitalist quite deliberately deprived of political authority. It was very much in the interest of monarchs to arrange loans with wealthy but otherwise politically marginal groups. Princes would often have a 'Court-Jew'. One king of Aragon explained in the mid-fifteenth century that 'our predecessors have [only] tolerated and suffered the Jews in their territories because these Jews are the strong box and treasury of the king'.[10] Few Jewish financiers would risk exploiting their hold over monarchs for political advantage, for fear of the sovereign stirring up pogromist popular hatreds in retaliation. Crown governments generally encouraged peoples ethnically distinct from the communities in which they operated to act as merchants, the better politically to isolate and weaken these important milch-cows of the state treasury. Thus German colonists were encouraged by the rulers of Poland, Bohemia, Hungary, and Russia to enter into trade. Similarly Jewish entrepreneurship was fostered in Poland, Greek traders in the Ottoman Empire, and Italians in the Habsburg dominions. Particularly in eastern Europe, the cities were ethnically demarcated from the countryside: Germans and Jews in a rural ocean of Slavs. The result was a developing bourgeoisie ethnically marked out and often resented as 'foreign' exploiters.[11] With the combined disability of economic, ethnic, religious, and political marginality, the early modern bourgeoisie may have played an important role in financing the state, but they could rarely dictate to it.

In the early modern period, technical changes in war and administration made permanent standing armies both possible and, given interstate competition, necessary. From the fourteenth century, gunpowder revolutionized warfare and massively increased its costs. Meanwhile, from roughly 1620 to 1740, European-wide inflation eroded in real terms the Crown's revenues. As the economic cake reduced in size, a struggle opened up between the centralized state on the one hand and the economic elites—particularly the aristocracy and gentry—on the other, over the disposal of the surplus product. Rising taxation was the main reason for European rebellions, both elite and popular, that stretched into the 1670s. Broadly speaking, centralizing states succeeded in limiting the independent political power of their aristocracies. As monarchs now claimed undivided political authority, they were recognized as 'absolutist'.

To increase their room for manoeuvre, early modern European states strove to downgrade the representative institutions (parliaments) of magnates, nobility, and urban burghers. The French Estates General was convened in 1615, but never again before the Revolution of 1789. While representative institutions in other realms struggled on, parliamentarianism only really entrenched itself vis-à-vis the Crown in seventeenth-century England. European contemporaries, however, 'were convinced', Peter Wilson notes, 'that absolute rule was more efficient at mobilizing resources than mixed monarchy or republican government'.[12] Thus the general tendency was towards the rise of absolutist monarchies.

While absolutist states did not have the ability to atomize civil society, they could dominate the taxable elites. Should the state possess a permanent armed force, it was able at least crudely to extract tax by sheer force or threat of force. The hundred or so years up to the American Revolution in 1775 was the highpoint of the standing army overawing the nobility in this way. France set the standard with Louis XIV's massive army, 360,000 men out of a population of 21 million by 1710. France's rivals, perforce, had to join in with the arms race. Eighteenth-century Brandenburg-Prussia was the extreme case, with an army of over 190,000 despite drawing from a population far less than half the size of France. The establishment of a standing army, often effectively mercenary in form, was seen by contemporaries as the death knell of civil society's independence from the state. A Württemberg historian wrote of his kingdom in 1783 that 'When finally the Estates consented to pay taxes for the maintenance of a few hundred guardsmen, this was as good as if they assented to 6,000 men; and as the guards grew in numbers, so, on the analogy of the history of nearly all German provinces, the memory of the Estates' liberties was bound to disappear.'[13] It was a vicious circle. The greater the fiscal resources of the state, the more formidable were its armed forces, and the more power it had to extract taxes from its subjects without their consent. Jacques Necker, eighteenth-century banker and French statesman, observed the knock-on effect that as European states 'turned into vast military barracks' there was 'a proportional rise in taxes'.[14]

In Europe, the absolutist executive states deployed their advantage over the nobility in a concerted effort to restructure the very social basis of the aristocracy. Absolutist kings wished to preserve their tax base by protecting the peasantry from egregious exploitation by tax-exempt nobles. As the Austrian empress, Maria-Theresa, said of the peasantry, 'The sheep should be well-fed, in order to make it yield more wool and more milk.'[15] Absolutist states, therefore, effectively bolstered the peasantry against their landlords. The state moved to emancipate peasants from their feudal servitude to the nobles, and were particularly swingeing in their reforms where nobles were considered to be disloyal, as in Russian-ruled Poland. Emancipation of the peasants in continental Europe came first in Savoy (incompletely in 1771, but definitively by the French occupation in 1792), and last in the Danubian Principalities (Rumania) in 1864. A total of thirty-eight European states went through the often tortuous and halting process. As Jerome Blum observes, peasant emancipation was the 'last great triumph of royal absolutism over nobility', ending 'the centuries-old struggle for supremacy between throne and nobility'.[16] The limits of absolutism, however, were evident in the inability of the early modern state to actually dispense with the aristocracy as a governing class. Professor Christian Jacob Kraus, of the University of Königsberg, remarked at the end of the seventeenth century that 'The Prussian state, far from being an unlimited monarchy, is but a thinly veiled aristocracy. The aristocracy rules the country in thinly disguised form as a bureaucracy.'[17] What was true for Prussia was true, *mutatis mutandis*, for all absolutist monarchies. Absolutist courts could not be really independent of aristocracy and gentry, for the landowners comprised the executors of state power throughout the realm. No independent royal civil service could hope to displace them.

Whilst fostering commerce as an easily taxed economic activity, absolutist states were easily tempted into over-enthusiastically taxing enterprise for short-term advantage, but to the detriment of long-term national economic vitality. Autocratic China presented an extreme example. The country's sheer size, and the low if usually self-subsistent productivity of its peasant population, made it exceptionally difficult there to harmonize an efficient state apparatus with a commercial civil society co-extensive with the realm. In 1760 the Qing dynasty limited the impact of the outside world, and maximized fiscal skimming of the flow of commodities, by streaming all foreign trade through the port of Guangzhou, where only a dozen Chinese merchant firms were officially licensed to trade with Westerners. States in eighteenth-century Europe, on the other hand, sponsored commercialism, in a policy known as 'mercantilism', with the intention that trade as far as possible be channelled through tax-visible nodes: the posts and border crossings. Still, tax evasion remained an acute problem for the mercantile central state.[18] Moreover, the subordination of commercialism to an irresponsible tax-state was widely held to reduce incentives for private investment. Imperial Spain in the sixteenth and seventeenth centuries was the heartland of the enormous Habsburg Empire. To finance a succession of Spanish wars, however, the commercial regions of Andalusia and Catalonia were squeezed relentlessly for resources. By 1800 Spain had fallen far from the first rank because forced loans and emergency taxes had over time devastated local economies.[19] Taxation by arbitrary fiat tended to kill the goose laying golden fiscal eggs. Absolutism, in sum, failed to emancipate the potential of commercial, capitalist property.

## BRITAIN AND CONSTITUTIONALISM

The most important European exception to the absolutist pattern of development was to be found in Britain. It was here, largely by accident, that the political infrastructure evolved in such a way as to liberate commercialism from the dead hand of state manipulation and aristocratic indifference. England's medieval heritage, as Alan MacFarlane argues, might well be considered 'feudal', but it was of a relatively peculiar type.[20] Land was held by freeholders, paying rent but otherwise disposing of their property as they saw fit. The countryside, thus, was organized around individual private possession, so that the surplus produced by those working the land was protected from arbitrary appropriation by landlords or state. Labour was relatively mobile and flexible, and from 1300 probably over a third of the country's inhabitants engaged full or part-time in wage labour. The existence of a substantial, if dispersed, semi-proletarian labouring population, with tenuous if any possession of productive property, was a real concern for the ruling elites anxious to maintain order. In response, a remarkably advanced system of public relief for the indigent developed: the 'Old Poor Law' system, as brought to a peak in 1601. This was run through the parishes, and so encouraged a thick texture of local self-governance, interacting with central government, and extending far beyond aristocracy to enfold gentry, burghesses, merchants, and even prosperous farmers and artisans.[21] By the seventeenth century the English Stuart monarchy was equally unusual in Europe in being without a substantial standing army, or a large local bureaucracy dependent on centralized power, or arbitrary powers of taxation and imprisonment. England, thus, was unique in the degree to which private property rights were protected from state interference.

The English Parliament—a House of Commons dominated by the gentry, and an aristocratic and hereditary House of Lords—saw itself as responsible for providing the Crown with funds, but also protecting private property and traditional law. Arbitrary taxation was seen as contrary to established practice. Sir John Fortescue, Lord Chief Justice under Henry VI, had written in his *c.*1470 legal treatise, *De Laudibus Legum Angliae* ('In Praise of the Laws of England') that:

> The king cannot at his pleasure change the laws of the kingdom...the statutes of England are established not only by the prince's will but by the assent of the whole kingdom...the king of England does not by himself or his ministers impose upon his subjects any tallage [new tax] or burden, nor change their laws nor make new ones, without the express consent or concession of his whole kingdom in his parliament.[22]

One MP, Sir Francis Seymour, declared in 1628 that the right of the Crown to impose forced loans and tax arbitrarily was incompatible with the security of property, and thus with the independence of subjects, for if the king 'is pleased to take what he thinks fit', then 'we do not know what we enjoy'.[23] The English gentry, squeezed by inflation eating away at rentals, could no longer easily live off their land in isolation from the court and City of London. A typical country squire, Sir John Oglander, complained in 1632 that 'It is impossible for a mere country gentleman to ever grow rich or grow his house. He must have some other vocation with his inheritance, as to be a courtier, lawyer, merchant or some other vocation.... By only following his plough he may keep his word and be upright, but he will never increase his fortune.'[24] Though most gentry did rather well precisely by engaging in such 'vocations', there rose a groundswell from the country (but no inevitable momentum) in favour of further opening state and commerce to all those with resources, ambition, and capability.

After much toing and froing, by the end of James I's reign (1625), the Crown could rely upon funds more or less adequate to meet ordinary expenses, but was still forced to ask Parliament for emergency grants in time of war. Preserving Crown independence from the legislature meant avoiding military entanglements. Tension was exacerbated by the accession of Charles I in 1625, who wished to pursue a vigorous foreign policy, unconstrained by parliamentary penny-pinching and its ideological bugbears (such as international promotion of Protestantism). Charles, when addressing Parliament, made it clear that he expected Parliament to vote supply whether or not the Crown was minded to take their views into account. He deplored 'tedious consultations'.[25] The Parliament of 1628 pressed on Charles a 'Petition of Right' condemning arbitrary unparliamentary taxation, and impositions arising from a standing army (arbitrary imprisonment, billeting of soldiers on civilian property, and martial law).[26] This was backed up by an attempted 'tax-strike', the majority in the Commons condemning those who paid taxes not authorized by Parliament as 'Capitall Enemies of the Kingdome and the Liberties of the Subject'.[27] Rather than concede, Charles I preferred in the 1630s to rule without summoning a Parliament at all. He imposed an illegal 'forced loan' in lieu of agreed tax, imposed the 'ship money' tax without parliamentary consent, and threatened imprisonment against those who would not pay. Generally speaking, civil society consented, if truculently. Still, without a peacetime standing army, or a state bureaucracy independent of the gentry at the local level, Charles I could not hope to rule as a tyrant even had he so wished.

In 1639 and 1640, Charles waged war on Scotland in order to force the English Prayer Book upon the Presbyterian Scots. He was disastrously defeated. The failed wars shattered the precarious finances of the Crown, and forced the king to summon Parliament. Defeat had left him disarmed before the political representatives of the elites, and the royal government was effectively deserted by the propertied classes in 1640. Rebellion in Ireland in 1641, however, made the raising of a new army imperative. The crucial question became: who would control it? Fearing the consequences of putting a counter-revolutionary weapon into the hands of the king, the parliamentary leader, John Pym, insisted that Parliament intrude upon the once incontestable executive privilege, the right of the Crown to command the armed forces. This was an unprecedented incursion on royal authority. Reflecting in a letter to his son in 1646, Charles I was strenuous on the matter:

> Next to religion, the power of the sword is the truest judge and greatest support of sovereignty, which is unknown to none (as it may be religion is to some). Whosoever will persuade you to part with it does but in a civil way desire you to be no king; reward and punishment, which are the inseparable effects of regal power, necessarily depending upon it.[28]

The choice between supremacy of executive or legislature was starkly posed in 1641. By attempting to deprive the monarch of his prerogative command of the army, Parliament was threatening to reduce the executive freedom of the government to its barest minimum.

A backlash against Parliament's pretensions led to the outbreak of Civil War in 1642. Pym's appeal to the London 'mob' secured the capital, but alienated much of the propertied classes. As parliamentary leaders geared up for war, they began to construct a centralized, 'absolutist' state structure, complete with standing army and coercive taxation. Seeing what their opposition to royalist overreach was bringing about in its stead, many constitutionalists switched sides to the king as the lesser threat to established liberties of the 'free-born Englishman'. Indeed, it was elements of the powerful peerage, hoping to impose their will on the Crown through the legislature they controlled, that tended to oppose the Crown, while the merchant classes overall were either neutral or sympathetic to its cause. However, while established monopoly companies, such as the Merchant Adventures and Levant Companies, who benefited from royal patronage, duly allied with the Crown, the independent merchants of London, those trading in India, the Mediterranean, and the Americas, chaffing at the system of royal monopolies, had swung decisively to the side of Parliament in 1641. Thereafter the City supplied the parliamentary cause with war-winning fiscal resources.[29] In protracted and sanguinary civil wars, in course of which the parliamentarian New Model Army led by Oliver

Cromwell (1599–1658) became the real power in the land, the royalists were destroyed as a force, and the king made a prisoner of the parliamentarians.

Charles I was executed in January 1649, and Britain and Ireland became a single republican 'Commonwealth'. This was, in effect, Britain's historical experiment with state absolutism. Before the eighteenth century the English state was weak and of little account internationally. The one exception was during the rule of Cromwell, when Commonwealth forces smashed resistance in Scotland and Ireland and defeated the United Netherlands in 1654. Cromwell's constitution, 'The Instrument of Government' (1653), guaranteed the regular election of parliaments with the power to levy taxes and make grants. Though formally parliamentarian, the most important provision of the Instrument was that maintenance of a permanent standing army of thirty thousand men was imposed as an inviolable duty. The army duly displaced Parliament, and imposed an onerous and rigidly Protestant regime on the country, reducing the aristocracy to its lowest political ebb. As the nineteenth-century Whig historian Thomas Babington Macaulay (1800–1859) pointed out, the Cromwellian legacy turned even ardent royalists against the armed independence of the executive: 'The very name of standing army was hateful to the whole nation'.[30]

The return of Charles II in 1660 was widely popular, representing as it did peace, the end of Puritan cultural intolerance, and the pegging back of the executive state—which latter had, after all, been the intention of pro-parliamentarians in the first place. The Restoration, however, started again the prolonged process of conflict between a state looking enviously at the French model of executive independence, and a gentry unwilling to pay for a Crown government that looked dangerously inclined to continental-style papism and absolutism. When the Stuart monarchy appeared, under James II, to be decisively moving towards the model of continental Catholic absolutism, the aristocratic and gentry elites invited and supported an invasion by the sovereign of the Dutch United Provinces, William of Orange, to found a new constitutional and Protestant monarchy.

By the settlement stemming from the 'Glorious Revolution' of 1688, the Crown was saved from continual recourse to the begging bowl for its very existence by the ring-fencing of a permanent 'civil list' sufficient for its regular needs and household expenses, and for the payment of judges, officials, and courtiers. Arbitrary monarchical rule was inhibited by the Bill of Rights of 1689, which ended the royal prerogative to suspend the operation of laws. The Crown's right to maintain a standing army in peacetime, without the dispensation of Parliament, was abolished. Now funding for the military depended upon the passage of annual 'Mutiny Acts' in Parliament. This ruled out the possibility of non-parliamentary periods of rule like those of 1629–40 and 1681–5. The 1694 Triennial Act required that a general election be held every three years (extended to seven years by the 1716 Septennial Act). This was to prevent the executive simply prolonging a sympathetic Parliament indefinitely, as had been Charles II's expedient between 1661 and 1679 (and the ploy of the nobility and Cromwellians between 1640 and 1648). Simultaneously, the territorial range of the state was extended and consolidated. The old Catholic landholding class in Ireland was almost entirely expropriated while the

Act of Union of 1707 absorbed Scotland to the polity. The Act of Settlement in 1701 secured the independence of the judiciary, whose offices could no longer be revoked at the will of the monarch. When Queen Anne died in 1714, Parliament intervened to settle the succession on the Protestant House of Hanover.

The Glorious Revolution, in all, allowed a Parliament of substantial property owners to exercise firmer control over the Crown's ability to raise and spend tax revenues, and limited the state's ability to overawe the political nation. Parliamentary sessions became regular and unavoidable for governments. The threat of unbalanced parliamentary supremacy, on the other hand, was nipped off from about 1720. The emergence of the office of prime minister—Sir Robert Walpole being the first—stabilized the executive. Party conflict died away as the government manipulated competitive elections, which themselves were much less frequent, and the electorate was reduced in size.

The Civil War and Glorious Revolution reinforced a settlement whereby the state was responsive to the taxpaying elites. Britain was able to resist the imperative of a huge standing army, and thus an absolutist state, because it was an island. It did not require a large standing army in normal times to ward off invasion. It had a powerful navy, of course, but ships are poor instruments for domestic revenue collection. Still, there was nothing inevitable about this revolutionizing of the British government. It was the outcome of a balance of power whereby the state was unable to accrue to itself overwhelming military preponderance over the citizenry, while Parliament proved itself incompetent to merge into itself the executive and legislative branches of government. The Glorious Revolution strengthened the executive state within its defined responsibilities whilst setting Parliament up as a constant monitor of the executive on behalf of the propertied nation. In these constitutional struggles between Crown and Parliament, the commercial middle class had never played more than a subaltern role.

Britain's settled dispensation of an executive subordinated to the wealthy elites seemed, at first blush, to doom her to military weakness. No such state, it was thought, could have the freedom and flexibility of an unfettered monarchy in the constant struggle for geopolitical advantage. However, paradoxically, the Crown in England found it was able to raise taxes and finance loans as it never had before. Because Parliament guaranteed regulation of government taxation and the property rights of subjects, creditors were confident in lending to the government. Moreover, citizens were content to concede higher taxes knowing that their level was set consensually and in exchange for control over government spending. Government 'weakness' actually increased its net income and overall fiscal strength.[31] While France and Spain were confronted by fiscal crises, Britain's Parliament meant that her ability to tax and borrow was unmatched.[32] The interest rate at which the government could borrow fell from 10 per cent under William III, shortly after the Glorious Revolution, to only 3 per cent under Prime Minister Walpole.[33]

The German philosopher Immanuel Kant wondered at and worried about Britain's impressive 'national debt' mechanism, 'the ingenious invention of a commercial people' by which the state borrowed almost 'without end' yet never had to fear defaulting 'since the creditors never make their demands all at one time'. Britain, thus, was laden with treasure, 'a means of military power, more efficacious perhaps than that of armies or alliances':

> Considered as a political engine, it is a dangerous means of monied power, a treasure for war, superior to that of all other states collectively, and which cannot be exhausted except by a default in the taxes (an exhaustion eventually certain, but long kept off by the favourable reaction credit has upon commerce and industry). This facility of carrying on war…is an invincible obstacle to a perpetual peace.[34]

Britain, indeed, was pre-eminently a war-making state in the eighteenth century, a terror to its European neighbours and farther-flung peoples. Between 1700 and 1815 the percentage of adult males in the armed forces fluctuated between 8 per cent and 15 per cent.[35] Through aggressive conquest, Britain by 1763 had acquired an enormous land empire, notably North America and Canada, and a string of naval and commercial bases giving her command of the seas. She was also extending her power over the Mughal Empire in India.

Popular suspicion of the Crown's war-making capacity continued through the eighteenth century. Adam Smith (1723–1790), however, contentedly defended Britain's limited standing army as permitting the Crown just enough independence vis-à-vis civil society to render it secure and thus tolerant.[36] For the British government there were solid practical reasons for keeping its home army in check. As Britain's population was much smaller than that of her main rival, France, a British standing army could not anyway compete in size with absolutist rivals. The Channel was Great Britain's decisive advantage, and it made British naval power crucial. A navy was outward-looking, clearing the seas for commerce, and incapable of being turned inwards as an oppressive tool in the hands of royal despotism.

The power of Parliament also meant that government and gentry actually cooperated in restructuring agriculture, in contrast to the competition between state and aristocracy characterizing absolutist Europe. Between 1727 and 1815, some 1,385 legislative measures enclosed 706,284 hectares, about 20 per cent of Britain's land surface. This massively facilitated the development of productivity per farm worker, which doubled between 1700 and 1800.[37] Capitalist mechanisms—facilitated by Acts of Parliament establishing statutory bases for bills of exchange, bank credit, joint-stock companies, and insurance—encouraged commercialism. The Bank of England was established in 1694, modelled on the precedent of the Netherlands. Colonial and slave trading, linking Britain, Africa, the Caribbean, and the North American colonies, did not directly accumulate capital on a scale sufficient of itself to launch the Industrial Revolution, though a million slaves working gratis in the British Caribbean for the benefit of well under ten million Britons was hardly to be sniffed at. The demands of the 'Atlantic triangle'—based around African slaves labouring in the West Indian 'sugar islands', victualled by the North American colonies, which in turn traded with Britain—helped develop the markets, consumerism, and institutions of a commercial economy.[38] By 1760, England had become the greatest trading nation and the dominant naval power in the world.

An expensive and elaborate poor-relief system—the cost of which multiplied sixfold over a hundred years—put a floor under wages higher than elsewhere in

Europe. Employers, therefore, had a strong incentive to increase productivity through capital-intensive exploitation of fossil fuels and machinery. A strong state with parliamentary backing was able to enforce transport routes across parcels of private property (canals and turnpike roads), so allowing for the conveyance of coal and other materials. As Robert Allen has pointed out, these were conditions for a turn to industrialization: 'Wages were high and energy was cheap.'[39] From about 1770 the country's cotton mills, ironworks, and coalmines began to be transformed by steam-powered mechanization. Cotton goods, working up the raw material produced by slave labour, made up about half of all British exports in the first half of the nineteenth century. Wage earners were key in these cutting-edge manufactures. The propertyless proletariat decisively moved from the margins of the economy to its centre, at least in the north of England.

Given the rule of law and a government that was without arbitrary prerogative power, eighteenth-century Britain was certainly the freest and most just country in Europe. The century saw a marked rise in the 'middling-sort': gentlemen, yeomen tenant farmers, professionals, merchants, tradesmen, businessmen, shopkeepers, clerks, and skilled craftsmen. This was a substantial, pro-property social presence, much larger and wealthier than its continental counterpart.[40] An autonomous public opinion developed on the basis of the middling-sort, associating in the rapidly spreading coffee houses, assembly rooms, libraries, and around provincial newspapers. It was able to articulate opinions at variance with the oligarchic elite. The middling-sort were far from being a revolutionary constituency, but they generally supported an integrated programme of economical government, reduced sinecures, and a reform of Parliament to emancipate it from government control.[41] Civil society was also the ideal sphere for cross-fertilization between scientific *savants* and practical *fabricants* that drove industrial innovation.[42]

The construction of 'bourgeois' Britain, therefore, was circuitous and largely unintended, a side effect of collision and compromise between the state and the aristocracy, and essentially a political process. It did not result in middle-class control of the government, nor did even the richest merchant wish to sideline the politically dominant nobility. Rather, there was a dialectic between bourgeois society and the (mostly) aristocratic state, a complicated choreography by which one came to rely upon the other. The Great Britain of Adam Smith was dominated by state and nobility, but rested upon a commercial civil society.

## THE AGENCY OF CONSTITUTIONAL MODERNIZATION

England in the seventeenth century had been wracked by constitutional conflict between a Crown aspiring to absolutist prerogatives that would allow it to punch its weight in war-making and diplomacy, and a political nation, generally led by its aristocracy, seeking to defend private property rights and civic traditions from state interference. With neither side winning a decisive victory, a settlement evolved whereby Crown and Parliament established a division of labour that protected the ability of civil society to accumulate capital without hindrance, whilst the state benefited from orderly and consensual taxation supporting a formidable credit rating. The Crown and aristocracy remained politically pre-eminent because, by the eighteenth century, both clearly saw the advantage of nurturing a middle-class civil society that buttressed a constitutional monarchism without itself seeking to bend political power to its own narrow class interest. Being reliant for its mode of economic existence on commerce and private contract, rather than public executive prerogative, middle-class civil society was a mutually acceptable pedestal, because of its political passivity, for a finely crafted constitutional settlement of accommodation between the Crown and the aristocracy.

What did contemporaries make of this emergence of a new kind of polity in Britain, and one world-beating at that? Faith in the rationality of the state, its ability to recognize the limits to its own competence, was central to the arguments of enlightened reformers. Adam Smith had advised statesmen that any attempt on their part 'to direct private people in what manner they ought to employ their capitals' would simply overload the government.[43] The assumption here was that the state, if rationally enlightened, would out of self-interest refrain from interfering capriciously in areas where it had no competence.

This was not a new idea. The English political philosopher Thomas Hobbes (1588–1679), writing in the shadow of the civil wars, had argued that a state sovereign, in pursuing its own interests, would usually refrain from exercising authority in a vexatious manner. This was not because the sovereign was constrained by contract with civil society. A sovereign power was 'neither…bound to the Civill Lawes…nor to any of his Citizens'.[44] Rather, while the sovereign power is self-seeking, it is also prudent. The sovereign does not seek unnecessarily to disrupt civil society. After all, the sovereign knows that its 'power and safety…hath no foundation but in the opinion and belief of the people'.[45] The sovereign may legislate on any matter, but otherwise subjects are free to follow their own discretion where the laws are silent.[46] Those areas of civil society where the 'silence of the laws' reign are not, in practice, unpredictable. While the sovereign keeps tight check on anything touching upon its essential interests—say, the conduct of international relations, or the suppression of political sedition—it will barely ever find it efficacious or necessary to intrude upon the subjects' 'commodity of living',[47] by which Hobbes meant the 'Contentments of life, which every man by lawfull industry, without danger or hurt to the Common-wealth, shall acquire to himself'.[48] A sovereign government insulated from aristocratic (or democratic) 'solicitation and faction', therefore, is most likely to nurture a peaceable commercial Commonwealth.[49]

Hobbes made a powerful case for the assumption that a rational government will leave the production, commerce, and trade of its subjects to fructify. It was obedience to rational sovereignty that best guaranteed an unmolested civil society, rather than any attempt to capture it. This argument was long influential amongst liberal thinkers. It meant that an assertive attempt by society, or any part thereof, to master the state was neither desirable nor possible. As such, it was an argument against revolution. In the *Fragment on Government* (1776), even the vastly more democratically minded Jeremy Bentham espoused a utilitarianism that echoed Hobbes in its assumption that the state, looking after its own interests, wishes to govern a passive rather than a turbulent people, and so will pragmatically seek to govern for the greatest happiness of the greatest number.[50] Built into liberal thought was the notion that the rational state would take a laissez-faire approach to the economy. 'Rationality' was itself a motivating force.

Still, it was apparent that the particular form of a state could constrain or emancipate commercialism to greater or lesser extents. As the French writer Baron de Montesquieu wrote in 1748, merchants would speculate to accumulate only if they felt confident that their property would not be seized upon by a capricious state. As a 'general rule', he concluded, 'a nation in slavery labours more to preserve than to acquire; a free nation, more to acquire than to preserve'.[51] This did not mean that absolutism on the European model was considered to be entirely inhibitory of commercial development. After all, as Jacques-Bénigne Bossuet, a theologian at the court of Louis XIV, pointed out in 1679, absolutist government was quite distinct from arbitrary government. While it was true that absolute government was 'not liable to constraint' in public policy, when it came to civil society, 'each man remains the owner of his property'.[52] Across the Channel, the Enlightenment Scottish thinker David Hume (1711–1776) agreed: 'Private property seems to me almost as secure in a civilized European monarchy, as in a republic'. However, he warned that the executive was only provisionally in favour of commerce. Whilst wealth and resources might be left to private individuals in times of peace, in times of war they were always liable to be appropriated to meet 'the exigencies of state'.[53] Hume, furthermore, felt that absolutism was fundamentally inimical to commercialism:

> Commerce...is apt to decay in absolute governments, not because it is there less secure, but because it is less honourable. A subordination of ranks is absolutely necessary to the support of monarchy. Birth, titles, and place, must be honoured above industry and riches. And while these notions prevail, all the considerable traders will be tempted to throw up their commerce, in order to purchase some of those employments, to which privileges and honours are annexed.[54]

By this reckoning, aristocratic culture remained key to absolutist state structures, and as such they remained essentially pre-capitalist and 'feudal'.

Hume's argument was echoed by a French author looking back on the *ancien régime* in 1819:

> Respect is the first requirement of the manufacturer and the trader; doubtless they can acquire it by irreproachable conduct, strict honesty and constant fidelity; but this distinction is insufficient for them; they still want respect for their profession, as such. The stupid prejudice which forbids the French nobility to engage in commerce and relegates the individual who is involved in any kind of industry into a lower class, has contributed not a little to the arrest of progress of public fortune. The son of a merchant scorned the status of his father; he tried to hide the source of his wealth; he aspired to live like a noble; in this way family fortunes were dissipated; establishments, hardly begun, disappeared; traditions were lost; development was stifled.... This fundamental institutional vice estranged the merchants and manufactures from the Government; they all felt how useful they were to their country, but they realised their

country did not care for them; from that moment they isolated themselves and separated themselves from the national interest, in order to concentrate entirely on their own interests.[55]

The problem highlighted here was that the slighted entrepreneur was not inclined to enter politics at all. So how might the state be made more rationally amenable to the interests of commerce? This brought into focus the concept of social agency: what classes or estates were best equipped to support the state at its most rational?

## 'THE PEOPLE' AND LAW

Hobbes had implied that a state intruding upon the property and customary liberties of its subjects exposes itself to revolution. John Locke (1632–1704), in more insistent terms, argued in *Two Treatises of Government* (1689) that rule by 'Absolute Will and arbitrary Dominion' was a dissolution of government justifying or even demanding a revolution to rectify the situation.[56] The moral basis for revolution was 'the People' who 'for the preservation of property' had formed 'one body politic, under one supreme government'.[57] Locke did not seek in theory to identify any social or political agency to enforce the people's will against the executive. In practice, 'the People' for Locke was a cipher endorsing the actions of the gentry, merchant elites, and foreign allies in the Glorious Revolution of 1688, not a self-liberating agency.

'The people' was an amorphous term, though its long career as the hero of liberal agency was only just beginning. Adam Ferguson (1723–1816), the Scottish enlightenment thinker, was rather more precise in identifying specifically the propertied classes as the agency best suited for fettering arbitrary government. People 'possessed of wealth, and become jealous of their properties' had in the past 'formed the project of emancipation', because 'great accessions of fortune, when recent...may render the owner confident in his strength, and ready to spurn at oppression'. However, it was Ferguson's view that the propertied classes only played a progressive role in fettering despotism in limited, one-off circumstances, when first in the flush of self-acquired wealth. Once wealth becomes established as inheritable amongst a class, it tends to 'support a tyranny'. The wealthy classes as such were not a sustainable counterweight to executive state tyranny. For Ferguson, periods of revolutionary upheaval, as a newly enriched class asserted itself against the old order, were transient, but they had the capacity to establish a self-sustaining rule of law. 'Liberty results...from the government of laws', such laws being a self-sufficing 'power' and a 'barrier which the caprice of men cannot transgress'.[58]

It was, however, more widely assumed that property owners acted as an ongoing limit on despotic government. 'Civic republicanism' shaped political thought in the early modern states, spreading from the northern Italian republics, and was significant in the American and French Revolutions. Its emphasis upon individual self-ownership reinforced the conception of private property as being the basis of civil society. Immanuel Kant in Königsberg argued that 'self dependency' was the only appropriate condition for full citizenship: the individual was 'his own master by right (*sui juris*)', if he owned 'property that supports him'.[59] Such 'Neo-Romanism', however, still tended to emphasize the agency of juridical structures rather than any particular class.[60] The property owner would support an orderly state, and spurn corrupting dependence on the government for income, but otherwise Enlightenment thought allotted no special state-bearing agency to those involved in commerce. Instead, Enlightenment thinkers championed education above all as the factor that would usher in a society and state based upon rationality.[61] For moderate Enlightenment intellectuals, it was the sovereign princes who should be educated; the radicals thought this strategy hopeless, and preferred to address the wider reading public.[62]

The disorders of the French Revolution partly discredited both schemes for civilizing barbarian passions in the multitude. Burke, De Maistre, De Bonald, and others argued strongly that reform schemes and rationality could not overturn engrained traditions organically evolved without shattering social stability. In this conservative view, the state was self-sufficient and at odds with commercial society. François-René de Chateaubriand (1768–1848) hoped for a reasonably self-sufficient state apparatus: 'A bishop, an army-commander, a prefect, a police chief; if these are for God and king, I will answer for the rest.'[63] Edmund Burke, the Irish-British statesman (1729–1797), expressed a common conservative suspicion of the commercial middle class. Those 'artificers and clowns, and money-jobbers usurers, and Jews' who, he thought, dominated the revolutionary French National Assembly, would injuriously subvert the 'next generation of the nobility'.[64] In this view, the very money-grubbing involved in commerce rendered its practitioners ill-educated and ill-prepared for governance, certainly in contrast to the aristocracy.

In restating the liberal case, the French constitution-monger Benjamin Constant (1767–1830) insisted that sufficient individual property was a prerequisite for citizenship supportive of a rational state. He wrote in 1814:

> Those whom poverty keeps in eternal dependence are no more enlightened on public affairs than children, nor are they more interested than foreigners in national prosperity, of which they do not understand the bases and of which they enjoy the advantages only directly. Property alone, by giving sufficient leisure, renders a man capable of exercising his political rights.[65]

The growth of commercial and monied wealth, he argued, because it could so easily evade the attentions of the tax-state in comparison to static landed property, spontaneously undermined 'despotism' and encouraged consensual governance.[66] Constant, however, again relied upon structures rather than class agency as the preserver of liberty. He was impressed by the architecture of the British constitutional tradition, particularly the limited autonomy of the executive from the legislature.[67] Any attempt by the legislature to intrude upon the prerogatives of the executive or judiciary he rejected as tending towards either plutocratic or democratic class rule.

A key point to emphasize, therefore, is that for contemporary thinkers constitutionalism favoured commercialism, but the agent for bringing about and maintaining constitutionalism seemed to be the state rather than any social class. While a broad middle class of property owners passively supported a rational state, the commercial bourgeoisie itself, at least in normal times, was likely to be too deeply engaged in trade and barter to develop the *noblesse oblige* and civic responsibility necessary for it to contribute directly to governance.

## THE COMMERCIAL-FISCAL STATE

Marx later remarked on the centrality of state finances for an understanding of the revolutionizing impact of bourgeois civil society.[68] This was the nexus that rendered constitutionalism rational. By 'constitutionalism' was historically and universally meant a system whereby the executive state—usually a monarch and his advisors—could not levy taxation, or at least could not levy new taxes, without consulting with the wider political nation, which generally meant the elites of aristocracy, Church, and city. Parliaments were no embodiments of abstract love of freedom. They were machines for raising money. The German saying was, *Landtage sind Geldtage*—'representative assemblies are financial assemblies'.[69] The ability to dole out monies to the executive state gave parliaments their power. "Tis money that makes a Parliament considerable, and nothing else', advised Sir Thomas Meeres, British Member of Parliament in 1677.[70]

The details of constitutional political struggle were highly complex. The general drift, however, was clear. The legislature, representing the elites (broadly, those with the capacity to deliver or withhold tax) wished to limit the ability of the state to dip into their pockets They demanded an accounting for the expenditure of public funds, and redress of grievances and an influence on policy in return for stumping up cash. The executive, for its part, wanted money, not just in quantity but regularly (to service its debt). But it was equally anxious not to find itself tangled up in negotiating and compromising with domestic parliaments when faced with an opportunity in foreign policy to 'seize events and profit from them as they happen', as Frederick the Great of Prussia put it in 1768.[71] Should the legislature have the money power, it was assumed that government policies would conduce to the safety of property and pro-wealth policies, but would also limit that traditional 'sport of kings', inter-dynastic warfare.[72]

The social content of this political struggle was determined by the class composition of the tax-controlling classes. In pre-capitalist societies, the wealth of the landed elites, the clergy, and a good many of the commercial classes derived from unequal exchange. More precisely, the surplus product of the labouring direct from producers was handed over to landlords in exchange for access to land and tools; to the military classes in return for protection of life and limb; to the Church in return for immortality and a relationship with God. Taxation was of a piece with these, being another category of tribute derived from monopoly privilege that was essentially a function of political power. Constitutionalism in the pre-capitalist economy, therefore, was primarily motivated by a struggle over the division of tribute levied from producers, conducted between the centralized executive state on one side and the decentralized aristocracy, gentry, and middle classes on the other.

Once the composition of the taxpaying classes changed, however, to encompass those engaged heavily in trade and commerce, the social content of the struggle over constitutionalism was transformed. It was the fiscal exigencies of the eighteenth century, for example, that shifted the social content of British constitutionalism decisively towards bourgeois commercial interests in a capitalist economy. Reliance on direct taxation in the form of the land tax began, during the expensive wars at the turn of the century, to be displaced by indirect taxes on commodities sold through the market, specifically excise and customs levies. The Seven Years War (1756–63) sent Britain's annual state borrowing requirement spiralling, from £2 million at the outset of the war to £12 million in 1762. By 1760, excise and customs taxes accounted for 68 per cent of the government's revenue. The executive was relying, as Nancy F. Koehn points out, on 'trade, trade, and more trade, both at home and abroad': '[This] carried significant consequences for the politics of imperial decision making. As the relative contribution of duties on ale, candles, sugar, tobacco, and other goods to state revenue rose, so too did the demands of manufacturers and merchants for a voice in how their country's commercial empire was to be governed.'[73] Particularly when reliant upon merchant communities involved in foreign trade, states were incentivized to extend to commerce maximum freedom to organize and accumulate, with important consequences for constitutionalism.[74]

Most important was the transition in production. The base of the tributary social economy was made up of direct producers labouring in a bifurcated manner, to satisfy their families' subsistence requirements on the one hand and to generate a surplus for paying rents or for trading on the other. Once direct producers laboured entirely for exchange, however, the disposal of surpluses devolved onto the organizers of this commodity production, that is, onto capitalists. In this situation, the tax-controlling classes derived their control of wealth from their strategic insertion in a money-mediated cycle of commodities, of capital. The state benefited from this capitalism, as a system by which social wealth was concentrated and made accessible for skimming as taxation. As the economic historian John Hicks pointed out, commercialism and the fiscal state would in the long run tend towards complementarity:

> It is because incomes arise out of legal contracts, enforceable at law, that they can be established at law, and can therefore be taxed. It is because profits—nowadays the great bulk of profits—are the profits of companies, which are complicated legal entities, operating under closely prescribed legal provisions, that profits are taxable, indeed so readily taxable. It is because so large a part of property is now in the form of transferable securities, with easily attached market prices, that capital taxes, of any degree of efficiency, are feasible at all. In all these ways the taxing power of the State has been fortified by mercantile development.[75]

In a capitalist society constitutionalism represented the bourgeois interest, and the state protected the interests of capital. The winning and consolidation of constitutional political authority, in this context, becomes bourgeois revolution.

Very broadly speaking, the eighteenth and nineteenth centuries saw direct taxation on land and visible wealth being displaced by indirect taxes on the circulation of commodities, led by customs duties (foreign trade) and in due course taxes levied on domestic trade (internal consumption). England, 'with a vigorous commercial economy and incipient industrialization', led the way in the eighteenth century, with most of continental Europe following in the nineteenth century. This rendered the fiscal state 'immediately responsive to economic fluctuations', as Carolyn Webber and Aaron Wildavsky put it, and so attuned to the capitalist system.[76]

Three comments might be usefully made at this point. First, as already noted, constitutionalism per se, in that it limits the ability (and indeed incentive) of the state to expropriate concentrations of wealth as they arise, encourages accumulation, investment, trade, and commerce. Constitutionalism secured under the banner of the aristocracy, therefore, tended to work to the benefit of bourgeois civil society, and in so doing accelerated the transformation of constitutionalism itself into bourgeois revolution. Secondly, trade and commerce in commodities, being highly monetized and usually funnelled through state-regulated ports, fairs, and toll roads, were generally of greater importance to fiscal planning than the size of the capitalist bourgeoisie in relation to the overall social formation would otherwise suggest. Parliamentarianism, therefore, tended to reflect bourgeois interests much earlier than the size, coherence, and political audacity of the middle classes would imply. Finally, the bringing to bear of influence from the bourgeoisie onto the state was not all at once. As the nexus between bourgeoisie and state was primarily focused on credit, taxes, loans, and bonds, it was naturally enough through high finance and banking that bourgeois civil society had its earliest impact on the state. These financial sections of the bourgeoisie, in turn, tended to be most closely assimilated to aristocratic values and interests.

## CONCLUSION

The process by which the world-changing destiny of the bourgeoisie came into focus was circuitous, and generally the commercial and entrepreneurial classes played a minor direct role. The middle classes were not concerned that the dispersed and largely powerless propertyless class of semi-proletarians threatened to realize a social vision contrary to their own. Naturally, however, fear of vagabondage and rioting amongst the desperate concentrated minds on the value of orderly, even if absolutist, government. In England, the 'poor law' underpinned a system that involved the middle classes in local governance, certainly giving them a stake in affairs of state, and an influence too. The relative bargaining strength of the English wage earner, as it happened, was important in setting the path to capital-intensive industrialization.

The bourgeoisie, primarily, benefited from the revolutionary struggles of others, because the securing of constitutional government in a commercialized society automatically gave their interests the whip hand. Most credit for historic battles against the state to assert constitutional liberties rested with the aristocracy, indeed the nobility. The assault on aristocratic (or mercantile) rent-seeking arose, on the other hand, to no little degree from pressure applied by the 'absolutist' state. It was bourgeois civil society, nonetheless, that benefited from this unwitting 'bourgeois revolution'. But until aristocratic privilege was subsumed into the equal rights of wealth, and until the state was firmly subordinated to the interests of commercial society, the revolution was not complete.

# 2
# Revolution, Restoration, and Reform

The French Revolution was considered by Marx and Engels as archetypically 'bourgeois'. Suitably elaborated, their reading of the Revolution became virtually orthodox in the post-Second World War academy until the argument was dismantled from the 1970s by successive waves of 'revisionist' historians. Now, perhaps, the Revolution is basically understood as having being initiated not by a rising capitalist bourgeoisie but by a broadly defined middle class seeking access to government jobs. Historians admit that the Revolution had a profound cultural impact, doing much to generate the 'language' of political modernity, but its impact on the development of French capitalism is much more debatable. In so far as it consolidated peasant proprietary ownership, it may have inhibited the development in the nineteenth century of capitalism, or at least British-style industrialization. However, it remains the case that the Revolution can be convincingly understood as an attempt to bring the state into line with the widely acknowledged developmental potential of the market economy. Concepts of property and legitimate state authority ran like red threads through the ascent, descent, and legacy phases of this Revolution.

## THE FRENCH REVOLUTION: BOURGEOIS?

The success of the British state in the Seven Years War (1756–63) further encouraged European absolutist powers to foster commercialism at the expense of aristocratic privileges. However, absolutism was itself parasitic on commercialism. If anything, absolutism accentuated political distortions of market rationality by dispensing trade monopolies and seeking short-term loans in return for long-term tax immunities. The French *ancien régime* was much influenced by the British model, but was painfully aware that it could not simply recapitulate its organic development adapted to the interests of the Versailles court and the aristocratic chateaux. Not least, its long land border denied France the political and social benefits of a navalist orientation. The *ancien régime* comprised an 'absolutist' king governing with and through the 'estates' of clergy and nobility. With the development of mass literacy and commercialism in France, as elsewhere, a civil society, or 'public sphere' distinct from court culture, emerged. The political expression of this was a hostility to overweening executive arrogance, or 'despotism'.[1] The French monarchy, however, had every interest in rationalizing its archaic and venal tax system. Of the eighteen men who occupied the position of *Contrôleur général des Finances* in the forty years before the Revolution, most were influenced by rationalizing *Philosophe* ideas and at least seven attempted substantial reform. The difficulty was that taxes could not easily be imposed upon the recalcitrant. The bureaucratic and coercive apparatus of the state was simply not up to the task of overseeing in detail the income and outgoings of the propertied classes, still less of extracting resources from them without some minimum degree of consent.

The monarchy planned to wrest consent for more taxes from a representative Assembly of Notables, drawing on the First Estate (clergy) and the Second Estate (aristocrats), which could be confronted by the state's looming bankruptcy. On 22 February 1787 the Assembly sat and the Crown put to it the demand that special tax immunities of certain social classes, corporations, and localities be ended. Added to this were positive proposals to ease a seigneurial shift further into the market economy: the abolition of internal customs duties and the removal of most restrictions on the movement of grain within the country. The Crown proposed provincial assemblies where they did not already exist, but Assembly members proved unamenable and would only countenance reform if the state submitted to ongoing monitoring by a national Parliament of Notables. The Assembly was dissolved but, with the state and the country's wealthy elites so publicly at odds, even the government's day-to-day operating credit collapsed.[2]

The Notables had pretension that they spoke for the nation. King Louis XVI now attempted to call their bluff. He called an Estates-General which would include representatives of the popular Third Estate, hoping that this would expose the narrow interests of the nobility, and isolate them amidst a mass more inclined to look upon the Crown as an honest broker. As representatives were selected, lists of grievances (*cahiers des doléances*) were drawn up for consideration by the state, as was customary. In many respects, the *cahiers* indicated that the mass of people did, in fact, accept the Crown's reform package of regal authority and rational market: 'one king, one law, one weight, one measure' was a frequent demand.[3]

The Third Estate representatives were not synonymous with the commercial bourgeoisie. Forty-three per cent of Third Estate members elected to the Estates General were holders of office in government administration, one quarter were lawyers, and only 13 per cent were in trade, industry, and banking.[4] The Third Estate did, however, voice bourgeois assumptions. While the nobles insisted upon defence of property against state reorganization, the Third Estate, as John Markoff says, 'tended to focus on freedom to participate in the market, unconstrained by state, communal or seigneurial barriers'.[5] The self-interested nature of their demand that aristocratic status be no longer a qualification for state employment was evident. But by justifying this with the rationale that economic success should be correlated with talent and hard work, not inherited titles, they presented themselves as spokesmen of moral and commercial civil society.

King Louis seemed to have reached a favourable settlement when he struck a deal with the First Estate and Second Estate. Their title to property was to be converted from 'feudal' privilege, arising from legally defined status, into bourgeois rights of private ownership, as applicable to 'all forms of property without exception'.[6] However, the Third Estate, once mobilized, could not easily be stood-down again.

A clergyman, Abbé Sièyes, declared the Third Estate to be the true representatives of the nation, not simply a sectional interest. As the nobility claimed prerogatives above the nation, it 'is not capable of being a part of it'.[7] On 17 June 1789 royal soldiers locked Third Estate representatives out of the Assembly. The representatives re-convened unofficially, and pledged themselves not to disband until they had been officially recognized as a National Assembly. The Parisian crowd supported this act of rebellion with an insurrection. Royal troops refused to fire on the crowd, and on 14 July many of them joined with the rioters in taking the symbol of royal authority (and arsenal) in the capital, the Bastille prison. A long-lasting precedent had been set. The power of the urban crowd in the capital city to overthrow the government was to be a central revolutionary motif until 1871.

Urban disorder sparked the 'Great Fear' in rural France. Anticipating aristocratic counter-revolution and vengeance, peasants struck pre-emptively to crush the seigneurs' capacity to resist. Chateaux were attacked and manorial records singled out for destruction. It would have required mobilization of the royal army to suppress peasant disturbances. The National Assembly would not countenance so empowering the executive state; instead it legislated the peasant revolution. The Assembly approved dismantling systems of exaction based upon custom, in the hope that relations based upon 'free' exchange could be ring-fenced. On 4 August 'feudalism', so defined, was abolished by decree. Further legislation sought to remove impediments to internal trade, by reducing or abolishing tolls and standardizing weights and measures. The heavy tax imposed upon noble land sales to commoners was abolished. The Declaration of the Rights of Man and of the Citizen, approved by the National Assembly on 26 August, explicitly replaced the principle of inherited status with that of advancement by merit: 'All citizens, being equal in the eyes of the law, are equally eligible to all dignities and to all public positions and occupations, according to their abilities, and without distinction except that of their virtues and talents.'[8]

The National Assembly insisted upon a single 'bourgeois' definition of property, owing nothing to inherited social status. Count Mirabeau, in defending the revolutionary confiscation of Church land in November 1789, offered a definition of property that abolished all justifications deriving from duty or obligation: 'each individual enjoys his property not by title of contract, since he can dispose of it; nor as depositary, since he can dissipate it; nor as usufructer, since he can destroy it; but as absolute master, just as he can dispose of his will, his arms, his thought'.[9] In this view, property was lodged with the possessor, and was not dependent on any historic privilege such as that claimed by the Church or nobility. This expressed a 'civil society' ideal, widely resonant amongst urban and educated citizens, of bourgeois property unencumbered by legal or customary social obligations.[10] By the Loi Le Chapelier, craftsmen's guilds and legal monopolies were outlawed (to the outrage of artisans). Between October 1789 and September 1790, there were no fewer than five National Assembly proclamations declaring freedom of commerce (though no worked-out commercial code).

The revolutionary road to bourgeois reconstruction, however, unleashed an escalation that was to loom over the European imagination for two centuries. Louis

XVI, the symbolic lynchpin of order and continuity, was also, unfortunately, the fulcrum of counter-revolution. With the royal family secretly appealing for foreign intervention, on 20 April 1792 the Assembly declared war on the counter-revolutionary powers, Austria and Prussia. A French Republic was proclaimed, and Louis XVI was placed on trial and executed on 21 January 1793. Peasant revolt broke out in the Vendée, protesting at the humiliation of the Church, the republican pretensions of the capital, monetary inflation, and conscription. In a savage civil war religious fanaticism clashed with the self-assured callousness of the 'Enlightened'.

An emergency centre of government, the Committee of Public Safety, was formed on 25 March 1793, and rule by a settled representative government was delayed indefinitely. As Antoine de Saint-Just, a radical Jacobin, put it, 'the Provisional Government of France is revolutionary until the peace'.[11] The Jacobin faction in Paris, led by Georges Danton and Maximilien Robespierre, made an 'implicit pact with street violence', in Ruth Scurr's words, to overthrow the more moderate Girondin republicans.[12] Jacobin street allies were the artisanal *sans-culottes*. These were not wage earners, and their ideal was a moral market geared towards protection of small property: as their representatives put it, 'the same citizen can have only one workshop, one shop'.[13] There was a difference, certainly, between the bourgeois ideal of a free market in property and the preference of *sans-culottes* for guaranteed security of tenure. But they agreed on the sanctity of individual possession of productive property. Still, pressure from the *sans-culottes* did help to deviate the revolution from bourgeois norms. In July 1793 a 'General Maximum' was set in an attempt to regulate prices and wages. Suspected profiteers were terrorized. By the Ventôse Decrees of 1794, it was proposed that the property of active counter-revolutionaries be redistributed to the patriotic needy. This corroded the recently secured bourgeois solidity of property. Robespierre in 1794 insisted that 'we must moralise trade', and considered limiting profit margins.[14]

The bourgeoisie, however, had no cause to fear a challenge from wage earners. Gracchus Babeuf (1760–1797) did attempt to lead a quasi-communist 'Conspiracy of Equals' to institute a dictatorship based upon common ownership. Babeuf had hoped, through a *coup de main*, to establish a collectivist 'community of Goods'. His justification starkly repudiated the bourgeois common sense of unequal rewards for unequal talents: 'It is both absurd and unjust to pretend that a greater recompense is due someone whose task demands a higher degree of intelligence, a greater amount of application and mental strain; none of this in any way expands the capacity of his stomach.' Babeuf argued for 'social institutions...[able to] eradicate within every last individual the hope that he might ever become richer, more powerful, or more distinguished because of his talents, than any of his equals'. Modern obsequiousness before intelligence and talent only bolstered those who benefited from the unequal distribution of wealth. Babeuf speculated that eventually 'equal distribution of knowledge among everyone would make all men nearly equal in capacity and even in talent'. Still, common good would require repression even of the over-industrious labourer: 'Wisdom imperiously demands of all the members of the association that they suppress such a man, that they pursue him as a scourge of society, that they at least reduce him to a state whereby he can do the work of only one man, so that he will be able to demand the recompense of only one man.'[15] This was anti-meritocracy, in the raw.

Babeuf's plan was to exploit a window of opportunity arising from the dislocation of revolution and war that had created a 'host of propertyless men'.[16] How these underemployed or unemployed legions of the desperate were to be organized was anyone's guess. There was no coherent proletariat who, being systematically denied individual property rights in the resources they worked, could provide a stable constituency supportive of collective control of production. Babeuf was isolated, exposed, and executed in 1797, and his movement had no great social resonance. His imaginary armies of the dispossessed were fodder more for France's armies than collectivist conspiracies.

The military mobilization of the revolution, however, was overwhelming its bourgeois nature. An enormous army was called up in the *Levée en masse* of 23 August 1793, and about 1,500,000 were serving by September 1794. Revolutionary war generated a 'war-addiction' state. French armies, being vast and labour intensive rather than small and capital intensive, were obliged to stand on and live off enemy ground. One French soldier noted of a typical campaign that 'Our expedition [across] the Rhine' was due 'entirely to pecuniary considerations.... Our incursion into a rich and defenceless country was to procure us the money of which we were in such dire need.'[17] The regime stabilized, with rebellion crushed and foreign armies defeated in Belgium at Fleurus on 26 June 1794. In July 1794, Robespierre and his faction were themselves led to the guillotine in the reaction of Thermidor. Militarization made it almost inevitable that a single dictator would emerge from the armed state. Napoleon Bonaparte filled this role with aplomb, coming to power in the coup of Brumaire in 1799. On 2 December 1804, Napoleon crowned himself 'Emperor of the French Republic', a move approved by plebiscite. Napoleon attempted to preserve the lineaments of bourgeois civil society, particularly a 'career open to talents', but without thereby restraining the state. The 1804 legal Code Napoléon enshrined religious freedom and equality before the law; but also reinforced centralized government through appointed 'prefects'. Under the Consulate, there were limited elections and plebiscites, but the Legislative Assembly could only vote on measures presented to it without discussing them. A new Imperial Nobility was established in 1808, but titles were handed out on the basis of military or public services, and they could only be passed to descendants if supported by sufficient wealth. Napoleon downgraded the bourgeois National Guard, and established the praetorian elite Imperial Guard, amply funded and privileged, eighty thousand strong. He centralized and reformed the collection of tax revenue, permitting something close to balanced budgets. Along with the prestige and opportunities for preferment derived from war booty, this gave Napoleon considerable power to lord over civil society.

While France was to be industrially retarded relative to Britain, it is likely that this was less to do with limitations to bourgeois property norms—peasant proprietorship, for example, limiting a free trade in land—than its being squeezed out of international maritime trade by Britain. The commercial reforms of the Revolution were retained and operated. 'Feudalism' was not restored. The new order of property and law was particularly effective in fostering capitalistic development in areas where natural resources abounded, but these were primarily in Belgium and on the left bank of the Rhine, areas detached from France after the fall of Napoleon in 1814.

The French Revolution had attempted to create a British-style balance of power, but in a manner that eliminated aristocratic privilege entirely. The aim was to balance the legitimate authority of the state against a political class constituted largely of government functionaries and legal professionals but claiming to speak for the sovereign nation. The revolutionaries, through a radical reform of property rights, tried to generate a dynamic commercial economy that would sustain a bourgeois civil society. As in Britain, such a civil society would be apolitical in itself but supportive of a compact between state executive authority and the political nation. With the collapse of the traditional aristocracy, however, the French Revolution was left with inadequate leadership for the political nation; lawyers and placeholders lacked the inherited social authority of aristocrats. The commercial and entrepreneurial bourgeoisie, though supportive of the emerging regime of property norms, had no inclination or talent for political organization analogous to that of the displaced aristocracy. The vacuum was filled by explosive outgrowth of state executive power in the form of the Napoleonic empire.

Napoleon dominated continental Europe. At the height of his empire there remained entirely outside of his power only the extremities of Europe: Great Britain and Ireland, Russia, Sweden, Sicily, Portugal, and the Spanish insurgents. With all of these he was at war. Napoleon's military system of despoliation, Paul Schroder notes, was directly measured against Britain's parliamentary fiscal state. The British model won out due to its 'superior financial resources, organization, and public credit'.[18] Its consensual taxation system permitted a fiscal revolution that allowed the British state to wage its wars with France largely on credit. Napoleon's empire finally crashed to the ground in 1815, laid low by an alliance of European monarchies subsidized by Britain. The lesson was not forgotten. Arthur Conan Doyle years later had one of his characters say 'The greatest monument ever erected to Napoleon Buonaparte was the British National debt'.[19] By 1815, the end of the Napoleonic Wars, therefore, Britain's was the model to emulate. It was an aristocratic nation so far as its governing elites were composed, but with a constitutional framework and economy driven increasingly by capital accumulation, Britain was the premier bourgeois society.

## RESTORATION EUROPE

Continental Europe, as restored in 1814–15, was predominantly absolutist. Sovereigns ruled personally, advised by ministers appointed and dismissed at royal will. The richest class remained the landed aristocracy, which wielded political power at court and in representative assemblies where these existed. Working in cooperation with the aristocracy were office-holders appointed by the royal executive. With demobilization, armies were consolidated into standing bodies of career soldiers kept distinct from civilian society and wielded as instruments of executive will. The clergy no longer challenged the political authority of the state. There was a concerted effort to bolster the authority of the Church as a counterpart to princely rule—'the union of throne and altar'—but the clergy remained subordinate, if privileged, and to a considerable extent functioned as an arm of government. Restored government thus comprised a tacit coalition between the bureaucracy, aristocracy, clergy, and army, all under the direction of the monarch.

Scandinavia was an exception to the overall pattern. Here a rural society of property-owning farmers provided the firm basis for a democratic tendency. Conservatism was based in the cities. Norway, attached to the Swedish Crown, was the most democratic state in Europe. By its constitution of 1814, sovereignty lay with the people represented by an elected Parliament. The economic benefits of constitutionalism were evident. The country's heavy debts were paid off by 1850, and as prosperity grew, Norwegians came to own no less than a quarter of Europe's merchant marine.[20]

Republics spread across Latin America following the collapse of the imperial power of Spain and Portugal under Napoleonic hammer blows. But they subsisted largely by the grace of the Royal Navy, as Britain in 1822 forbade any attempt at recolonization. Latin America began its long career of largely faux constitutionalism. Peasants were bound to the tribute-exacting *hacienda* system, and their mighty landlords shared power with the Church and the military. A privileged minority monopolized land and public office, and by accepting foreign capital and goods they destroyed domestic manufactures. British merchants and financiers replaced those of Spain. Though slavery slowly died away, the colonial societies survived largely intact, with rigid social stratification, economic underdevelopment, *caudillos* (military strongmen), army governments, and impermeable ruling classes.

The norm was restored absolutism. Opposition to the absolutist state was weak but its potential was growing due to the beginnings of profound economic change. In the first decades of the nineteenth century, manufacturing in the European countryside expanded considerably, via the putting-out system. Capitalists sold raw materials to peasants, who processed them in their cottages or workshops, and the capitalists then bought back the worked-up commodities for further processing or re-sale. Such cottage industries produced textiles in particular, but also metal goods. Hundreds of thousands in rural areas lived entirely or substantially by their labour in cottage industry. Such proto-industry often allowed for dense population in land-poor areas. This could lead to industrialization proper, but also to disaster when swamped by British competition, as for the Flemish linen industry in 1846.

In the years after Napoleon's fall, Great Britain's industrialization proper began to spread out to Ulster in Ireland, northern France, Belgium, and the Rhineland, picking up pace from about 1830 (when the British economy surpassed 3 per cent annual growth for the first time). Cotton textile production proved rapidly amenable to revolutionized industrial production. Usually the transition to industrialized textile production lasted only a decade, rapidly assimilating or ruining domestic spinners and weavers working from their cottages. Industrialized cotton production had taken over in Britain by 1800, in France and Belgium by 1830, in Germany by 1840. 'Hot-spots', where good transport links, traditions of wage labour, networks of entrepreneurs, and abundant natural resources coincided, developed as integrated centres of industry, fostering coal extraction and metallurgy as well as textiles. The Belgian/French Ardennes, Upper Silesia, South Wales, and the German Saar were centres of innovation. The processing of food, building, tailoring, cobbling, and soap production remained skilled artisanal professions and resisted industrialization well into the latter half of the nineteenth century.

Alexis de Tocqueville (1805–1859) observed that as wealth commodified, circulating 'with inconceivable rapidity', the social and political power of the stable landed aristocracy inexorably receded.[21] The early pioneers of industrialization tended to come from the ranks of improving artisans, wealthy farmers, and organizers of domestic manufacture. Both the aristocracy and the lower classes were notably under-represented. The entrepreneurial capitalist class were not, in fact, particularly close to political power, but nor were they seeking to gain it. They were disproportionately made up of out-groups, excluded from mainstream society and at best marginal within the political nation, but with strong community bonds of trust. So it was nonconformists in England, Presbyterians in Ulster, Calvinists in Alsace, Catholic Belgians in the United Netherlands, Protestants in northern France, and Old Believers in Russia who were in the vanguards of entrepreneurial capitalism.

Certainly in the first decades of the nineteenth century the middle class grew in number and social weight. Their political identity, however, remained complex. On the whole, the middle class in this century amounted to between 5 and 20 per cent of the population, depending on time and place. The percentage was higher in the industrially developed north-east of Europe, lower in the east and the south.[22] The bourgeoisie was a fairly closed group. While all classes got richer, there were few transfers between them.[23] Within the middle classes, however, social mobility was considerable, both up and down. Despite certain complications, the distinction between bourgeoisie on the one hand and workers on the other was clear enough. Even the average shopkeeper in a big city possessed at least twenty times as much capital as the average artisan.[24]

The intellectual leaders of the bourgeoisie were generally professionals, often sons of clergymen, private employees, or petty officials. Professions were keen to see the destruction of manorialism and the aristocracy-dominated civil service in the expectation that they would fill the bureaucratic and judicial posts thus opened to talent rather than birth. Such professionals functioned as the political arm of the bourgeoisie and as standard-bearers of the demand for a reconstruction of the state on the basis of merit, and they tended to dominate the lower houses of such parliamentary legislatures as existed. Prince Metternich (1773–1859), chancellor of Austria during the 'Vormärz' (pre-1848) years, wryly identified the promoters of subversion in a memorandum to the Tsar of Russia:

> The great mass of the people are tranquil spectators of... revolutions.... A few are carried off by the torrent, but the wishes of the immense majority are to maintain a repose.... It is principally the middle class of society which this moral gangrene has affected.... In all four countries [France, Germany, Spain, and Italy] the agitated

classes are principally composed of wealthy men—real cosmopolitans, securing their personal advantage at the expense of any order of things whatever—paid state officials, men of letters, lawyers, and the individuals charged with the public education.... This cry, since 1815, has been Constitution.... Everywhere it means change and trouble.[25]

It was not the case that the middle class was uniformly or even by majority subversive. Many who joined the subversive groups of Restoration Europe, such as the *Carbonari* in Italy and the *Burschenschaften* in Germany, were young men trained for over-subscribed professions, notably law and medicine, which were overwhelmingly bourgeois rather than noble professions.[26] *Carbonari* recruiters, however, were certainly aware that the 'unprejudiced peasant is more enthusiastic than the rich man, the property owner'.[27] Peaceable Masonic Lodges were more congenial liberal haunts (and well organized even in Latin America, even if more or less null politically). In Spain and Italy liberal revolutionaries were disproportionately military men; in Poland and Hungary they were aristocratic. Many of Russia's revolutionaries were in the official and military classes, numerous liberals in Germany were in the lower reaches of the state bureaucracy, while everywhere liberalism was strong amongst the professions and literary trade (newspapers and academics). Actual entrepreneurs were not conspicuous in political activity of any kind. Richard Cobden, British free-trader and liberal, praised 'the great capitalist class' for their 'inexhaustible purses, which they opened freely' when 'their pecuniary interests' and 'pride as an order was at stake'.[28] Nevertheless, Cobden remained unconvinced that wealthy capitalists in particular were capable of giving a lead to the 'People', where 'a great and impassable gulf separates the workman from his employer'.[29]

This gulf was tending to grow. By the 1830s, the proletariat had become an obviously permanent feature of industrializing societies. For the first time, those labourers without hope of owning individually the means by which they made a living had moved from the economic margins (carrying out casual work, portering, and so on) to the very forefront of the most dynamic sectors of the economy. The apprentices and smallholders that had, like the *sans-culottes*, shared with the bourgeoisie an intense commitment to living by private property were being slowly displaced by wage workers. These proletarians, because they needed to prioritize the stability of paid work, could not blithely accept the sanctity of private ownership of the means of production. To be sure, only in Britain did factory workers approach half the manufacturing labour force by the mid-nineteenth century. But across Europe, the artisanal condition was being steadily proletarianized, in that labour was being treated more and more as a commodity to be hired, fired, and remunerated in line with market conditions.[30] The liberal economist, Bruno Hildebrand, in 1848 claimed that the bulk of artisans 'must at present be considered proletarians' because they lived 'from hand to mouth just like the day labourers'.[31] In fact, this proto-proletarianization was in respects arrested and sometimes even reversed after 1848, but it was a striking feature of first-wave industrialization. 'Master' artisans survived, but 'journeymen', working for these masters in small workshops, proliferated.

As early as 1830, the French journalist and Deputy Secretary of State, Louis-François Bertin de Vaux, warned deputies in the French National Assembly:

> The barbarians threatening society are most definitely not in the Caucasus; neither are they on the steppes of Tartary. They are in our manufacturing cities' slums.... The bourgeoisie needs to know well the real state of things; it needs to know well its own place. Beneath it, the bourgeoisie has a malcontent population of proletarians, a population that wants to change. This then is the danger in modern society: it is from there that the barbarians might emerge to destroy it. Let us not give political rights or national arms to those that possess nothing.[32]

Most European liberals, however, evinced sympathy as much as fear. They looked with concern at the growth of insecurity and destitution amongst the burgeoning wage-earning class.[33] As 1848 approached, liberals were often conceding the necessity for progressive taxation on grounds of equity.[34] Liberalism, thus, was not a narrow creed of the thrusting bourgeoisie, intent upon amassing wealth beyond memory. As Richard Cobden said, 'mine is that masculine species of charity, which would lead me to inculcate in the minds of the labouring classes the love of independence, the privilege of self-respect, the disdain of being patronized or petted, the desire to accumulate, and the ambition to rise'.[35] Because of disillusion with Enlightened absolutist monarchs and popular revolutionary violence, however, Restoration Europe saw a new liberal interest in the bourgeoisie as the class who, in emancipating themselves, would emancipate society.

Liberal celebration of the importance of the middle classes, paradoxically, owed much to its perceived passivity. It was precisely their desire to be left in peace that distinguished them from chateau-burning peasants, rioting urban workers, and (most particularly) conniving aristocrats. The German philosopher Georg Hegel (1770–1831) argued that while the bourgeoisie certainly desire good government—'sense of freedom and order has...arisen mainly in towns'—it was as a means to private activity, because in 'the estate of trade and industry, the individual has to rely on himself'.[36]

Liberal political theory consciously rejected the idea that political power should be focused on any one class.[37] Discussions of the middle class vaunted their power to permeate state and society with bourgeois values without the need to behave as a directly governing elite.[38] Thomas Macaulay, the English liberal Whig, rhapsodized on the middle classes as the crucial buffer between 'narrow oligarchy above' and 'infuriated multitude below'. They served more as a still centre rather than an active political power in their own right.[39] The model of 'organic development' was adopted. National histories became lengthy stories of advancing liberty, rationality, and commerce. As such, numerous historical agents were recruited by the historians as unwitting actors in the great drama of liberal emergence. The 'bourgeoisie' were celebrated in such narratives, but as only one element of 'the people', alongside monarchs, aristocrats, and the masses. Though allowed certain crucial virtues—moderation, commercial instincts, economic dynamism—the bourgeoisie were not attributed sole custody of the liberal cause.[40]

The insistence of civic republicanism that free citizens should participate in governance was replaced by liberal thinkers with a more passive desire that citizens be 'left alone'—laissez-faire.[41] The French liberal, Benjamin Constant, defined 'modern' liberty as a partnership in which civil society had the right to 'influence', and the state an obligation to take such influence, to a 'greater or lesser degree...into account'.[42] As Macaulay similarly wrote:

> Our rulers will best promote the improvement of the nation by strictly confining themselves to their own legitimate duties, by leaving capital to find its most lucrative course, commodities their fair price, industry and intelligence their natural reward, idleness and folly their natural punishment, by maintaining peace, by defending property, by diminishing the price of law, and by observing strict economy in every department of the state. Let the Government do this: the People will assuredly do the rest.[43]

This notion of distinct spheres reinforced the idea that the virtue of the middle class lay particularly in its being averse to ruling politically. Liberals did believe that governments should be responsible to taxpayers and property owners. This appealed as a means of influencing and constraining the state without reconstituting it. The relationship between government and propertied tax-classes would be mutually supportive, not antagonistic. Giacomo Durando (1807–1894), an Italian soldier and liberal politician, argued in 1846 that 'in the mutual pact established by representative institutions between sovereigns and nations, taxpayers find a guarantee of the right employment of the new taxes, and creditors a moral security for their loans. Whereas, if the cause of dynasties is separate from that of peoples, the force of public credit is diminished by half'.[44] Constitutionalism, therefore, would increase state credit. Moreover, liberalism was best calculated to absorb popular political pressures into a party system. Said the Italian patriot Massimo d'Azeglio (1798–1866) in 1857:

> Free governments in general have the virtue of converting factions into parties, representative governments the virtue of leading these parties from the market-place to the chamber. Another virtue of these same governments, but especially of monarchies, is to reduce the complex series of parties to the smallest possible number, or even to two, the ministry and the opposition.[45]

Liberals favoured a strong executive government bound by law. 'Who should rule?' a German liberal asked rhetorically, answering: 'Legality, the law, and the king as the law's guardian and fulfilment.'[46] Liberalism, thus, made two key related claims. A middle class rooted in commercial society would support a strong state fiscally so long as its interests were protected through some form of constitutionalism. Constitutionalism, in turn, would regulate the political sphere, protecting against a palace coup or a popular revolution. Bourgeois civil society, eminently commercial, was seeking a mutually beneficial trade with the *ancien régime*, not a hostile takeover. The liberal expectation was that constitutionalism would benefit all classes, while gifting the state 'the necessary strength to do good'.[47] The middle classes were seen not as a new political ruling class but that stratum most moderate in political appetite and most energetic in commerce.

## THE BRITISH MODEL

In Britain the Crown and gentry respected commercial civil society as mutually beneficial and necessary to their consensual coexistence. The urban middle classes themselves, however, were definitely excluded from political power. English politics was certainly far more liberal than in any other power. However, it was not clear whether this liberalism was tenable in the long run. The hitherto successful British model, established by the Glorious Revolution, rested upon a commercial middle class limited in wealth compared to the landed classes, and thus easily kept in its place. But with burgeoning industrialization redistributing the balance of wealth, an uncertain future now stretched ahead. One possibility was that the middle classes would continue to be marginalized politically, but to the long-term cost of Britain's capitalist dynamism. Another possibility was that industrial and mercantile growth would overwhelm the aristocracy and shatter the stability of the constitutional monarchy. Whether a capitalist society could remain stable in the long term was at issue in Great Britain.

By the end of the Napoleonic Wars, it was evident that a gentry-banking nexus wielded disproportionate power in England. The state apparatus was principally in the hands of Justices of the Peace, appointed by the government from among the gentry, who, unpaid, managed policing, dispensed most local justice, and organized the assessment of taxes. These local elites were the backbone of the electoral process, and as magistrates recording votes cast in public they were in a position to intimidate the electorate. In 1829, at Newark, the Duke of Newcastle evicted 587 of his tenants for having voted against his preferred candidate. 'Is it presumed then that I am not to do what I will with my own?' he retorted to critics.[48] Though an egregious example, in general the control by gentry of electoral constituencies allowed it to sell parliamentary votes to the government in return for sinecures and influence.

The British government had initially paid for the war against France with loans, before adopting the income tax. Still, the annual debt charge, which had to be serviced by taxes on basic consumption goods, stood at £30 million in 1815, greater than the entire government outlay in the last year before the war. This was a massive and (given the revealed capacity of income tax) unnecessary diversion of money from the ordinary family budget to a small group of rich fund-holders. The executive state was worried, indeed, that it was losing power to the bankers, and insisted upon a return to the Gold Standard in 1819 to limit their political power. Robert Peel (1788–1850), a Tory MP, approved the resumption of gold convertibility as no less than 'a tactical blow against City and Bank in a constitutional battle for power and responsibility'.[49] It may have been a tactical strike but it was no strategic knock-out blow.

A provincial capitalist gentry and a metropolitan fiscal elite exercised a substantial grip on the British state. With the war concluded, two Acts were passed by Parliament that served this power bloc. The 'Corn Laws' reinforced the agricultural interest by ordinarily shutting out foreign wheat from the domestic market. Secondly, Parliament, in an act of 'ignorant impatience', as the Foreign Minister Lord

Castlereagh put it,[50] abolished the income tax. The very success of the gentry-financier nexus exposed it to popular opprobrium as 'The Thing'.[51] William Cobbett, a tribune of the labouring classes, attacked 'the unproductive classes', fund-holders, and clergy as responsible for imposing exactions; William Hazlitt sarcastically labelled them 'state paupers'.[52] Radicals hoped to break their political monopoly, which they held to be corrupting the state, with a reformed Parliament and universal male suffrage.

The post-war moment of triumph for the gentry-finance nexus exposed its inadequacy. It became increasingly apparent that this network was unable to keep the central state on starvation rations without imperilling its social hegemony. This was due, primarily, to the thinning and fracture of gentry-run local government outside its south-east England redoubt. In the north and west, centres of expanding manufacture, systems of gentry control were increasingly inadequate. Though clearly on a steep upward incline, English industrialization was prone to acute periodic crises (1816, 1819, 1826–9, 1837, 1842, 1848). Each downturn in the market threw into penury numerous workers, especially spinners and weavers of wool and cotton. The local gentry-controlled system of poor relief was evidently self-serving and breaking down.

Widespread popular agitation from 1816 to 1820 was met with state force (the Peterloo Massacre and repressive 'Six Acts' of 1819). It was noticeable that the coercive reserves of gentry authority—constables and watchmen—were wholly inadequate. On numerous occasions, following desperate appeals to central government by Justices of the Peace, the army was mobilized, exposing the inability of the gentry to maintain order. A more immediate revolutionary threat to gentry autonomy was evident in Ireland. Here the local elites—Justices of the Peace, town councils, juries—were Protestant, whereas the great mass of tenant farmers and many of the urban classes were Catholic. The Catholic Association, established in 1823 and led by the charismatic and hugely capable lawyer, Daniel O'Connell (1775–1847), demanded Catholic 'emancipation', that is, the right of Catholics to sit in Parliament. A massive mobilization of the large Catholic peasant electorate, led by the urban middle classes and buttressed by parish priests, defied gentry intimidation, and a revolutionary crisis loomed. Coerced, the government pressed for, and Parliament passed, an Act in 1829 removing most civil and political disabilities from Catholics.

With the July 1830 Revolution in France, advocates of franchise reform in England were emboldened. Some two hundred political associations, thickest on the ground in the industrial areas of the Midlands and north-east, sprang up to win Parliament from the gentry-financial nexus by pressing for franchise reform. They united workers and the middle class, comprising as they did artisans, shopkeepers, industrial workers, commercial and banking interests, military and other officials, and some progressive gentry. Birmingham was the epicentre, where a formidable Political Union coordinated vigorous agitation. A new government, led by Lord Grey and committed to an electoral Reform Bill, was supported by a coalition of liberal Tories and Whigs. There now followed a prolonged battle between government and opposition. The Whigs won a solid majority in the House of Commons, their first since

1783, but the aristocratic House of Lords continued to oppose Reform. Outraged popular opinion became semi-revolutionary. Workers and artisans rioted, while a more middle-class meeting in Birmingham announced plans to refuse the payment of taxes if the Reform Bill was not passed. It was hoped that by withdrawing deposits from banks, partisans of Reform could intimidate Wellington, leader of the obdurate Tories, by sparking a run on the pound: 'To Stop the Duke, Go for Gold'.[53] Thus did commercial civil society hope to bring pressure to bear.

It took a threat to pack the House of Lords with pro-government peers to finally pass the Great Reform Act in 1832. The electoral franchise was standardized and, to a degree, extended, though the property qualification was set at a substantial level. The electorate increased in the counties from 247,000 to 370,000, in the boroughs from 188,000 to 286,000. The Tories under Sir Robert Peel declined to attempt Repeal of the Act for fear of unsettling the 'peace' of the country.[54] In a minor-key second act, it was established that the executive would be responsible not to the monarch, but to the Reformed Parliament. When King William IV in 1834 dismissed the Whig ministry and asked the Tories to form a minority government, Tory leader Peel ultimately refused to serve on the grounds that executive government was untenable 'without control over the House of Commons'.[55] A Parliament responsive to commercial civil society, and a government responsible to the elected chamber of Parliament, had been achieved.

The Reformed Parliament set about cutting gentry governance down to size. By the Municipal Corporations Act (1835), it gave to all local taxpayers the right to vote for urban councils in nearly two hundred cities and towns. The New Poor Law Amendment Act of 1834 established Poor Law Unions, with their own elected officers and paid functionaries, to administer indoor relief for paupers. These Poor Law Unions exercised their powers independently of the Justices of the Peace, undermining local government by landed elites. The regular police force, organized in London since 1829, was in the 1840s rolled out across the cities. To oversee the overall system, a Local Government Board was established.[56] Thus was Victorian governance rebalanced away from the gentry. It was a key episode in constitutional history. Commercial civil society was no longer simply the passive base of a political nation comprising the executive state and the landed elites: the middle classes were made co-partners within the political nation.

## THE MODEL OF THE UNITED STATES

A more radical example of a modernizing country, though far less influential, was the United States. Here the primary problem was whether an executive state resting upon a commercial, bourgeois economy could maintain its vital interests. In the eighteenth century, the British government wished to see her colonies in North America contribute more substantially to their own defence, but this raised sharply the issue of whether the British Parliament had the authority to impose taxation on Americans. The famous rallying cry became 'No taxation without representation!' Campaigns for non-consumption of goods imported from Britain invoked, it is argued, a bourgeois ethic of virtue, in which the marketplace became the locus for active citizenship.[57] During a process of revolutionary radicalization, culminating in war against the Crown (1775–83), an American national consciousness coalesced and, with the help of French arms, British rule was ended and the United States of America established. The origin of revolutionary attitudes lay in the strong sense of local independence from the centralizing executive. This legacy meant that the original Confederation unifying the various colonies into the United States was particularly loose. The national government had very little capacity to finance itself and was nugatory in international relations, unable even to negotiate commercial treaties.[58] Replicating in less traumatic form the experience of the English Civil War and the French Revolution, North America had careered from an over-mighty executive to over-mighty representative institutions.

Support for a remedial strengthening of central government was particularly strong among the professional and propertied classes.[59] Their influence profoundly shaped the new Constitution drawn up in 1787, which created a strong central executive government contained within a framework of 'checks and balances'.[60] Overall, the framework was characterized by a substantial mistrust of unmediated public influence. Fisher Ames, a leading politician of the early republic, in an essay entitled 'The Mire of Democracy' (1805), wrote that the framers of the Constitution 'intended our government should be a *republic*, which differs more widely from a democracy than a democracy from a despotism'.[61] However, the Federalist party anticipated that a wide suffrage in a commercial economy would produce a bourgeois hegemony as workers and master artisans deferred to the organizers of trade and credit:

> Mechanics [workers] and manufacturers will always be inclined, with few exceptions, to give their votes to merchants in preference to persons of their own professions or trades.... They know that the merchant is their natural patron and friend; and they are aware that however great the confidence they may justly feel in their own good sense, their interests can be more effectually promoted by the merchant than by themselves.[62]

This observation that American democracy spontaneously defers to the wealthy elites was to have validity for a long time to come.

The new country set to consolidating its domestic market. A protective tariff was established and a national mint regularized currencies across the states. Thomas Jefferson (1743–1826), a champion of 'yeoman' property against the Northern merchant elite, led the Democratic Party. Jefferson argued that the Constitution should be interpreted so as to be sensitive to the local market and cultural conditions of small producers, not simply the nationwide interests of big producers and financiers. 'To the united nation belong our external and mutual relations,' he recommended to the Rhode Island Assembly in 1801, 'to each State, severally, the care of our persons, our property, our reputation and religious freedom.'[63] In 1800, Jefferson was elected president. He proved not at all averse, as it turned out, to using the national executive power in a most activist manner. He negotiated the Louisiana Purchase in 1803, which bought from the French a substantial swathe of territory. This expensive acquisition was itself indicative of the state's vastly improved credit, a side effect of stable constitutionalism. Expansion westwards greatly increased the scope for small property worked by free labour, and it was possible now for Democrats to favour a strong national government regularizing property rights without fear that it would destroy independent producers. Over the course of the 1820s, universal male suffrage spread, both in state and presidential elections. The election as president of Andrew Jackson (1767–1845) in 1828 was a milestone. Jackson was identified as representative of the common, hard-working, self-sufficient small property owner. He stood up for economic individualism, a property-owning democracy, as against the sway of landlords and capital. Jackson was hailed as a symbol of the 'new democracy'. The United States proved its case by demonstrating that democracy, capital accumulation, and class hierarchies could indeed coexist.

## CONCLUSION

The French monarchical state had been keen to apply *idées anglaises* in a controlled fashion, to foster commercialism and bolster its rickety fiscal base. Once the gyre of revolution took hold, however, it became imperative to smash and rebuild the *ancien régime* state apparatus for fear of its counter-revolutionary vengeance. The artisanal *sans-culottes* provided a formidable force with which to secure the urban areas, but at the cost of alienating much of the peasantry who feared a tyranny of the towns. The bourgeoisie—being only partly engaged in time-consuming production, because particularly reliant on investments in government bonds, and long integrated with the ennobled but mostly administrative *noblesse de robe*—perhaps felt itself to be peculiarly well adapted for taking up the reins of governmental power directly. However, in the end, they could not fill the gap left by the collapse of the aristocratic governing elites, and Napoleonic militarism colonized the state. Britain bankrolled the anti-Napoleonic coalition, but faced its own difficulties thereafter in recalibrating the alliance of aristocracy, gentry, and bourgeois civil society. The Great Reform Act, achieved without revolution, was an impressive model for attentive continental liberals. Across the Atlantic, American democracy relied upon a natural linkage of interest between the labouring masses, with eyes still fixed on the prospect of owning small property, and the elites of merchants, manufacturers, and sundry plutocrats. At least in the absence of a 'parasitic' aristocracy, free-market commercialism appeared to encourage pan-class politics.

# 3
# Holding Back the Tide

Between 1815 and 1848, Britain (and to a lesser extent America) were widely recognized in Europe as being highly successful. Their examples of free-market commercialism, laissez-faire, a strong middle class, and a constitutionalism that circumscribed the state but strengthened its fiscal sinews, were unquestionably impressive and acknowledged as such. Nonetheless, the applicability of their constitutional models, having emerged adventitiously and behind the natural defences of the Channel and Atlantic Ocean, were not considered to be easily exportable. They inspired liberalism and intrigued statesmen, but provided models of dubious applicability to European sovereigns.

## HOLY ALLIANCE EUROPE

Liberalism, on the British, utilitarian model was widely accepted as a doctrine conducive to economic growth and modernization. England was praised by an Italian periodical as 'so industrious, commercially so active, so enterprising, in a word, mistress of the earth', but the writer also admitted ruefully that Britain's development had been fortuitously organic.[1] Given the experience of the French Revolution, European elites were not anxious to experiment with constitutional reform. They mostly assumed that the British experience of accidental, gradual evolution could not be replicated. Metternich, Austria's chancellor, was convinced that destabilization of any kind could only be for the worse. 'The basis of modern policy is and must be repose,' he wrote in 1817. 'Among the causes of the tremendous confusion characterizing present-day Europe', he argued:

> is the transplantation of British institutions to the continent, where they are in complete contradiction to existing conditions, so that their application becomes either illusory or distorted. The so-called 'British school' has been the cause of the French Revolution and the consequences of this revolution, so anti-British in tendency, devastate Europe today.[2]

He was even more convinced that the United States model was not exportable. While the subordination of government to representative institutions demonstrably encouraged a vibrant, competitive civil society, it made for weak executive state action. While this might be tolerable in the Americas, where space and the overwhelming preponderance of the United States made international collisions less likely, it would never do in Europe where war and revolution were intimately entwined. 'Democracy is a truth in America,' Metternich averred, but 'in Europe it is a falsehood'.[3] Perhaps in the future the advantages of the British and American models could be reproduced in continental Europe. In the medium term, however, only the protection of Crown prerogatives, aristocratic authority, and churchly influence under the carapace of absolutism could ensure that the disastrous spiral of revolution would be avoided.

Whilst the European absolutisms looked enviously at British economic performance in particular, they saw no way of allowing commercial civil society anything like the same scope without undermining the authority of Crown, aristocracy, and Church. As one industrialist cheerfully put it, 'the locomotive is the hearse that will carry absolutism and feudalism to the graveyard'.[4] European absolutisms, thus, were prepared to forgo economic development rather than risk a political liberalization. Pope Gregory XVI (1831–1846), for example, refused to permit the building of railways in the Papal States of central Italy for fear that they would 'carry fewer goods than ideas'.[5] Similarly, absolutisms had to forgo the fiscal strength and credit that came with consensual taxation agreed through free parliaments. They consciously chose fiscal weakness as the necessary price for refusing legislative independence to representative assemblies. In 1837 the King of Hanover even cancelled new taxes so as to rescind a recently conceded Constitution.[6]

Constitutionalism was granted by absolutist states only in exceptional circumstances. So, while the Tsar was an autocratic ruler with illimitable sovereignty, that part of the Polish Kingdom incorporated in the Russian empire was permitted a version of its original constitution. Not coincidentally, it was economically vigorous and the most productive fiscal resource for the autocracy.[7] The most important European absolutism in the years after 1815 was based round Austria. Here the strengths and weaknesses of absolutism were perhaps most evident. The Hapsburg emperor, Francis II (ruling, inter alia, Austria, Hungary, and north Italy), disposed of absolute governing authority. Much of the administration of the empire, however, relied upon the free service of the aristocracy. Customs duties were so high as to be almost prohibitory, but in practice officials allowed massive smuggling. Trade was simply not being formally recorded: in the three years to 1844, official statistics purported to show only one silk garment entering the country.[8] The potential advantages of constitutionalism were widely understood. Baron Victor von Andrian-Werburg, an official of the Imperial Chancellery, published anonymously in 1841 a book, *Austria and Her Future*, in which he bemoaned the empire's recourse to private loans which left her deeply indebted. He urged the necessity of a parliamentary imperial Diet to authorize adequate domestic taxation.[9] It was not at all clear, however, that the House of Habsburg could survive such an initiative; it was certainly not inclined to take the chance.

The Habsburg empire, typically of absolutisms, ruthlessly exploited commercial civil society where it had developed within its domains. Politically oppressed and relatively commercialized, Austria's recently expanded north Italian territories were in the unfortunate position of being a classic absolutist milch-cow. Despite comprising less than an eighth of the population of the empire, Lombardy-Venetia provided about a third of the emperor's revenues. Cesare Correnti, a revolutionary of minor noble background, complained that 'thirty-three millions are taken out of the country [Lombardy] every year without it receiving anything in exchange but contempt and insults. These thirty-three millions, together with the rich takings of the sister province of Venetia, sustain the dying credits of the empire.'[10] If bourgeois civil society had little ability to fend off the absolutist state, a well-established aristocracy could much more successfully contend with the Crown. Austria struggled to overawe its Hungarian possessions where aristocratic 'historic rights' had to be taken into account. The imperial government's attempts to take control of the kingdom's administration directly by sending in commissioners foundered as local officials concealed records, seals, even keys to archives. The emperor was forced to back down, and convene a mostly aristocratic Hungarian Diet (a parliament) at Presburg in 1825.[11] The failure of Vienna to extract taxes without conceding representation provides a stark example of the limits of early nineteenth-century absolutism.

Monarchs might occasionally brag that their soldiery could levy taxation non-consensually—'the soldiers are mine, and if I want money, I shan't ask you twice,' Francis I of Austria was supposed to have loftily rebutted petitioners—but in reality there was a trade-off between executive state power and absolutism.[12] The states of Restoration Europe deliberately 'downsized' their military capability to reduce the need for a convincing fiscal mechanism in the form of a representative legislature. A stern policy of inoculation against revolution meant, in effect, a pacifist attitude to international relations.

A partial yet instructive exception was Prussia. This German kingdom took considerable risks to develop its fiscal capacity and commercial civil society to the maximum extent compatible with the continued existence of an absolutist executive state. It attempted a controlled revolution from above. After catastrophic defeat at the hands of France in 1806, leading state bureaucrats, Gerhard von Scharnhorst, Karl von Hardenberg, and Karl von Stein, overhauled the structure of the state. Stein made clear that the aristocracy as a governing class had failed: 'The aristocracy of Prussia is a burden to the nation, because the members of this caste are found in great numbers, are poor and full of claims, receiving emoluments, occupying official posts, and demanding privileges and precedence of every kind.'[13] The spirit of reform, according to Hardenberg, was 'revolution in the good sense of the word', to introduce 'democratic principles in a monarchical state'.[14] The aim was to strengthen the fiscal sinews of the state. This amounted to the lifting of mercantilist restrictions on commerce, and the rationalization of taxation so as not to penalize the accumulation of capital. Formerly strict classifications, which barred nobles from commerce and prevented peasants moving into wage labour, were largely abandoned by decrees in 1807 and 1808. In 1811 peasants on private estates were made full owners of the land they worked, but at the heavy price of giving up a portion of it to their former landlords. The 'junker' aristocracy retained a good deal of judicial and police power over the localities. This was an attempt by the executive state to triangulate between aristocratic authority in the provinces and commercial civil society. The scheme was designed to improve tax collection so as to refurbish the military power of the state. Thus all able-bodied men were made liable for conscription. Because the Prussian army was limited, by a treaty imposed by Napoleon, to forty-two thousand men at any one time, repeated levies were cycled through three years' service with the colours to build up a trained reserve. Quite by accident Prussia had stumbled on the ideal balance, in terms of military efficacy in the coming circumstances of the nineteenth century, between that professionalism and loyalty to the regime characterizing a standing army, and the large numbers and popular enthusiasm of a national militia. This system would prove to be a war-winner, and would eventually be adopted by all Europe.

In 1820, 'in order to give every security to the native and foreign holders of Prussian stock', the king pledged not to contract a further loan without the consent and guarantee of a future assembly of the Estates of the Kingdom.[15] The logic was state adoption of constitutionalism to build up its credit rating with the money markets. The king, however, was particularly frightened by the 1820–1 revolutions in Spain and Italy, and rather than risk a parliament, he disavowed new loans. New income could be raised from commercialism without parliamentary sanction. In 1818 a royal official, Karl Georg Maassen, was charged with setting up a single customs zone for the whole kingdom. To discourage smuggling, Maassen set tariffs very low by the standards of the time and region, at 10 per cent. It was no easy task to consolidate and protect a kingdom-wide market, as Prussia's territory was divided and pockmarked by sovereign statelets independent of the Prussian Crown. These and contiguous sovereign entities, therefore, were enticed into an expanded customs union, formally inaugurated as the Zollverein in 1834. Prussia found itself coordinating the market integration of the pan-German zone, and fostering the expansion of bourgeois civil society. Prussia's experiment, a relatively little remarked third way in contrast to British-style constitutionalism and Austrian-style absolutism, prefigured the state- building strategies adopted much more widely in later decades. It demonstrated that an absolutist executive state could encourage commercialism and adopt elements of constitutionalism without thereby abandoning altogether a powerful aristocratic state responsible only to itself.

## INTERNATIONAL RELATIONS

In general, continental powers abandoned expensive expansionist policies that would have required pacts with parliaments (with the major exception of France's conquest of Algeria from 1830) and Britain was left nearly alone to command the oceans. Armies became instruments turned inwards, which, as Geoffrey Best observes, 'unprecedentedly made "policing" seem for many their *raison d'être*'.[16] The states of Europe sacrificed full-scale military capability for counter-revolutionary stability, and war as a tactical weapon of dynastic aggrandisement was virtually disavowed.[17] The anti-revolutionary German thinker, Fredrich von Gentz, admitted that, in the absence of strong, tax-raising representative assemblies, 'financial distress' was 'the common malady of all European governments'. This 'penury of all the governments' meant that the Great Powers were intent on avoiding war: by maintaining the 'general peace' they protected 'the political system'.[18] A reactionary peace settled on post-Napoleonic Europe.

Counter-revolutionary expeditionary forces were internationalized, so as to cheapen their costs. As early as 1817, Metternich called on states to 'openly pool their resources and their energies to stifle everywhere that revolutionary spirit'.[19] Indeed, a series of Great Power congresses, all held on Austrian territory—at Troppau in Silesia in 1820, Laybach in Carniola in 1821, and Verona in Venetia in 1823—arranged for the armed quashing of revolution. Austria, Prussia, and Russia (the 'Holy Alliance') asserted that 'the overthrow of a Government . . . by revolution' would itself be treated as a hostile act against their sovereignty by virtue of its example propagating 'revolution and confusion'.[20] However, Foreign Secretary Lord Castlereagh, for Britain, rejected reactionary interventionism altogether. He admitted the dangers of revolution, but insisted that Britain's 'System of Government, strongly popular, and National in its character' meant that public opinion would never stand for intervention in foreign affairs 'upon abstract and speculative Principles of Precaution'.[21] Nevertheless, when in 1820 no fewer than four revolutions broke out in Spain, Portugal, Naples, and Piedmont-Sardinia, they were crushed by foreign interventions authorized by the Holy Alliance.

There was a further wave of revolution between late 1829 and the winter of 1832, a fifty-month crisis, which affected Britain, Spain, Poland, and the Balkans, but most dramatically France and the Netherlands. Constitutionalism was at the centre of this upheaval.[22] Revolution in Belgium led to secession from the United Netherlands. Here, liberals and Catholics had warily moved into alliance against their Protestant Dutch rulers. Royal forces in Brussels, on 23 September 1830, overreacted to fairly mild bourgeois agitation by seizing the upper part of the city with ten thousand troops and attacking the plebeian lower city. They were repulsed by barricades and street fighters, and the Belgian provinces rose in revolt. A rebel Constitutional Congress was elected on a mostly bourgeois wealth franchise, some forty-four thousand voters out of a population of about two and a half million. The Congress finally proposed a constitutional Belgian monarchy. Sovereignty was to be vested in 'the people', the monarch ruling through ministers who were responsible not to him but to the elected parliamentary chambers. Both the Senate and the Chamber of Representatives were elected by a property-based franchise, which was quite wide for the time. Personal and civil liberties were defined and guaranteed, and Church was separated from State. The Belgian constitution became a new model for European liberals to add to those various adopted by France since 1789.

Britain and France, acting as a counterweight to the Holy Alliance, ensured that Belgian independence was recognized. Austria, Prussia, and Russia publicly restated their right to counter-revolutionary intervention in the Münchengraetz Convention of September, 1833. The following year, Britain, France, Spain, and Portugal joined in a league of the four constitutional monarchies of the West. The British Foreign Secretary, Lord Palmerston (1784–1865), posed both as the champion of British national interest and of liberal ideals. He lost no opportunity to lecture the dynasties of Europe that there would be, in L. C. B. Seaman's paraphrase, 'no stability (and certainly no progress) in Europe while rulers refused to adopt a constitutional, representative system of government on the English model'.[23] Britain even secretly negotiated with liberal oppositionists in absolutist countries. Nonetheless, Britain saw itself as promoting European civilization in general on a global scale. While there was enormous and growing demand in Europe for Chinese tea, for example, China had little need for Western goods. Britain, therefore, exported to China raw cotton and opium acquired from India. When, in 1839, the Qing government attempted to prohibit the import of opium, and detained the entire foreign community at Guangzhou, Britain retaliated militarily, in what became known as the Opium War (1839–42). By the Treaty of Nanjing (1842)—the first of what later Chinese nationalists called the 'unequal treaties'—China ceded Hong Kong, allowed British nationals 'extraterritoriality' (exemption from Chinese laws), and substantially opened up its markets. This was the beginning of a process by which the Qing state progressively lost control of its tax base, and foreign interests protected, oversaw, and benefited from the development of Chinese markets. Britain having opened the door, Japan, Russia, Germany, France, and Belgium each eventually demanded and gained 'spheres of influence' in China, which involved extra-territorial rights and command of regional market economies. Constitutionalism allowed Britain to punch above its weight in world affairs, whereas absolutist powers punched below their weight.

## BOURGEOIS MONARCHY IN FRANCE, CARLISM IN SPAIN

France remained the key continental country for liberalism. Here an expansive bourgeois civil society provided the base on which a restored semi-absolutist monarchy manoeuvred with liberals on the left and aristocratic reactionaries on the right. Ironically, the victorious allies preferred for France a constitution (or Charter, to emphasize that it was a gift from the king) to rein in excitedly vengeful counter-revolutionaries. France, therefore, provided the second model after Britain of constitutional monarchy.[24] Louis XVIII, re-established by force of foreign arms, conceded a legislature. The Lower Chamber would have primary control of the budget, approving taxation. The king would choose his own ministers, but they would be 'responsible', presumably to the legislature but this was left rather vague.

The Revolution and Napoleon had massively built up the already powerful *ancien régime* state apparatus. The tax system of the Revolution was retained in 1814, and indirect taxes were reintroduced on salt, wine, and tobacco. The standing army based upon conscription was also retained, though its loyalty to the regime was vitiated by its strong Bonapartist sympathies. While Britain was largely ruled by a decentralized gentry elite, France was administered exclusively by officials appointed centrally from Paris. Who controlled the ministers controlled the executive power. Throughout the Restoration period, political contestation in France centred on a struggle to control the selection of ministers, the scope of the franchise, and regulation of the press.

The 'Ultras', who took control of the legislature, were more reactionary than the king. 'Long live the King in spite of himself!' was their slogan. Their proposals to abolish the national debt, replace centrally appointed permanent prefects with seigneurial justice, and restore confiscated estates, would have created a gentry rule independent of —and far more conservative than—the central state. As a means to an end, the Ultra Chamber sought to make the king's ministers responsible to itself, the better to destroy the Charter. Further, they argued for a form of conservative 'democratization': an extension of suffrage coupled with indirect elections, in the expectation that this would mobilize richer peasants behind the gentry. Constitutional liberals rallied in defence of the king's right to appoint and dismiss his own ministers. Liberals were known as *doctrinaires*, as they cleaved to the 'doctrine' of the 1814 Charter. Pierre Paul Royer-Collard, the constitutionalist leader, insisted during the early years of the Restoration that 'the day it is established that the Chambers can reject the king's ministers and impose others on him, our royalty is lost'. Only by 1826 was he moved to declare that 'the Chamber can withdraw its support from a minister when he violates the Charter'.[25] It was this rather unusual political division, with the liberals supporting constitutional monarchy against the excessive parliamentarianism of the Ultras, which encouraged liberals to promote a myth of the 'bourgeoisie', hitherto an amorphous term.[26] The *doctrinaires*, at whose head were Royer-Collard and François Guizot (1787–1874), developed a theory of the *juste milieu*.

For the nineteenth-century bourgeois, Guizot argued (echoing Benjamin Constant), the expanding state as a taxing and organizing power had at last become inescapable. The bourgeois could no longer limit himself to private affairs; he had to parley with government.[27] But this was all to the good. The moneyed middle classes were demarcated both from the aristocracy seeking privileges and jobs at court and in government, and from the unruly urban plebeians. 'In the class above,' Guizot declared, 'there exists a tendency to dominate against which we must be on guard. In the class below there is ignorance and the lack of independence as a result of which there is a complete lack of political capacity.'[28] The bourgeoisie celebrated by the *doctrinaires* were not practitioners of the political arts like the aristocracy, nor were they a socially radical threat. Their precise virtue was that they would let the government get on with the job of governing so long as it did not interfere with civic and commercial freedom. As a class, thus, they squared the circle, being a basis for constitutional government but not thereby interfering with the necessary prerogatives of state-executive decision-making and action. Their modus operandi was in contrast (it was argued) to the self-seeking aristocracy who used the political sphere as a mode of wealth appropriation. So, as Guizot argued, the bourgeoisie did not conspire to impose itself, but was simply 'a powerful and formidable fact' that the state disrespected at its peril. The pre-eminent class of commercialism presented a 'a theory in action, capable of defending itself against opponents. Past centuries had prepared the way for it; the French Revolution proclaimed it. All new interests promptly attached themselves to the bourgeoisie, whose security could not be disturbed without danger to the established order.'[29] The point here was that bourgeois interests coincided with good order, not that the bourgeoisie as such was an active political agent equivalent to the aristocracy. The political concept of the bourgeoisie, thus, was fully fleshed out in the somewhat peculiar circumstances of Restoration France. Liberals, anxious to defend the executive state from aristocratic engrossments, refined the ideological construction of the bourgeois as a pre-eminently 'apolitical class', the ideal basis for a rational state. Francois Guizot and his *doctrinaire* colleagues did much to 'invent' the bourgeoisie as such. *Juste milieu* came to define the bourgeoisie politically.

*Doctrinaire* reasoning was apparent, in strikingly heterodox form, in the writings of Henri Comte de Saint-Simon (1760–1825), a peculiar hybrid of absolutist, liberal, and socialist. Saint-Simon perceptively observed that a commodified society, in which 'the producer will depend solely on the consumer for his salary', was inexorably emerging. The power of the 'industrial class' consisted in its 'being taxed only with its consent'.[30] The future, he thought, lay in the eclipse altogether of the political sphere by an efficiently administered civil society dominated by these industrial managers. The logic he applied was classically liberal in a sense, but without liberalism's eschewal of direct bourgeois control of the state:

> the political inclination of the vast majority of society is to be governed as cheaply as possible; to be governed as little as possible; to be governed by the most capable men, and in a manner which will completely ensure public tranquillity. Now the only means of satisfying in these various respects, the desires of the majority, consists in entrusting to the most important industrials the task of directing the public function; for the most important industrials are most interested in the maintenance of tranquillity; they are most interested in economy in public expenditure; they are most interested in restricting arbitrary power.[31]

For most social radicals, however, a decisive shift in their thinking came with the publication in 1828 of Philippe Buonarroti's memoir of Babeuf and his 'Conspiracy of Equals'. This lauded propertyless workers as selfless. Being without hope of individual advancement through acquisition of private productive property, they lacked particular interests distinct from universal interests.[32] Though rough in argument, it set socialism on its feet as a specifically proletarian cause.

\* \* \*

When Charles X, himself an Ultra, succeeded Louis XVIII in 1824, he applied the creditworthiness of the constitutional state to the benefit of his returned émigré loyalists. The émigrés were granted a thousand million francs as compensation for estates confiscated by the Revolution.[33] This was financed by a new issue of government bonds, making necessary a reduction of interest repayments on all bonds—old and new—from 5 per cent to 3 per cent. Government securities were a major source of income for the bourgeoisie, and so by this means opposition to the Crown was solidified. The new Chamber elected in 1827 was anti-Ultra. The liberal majority in the Chamber contemplated refusing to approve any subsequent budget and to call on the public to withhold taxes. The *Journal des Débats*, a newspaper of the liberal left-centre political faction, threatened tax rebellion in August 1829: 'The Charter has now an authority against which all the efforts of despotism will fail. The people will pay a thousand millions to the law; they will not pay two million to the ordinances of a minister. If illegal taxes were demanded, a Hampden would arise to crush them!'[34] The tax-strike was the bourgeois political weapon par excellence, while Hampden's name was invoked as an ominous reference to the champion of the English Parliament against Charles I in 1640.

Charles X decided upon a coup d'état. Four ordinances proclaimed on 26 July 1830 dissolved the recently elected Chamber even before it had met, tightened censorship, and called elections for a new Chamber reduced in size and tied more tightly both to the landed interest and manipulation by the ministry.[35] Despite the coup, duly elected Constitutionalist deputies had already arrived in Paris. They met and agreed on legal resistance but no program of action. It was in fact revolutionary republicans leading artisans who made the revolution of 1830. Street fighting erupted on 27 July, and after three days a demoralized army evacuated the capital. The Constitutionalist deputies, terrified that social revolution would develop, established a committee to 'guard the safety of person and property'.[36] On 7 August, by a vote of 219 to 33, the Chamber proclaimed Louis Philippe, Duke of Orléans, King of the French. François Guizot, liberal and Orléanist, said: 'He will respect our rights, because it is from us that he will hold his.'[37] The Chamber of Duties gained new prerogatives, notably the right to take the initiative in proposing legislation. The tax threshold for voters was lowered from 300 to 200 francs. The amended Constitutional Charter guaranteed civil and political liberties, and the permanent establishment of a National Guard made up of all taxpayers who could afford to provide their own uniform: 'The Charter, and all the rights which it consecrates, remain entrusted to the patriotism and courage of the national guards.'[38] This centrality of a political and solidly middle-class National Guard was the most novel feature of the 'July monarchy'. 'I desire, I strive for, I serve with all my might, the political preponderance of the middle classes in France,' said Guizot, now a leading minister, in May 1837.[39] In practice, as Pamela Pilbeam notes, 'France was still run by a traditional bourgeoisie, not a new entrepreneurial middle class.' The number of businessmen in the Chamber actually fell from 17 per cent to 14 per cent.[40] The July Monarchy was, nonetheless, indulgent of French business concerns. It maintained very high tariffs, whilst levying only very low taxes on commerce and industry. Bankruptcy laws were made less onerous, and the government encouraged investment in railways by purchasing land and guaranteeing returns. Strikes remained illegal.

The politics of Restoration France defined for observers the lineaments of bourgeois liberty. The bourgeoisie were lauded by its *doctrinaire* champions as the quintessential constitutional class, loyal to the rule of law and protection of private property and commerce. Bourgeois entrepreneurs disdained to exploit the state as a direct source of income, in contrast to the aristocracy and, potentially, the propertyless proletariat. The state's reliance on civil society for tax income and credit gifted the bourgeoisie its class-specific weapon of struggle: the tax-strike. Whilst it was the urban mass that took to the barricades, respectable bourgeois property brought order to the streets as a National Guard, and disciplined the government by insisting upon a representative assembly with teeth and government transparency in return for credit.

\* \* \*

The 1830 French Revolution resounded in Spain, where liberalism and a form of populist absolutism violently contended. In 1831 King Ferdinand, in order to secure the succession to his daughter, disinherited his brother Carlos. The rank and file of Catholic clergy and monks, fearing absolutist executive overwhelming Church prerogatives, rallied to Carlos. In September 1833, Ferdinand suddenly died and his widow, Christina, took over as regent until Isabella came of age. The country sharply divided, between the traditionalist partisans of Carlos (the Carlists) and the defenders of Christina. Feeling her weakness, Christina turned to the liberals. Martinez de la Rosa, a previously imprisoned liberal, was called in to form a ministry. By the Statute of 1834, constitutional government was established, but the centre of political power remained focused on the executive and army.

Anti-liberal Carlism was not merely the last stand of an obsolete ruling elite. It had a substantial popular component, notably the hardy peasants of Catalonia and Aragon in the east, and Navarre and the Basque country in the west, where liberal centralization meant the loss of liberties (*fueros*) from centrally imposed officials, taxation, and military conscription. Here absolutism meant a distant central government and considerable local autonomy, whereas liberal constitutionalism meant subordination to the market and the state. While the Carlists of central Spain were quickly routed, and the cities of the rebellious peripheries fell under radical national guards fiercely opposed to rural 'obscurantism', the tenacious guerrilla warfare of the mountaineer peasants, rallied by their priests, took five years to suppress. Brutality was marked on both sides. As ever, the sovereign's main concern in accepting constitutionalism had been fiscal.[41] First minister Juan Álvarez Mendizabal, advised by English experts, with a decree in 1836 seized and sold the monastic strongholds of Carlism, ousting some ninety thousand monks and realizing a government windfall to pay off national debt. In practice, this blunt instrument failed to yield the expected income: in the long run it served only to attach the Church closer to its wealthy patrons. Though a sidelight of European affairs, Spain's experience (closely parallelled in Portugal) was indicative of wider trends. The executive state tried to use a limited constitutionalism to balance liberals and conservatives, the better to secure fiscal solidity and independence. A 'democratic' absolutism, deeply religious in nature, resisted state centralization. The international powers backed proxies and connived to advance their vision for the future.

## CONCLUSION

Liberated from the oppression of Napoleon's militarized empire, European states after 1815 had lived in mortal fear of any innovation that might once again open the gates to revolutionary turmoil and international anarchy. For Metternich and his allies, any move towards constitutionalism must be untimely. Monarchies bolstered aristocratic and churchly powers as conduits of stable, if archaic, rule. There were heavy costs to such stasis: civil society was suffocated and commercialism treated with utmost suspicion as more a danger than an opportunity; state structures were downsized to cheapen governance and thus relieve pressure on revenue-raising parliaments; dynastic warfare, 'the sport of kings', was disowned and military adventures limited to counter-revolutionary police duty. Two countries that unquestionably had crossed the line to liberal constitutionalism and commercialism, Britain and the USA, did prove that the new dispensation could prosper, at least given congenial circumstances. Suitably comforted, liberalism as an ideology developed—particularly in France, where the bourgeoisie was apotheosized as a class that in liberating itself would liberate the state, both from fiscal weakness and capture by narrow class or estate interests. Moreover, a free middle class would protect civic and political freedoms for all, and hold out hope for an expanding, independent, property-owning citizenry. It was beginning to become apparent, however, that the newly proletarianized artisans were beginning to doubt whether liberal economics, destroying their independence today, could somehow restore it tomorrow.

# 4

# The Turning Point

In Europe by the 1840s, the requirements for liberal transcendence of absolutism were widely understood: representative assemblies should pass legislation, vote taxes, scrutinize state budgets, and perhaps appoint or dismiss ministers. With fiscal transparency established, states would be required to respect private wealth and capital accumulation to guarantee their probity in the eyes of the money markets. A middle class would be encouraged by the diffusion of property and freedom of commerce. Liberty of association and the press would ensure accountability and openness. The outcome would be well-provisioned states benefiting from national prosperity. Few thought that absolutism would capitulate without some sort of struggle, but most were convinced that the tide of constitutional modernity was irresistible.

The wage-labouring working class assembled by expansive manufactures, however, complicated the picture. Still, most observers, whether liberal or socialist, saw the working class as objects of pity, and perhaps raw material for revolutionary violence or zeal. They did not, however, generally suspect them of harbouring political inclinations, other than a wish to be saved by patrons, visionaries, or demagogues. Exceptions were rare. Even the pioneer Irishman, William Thompson (1775–1833)—unusual amongst early socialists in being a fervent democrat and believer in self-emancipation by the 'industrious classes'—worried that workers were befuddled by the 'higglers in the market': 'When will the industrious perceive that...it is their imperative interest to seek out for a system of industry...giving to all abundantly and equally the means of acquiring happiness?'[1]

Flora Tristan (1803–1844), the French trailblazer of feminism and socialism, was more optimistic that socialist inclinations arose spontaneously from proletarian conditions of life. Though her 'catechism' is usually dismissed as merely exhortatory—perhaps because of her sex—it actually proposed a sophisticated theory of proletarian 'socialist preference formation':

> ...for the poor worker who possesses neither land nor houses, nor capital, nor absolutely anything except *his arms,* the rights of man and citizen are of no value (and in this case they even become for him a bitter mockery), if first one does not recognize *his right to live,* and, for the worker, the right to live is *the right to work,* the *only one* that can give him the possibility of *eating,* and consequently of living.
>
> ...What, in fact, does the working class demand?...

Its own property, the only one that it can ever possess, is *its arms*. Yes, its arms! They are its patrimony, its unique wealth! Its arms are the *only instruments of labour* in its possession. They therefore constitute *its property*...

...for the working class to be *secure* and *guaranteed* in the enjoyment of its property... the *free use* and guarantee of that property must be recognized *in principle* (and also in reality). Now the actual free use of this property would consist, for the working class, in being able to *make use of its arms,* whenever and however it wished, and to make this possible it must possess the *right to work*. And as for the guarantee of this property, it consists of a wise and equitable ORGANIZATION OF LABOUR.

The working class has therefore two important claims to make: (1) THE RIGHT TO WORK; (2) THE ORGANIZATION OF LABOUR...

Workers, you see the situation. If you want to save yourselves, you have only one means: you must UNITE.[2]

Tristan's argument was that the class-specific nature of proletarian productive property—the ability to work on and with material resources provided by others—was such that it required a social contract, mediated either by the market or otherwise, to be realized. Wage workers, moreover, imperatively desired full and stable employment protected from the caprice of the market. That this meant the organization of labour was intuitively obvious for proletarians.

In 1843, Karl Marx, a young German philosophical radical, converted to the socialist belief that only common ownership of the means of production could reconcile individual freedom with the necessary association of humans in society. Gracchus Babeuf, in 1790s France, had called for a forcible levelling of aptitude and effort to undercut inequalities of income. Marx, on the contrary, believed that abolition of private property in the means of production would serve to redeem individual merit. Personal aptitudes would no longer be twisted and reduced into mere keys to class privilege. They would develop naturally, even luxuriantly, with each individual finding their own path to fulfilment in a cooperative social context. He envisaged a society where 'the free development of each is the condition for the free development of all', based upon the creed: 'From each according to his ability, to each according to his needs!'[3] Innate talent would be reconciled with social solidarity.

Marx remained sceptical, however, about most socialists' faith that philanthropists or the state could be persuaded by reasoning intellectuals to finance experiments in cooperative production. In 1844 he adopted the idea that the modern proletariat is the only great social force systematically inclined to socialist politics. To win his individual security, the wage worker requires guaranteed remunerative work. This in turn, Marx thought, ultimately requires a transcendence of the market, and a collective ownership of the means of production, which he believed laid the basis for a truly human liberation.[4] About this time, Marx met with Engels, who adopted the same viewpoint. Whatever the validity of Marx's general prognostications, the 'right to work' *was*, in fact, perhaps *the* central demand of workers in this period. Marx (and Tristan) were not mere quasi-religious prophets, as sometimes they are depicted; they were responding to, and championing, the emergence of proletarian democracy.

## CHARTISM

In Britain, middle-class presence near government was secured and marked by the 1832 Great Reform Act. The working classes, however, felt betrayed. Lord Salisbury, later a Conservative prime minister, reflecting on the Reform Act in 1869, concluded that:

> Except when fired by genuine oppression, the working class alone cannot make a revolution. The middle class has often fought its way to power with their help; and on such occasions very democratic theories have found their way into very exclusive company. But as soon as the middle classes are inside the citadel instead of outside, their former allies find that democracy goes with marvellous rapidity out of fashion.[5]

However, the working class did not recede quietly. The prominence of wage-earning workers had put new strains on the social order. As Johann Caspar Escher, a German living in England, observed in his diary on 20 August 1814, 'In England a heavy fall in the sale of manufactured goods would have the most frightful consequences. Not one of the many thousand English factory workers has a square yard of land on which to grow food if he is out of work and draws no wages.'[6] Wage fluctuations were a continual pressure for workers in early industrializing Britain, inclining them towards solutions of collective security. In 1824, Robert Owen founded 'co-operative societies', which tried to organize production so that labour was no longer treated as a commodity.[7] His later Grand National Trades Union, which attracted a membership of half a million, was broken by emergency legislation (as recommended by the liberal economist Nassau Senior) by 1834.[8]

The New Poor Law (1834), which moved from a system of supporting labourers' wages through times of dearth towards one in which paupers were corralled in prison-like workhouses, so as to remove them from the labour market altogether for so long as they were surplus to requirements, caused outrage amongst labourers and artisans. It seemed a vindictive act by the new gentry/middle-class Parliament, criminalizing poverty, and it contrasted with the effective outdoor relief afforded to landed property by the protectionist Corn Laws. In 1837, William Lovett established the London Labourers' Association, with the aim of gathering signatures for a petition to Parliament demanding universal (male) suffrage. This 'People's Charter', published in May 1838, was significant in that it demonstrated that—especially since 1832—Parliament had been accepted by the disenfranchised as the legitimate locus of national political life. Chartist agitation continued with greatly fluctuating intensity for ten years (1838–48). Peaks of activity, when huge petitions were organized and presented (1838–9, 1842, 1848), generally coincided with periods of industrial depression. The novelist Elizabeth Gaskell compared the Chartists to a Frankenstein's Monster who 'in the moment of our [middle-class] triumphant power...gaze[s] on us with mute reproach'.[9] In contrast to Owenism, Chartism was not ideologically socialist, but it did reflect wage-worker class ideals. Democratization of Parliament was a necessary preliminary to the collective, state-organized buttressing of wage labour as a secure mode of existence: 'Nothing short of political power to *protect* our *labour* will satisfy us, the working classes of this country.'[10] In 1848 the much-alarmed ministry banned a planned Chartist march on Parliament. This move had the support of commercial civil society: eighty-five thousand of London's middle class were enrolled as special constables, joining the army on the streets.[11] The procession was stopped, and so ended the Chartist agitation. The state apparatus had never looked close to breaking.

It was not simply repression that defeated Chartism, however. The discontent that Chartism revealed was clear evidence of the political limits to the policy of screwing down on the poor, and anyway such a policy left the state's finances precarious. While bourgeois property was the foundation of the state's fiscal strength, in that indirect taxes on trade provided most exchequer revenue, this was a burden passed on to consumers. Lord Grey, Secretary of State for the Colonies, in an 1848 memorandum on colonial taxation, elucidated the basic assumptions on which taxation was based in the commercial metropolis. Grey's key point was that tax revenue must derive principally from the proletarianized mass of society, 'those whose only income is derived from their labour, and who form the great majority of every community'. Therefore, indirect taxes on articles of consumption were appropriate.[12] By the time Grey wrote his memorandum, in fact, its stated principle that taxation on workers' consumption should provide almost alone the fiscal resources of the state had actually been abandoned. But until the 1840s, taxation did indeed focus on 'those whose only income…derived from their labour'. About half a labourer's income was taken in taxes on liquor, sugar, tea, soap, housing, bread, meat, and clothing.[13] The most notorious fiscal instrument, however, was the Corn Law, because it so obviously benefited the landowner at the expense of consumers, by artificially inflating the price of food imports when market prices fell to a level that might discomfort the agricultural interest. The Anti-Corn Law League, in urging repeal of the Corn Laws as a burden placed on bourgeois civil society, was able to appeal both to entrepreneurs and workers. 'Who that is endeavouring to support himself and his family by commerce has not an interest in Free Trade?', asked an Anti-Corn Law League orator in 1843.[14]

When the Conservatives returned to power in 1841, Prime Minister Robert Peel re-established the income tax, abolished in 1816, on all incomes exceeding £150. Income tax became thereafter one of the foundations of English finance. Between 1843 and 1870, income tax brought in between 10 and 14 per cent of annual revenue, while the take derived from indirect taxes fell from 76 per cent to 62 per cent.[15] The weak Factory Act of 1833 was strengthened in 1844, and a Labour in Mines Act was passed in 1842. These employment laws in theory only protected women and children, but as labour-market control reduced pressure on male wages, as men working with women and children could not easily be organized onto separate and longer shifts, they ratcheted up male working conditions. More controversially, Peel abolished the Corn Laws in 1846, a presumed blow against the landed interest that sheared the Peelite 'economical reformer' Members of Parliament away from the landlord and gentry base of the Tory Party. Together, these measures were a wager on a dynamically growing capitalist economy that would be sufficient to preserve the landed interest, satisfy the middle classes, keep the working classes quiet, and maintain adequate finances for determined executive government.[16]

Peel was a semi-willing agent of bourgeois transformation. Walter Bagehot (1826–1877), an important writer on the British Constitution, reflected on Peel's relationship with the middle class in remarks that deserve extensive quotation:

> Of course it cannot be said that mill-makers invented the middle classes. The history of England perhaps shows that it has not for centuries been without an unusual number of persons with comfortable and moderate means. But though this class has ever been found among us, and has been ever more active than in any other country, yet to a greater extent it was scattered, headless, motionless. Small rural out-of-the-way towns, country factories few and far between, concealed and divided this great and mixed mass of petty means and steady intelligence. [But] the huge leaps of [new] manufacturing wealth were not to be concealed. They at once placed on the level with the highest in the land—in matters of expenditure, and in those countless special relationships which depend upon expenditure—men sprung from the body of the people, unmistakably speaking its language, inevitably thinking its own thoughts. It is true that the first manufacturers were not democratic.... [But] the grain of the middle class will surely show itself in those who have risen from the middle class.... The habit of industry is ingrained in those who have risen by it; it modifies every word and qualifies every notion. They are the βάναυσοι [vulgarity] of work. Vainly, therefore, did the first manufacturers struggle to be Conservative.... The new class have not, indeed, shown themselves republican. They have not cared especially to influence the machinery of government. Their peculiarity has been, that they wish to see the government administered according to the notions familiar to them in their business life...they wish to see plain sense applied to the most prominent part of practical life. In his later career, the second Sir Robert Peel was the statesman who most completely and thoroughly expressed the sentiments of this new dynasty;—instead of being the nominee of a nobility, he became the representative of a transacting and trading multitude.[17]

By reintroducing income tax as a permanent fiscal instrument, and abandoning the Corn Laws, Peel effected an important transition. The taxation of trade, which had ensured a government sympathetic to commercial interests, had borne down heavily on the consumer, and a consequence had seen rising popular discontent expressed through Chartism. Under Peel, direct taxation had taken the place of indirect taxation in order to assuage popular protest and to give the state room for manoeuvre. This certainly did not mean that bourgeois or landed interests were eclipsed in government. Bourgeois civil society dominated, and social transactions were almost completely commodified. The re-establishment of government finance was not a challenge to middle-class economy. It did mark, however, a definite assertion of state autonomy from bourgeois civil society that was to be reflected in the long domination of senior political ranks by the aristocracy, and in all circumstances a dedicated 'political' elite beholden to no single class interest. Britain weathered the storms of the early nineteenth century. It emerged with a liberal constitutional structure run, to a large degree, by aristocrats, a free-market economy that nevertheless supported a strong state, and a sufficient suggestion of 'class fairness' to incorporate the working classes. The Great Reform Act and the Peel ministry of the 1840s did not subordinate the state to the middle classes, but reinforced the state sufficiently so that it could, in looking to its own interests, defend and preserve bourgeois civil society.

In the decades after the Napoleonic Wars, Britain had steered between the Scylla of a gentry-banking nexus suffocating bourgeois dynamism and the Charybdis of popular rebellion against the ruthlessness of the capitalist cash-nexus. Constitutional monarchy had been consolidated by the rationalization of the franchise and the clear assertion of ministerial responsibility to Parliament rather than to the Crown. The priority of free-market commercialism over protectionist buttressing of landed wealth had been admitted. The government was not altogether convinced at heart that middle-class manufacturing goals were always best; but as Peel confessed, the dynamic of the capitalist economy could not be gainsaid: 'If you had to constitute new societies you might on moral or social grounds prefer cornfields to cotton factories, an agricultural to a manufacturing population. But our lot is cast and we cannot recede.'[18] The wage-labouring population had been given some remission from the tax burden, and by the mid-nineteenth century were clearly benefiting from national economic growth. Britain was more stable than any European competitor. The long-term viability of a bourgeois political economy had been proven.

## PRELUDE TO REVOLUTION

Meanwhile, amongst the king's ministers in the post-1830 monarchy in France tension existed over the rights of the executive. Guizot argued that ministers should only be chosen or dismissed by the king. Adolphe Thiers (1797–1877) opposed to this the doctrine that ministers required the confidence of a majority in the Chamber and that the king should leave the ministry to govern without his interference. King Louis Philippe did attempt to direct his ministers and in particular insisted that foreign policy was his personal responsibility. Duvergier de Hauranne, for the reformists, complained that so-called *députés fonctionnaires*, those elected representatives paid off with various state offices, made up about two-thirds of the pro-government contingent in the Chamber of Deputies. The substance of parliamentarianism, by such means, was being hollowed out.[19] Elections, moreover, were openly manipulated by government prefects. Guizot tried to defend this arrangement, arguing that the ability of the administration in France to influence the electorate was equivalent to, and as healthy as, the influence of the aristocracy in Great Britain.[20] This was the nature of the French 'bourgeois monarchy'.

Democratic republicans, hoping to seize power by conspiracy and insurrection, organized in successive 'Societies'. A manifesto issued in 1836 by one incorrigible conspirator, Louis Auguste Blanqui, adopted the cause of the 'proletariat' (widely defined), and made clear that the extension of political rights, electoral reform, and universal suffrage were a means to achieving the 'complete...reign of equality'.[21] Although, by the 1840s, repressive legislation had crushed insurrectionism, Louis Blanc (1811–1882), the editor of a democratic paper, had a substantial impact on the political consciousness of workers. His newspapers popularized Blanc's 1839 book, *L'Organization du Travail* (*The Organization of Labour*). This proposed that *ateliers sociaux* (national workshops) be established at government expense, and thereafter be directed on a profit-sharing basis by the labourers employed. Blanc supported a parliamentary democracy with a dynamic 'proletarian' component. He wrote in 1839 that 'The logic of history demands the creation of a Ministry of Progress, having as its special purpose the energizing of the Revolution, the opening of the road that leads to dazzling horizons.'[22] By the 1840s, such ideas had outstripped Jacobin-style radicalism.

The French monarchy was not easily tamed, and the Crown remained a formidable power in its own right, resistant to dictation. As Guizot pointed out, without a politically authoritative gentry, France's was a lopsided state of affairs. The radical republican street was increasingly in competition with bourgeois respectability, and the executive state, buttressed with its own powerful bureaucratic apparatus, threatened to subordinate both the street and bourgeois civil society to its own interests. France little anticipated its near fate, but the structures were there to support it.

\* \* \*

As the 1840s opened, it appeared possible that a liberal breakthrough on the continent of Europe might be possible without revolution. In February 1847 a new king, Frederick William IV of Prussia, conceded a consultative and disproportionately aristocratic National Assembly, or United Landtag, to authorize new taxes and loans. At its opening session on 11 April, Frederick William waxed lyrical on his traditionalist objections to liberal constitutionalism. In a section to become famous, he insisted that 'no power of the earth will succeed in moving Me to transform that natural relationship between ruler and people...into a legalistic or constitutional one'. In a more pragmatic register, he reminded his audience that executive power, particularly in a state confronted by continuous foreign-policy challenges, required direction 'by One Will', and that sovereignty be undivided.[23] This was the authentic voice of absolutism. But by summoning the United Landtag at all, Frederick William had invited a challenge. When the government proceeded to its business, and asked the Landtag to guarantee a railway loan, the deputies refused to vote funds for the Berlin-Koenigsberg railway unless the government agreed to turn the united Landtag into a regular national Parliament. The king refused to yield. When the Landtag was broken up in June 1847, the government was without its loan and the deputies without their constitution. Only in January 1848, when revolution was obviously imminent, did the king decide to concede guaranteed periodic meetings of the Landtag. By then, it was too little, too late.

This struggle clearly had a formative influence on Marx and Engels' assumptions regarding bourgeois liberal interests and capacities. Though a relatively obscure episode, it influenced their understanding of what 'bourgeois revolution' meant in contemporary politics. The United Landtag, Marx argued, was made up of the 'big landowners and capitalists', the aristocracy having been 'largely bourgeoisified' in its economic interests. As such, it was necessarily opposed to;

> the absolutist state, which in the course of development lost its old social basis, became a restrictive fetter for the new bourgeois society with its changed mode of production

and its changed requirements. The bourgeoisie had to claim its share of political power, if only by reason of its material interests. Only the bourgeoisie itself could legally assert its commercial and industrial requirements. It had to wrest the administration of these, its 'most sacred interests' from the hands of an antiquated bureaucracy which was both ignorant and arrogant. It had to demand control over the national wealth, whose creator it considered itself… the bourgeoisie had also the ambition to secure for itself a political status in keeping with its social status.

Bourgeois social interests were generalized, however, as liberal goals applicable for all society:

> To attain [its] aim it [the bourgeoisie] had to be able freely to debate its own interests and views and the actions of the government. It called this 'freedom of the press'. The bourgeoisie had to be able to enter freely into associations. It called this the 'right of free association'. As the necessary consequence of free competition, it had likewise to demand religious liberty and so on. Before [revolution in] March 1848 the Prussian bourgeoisie was rapidly moving towards the realization of all its aims.

The pressure the bourgeoisie and bourgeoisified aristocracy were able to bring to bear was first and foremost fiscal—'The Prussian state was in financial difficulties. Its borrowing power was exhausted. This was the secret reason for the convocation of the United Provincial Diet.' Indeed, no violent revolution, Marx averred, was necessary for liberal victory: 'Although the government struggled against its fate and ungraciously dissolved the United Provincial Diet, lack of money and of credit facilities would inevitably have driven it gradually into the arms of the bourgeoisie.'[24] Clearly, therefore, Marx conceived the possibility of a peaceful 'bourgeois revolution', though he understood that absolutist reaction made a violent confrontation more likely than not.

We can see that Marx and Engels' theory of the constitutionalist state was, in reality, not so different from that of the liberals. The threads of taxation and credit tied the government to commercial interests. They wrote in *The German Ideology* in 1845 that:

> the modern State, which, purchased gradually by the owners of property by means of taxation, has fallen entirely into their hands through the national debt, and its existence has become wholly dependent on the commercial credit which the owners of property, the bourgeois, extend to it, as reflected in the rise and fall of State funds on the stock exchange.[25]

This allowed for a division of labour between the bourgeois government, who paid for government, and those bureaucrats and aristocrats who exercised it. In England, the richest sections of the bourgeoisie, said Engels in 1847–8, 'have left the nominal rule to their dependent debtors, the aristocrats'.[26] Marx and Engels substantially understated the continuing structural distinction between aristocracy and bourgeois civil society, certainly in central Europe and even in Britain. They also were inclined to downplay the autonomy of the state. Their tendency, indeed, was to define 'bourgeois revolution' as virtually a done deal, with state debt umbilically connecting the state to the interests of bourgeois commercialism. Like many observers, they were rather Pollyannaish about the prospects of constitutionalism.

Marx and Engels' theory of bourgeois revolution, as it emerged in the early 1840s, emphasized that constitutionalism best fitted the bourgeois mode of existence. They trusted that the state was more or less forced to come to terms with bourgeois constitutionalism if it wished to establish the fiscal resources necessary to compete with established constitutional states.

\* \* \*

Little observed by Marx and Engels was the crucial role played by mass Catholic mobilization, democratic in spirit but socially conservative, as a counterpart to bourgeois liberalism. From 1814, the Catholic Church had striven to shore up its authority in conjunction with the absolutist state. Against this ran a temptation, particularly marked amongst the Catholic lower clergy and laity, to win religious independence from state dictation, particularly in countries where the government was Protestant. From about 1828, particularly in Ireland and Belgium, Catholic mass movements added a freight to liberalism that both neutralized peasant suspicion of the urban classes and mitigated tendencies towards unsustainable radicalization. Pius IX, elected as Pope in 1846, had seemed at first to be sympathetic to this liberal Catholicism. But the traumatic revolutions of 1848 completed his disillusionment and were to rupture Roman Catholicism and liberalism definitively for a generation and more.

Switzerland provided a striking, if indirect, example of democratic mobilization retained within constitutionalist limits by Catholic agency. Switzerland's era of revolutionary crisis and civil war lasted from 1829 until 1847. Liberalism of an urban, radically democratic mould vied for mass support with Catholicism reaching out to the peasantry. From two directions formidable democratic movements—often in tactical alliance, notably in Geneva—squeezed the conservative and liberal aristocracies and oligarchies alike. As catonial *ancien régimes* toppled, politics began to polarize between the two democracies, liberal and Catholic. In 1845 the Catholic cantons formed a separate union, the Sonderbund. Though easily outmatched in terms of resources and military strength, the Sonderbund hoped for armed support from the Holy Alliance. Britain, however, egged on the Radical Diet to achieve a fait accompli, and in a brief military campaign in 1847 the Sonderbund was crushed before the Great Powers could come to its aid. The Radicals thus won the spoils of democratic revolution in Switzerland. Powerful communalism and democratizing pressure from both liberal and Catholic directions gave Switzerland a sold basis for its constitutionalism, a basis that individualistic liberalism alone was not able to replicate adequately, as the coming year was to show.

## 1848: REVOLUTIONARY HIGH TIDE

The age of 'bourgeois revolution' reached a climax in 1848 when absolutisms in Europe were swept away by constitutionalist movements seeking to establish representative assemblies, civic and political freedoms, transparent state budgets, a rule of law, and rationalized commercial codes. The 'great question' in dispute, observed a contemporary correspondent for the *Illustrated London News*, was 'the right of the middle classes to a share in their own Government'.[27] Aristocracy and clergy, both as personnel administering government in the localities and as bulwarks of 'legitimist' ideology, were swept to one side by the revolutionary wave with ease; not infrequently, they sided with the revolutions, thus earning the lasting contempt of embattled absolutist governments. While the revolutions certainly exposed the exhaustion of clerical and aristocratic authority, however, the executive states quickly recovered their power more or less intact. By and large, the standing armies and senior office-holders of absolutist governments remained loyal to executive government and their sovereigns. They proved capable of stemming and reversing the constitutionalist flood. The outcome of 1848, therefore, was by no means the political domination of the middle classes. Rather, refurbished executive states were emboldened to foster bourgeois civil society on their own terms.

With severe economic recession and failure of the potato crop (which, partly in deference to the triumphant British theology of free-market liberalism, was permitted to kill in Ireland at least a million of Europe's most restive and democratically sophisticated population; the apocalyptic Gorta Mór), the desperation of hunger spurred the street fighters. But the early and dramatic success of the 1848 revolutions was substantially due to the weakness of state structures. Monarchies had thinned their repressive and military apparatus precisely because these could not be afforded without conceding the Constitution. Political administration was concentrated in the cities and these were peculiarly prone to insurrection. In street fighting, with small numbers of combatants on both sides, the army often had no decisive initial advantage.

Significantly, the revolutions of 1848 began as a tax revolt, that instrument of struggle best adapted to the exigencies of bourgeois civil society. From January 1848, Lombardy-Venetia, Austria's Italian possession, was convulsed by protests refusing taxes on goods, and the government's tobacco monopoly. As revolutions erupted across Italy, the independent Kingdom of Piedmont-Sardinia conceded a Constitutional Statute on 8 February (which later became the basis for the Constitution of the Kingdom of Italy). Revolutionized Piedmont-Sardinia sent its army into Austrian-occupied Lombardy, where it was set to be joined by the armies of Tuscany, the Pope, and Naples in a war of national liberation. France, however, was the epicentre of revolution in 1848. Barricades sprang up across Paris, and on 24 February, Louis Philippe abdicated and the Republic was declared. News of the successful uprising sparked the 'days of March' in Prussia. There demonstration followed demonstration, and a bourgeois civic guard took over Berlin, effectively holding the government hostage. King Frederick William seemed positively to embrace his new role as constitutionalist monarch of the incipient German-wide nation.

The Austrian empire's repressive apparatus was pummelled on all sides. From January 1848, the tax revolt and revolution in Lombardy-Venetia immediately cut off a quarter of the imperial Crown's revenues. Worse, the independent Italian states, Piedmont-Sardinia foremost amongst them, rushed or were dragged into a war to wrest Italian territory from the empire. Austria thus effectively lost its richest tax base just as it was confronted by conventional warfare in the Italian peninsula. The

Austrian commander-in-chief, Joseph Radetzky, evacuated revolutionary territory and built up imperial armed forces in the security of the Quadrilateral, a redoubt formed by four strongholds in Lombardy-Venetia. The empire, therefore, was confronted by a major challenge on its Italian periphery just as revolution erupted in its heartlands. Vienna was taken over by its revolutionary middle class, backed by workers, and the emperor fled to the Tyrol, under the protection of the imperial armies in the Quadrilateral. A Constituent Assembly elected by universal male suffrage met at Vienna, in the famous Spanish Riding School, on 22 July, and after a month's discussion the Assembly voted unanimously to abolish seigneurial *corvée* (forced labour), rents, and gentry courts. All legal distinctions between nobles and commons were suppressed. Hungary, meanwhile, established its own government, leaving it only nominally under the authority of the Austrian Crown.

From the outset, the spectre of Red Revolution perturbed the ranks of middle-class revolutionaries everywhere. Alexis de Tocqueville commented on the immediate aftermath of the February revolution in Paris:

> The people alone bore arms, guarded public buildings, watched, commanded, and punished. It was an extraordinary and a frightening thing to see the whole of this huge city... rather the whole of this great nation, in the sole hands of those who owned nothing; for, thanks to centralization, whoever reigns in Paris controls France. Consequently the terror felt by all the other classes was extreme.[28]

The French provisional government in the Hotel Hôtel de Ville was under the immediate influence of the revolutionary workers of eastern Paris, and it threw the National Guard open to workers. On 25 February armed workers petitioned for and secured a declaration of the Rights of Labour. Louis Blanc, as the new Minister of Labour, issued a decree reading: 'The government of the French Republic undertakes to guarantee the workers' livelihood through work. It undertakes to guarantee work for every citizen.'[29] To this end, the following day, it was resolved to establish 'national workshops'. The provisional government tried to sideline 'Social Republicans' into a Government Committee for the Workers 'with the express and specific task of concerning itself with the workers' problems'.[30] Blanc and the workers' minister, Albert (Alexandre Martin), were put in charge of the committee and it was dispatched to the Luxembourg Palace. This became a kind of workers' parliament, with delegations from the diverse trades presenting demands. The programme eventually submitted by the Luxembourg Commission to the provisional government proposed state support for workers' cooperatives and condemned 'liberticide *laisser faire*'.[31]

French elections on 23 April, however, saw signal defeats for socialist candidates in France. Defying the ballot box, a workers' demonstration marched to the Hôtel de Ville. Alexandre Ledru-Rollin, the moderate Social Republican and Minister of the Interior, who had hitherto equivocated, mobilized the National Guard. The demonstration fizzled and Social Republican influence on the government immediately dissipated. It was a turning point. Still, outdoor relief and work schemes for the unemployed workers of Paris were considered for the time being to be a political necessity. Due to the uncertainty of revolution and the provisional government's apparent deference to the urban masses, state credit dried up—indicative of bourgeois civil society's lack of confidence. The provisional government was unable to raise a loan to continue relief payments, and it was forced to institute an direct tax of 45 centimes in the franc. At a stroke this alienated the middle class and peasantry, who despised a Republic apparently committed to coddling the urban *canaille* at their expense.

In the 'Days of June', an uprising erupted in response to the provisional government's decision to close the national workshops. Workers armed and seized control of eastern Paris. General Louis-Eugène Cavaignac was invested with dictatorial powers by the Assembly to bring revolutionary Paris to heel. The insurgent population of the eastern quarters of old Paris was confronted by the National Guard drawn from the rest of the city, the surrounding country, and neighbouring cities, also by the mixed-class Garde Mobile, and the regular army garrison of twenty thousand men. The battle was desperate but one-sided. The Faubourg Saint-Antoine held out for three days (24–26 June), but defeat was total. These 'June Days' were a stunning moment for partisans of the Social Republican left. The leftist Russian observer, Alexander Herzen, saw it as the bourgeois republicans effectively deserting to the side of counter-revolution: 'Such moments kindle hatreds for a dozen of years, call for lifelong vengeance. *Woe betide those who forgive such moments.*'[32]

In France, the provisional government had perforce accommodated the interests of the wage-earning population, whose class interests inclined them towards support for guaranteed employment over the free labour-market requirements of bourgeois civil society. This had sapped the creditworthiness of the state, as such economically 'irrational' expectations could not be countenanced by the nation's creditors. The state's attempt to fill the gap by imposing swingeing taxation simply alienated the property owners, both bourgeois and peasant. The politically radicalized workers of Paris showed precious little obeisance to the voice of the nation, as expressed through the ballot box, and it was to palpable public relief that they were provoked and bloodily suppressed by the Republic. The bourgeois nature of the revolution seemed assured, but at the heavy price of empowering the military and alienating the insurrectionary crowd that had actually made the revolution.

While the French military was at least non-royalist, in Prussia the army remained deeply hostile to the revolution. As the National Assembly radicalized, Frederick William imposed counter-revolution by force. The army re-entered Berlin and placed it under martial law between 10 and 12 November 1848. The Assembly protested and, in an attempt to bring to bear the weight of commercial civil society, called for a tax strike. In practice no taxes went unpaid, and of the thirty thousand rifles that had been distributed to citizen militias in March, all but 150 were meekly returned to the government.[33] The weakness of bourgeois civil society unable to call upon effective military forces was ruthlessly exposed.

The Frankfurt Parliament had the unenviable distinction of becoming the outstanding symbol of liberal impotence in the face of counter-revolution. Elected in 1848 by universal suffrage across Germany to draw up a Constitution for a united Germany, in the Parliament sat figures prominent in established liberal oppositions, predominantly professors, lawyers, writers, and government officials. Carl

Theodor Welcker, member of the Constitutional Committee of the Parliament, voiced the opinion of most deputies:

> I have not received a mandate to tear governments from the throne. Or to rob them of their dignity and honour in order further to open the maw of the revolution. My mandate says: use the legal basis of a constitutional situation to close off the unhappy road, the abyss of the revolution. Re-establish trust, mutual respect for the law, peace and calm, so that the businessman can once again enjoy wealth and freedom in his enterprises.[34]

Proletarianized German journeymen, in so far as they found a voice at all (a conference in Hamburg in May 1848 was perhaps the most representative), were hostile to capitalist disruption of traditional labour markets and security of work, and favoured a restoration and enhancement of the corporate guild system. This would save them from the fate of workers in Britain and France, and be preferable to the 'dangers of communism', as their main intellectual leader, Karl Marlo, put it.[35]

Marx and Engels were concerned that the Frankfurt Parliament, being located in a relatively small city and thus isolated from the revolutionary crowd, would be timid in the face of counter-revolutionary aggression. In essence, they hoped that the urban revolutionary crowd would harass the Frankfurt Assembly in order to counteract the pressure of the princely governments and armed forces: 'Intimidation by the unarmed people or intimidation by an armed soldiery—that is the choice before the Assembly.'[36] In September 1848, indeed, republican deputies summoned oppressive mass demonstrations as a prelude to purging moderates from the Parliament. The Parliament understandably feared dictation from the street, but without its own forces it had to call upon the aid of Bavarian, Prussian, and Austrian royal troops. Fighting broke out, but this time the army was unyielding: artillery was brought into play and 'shattered the barricades in every direction'. The insurrection was crushed.[37] Royal armies defending the Parliament were in no way loyal to its political aims. The King of Prussia refused the indignity of the Frankfurt Parliament's offer of a pan-German constitutional monarchy as a 'crown from the gutter'.[38] Republican risings in Prussia, Saxony, Baden, and the Bavarian Palatinate were suppressed by royal forces and the Frankfurt Parliament closed down.

Most importantly for central Europe, the Austrian state apparatus stayed intact and vehemently counter-revolutionary. Radetzky commanded the imperial army in Italy, Prince Alfred Windischgraetz commanded the armies on the Danube, while Franz Jelačić led forty thousand (much feared) Croat soldiers. Again, the Vienna National Assembly had no forces of its own. As the liberal deputy Ludwig von Löhner admitted fatalistically in September 1849, the 'twenty millions' in taxation voted by the Assembly had in no way tied the government to the revolution, but simply 'paid the army of Jelačić': 'real horses will be rearing again in this riding school instead of the Pegasus of liberty which already seems to me somewhat lame'.[39] True enough, the emperor formally raised the imperial standard against domestic revolution, and revolutionary Vienna was reduced by an overwhelming pincer movement: Jelačić with his Croat army from the east, Windischgraetz leading a Bohemian army from the north. Windischgraetz placed Vienna under martial law and the leaders of the democratic resistance were shot.[40] Without their own military force, the tax-supply voted by the Austrian Assembly, intended to be golden manacles fettering the absolutist government, simply paid for the constitutionalists' own suppression.

Only in Italy, and especially in Hungary, where Magyars in the imperial army rallied to the revolutionary government, was there sustained and effective resistance against the revitalized forces of the empire. It took help from a substantial Tsarist army for Austria to finally suppress the Hungarian republic in August 1849. Outside Sicily, where the Bourbon dynast, Ferdinand, crushed the revolution himself, earning the sobriquet 'Re Bomba' (King Bomber), it was foreign armies that effected the restoration in Italy. Austria defeated Piedmont-Sardinia at the battle of Novara (22 March 1849) and North Italy was clamped under the close supervision of absolutist Austria. Three foreign Catholic powers—France, Spain and Austria—offered their armies to overthrow the Roman republic and restore papal power. Rome finally fell on 30 June 1849. Revolution in Italy and Hungary had a chance at least to contend with reaction because it could call upon conventionally organized national armies called up through pre-existing state structures; but in so appealing to national egotism the revolutionaries inflamed their own nemeses, in the form of German or South Slav chauvinism.

In France the 1848 revolution had gone furthest, with the state apparatus falling into republican hands. The old monarchy had been definitively defeated and bourgeois rule consolidated by the 'June Days'. The real—if passive—force in France was the peasantry. Unenthusiastic about the working classes, who seemed intent on taxing rural property to pay for urban welfare, the peasantry gravitated more naturally to the idea of a strong state that could defend them against the depredations of workers, capitalists, and landlords alike. In the presidential elections of December 1848, Louis Napoleon, nephew of Bonaparte, attracted the votes of the former royalists and the peasantry to defeat two republican candidates. When elections to the Legislative Assembly were held in May 1849, of the 750 members returned, more than 500 were monarchists. The monarchists launched a legalist offensive, suppressing the Social Republicans and disenfranchising about three million citizens as transients or inveterate revolutionaries. President Louis Napoleon presented himself as a democratic restraint on the Assembly's vindictiveness, and he demanded that the restrictions on universal suffrage be rescinded. Bonapartists set in motion a mass-propaganda campaign in favour of changing the Constitution to allow Louis Napoleon to stand for re-election. When the Assembly refused to cave in, the Bonapartists launched a coup d'état on 2 December 1851. The Assembly was dissolved by the soldiery.

## NEO-ABSOLUTISM

The new Napoleonic Constitution in France settled all executive power upon the president, who appointed his own ministers. There was a 'Legislative Body', elected by universal suffrage, to vote on bills and the budget, but supervised by a 'Council of

State' and a Senate appointed directly by the president. The constitutional system was approved by plebiscite on 21 December 1851. When Louis Napoleon had himself elevated to the imperial throne, becoming Napoleon III, emperor of the French, this too was approved by plebiscite (10 December 1852). The royal executive power, thus, had triumphed over the representative Assembly's legislature using 'democratic forms'. Louis Napoleon had long argued that, while aristocratic republics historically had sustained a genuinely collective ruling class, 'the nature of democracy is to personify itself in one man'.[41] He had apparently proven his own case.

Outside France, of course, the pre-1848 old regimes had survived the revolution. They were not unchanged, however. A tendency towards a strengthening of the executive state vis-à-vis aristocracy was general in the decade after 1848. An exception was southern and central Italy, where simple reaction reigned, liberal ideas were repressed, and the bourgeoisie were treated with hostile suspicion and contempt. The decrepitude of these restored regimes, however, was evident in their increased reliance on foreign garrisons (the Austrians protecting the regime in the Duchies and the Romagna, and the French in Rome) and their growing deficit in state finances. The Italian exception to this dismal picture was the Kingdom of Piedmont-Sardinia. Here the liberal Constitution was preserved, as was even the revolutionary tricolour flag. The king only appointed ministers who were acceptable to a majority in the Chamber of Deputies. Sovereignty still lay with the monarch, but this in fact made for flexibility: as the Constitution was merely a royal grant, it could be flexibly amended. In characteristic modernizing fashion, the state tilted against the power of the Church. Having failed to reach a concordat with the Roman Catholic Church, the 'Siccardi laws' of 1851 (named after the minister of justice) suppressed many privileges of the Church and clergy. Despite suffering military defeat twice at the hands of Austria, the monarchical government of Piedmont-Sardinia emerged stronger than ever after 1848.

In Prussia, having dispersed the National Assembly, Frederick William proclaimed unilaterally a Constitution handed from above and, while keeping universal male suffrage, divided the electorate into three 'classes' weighed by liability for direct taxation. The richest of the three voting classes accounted for no less than 89 per cent of the electoral college. With a tax-raising Parliament firmly under royal control, the Prussian state was able to build up its civil service and so had to rely less upon aristocratic landlords in the localities. Private enterprise was more or less emancipated from the interference of over-mighty officialdom.[42] A semi-constitutional absolutism prospered in post-1848 Prussia. Even where the constitutions of 1848 were simply abolished, there was not a return to the status quo. The revolution in the Austrian empire, for example, had destroyed manorialism and weakened substantially the aristocracy. In the 1850s, government neo-absolutism in the Habsburg dominions sidelined the aristocracy and attempted direct rule through the bureaucracy.

The executive states, therefore, were relatively strengthened by the experience of 1848. Their fear of revolution had been exorcized—against all expectation they had survived—and traditional aristocratic limits on bureaucratic power had been greatly lessened. There opened up, therefore, an era of neo-absolutism. It was now possible to make concessions to bourgeois civil society without fear of a revolutionary escalation. Obstacles to commerce and trade could be removed in the reasonable expectation that the gates of revolution would not thereby swing open. Financial capital was happy to see order restored, and duly supported the counter-revolutionary regimes. The banker Thomas Baring, as a Tory Member of Parliament in Britain in 1852, spoke for his calling when he reminded listeners that 'in dealing with the great commercial questions and with great interests sudden revolutions are the worst and most dangerous experiments'.[43] It seemed like an eminently sensible option, as it had not in 1815, to brazenly copy the British economic model without fear of unintended political consequences. Alexis de Tocqueville maintained that princes were now centralizers:

> All endeavour, within their own dominions, to destroy immunities and to abolish privileges. They confound ranks, they equalise classes, they supersede the aristocracy by public functionaries, local franchises by uniform enactments, and the diversities of authority by the unity of a Central Government. They labour at this revolutionary task with unwearied industry, and when they meet with occasional obstacles, they do not scruple to copy the measures as well as the maxims of the Revolution. They have even stirred up the poor against the rich, the middle classes against the nobility, the peasants against their feudal lords.[44]

The revolution, willy-nilly, had broken aristocratic power, but left the executive state regnant.

## REVOLUTION BETRAYED?

The year 1848 was an object lesson for revolutionaries and their opponents everywhere. Naturally, they had an enormous influence on Marx and Engels' understanding of the dynamics of bourgeois revolution. They developed, not without contradiction and qualification, a theory of bourgeois betrayal of the revolution. However, such a theory had to efface certain problems. Notably, whereas in France the working class had played an independent role in the revolution, and been crushed for its pains in the 'June Days', the bourgeoisie could hardly have been said to have betrayed the revolution. On the contrary, they had been keeping it within the bounds of bourgeois civil society, and as such were faithful to the historic essence and limitation of the revolution, as even Marx and Engels saw it. Elsewhere, in the German lands and the Habsburg sphere of influence, it is certainly true that absolutism was not defeated. But it is not at all evident that this was because of any bourgeois betrayal as much as a reflection of the balance of forces. The royal state machines were simply too strong to be overthrown.

Over the summer of 1848, working-class and radical agitations, in Berlin, Vienna, Prague, and Milan, had demanded a general arming of the (urban) masses to defeat counter-revolution. They had been crushed, ignored, or sidelined by a frightened middle class. The revolutions failed, Peter Jones concludes, because of divisions of interest 'between the respectable middle class and the tradesmen on the one hand and the craftsmen and workers on the other'.[45] Engels, writing to

Marx, and speaking rather presumptively as a representative of European working-class opponents to bourgeois civil society, concluded that 'the heart of the matter is this, that even the radical bourgeois see in us their chief enemies of the future and therefore refuse to put any weapons in our hands that we would turn against them'.[46] Whilst a general arming of the masses might have been a plausible or least an honourable strategy, even in retrospect,[47] there was in fact no middle-class stomach for popular revolution and the disintegration of state forces, particularly after the fearful spectre of worker rebellion in the Paris 'June Days'. Gustav Mevissen, a German banker and liberal politician, warned in 1849 that evidence of worker presumptuousness 'would soon lead all propertied strata to support the government. They will give preference to an absolutist monarchy over a red republic'.[48] More to the point, it is a certainty that militias alone would not have been able to defeat conventional armed forces. It is true that the armed forces could be subverted. In Hungary, the locally recruited imperial garrison of thirty thousand defected and made up the hard core of the new revolutionary national army. Ten thousand Italian troops of the imperial army in North Italy deserted to Piedmont-Sardinia, while virtually the entire imperial fleet, being made up almost entirely of Italians, sympathized with the revolution in Venice.[49] Still, counter-revolutionary armies remained solid so long as national loyalties did not conflict with military discipline. And this was usually the case.

Engels had to admit that a military force actually capable of taking on the regular soldiery was a requirement of revolutionary victory.[50] Organizing a revolutionary army out of nothing seems a tall order. He tacitly conceded this, perhaps, when he reflected years later that it was the revolutionary determination of the mostly bourgeois national guards, standing between insurgents and the military, which was key in deciding whether the regular soldier could be neutralized or won over.[51] This effectively admitted that trying to break a loyal and determined government army by frontal assault would be suicidal. Rather than acting as a counterweight to reaction, however, national guards generally eased the path of the soldiery. Marx was disgusted, writing in July 1848, at the sight of the ostensibly revolutionary citizen militias being transformed into a 'hybrid between a Prussian policeman and an English constable!'[52] Siding with the urban crowd, however, would hardly have been congruent with the liberal belief in the rule of law and the emancipation of the state from dominion by any one class. A National Assembly beholden to workers demanding the 'organization of labour' was hardly preferable, so far as bourgeois civil society was concerned, to absolutist reaction.

The main complaint of Marx and Engels was that the revolutionaries had failed to establish an emergency 'dictatorial' regime, resting upon the armed urban workers in particular, that could effectively anticipate and confront the reactionary dictatorship of the counter-revolution. Any public authority in the throes of revolution, they insisted, was necessarily 'provisional', and the revolutionary assemblies had to face the reality that the forces of reaction were not defeated merely by the initial granting of a Constitution or change of ministers. Reaction remained entrenched 'within the bureaucracy and in the army', as Marx put it.[53] When revolution and counter-revolution contended, it was idle to believe that liberal assemblies could rein in the state executive by legality. Certainly the reactionary opposition would respect no such distinction.[54] This was Marx and Engels' argument. A revolutionary dictatorship, however, was contrary to the very bourgeois constitutionalism that was the most progressive possible outcome for most, if not all, of Europe. Submitting to a mood of revolutionary fervour, Marx and Engels embraced dictatorial means without explaining how they could lay the basis for a regime of civic and political liberties. Liberals were perhaps more realistic in assuming that revolutionary dictatorship could only end in dictatorship *sans phrase*.

National differences had also riven the revolutionary movement. Germans were disinclined to support Italian claims, and supported the royalist suppression of the Czechs and Poles, while the 'south Slavs' were keen to support a counter-revolution against chauvinist Magyar claims in Hungary. Marx and Engels' newspaper, the *Neue Rheinische Zeitung*, echoed the 'historic nation' egotism of liberalism: 'the Germans, Poles and Magyars took the side of revolution,' remarked Engels, 'the remainder, all the Slavs, except for the Poles, the Rumanians and Transylvanian Saxons, took the side of counter-revolution'.[55] Nevertheless, both Marx and Engels were deeply concerned by the debilitating impact of national chauvinists who 'sought to paralyse democratic energies...to dig conduits for the fiery lava of the revolution and forge the weapon of suppression within the country by calling forth a narrow-minded *national hatred*'.[56] This is not to say that Marx and Engels were opposed to international war per se. Rather hair-raisingly, they called for a western European 'world war' against reactionary Russia. They were certainly in favour of Polish national revolution, even though this meant the loss of 'German' territory, not least because it would undermine Russian power.[57] On balance, however, Marx and Engels' lack of sympathy for the 'nationalities' left them ill-equipped to confront with due seriousness the reality of national fractiousness debilitating the revolutionary front. Blaming bourgeois 'betrayal' seemed both easier and, for patriotic Germans, more congenial.

Whilst the thesis of 'bourgeois betrayal' was the dominant theme of Marx and Engels' reflections on 1848, and certainly that taken on by subsequent socialists and radicals, in detail their reflections on the revolutionary experience were rather more nuanced. Marx believed, in the end, that modern government was disciplined by the necessity to raise money. In a developing bourgeois economy, government reliance on credit directly constrained the most absolutist of monarchies and insensibly brought them into complementarity with financial capital.[58] By 1850, therefore, Marx and Engels had concluded that, contrary to appearances, the outcome of the revolution had not been the triumph of the *ancien régime* in its pristine form. The absolutist states had, by abandoning governance through the aristocracy in favour of direct, and expensive, bureaucratic and military rule, tied themselves inextricably to the credit markets that constituted the power of the upper bourgeoisie. In effect, the absolutist state and the wealthiest bourgeoisie had merged. 'Who profited by the revolution of 1848?' asked Engels in 1850: 'The big princes, Austria and Prussia. Behind [them] there stood the modern big bourgeoisie, quickly subjugating them by means of the State debt.'[59] Marx, speaking of the German revolution in March 1850, evidently agreed:

it was the bourgeois who, immediately after the March movement of 1848, took possession of the state power and at once used this power to force back the workers, their allies in the struggle, into their former oppressed position. Though the bourgeoisie was not able to accomplish this without uniting with the feudal party, which had been disposed of in March, without finally even surrendering power once again to this feudal absolutist party, still it has secured conditions for itself which, in the long run, owing to the financial difficulties of the government, would place power in its hands and would safeguard all its interests.[60]

Marx and Engels by 1850 had come to argue that the restored *ancien régime* states were now seeking to govern in cooperation with the interests of bourgeois civil society, or at least the financial sections thereof.

This was not to say that Marx and Engels thought that the liberal revolution as such had triumphed. Constitutionalism, after all, had not been secured. In a circular to fellow socialists, written in 1850, Marx predicted that 'the democratic petty bourgeois' (and those of the broader bourgeoisie still committed to thoroughgoing constitutionalism) would play the leading role in the coming struggle against the bourgeois-absolutist amalgam state. Ongoing revolution would, in Marx's term, become 'permanent':

> While the democratic petty bourgeois wish to bring the revolution to a conclusion as quickly as possible... it is our interest and our task to make the revolution permanent, until all more or less possessing classes are forced out of their position of dominance, until the proletariat conquers state power... not only in one country but in all the dominant countries of the world.[61]

This ultimate vision of global revolution, however, implied that in the short to medium term, bourgeois revolution remained the order of the day in national states, even if workers forced themselves into government. 'Louis Blanc offers the best example of how you fare when you come to power too early,' said Marx, rather ungenerously, when glossing his 1850 circular. 'Anyway, in France it is not the proletarians alone that will come to power but along with them the peasants and the petty-bourgeois, and it is not their own measures but the latter's that they will have to put into effect.'[62]

Marx and Engels thus developed a rather complex, even contradictory analysis of 1848. The revolution had been 'betrayed' by the bourgeoisie, who failed to secure constitutionalism, but was successful from the point of view of most of the bourgeoisie, in that it consolidated the influence of civil society on the state. The aristocracy had been discredited as the administrative class. The restored monarchies, needing to fund a royal bureaucracy to replace the free services of the aristocrats, could not fail to appreciate the increased importance of the national debt, which relied upon the confidence of bourgeois civil society. If the revolution resumed, it would complete the work of establishing constitutionalism. However, with much of the bourgeoisie content with the status quo, the revolutionary front would be proportionately influenced by those social classes striving to resist the commercial imperative: the petite bourgeoisie and the proletariat. For Marx and Engels, this was to be welcomed as the wave of the future, negating capitalism. For liberals, however, such a development would threaten to crush out the associational life characteristic of commercial modernity. It was hardly to be expected that many of the middle classes would take such a chance on renewed revolution.

In any case, the revolution was exhausted. Following the failure of 1848 to overthrow absolutism, there was a general lack of faith in the ability of the bourgeoisie to provide the personnel for governing elites directly. The liberal German, Georg Gottfried Gervinus (1805–1871), in a generally optimistic history published in 1853, concluded starkly that 'the middle class has seldom proved itself capable of political rule. As a separate body it is neither ambitious, nor has it the leisure for the occupation, nor the inclinations or habits to assert its political position with the hand of power.'[63]

## CONCLUSION

During the revolutions of 1848, fear of the 'red republic' certainly struck fear into the middle classes, as it had not in the 1790s. The social *imaginaire* of the proletariat or proletarianized artisanate (factory workers having played very little role at all), whether articulated as 'social republicanism' or 'guild' nostalgia, was sufficiently coherent to encourage bourgeois and liberal retreat from revolution. Writing in November 1848, the English Whig politician and historian Lord Macaulay had reflected dolefully on the 'antipathy of class to class, of race to race' wracking the continent of Europe. If plebeian interests triumphed, he grimly predicted, thirty years of misrule would undo thirty centuries of progress. This life-long liberal contemplated a flight to reaction as a response to revolutionary turmoil: 'Europe has been threatened with subjugation by barbarians, compared with whom the barbarians who marched under Attila and Alboin were enlightened and humane. The truest friends of the people have with deep sorrow owned that interests more precious than any political privileges were in jeopardy and that it might be necessary to sacrifice even liberty in order to save civilization.'[64] But outside of France the threat from radicalized workers was minor, and in France a rising by a minority section of Social Republicans was put down with dispatch. More important in explaining bourgeois timidity, at least outside of France, was the sheer difficulty of taking on the unbroken governing and military apparatus of the old regimes. While aristocratic and churchly authority did, indeed, prove largely impotent against the hurricane, the state apparatus of absolutism turned out to be more than sufficient to suppress revolution.

It became almost immediately apparent that the restored absolutisms, having faced the worst of revolution and survived it, enjoyed vaunting new confidence. They were willing, as we shall see, to foster commercialism, and experiment with semi-constitutionalism, to win the best of all worlds: fiscal strength, national prosperity, and governmental freedom of manoeuvre. It was doubtful whether these could be described as bourgeois states as such—but then the unwillingness of the entrepreneurial middle class to govern directly, preferring trade and commerce, was their defining liberal characteristic. It was evident, however, that the states of post-1848 were definitively capitalist.

# 5

# Liberalism and the State

The post-1848 period saw an overall expansion of the capitalist economy, as executive states were able to experiment with controlled constitutionalism and sweep away feudal restrictions on commerce. From about 1850 opened the era of 'second-wave' industrialization as metallurgy displaced textiles at the cutting edge of capitalist growth and innovation. Railway building from the 1840s contributing to the decisive breakthrough. Production of coal in Europe increased by 400 per cent between 1841 and 1870. Output of pig iron in England increased from 1.4 million tons in 1840 to 6.7 million in 1870. Between 1845 and 1875, pig-iron production in Germany increased by a massive 950 per cent.[1] Industry was heavier, plants were bigger, and investment no longer came primarily out of profits, but now from bank loans. Great Britain increasingly specialized in services, especially international finance. Her manufacturing workforce climbed and plateaued at about one-third of the working population by 1871 (a proportion that thereafter remained steady up to the First World War). France remained the world's second greatest industrial power until the 1860s. While Germany was catching up quickly, on the eve of the Franco-Prussian War (1870) she remained mainly agrarian. Still, across Europe manufacturing production was well on the way to outstripping agricultural production in terms of value.[2] Factories and mines absorbed a greater percentage of the wage-labour workforce, but small workshops were still the norm, and at least until 1870 or thereabouts, artisanal work patterns remained substantially different from the factory experience. A strong artisanal ethic of personal independence and mutual solidarity persisted, and seeded the fledgling workers' movements. But labour organization remained much in the shade in these decades.

## THE STRENGTHENED STATE

State finances were much improved after 1848. Indeed, counter-revolutionary stability meant that the middle classes became ever more confident in buying 'securities', and these included government bonds. Governments were able to benefit from this extension of market power. In 1854, for example, a 5 per-cent loan issue brought half a billion gulden to the Austrian treasury from bonds sold in denominations as low as 20 gulden. Loans raised in 1854 and 1855 by Napoleon III's government attracted half a million subscriptions. Count Cavour, prime minister of Piedmont-Sardinia, was able to finance war with Austria through publicly subscribed loans, turning down more expensive credit from the Rothschilds. Such state debts financed by relatively small investors were described in the press of the time as 'the universal suffrage of capital'.[3] The extension of the market, thus, certainly did subordinate governments to market discipline, but equally released them from dependence on decaying aristocratic structures of governance, and held off pressures for thoroughgoing constitutionalism.

Commercialism and industrialization strengthened the middle classes, which nonetheless remained politically chastened and timid. The upper middle classes were rather less distinct from traditional elites than had been the case. In his 1867 magnus opus, *Das Kapital*, Marx described how the pioneer capitalists up until roughly the 1830s had been so zealously committed to sustaining their enterprises in a cut-throat market that they considered even their 'own private consumption' as being 'a robbery' committed against their accumulation of capital. However, by the 1860s, as capitalism had generalized and developed a sophisticated credit system, investment no longer needed to be self-financing out of profits. To ensure good credit lines, in fact, capitalists now needed to display conspicuous personal wealth as evidence of their creditworthiness. 'Luxury,' as Marx put it, had entered 'into capital's expenses of representation.' So, while capitalists' personal self-enrichment was still a good way short of 'the *bona fide*...feudal lord's prodigality', there had developed in the modern capitalist 'a Faustian conflict between the passion for accumulation and the desire for enjoyment'.[4] To this extent, Marx implied, capitalists were gradually shedding their culture of abstinence, and converging with traditional forms of ostentatious wealth.

Liberalism had ceased to be an insurgent creed. It had been adopted in large part by the governing elites as a developmental model that could be shorn of its subversive potential. Liberals, always wary of revolution, were more than happy to accept this; the prospering commercial bourgeoisie, who had no time for the complications of direct political involvement, were still more content. Charles Morazé's overview argues that for France, 'The middle-class business world allowed itself to be edged out of power' whilst enjoying a 'firmer grip on the reins of economic life.'[5] This view, perhaps, implies too hard a distinction between civil society and state. The state was becoming implicated in bourgeois civil society through the threads of fiscal policy. State financing was evolving, as borrowing rather than simple taxation became the accepted norm of public finance; and the more constitutional a state was—that is, the greater was Parliament's control over the executive government—the lower was its borrowing cost.[6] However, it was not only governments responsible to Parliament that enjoyed good access to credit. Having survived and suppressed the revolutionary upheaval, and so proving their stability and ability to weather storms, the post-1848 neo-absolutist states had automatically improved their credit rating.

Quite suddenly, the importance of the executive state's capacity to act decisively leapt to the forefront of international diplomacy. This was as a consequence of the Crimean War (1853–6), which opened up an era of territorial rearrangement in central Europe. Russia's defeat in this conflict at the hands of Britain and France diminished her prestige and capacity. While Russian forces had helped to suppress revolution in Hungary in 1849, after the Crimean War she could no longer be expected to intervene in central Europe in defence of the status quo. Piedmont-Sardinia's army fought with British and French troops in the Crimea, bolstering her military credibility and winning friends in preparation for a renewed struggle against Austria for hegemony over the Italian peninsula. France, led by an emperor determined finally to destroy the anti-Napoleonic settlement of 1815, came out of the Crimean War with more prestige than Britain, having played a more glorious military role. To take advantage of these shifting sands required agile and fast-reacting statesmanship. The crucial importance of an executive state with freedom of manoeuvre was evident. The patriotic generation after 1848, therefore, was inclined to find reasons for stopping short of demanding governments entirely responsible to the legislature. German liberals such as Gneist, Laband, Meyer, and Jellinek took to rejecting the 'French' ideal of parliamentary supremacy, preferring instead a balance between Parliament and executive. In their view, Parliament was responsible for legislation but government should be as little restrained as possible.[7] Liberals saw themselves as working in tandem with governments, not trying to take them over, and they saw their natural sites of power as parliaments and municipal government, rather than in ministerial cabinets.[8] Still, the middle classes hoped for and expected a drift to constitutionalism so long as they did not present themselves as seeking to usurp state prerogatives.

## BRITISH EQUIPOISE, AMERICAN CRISIS

Britain remained by far the premier country. It led the way, for example, in crushing the Chinese millenarian Taiping Rebellion (1851–64), during which maybe 30 million had perished. It was not clear, however, how Britain's economic weight might effectively be translated into diplomatic clout amongst the great powers. The pre-eminent middle-class liberal association of the 1840s had been the Anti-Corn Law League. After seeing its immediate goal won, the League evolved thereafter into the more diffuse 'Manchester School'. This tendency promoted Free Trade not simply as a pragmatic economic policy but as an entire system of policy appropriate for a commercial country. Maybe one third of Members of Parliament subscribed to this 'radical' agenda. By fostering trade and commerce between nations, 'Manchesterists' argued, Britain could help to make warfare increasingly redundant. In their view, conducting war so as to seize upon material wealth and resources was an aristocratic relic, being the logical outcome of a tributary economy whereby ruling elites engrossed wealth by force. In a commercial economy wealth was produced through trade and investment. This tied together the interests of economically useful classes: farmer, wage labourer, and capitalist. As war could only disrupt complex networks of contract and the division of labour, and in so doing undermine the fiscal bases of modern states, it must in time fall into misuse. Free trade, therefore, was democratic and peaceful in tendency, opposed to dynastic militarism and aristocratic privilege. Richard Cobden and John Bright, as leading radicals of the Manchester School, vehemently opposed traditional British foreign policy in favour of the 'Balance of Power', as serving only to maintain aristocratic power at home and abroad. 'War is not the disposition of the people,' insisted Cobden in December 1849, 'on these grounds...I wish to see a wide extension of the suffrage, and liberty prevail over despotism throughout the world.'[9] Bright in 1865 condemned the theory of the Balance of Power as a 'foul idol—fouler than any heathen tribe ever worshipped':

> during 170 years [it] has loaded the nation with debt and with taxes, has sacrificed the lives of hundreds of thousands of Englishmen...and has left us, as the great result of the profligate expenditure which it has caused, a double peerage at one end of the social scale, and far more than doubled pauperism at the other.[10]

For the radical 'Manchester School', commercialism, democracy, and peace were closely intertwined.

Cobden and Bright, however, commanded diminishing support in the 1850s. In the election of 1857, Cobden was defeated at Huddersfield and Bright in Manchester itself. For a middle class that felt it had secured an honoured place in the political nation, radicalism's critique of the status quo made them feel increasingly uncomfortable. Unsystematic liberalism and confident nationalism, as espoused by the urbanely aristocratic prime minister, Lord Palmerston, was much more to their taste. Palmerston promoted Britain as 'a political, a commercial, a constitutional country'.[11] In declaring war on Russia in February 1854, a policy encouraged by Palmerston from within the Cabinet, Britain appeared to be promoting liberalism internationally, even if Balance of Power was the overriding consideration. The Crimean War enthused the great bulk of the British middle classes and sidelined the Manchester school of free-trade pacifism. Poor British performance in the war, widely blamed on aristocratic domination of the army, brought Palmerston to the premiership for the first time in 1855. He set as his goal a refurbishment of the reputation of Britain's aristocracy. In this he was substantially successful, though at something of a price; aristocrats in high office were increasingly expected to justify themselves at least partly by talent rather than simply by birth.

The middle classes, therefore, remained politically in the second tier in Britain. Cobden certainly took a positive view of the influence of the middle classes but he depicted them not as politically dominant but rather as offsetting the overweening governing power of the aristocracy: 'our mercantile and manufacturing classes as represented in the chambers of commerce are after all the only power in the state possessed of wealth and political influence sufficient in part to counteract in some degree the feudal governing class of this country'.[12] Another redoubtable champion of small government, Robert Lowe, was still less impressed with middle-class activism: 'I was one of those—and they were very few indeed—who lifted their voices in favour of the middle-class not so much for their own sake as for the sake of the country...I never met with the slightest encouragement or support from those whose cause I was pleading.'[13] The middle classes, in fact, were quite happy with aristocrats of the mould of Palmerston, who was certainly far more liberal than almost all statesmen on the European mainland. 'Reaction' simply did not exist as a politically important constituency in Britain.

Palmerston died in 1865, and after a brief interlude, William Ewart Gladstone (1809–1898) succeeded to the leadership of the Liberal Party, itself a coalition of Whigs and radicals. Gladstone, as a former Chancellor of the Exchequer, was inclined to see fiscal rectitude and a light tax burden as vital both for economic prosperity and the freedom of civil society. He had never reconciled himself to Palmerston's occasional bombast about international relations. For Gladstone, Britain best promoted liberalism abroad by practising it at home. His government included John Bright at the Board of Trade, and for the first time represented all sections of Liberal opinion, including radicalism. Gladstone felt able to twit his Conservative opponents smugly in 1866:

> You cannot fight against the future. Time is on our side. The great social forces which move onwards in their might and majesty, and which the tumult of our debates does not for a moment impede or disturb—those great social forces are against you; they are marshalled on our side; and the banner which we now carry in this fight, though perhaps at some moment it may droop over our sinking heads, yet it soon again will float in the eye of heaven, and it will be borne...perhaps not to an easy, but to a certain and to a not distant victory.[14]

Under Gladstone, Liberalism succeeded in reaching far beyond its middle-class core. As a social philosophy promising individual freedom, economic opportunity, low taxes and morality in foreign policy, it appealed to workers and gentry as well as to bourgeois interests. As Chancellor of the Exchequer from 1859 to 1865, and prime minister from 1868 to 1874, Gladstone promoted free trade, education of public opinion through the abolition of the paper duties and the 1870 Education Act, and reduction of state expenditure and taxation. He attacked entrenched privilege by disestablishing the Irish Church, opening the universities to nonconformists, introducing competitive examination for Civil Service posts, and instituting promotion by merit in the army.

However, in some respects Britain seemed to be tending towards domestic involution. Class politics were contained, but the 'social question' absorbed governmental energy. Conservatives feared the democratization of genuinely parliamentary governments. Democracy, they predicted, must mean the relatively poor majority despoiling the industrious minority through extravagant government expenditure, and irrationality in foreign policy as popular nationalism took charge. Insecurity of property and of liberty would result in a reversion to despotism.[15] This was not, however, a widespread dread in post-Chartist Britain. The liberal thinker John Stuart Mill (1806–1873) was less concerned that the working classes might despoil the rich, than that unfettered democracy would lead to rule by the mediocre 'common herd', and a sidelining of that 'leisured class' where was to be found talent, cultivation, and creative eccentricity. The goal, Mill wrote, was to extend the franchise in a controlled fashion, so as to educate the masses in 'responsibility' and deference to elite political authority.[16] It was the Conservative Party, in fact, that enfranchised much of the urban working class in 1867, roughly doubling the electorate, from about 1 million to about 2 million, in a manner calculated to reinforce the division between the 'respectable' secure working class and the 'rough' insecure working class.

This was a pivotal period for the development of class relations in Britain. Strikes and lockouts in the prosperous years of the 1860s occasionally led to violent clashes. In 1866 workers in Sheffield used violence to intimidate employers and scabs: the 'Sheffield Outrages'. Though trade-union officials loudly disavowed such tactics, a good deal of middle-class opinion was suspicious that trade unions were by their nature dangerous and violent. A Royal Commission on Trade Unions in 1869, however, reported that organized labour was effectively being forced to go outside the law simply to bargain with any effectiveness at all.[17] Eventually, in 1875, Disraeli's Conservative ministry radically reformed labour legislation. Workers could no longer be found guilty of criminal conspiracy for agreeing to acts that would be perfectly legal if carried out individually. This gave workers in Britain a protection unparalleled in Europe. It was proof that Liberalism in Britain not only accommodated landed wealth and aristocratic honour within a broadly commercialized civil society, but it also made room for the peculiar requirements of organized labour.

Britain's Liberal apogee coincided with that country's marked weakness in continental affairs. Britain had, of course, allied with France to defend the Ottoman empire from presumed Russian hostility. The subsequent Crimean War brought little territorial reconfiguration and exhausted Britain's appetite for war against peers (wars against primitive peoples remained acceptable). By the time of Palmerston's death in 1865, Britain's impotence materially to affect the international relations of the great powers had become painfully apparent. Her attempts to avert a war between Sardinia and Austria in 1859 failed (partly because of Austrian diplomatic blundering). Britain rhetorically favoured the Poles when they rose against the Tsar in 1863, but she refused Napoleon's proposal that they jointly wage war on Russia. Britain was theoretically committed, since 1852, to defending Danish sovereignty over the duchies of Schleswig-Holstein. When Austria and Prussia confronted Denmark, however, the British government baulked at sending an ultimatum. Thereafter, Britain was a helpless observer to the process of German unification under Prussia, the defeat of Austria, and the defeat of France. Bourgeois civil society consolidated domestically, but British ability to project power in competition with peer countries was attenuated.

The British model, therefore, was not entirely enticing. Could its model of economic growth be better reconciled with executive governmental power? The United States was not a reassuring counter-example. J. S. Mill anxiously studied the gleeful coverage of US affairs by British newspapers hostile to democracy. The outbreak of the American Civil War in 1861 caused him particular angst.[18] Since the 1840s, substantial economic chasms in America had gaped ever wider. Broadly speaking, in the North manufacturing and commerce dominated. Because of the difficulty in holding onto free labour, wages were quite buoyant. In the South, however, with Alabama, Louisiana, and Mississippi at its core, the growing of cotton for export had developed as a mass-production industry. Here slave labour was employed. The surpluses produced helped sustain an oligarchy that was aristocratic and militarist in its social attitudes. These parallel societies competed to colonize in their own image the new states being acquired through Western expansion.

Slavery became the main line of political division in the country with the establishment of the Republican Party in 1854. For abolitionists the destruction of slavery was a moral imperative. This was a struggle over the nature of property itself, as Gregory S. Alexander points out: 'The commodity conception is the product of a modern commercial social order that was in many ways the antithesis of what proslavery theorists valued.... [It] threatened to transform Southern order into the fluid sort of society that existed in the bourgeois communities of the North.'[19] In 1860, Abraham Lincoln (1809–1865) won the presidency on a Republican Party ticket. This was treated by the South as tantamount to a capture of the federal state by a revolutionary faction. Most Southern states seceded to form a new sovereign state, the Confederacy. Lincoln determined to wage war to maintain the Union. The war tested whether government responsible to elective representatives was compatible with firm and state-maintaining executive action. Lincoln posed the question to be proved by the sword: 'Must a government, of necessity, be too *strong* for the liberties of its own people, or too *weak* to maintain its own existence?'[20]

As it happened, the North was able to finance the war effort by drawing upon the resources of its commercial civil society through taxation, loans, and treasury notes. The South, in contrast, suffered ruinous inflation peaking at 9,000 per cent. In the course of the conflict (1861–5) slaveholders were expropriated of their property, without compensation, by the emancipation of slaves. The post-war forces of reaction permitted the survival of pre-war Southern society in modified form—notably, Southern blacks were tied by debt into sharecropping schemes, denying them both the status of genuinely free labour or genuinely independent petty proprietorship. This was reinforced by the 'Jim Crow' system, which systematically denied blacks in the South either the suffrage or access to justice. The Civil War, nevertheless, was a key turning point in the emergence of modern America, representing the triumph of bourgeois society and (as Charles Sellers puts it) a 'market revolution...commodifying the family labor of subsistence producers'.[21] America was a test case for those concerned that constitutionalism and firm state action were incompatible. But it had seemed a close-run thing.

## AUSTRIA-HUNGARY AND THE SECOND FRENCH EMPIRE

The Habsburg empire for the first decade after 1848 went to the other extreme from Britain. Here the state attempted to rule virtually regardless of civil society. Austria's bold attempt at bureaucratic absolutism in the years after 1848, however, stretched the resources of the executive to breaking point. With the aristocracy discredited by failure to prevent revolution in 1848, first minister Baron Bach, appointed in 1852, proposed to draw instead upon the Catholic clergy as anti-liberal and anti-German-nationalist supports of the executive. To secure the clerical alliance, the neo-absolutist form of 'Josephism' inherited from the Enlightened eighteenth century, which established the complete subordination of the Catholic

Church to lay authority, was abandoned for a concordat, formalized in 1855, that divided spheres of interest between Church and state. The bishops were accorded official authority over believers, schools, and censorship. Church property was declared inviolable. This bureaucratic/ecclesiastical system managed the empire until 1859. The state, it was said, was now ruled by a standing army (of soldiers), a sitting army (of officials), a kneeling army (of priests), and a crawling army (of informers).[22]

Revamped absolutism created an environment congenial to some degree of modernization. However, the fiscal problems of the empire remained unresolved. The total state deficit between 1848 and 1853 amounted to 920 million gulden (annual income being less than 240 million gulden).[23] This had to sustain both court and the standing army of six hundred thousand men, though money was also found for investment in railways. The state relied heavily on loans: 'it could be said that the proud empire was financed mainly by the Rothschilds'.[24] Due to its precarious fiscal position, the Austrian government was not able to put into place a much-needed program of military reform and refurbishment, and by 1859 Austria's credit was exhausted.

Austrian neo-absolutism, founded in 1849, collapsed as a direct consequence of the disastrous Italian war of 1859. War cruelly exposed the weaknesses of the regime. Austria was defeated, if not overwhelmingly, by French forces and Italian auxiliaries at the bloody battle of Solferino in June 1859. This was partly due to years of under-funding for Austrian armed forces, and even a short-term loan to cover operations in Italy was only 40 per cent subscribed despite onerous official pressure on banks.[25] In August 1859, shortly after the war's conclusion, Emperor Franz Joseph in August 1859 issued the Laxenburg manifesto, in which he was forced to confess that 'hereditary abuses' had led to the defeat, and he offered an 'effective control' over taxation and expenditure. In so doing he held out the prospect of a Parliament with tax-voting and oversight powers in return for widespread public subscription to a domestic loan to the imperial Treasury. Even with this promise, in 1860 a mere 75 million florins were subscribed in response to a call for a loan of 200 million.[26] Franz Joseph then convoked an augmented Council of State (*verstärkter Reichsrat*), made up of prominent office-holders and aristocracy, specifically to give its opinions on financial questions. Its report condemned 'the system of internal organization in the monarchy' and made it quite clear that state fiscal solvency depended upon properly representative institutions.[27] Emboldened, Hungarian patriots refused to pay taxes, while the German liberal majority in the new parliamentary Reichsrat demanded in 1864 a balanced budget and in 1865 a budget reduction. Finally, the Reichsrat liberals refused even to sanction a loan, threatening the state, as a parliamentarian put it, with 'a financial Solferino'.[28] In 1865, Franz Joseph authorized negotiations with the Magyar leaders of the Hungarian patriotic campaign of civil disobedience.

The compromise (*Ausgleich*) of 1867 divided the empire, now known as Austria-Hungary, into two equal states: a union, not between the two states, but between each of them and the Crown. In Austria the Germans were the ruling race, in Hungary the Magyars were. The Hungarian statesman Count Andrássy told

Francis Joseph: 'You look after your Slavs, and we will look after ours.'[29] Each state separately had restored constitutionalism and elected representation under a limited franchise. The emperor remained 'sacred, inviolable, and irresponsible [to the legislature]', meaning that he could appoint his own ministers.[30] The impact of defeat in war and fiscal crisis, therefore, made for a marked if not total shift towards constitutionalism, though vitiated by ethnic supremacism. The limits of neo-absolutism had been starkly revealed by Austria's diplomatic and military weakness, and her subsequent retreat to a form of constitutionalism based upon national 'historic rights'. The clear lesson was that neo-absolutism could not match parliamentarianism for a state's fiscal strength. The forces pushing for reform had been as much from within the state structure and the traditional German and Magyar aristocracies as from the middle classes as such.

\* \* \*

While Austria provided comfort for the liberal assumption that a state denying political freedom to civil society paid a price in revenues, France was a much more worrying case. The Bonapartist regime here appeared to be squaring the circle of executive supremacy, buoyant state finances, and economic modernization. The politician Duc Albert de Broglie came to regret the action of his fellow liberals in helping to hoist Napoleon III into power as president:

> We were slow to admit that we had been mistaken; nobody likes to confess that he has been caught out, but we realised that an army of four hundred thousand men, and all the resources which the administration of France provides for the man in power, joined to immense popularity, made this candidate for Empire a very redoubtable adversary for those who remained faithful to liberal and constitutional principles.[31]

The formidable bureaucratic and military resources available to the head of the executive power threatened to untether the state from civil society. Napoleon III's *intendants* had the capability to control elections to the legislative assembly, whilst maintaining a level of formal constitutionalism sufficient to authorize and oversee state budgets, and in so doing satisfy the money markets that loans to the government were safe. Napoleon III's aim was to marry the fiscal strength of parliamentarianism with the flexibility—particularly in foreign policy—of an absolutist executive.

While the Bonapartist state was far from being totalitarian, an unprecedented police surveillance of subversive individuals was instituted. This was quite open: an official system of 'warnings' was carefully calibrated to degrees of dissidence. All male citizens had the vote, but electoral boundaries were extensively manipulated. In elections the government machine, both central and local, openly threw its weight behind the 'official candidate' in each department. The opposition newspaper, *L'Atelier du Gers*, complained that 'In each commune the official candidate has the services of ten civil servants, free and disciplined agents who put up his papers and distribute the ballot papers and his circulars; one mayor, one deputy-mayor, one school-master, one constable, one road man, one bill sticker, one tax collector, one postman, one licensed innkeeper, one tobacconist, appointed, approved and authorised by the Prefect.'[32] Election meetings were banned and opposition candidates were forbidden to present themselves under a party ticket. The Chamber met for three months every year to pass the laws put to it by the government. It also voted the budget, but as a lump sum for the ministry to dispose of, rather than as an itemized list of appropriations open to debate and amendment on particulars. This was the kind of parliamentarianism to gladden the heart of any self-willed emperor.

The Napoleonic regime also had to concern itself with the oft-demonstrated power of the insurgent barricade. The resources of the state allowed for a bold attempt to remodel the street politically and physically. From 1854, Baron Georges-Eugène Hausmann, prefect of the Seine *département*, set about transforming Paris's layout, to beautify it, and to create a cityscape better suited to the army than the insurrectionary crowd. Driving boulevards through the slum *quartiers*, Haussmann had twenty thousand houses demolished, and 135 kilometres of straight, wide, tarmac-covered roads replaced winding slum streets, sites of previous revolutionary battles. Exhausted by revolution and reaction, and dazzled by the new Napoleon, Social Republicanism was reduced to a low ebb in the 1850s.

Independent bourgeois society was suppressed, even compared to the years of the July Monarchy, and a decree in 1852 dissolved the national guards. However, the middle classes were liberated in the economic sphere. The burden of taxation in imperial France fell on the working class and on ostentatious consumption, with rents, business profits, stocks and shares all left off lightly.[33] This was a period of marked economic growth. There was a boom in railroad construction and the joint-stock company emerged as the increasingly standard repository of capital. The government increased the public debt to fund numerous undertakings but had no trouble in floating its bonds. In 1868 a loan floatation of 400 million francs attracted no fewer than 830,000 subscribers together offering 15 thousand million francs.[34] Napoleon III's regime traded off its political stability by encouraging public investment in the Crédit Mobilier, founded on 18 November 1852 to support new industrial enterprises. By lending in turn to the government it thereby made investors, both domestic and international, 'sleeping partners in the public works'.[35] Though credit was damaged by excessive speculation in the long run, the Crédit Mobilier was able to invest funds abroad, considerably adding to France's international weight. Napoleon III was genuine in his support for a bourgeois civil society to underpin the imperial state. He favoured free trade and the 'democratization of capital'. In January 1860, Napoleon used his constitutional powers to authorize the 'Cobden-Chevalier' free-trade agreement with Britain without seeking the authority of the Chamber. Much of the bourgeoisie, ironically, were unhappy with these innovation, which, they maintained, increased speculation and irresponsibility. Napoleon III was soon obliged, due to pressure from manufacturers and bankers, to tighten budgetary control and rescind the right to raise state loans without the agreement of the legislature. The appointment of Achille Fould, a fiscal conservative, as Minister of Finance in 1861, marked a turning point in which the state was brought back under a closer degree of bourgeois control.[36]

Being a new dynast trading on Bonaparte's reputation, Napoleon III's domestic credibility relied disproportionately on diplomatic and military success: on *gloire*. In a sense, the times were propitious for Napoleon III. Following the Crimean War, he was 'Arbiter of Europe', at least between 1857 and 1863. He abandoned the monarchical conservatism dominant since 1815, which favoured peace for fear that war and its discontents would unleash revolution. His foreign policy embraced revolution in so far as its emancipatory nationalism challenged the Vienna settlement designed to hem France in. By helping liberate oppressed peoples—the 'policy of nationalities'—Napoleon III hoped to gain gratitude and allies, even client states, not to mention grants of territory as *pourboire* (the 'waiter's tip', in Bismarck's sarcastic coinage).

Until 1857, Napoleon III's government was supported by the clergy, both as a bastion against liberalism and as the protector of the Pope's temporal power in the Papal States. The wars in Italy, in which France and Piedmont colluded to expel Austria from the peninsula, sparked a process of national unification that lost the Papacy its territory. The Catholic clergy in France were duly alienated from Napoleon III's regime, and the liberals were enthused. Turning adversity to advantage, the emperor moved to transform the absolutist empire into a parliamentary one. In November 1860 the Chamber's powers of oversight were increased, with the right to draw up an address in response to the speech from the throne, and to publish its proceedings in the official organ, the *Moniteur*. The following year, the annual budget was divided into sections on which the Chamber voted separately. Opposition in the Chamber, expressed quite freely, criticized government expense, particularly military spending. France was, indeed, overstretched. An attempt from 1864 to set up Archduke Maximilian of Austria as client emperor of Mexico collapsed in 1866–7, exposing the limits of French military power. Cognizant of the relatively weak fiscal and military position of the state, Napoleon III hurried to concede substantial measures of liberal constitutionalism. Deputies were given the right to question ministers on every policy issue, and fairly free political organization and agitation was permitted.[37]

The quid pro quo was military reorganization. The army had a small professional core but was filled out by various categories including conscripts drafted for seven years' service and substitutes for those rich enough to pay. A reserve had been created in 1861, though it was not thought that it could provide competent front-line troops. Even with the reserve called out, the French army could muster only six hundred thousand men. After the stunning success of Prussian arms against Austria in 1866, the minister of war proposed Prussian-style universal military service. This was not enforceable without the Chamber's consent, however, and consent was not forthcoming. The fear was that, although the emperor was now forced to come begging to the Chamber, once he had his army, and a successful war under his belt, he would again be in a position to govern without the consent or interference of civil society. Indeed, deputies who favoured absolutist government, known as the Arcadiens, favoured a war with Prussia for precisely this reason.[38] Nevertheless, liberals could hardly ignore the requirements of national defence. A compromise was arrived at: conscripts would serve for nine years, five years with the active army and four with the reserve. This was expected to yield a force of eight hundred thousand men. The liberal opposition, however, to protect the reserve Garde Mobile from militarist indoctrination, voted funds only for very inadequate training.[39]

The general elections of 1869 saw the opposition gain a million and a half votes compared to 1863. The government had lost a million. Liberal imperialists, that is, those intent on turning the regime into a liberal parliamentary state without overthrowing the dynasty, were numerous in the new Chamber. When deputies of the left were added, there was a clear majority opposed to an absolutist executive. Theoretically, Napoleon III conceded a ministry responsible to the legislature in a decree issued in September 1869. These were real and substantial changes. However, the Napoleonic system of executive supremacy survived yet. Ministers were still appointed by the emperor, and they could only be forced out of office—impeached—by the unelected upper House, the Senate, itself appointed by Napoleon III. The lower Chamber was certainly a real Parliament, able to propose laws, discuss amendments, demand explanations from ministers, and to vote on the budget item by item. But the imperial executive still focused on the person of the emperor.

Marx's fearful derision of the French empire, as a melange of soldiers, bureaucrats, lumpen-proletarians, and courtly lick-spittles exploiting the ignorant narrow-mindedness of the peasantry to lord irresponsibly over urban civil society, was a gross exaggeration of both its capacity and, in fairness, the emperor's own intentions.[40] Louis Napoleon's regime had never been more independent of civil society than, for example, the Habsburg monarchy during its first ten years after 1848. Once the exhaustion of 1848 had passed, Napoleon III had to come to terms with civil society and constitutionalism, and did so with some conviction and skill, if incompletely. The stability and capability of the Second Empire had been impressive. Its most significant advantage over Austria was in the reach of its relatively large and centrally directed government bureaucracy. Napoleon III did not have to contend with the almost continual tax strikes and evasion faced by the Austrian regime. Certainly, the state administration in France was very far from omnipotent. It could not function without 'the co-operation of local notables', as Roger Price has demonstrated.[41] Nonetheless, in an age of bureaucratic ramification in all countries, the Napoleonic state apparatus signalled dangers for the liberals' trump card: the necessity for a modernizing, activist state to govern through consensus. To this extent, Marx's tendency to caricature the Second Empire is understandable as a fearful premonition of the future.

## WARS OF ITALIAN UNIFICATION

Piedmont-Sardinia in northern Italy balanced quasi-constitutionalism and executive flexibility in their pursuit of adventurous foreign policies more successfully than did France. Such risk-taking would have been inconceivable before 1848, when war was widely feared by conservative elites as the midwife of revolution.

After 1848, however, it became the art of the possible to build up military machines, harness nationalist enthusiasm, and launch wars of choice. Piedmont-Sardinia carefully balanced executive-state initiative, dynastic independence, and degrees of constitutionalism to construct mobilized polities for waging war, not promiscuously but strategically. Though considered a minor power at mid-century, certainly compared to Britain, France, and Austria, the success of Piedmont-Sardinia at harnessing the diplomatic flexibility of executive-led governments to the motor of constitutionalism and commercialism meant that it emerged as an exemplar of the modernizing, realpolitik power.

The union of Italy was led by Sardinia-Piedmont. The Piedmontese king, Victor Emmanuel, was little interested in politics, and executive policy was effectively conducted by his prime minister, Camillo Benso di Cavour (1810–1861), an aristocrat who spoke Piedmontese and French more fluently than literary Italian. Cavour had been discharged from the army as a sympathizer with the French revolution of 1830. On his subsequent travels, he absorbed the political liberalism of the French bourgeoisie and the economic reformism of German state-led modernization. He greatly admired the 'balance' of the English constitution. In 1847 he helped found a liberal monarchist newspaper, the *Risorgimento*, in Turin. During the 1848 revolution, Cavour vigorously opposed democratic opinion, but when reaction set in he turned his energies to defending the Constitution and freedom of the press. Cavour led the right-centre faction that first entered government in 1850 under a Conservative prime minister. In 1852 he formed his own ministry based upon an alliance with the centre-left, which lasted until 1859.

Cavour was of the view that, post-revolution, the danger to effective government in Piedmont came not from the left but rather from reaction. In a speech to the Piedmontese Parliament, delivered on 6 February 1855, he made clear his preparedness to mobilize liberalism behind the military resources of the Piedmontese state: 'Two things are necessary: firstly to prove to Europe that Italy has enough civil sense to govern herself in an orderly manner, to rule herself with liberty, that she is capable of assuming the most perfect forms of government that are known; secondly that her military valour be equal to that of her ancestors.'[42] Cavour's strategy was to leverage the fiscal authority of the constitutionalist state, and the creditworthiness of bourgeois civil society, to build up the armed forces of Piedmont, in preparation for a showdown with Austria. To this end, he laboured to strengthen the sinews of the state. Characteristically of post-1848 regimes, he approved economic liberalization to increase the flow of taxable commerce. Doctrinaire adherence to free markets may have actually impeded Italian growth, reducing her to providing raw materials to more industrialized economies. However, by committing his country to, in B. A. Haddock's words, 'a very specific vision, both liberal and capitalist',[43] Cavour's reforms attracted foreign loans from the money markets of London and Paris. These measures were designed to increase resources for the military, which was reorganized along Prussian lines.

When the Crimean War broke out in 1854, Cavour allied Piedmont-Sardinia with France and Britain. This was a matter of prestige. Cavour was anxious to display his country's capabilities as an ally, and the Sardinian expeditionary force was paid for by the state, English subsidies being ostentatiously refused.[44] As a victorious power, Sardinia was able to participate in the Paris Congress of 1856. All this was sufficient to impress Napoleon III that Piedmont could be a valuable ally in his attempt to destroy the settlement of 1815. Both powers agreed to wage war on Austria to break its hold over Italy. When it appeared that English mediation would prevent war with Austria, Cavour contemplated suicide, not only because Piedmontese geopolitical ambitions faced frustration, but also because it put in peril the entire experiment of coalition between liberal constitutionalism and dynastic state-executive diplomacy. He wrote to Louis Napoleon in desperate words:

> Your Majesty knows the difficulty of our position. We concerted a plan with your majesty by which we would group around us all the live forces of Italy but without allowing our cause to be contaminated by the revolutionary element.... If we are now made to wait outside the door while others discuss the fate of Italy...the rest of Italy will see us as feeble and powerless. Even in Piedmont opposition will grow and it will be hard to go on governing without exceptional measures and the use of force.[45]

An untimely Austrian ultimatum requiring Sardinian disarmament provided a *casus belli*, however. The Chamber of Piedmont-Sardinia, in an act of self-abnegation, conferred powers of 'dictatorship' onto the monarch, effectively giving the executive complete freedom of manoeuvre for the duration of the war.[46] This was an expressive acknowledgement of the unique capacities of the executive-military state in time of crisis and opportunity. To an extent, it made constitutionalism revolutionary until the peace. There was a still more obvious revolutionary process outside the Piedmontese dynastic state, however, with Giuseppe Garibaldi (1807–1882) raising an autonomous revolutionary detachment of fighters to attack the Austrian flank. Cavour was willing to use Garibaldi, but Garibaldi's revolutionary instincts jarred with Cavour's careful constitutionalism.

When Austrian garrisons supporting client statelets in central Italy were withdrawn at the outbreak of hostilities (1859), revolutionary provisional governments filled the vacuum. French victories at Magenta and Solferino forced Austria to give up Lombardy. The new revolutionary regimes of Tuscany, Modena, and Parma, and Romagna, approved their absorption by Piedmont in January 1860, as a step towards Italian national unification. The parliamentary Chamber at Turin in Piedmont-Sardinia accepted representatives from the new territories, and was renamed the National Parliament. The remaining despotisms of southern Italy depended upon increasingly discontented Swiss mercenaries. A revolutionary uprising began in Sicily in 1860, reinforced on 11 May by the famous landing at Marsala, on the westernmost part of the island, of a volunteer revolutionary army led by Garibaldi: the 'Marsala Thousand'. Garibaldi's forces, who were secretly aided by Cavour, crossed the straits to mainland Naples and defeated the disintegrating Papal armies. Agents of Cavour's government quickly rushed in to pre-empt Garibaldi's forces. They organized a referendum in the liberated Papal States (excluding Rome, defended by a French garrison), securing by fair means and foul nearly unanimous support for annexation to Piedmont. Garibaldi still held southern Italy and at first he resisted absorption into a monarchical Italy. Public opinion in Naples, however, clearly favoured annexation to Piedmont: when Garibaldi put it to referendum, 1,302,064 Neapolitans voted in favour against only 10,312; in Sicily the vote was 432,053 to 667.[47] The expanded National Parliament, combining dynastic and revolutionary principles, proclaimed Victor Emmanuel King of Italy, 'by the grace of God and act of the people', in March 1861.

Thereafter, the Italian state strove to sideline revolutionary impetus. Italy allied opportunistically with Prussia in its war with Austria in 1866, in the hope that Venetia could be liberated while Austria was distracted. Italy's military fared poorly, however, its army being repulsed at Custozza, and much of its fleet sunk at Lissa. Still, when Austria was defeated, Venetia was handed over to Italy. Now only Rome remained at issue. The Pope's French protectors left for good at the outbreak of the 1870 Franco-Prussian War. After Napoleon's capitulation at Sedan, the Italians occupied the Papal territory. In a referendum, annexation to the Kingdom of Italy was approved by 133,861 to 1,507.[48] Throughout the eleven-year process of Italian unification, referenda had been used to authorize annexations; executive action, revolutionary *coups de main*, diplomacy, and limited war had driven the process. Between 1848 and 1866, nearly twenty-eight thousand Italians lost their lives in the Risorgimento struggle. Cavour, the architect of profound victories, died in 1861.

Still a republican at heart, Garibaldi versified poignantly about his role in replacing Re Bomba, Naples' hollow monarch, with the Piedmontese dynasty: 'We drove the Bourbon out and took that other/Dethroned a corpse, and set up its sick brother!'[49] He reflected the widespread sense, particularly in the south, that the national revolution was in effect not much more than a successful conquest of the peninsula by the Piedmontese state, aristocracy, and bourgeoisie. The new state, indeed, was administratively centralized on the French model to suppress regionalism. Law and order proved particularly difficult to enforce on the former Kingdom of Naples. Political brigands—including the *Camorra* in Naples and the *Mafia* in Sicily—operated in the name of the deposed Ferdinand and Catholic absolutism, much in the style of populist Spanish Carlism. Brigandage disrupted payment and collection of taxes, and terrorized liberals. The ideal of the archaic absolutist state, ironically, could be romanticized as a form of freedom precisely because it had so little practical ability to disrupt for long the traditions and procedures of long-standing village communities. The Italian army waged pacification warfare over several years in the mountain districts, and was seen as being firmly on the side of the landowner and the exploiter.

Burdened by the costs of the Risorgimento, Italy by 1864 faced bankruptcy. Francesco Ferrara, Italy's leading economist, pointed out the harsh reality of overstretch in 1866:

> In foreign eyes the very name of nation...seems something like a mockery when applied to our Italy which we admire so much. She seems a beggarwoman knocking at the door of every banker in turn, a girl at the beck and call of any strong man, a bankrupt country which could at any moment involve in her own ruin anyone simple enough to accept her pledges.... our country is getting a bad name.[50]

Francesco Crispi, when Premier, admitted, in a speech delivered on 10 March 1881, the long-term debilitating impact of nationalist idealism combined with the indifferent success made of sovereign independence: 'It is a fact that the further we travel from the days of the great revolution the colder and narrower our hearts grow until they become almost unpatriotic!'[51]

This mood of disillusion owed ironically not to failure but to the extraordinary success of Italian nation-builders in overcoming their intrinsic weaknesses through judicious alliance. The Italian state could hardly be anything other than somewhat jerry-built, given the many and disparate hands involved in its construction. Its residents were justifiably bewildered by the rapidity at which the edifice was put up. They were left with a heavy mortgage, not easily paid off. Antonio Gramsci, a Communist intellectual, would later characterize the Risorgimento as a disappointingly 'passive revolution', because the state rather than social classes as such played the most important role. As a consequence, social transformation was piecemeal, and the powers of the traditional governmental apparatus were preserved, even augmented. This reading, however, was from the jaundiced perspective of Leninist contempt for the bourgeoisie. To be sure, without the support of France and without the popular movement against Austrian influence in Italy—partly nationalist, partly regionalist in inspiration—Piedmont-Sardinia could hardly have succeeded in annexing most of Italy. But there was no 'true' revolutionary alternative, for bourgeois civil society in Italy was no more capable (or desirous) of decisive political action on its own behalf, against all-comers, than middle-class movements anywhere else. Constitutional liberalism, even where capitalism was much more developed, always worked with established elites, state structures, and the popular movement where it could, and rarely insisted upon political command. Entrepreneurs made for poor politicians in Italy, but no more than elsewhere. State initiative, aristocratic mediation, popular energy, and commercial dynamism was the norm for constitutional revolution, and in fact rather more effectively compounded in Italy than in most instances. Cavour's skilful welding together of traditional aristocratic militarism, executive state 'dictatorship', constitutional liberalism, and commercialist economic modernization, raised the credibility and punching power of the dynasty he served, making the expansion of Piedmont-Sardinia the only credible alternative to Austrian hegemony in Italy. This was hardly a 'passive' revolution; it was, on the contrary, executed with at times consummate skill.

## CONCLUSION

In the decade after 1848, European states encouraged the spread of commercialism and industry within their borders. They were confident that political liberalism could be contained, and increased trade and prosperity turned to the fiscal advantage of government. When the Crimean War weakened Russia and Austria—the two major empires of the axis of international order as constructed in 1815—it was evident that forceful diplomacy and war-making to advance dynastic interests was back on the agenda. In this newly competitive international environment, it made sense for executive states to be left a great deal of latitude by their respective legislatures. Placated by a strengthening of the rule of law and market domestically, liberals were increasingly willing to support governmental power of initiative, even as this meant moderating their support for parliamentary sovereignty and control over the executive.

In 1864 an International Workingman's Association was set up, to link organizations dedicated to working-class self-representation. Karl Marx was secretary and the most influential individual on the General Council. The first Congress in 1866 adopted the general principle that 'emancipation of the working classes must be conquered by the working classes themselves'. An important strain within the International, influenced by Pierre-Joseph Proudhon (1809–1865), opposed working-class participation in parliamentary politics; the state was the enemy. The 1867 Congress, however, declared 'that the social emancipation of the workers is inseparable from their political emancipation', and so 'the establishment of political liberties' was accepted as being 'a measure of absolute necessity'.[52] This put the International in the camp of radical political liberalism, as it prioritized the winning of democratic representation, again at Marx's urging.

That socialism after 1848 re-emerged flying the banner of radical democratic constitutionalism is not surprising, for liberalism permeated both left and right in this period, without ever quite dominating on its own behalf. Cavour's statecraft was only one example, if undeniably impressive and assured, of how a monarchy that had been timid and obsessed with fending off revolution in the first half of the century could turn to political finesse at home and diplomatic adventuring abroad in the third quarter. The years between 1848 and 1867 had seen the rapid exhaustion of neo-absolutism in Europe and the impressively rapid spread of liberal civil society and constitutionalism. But rather than sweep away the old state regimes, those bold enough to take control and advantage had been immeasurably strengthened. The period 1850 to 1865 was not characterized by bourgeois betrayal of liberalism for fear of the working class. Rather, it was an era in which liberalism colluded with pre-existing state structures, because the latter were advancing the interests of bourgeois civil society, if for their own purposes, and conceding significant constitutional reforms.

# 6
# Bismarck, Liberalism, and Socialism

German unification, led by an authoritarian, conservative, and aristocratic ('junker') Prussia, is remembered as the definitive example of 'revolution from above', and the most ominous example of national modernization without a concomitant movement of bourgeois liberalism. In fact, the Prussian experience came closest to being the most striking example of an archetypal bourgeois revolution. The Constitutional struggle between Crown and Parliament that broke out in Prussia in 1860 combined in almost pure form the demands (government responsible to the legislature, economic liberty), the modes of struggle (resistance to 'illegal' levying of taxation), sites of struggle (urban local government, Parliament), and the class composition (strongly middle class) of abstract 'bourgeois revolution'. In practice, it was too theoretically 'pure' for its own good: the weakness of a bourgeois Constitutional movement lacking sufficient aid from sections of the state, aristocracy, or masses was highlighted by its defeat and the Crown's triumph. This was a movement too straightforwardly bourgeois to win; but its defeat was honourable by its own terms. Bourgeois 'betrayal', such as it was, emerged only as a recognition of defeat. It did not precipitate that defeat.

Like Piedmont-Sardinia, Prussia preserved a Constitution of sorts from 1848, but it reserved much more power to the royal executive. By convention, budgets were only presented to the Landtag (House of Deputies) for approval retrospectively, after the money had been spent, and only as a bloc, without individual items being debated. By 1854, King Friedrich William IV had secured the replacement of an elected Upper House with a Herrenhaus, or House of Lords. This degree of constitutionalism, though limited, when taken with economic prosperity and fiscal discipline was sufficient to augment significantly state finances. With an income tax introduced in 1851 and reforms to the land tax in 1861, the kingdom was, as Christopher Clark notes, 'flush with new cash'.[1]

The Prussian government wished to maintain maximum freedom of executive action, combined with a Constitutionalism credible enough to underpin fiscal strength in depth and liberal enough to appeal to progressively minded German nationalists beyond the borders of the kingdom. Prussia was positioning itself for a struggle that had opened up in the revolutionary year of 1848, and which never completely receded in the reaction. A German nation seemed to be coalescing, and in the absence of a cataclysmic republican revolution from below, it was evident that a pre-existing state power would effectively absorb a greater or lesser part of the central European German milieu. The question was, which of the two largest German powers would prove to be the beneficiary—Prussia or Austria? There were a good number of Germans in the Austrian empire, but still they amounted to no more than 8 million out of an imperial population of 36 million. Prussia was much more completely German (though it had a significant Polish minority), and it bordered no fewer than twenty-eight other German states. Her claim to German leadership, thus, was naturally strong. The question was whether this could be reinforced by military and economic hegemony.

## THE CONSTITUTIONAL STRUGGLE IN PRUSSIA

As the Prussian King Friedrick William lost his mental faculties, his brother, Wilhelm, became regent in 1858. This seemed to mark the end of the reaction: Wilhelm discarded the 'Feudal party' who had advised his brother, and he openly accepted the Constitution, though he still assumed higher responsibilities, to God and, in his capacity as commander-in-chief (Kriegsherr), to the army. Liberals felt that a 'New Era' had begun, and the elections of 1858 saw a strong constitutional liberal majority returned to the Landtag. At first, they hoped to work cooperatively with the king's ministers. Gradually, however, conflict emerged between legislature and king over the question of the army.

Marx observed that the professional standing army was constitutive of dynastic supremacy, 'the true prop of...kingly power' being a soldiery 'separated from the mass, opposed to it, distinguished by certain badges, trained to passive obedience, drilled into a mere instrument of the dynasty which owns it as its property and uses it according to its caprice'.[2] This was Wilhelm's view too. In 1861, aged sixty-three, the regent succeeded to the throne as King Wilhelm I. His immediate priority was to refurbish the military system. He was determined to build a professional standing army, fully inculcated with loyalty to the dynasty and state. Wilhelm distrusted the Landwehr, a militia made up of older family fathers, as 'civilians in uniform' irredeemably subversive of the Crown's will.[3] Only 'long familiarity' with barracks life, Wilhelm insisted, could infuse men with the soldierly qualities of 'discipline' and 'blind obedience'. Albrecht von Roon, the king's minister, doubted whether the Landwehr militiaman, 'his soul clung to his farm, his chisel, his work at home, not to the flag', could ever be made amenable to 'the iron screws of military discipline'.[4] A disciplined, militarily effective army, both men were sure, could not depend upon a civilian militia.

Wilhelm used his prerogative as Kriegsherr to increase the active army to nearly 200,000 soldiers, with another 220,000 in the reserve, while the Landwehr was downgraded. This, of course, was expensive and controversial. The king was forced to propose to the Landtag an increase in the land tax to pay for army reorganization. In May 1860, however, the Landtag agreed only to renew funding for a single year, a compromise it approved again (narrowly) the following year. New elections were held in 1861. Radicalized by the struggles over the army bills, liberals coalesced into a new German Progress party (the Progressists, or Fortschrittspartei). This was a middle-class formation, though with officials employed by the government rather than capitalist entrepreneurs prominent in its leadership.[5] The Progressists demanded a more fully constitutional state and favoured a liberalized Prussia consensually merging with other German lands by bilateral agreement, on the Sardinian/Italian model. Crucially, the Progressists insisted that compulsory service with the army be cut from three to two years. This was a direct challenge to the authoritarian Crown government. The Liberal politician Franz Schultze-Delitzsch declared in July 1862 that 'the question of a permanent development of a liberal Constitution could not be solved under existing conditions, unless the National Army, being, in fact, the nation armed, were to stand behind this Parliament'.[6] Whether the army would be a tool of the executive or of the Parliament was the issue at stake. The Progressists gained the majority in the 1861 election, drawing particular strength from the larger towns and the manufacturing districts—Saxony, Silesia, and the Rhine Province. The old Liberal party, which had been pro-ministry since 1858, was nearly wiped out. The Landtag was no longer a supine tool of government. Seeking a showdown, it refused to renew the additional spending on the army for another year.

Twice, King Wilhelm dissolved the Landtag, twice a Progressist majority was re-elected. The king had even drawn up an act for his abdication before changing his mind and calling on one of his diplomats, Otto von Bismarck (1815–1898), to form and lead a 'fighting ministry' as Minister President. Bismarck, a scion of the landed gentry of Prussian Saxony, had come to the government's notice in the Landtag of 1847, where he had vigorously opposed the concept of parliamentary government. In 1849 he had deprecated with rhetorical relish the 'Western' arrangement of parliamentary control of the budget. He believed that Prussia should indeed challenge Austria for national mastery, but, he said, 'Germany does not look to Prussia's liberalism, but to her strength. The South German States—Bavaria, Wüttemberg, and Baden, would like to indulge in liberalism, and because of that no one will assign Prussia's role to them! Prussia must collect her forces and hold them in reserve for an opportune moment.... Not by speeches and majorities will the great questions of the day be decided—that was the mistake of 1848 and 1849—but by iron and blood.'[7] This was a plea for an unencumbered state, fiscally secure, but left free and self-willed, focused and flexible in international affairs. Whilst, as Bismarck said later, he was 'perfectly aware that, in Germany, in the second half of the nineteenth century, absolutism and autocracy would be impossible', he nevertheless was determined to prevent the emergence of a fully fledged 'parliamentary regime' as making for 'weakness and incompetence at the top...bumptiousness and ever new demands from below'.[8] Already convinced that war with Austria was inevitable, Bismarck was as certain as the king that the army reorganization must be made permanent.

Bismarck determined that full spending must be authorized for the army whether approved by the legislature or not. The Deputies protested that it was 'a breach of the Constitution if the Royal Government directs expenditure to be made which had been definitely and expressly disallowed by a resolution of the House of Deputies'.[9] Bismarck, nonetheless, had the House of Lords pass the necessary budgets. The Lower House in October 1862 declared this to be unconstitutional as any budget must be approved by the representatives of the taxpayers.

Bismarck, in response, proffered the legalistic theory of an 'omission' (Lückentheorie) in the Constitution. The Constitution of 1850 had given the king, the Chamber of Deputies, and the House of Lords co-equal legislative authority, even in budget matters. It had failed to specify the ultimate authority in case of deadlock. In the absence of positive direction from the Constitution, the law must revert to the status quo prior to 1850. As Bismarck put it in 1863, 'If...compromise is thwarted...in its place will occur conflicts. And since the life of a state cannot remain still, conflicts become questions of power.'[10] Bismarck's opponents polemically shortened this to the brutally simple maxim, 'Might before Right.'[11]

The Landtag certainly enjoyed wide public support, and they could credibly call on citizens to resist paying unconstitutional and illegal taxes. The Ministry, however, had the backing of the army and of the government bureaucracy with which to actually collect the tax. Otto Pflanze has commented:

> The best weapon of any parliament against the executive is financial. By finally denying the funds needed to carry out the military reorganization, the deputies had taken the first step.... It was the misfortune of the deputies that the period of the constitutional conflict was one of steadily rising national income and increasing tax yields. While the deputies struggled against the crown, their political supporters were piling up the profits and paying the taxes which were to bring about their defeat.[12]

Due to economic upsurge in the second half of 1861, for example, revenue from indirect taxation (which made up well over half of the total) surged, as did revenue from state enterprises (forests, railways, mines, postal services, etcetera). Rather than the expected deficit of 3.5 million thaler there was a surplus of 5 million thaler. 'Ironically,' as Mosse puts it, 'the very success of the Prussian bourgeoisie in the economic sphere contributed to its political discomfiture.'[13]

By 1862, Ferdinand Lassalle (1825–1864), a talented if egocentric Jewish intellectual then on the left wing of the Progressists, was calling for an all-out tax strike. This was the appropriate form of struggle, he argued, in modern society where state dependence on the industrial resources of bourgeois society made outright absolutism an impossibility. The authoritarian executive-state was forced to affect a sham constitutionalism because 'a government which has its hands continually in everyone's pocket must assume at least the appearance of having everyone's consent'. Lassalle's proposal that the House of Deputies adjourn indefinitely, however, was rejected by the liberal press as being tantamount to initiating an armed rebellion that must certainly be crushed in blood. The one Progressist Deputy who came out in agreement with Lassalle was so isolated that he felt obliged to resign his seat.[14]

Bismarck had the king dissolve the Lower House again in 1863. Following the example set by Napoleon III, 'official candidacy' in Landtag elections was formally established. The king issued a directive to all officials declaring that their oath of loyalty and fealty to the Crown obliged them 'to follow as voters the course indicated by the King'.[15] Nonetheless, another Progressist majority was returned. After this, the government simply stopped presenting budgets for approval to the Chamber of Deputies, and sessions of the Landtag were made as brief as possible.

For three years, the ministry levied taxes authorized only by the House of Lords. Prussia's liberal bourgeoisie was now engaged in a decisive confrontation with the conservative monarchy. In 1863 the Landtag passed a bill to enforce the responsibility of ministers to itself rather than to the Crown. The House of Lords and king refused to ratify it. Cities organized meetings in support of the Landtag deputies, many of which the government prohibited; citizens in retaliation refused to celebrate the royal anniversaries. Liberal physical training and rifle clubs were formed, consisting mainly of merchants and artisans: they symbolized constitutionalist intent to reduce the reactionary standing army.[16] The mood was bitter: years later Bismarck recalled with wonder that 'men spat on the place where I trod on the streets'.[17] It was stalemate between a semi-absolutist state and bourgeois constitutionalist revolution. Moderate liberals, however, grew increasingly discomfited. By October 1863, Johann Gustav Droysen, a former member of the Frankfurt Parliament and eminent Prussian historian, was fearful that the liberal centre ground risked being squeezed between the 'brutality' of Bismarck's government and the extreme Left: 'For me the absolutism of the democrats is as unacceptable as that of the courts.'[18]

## GERMAN UNIFICATION

Seeing Bismarck's struggle for mastery in Germany as little more than Prussian aggrandizement and an excuse to maintain an unconstitutional army, the Progressist Chamber deprecated Bismarck's efforts in international diplomacy. With the Prussian Landtag refusing funds, Bismarck turned to his confidant, the brilliant Jewish financier Gerson Bleichröder, to orchestrate (probably unconstitutionally) a conversion of government rights to shares in the Cologne-Minden Railway in order to raise the necessary funds to fight a war.[19] Bismarck did not pay much attention to winning over German national opinion. He manoeuvred between the Great Powers to isolate Austria. It was through three wars—with Denmark in 1864, with Austria in 1866, and with France in 1870–1—that Prussia secured united Germany. In their conflict with Denmark over the duchies of Holstein and Schleswig, Austria and Prussia studiously avoided reference to popular principles of nationality. Liberal opinion throughout Germany was troubled by the duchies being claimed simply as dynastic spoils of war, a contrast to the referenda employed to legitimize annexations to the Italian state.

Anticipating a military contest with Austria, Prussia in April 1866 proposed radical plans including a German-wide Parliament elected by universal suffrage. Nevertheless, most liberals and governments favoured Austria, which had been domestically liberalizing since 1859. Prussia struck first, having secured an alliance with Italy that tied-up Austrian forces in Venetia. The Prussian military machine was far more effective than its rivals, rapidly moving a large number of men and pitching them early into the contest. A single battle at Königgrätz, Bohemia, on 4 July 1866, broke the Austrian army. Prussia's army of citizens, hammered into shape by a professional army officer caste, proved its worth against the Austrian model of a large professional establishment disdaining mass civilian levies. Prussia's triumph announced a revolution in military technique.

Austria accepted that it had been pushed out of the political life of Germany, and it consented to the dissolution of the loose pan-German Confederation. Austria's 8 million German citizens found themselves expelled from national life. A new North German Confederation (Norddeutsche Bund) brought all states north of the River Main within a Prussian-dominated union. The Parliament of the North German Confederation, the Reichstag, elected by universal male suffrage, was no lapdog of the government. However, the new state structure went a considerable distance to insulate the fiscal resources of the executive from parliamentary pressure, whilst maintaining sufficient constitutionalism to convince bondholders that the government ruled broadly by consent. Federal revenues, to pay for military forces, foreign diplomacy, commerce, and public-transportation infrastructure, derived not from parliamentary appropriations but from customs, indirect taxes on consumption, and fees for post-office services and telegraphs. Any deficiency was made up by subventions paid in by the constituent princely states in fixed proportions (Matrikel). This arrangement sharply limited the Reichstag's control of the purse strings. Moreover, the military budget was fixed for five-year periods. Bismarck's introduced universal suffrage for Reichstag elections, to balance the particularist tendencies of the state governments and the aristocratic elites, and to 'do away with the influence of the Liberal bourgeoisie', as he put it.[20] The new Bundesrath Upper House, made up of princely delegations, in turn, would negate the Reichstag's democratic tendencies and parliamentary claims. Bismarck was following Napoleon III in mobilizing universal suffrage in order to smother aristocratic or bourgeois resistance to executive domination, whilst simultaneously ensuring that the democracy had no real access to the levers of state.

Prussia's triumph in 1866 decisively ended the constitutional conflict between the Progressist liberals and Crown government to the latter's advantage. It marked, says Wehler, 'the second great turning-point in Prussia's domestic politics [after 1848] and, consequently, in German history as a whole.... The outcome of this conflict was to seal the political impotence of the bourgeoisie up to 1918.'[21] The Progressist party was deserted by the voters. Liberals split, with more than half admitting that demands of constitutional transformation were now only 'ultimate goals', and re-forming themselves as 'National Liberals' to offer support to the ministry.[22] Bismarck was slow to accept the entreaties of the National Liberals to be allowed to act as the 'government party' in the Reichstag. Only in December 1869 were two National Liberals finally admitted as ministers. Already by 1868, however, Bismarck was adopting much of the administrative and economic reform programme of Liberals. Economic reforms were instituted particularly rapidly. Usury laws, which inhibited capitalist finance and commerce, were repealed. Restrictions on business enterprises were abolished. Imprisonment for debt, a disincentive to risk-taking in business, was done away with. There were also reforms conducive to personal freedom, as in marriage law, and a new penal code. David Blackbourn and Geoff Eley judge these changes, taken together, to have been a 'silent bourgeois revolution'.[23] Considering the evidence comparatively, John

Breuilly concludes that 'there is a good case to be made for the argument that the decade of the 1860s in Germany saw the most dramatic victories won by a clear and coherent liberalism at any time in nineteenth-century Europe'.[24]

Liberal opinion hostile to Prussianism in the late 1860s remained formidable across Germany. The consolidation of a separate, markedly liberal, southern German federation seemed a distinct possibility. A French declaration of war against the northern Confederation in 1870, however, aroused German patriotism north and south of the river Main. Within eighteen days Prussia mobilized 1,183,000 men and after two weeks had an invasion force of 462,000 poised. France, in contrast, mobilized only 230,000 (not the expected 385,000) after a fortnight, of whom fewer than 200,000 were battle-ready.[25] The French Second Army was surrounded and cut off at Metz, bottling up the principal French strike force. A patched-together relief force was trapped and defeated at Sedan. The entire army, including Louis Napoleon himself, surrendered on 2 September 1870. Prussian victory over France massively boosted her national credentials and made German unification under Prussian auspices inevitable. It was by suggestion of the King of Bavaria that the old historical names of Reich and Kaiser—empire and emperor—were revived for the united Germany. Rather than construct a new Constitution, the four southern states joined the union by treaty between sovereigns (again, in contrast to Italian referenda). In January 1871, the King of Prussia was crowned emperor in the presence of the German sovereigns. Humiliatingly for France (and, indeed, for the Reichstag), the ceremony took place not amongst the German *volk* but in the monarchical Palace of Versailles.

Thus the German Reich came into being. It was a strongly monarchical constitutionalism, with the chancellor and his ministry dependent on the goodwill of the monarch rather than the legislature. Jacob Burckhardt, the Swiss historian, in a 1872 letter, reflected soberly on the circumstances of German unification:

> Bismarck has only taken into his own hands what would have happened anyhow with the passage of time, but without his aid and against his interests. He saw that the growing democratic-socialist wave would somehow provoke a state of absolute power, whether through the Democrats themselves or through the governments. So he spoke: '*ipse faciam*'—and waged the three wars of 1864, 1866 and 1870.... The external apparatus of so-called freedom has been allowed to come into existence, but they ['our Berlin masters'] are secretly resolved to act for all time according to their own will—not that I would deem absolute government an especial misfortune as compared with the consequences of universal suffrage. I have become extremely cool about such things.[26]

This was the opinion of not a few liberals, who overstated the risk that a constitutional struggle could spin into democratic red-republicanism, if only to convince themselves that Prussian-led unification of Germany was the best outcome on offer.

Liberals did succeed in preserving the Constitution, such as it was, against a coup d'état. Though the Constitution, as adapted for the unified German Reich, fell well short of liberal ambitions, even National Liberals did not disavow the ultimate goal of ministerial responsibility to the representative legislature. In the short term, civil and personal liberty was more or less secured in a law-bound

Rechtsstaat, and the interests of commercial civil society were clearly paramount, even if the junkerdom remained powerful. But given the bold hopes and indeed tenacious liberal struggle of the first half of the 1860s, it is not perhaps surprising that socialists sniffed betrayal in the liberal reconciliation by 1870 with the reality of the Bismarckian Reich. Still, it is hardly fair to accuse liberals specifically and the bourgeoisie in general of easily capitulating to Bismarckian authoritarianism. While it would have been possible to boycott parliamentarianism altogether until a fully liberal Constitution was conceded, the only possible next step thereafter, without a disintegration of the ruling order, was armed revolution. The years 1848–9 had indicated well enough that the chances of this working against a determined state-executive were not good. Indeed, as we shall see, the Socialist Party itself in Germany soon explicitly disavowed any attempt to 'make revolution', as opposed to making use of it should it arrive spontaneously. The failure of liberals to make revolution, therefore, cannot be a special mark to their discredit.

## SOCIALISTS AND GERMANY

In a booklet on German affairs, *The Prussian Military Question and the German Workers' Party* (1865), Engels was highly critical of German liberal tactics, though not always from the perspective we might expect. As an influential and clear conspectus on the contemporaneous bourgeois revolution from the perspective of mature Marxism, it is worth sustained attention. Engels highlighted the centrality of representative parliamentarianism as being the specific political form for securing the hegemony of those classes with their locus in civil society:

> The feudal aristocracy and the bureaucracy can retain their real power in Prussia even without parliamentary representation. Their traditional position at the court, in the army and in the civil service guarantees them this power.... They would therefore dearly like to consign parliament and all its trappings to oblivion. On the other hand the bourgeoisie and workers can only exercise real, organized, political power through parliamentary representation; and such parliamentary representation is valueless unless it has a voice and a share in making decisions, in other words, unless it holds the 'purse-strings'.[27]

Here, parliamentarianism is defined as the only means by which those classes, the bourgeoisie and the working class, that lack the juridical and local governing authority of the traditional landowner, or the privy access power of the courtier, may in practice exercise political power. They do so specifically because Parliament authorizes the tax-state, which in turn requires that the state pays due regard to the interest of the taxpayer, the credit market and, at a further remove, the producers of wealth. Parliamentarianism is not simply an expression of bourgeois class dictatorship. Rather, the logic of the bourgeoisie's social condition implies a universal and consistent political freedom:

> As distinct from the old Estates, distinguished by birth, it must proclaim human rights, as distinct from the guilds, it must proclaim freedom of trade and industry, as

distinct from the tutelage of the bureaucracy, it must proclaim freedom and self-government. To be consistent, it must therefore demand universal, direct suffrage, freedom of the press, association and assembly and the suspension of all special laws directed against individual classes of the population.[28]

Liberty for bourgeois conditions of existence requires freedom of information and contact, as conditions for a commercialized economy. This, in principle, is not limitable to one class, and so means freedom for all citizens, including workers.

The bourgeoisie as a class, argued Engels, were not adequate of themselves to make a revolution, being insufficient in numbers and hardly best situated for street revolution. They were an 'army of officers without any soldiers' and to remedy their lack of coercive force 'must either ensure that the workers are its allies, or it must buy political power piecemeal from the powers opposing it from above, in particular from the monarchy'. Engels had little doubt which strategy the bourgeoisie favoured: 'holy fear of the workers had become a habit with the bourgeoisie' such that they would wish to cut a deal with the junker state.[29]

Before rushing to ascribe to Engels a theory of bourgeois 'betrayal', however, it is important to register that he thought that a bourgeois deal with the junker state was both realistic as a strategy and congruent with the historic 'tasks' of the bourgeois. The prospects for liberalism cutting an advantageous deal with the Prussian state were entirely promising because the strength of the bourgeoisie, its '*real* power in the state, consisted...in the right to approve taxation'.[30] Bourgeois civil society, in Engels' view, could bargain with the state from a position of some strength. From this proposition, however, Engels' argument took an unexpected turn. He criticized the liberals not for *refusing* the state taxes but rather for failing to supply *enough*. The 'bourgeois opposition in Prussia,' he insisted, had foolishly attempted to 'bargain for power *without* paying any money for it'.[31] The mistake of the Progressists, indeed, had been to resist the Prussian state's attempt to reform its military apparatus. Given that the 'New Era' government was determined on nothing more than augmenting the army, and so willing to make concessions in return for tax funds, the liberals should have 'seized [the opportunity] with both hands; such a chance for the bourgeoisie could not be expected again in a hundred years. What might not be extracted from this ministry, in point of detail, if the progressist bourgeoisie viewed the situation not as misers but as great speculators!'[32] Furthermore, the extremely rapid recruitment of professionalized elements to the army offered opportunities decisively to bolster its bourgeois credentials and sideline the aristocratic officer class: 'with *this* military system Prussia can neither wage an unpopular war nor carry out a coup d'état which has any prospect of permanence'.[33] Engels was blithely confident that no modernizing state attempting to keep up with international rivals could afford to resist constitutionalist pressures from civil society. The state's expensive project of military augmentation and modernization, Engels argued, played to the enduring strength of the bourgeoisie, which was fiscal:

> Ultimately...the main safeguard against a coup d'état...is to be found in the fact that no coup d'état can enable a government to convene a Chamber which will approve

new taxation and loans for it; and that, even if it did manage to find a Chamber willing to do so, no banker in Europe would give it credit on the basis of resolutions passed by such a Chamber.... [I]t is generally accepted that no one may lend Prussia a penny without the legal and unimpeachable approval of the Chamber.... And this is where the strength of the bourgeoisie lies: that if the government gets into financial difficulties—which sooner or later it is bound to do—it is *itself* obliged to *turn to the bourgeoisie for money.*

The problem with the Prussian bourgeoisie had not been timidity but that by 'overestimating its own strength [it had] got itself into the situation of having to use this military question as a test-case to see whether it is the decisive force in the state or nothing at all'.[34] This was far too risky a strategy: 'If it wins, it will simultaneously acquire the power of appointing and dismissing ministers, such as the English Lower House possesses. If it is vanquished, it will never again achieve any kind of significance by constitutional means.'[35]

Given the relative social weakness of the German bourgeoisie, compared to that of France and Britain, Engels anticipated that its courage would fail once a long-term struggle became the only evident path to success, particularly as it relied upon the authoritarian state for economic reforms congenial to its interest. A protracted struggle, moreover, must serve to mobilize the working-class movement. Thus would bourgeois conservatism and fear of outright revolution proportionately grow. The risk was that the bourgeoisie would learn to forgo civil liberalism just as civil liberalism began to advantage the working class, who were necessarily much more dependent upon the resources of political and civic rights to promote their interests. While 'a timid bourgeoisie' could 'manage passably well' without freedom of the press, freedom of association and assembly, universal suffrage, and local self-government, 'unless there is freedom of the press, the right of association and the right of assembly, no workers' movement is possible'.[36] The task of the workers, therefore, was to ally with the bourgeoisie and drive them on.

This was a striking discussion of bourgeois revolution in process. It made clear that, in the Marxian schema, the consolidation of bourgeois political influence was marked by constitutionalism, that the principal lever of civil society to turn the modern state was fiscal, and that constitutionalism was no regime of narrow bourgeois benefit but rather benefited workers at least as much.[37] Engels' brochure was rather ambiguous in tone. He certainly argued that the workers' movement should ally with the liberal middle class in pursuit of constitutionalism. On the other hand, he evinced clear regard for the hard-headedness and national spirit of the state, and even applauded the goal of an expanded army. It is little surprise to find that this tension, between supporting the bourgeoisie as progressive and sympathizing with even the semi-authoritarian state for its national perspective, to some degree at least 'above class', could be found in yet starker forms in the embryonic socialist movement itself.

German liberals, for their part, were far from irredeemably hostile to working-class interests and organization. They were strongly of the view that in time all citizens could be brought within the *mittelstand* (middle class), particularly if workers were encouraged to join together in cooperative enterprises operating within the market.[38] This interest in cooperatives, however, naturally encouraged socialist ideas amongst workers. In March 1863, Lassalle published an open letter in which he called for a workers' party independent of middle-class leaders. He emphasized the struggle for universal suffrage as a key stage on the way to the working class winning systematic support from the state for workers' cooperatives.[39] He promised workers leadership provided by serious, modern-minded intellectuals; not the idealistic pipe-dreamers of old, but rather 'men who understand your position and are devoted to your cause—men, armed with the shining sword of science, who know how to defend your interests'.[40] Lassalle, of course, had himself first in mind as leader-saviour of the proletariat, but this 'great man' theory also played on the widespread admiration for Bismarck's masterful role. Lassalle's 'General Union of German Workingmen' was strongly, even dictatorially, centralized under his personal control.

Lassalle passionately opposed the Progressists as irredeemably wedded to middle-class interests. He hoped that Bismarck could be convinced to institute simple universal male suffrage, so as to swamp the liberals. There was less intrinsic conflict of interest, he believed, between workers and the state, rationally maximizing its resources and minimizing domestic discord, than there was between workers and the free-market bourgeoisie. Lassalle even had secret negotiations with Bismarck, the latter curious as to whether the incipient workers' movement could be an ally against the liberals.[41] Lassalle, always a flamboyant and mercurial leader, was killed in a duel in 1864, to be succeeded by Johann Schweitzer. When Schweitzer criticized 'parliamentarianism' as 'mean empty wordiness...the rule of mediocrities', and expressed a preference for the 'masterful initiative' and 'overwhelming action' of 'Caesarism' in the Bismarck style, Marx repudiated him.[42] But attraction to strong executive government in contrast to bourgeois vacillation was far from banished from the socialist movement.

The Lassallean party, due to its willingness to treat with Bismarckian authoritarianism against liberals, was opposed by those German socialists hostile to 'Prussianiasm'. They were led by Wilhelm Liebknecht (1826–1900), a former '48 refugee under the influence of Karl Marx, and August Bebel (1840–1913), a Saxon lathe-worker and Catholic democrat, who in 1867–8 was won over by Liebknecht to the Marxian socialist camp. This party had much more faith in liberalism. They drew their recruits from workers' educational societies (Arbeiterbildungsvereine) established by Progressists, in the main, on liberal principles of self-help and individual betterment.[43] Their strongholds were in non-Prussian parts of Germany where liberalism most vehemently opposed the victory of Prussian militarism, notably Saxony. By 1867, Liebknecht and Bebel had each won seats in the Reichstag of the Prussian-organized North German Confederation. A meeting of workers' educational societies at Nuremberg the following year, by a two-thirds vote, came out in favour of the International Workingman's Association, organized by Marx from London.

In 1869 the German 'Marxists' founded the Social Democratic Workers' Party. Its 'Eisenach Program', named after the central German town where it was drawn up, was effectively a combination of the advanced democratic politics of left-liberal radicalism and a denunciation of capitalism and hope for its transcendence, as derived from an imperfect assimilation of the doctrines of Marx. In contrast to Lassalle's centralized party structure, the Eisenach party was federative. It rejected strategies that dismissed parliamentarianism as if of no interest to workers: 'Political freedom is the essential prerequisite for the economic emancipation of the working classes.... [A solution to the] social question... [is] possible only in a democratic state'.[44] The 'Marxian' party in German socialism, therefore, tended towards support for the 'bourgeois liberty' when it came to a contest with junker authoritarianism. This was, perhaps, more of a party shibboleth, distinguishing the Eisenachers from a Lassalle party that retained formidable sympathy amongst the fledgling socialist movement, than a deep-set conviction. As evidenced by Engels' sneaking regard for a strong state, discussed above, and by Marx's flinty promotion of 'dictatorial' methods in time of revolution ever since 1848, orthodox socialism retained an undertow of sympathy for dynamic executive-state action. This contributed to setting it apart from the limited ambition of parliamentary liberals to emancipate civil society from undue interference. Statism, perhaps, was ineradicable from a socialist movement whose putative working-class constituency felt fully the insecurities of commercial civil society.

Socialists were suspicious of bourgeois antipathy to the political public sphere, and preference for a commercial civil society. It must, they reasoned, make for a middle-class liberalism ill-suited to contest the state on the terrain of politics, and ready to betray the struggle for constitutionalism as long as private economic interests were promised protection. Thus German socialists were predisposed to interpret a defeat for constitutionalism as due to betrayal by the bourgeoisie. Engels, seeing parallels between Bismarck and Louis Napoleon, was increasingly convinced that the bourgeoisie was not destined by normal development to become a political ruling class. In 1870 he published a new edition of his 1850 work, *The Peasant War in Germany*. In the first edition he had argued that the 1848 revolution, despite appearances, had led to a real victory for the bourgeoisie in Prussia because the executive-state admitted its dependence on parliamentary taxation levied on a basically capitalist economy. He now radically revised this view. While the bourgeoisie had, during the constitutional crisis of the 1860s, been confronted with the opportunity of taking the Prussian political executive in hand, this 'opportunity of "quickly subjugating" the monarchy by means of the State debt' had been fumbled. The bourgeoisie had, it is true, secured a constitutional state in Austria following the defeat of monarchy in war, but it proved incapable of a decisive governing will, and real power was remorselessly devolving back towards court circles. In Prussia the state debt had 'increased by leaps and bounds', and the liberal bourgeoisie had a majority in the lower Chamber so that 'No taxes can be increased and no debts incurred without their consent.' Still, the executive state run by Chancellor Bismarck maintained its supremacy over the Reichstag.[45] This outcome, Engels argued, was due to a structural inability of the bourgeoisie to govern directly:

> It is a peculiarity of the bourgeoisie, distinguishing it from all other classes, that a point is being reached in its development after which every increase in its power, that

is, every enlargement of its capital, only tends to make it more and more incapable of retaining political dominance. *'Behind the big bourgeoisie stand the proletarians.'* In the degree as the bourgeoisie develops its industry, its commerce, and its means of communication, it also produces the proletariat. At a certain point, which must not necessarily appear simultaneously and on the same stage of development everywhere, it begins to note that this, its second self, has outgrown it. From then on, it loses the power for exclusive political dominance. It looks for allies with whom to share its authority, or to whom to cede all power, as circumstances may demand.... These allies are all of a reactionary turn. It is the king's power, with his army and his bureaucracy; it is the big feudal nobility; it is the smaller junker; it is even the clergy.... And the more the proletariat developed, the more it began to feel as a class and to act as one, the feebler became the bourgeoisie.[46]

Nonetheless, Engels concluded that the tendency was still for embourgeoisification of the state in so far as it inevitably reflected the triumph of capitalism in civil society: 'the non-bourgeois elements are becoming more bourgeois every day.... In all economic questions the Prussian state is falling more and more into the hands of the bourgeoisie.'[47]

By 1871, Marx similarly had come to suspect that the Napoleonic-type state did not, as he had argued previously, constitute an exceptional freeing of the executive from civil society, but was in fact the form appropriate to generalized bourgeois civil society:

> The modern bourgeois State is embodied in two great organs, parliament and the government. Parliamentary omnipotence...from 1848 to 1851, engendered its own negative...and imperialism [meaning rule in the mode of Napoleon III], with its mere mockery of parliament, is the *régime* now flourishing in most of the great military States of the continent. At first view, apparently, the usurpatory dictatorship of the governmental body over society itself, rising alike above and humbling alike all classes; it has in fact, on the European continent at least, become the only possible State form in which the appropriating class can continue to sway it over the producing class.[48]

Marx and Engels here were generalizing from their reflections on 1848–51. Then, they argued, the bourgeoisie had let constitutionalism slip though their fingers for fear that otherwise the worker movement would be empowered. In the decades since, the proletariat had grown in number and confidence as capitalism had grown. The bourgeoisie were now at least ambivalent about constitutionalism, and positively averse to determined revolutionary struggle to achieve it. They were haunted by the spectre of communism.

## THE PARIS COMMUNE

Marx and Engels were revisiting the question of bourgeois accommodation with authoritarianism in the context of the Paris Commune of 1871, a brief civil war between classes arising from France's catastrophic defeat at the hands of Prussia. It is little surprise, therefore, that their attention was focused on the hostility between bourgeois liberalism and plebeian militancy. The French Third Republic that arose from the ashes of Napoleon III's defeat was in many respects the quintessential bourgeois republic. Its first priority was to stamp its authority with force on the capital of Paris. Since the French Revolution of 1789, the urban crowd of journeymen artisans had in times of turmoil held governments to ransom and bent entire countries to their will. The Paris Commune of 1871 was the last and perhaps most operatically tragic of these astonishing *journées*.

In a familiar pattern, the people of Paris suspected that the newly elected National Assembly was seeking to destroy the Republic, understandably given its mostly royalist composition. When soldiers of the government—located at Versailles, safe from the intimidation of the revolutionary crowd—attempted to seize several cannon in the Parisian suburb of Montmartre, the city's National Guard resisted. Two Versailles generals were captured and shot. With the die cast, a National Guard Central Committee installed itself in the Hôtel de Ville. Universal suffrage elections to the Parisian Commune ('commune' was simply the name given to French units of local government) were held on 26 March. The Commune declared that the writ of the 'Versailles government' did not run in Paris, and it adopted the red flag. Known to the world as the Communards, they called themselves Fédérés, reflective of their desire to bring about maximum decentralization, and devolution of self-rule. A Paris Commune proclamation on 19 April announced its commitment to 'absolute independence of the Commune extended to all places in France'. Nationally, 'the unity of France' would be limited to a 'contract of association' between Communes.[49] From the outset, the Versailles government treated the Communards not as belligerents, but as rebels. They were liable to be shot on capture. As Versailles troops advanced they relentlessly executed prisoners. Communards burnt buildings and latterly shot hostages, but to no avail. The revolutionary party was crushed in blood.

Marx used the example of the Commune to stress certain points. He hailed the Paris Commune as a model that resolved some of the contradictions which had aborted the 1848 Revolutions, particularly the tension between town and country, and showed how a reactionary state apparatus might successfully be displaced. Particularly in France, the left usually dismissed the countryside as backward, and 'universal suffrage' as a passive and bribed populace upon which state despotism rested. One anarchist prominent in the 1860s and 1870s, Michael Bakunin, approvingly quoted another whose heyday had been in the 1840s and 1850s, Pierre-Joseph Proudhon: '*Universal suffrage is the counter-revolution*'.[50] Marx was certainly aware that the Parisian masses were a revolutionary vanguard, but he was impressed precisely by the federalism of the Commune, which insisted only on the self-government of Paris, trusting that its example would spread the model of decentralized, bottom-up government across France. This seemed to square the circle: it allowed Paris to lead the way without imposing its will dictatorially on the country. 'The Paris Commune,' Marx wrote, would 'serve as a model to all the great industrial centres of France. The communal regime once established in Paris and the secondary centres, the old centralized government would in the provinces, too, have to give way to the self-government of the producers.'[51] Here we can see

Marx attempting to break from the straightjacket of plebeian 'intimidation' as the only thoroughgoing revolutionary strategy. Marx did also, however, berate the Commune for 'not at once marching upon Versailles', after the Montmartre episode.[52] As in 1848, he was averse to decorum or reticence in revolution. It seems likely, however, from Engels' later preface to Marx's *Civil War in France*, that he and Marx had hoped for a compromise 'peace' between the Commune and Versailles, not a Parisian armed conquest of the country.[53] Behind the understandably heated rhetoric, Marx was struggling to reconcile revolutionism with due deference to majority opinion.

The second major lesson that Marx drew from the Commune was its model of an alternative to the permanent state apparatus. Experience had shown that the introduction of constitutionalism left intact the power of the conservative civil service, judiciary, and armed forces. Such an inheritance prevented any decisive break in governance, lying behind parliamentary forms of government and circumscribing them, often to the point of negation. The Commune showed that the self-organization of workers and radical democratization could decompose the counter-revolutionary state apparatus in a manner (he thought) that would prevent a subversion of the revolution.[54] Marx was trying to come to terms with the problem revealed by the experience of the years since 1848, when pre-existing state structures had adopted degrees of constitutionalism without thereby being subordinated to civil society. He was canvassing a much more radical project of displacing the traditional state apparatus altogether.

The Paris Commune was to become a founding legend for European socialism, and the writings of Marx and Engels in its shadow were soon canonical. Given the circumstances of their composition, whatever their sophistications, these widely distributed writings tended to overstate Marx and Engels' view that the bourgeoisie and the proletariat were politically at daggers' drawn, relative to many other of their observations on the topic. They overemphasized the tenuousness of the attraction of constitutional legality for the bourgeoisie when confronted by insurgency, and they diminished the utility of constitutionalism for the revolutionary working class. These fairly late works by the founders of 'scientific socialism' promoted the idea that the bourgeoisie betrayed political liberalism in proportion to the militancy of the proletariat. For subsequent socialists, two diametrically opposed conclusions could be and were drawn: either that the working class alone were the politically progressive class, the bourgeoisie having passed over into the camp of reaction; or that socialists must temper their radicalism so as not to frighten the bourgeoisie into abandoning the cause of civil and political liberty.

## CONCLUSION

Marx and Engels' analyses were problematic. There is little doubt, as they argued, that the middle classes were suspicious of political movements or forms that might empower the propertyless democracy, but this was not a novel development. Liberalism and its progenitors had always condemned on principle the state being used as an instrument of enrichment for any class interest. This meant opposing the continuing legacy of state power being monopolized by aristocrats or caste, who would use its coercive power to extract tribute from the productive economy. Equally, however, it meant resisting any attempt to convert the state into an instrument of wealth redistribution from the rich to the poor. Liberals held that such instrumentalization of the state by the propertyless would re-institutionalize the state as a rent-seeking parasite on productive civil society. Hostility to socialist political economy was engrained in bourgeois liberty. This hostility unquestionably had an impact in circumscribing liberal adventures in 1848–51, particularly in France where Social Republicanism was a real force. However, even in France, the working class left was fairly easily defeated in the June Days of 1848, and certainly elsewhere, socialism and the workers' movement had been politically marginal. Liberal defeat in the 1848 revolutions had been more a result of the strength of reaction than the betrayal of the bourgeoisie.

In the decades after 1848 until at least the Paris Commune of 1871, despite the limited revival of socialism in the 1860s, the workers' movement was never sufficiently threatening to inhibit the political ardour of the middle classes decisively. Moreover, Britain was an impressive example of how a liberal constitutionalist state, at least once fairly set, could placate and absorb working-class demands without imperilling bourgeois civil society. Indeed, European liberals (and politicians of all temperaments in the United States) were quite genuine in their efforts to encourage working-class organization in self-help societies and cooperative enterprises. They saw this as the means by which the worker could be given a stake in commercial civil society, and inoculated against the despotic temptation to plunder productive wealth through state power.

Prussia's success, however, made governments responsible to Parliament much less appealing for those who wanted their nation states to cut a dash in the world; strong, uninhibited executive action had been vindicated. Certainly the middle classes were increasingly content to accept this state of affairs, though most liberals evinced continuing determination that some day all countries would take the British and American road. To justify their pragmatic coming to terms with remaining aristocratic privilege and statist pretension, however, many erstwhile fire-breathing radicals were inclined to explain their new-found 'realism' by reference to the fearful prospect of democratic overheating and socialistic revolution. The Paris Commune, unquestionably, reinforced this politics of fear.

# 7

# Capitalism and Socialism

Towards the end of the nineteenth century, 'third-wave' industrialization, with an emphasis on light engineering—particularly electrics and chemicals—became marked. Coal, iron, heavy engineering, and textiles industries continued to expand impressively, but they were joined now by developments in steel, chemicals, and electrics. Britain remained an economic colossus and world power. Coal, textiles, iron and steel, and engineering accounted for about half of total British output and three-quarters of her exports by 1907, and employed a quarter of the workforce. The proportion engaged in public and professional services rose by two-fifths over the same period.[1] From about 1870, however, new serious competitors to Britain emerged in Germany and the USA. Whereas in 1871 half of the German population was engaged in agriculture, by 1914 it was less than a third. Germany became the largest producer outside America of coal and pig iron. Her steel production increased nearly ninefold, being twice the level of British output by 1914. The year previously Germany steel output exceeded that of her European rivals combined, as did the amount of electrical energy it produced. German dyestuff production totalled four-fifths of the world output. Post-Civil War, American industrialization took off almost vertically. Railways were constructed by private enterprise, but with the ample subsidy of federal land grants, and the country knitted together into one market. Manufacturing outstripped agriculture in terms of value in the early 1880s, and by 1900 contributed almost twice as much in value. An economy based upon steel, oil, railroads, and machinery was soon challenging and then outstripping European rivals. The US accounted for about 30 per cent of world manufacturing in 1900, compared to 22 per cent for Britain, 19 per cent for Germany, 7 per cent for France, 5 per cent for Russia, and 7 per cent for all other countries combined.[2]

The aristocracy entered a long period of economic crisis from about 1873, as huge imports of grain from the Ukraine in the east and from the United States' prairies, plus the import of meat from the New World ranches in refrigerated transport ships, undermined food prices and land values in Europe. The aristocracy turned increasingly to the state to bolster its position, both by securing tariffs against foreign foodstuffs, and indeed by seeking employment in the state's burgeoning bureaucratic ranks. Not to be outdone, industry looked to receive similar protection.

The free-trade global economy accommodated such protectionism. Countries could adopt protectionism whilst still having access to foreign capital and markets. International credit was freely available and multilateral because of the (relatively brief) international triumph of the 'Gold Standard' of currency convertibility. Britain maintained the 'Gold Standard' by sticking to free trade, but it was able to do this precisely because of its de facto control of colonial markets. Huge and integrated British merchant corporations, acting as 'virtual monopolists', were able to dictate terms of trade to colonial producers.[3] Britain's consequent balance of payments surplus with India (and China) allowed her to maintain trade deficits arising out of free trade with peer competitors, and so prevented the world economy breaking up into autarchic trading blocs. It was partly Britain's hold on India that made the limited protectionism of her rivals possible.[4]

At the top of society, big business and the aristocracy became entangled. Businessmen would buy land and pay for expensive educations to acquire for their children the social distinctions of gentility. Aristocrats were often brought onto the boards of directors in corporations for their cachet and their contacts. Big business and the aristocracy in common called for tariffs and higher military spending. Particularly from the 1890s, as working-class mobilization disconcerted property owners of all kind, the political interests of the upper bourgeoisie and the aristocracy cohered. In effect, a new, oligarchic upper class emerged.

Higher education expanded rapidly, so that usually 2 to 3 per cent of the population attended university. Traditional professions—in medicine, law, and so on—did not expand as quickly, and many graduates entered state bureaucratic service and party politics. These political service professionals developed an affinity and identity of interests with that political class par excellence, the aristocracy. Style became a prerequisite for professionalism, and increasingly this implied an affectedly patrician mien, and usually a reactionary cast of politics. Under upper-class leadership, traditionalist doctors, lawyers, and students filled the ranks of right-wing nationalist and imperialist organizations, such as the Pan-German League. More importantly, of course, they staffed most political parties, the parliaments, and many positions in the government bureaucracy.

Even outside Europe, the bourgeoisie could be harnessed to the aristocracy. From the 'Meiji Restoration' of 1868, under the slogan of 'fukoku kyohei' ('rich country, strong army'), Japanese elites had consciously sought to integrate with the economic and political forms of the West. They combined forceful militarism and a rigidly hierarchical social structure with carefully calibrated constitutionalism to foster commerce and industrialization. The fierce *bushido* warrior code of the samurai caste was allied to the productive and organizational power of a modern industrial state. Japan's startling success, the only nineteenth-century break-out into industrial modernity by a non-European or European settler society, paid the expected dividends in sovereign power. In 1894 Japan invaded and occupied Korea, and it successfully fought a war with Russia for influence over the Manchurian province of China in 1904–5. China, on the other hand, warned of the fate of those countries unable to execute revolution from above. The decline of state capacity there helped provoke serious domestic disorder, which in turn added to the crisis of state capacity in a vicious spiral. Centralized imperial power began to fragment, and de facto 'warlords' took over functions of government and the taxes that came with them. The elites in China were painfully aware of the far greater ability of Western constitutional and socio-economic forms to project state power. Western-style parliamentarianism, however, was widely considered inapplicable in a country where, as one Chinese conservative put it, 'merchants rarely have much capital'.[5]

## 'STATISED CAPITALISM'

The prime duty of the state remained military rather than economic, as the war of 1870–1 made all too clear to a stunned Europe. Britain straddled the globe with its navy, which also provided a near-impregnable barrier against invasion. America's economy was orientated to domestic markets, but with the USA hegemonic on its continent, the homeland was even more secure from invasion. The Secretary of State, Richard Olney, boasted in 1895 that America's 'infinite resources combined with its isolated position render it...practically invulnerable against any or all other powers'[6]. Britain and America were liberal empires based upon commerce, constitutionalism, and rather smug navalism. European continental powers, however, could not be so sanguine.

On the outbreak of the Franco-Prussian War, both sides had rushed to take the offensive. The Prussians were victorious because, as one observing American general put it, they got their forces into action 'fustest with the mostest'.[7] War-winning strategy now depended upon a mass service army, based upon young men trained adequately to respond to iron discipline exercised by an elite officer core. This model definitely displaced both the long-service professional army of grizzled warriors and the citizen militia minimally trained and retaining a civilian ethos. The only kind of modern armed force that could be limited in size and social weight and still be militarily effective was likely to be stationed outside the country: colonial or naval. Britain combined these as did no other power. For modern continental warfare, however, the mass army, based upon a barracks-drilled and trained civilian levy, was a *sine qua non*. The Prussian model was state of the art. Its triumph set the seal on the state-building lesson of the post-1848 period. The Austrians adopted Prussian-style mandatory military service in 1868, France in 1872, Japan in 1873, Russia in 1874, and Italy in 1875. By 1900 it was virtually universal, excluding only Britain and the United States.

Mass armies in Europe were, as the Franco-Prussian War had shown, a necessity. This put liberals in a quandary. Traditionally they had vehemently opposed militarism as acidly corrosive of civil society's freedom. As the state extracted revenue in order to build up the military apparatus, it became increasingly independent of civil society, and less in need of consensus to assure fiscal solvency. The French liberal Frédéric Bastiat in 1863 bitingly characterized statist reckoning: 'Let's overburden the taxpayer to have a big army, then let's have a big army to contain the taxpayer'.[8] The clear-cut success of mass arms in 1870, however, meant that liberals, when confronted by governments seeking direct taxes, tariffs, and state monopolies for military purposes, felt unable to refuse supply without imperilling national defence.

In Engels' view, militarization made the development of national capitalisms all the more inevitable:

> From the moment warfare became a branch of the *grande industrie* (ironclad ships, rifled artillery, quickfiring and repeating cannons, repeating rifles, steel covered bullets, smokeless powder, etc), *la grande industrie*, without which all those things cannot be made, became a political necessity. All these things cannot be had without a highly developed metal manufacture. And that manufacture cannot be had without a corresponding development in all other branches of manufacture... in one form only: the *capitalistic form*.[9]

It is certainly true that industrialization was necessary for modern militarism. The armaments industry, indeed, was at the cutting edge of engineering and chemicals. Militarism was not just a matter of industry and expenditure, however. It tended, at least outside the navy, to inculcate an anti-democratic, hierarchical ethos. Liberals feared the militarization of society. The radical journalist Urbain Gohier, in his *L'Armée contre la Nation* (1899), polemicized against the barracks culture of the emulated Prussian model as 'a school for all the dissolute vices'. He ascribed the 'vitality of the Anglo-Saxon race' in Britain and America to 'the fact that its members escape the corrupting, degrading influence of the barracks'.[10] The French republican Jules Simon, in the debate on Draft Law of 1867, put the classic radical point of view against militarism: 'We want an army of citizens who would be invincible on their home soil, but incapable of carrying a war abroad.'[11] Attacking across borders, however, was universally acknowledged as the best form of defence by all European military professionals.

Radical liberals had good cause to fear the political effects of militarism. It was evident even in liberal republican France. Between 1886 and 1889, General Boulanger won huge popularity, across the left and the right of the political spectrum, as a 'man on horseback' to redeem the martial pride of the French nation. Had he been made of sterner stuff, Boulanger could have put up a credible bid for authoritarian power. As it was, he rankled the republican establishment and fluffed his chance. Within a decade of the Boulanger scare, the military subverted republican legality in the infamous Dreyfus affair. In October 1894, Alfred Dreyfus, a Jewish officer in the army, was found guilty by court martial of treasonously transmitting documents to a foreign power, presumed to be Germany. It soon enough became apparent that the evidence against Dreyfus was wholly inadequate, indeed forged, but to protect the integrity of the army the establishment sabotaged a proper re-examination of the case. Mass anti-Dreyfusard opinion impugned Jews as inveterate traitors to national honour. It was only in 1905 that Dreyfus was exonerated. French militarism, understandably, was seen as such a threat to the Republic that the army was subordinated to a civilian-dominated Conseil Supérieur de la Défense Nationale in 1906, and generals were normally limited to three years in a corps command.[12] An act in 1905 cut the national service in France from three years to two, reducing the army from 615,000 to 504,000. The military apparatus of the state, by these measures, was gravely weakened, and the restoration of three-year service (Loi de Trois Ans) in 1913 was just in time, perhaps, to save France from being overrun at the outset of the First World War the following year. The trade-off between anti-militarism and adequate defence was a fine one.

Germany was widely held to be the country most infected by militarism. When, in 1913, an army commander briefly imposed something like martial law on the town of Zabern in annexed Alsace, this was taken as a revelation of where the real balance of power lay between military and civilian authority in the Kaierreich. Still, the army's action was condemned by the majority of Reichstag members. As David Schoenbaum points out, what 'Zabern did not prove was that imperial Germany was particularly violent or autocratic, though there was not much evidence that it was easily reformable, let alone a closet democracy, either'.[13] Baron Beyens, writing in 1916 when much of his country was under German occupation, recalled his impression, from his pre-war days as a Belgian ambassador living in Germany, that all classes there—from proletarians and peasants, to industrialists, financiers, and even aristocrats—evinced little bellicosity and favoured peace.[14] Indeed, Admiral Tirpitz, who from 1898 promoted in Germany the need for a larger fleet through his Navy League, consciously shaped his propaganda to flatter the prejudices of the parliamentarian bourgeoisie against land armies, and in favour of commerce and colony-protecting sea power.[15] Whilst standing armies were seen as a potential tool of authoritarianism at home, navies and colonial expeditionary forces encouraged commerce and the 'civilizing mission'. Much of Germany wanted a great navy not to confront Britain but to emulate her conjunction of liberalism, imperialism, and navalism.

So, militarism was not as extreme in Germany as was often suggested, nor was it absent elsewhere. Britain, of course, could rely on its navy, and so had a proportionately weak (and poorly regarded) army. The shock of the Boer War (1899–1902) and the developing naval arms race with Germany (*c*.1898–1914), however, meant a considerable hike in British military spending. Lord Salisbury as prime minister, speaking to the Commons in 1900, cast doubt on the liberal 'night-watchman' state in the context of modern international challenges: 'I do not think that the British Constitution as at present worked is a good fighting machine.'[16] After 1900, Britain's military spending was actually the highest per capita in the world.[17] Germany, in contrast, found its military spending to be inelastic and in the long run lost the arms race.[18] It was with nostalgic regret that General Friedrich von Bernhardi recalled in 1914 the glory days when Bismarck 'extorted' tax funds from an unwilling public to further Prussia's foreign-policy goals. He feared that such executive boldness was a thing of the past.[19]

It remains the case that Germany was the country where the army was most solidly organized and protected, the values of civilian society most militarized.[20] The large standing army remained suspect in the Anglo-American world, and militarism was constrained by powerful republican forces in France. Still, contrary to earlier expectations that the rise of commercial civil society would proportionately diminish the influence of the armed forces, militarism was a near-universal and growing phenomenon in all industrial countries. If Germany had its Zabern Affair, France had the far more momentous crises of Boulanger and Dreyfus, when militarism threatened to run riot. Even in Britain, by 1914, the army teetered on the brink of mutiny. Backed by the Conservative opposition, the army made clear that it would refuse to enforce an Act of Parliament legislating Home Rule for all Ireland. The Liberal government privately conceded that if they tried to order the army, 'the instrument would break in their hands'.[21]

Bourgeois civil society was finding itself obliged by geopolitical reality to accept militarism, but it also directly benefited from the huge government contracts and infrastructural support it sluiced towards private enterprise.[22] This intertwining with the state only reinforced the impact of wider changes in the structure of capitalism. In order to secure their creditworthiness, companies increasingly took the form of a corporation. This distanced capitalist enterprises from the ownership and management of single entrepreneurial families. The shift in industrial property from private ownership to company shares and bonds facilitated the merging of agrarian and business interests.[23] Cartels—associations in which companies divided up markets into pre-agreed shares—emerged during the 'Depression' of the 1870s, as a way of avoiding the excessive turbulence and insecurity of cut-throat competition. German capitalism took the particular form of bank-led cartels. There were two hundred cartels in Germany in 1890, nearly four hundred by 1906, and six hundred in 1911.[24] The banks took a hands-on role in managing its loans to industry. By 1914, sixteen of Germany's top bankers held between them 437 industrial directorships.[25] In Britain, by contrast, despite the mighty London money market, industry in the provinces remained more or less self-financing.[26] The overall picture was complex, but at least in sectors with high fixed-capital costs, corporations were growing in size and relying on the state to rig the market.

Global markets themselves were being carved out into regions: Great Britain was preponderant in East and South Africa, and in South Asia; and France dominated in West Africa, the Balkans, and Russia. The British liberal John A. Hobson (1858–1940) argued that imperialism arose from the distorted mode of finance capitalism, in which investments were not used to their potential to develop the domestic market, by increasing wages to encourage consumption, but were instead invested overseas for quick returns. (The United States, as it grew in power, was not immune to overseas interfering, but it was driven mostly by requirements of military security, as well as by a mission of 'liberal interventionism'. America had much less of an economic impulse to imperialism. With a high-wage domestic market, it exported only 8 per cent of its gross national product in 1913.[27] Much of this comprised raw materials.) The baleful results of finance-capitalist imperialism, argued Hobson, were suppressed wages at home; speculation, embroilment, and annexation abroad.[28] Hobson's picture was apposite, if perhaps inverted. It was not so much that suppressed wages in the domestic labour market led to imperialism; rather that imperialism permitted capitalists to hold wages down. The European powers were heavily export-orientated, using protected home markets as a base to penetrate foreign ones. In these years, world trade grew faster, at 3.4 per cent per annum, than world production, which grew at 2.1 per cent per annum.[29] Most of this increase was captured by European countries, which relied upon strict wage restraint at home to sell competitively priced goods abroad. Imperialist seizure of territory was more a fail-safe complement to this export orientation than a cause of it.

By the First World War, almost the entire globe was subjugated to the capitalist nation states, all of European origin with the exception of Japan. Europe itself remained largely divided between nation states, but Albert Ritter spoke for many in Germany when he looked forward to a *Mitteleuropa* as a bloc, organized internally as a free-trade zone but fenced against its external counterparts of 'Greater Russia, World Britannia [and] pan-America'.[30] It was far from certain that Europe could indefinitely be preserved from the empire building it inflicted on the rest of the globe.

\* \* \*

Liberal supporters of laissez-faire worried that the rise of financial investments and intertwining of commerce, aristocracy, and state was replacing the bourgeois entrepreneurial ethic with oligarchic dependency culture. For the French liberal journalist Jules Huron, writing in 1897, the idle rich living off rentier investments were inverted 'socialists', refusing to work for a living.[31] Luigi Einaudi, an Italian liberal economist, wrote fretfully in 1900:

> It is important for our country that the possessors of capital do not just settle back and enjoy the 4 percent return they can get with long-term government bonds or ground rents; they have to take more risk in enterprises beneficial for themselves and the whole nation. For the good of the country, the ruling class ought to steer their offspring to seek their fortunes in the fields of industry and commerce, instead of continuing to steer them towards professional and bureaucratic careers that are already clogged with frustrated aspirants.[32]

Georges Sorel, a maverick French intellectual who progressed from Marxism through revolutionary syndicalism and then Leninism, arriving finally at an ambivalent fascism, felt that the bourgeoisie had become soft and flabby, unsure of its own mission and running down into a welfarist 'capitalist degeneration'.[33] The statist dependencies of the bourgeoisie, he felt, corrupted society as a whole, hollowing out the self-reliance of civil society.[34]

If the bourgeoisie were going soft, the landed aristocracy, despite the travails of falling food prices from 1873 to 1896, which they bemoaned as the 'Great Depression', remained politically prominent. They were the 'class dirigente', as Arno Mayer puts it, who condescended to 'let the bourgeoisie make money and pay taxes'.[35] Certainly the aristocracy continued to play a prominent role in government and the armed forces.[36] The traditional argument for aristocratic governance had been historicist. A genealogically established title to rule, symbolically expressed most potently in the institution of monarchy, was powerful because in principle it was less disputable and divisive than claims of merit or representativeness. A hereditary ruling class, moreover, was an efficient socialization process for the habits and arts of governance, transmitted generation to generation through family upbringing. As a class, the British Conservative James Anthony Froude argued in 1876, the aristocracy were tenacious, politically skilled and bound to real communities by their stewardship of the land; in contrast, 'successful men of business' comprised an apolitical and deracinated capitalist plutocracy.[37]

Nonetheless, the rise of commercial civil society as the yardstick of public utility gravely weakened an aristocracy that constituted itself as the antithesis of the grubby producing classes. The aristocracy did not collapse in face of modernity's implied critique but rather, in the latter half of the nineteenth century, reconstituted its claims to authority. This was achieved by recasting dynastic genealogy, from an elitist narrative of separation from and lordship over the masses, to a mythology in which monarchical and aristocratic forebears were depicted as bearers of nationality, culminating in the nation state. In a stark inversion, the historical aristocracy's pride of caste, warmongering, and contempt for the slavish peasantry was transmuted into nationalist ideology, a historicist creed compounding the written records of court and country house with bowdlerized renditions of rural folklore. Nationalism of this kind was the foremost and aggressively promoted state ideology in Europe by 1914.

Still, the pretensions of the old regime to modern relevance were already on the slide as oligarchic wealth and party-political power encroached on the nexus of landed wealth and the glamour of the titled nobility. It was not simply the case that the aristocracy dominated the bourgeoisie. Rather, distinctions between the classes were fading, as the upper bourgeoisie aped aristocratic airs, and aristocrats committed themselves increasingly to pragmatic values of business and efficiency. 'It is altogether preposterous, nowadays,' wrote former German Chancellor Prince Bernhard von Bülow in 1914, 'still to contrast the nobility and the bourgeoisie as separate castes. Professional and social life have so fused the old classes that they can no longer be distinguished from each other.'[38] To a certain extent, at least at the upper reaches of wealth and power, a unified oligarchy was crystallizing.[39]

By the turn of the century, corporate capitalism was well established in Europe. Previous generations of commercialism had been founded upon risk-taking, privately owned enterprises. These had been the basis for a civil society distinct from the state and the aristocracy. The new era of large-scale industry, corporations, and stock ownership, in contrast, appeared to blur the boundaries between productive property, aristocratic privilege, and the militarized state. The wealthiest bourgeoisie and aristocracy combined into an oligarchy of such weight as to influence governments for its own ends, threatening to revive politically constituted power as an instrument of direct enrichment for elites. Further down the social chain, the bourgeoisie of professionals, state officials, and small businessmen, and the petite bourgeoisie of shopkeepers, workshop owners, and farmers, endorsed statist ideologies of nationalism and imperialism. Wage earners, resentful of the oligarchic stitch-up of the state, were increasingly motivated to level the playing field by having the state for a change act to protect wage labour.

## THE CRISIS OF LIBERALISM

Classical liberalism came under pressure as its historic social bases—not just the urban bourgeoisie, but petite-bourgeoisie elements of the working class, and sections of the rural gentry—abandoned the cause, veering off either right or left.[40] An international crash in the world's stock markets in 1873 did much to discredit the laissez-faire politics of liberalism. Liberalism, indeed, was as a party label increasingly freighted with doctrinaire connotations ideologically, and Liberal parties steadily retreated to a narrower, more purely bourgeois social base.

Classical liberal constitutionalism was everywhere under pressure in the last quarter of the nineteenth century. Bismarck's unwillingness to pay the traditional price for a strong domestic tax basis—a fully constitutional government—meant that he increasingly turned away from the National Liberals and towards protectionism, so as to raise state funds by taxing foreigners. In 1878, Bismarck proposed a 'revision of the tariff on as broad a basis as possible'.[41] The National Liberal Party forlornly demanded that in return Bismarck accede to the creation of a formal cabinet government. Bismarck refused and introduced his protective tariffs. These did not evidently inhibit economic growth. Between 1887 and 1912, the value of Germany's exports rose by 185.4 per cent per annum, while the value of her imports rose even more steeply, by 243.8 per cent.[42]

Towards the end of the nineteenth century, indeed, it was becoming increasingly apparent that there was not a straightforward correlation between bourgeois constitutionalism (restricted franchise, parliamentarianism, and a responsible executive) and economic growth.[43] The very success of international capitalism rolling out from the states where bourgeois liberty was well established meant that credit both for private enterprise and governments was available in unprecedented volume from international banks and governments. There was a convergence of long-term interest rates internationally at which the Great Powers could borrow.[44] This progressively reduced the fiscal advantages enjoyed by constitutional states. The competitive margin of constitutional states in creditworthiness and economic development was eroding. Governments, moreover, were better placed by the end of the century to resist constitutionalism without imperilling their tax base and ability to service loans, because of vastly improved government revenue-collection machines.[45] Even archaically authoritarian governments could secure loans on the international money markets, so long as they were prepared to pay premium interest rates and run the risk of a complete or partial loss of sovereignty if they defaulted.[46]

States were thus in a much better position than before to support quasi-mercantilist strategies of national capital accumulation. Free trade, which had advanced steadily in Europe since the 1840s, gave way to protectionism. The McKinley Act of 1890 and the Dinley tariff of 1897 completed a rigid protectionist wall around the United States: tariffs amounted to no less than 57 per cent of the value of imported goods. Germany introduced moderate agricultural and industrial tariffs in 1879, and erected a solid protectionist wall against finished goods in 1902. Italy introduced substantial tariffs in 1887, Switzerland in 1884 and 1906. French general tariffs, introduced in 1892, and reinforced in 1910, rewarded royalist businessmen and landed interests, helping to solder them to the Republic after the

Boulanger episode.[47] Russia was the most protectionist country of all. By the First World War, only Britain, Holland, and Denmark were still operating free trade. Despite liberal disquiet, there is no evidence that protectionism was economically harmful for those countries that adopted it.[48]

All this was deeply disconcerting for liberals. Liberalism had offered a pact between state and bourgeois civil society. If government left commercial and private interests alone, protected by the rule of law, and if it permitted public oversight and restraint on its taxing and spending, then prosperity would ensue and the fiscal basis of the state would be secured. This tacit deal, however, was being undermined. The modern state secured its tax basis less through consensus and more through bureaucratic coercion. It could secure loans on the international market without reference to Parliament. And it could even drive economic development actively, rather than simply delegating the economy to the 'hidden hand' of market forces. The compact of mutual benefit between a strong state and a free commercial civil society seemed to be breaking down.

The enduring strength of Russian Tsarism was evidence of the ability of absolutist states to benefit from the internationalization of credit. First German then French loans were used to encourage capitalist development, particularly in railways. About 30 per cent of Russia's national debt was held abroad in 1895; by 1914 this had risen to 48 per cent, making Russia Europe's largest debtor nation.[49] In the early twentieth century, about one-third of private enterprises in Russia were foreign owned.[50] Tsarism, thus, to the frustration and consternation of liberals and socialists alike, could support itself on the basis of international loans and investment, switching from one foreign source of credit to another if need be. Sergei Witte, Minister of Finance from 1893 to 1903, was able to finance, through international loans and heavy domestic taxation, a 'state capitalist' development of railway construction that in turn facilitated a 'great spurt' of economic growth. Statist leadership in the economy weakened the financial independence and leverage of Russia's small bourgeoisie. The Liberal leader, Paul Miliukov, writing in 1904, was pessimistic that the Russian bourgeoisie could be an agent of liberal transformation:

> Until very recent times there was no bourgeoisie in Russia worthy the name. The dependence of the Russian trading and commercial class on the government was still greater than that of the gentry; and this could but be expected, since the cherishing and fostering of Russian industries are entirely due to state measures. Thus we were obliged to conclude that there was on the stage no social force which could influence political life and take part in the development of political ideas.[51]

Russian liberalism lacked a 'solid bourgeois core'. Heavy industry, metallurgy, engineering, and the banks were reliant upon foreign capital for investment (in contrast to Moscow textiles) and on the Tsarist state for contracts. Capitalists did not need constitutionalism, and they showed precious little inclination to press for it.[52] Russia was an extreme example, perhaps. But the apparent strengthening of the Tsarist absolutist state confounded the hopeful predictions of liberals that only through constitutionalism, a strong middle class and laissez-faire could a path to modernity be hewn.

## THE RISE OF SOCIALISM

With liberalism in crisis, the socialist movement dramatically broke though politically in the 1890s. By 1900, socialist parties contesting elections were established in most European countries, and in Denmark and Germany they were within striking distance of 20 per cent of the vote. In Belgium, socialists had just under 10 per cent, and in Italy just under 7 per cent. By 1914, in Sweden the left workers' party had 36.7 per cent of the vote, in Germany 34.8 per cent, in Belgium 30.3 per cent, in Denmark 29.6 per cent, in Italy 17.7 per cent, in France 16.8 per cent, and in Great Britain 7.0 per cent. The socialist vote in US presidential elections rose from under one hundred thousand votes in 1900 to nine hundred thousand in 1912.

The commodification of wage labour underpinned the rise of European workers' movements, but its national and regional expressions depended upon the cultural construction of the labour process. At one pole, militant Marxism had greater purchase in Germany where workers perceived a commodification of labour power, thus suggesting the need for the labour process to be brought under conscious social control. In Britain workers saw a similar process as the commodification of the goods produced, which lent itself to the labourist solutions of organized markets.[53] That the proletarian *imaginaire* of de-commodified wage labour uniformly inclined towards some degree of socialization of the means of subsistence is evident, but it found political expression within substantially different frameworks.

Working-class and artisanal self-organization was often in its early days nurtured by bourgeois liberals, and in general the progress of labour depended upon such liberal constitutionalist reforms as had been won. But it was the linking of capitalism to the oppressive state apparatus and oligarchic privilege, the disordering of liberalism unable to deny the growing demands of the militarized state, and the collapse (outside the United States) of radical, anti-state liberalism, that really opened up a vacuum which in most of Europe was filled by workers' parties.

The Paris Commune of 1871 was not a result of the International's planning. After its defeat, however, Karl Marx, on behalf of the General Council, issued a stirring defence of the Commune. The French Assembly banned the International in 1872, while the moderate trade unions in England disassociated themselves. Just as its support ebbed, a struggle between Marxists and Bakunin's anarchists shook the International's structures. The Russian Mikhail Bakunin (1814–1876) set anarchism on its feet as a militantly revolutionary discipline. Bakunin saw anarchism as already inherent in human psychology, and as such it required an act of destruction to tear down the hypocritical and oppressive civility that stifled natural freedom. He argued that the bourgeoisie had been revolutionary in the eighteenth century, and at least 'full of spirit' up to 1848. Fear of the proletarian 'red spectre' since then, however, meant that the bourgeoisie had definitively 'submitted itself to the protection of the military, and gave itself over, body and soul, to the most complete reaction'.[54] Any progressive role for the bourgeoisie, thus, was at an end. Bakunin's anarchist tendency, strongly hostile to parliamentarianism, and supportive both of the autonomy of local producers and the efficacy of violent direct action in the course of struggle, was particularly well established in Spain, Italy, Belgium, and the Italian and French portions of Switzerland. At the Hague Congress of 1872, Marx—fearing that the name of the International stood to be hijacked by numerous revolutionary groups and ideologies—successfully moved that the General Council relocate to New York. This effectively ended the International, which was formally wound up in 1876.

The bloody suppression of the Paris Commune, however, did have a galvanizing effect on left-wing anti-constitutionalism. Anarchism had a vogue in southeast France, and Paris, from 1872 to 1882, where the writings of Élisée Reclus were influential. Reclus, like many of his type, was alienated from parliamentarianism by the Republic's savage repression of the 1871 Paris Commune.[55] Where constitutionalism was particularly fake, anarchism tended to thrive. In Spain, Portugal, and Italy, the local political bosses (called *caciques* in Iberia) manipulated local taxation, patronage, public works, and even conscription to ensure that elections produced the right result for the national political elites.[56] Parties alternated in power without effecting any real discontinuity in policy or even much by way of personnel: the process was called the *turno pacífico* in Spain, *rotativism* in Portugal, *trasformismo* in Italy. Mediterranean constitutionalism appeared nothing more than an ersatz simulacrum of the real thing. The Spanish socialist leader, Pablo Iglesias, in 1898 complained of his country's 'inept' bourgeoisie, 'lacking in education, dominated by routine, without even the gift of being able to imitate good things done in other nations'.[57] Anarchism in Spain, seeing nothing worthy of defence in the parliamentary monarchy, turned to terrorism. The Liberal ministry was unsparing in its response: executions, repressive legislation, and even torture of suspects. Catalonia, where both anarchism and bourgeois nationalism was powerful, was effectively placed under military rule. For two years, from 1907, Barcelona was terrorized by gunmen. A semi-insurrectionary general strike in 1909 was crushed violently. This *Semana Trágica* looked to observers like a spontaneous social revolution, a popular 'week of intoxication, of holy rage'.[58] Visceral insurrectionism and anti-parliamentarianism had deep roots in popular politics.

If anarchism represented a tendency amongst labourers to reject bourgeois civil society and constitutionalism as a hypocritical fraud, the development of mainstream socialist parties had a more complex relationship to liberalism. Parliamentary socialism developed a mass basis first in Germany. The two German socialist parties finally united into one Sozialdemokratische Arbeiterpartei Deutschlands (SDAP). Their common platform, agreed at Gotha in 1875, carried a heavy Lassallean dose, particularly in its lumping the bourgeoisie into one 'reactionary mass' confronting the proletariat. This, complained Marx, failed to acknowledge the continuing progressive struggle that the smaller bourgeoisie at least was capable of waging in the face of the quasi-feudal state.[59] Nonetheless, for the first time in a major state, a socialist workers' political party, constitutionally tolerated, had taken its place in regular democratic life.

Most national socialist parties, following the demise of the First International, modelled themselves on the successful German Party. In Denmark, socialists won their first two seats in Parliament in 1884, the Belgian Labour Party, Parti Ouvrier Belge (POB), formed in 1885, and the Swedish Social Democratic Party in 1887. The year 1888 saw the unity congress of the socialist Sozialdemokratische Partei Österreichs (SPÖ) in Austria. An Italian Socialist Party (Partito Socialista Italiano, PSI) definitely constituted itself in 1892. Jules Guesde, amnestied for his part in the Paris Commune, from 1880 organized a fairly orthodox Marxist Socialist Party in France. The Guesdists, however, were never hegemonic, and they competed with other socialist groups: the reformist Possibilists, the syndicalist Allemanists, the insurrectionist Blanquists, and various Independents. The factions finally united into one Section Française de l'Internationale Ouvrière (SFIO) in 1905. The first organized group of Russian Marxists, in 1883, took the name Osvobozhdenie Truda—Emancipation of Labour. The Russian Social-Democratic Labour Party (RSDLP) was formed in 1898.

These parliamentary socialist parties were barely tolerated. In 1878 two attempts were made on the life of the German Kaiser. Bismarck took this opportunity to dissolve the Reichstag and have the new Reichstag (including the Liberals) vote through emergency anti-socialist laws. The German general and politician, Helmuth von Moltke, was able to persuade liberal members of the parliamentary Reichstag to vote for repressive anti-socialist laws on just this basis. So long as red revolution was a threat, he insisted, normal liberal suspicion of the heavy-handed state must be moderated:

> Gentlemen, we should cease to look upon the government as, in a certain sense, a hostile power which is to be held in check, and hampered as much as possible. Let us invest the government with that fullness of power which is indispensable to the safeguarding of all interests! The history of the [1871] Commune in Paris attests to the consequences that follow when a government allows the reins of authority to slip out of its hands, and when the direction of affairs is controlled by the masses.... Nothing…was gained; much, on the contrary, was destroyed…[in] an abyss of depravity.…Gentlemen, our labouring classes, even the most misguided amongst them, do not contemplate such consequences as these, but, on the downward road, it is always the better elements who are carried along by the worse. Behind the moderate liberal comes the man who is prepared to go much further than he. This is the mistake that so many make; they believe they can, without danger, bring things down to their own level, and there stop, just as if they could abruptly arrest the rush of a train going at full speed—without peril to the necks of the passengers. Gentlemen, from behind the honest revolutionist those dark shapes may be descried emerging, the…apparitions of 1848, the *professeurs des barricades* and the *pétroleuses* of the Commune of 1871.[60]

Twice extended, these emergency measures remained in force until 1890. In this time, about 1,300 publications and 332 organizations were banned, 900 persons banished, and 1,500 imprisoned.[61] The SDAP, however, may have benefited, in that it was forced to organize under the guise of local fronts, such as choral societies, smokers' clubs, mutual assistance unions, and so on. This implanted the party in working-class culture probably more firmly than any number of purely propagandist societies would have done. While the party (which was still allowed to contest elections) polled only 310,000 votes in 1881, this rose to 550,000 in 1884, and 1,427,000 in 1890. Socialists were understandably predisposed to look favourably upon electoralism, with all its imperfections.

The German Socialist Party was able to organize openly after anti-Socialist laws were dropped in 1890. They took the name, Sozialdemokratische Partei Deutschlands (SPD), and built up its local groups, which were electoral committees rather than combat-oriented cells plotting riot, paramilitarism, or insurrection. In 1891 the SPD had its first Congress since legalization, in Erfurt. Here the party programme was revised to suppress the influence of Lassalle's doctrine, though the vision of socialism as state ownership and centralization of production to a top-down plan remained pronounced.[62] The SPD saw itself as bringing the art of politics and theory to an instinctively socialist working class. Said Karl Kautsky (1854–1938), the party's theoretician: 'the class condition of the proletariat produces socialist *inclinations*, but not socialist knowledge'.[63] The Erfurt Programme was essentially a radically democratic programme, directed particularly against residual manorialism and burgeoning militarism, with socialism to supersede capitalism after a democratic revolution. The undercurrent of socialist sympathy for authoritarianism, strong in Germany because of Lassalle's legacy, and indeed the intractably anti-worker bias of most local and state government franchises, inclined the SDP to envisage political revolution as being highly centralized. They anticipated a remaking of Germany by a democratized imperial centre expeditiously taking the property of landlords and big business into state ownership, and crushing 'reactionary' resistance in the provinces.

A contrast to the Erfurt Programme's centralism was the programme of the Belgian POB, formulated under the influence of Cesar de Paepe and adopted in 1893. In Belgium, there was little feudal aristocracy of political significance. There was less concern, therefore, with centralizing in order to break down the reactionary particularisms and regional power bases of landlords. Rather there was an unwillingness to empower a state that might well be run by political Catholics. While the Belgian POB, like the German SPD demanded common ownership of the means of production, public services were to be delivered not through the state, as such, but by the 'commune' (the basic unit of local administration—a town being made up of a 'federation of communes').[64] This model of decentralized socialism was influential, and was echoed, for example, by the French Socialist leader Jean Jaurès (1859–1914) in 1901: socialism would make 'the nation' the 'sovereign of property and guardian of the social right', while democracy would operate through 'innumerable organs—communes, cooperatives, unions'.[65] The long tradition of political centralization in France had soured many on the left of the unitary Republic.

Of course, socialists were distinct from the working class and even the organized labour movement as such. In Germany, Austria-Hungary, Belgium, and Italy, socialist parties in the later nineteenth century tended to grow more rapidly than did workplace combinations, and here the socialist political parties fostered and politically led most trade unions. In Britain, the United States, and France, however, trade unions were not subordinated to party-political socialists, as workers were legally permitted to self-organize with minimal state harassment. Only slowly and incompletely did British trade unionists abandon liberalism. Liberal 'radicalism', which offered a future of 'social legislation', appeared quite sufficient for the bulk of progressively minded workers. 'Radicalism' was destabilized by the desertion of its leader, Joseph Chamberlain, to the Conservatives in protest at Liberal adoption of the policy of Home Rule for Ireland in 1886. Even then, the Independent Labour Party, established in 1893 and led by Keir Hardie, found the going hard. Nonetheless, even in Britain democratic politics were turning to the 'social question'. The Conservative Party leader Arthur Balfour, after his heavy defeat in the election of 1906, bemoaned 'the mob of ignorant voters who now elect our parliament' and warned of the osmotic influence of 'the Labour and Socialistic movements on the Continent'.[66]

In general, however, where liberalism accorded organized labour a secure position in the political nation, socialists of a radical hue had less purchase. Socialists adopted revolutionary phraseology, and won worker support for doing so, in those countries where the state and the middle classes were most inclined to treat worker self-organization as inherently subversive of public order. Socialists and trade unionists labelled 'revolutionary' by a disapproving official society reacted by wearing the accusation as a badge of pride. In Britain and the United States, where there was much less inclination to paint all worker opposition as dangerously 'red', workers and socialists generally abjured revolutionary rhetoric. Indeed, with democracy more or less achieved in the US and Britain, an 'act' of revolution, as understood by the Marxist mainstream, was barely warranted.

France was something of an exception, for while this was a democratic republic, it was very narrowly 'bourgeois', drawing an electoral mandate from the numerous farmers and urban property owners, and unresponsive to proletarian interests. The Third Republic had been born in fear of both left-wing revolution and right-wing reaction. It stuck thereafter to a rigorously middle road. Its first president, Adolphe Thiers, had insisted that 'The Republic will be conservative or it will cease to exist.'[67] The executive power of the presidency was whittled away, for fear of a new Napoleon, and parliamentary supremacy produced, in constitutional terms, an almost purely bourgeois republic. Executive government was reduced to near domestic impotence, penny-pinching while private fortunes accumulated. (Between 1872 and 1907, there were no fewer than sixty-five bills moved in the National Assembly to introduce income tax; all failed.)[68] With executive government so unenticing a prize, broad-church parties to capture it did not really evolve, and the 'party' system in the Assembly was little more than a bewildering system of shifting alliances between deputies representing narrow constituency interests. As socialists shared in the general factionalism, many trade unionists were repelled by their apparent sectarianism.

French anarchists, disillusioned with terroristic 'propaganda of the deed', entered the trade unions between 1895 and 1900, and organized the General Confederation of Labour (Confédération générale du travail, CGT). By 1904 the CGT cadre had developed the doctrine of Revolutionary Syndicalism, which rejected parliamentary action as tending to obscure the 'class struggle'. Rather than conquer state power, the idea was to destroy both state as well as private property. Ultimately, they put their faith in a general strike to overthrow the capitalist order. The Charter of Amiens, adopted by the CGT in 1906, advocated a revolutionary 'general strike' to overturn capitalism. Until then, the union was to be a 'nucleus of resistance', thereafter, 'the nucleus for production and distribution, the foundation of social reorganization'.[69] When the CGT trade-union federation launched a general strike for an eight-hour day on 1 May 1906, two hundred thousand workers responded, a state of siege was declared, and many of the bourgeoisie, fearing another Commune, temporarily left Paris.[70] Syndicalism rejected insurrectionism as such, without embracing parliamentarianism.

In Britain, political Labourism only slowly evolved, and was firmly antirevolutionary. In France, anarcho-syndicalism was significant. In the United States, 'Business trade unionism' looked to increase the workers' share without questioning capitalism and fully sharing in the constitutionalist consensus. Otherwise, Marxism was widely adopted as the 'theory' of socialism, not least due to the indefatigable correspondence with disciples conducted by Fredrick Engels. Most sophisticated was Karl Kautsky, the 'Pope of Marxism', the son of a Czech father and a German mother, and a citizen of Austria. Jules Guesde mechanically and Paul Lafargue idiosyncratically popularized the system in France. George Plekhanov espoused an intellectually overbearing Marxism for Russia, while Filippo Turati (pragmatically) and Antonio Labriola (more academically) spread the gospel in Italy. More marginal were the indefatigable popularizers H. M. Hyndman in Britain and Daniel de Leon in America. The Erfurt Programme, and Kautsky's 1892 commentary thereon, *The Class Struggle*, which presented modern Social Democracy as the amalgamation of the spontaneous workers' movement and socialist intellectuals, became the standard of Marxist orthodoxy.[71] At a popular level, class-struggle socialism spread invisibly through the proletarian and artisan social networks of the time: taverns, pubs, and 'agitation at the beer table' as one activist put it.[72]

In 1889 two international socialist congresses were held in Paris. One was convened by the 'Possibilists' (who wished for reform within the existing political setup), and the other by those styling themselves as revolutionary. The latter 'Marxist' Congress proved more significant. Regular international socialist cooperation—the Second International—was agreed. The International was rather ad hoc until, in 1900, an International Bureau was established in Brussels. An international Congress of socialist parties held in Brussels in 1891 excluded all parties that did not recognize 'the necessity of political struggle'. This was designed to shut out the anarchists altogether. Socialism was committed to constitutional struggle, and so accepted the terrain established by 'bourgeois revolution', even if it retained the socialist goal. Marxism, as an orthodoxy, balanced acceptance of constitutionalism with a faith that, as bourgeois liberalism declined, the worker movement was the inheritor of the struggle for civil and political freedom. This Marxist 'centre' attempted a balance between anarcho-syndicalist revolutionism and 'opportunist' reformism.

Wilhelm Liebknecht, the German socialist leader, had, it is true, in an 1869 speech soon published and notorious, assailed parliamentarianism: 'Socialism is no longer a question of theory: it is simply a question of force which cannot be resolved in a parliament, but only on the street, on the field of battle, like any other question of force.... For the peoples as well as the princes, it is violence that has the last word.'[73] His colleague August Bebel was worried by this. At the party's Stuttgart conference the following year a compromise resolution was adopted. The party would take part in elections 'chiefly for propagandist reasons' but in general 'maintain a negative attitude towards the work of parliament'.[74] This was primarily an attack upon Germany's sham parliamentarianism, however, rather than upon parliamentarianism as such. Because of the three-class voting system for the Prussian Landtag, for example, 333,000 socialist votes were inadequate to get one socialist elected, while the same number of Conservative voters returned 143 members.[75] It was generally felt, however, that socialism could be achieved via a properly democratic franchise and a government responsible to a national Parliament of elected representatives. Kautsky's *Parlamentarismus und Demokratie* (1893) polemicized against one Moritz Rittinghausen, who had written to propose thousands of popular assemblies, with the right of initiative, as the basis of socialist democracy. Kautsky made clear his view, shared by most socialists, that while direct democracy might complement representative parliamentary democracy to some extent, it could not supplant it.[76]

In practice, as Wilhelm Liebknecht put it in 1899, 'the German Social Democracy...consistently and consciously followed the tactics prescribed in the *Communist Manifesto* to direct its main attack against political reactionism and to lend aid to the bourgeoisie, so far as it is liberal or democratic, in its struggle against political reactionism and in no case to throw itself on the side of political reaction in its struggle against the bourgeoisie'.[77] The SPD did not even call for nationalization of industry before democratization, because that would benefit the reactionary Prussianized state.[78] The task of the SPD, therefore, was to agitate for the complete reconstruction of the state, the thorough democratization of the franchise, and the subordination of the government to the legislature. Until that point, any so-called progressive reforms, whether in terms of welfare legislation, or even more dangerously, the extension of state economic power, were a positive danger in that they would be calculated to strengthen the state.

## TAKING ON THE STATE

If the Marxist 'centre', in stark contrast to anarchism, accepted such constitutionalism as had emerged from the evolution of bourgeois civil society and the state, it was still confronted with the problem of how this constitutionalism could be driven to its conclusion: a Parliament elected by universal suffrage, with a government entirely responsible to it. The problem was how obdurate state power, refusing the right of democracy to dictate government policy, might be faced down. In 1830 and 1848 urban insurgents, wielding fowling pieces, were scarcely less well armed than the soldiery armed with flint-lock and muzzle-loaded cannon. In a street fight the rebel, having shelter and barricade, might even have the advantage.[79] The evolution of military technology, however, had by the 1870s changed the picture utterly. With unprecedented ability to manoeuvre and concentrate, due to rail, metalled roads, and urban street planning, huge peacetime forces of police and army, equipped with rifles, smokeless powder, and breech-loading cannon, had every advantage over the insurgent. As Charles Seignobos put it in 1898, 'There is no longer any way to overturn a legal government, not even to defend a constitution against the executive power. The civil population has lost its only effective means of resistance to abuse of power by the government.'[80] Could any revolution against state power actually succeed? This was not just a question of the 'socialist' revolution, but, for most countries in Europe, of immediate relevance in the struggle to secure governments properly responsible to parliaments, and parliamentary suffrages fully democratized. To this extent, it restated the essential conundrum of 'bourgeois' political struggles against absolutism. It was no longer sufficient for left-wing critics simply to say that the bourgeoisie had, in previous abortive revolutions, temporized. What better strategy for overcoming state power did the workers' movements have to offer?

Most socialists argued that while immediate reforms could strengthen the morale of the workers, the main thing was to trust in the rapid growth of socialist parties and the imminence of majorities in the national parliaments, allowing workers' parties to assume government responsibility and undertake the reorganization of economic and political life on a socialist basis. Insofar as revolution was a 'struggle for power', therefore, it was a democratic revolution, the securing of a popular government and as such a left iteration of bourgeois constitutionalist revolution. The socialist 'transformation' would unfold thereafter as a more or less rapid series of reforms. Marx himself, in 1872, had quite publicly stated that in countries with appropriate institutions and traditions, such as America, England, and similar liberal-constitutionalist countries, workers could 'attain their goal by peaceful means'.[81] But elsewhere, Marx had admitted that a duly elected workers' government, even in the most constitutional country, was likely to be confronted by a capitalistic 'slave-owners' war', analogous to the American Civil War.[82]

The Marxist 'centre' warily acknowledged that in practice a reactionary counter-coup against parliamentary constitutionalism was likely in the event of socialists coming within reach of a parliamentary majority. Then the only hope would be the unwillingness of the state and army personnel to follow the bidding of the government. They suggested that if the state, in order to head off a socialist majority, attempted a reactionary coup d'état against the existing suffrage arrangements, it would provoke a backlash in support of the integrity of the Constitution, and socialists would sweep to power on a tidal wave of popular support extending far beyond the heartland of organized labour. This was a prophecy sustained by heroic, indeed unrealistic, assumptions, and the SPD knew it. The party leadership was deeply unhappy when Karl Kautsky speculated openly on the subject in 1909.[83] They were justified in fearing the consequences of even verbally predicting an uprising in this way.

The electoral 'coup' was a lived reality for the German SPD. Even after legalization, for example, when the SPD did particularly well in the Saxony state elections, the other parties (including the bourgeois liberals) in 1896 combined to alter Saxony's electoral law along the lines of the discriminatory three-class Prussian system. Socialist representation was wiped out in the Diet.[84] More brutal forms might be expected should the Social Democrats overstep the mark of legality. Wilhelm II, who ascended to the German throne in 1888, was steeped in Prussian traditions of militarism, and idealized hierarchies of patronage and deference. Addressing army recruits at Potsdam in November, 1891, he advised them where their duty lay in the event of revolution:

> You are now my soldiers, you have given yourselves to me, body and soul. The only enemy you have now is my enemy. With the present subversive activities of the socialists it could come about that I order you to shoot down your own relations, brothers, even your parents. God forbid that this should happen, but in the event you must obey my orders without a word.[85]

Count Waldersee, Chief of the General Staff, in 1896 openly advocated the abolition of the universal male suffrage for Reichstag elections, hoping that socialists would be provoked into street fighting, to be easily crushed by the army.[86] The risk of provoking a militarist backlash was ever present, especially as spontaneous 'suffrage riots' became increasingly common from the 1880s to the Great War.[87]

It was hardly clear, therefore, how the Marxist 'centre', whilst rejecting timid reformism and foolhardy ultra-leftism, expected the state power to be overthrown, should it not simply fall apart. There was no mention of violent revolution in the Erfurt Programme, and indeed Engels admitted in 1892 that 'the era of barricades and street fighting has gone for good; if the military fight, resistance becomes madness.'[88] In a new introduction to Marx's pamphlet on the Paris Commune, published in 1895 as a kind of 'last testament', Engels argued that workers and ultimately socialists would have to penetrate and subvert the mass armies (to avoid enraging the German censor, and getting the SPD into hot water, he outlined this in the form of a historical analogy with early Christian permeation of Roman Imperial Legions).[89] However, there was a realization, particularly in Germany, that mass standing armies were protean, as likely to infuse mass society with anti-democratic militarist sentiments as to be subversively democratized. The SPD radical Karl Liebknecht warned in 1907 that:

> [Modern militarism] wants neither more nor less than the squaring of the circle; it arms the people against the people itself; it is insolent enough to force the workers… to become oppressors, enemies and murderers of their own class comrades and friends, of their parents, brothers, sisters and children, murderers of their own past and future. It wants to be at the same time democratic and despotic, enlightened and machine-like, at the same time to serve the nation and to be its enemy.[90]

Indeed, the German state was careful in its recruitment policy, calling up on average only 57 per cent of eligible males, so that few recruits came from urban and industrial districts infused with socialist ideology, and many from the agricultural and rural provinces considered naturally loyal to the regime.[91] (In contrast, by

1914, Republican France called up 80 per cent of those eligible.) Chancellor Bethmann Hollweg agreed with the brass that the army should not be expanded, for fear that it 'would expose the army to democratization'.[92] This demonstrates that, contrary to the SPD's worst fears, workers were relatively resistant to militarism. It was principally the middle classes who were 'becoming feudalised and militarised', as an SPD speaker put in 1914.[93] However, the principal point remained: there seemed little chance that a mass citizen army, at any rate outside a major crisis of military defeat, could be subverted from within. Engels' 'last testament' offered no way out of the conundrum of revolution in conditions of the state's clear military supremacy over the citizenry.

However, if the bourgeoisie's class-specific forms of struggle—the tax-strike, withholding of credit, and the production standstill—were insufficient to overthrow a determined authoritarian state, perhaps the forms of struggle peculiar to the wage-labouring class might be more effective. Certainly socialists were attracted to the possibility. Revolutionary syndicalists, in particular, pressed the novel potential of characteristically proletarian struggle. Eugene Guerard explained syndicalist reasoning in 1896:

> In an attempt to defend factories, workshops and warehouses, the army would disperse its forces. The mere threat by the workers to destroy railway lines and signalling equipment would compel the government to spread its troops over 39,000 kilometres of the French railway system.... In these conditions the government would be unable to protect the warehouses and factories. The factories would be left undefended and the revolutionary workers in the towns would have the field to themselves.[94]

Though ingenious, this rather underestimated the tactical capacity of the state to concentrate forces, arrest workers' leaders, and demoralize the movement through sanguinary oppression. Guerard himself later abandoned his syndicalist idealism.

Still, the 'general strike' was a beguiling notion. In the early days of the Second International there was some enthusiasm amongst French and Dutch adherents for a general strike as an effectual way by which war could be prevented and democratic revolution achieved. The great majority of socialists, however, were convinced that the repression provoked by such a revolutionary action would be unrestrained and quite brutal enough easily to break strikers' resistance. In general, Second International parties adopted the form of regular parliamentary political parties, and restricted themselves to labour organization, propaganda, and fairly cautious agitation, for fear that imprudent action would simply provoke a state coup against constitutionalism, and the smashing of the workers' movement. As Karl Kautsky put it, 'the three great branches of the class struggle' were 'parliamentarianism, trade unions, press'.[95]

It was most clearly amongst the Russian socialists that an insurrectionist form of revolutionary organization was canvassed: a party organized as a network of combat cells. To be sure, this was supposed to arise out of proletarian struggle. V. I. Lenin (1870–1924) in 1905 argued that once mass political strikes broke out, and the regime tottered, the party had to arm the proletariat, train and coordinate insurgent groups, suborn the army, and systematically plan for insurrection.

A period of revolution, Lenin insisted, was 'a period of civil war', and in these circumstances, 'the ideal party of the proletariat is the *fighting party*'.[96] The notion of 'civil war' as the royal road to revolution, with all that it implied for the militarization of revolutionary politics, was not a strategy that found favour in the Marxist centre, however much they (and most European liberals) might indulge it for those caught in the toils of the hated Tsarist 'despotism'.

Still less attention was paid by the Second International to how a socialist government in power might sustain itself against a reactionary rebellion. Perhaps because the violence of reaction was so stark in Russia, Marxists there drew the most ominous conclusions. The 1903 conference of the Russian SDLP agreed that 'An essential condition for the social revolution is the dictatorship of the proletariat—that is, the conquest by the proletariat of such political power as to allow it to suppress all attempts at resistance on the part of the exploiters.' Plekhanov glossed this as follows:

> If it were necessary for the success of the revolution to restrict the effect of one or another democratic principle, it would be criminal to stop at such a restriction.... Hypothetically it is conceivable that we, Social Democrats, may have occasion to come out against universal suffrage.... The revolutionary proletariat could restrict the political rights of the upper classes the way these classes once restricted the political rights of the proletariat. The fitness of such a measure could only be judged by the rule: *salus revolutionis suprema lex*. The same point of view should be adopted by us on the question of the duration of parliaments. If, on an impulse of revolutionary enthusiasm, the people were to elect a very good parliament, a sort of *Chambre Introuvable*, we should try and make it a long parliament; and if the elections turned out to be unfavourable, *we should try and dismiss it not in two years' time, but if possible in two weeks*.[97]

This clearly owed much to Marx's view that legality lapses when revolution and counter-revolution contend for influence over Parliament. It was a language alien to the Marxist 'centre' of the Second International, however, and pregnant with consequences for Russia.

CONCLUSION

With capitalism pervasive and international, the political importance of bourgeois civil society paradoxically declined from about 1870. Capital itself was, at least in high-investment industries, increasingly anti-competitive in organization, and tied via banking and state connections to strategies that deployed state and political power as protection against the market's invisible hand. The ability of the state to range widely in the international markets for its credit, and to use business and accounting practices to improve its revenue collection massively, refreshed its capacity to operate autonomously of civil society.

For all their insistence that capitalism was established and ripening towards working-class collectivism, European socialists found themselves chewing over the same old problems of constitutional revolution. They asked essentially the same questions liberals had asked and failed to answer in 1848: how to force an executive state to accept responsibility for a democratically elected Parliament? And could a constitutional government protect itself against counter-revolution? Socialists thought of themselves as more determined than the vacillating bourgeoisie, but they essentially failed to come up with more convincing strategies for victory. Syndicalists and leftists fetishized the 'mass strike' without acknowledging that its provocative bark would be worse than its bite. The Marxist 'centre' counselled building the party and trusting that a spooked authoritarian regime would miscalculate, and in attempting untimely repression so discredit itself. But this essentially misidentified the problem by playing down the vast reservoirs of popular hostility to socialist parties, particularly amongst small property owners outside the big cities. The incipient Leninist strategy of 'civil war', which effectively meant launching an armed minority insurrection amidst the turmoil of a popular movement, and using repression to secure and hold onto power, was realistic only in conditions of societal breakdown, and incompatible with democratic consolidation.

Mainstream socialism had set itself the task of completing and superseding the 'bourgeois revolution' by campaigning for governments responsible to democratic electorates, which would then go on to end the turbulence of the capitalist economy. The existence of anarchism indicated that there subsisted a leftist rejection of parliamentarianism, however, and the powerful statist trend within socialist orthodoxy made it clear that liberalism was by no means fully assimilated by the worker movement. It was certainly the case, however, that the identification of the bourgeoisie with liberalism had weakened, and campaigns for democratic reform of the franchise were primarily working-class movements organized by the socialist left.

# 8

# Democracy and State Power

By the late nineteenth century, the traditional liberal reliance upon bourgeois civil society was being challenged by the rise of democracy, or at any rate wide electoral suffrage. Liberalism had long opposed universal suffrage, as either the path to socialistic excess or a ruse by executive states seeking to avoid genuine parliamentary constitutionalism. France and Prussia, however, had led the way with universal (male) suffrage, and this example gradually spread. Switzerland enfranchised its male population in 1874, Spain in 1890, Belgium in 1892, the Netherlands in 1896, and Norway in 1898.

Under limited franchise, elite and usually liberal political parties in the mid-nineteenth century had dominated parliaments. They had been based around small, often aristocratic cabals and attracted bourgeois votes. With the arrival of extended suffrage, these liberal parties were often slow to adapt. Instead, elaborately organized mass-membership parties, based upon class or confessional electorates, and often of the left, rose to prominence. However, class-based mass parties of the left were generally excluded from polite, commercial, and legal society. They were at a disadvantage, therefore, when confronted by 'catch-all' pan-class parties of the centre and right.

## MASS SUFFRAGE AND PARTY POLITICS

Catch-all parties, relying on the resources of the wealthy to propagate their message amongst the masses, were successful at blocking the emergence of a class-based party of the left in the democratic and non-aristocratic United States.[1] Even in the late nineteenth century, America's 'gilded age' of 'robber capitalism', when per-capita income growth outpaced wage increases, Republicans and Democrats were able to bolt labour-movement issues to their pan-class programs. Progressive measures protecting labour and consumer rights were passed in many states. 'Populist' politics constructed alliances to constrain the tax-state of 'Big Government'.[2] This generated curious but persistent class alliances. William Graham Sumner (1840–1910) of Yale University spoke frequently of the 'forgotten man' of the 'middle class' (a US category considerably larger than that of the bourgeoisie proper). The 'forgotten man', neither impoverished nor very wealthy, was always at risk of being gouged by special interests, monopolists, and the tax collector. Sumner placed in the vanguard of middle-class interests, however, the very richest in society, because of their concentrated power: 'The reason I defend the millions of the millionaire is...that I know of no way to get the defence of society for my hundreds, except to give my help...to protect his millions.' (There were 4,047 American millionaires in 1893).[3] This apparently quixotic formulation remains the very basis of United States politics: the prostration of the mass electorate before extraordinarily wealthy elites in effective control of the political process. Sumner's was a pellucid description of an effectively operating bourgeois political system in the context of mass enfranchisement.

In much of Europe, however, the anti-socialist 'catch-all' parties could not construct alliances ranged against statism. They needed to mobilize broad constituencies that relied upon it: the armed forces and their families and suppliers, the protectionist landlords with still-potent political influence over their tenants, and the small property owners who looked to the state to defend them against dispossession at the hands of socialists or the unfettered market. Liberalism in its own right, outside Britain and France, failed to secure a sufficiently substantial constituency. Instead its core constituency contracted, which only served to identify it more strongly with narrow class interest. 'Liberalism became more "bourgeois", but the bourgeoisie did not become more liberal', notes Dieter Langewiesche: 'The embourgeoisement (Verburgerlichung) of liberalism was accompanied by a de-liberalisation of the middle classes'.[4]

The difficulty of promoting bourgeois civil society through democratized politics was addressed by Max Weber, who rose to intellectual prominence in Germany in the 1890s. Weber pointed out that because capitalism requires calculability and reliability in government and law, the 'middle classes' had been historically enthusiastic for parliamentary control of 'administration and finance' to check capricious monarchs and feudal aristocrats. However, 'with the rise of class parties to power, especially the proletarian parties, the situation of parliaments has changed radically'.[5] In his inaugural lecture as Professor of Economics at Freiburg in 1895, Weber anatomized the bourgeoisie confronted by 'proletarian democracy': 'Part of the upper middle class longs only too obviously for the appearance of a new Caesar who will protect it—against the emergence of classes from below....Another part has long become submerged in the political philistinism from which the broad mass of the lower middle class have never emerged.'[6] For Weber, the main problem was to form a political class that went beyond the fragmented parties encouraged by parliamentarianism (notably in France). Weber's important writings on the 'vocation of politics' and the 'vocation of science' were not simple works of methodological sociology. His argument was that political ends, such as a preference for greater equality of outcome between individuals, or a preference above all for rewarding hard work and talent, were values adopted on purely ethical grounds that could not be adjudicated between objectively. However, the means by which ends might be approached, or the practicability of consistently realizing ends, were indeed amenable to scientific guidance by a suitably trained intelligentsia. For Weber, therefore, intellectuals were 'theoreticians orientated to *Realpolitik*'.[7] It was a matter of urgency for Weber to understand how such an intellectually guided political class might come to assert its beneficial influence. He concluded that under modern conditions it was best served by charismatic leadership providing focus within a system of electoralism and bureaucratic legalism.

Weber favoured a kind of 'plebiscitary dictatorship', by which he meant a strong executive state with a democratic mandate. This had been realized, he thought, in the presidential system of the United States, and in the United Kingdom, where the prime minister dominated government through use of powerful prerogative powers and a disciplined party structure that whipped Members of Parliament into a unified phalanx.[8] Thus Weber's theorization of 'charismatic leadership' was partly occasioned by his strong belief that class tensions were best contained by a political structure that unified national will around a popular leadership. The rule of law and property rights required a passive citizenry alienating its political volition to a democratically mandated executive. Weber's diagnosis echoed that of Moisey Ostrogorski, who observed that it was not the bourgeoisie who were replacing the aristocracy as the ruling elite, but rather a full-time and professional political class organized in the party, or 'caucus'. Political organization was maintained by wealth, argued Ostrogorski, but otherwise the bourgeoisie remained aloof: 'Shopkeepers, clerks, and superior artisans, this is the sphere from which most of the active members of the Caucus are taken.'[9] The potential for these social strata to embrace a politics of rage became evident in the inter-war period.

Weber was seeking to find a basis for the replication within continental Europe of Anglo-American mass politics, strong executive government, and the supremacy of commercial civil society. Cultural differences between the two worlds were profound, however. The intense voluntarism of associational culture in Britain and the United States owed much to a peculiar history of relatively fragmented religious confessionalism since the early modern period. In the United States, Church and state were formally separated, while in Britain the established Anglican Church was fairly latitudinarian, and had no spiritual authority over a large nonconformist community. Religious conformity in both countries was not easily enforceable, and citizens were used to a pluralist marketplace of ideas. They enjoyed the freeborn right to choose as consumers, whether of goods, of religious affiliation, or of political allegiance. The vote, though of negligible weight for each individual in actually influencing government, was valued as a warrant of citizenship, a recognition of competence to associate politically. Such a culture was easily congruent with the contractual ethic of bourgeois civil society, whereby buyers and sellers meet on legally equal terms for satisfaction of individual needs.

These conditions were not so easily translated into a continental European idiom. Europe had been divided into a patchwork of religious blocs—Roman Catholic, Lutheran, Calvinist, Orthodox—legitimizing dynastic authority on the principle of *cuius regio, eius religio*. Religious sectionalism structured the public sphere. Even as civil society gained traction in the nineteenth century, religious identity often formed the core of secular nation-building ambitions (for example, the secession of the Christian Balkans from the Muslim Ottoman Empire, Catholic Belgian secession from the Protestant Netherlands, Catholic Polish hostility to Orthodox Russian rule, Catholic Irish rejection of union with Protestant Britain). Religious sectionalism in most European countries thus habituated citizens to seek representation for their group identities. Political parties were often based upon confessional blocs (particularly Catholicism), or their secular homologues: ethno-national blocs. Class-based parties, speaking for defined middle-class, proletarian, or peasant interests, were natural analogues to this form of sectional politics. Anglo-American 'catch-all' parties, competing to represent a mass of individual voters, were not easily transferable.

As Protestant allegiances tended to align with national-liberal or state-conservative parties, the Catholic Church was especially prominent in mobilizing popular opinion for political ends. This could be politically progressive and liberal, as was markedly the case in Ireland and Belgium in the 1820s, but particularly after 1848 the Church was alienated from any tincture of 'progressive' politics by the anti-clericalism of the liberal left, and the seizing of Church assets by modernizing states. In 1864, Pope Pius IX, in a bold repudiation of modernity, issued a 'syllabus of modern errors' denying that 'the Roman Pontiff can, and ought to, reconcile himself, and come to terms with progress, liberalism and modern civilization'.[10] This was a theoretical counter-blast both to bourgeois civil society and to the realist executive state. In practical terms, the Catholic faithful were warned to abjure secular politics entirely in Italy and France, and in Germany the Church battled against attempts by Bismarck to interfere with Catholic schooling and ecclesiastical appointments (the Kulturkampf of 1871–7). Anti-clericalism was, and is, a well-worn path by which former liberals and radicals conform to power whilst retaining an image of themselves as daring iconoclasts. The National Liberals proved to be Bismarck's chief support during the Kulturkampf. Pope Leo XIII's condemnation of socialism in 1878, in the encyclical *Quod Apostolici Muneris*, helped bring the struggle to an end.

The parliamentary Centre Party proved itself a competent representative of Catholic interests in the united Germany. Impressed, Pius' successor Leo XIII softened the abstentionist line by allowing that democratic and republican regimes could be acceptable to the faithful, so long as the interests of the Church were protected. If the interests of the faithful could be represented corporately, so might the worker have a place of respect in an organic society. In 1891, Leo issued *Rerum Novarum*, which urged that labour's collective interests be recognized and acted upon. Trade-union organization was given the papal imprimatur as 'the natural right of man'.[11] Still, continuing sharp distinctions between Church and secular society—bitter Church-state collisions in France in the 1890s and early twentieth century, and the extreme anti-clericalism of the left in Spain, for example—made any modus vivendi of confessionalism and profane politics fraught. Nevertheless, there was evolving, if painfully slowly, a mode of Christian democratic politics willing to look for support outside the Catholic faithful by promoting a vision for society as a whole, rather than just the discrete interests of the Church. Christian democracy provided an alternative to socialism as a sectional interest with ambitions to integrate society. In continental Europe, it was in many respects potentially a better fit for existing civil society than the Anglo-American example of laissez-faire liberalism.

In this period, however, Christian democracy was prey to far-right radicalism, ultra-nationalism, and anti-Semitism. Jews, in particular, were victimized because of their prominence in finance and department stores; as such they were lightning rods for hostility to big business. Anti-Semitic riots accompanying the Dreyfus affair in France attracted the participation of the master artisans, notably shopkeepers, butchers and their assistants, grocers, *pâtissiers*, small investors, waiters, and medical and law students. Nevertheless, political parties that organized on a primarily anti-Semitic platform made relatively little headway before 1914. Adolf Stöcker's Christian Social Party attracted only 1 per cent of the vote in 1878 in Germany, and he finally took refuge in the Conservative Party. In Vienna, Karl Lueger, who served as mayor between 1897 and 1910, cynically and rather insincerely deployed anti-Semitism to appeal to his 'Grocers' and Tailors' Party', but it was mainly populism and administrative competence that united Lueger's alliance of bourgeoisie and small propertied 'mittelstand' against wage-earner based socialism.[12]

Generally speaking, catch-all parties superseded small liberal cliques on the right, and while these new parties were as vehemently in favour of private-property as purist liberals, they were less attached to the values of freely alienable commercial property as the foundation of a liberal civil association. Along with capital, they stoutly defended, even from market pressures, the freighted property of landed estate, small farm, workshop, and small shop, all of which was tied up with non-marketable status and traditional hierarchies.

## SOCIALISTS AND LIBERALS

Liberal politics by no means disappeared, however, and given the lack of convincing revolutionary strategy for taking the state by storm, socialist reformists came to believe that democratic advances might best be secured in alliance with bourgeois liberal parties. The Belgian POB allied with Progressive liberals in its struggle for a wider suffrage. In Italy, after the 'terrible year' of 1898, when artillery had been used against workers in Milan, socialists entered into an electoral bloc with the bourgeois left. In 1901, socialist deputies in Parliament supported the Giolitti government from outside in return for ending the repression in North Italy. Spanish socialists entered a pact with the republicans following the violent military repression of Barcelona in the *Semana Trágica*; even the anarchists brought workers to the polls for socialist and republican candidates. Because of this, the first socialist was elected to the Cortes; Pablo Iglesias in 1910. Russian Marxists around the turn of the century veered between dismissing bourgeois liberals and, more often, seeking to support their struggle for constitutionalism.[13] From 1903, however, Russian Social Democrats divided between Mensheviks, inclined to cooperate the liberal bourgeoisie, and the Bolsheviks, who preferred an alliance with the poorer peasantry.

In France, the socialist movement was divided over the notorious Dreyfus affair. The Guesdist and anarchist elements within French socialism were inclined to dismiss the affair as a spat within the bourgeoisie. A majority of the socialist movement, however, felt that on principle Dreyfus must be defended as otherwise a signal defeat would be visited upon civil liberties for all. Jean Jaurès insisted that:

If Dreyfus has been condemned contrary to all law, condemned falsely, what an absurdity to count him among the privileged class!... He is a living witness to military lies, to political cowardice, and to the crimes of the authorities.... And who is most menaced today by the arbitrary action of the Generals, by the constantly glorified violence of military repression? Who? The proletariat, I tell you. It is the first interest of the working class to hasten the discredit and the fall of those high reactionary officers who are ready to turn their guns on the proletariat tomorrow.[14]

The Radical party in France—a fairly moderate, increasingly bourgeois party, zealously defensive of laissez-faire economics and property rights—was genuinely concerned at the revival of the right during the Dreyfus affair. In 1899, Waldeck-Rousseau established a government of 'republican defence' to respond to the 'insolent challenge' of the ultra-nationalists, and to guard against any juncture of the anti-Dreyfusard mob with the army.[15] Socialist Independent Alexandre Millerand accepted the post of Minister of Industry. While many socialists distanced themselves, particularly as the government's Minister of defence had played a leading role in suppressing the 1871 Commune, Jaurès, not without misgivings, supported Millerand's decision as a legitimate concentration of forces to defend established liberties from reaction. As the government soon proved itself repressive of workers' rights, international socialist sympathy for Millerand ebbed away. Still, even as Rosa Luxemburg (1871–1919), the firebrand Polish-German Marxist, condemned Millerand's decision, she admitted the principle that socialists might legitimately join a bourgeois government to defend the 'common cause' of 'liberty of the country or...democratic achievements of the people'.[16] Jaurès drew the logical conclusion from his republican defencism that French liberties required armed defence from foreign attack too. The Dreyfus affair itself clearly revealed that the professional standing army which trained up the reserves was imbued with reactionary hostility to the republic. Jaurès, consequently, put much effort into drawing up plans for a national militia system with a democratic culture: *L'Armee nouvelle* (1910).

The Dreyfus affair, on the one hand, convinced many socialists that bourgeois liberty was decomposing (as it did Theodor Herzl, who began promoting a Zionist escape from Europe for Jews). Kautsky saw the affair as part of 'the great reactionary movement' in Europe characterized by the bankruptcy of liberalism and the advance of militarism.[17] On the other hand, Émile Vandervelde (1866–1938), President of the Second International and leader of the Belgian workers' party, suggested that precisely this weakening of liberalism required the socialist left to buttress progressive bourgeois parties. He put it thus at the 1900 International Congress in Paris: 'A coalition is legitimate in the case where liberty is threatened as in Italy: it is legitimate again when it is a question of defending the rights of the human personality, as recently in France. It is legitimate finally when it is a question of winning universal suffrage as in Belgium.'[18] The Marxist centre in general did reject participation in bourgeois governments, even as they involved themselves in electoral pacts with liberal parties, because they fully expected to inherit the state, and argued that building up to this consummation required utmost fidelity to a pure, proletarian class basis. However, they left the door firmly ajar for participation in bourgeois governments to protect established freedoms against outright reaction. A resolution, written by Karl Kautsky, was passed at the Paris Congress of the Second International in 1900:

> The winning of political power by the proletariat in a modern democratic state cannot be the result of a *coup de main*, but can come only as the conclusion of long and patient activity.... The entry of a single socialist into a bourgeois ministry cannot be considered as the normal beginning for winning political power: it can never be anything but a temporary and exceptional makeshift in an emergency situation.[19]

As Kaustky explained, socialists should not 'seek' ministerial appointment, but they might 'accept' it as a duty 'in purely exceptional cases, for example in the event of war or invasion'.[20]

It would be wrong to overstate the eclipse of liberalism's progressive credentials by socialism. It was not unusual for professionals and the petite bourgeoisie to lend aid to workers' struggles against big business which, after all, was often seen as a common enemy. Indeed, professionals and the petite-bourgeoisie made up a significant component of the socialist cadre at all organizational levels. Often socialists and liberals agreed on voting rights, on parliamentary supremacy, on separation of Church and state, on public education and secular schools, and on the social responsibility of the state.[21] Indeed, in 1901, the Austrian socialist Karl Renner advised the Austrian bourgeoisie to embrace universal suffrage in their own interest, rather than cling to the neo-absolutist hulk: 'The bourgeoisie must learn to swim and really swim in the stream. A boat made out of legal privilege is only a paper boat, on which only fools would rely.'[22] Even on social issues, liberals and socialists found common ground. The 'new liberalism', as espoused for example by Johannes von Miquel in Germany, admitted a role for the state in assisting 'self-help' for those disadvantaged by the precariousness of poorly paid and irregular employment.[23] The British liberal T. H. Green insisted that the historical emergence and continued degradation of the propertyless proletariat owed not to capitalism, but rather to feudalistic landowners, who had historically ejected the tenantry into burgeoning cities, which they then refused to provide with amenities. This implied, of course, a common front of worker and bourgeois against landlords disposing of unearned ground rent.[24] British Labour, indeed, supported the Liberals in their struggle for higher taxes on unearned income and against the power of the House of Lords, from 1909 to 1912. The Belgian Socialists formed a united front with Liberals in 1911–12 in support of *laïcité* (secularism), universal suffrage, and social reform, though in a general election the following year many Liberal supporters deserted to the Catholic party in protest.

Even in unpromising Germany, liberal-socialist alliances made real headway. In Baden, South Germany, the Liberals allied with the SPD to keep the Catholic Centre from taking control of the Landtag. The Social Democrats helped to draft and voted for the state budget, and lifted its ban on meeting with the Grand Duke.[25] The Reichstag elections of 1912 saw formal cooperation between the Social Democrats and the Progressist Liberals. The SDP emerged as the largest single party, with 4.5 million votes and 101 seats in the Reichstag. What the

Liberals lost to the Socialists they almost entirely recouped from the Conservatives.[26] Kautsky (rather half-heartedly) defended this alliance, which he justified by asserting that the growth of white-collar workers—proletarian in its economic position but bourgeois in its social intercourse—had revitalized the bourgeoisie from below.[27] The leader of the National Liberals, however, repudiated any 'death-dealing alliance with Social Democracy'.[28] Indeed, the very successes of liberalism and socialism complicated their interaction. Max Weber complained that social democracy had, 'by opposing the bourgeoisie, paved the way to reaction'.[29] This raised the question of whether socialists should set liberal minds at rest.

The German socialist Eduard Bernstein (1850–1932), who had been a close colleague of Engels, at the turn of the century openly queried whether the exclusively proletarian orientation of the socialists inhibited constructive cooperation with the liberal bourgeoisie. Bernstein was convinced that bourgeois society was moving under its own weight towards socialism. Socialism, for Bernstein, was not only an ultimate end, but the ongoing, pan-class 'movement towards...a cooperative order of society'.[30] Revolution was redundant because the ruling class were no serious obstacle to reform.[31] Bernstein admitted that contemporary Liberal parties were temporarily cut off from this moral teleology, having become doctrinaire 'guardians of capitalism', but he favoured 'historical' liberalism and considered 'the middle class, not excepting the German, to be in the main fairly healthy, not only economically, but also morally'.[32] Bernstein's was a highly optimistic wager on constitutional democratic evolution. Unconvinced, the orthodox Marxist centre doubted whether the liberal bourgeoisie would be any more willing to cooperate with socialists if the latter ceased to present themselves as champions of the proletarian class interest, and doubted even more whether the authoritarian state would so easily accept democratization.[33]

Socialists opposed to Bernstein agreed that their movement inherited liberal traditions. As Wilhelm Liebknecht wrote in 1899, history had 'assigned to the German proletariat the mission not only of solving its own strictly proletarian problem, but also of accomplishing the work left undone by our bourgeoisie'.[34] They did not agree that the bourgeoisie were likely allies in this constructive work. 'German liberalism, given the opportunity,' wrote Kautsky, 'prefers the conservatives to the Social Democrats... [and this] can henceforth be considered an irrefutable rule which is only confirmed by the rare exception'.[35] Bernstein believed that the bourgeoisie was basically liberal and progressive, and socialists should cooperate with them. Orthodox socialists agreed that such cooperation was worthwhile (so long as it did not dilute the class basis of the socialist movement), but they were far less optimistic about the strength and tenacity of bourgeois liberalism.

On the 'left' of Social Democracy, the Polish Marxist, Rosa Luxemburg, went further to insist that democracy and liberalism were not consummations of capitalism, but only a passing phase:

> To Bernstein, democracy is an inevitable stage in the development of society. To him, as to the bourgeois theoreticians of liberalism, democracy is the great fundamental law of historic development, the realisation of which is served by all the forces of political

life. However, Bernstein's thesis is completely false.... No absolute and general relation can be constructed between capitalist development and democracy. The political form of a given country is always the result of the composite of all the existing political factors, domestic as well as foreign. It admits within its limits all variations of the scale from absolute monarchy to the democratic republic.[36]

More worrying still, Luxemburg argued, was that the fragile equation between the bourgeoisie and democracy was coming to an end. Rather, the tendency now was the 'abandonment by bourgeois society of the democratic conquests won up to now'.[37] Economic integration and market functions could take place without democracy. Moreover, the modern state no longer required the fiscal authority given it by parliamentarianism. Liberalism and pressure from the masses had transformed the administrative state machinery so that it complemented capitalist economic order, but this only meant that democratic forms could now be suppressed without risk of the administration, finances, or the military organization of the state reverting to the antiquated conditions that had pertained under the absolutisms of pre-1848.[38]

Luxemburg's was a penetrating and sombre commentary. She had highlighted the ironic outcome of internationally mature industrial capitalism and developed bond markets. Now executive states could sustain their fiscal base, creditworthiness, and economic prosperity without surrendering to commercial civil society and parliamentarianism domestically. Moreover, as the bourgeoisie shaded into an oligarchy, based upon cartelized capital of an increasingly anti-competitive bent closely connected to the militarized state, it was structurally distanced from its historical liberalism. Luxemburg overstated the decline of middle-class liberalism, as we have seen, and underestimated the continuing vigour of competitive commercial civil society outside the cartelized sectors of heavy industry. Having said that, she had highlighted a real and potent trend. Constitutionalism of a sort, it is true, had become the norm west of Russia, but outside of those states that had made a breakthrough before 1848—Britain, France, Belgium, Scandinavia, and Switzerland—parliaments could oversee budgets and approve legislation, but they could not direct the executive government or determine ministerial appointments. A deadlock had been reached, and there was evidence of incipient regression.

The 'revisionist' controversy in international socialism, provoked by Bernstein's intervention, ended ambiguously. At the Amsterdam Congress of the Socialist International in 1904, the German delegation presented a resolution condemning revisionism. Jaurès criticized the resolution's celebration of isolation from bourgeois liberalism as an alibi for 'inaction'. German socialism, argued Jaurès, inherited a quietism deriving from Germany's lack of 'revolutionary tradition'; reforms such as universal suffrage had been handed 'from above'. August Bebel inadvertently conceded the point when he replied for the German socialists that 'we don't intend to get our heads smashed' for the sake of the democratic republic and representative government.[39] Despite Jaurès' debating flair, the resolution was passed, following which Millerand was formally expelled from the International in 1904. Conditions for cooperation with bourgeois liberalism in pursuit of democratic reform, however, were not much clarified.

Most socialists saw revisionism as being an expression of the white-collared and salaried 'new middle class'. The 'new middle class', as Louis Boudin, an American critic of Bernstein put it, was not properly speaking capitalistic. Being salaried, 'it has no love of property as such, because it does not possess any' and it lacked 'that love of economic independence and individual enterprise which is the characteristic of the true bourgeois'. The 'new middle class', therefore, was at least as insecure as the proletariat in its conditions of existence, and anxious for government employment:

> It has no veneration for property or property rights, no love of economic independence, and consequently no constitutional abhorrence of 'paternalism' or of socialism.... [I]t is, because of the very nature of its social existence, extremely restless, ever ready to change, and ever longing for a change that will finally do away, or at least alleviate, its unsettledness, give it a rest. 'Governmental interference' has no terrors for it. It feels the need of a stronger hand.... If such a makeshift can be dignified into an ideology, its ideology is State Socialism.[40]

Kautsky similarly had refused to identify revisionism with a 'corrupted' working class. He divined, instead, an international trend—comprising German revisionism, Jaurès' following in France, and British labour—as representing a 'renaissance of bourgeois radicalism' which borrowed eclectically 'from socialism and liberalism'.[41] Luxemburg, likewise, identified bourgeois intellectuals seeking to reconcile the German state and the working class through ameliorative reform, the so-called Kathedersozialisten, as the transmission belt for bourgeois ideology into the workers' camp.[42] The point for all of these authors was that 'reformism' represented a revival of bourgeois libertarianism, and to that extent it was a progressive tendency somewhat countering the general decline of bourgeois liberalism. Revisionism was problematic only insofar as it infected the workers' movement.

## THE 1905 REVOLUTION

The events in Russia in 1905–6, ultimately abortive, brought into sharp focus the possibilities and limitations of revolution against a determined and militarily powerful state, and whether in the presence of a substantial worker interest it would be a 'bourgeois revolution' or something more. Certainly, it began in many ways as a classic 'bourgeois revolution'. The international situation clearly provided an important context. The Tsarist state was weakened by unsuccessful war with Japan, and a temporary crisis in European stock exchanges reduced the flow of credit to the regime. A reform campaign mounted by liberals in the autumn of 1904 accelerated into revolution with the Bloody Sunday massacre of workers peacefully processing to petition Tsar Nicholas II on 9 January 1905. The Minister of Finance, Count Kokovtsov, warned his tsar that the shockwaves of the event had real implications for the state's fiscal stability: 'The impression it created abroad was tremendous, and this was just as I was negotiating for two independent loans, one in Paris and the other in Berlin.'[43] Revolution erupted throughout Russia and its dependencies. Opposition to the regime was centred upon school and university students, the intelligentsia, peasants, the rural (*zemstvo*) and municipal (*duma*) local-government leaders, merchants and industrialists, and the workers, who 'had fallen completely under the sway of revolutionary leaders and could be counted on where physical force was called for', as tsarist statesman Sergei Witte put it. Finally, all non-Russian nationalities (35 per cent of the population) joined the agitation. Even the civil service and soldiery were doubtful in their loyalty.[44] Most importantly, soldiers resisted the authority of their officers. Riots spread from the army to the navy, and socialist agitators encouraged the formation of soldiers' councils, 'an idea which in 1917 proved fatal to the Russian army'.[45]

The revolution began with fiscal crisis, analogous to the ruptures between state and commercial civil society typical of previous 'bourgeois revolutions'. However, in contrast to France in 1789, for example, it was turmoil in the international money markets rather than the weight of domestic civil society that was being brought into play. The autocracy may be 'at the mercy of the cool, hard hand of the banks and stock exchange', as Max Weber observed at the time, but this 'specifically 'bourgeois' instrument' was 'controlled by 'foreign financers' and 'not in the hands of the Russian liberals'.[46] Within Russia itself, therefore, the real motive force seemed to lie with the industrial working class rather than the bourgeoisie. Councils, or 'Soviets' of Workers' Deputies spontaneously formed (the first established in Ivanovo-Voznesensk) and put forward radical demands. These demonstrated the potential power of the industrial working class, which had grown rapidly in the previous decade, particularly in Moscow and St Petersburg.

Liberals, frustrated with government inflexibility, supported a general strike organized in October by socialists. The workers' general strike compelled the tsar to make major concessions in his October Manifesto, which proclaimed that a national representative assembly, or Duma, would be elected on a wide franchise, and as 'an unshakeable rule that no law can come into force without the approval of the State Duma'.[47] This clearly would amount to something close to a constitutional revolution, though the tsar could still veto legislation. However, a further decree established a Council of the Empire, made up of nominees and creatures of the autocracy, as an Upper Chamber of the legislature. Laws would have to be passed by both Council and Duma before being submitted to the tsar for approval. 'Octobrist' liberals, based mainly on financial and business interests, generally supported the government after the Manifesto. Most liberals, organized around the Constitutional Democrat (Kadet) Party were certain that the state apparatus remained unreformed, and were unwilling to abandon their hostility toward the government.

The prime minister, Sergei Witte, alienated reform-minded elements by his holding to reactionary ministers such as Pyotr Durnovo at the Ministry of the Interior. 'The deepening conflict between the government and the revolutionary left placed the liberals in a precarious position,' writes Abraham Ascher, historian of the revolution, and a growing number of liberals, while opposing the government, grew fearful of the outcome of any armed revolt.[48] With some difficulty, through bribery and repression, the regime secured the loyalty of its military forces. The December 1905 Moscow insurrection, supported by most socialists, broke out just as army mutinies were subsiding, allowing the full weight of heavy weapons to be turned on the insurgents and civilian population. Large parts of the Moscow textiles centre, a working-class stronghold, were destroyed.[49] This demoralizing dead end shattered the revolutionary alliance between bourgeoisie and workers. While the Kadets continued to place most blame on government repression, many other liberals were frankly celebrating that the uprising had been suppressed.[50] Savage government reprisals after the uprising, continuing into the winter and spring of 1906, ended the chance for a reconciliation between liberals and the government.

Prime Minister Sergei Witte's last major achievement in office was his securing of a long-term loan from France. 'With financial stability achieved,' writes Robert D. Warth, 'the tsarist regime became more confident of its ability to rule and less respectful of its critics.'[51] The fiscal ship of state had been steadied, as the international money markets discounted the potential for full-blooded revolution in Russia. When elections to the Duma were held in March and April 1906, a large majority of seats were won by the liberal Kadets. Opening on 10 May 1906, the Duma pressed for completion and consolidation of Western-style liberal revolution. The Duma was shut down, by government coup, after only two months. The Kadets repaired to Vyborg in Finland and, in classic style, called for a tax strike and refusal to serve with the military.[52] They did not call for armed rebellion, though sailors at the Kronstadt naval base did mutiny, and there was mass unrest especially amongst the peasantry. The Kadets, indeed, explicitly repudiated 'violence as a means of political overturn', relying instead on 'the organization of public opinion through agitation and propaganda' as its strongest weapon.[53] In 1907 a unilaterally imposed imperial decree altered the franchise giving the greatest weight to the votes of only one hundred and thirty thousand landowners. The Duma continued to exist only as a consultative body, and the first Russian revolution had definitely concluded with the survival of tsarist autocracy.

In his memoirs, Witte concluded that:

> It is noteworthy that the nobility was willing to share the public pie with the middle class, but neither of these classes had a sufficiently keen eye to notice the appearance on the historical stage of a powerful rival, who was numerically superior to both and possessed the advantage of having nothing to lose. No sooner did this hitherto unnoticed class, the proletariat, approach the pie than it began to roar like a beast which stops at nothing to devour its prey.
>
> Anticipating upon the course of events, I may say that when the nobility and the bourgeoisie beheld the beast, they began to fall back, or rather face to the right.[54]

Certainly, liberal radicalism rapidly ebbed from about 1907. Up until the eve of revolution in 1917, the Kadets declined to call even for a ministerial responsibility to the Duma, proffering instead a vague demand for 'government enjoying the confidence of the nation'.[55] The Russian industrial bourgeoisie generally held aloof from the liberals, either Octobrists or Kadets, who were staffed primarily by the gentry and the intelligentsia. Industrialists preferred to work through the 'apolitical' Council of Congresses of the Representatives of Industry and Trade.[56] However, the liberals had put up a much stiffer fight than Witte implied, and the bourgeoisie by no means adopted a reactionary nostalgia for unreformed Tsarism. The autocracy's continued encouragement of commercial and industrial development, combined with such powers of oversight allowed the Duma, offered at least the prospect of a bourgeois-friendly state by instalment plan. With Prime Minister Pyotr Stolypin's agricultural reforms, from 1906, fostering a rural farmer class above the peasantry, many moderates gave up advocacy of immediate constitutionalism, trusting instead in the development of a stable pro-capitalist caste in the countryside.

The humbling of liberalism had a profound impact on Lenin, who after 1905 was repetitively insistent that the bourgeoisie had become settledly opposed to democratic revolution, because it was confident that it could come to an agreement with the tsarist state.[57] 'The Stolypin Constitution and the Stolypin agrarian policy mark,' he argued, 'a new movement towards...a middle-class monarchy'.[58] Lenin predicted, therefore, that a future democratic revolution would be carried out without the bourgeoisie, by 'the revolutionary-democratic dictatorship of the proletariat and the peasantry'.[59] The wish was no doubt fathering the thought here; Lenin was temperamentally unwilling to see the socialist movement as an adjunct to bourgeois liberalism. He was flat-out wrong to argue that middle-class opinion was content with slightly reformed autocracy as an indefinite settlement, as its desertion of tsarism in 1917 was clearly to reveal. However, while the experience of 1905 was no evidence of a general bourgeois repudiation of the aim of constitutionalism, it did strongly suggest that in the struggle against the authoritarian state, the worker movement was by no means fated to be the junior partner.

The 1905 Revolution reinvigorated European debates about the feasibility of revolution against modern armed states. Inspired by the Russian Revolution, the German SPD in 1905 adopted a resolution contemplating a mass strike as a counter-measure to a government coup d'état. Rosa Luxemburg, generalizing from the Russian experience, argued that a revolutionary movement would be spontaneous, the party only providing slogans and defining the goal. The general strike would arise 'of its own accord and at the right time'.[60] Whilst Luxemburg agreed with Russian socialists that insurrection was the unavoidable next step after the mass strike in the face of obdurate state power, she unrealistically insisted the decision for a rising would be made not by 'a little minority of the working class organized into fighting groups' but by the 'entire mass of the proletariat'.[61] Luxemburg's faith in proletarian spontaneity over party organization was much against the mood of German Social Democracy as a whole, particularly as the Russian revolution stalled and fell back. The ease with which the December 1905 rising in Moscow was crushed by modern artillery was a sobering reminder of harsh reality. The German 'free' (socialist) trade unions were first to reject the tactic of the mass strike, and at the Mannheim Socialist Congress of 1906 they imposed a trade-union right of veto on any attempt by the SPD to call a mass strike on their own cognizance.

The fate of the Moscow rising suggests that it was hardly fair to berate the Russian liberal bourgeoisie for its failure to overthrow the tsarist state when the state's capacity for military repression remained intact. Still, for Kautsky, the main point was that the Russian bourgeoisie was in no position to take the lead in the revolution, the workers being far more prominent in radical rebellion. The urban workers, as Russia's only 'strong, organized class', were in a position to lead a broad class front against foreign finance and tsarism.[62] This, Kautsky speculated as the revolution unfolded, could 'eventually lead to the point that Social Democracy' took governmental power for a period.[63] While such a government would likely nationalize natural monopolies, such as railways, mines, and oil wells, there could be no introduction of full socialism, as least without international revolution; the peasant majority would constrain the proletarian government. The outcome would be an 'American'-style society, a democratic society with property well distributed and feudal remnants eliminated, allowing rapid economic development and 'important concessions' to workers. As such, it would be a 'preparatory stage' to socialism.[64]

Leon Trotsky weighed in provocatively. Trotsky borrowed much of his theory from Kautsky, particularly his analysis of the consequences of foreign ownership of much capital in Russia, the weakness of the bourgeoisie, the inability of the peasants to maintain a government in its own social image, and the strength of the proletariat gifting it the leading role in bourgeois-democratic revolution. He disagreed with Kautsky and Lenin, however, in insisting that a workers' government could not be expected to be self-restraining just because the revolution was theoretically 'bourgeois-democratic' in content: 'there can be no talk of any sort of *special* form of proletarian dictatorship in the bourgeois revolution.... Any illusions on this point would be fatal. They would compromise Social Democracy from the very start.'[65]

Trotsky argued that the proletariat was instinctively propelled towards socialism, and a Social Democrat government, even if overseeing a constitutional and so 'bourgeois' revolution, must respond to 'the steel-hard logic of class interest'.[66] A workers' government, irrespective of the development of the economy, would attempt to construct socialism so long as it remained true to its social base. Here Trotsky relied upon Kautsky's pamphlet, *The Social Revolution* (1903), in which Kautsky had argued that a workers' government, even if not consciously socialist, must, in its own class interests, and to preserve economic order, begin nationalization and communalization of the existing business monopolies.[67] As Kautsky put it, a workers' government 'at first fighting only particular phenomena of capitalism such as unemployment or the trusts [cartels]...would soon be driven to adopt measures that would result in the socialist organization of production'.[68] Kautsky was speaking of advanced countries with few socialist ideologues but a vast proletariat (specifically Britain and the US), but Trotsky extended his reasoning to Russia, where precisely these conditions were inverted. 'When it has come to power,' Trotsky argued for Russia, 'the proletariat will inevitably, by the logic of its position, be driven to introduce nationalized economic production.'[69] He meant that, to protect the jobs and wages of its supporters, and to break the lockouts, tax strikes, and production standstills of its bourgeois opponents, a Russian workers' government would inexorably be forced into expropriating the larger means of production and repressing the bourgeoisie, or lose its proletarian support. Of course, such a government would have a narrow social base. Whilst it must eventually fall to peasant reaction so long as the revolution remained isolated, Trotsky confidently predicted that such a regime would first inspire socialist revolution internationally. With equanimity he contemplated a minority workers' government exercising dictatorial power to hold onto Russia whilst it awaited international rescue.[70] It was this conception of the revolution's historic tasks, rather than its class nature, that comprised the novelty of Trotsky's theory of 'permanent (uninterrupted) revolution'. While socialists had long suggested that workers would take the lead in democratic revolution, the idea that such involvement must inevitably tend to push bourgeois revolution beyond its outer limits was radically new.

## THE QUESTION OF WAR

The revolution of 1905 had taken place in the context of Russia's failure in war against Japan, and had been repressed once the war had been concluded and the army recomposed. War had been shown to be the midwife of revolution, for calamitous international armed conflict and defeat were the only realistic means by which a mass army might be thrown open to subversives and broken as a tool of reaction. International war, however, was also a terrifying source of mass nationalist intoxication and brutalization. The socialist position on war, until the 1890s, had been essentially a continuation of that of radical bourgeois liberalism. In general, Marx and Engels had believed, with liberals, that free trade and capitalism in general made wars less rather than more likely. So, in the *Communist Manifesto* (1848): 'National differences and antagonism between peoples are daily more and more vanishing, owing to the development of the bourgeoisie, to freedom of commerce, to the world market, to uniformity in the mode of production and in the conditions of life corresponding thereto.'[71] Where international trade prospered, they argued, peaceful relations became a priority for capitalists. Indeed, the more mobile the capital, the less likely that war would break out. J. A. Schumpeter later defined imperialism as 'the objectless disposition on the part of a state to unlimited forcible expansion', rooted in the atavistic militarism of those economically redundant classes still prominent in the armies and governments of the modern state, particularly the aristocracy. This position was something akin to that held by Marx in the mid-nineteenth century.[72]

Marx and Engels had been of the opinion that each war should be judged on the basis of its contribution to the progressive cause. They supported Britain and France against Russia in the Crimean War (1853–6), for example, and Germany against Napoleon in 1870, before switching to support the French Republic against Bismarck. Thus the attitude of Marx and Engels was far from being ethically pacifist, still less a 'pox on all' capitalist warring parties. They were motivated by strategic consideration that allowed for considerable flexibility: partisanship, however, never implied confidence in the war-making states.

For the Second International, however, something close to pacifism became almost an article of faith. A resolution passed at the Brussels Congress in 1891 condemned the 'archaisms' of war as being the product of 'the exploitation of man by man'.[73] From 1900, imperialist and colonial ambitions were designated by the Second International as the principal causes of war, a shift away from their earlier tendency—in common with radical liberalism—to see arbitrary despotism and feudal irrationality transmuted into bellicose nationalism as the taproot of international aggression. The Moroccan crisis of 1905—a stand-off between Germany on one side, France and Britain on the other—suggested that an inter-European war might be sparked by colonial issues of little moment to European workers. In this context, the French Gustave Hervé, at the 1907 Congress of the Socialist International in Stuttgart, advocated the general strike, even a proletarian insurrection, as an ultimate response to an irresponsible outbreak of war; he was backed by Jaurès. Bebel and Georg von Vollmar of the German delegation, however, countered that even a war sparked on the imperial periphery was likely to escalate into a war of national survival in Europe. A general strike would be impracticable in these conditions of national emergency. The consensus of the Congress was for the right of national self-defence combined with continuing class struggle against the bourgeois state. Jaurès summarized this attitude as 'Treachery neither to the fatherland nor to socialism'.[74]

The resolution ultimately passed at Stuttgart insisted that wars are 'inherent in the nature of capitalism', but the International proclaimed itself to be incompetent to prescribe in 'exact form' methods of resistance to war. The main body of this resolution was drafted by Bebel. The last paragraph, hypothesizing revolution as an outcome of war, was composed by Lenin, Luxemburg, and the Menshevik Julius Martov. This called upon socialists to 'strive with all their power to make use of the violent economic and political crisis brought about by the war to rouse the people, and thereby to hasten the abolition of capitalist class rule'.[75] There was, therefore, a certain tension in the socialist position, between opposition to war and hope that it would spark revolution. Jules Guesde in France, indeed, became rather frustrated with his colleagues' bent towards pacifism: 'I don't understand your fear of war. War is the mother of revolution.'[76]

The assumption of the resolution in Stuttgart that proletarians were naturally pacifistic was weakly argued. The British liberal thinker, Norman Angell, pointed out some of the flaws:

> The forces, both economic and psychological, making for war, cut clean athwart class division. Large sections of the bourgeoisie, both by interest and temperament, are anti-militarist, just as some sections of the democracy are militarist.... Capitalism in its economic theory is just as international as Socialism; in its practice, it is a good deal more so. The definite repudiation of the doctrine of Universal Brotherhood, a repudiation embodied in the legislation of a rigid, harsh, and sometimes cruel character, has come first from the advanced democrats—I refer to the anti-Alien, anti-Chinese, anti-Japanese legislation of Australia, Canada and the United States. The capitalist classes oppose such legislation; the working class imposed it.... In this, as in so many other respects, it is capitalism which is non-nationalistic, universal, cosmopolitan; Socialism or organized Labour which is racial, nationalistic, exclusive.[77]

This was pertinent. Whilst the disruption of trade and credit occasioned by war were in many obvious ways contrary to the interests of laissez-faire commercial society, industrial warfare, in fact or in prospect, tended to improve the bargaining power and job security of industrial labour. British Labourites, indeed, usually championed the 'general strike' as a weapon against unjust war in no small measure because so many British workers clearly benefited from jobs in munitions factories and in the shipyards, docks, and coalmines servicing the Royal Navy; and so the usual socialist tactic of opposing military estimates in Parliament was proportionately unpopular in Britain. Still, working-class chauvinism was not the principal promoter of militarism and imperialism as such: Australia, Canada, and the United States were hardly the primary culprits in this regard. Generally, European workers resented as an imposition the high taxes on basic consumables used to fund the army, and they often despised the conscription of their sons and the frequent use of soldiers as strike-breakers. Indeed, military taxation and conscription were probably the two most potent issues winning electoral support for socialists on the continent of Europe. Militarism, therefore, was not the creation of a popular nationalism. As discussed above, it was a matter of national survival for counties with land borders in an industrializing Europe.

Socialists around the turn of the century understandably discussed the militarization of capitalism as a relatively recent phenomenon. They distinguished between an early stage of 'competitive capitalism', up until roughly the Franco-Prussian War, and its subsequent supersession by a 'state monopoly capitalism'. The leading theoretician on this matter was Rudolf Hilferding (1877–1941), whose *Finance Capital* (1910) argued that state capitalism, from around 1870, had displaced competitive capitalism. The processes of concentration within the capitalist economy identified by Marx, Hilferding argued, had culminated in the formation of cartels and trusts that progressively eliminated free competition. Moreover, the same process had tightly bound together bank and industrial capital, with the former predominating. In turn, finance capital put enormous pressure on the state, its debtor.[78] Hilferding argued that common share-ownership, and common fear of the proletariat, integrated capitalists, the aristocratic elites, the state bureaucracy, and sections of the professional 'new' middle class into an oligarchic 'possessing class'.[79] This imperialist oligarchy was distant from the pacific bourgeois civil society of old:

> The demand for an expansionist policy revolutionizes the whole world view of the bourgeoisie, which ceases to be peace-loving and humanitarian. The old free traders believed in free trade not only as the best economic policy but also as the beginning of an era of peace. Finance capital abandoned this belief long ago. It has no faith in the harmony of capitalist interests, and knows well that competition is becoming increasingly a political power struggle. The ideal of peace has lost its lustre, and in place of the idea of humanity there emerges a glorification of the greatness and power of the state.... The national idea... is now transformed into the notion of elevating one's own nation above all others.[80]

By this view, the modern bourgeoisie were shedding their historical class preference for liberalism. Hilferding chose not to emphasize that the impetus given to heavy industry by militarism also served to strengthen the organization of the working class, and fear of war was a powerful incentive for ruling elites to organize production and protect the industrial workforce. In so far as Hilferding saw organized capitalism as a precursor to socialism, however, he implicitly conceded that militarism was of advantage to the working-class labour-market economy, though the horrors of industrial war were an egregious price to pay.

## CONCLUSION

The strategy of allying with liberalism outside episodes of crisis to win reforms was tempting for socialists, but it was not self-evident that incremental reform could achieve what revolution could not. Indeed, the winning of a government responsible to a democratic Parliament meant crossing a Rubicon, and hardly to be achieved without the old order noticing what was at stake. More significantly, such 'reformism' relied upon a bourgeois liberalism that to many observers appeared to be on the decline, and this precisely because of the rise of socialism. Did liberal-socialist alliances not threaten to frighten the middle classes into abandoning their remaining liberalism, and to undermine the crusading élan and class solidity of socialism?

This is not to say that constitutionalism was on the wane. On the contrary, it spread throughout the Western world (and to Japan), and even made inroads in Russia. Scandinavia was democratizing, largely because small farmers could now appeal to new urban allies in the emerging worker movement. Here the state bureaucracy and bourgeoisie were steadily pressured into granting concessions. Even outright constitutionalist revolution was still possible, at least where the state apparatus disintegrated. By the twentieth century, for example, disillusionment with the imperial Chinese state was widespread, and in the commercial Chinese diaspora, vocal. On 10 October 1911, republican revolution broke out when army units rose in rebellion in the city of Wuchang in Hubei Province. The revolution rapidly spread and, the dynasty having clearly lost the army, on 12 February 1912 the last Qing emperor abdicated. The Republic's titular president, Sun Yat-sen, had already propounded principles for the Chinese people, 'nationalism, democracy, and livelihood', which were explicitly analogous to the principles of radical liberalism as derived from the French Revolution.[81] In August 1912, Sun's comrades established the Guomindang (Kuomintang or KMT) as a nationalist, republican political party. Similarly, the Mexican Revolution from 1910, though tumultuous and divisive, did succeed in winning a constitution in 1917 that established democracy and acknowledged the interests of workers and peasants, at least in theory.

However, while repercussions from the French Revolution echoed on the global periphery, the stasis of socialism in Europe told a different story of deadlock. The revolutionary drive seemed to have stalled. In Britain, France, and the United States government was responsible to the electorate. Elsewhere, representative assemblies were usually limited to monitoring, auditing, and legislating for self-sustaining royal executives. In Austria, the spool even appeared to be unwinding, with emergency decrees to strong-arm fractious parliamentary nationalists becoming the norm from 1897. Impetus seemed to have run into the sand. With the outbreak of the First World War, stasis became unendurable: democracy had to move forward or move back.

# 9

# Revolution and the 'Dictatorship of the Proletariat'

The wars of Italian and German unity from 1859 to 1870 had been orchestrated by statesmen exercising a governmental right to conduct foreign policy unconstrained by parliamentary dictation. Bismarck led a 'fighting ministry' authorized by the king's prerogatives as Kriegsherr. Cavour conducted policy through powers of 'dictatorship' vested in the monarch by Parliament for the duration of war. Both statesmen also consciously cultivated a limited constitutionalism calculated to improve the fiscal and material preparedness of their monarchies for war. The conflicts they engaged in were bloody, but limited in scope: they were calibrated strategies of dynastic aggrandisement orchestrated by politicians.

The Great War of 1914 to 1918, in contrast, erupted and was waged as if by machines under their own momentum. Military-industrial juggernauts smashed into each other, and the blood flowed unstaunched until one side collapsed. The mobilization of war resources was organized via direct engagement between military and state bureaucracy, and cartelized industry and agriculture. Ministers and parliaments were marginalized. Civil society was drawn up into a single rank as never before, nationalist fervour and will to complete victory comprising the very bedrock of morale. 'The wars of peoples will be more terrible than the wars of kings,' Winston Churchill had predicted in 1901.[1] He was right. Total deaths amounted to some 9.7 million military personnel and 6.8 million civilians.

Industrial war and nationalist passion contrasted starkly with the mundane peaceability, civility, and order of commercial civil society. The 'last summer' of 1914, before war broke out, was long remembered as a kind of bourgeois idyll: commerce, prosperity, and elegant middle-class leisure recalled as through a sun-dappled haze.[2] The eruption of war in 1914, however, while not inevitable, was predicated upon those features hardwired into European society since 1870: industrialized munitions, mass citizen armies, popular nationalism, and the unarguable demands of military commanders. The juggernauts of war were on a permanent hair-trigger. In an attempt to avoid huge and unwieldy armies bogging down, it was vital for every side to attempt a quick victory by taking the offensive before the enemy had a chance to dig in. This was truly a war machine, and once switched on it operated under its own power. The result was that the military dictated to the diplomats, who dictated to the governments, who dictated to parliaments. Such structural irrationality led Jean Jaurès to prophesy that ruinous war would discredit and overthrow such mindless militarism in all nations.[3] He fell victim first, and was assassinated by an enraged French militarist on 31 July 1914. This was also, however, an ideological war: France and Britain—the 'Entente' powers—representing 'civilization' (commercial, liberal, plutocratic), versus German 'Kultur' (junker-monarchical, hierarchical, militarist). Both the French Premier René Viviani and the British Prime Minister Herbert Asquith explicitly defined their war aims as the 'crushing of Prussian militarism'.[4]

The war dragged on because, against all expectations, governments proved capable of financing protracted industrial warfare without plunging into economic crisis and revolutionary turmoil. This was a war fought on credit that would not have to be repaid until after the conflict was over. All belligerents avoided heavy taxation; Britain, for example, raised only 18.2 per cent of war costs through taxes, while for Germany the percentage was only 13.9. Instead, inflation was allowed to take the strain.[5] Still, in absolute terms, taxation went up and stayed up. By 1925, governments collected and spent roughly between 20 and 25 per cent of national income, compared to about half that before the war.[6] Government spending bought off organized labour and shored up domestic capital. The already tottering compact between commercial civil society and the state, mediated by taxation and parliamentarianism, was radically destabilized. The impact of the war was to establish the virtually autonomous fiscal state, far more independent of civil society than had been thought possible. It also proved the potentialities of state direction of the economy.

The war tightened the bonds between state and capital, whilst for the first time incorporating organized labour in an admittedly subordinate role. A tripartite 'corporatism' was the result. This was at the expense of parliamentary power, the traditional locus of liberalism. During the war, munitions ministries took on board experts from the business world and expanded to become centres of economic coordination, planning the allocation of scarce resources and directing labour. Even after demobilization high-powered planning bodies, drawing personnel from business and negotiating with organized labour, survived and sometimes revived— as with the Inter-Party Committee and Ministry of Labour in Weimar Germany, the Ministry of Corporations in Italy, the Ministry of Commerce in France, and the Department of Commerce in the US. This represented, Charles S. Maier argues, the growth of the 'private power' of capital, as corporations and governments bilaterally negotiated and cut deals, bypassing parliaments. Corporatism was 'the twilight of [parliamentary] sovereignty'.[7] Capitalists and state bureaucrats were short-circuiting bourgeois civil society. Élie Halévy, writing in the 1930s, dated the 'era of tyrannies' not from 1917 or 1922 (when Benito Mussolini took power), but from 1914, for this was a turning point when the state 'extended control over the economy, bound the workers' movement in a corporate alliance, suppressed dissent and whipped up pro-state enthusiasm'.[8] The liberal middle classes, already harmonizing with the militarized state in the two generations after 1870, now seemed copper-fastened to the authoritarianism of war. The demands of total war and fever-pitch nationalism even sealed the labour movement into a pan-class *union sacrée*.

## SOCIALISTS AND THE WAR

Socialists had not been able simply to dismiss the war as opposed to workers' interests. They were obliged to decide whether the conquests of bourgeois liberty—constitutionalism and national self-determination—should be defended by socialists in a compact with bourgeois and oligarchic elites. The Entente socialists saw themselves as in an ideological alliance with their own liberal bourgeoisie against German junker-militarism. Belgian socialists pledged themselves to 'the cause of democracy and political liberties in Europe' and against 'militaristic barbarism'. Emile Vandervelde, socialist leader and secretary of the International, became the first minister to take a ministerial post in a wartime 'bourgeois' government when he joined the Belgian government of national defence on 5 August 1914. For the majority of French socialists, the war was ideological, the democratic values of the French Revolutionary tradition pitched against German and Austrian 'feudalism'.[9] Socialists joined a French government of national defence on 26 August. The British Labour Party took a similar view: 'the victory of Germany would mean the death of democracy in Europe'.[10] In Britain, Labour was represented in the National government formed on 25 May 1915.

The German socialists, for their part, relied upon national self-defence as a justification for supporting their country in war. A special issue of the party newspaper *Vowarts* argued from *force majuere*:

> We are face to face with destiny... the inexorable fact of war. We are threatened by the horror of hostile invasion. Today it is not for us to decide for or against war but to consider the means necessary for the defence of our country.... We demand that as soon as the aim of security has been achieved and our opponents are disposed to make peace this war shall be brought to an end.... With these principles in mind we vote for the desired war credits.[11]

Even Vandervelde recognized the German socialist dilemma: 'Had they voted against the war credits they would have given up their country to invasion by the [Russian] Cossacks. Yet in voting for the credits they provided the Kaiser with weapons for use against republican France and against the whole West European democracy. Between these two evils they chose what they judged to be the lesser.'[12] Leon Trotsky, though opposed to the 'chauvinist betrayal' of the Second International, was quite sensitive to the strains that had led to national parties supporting war efforts. Given their isolation, Trotsky argued that socialists could at best only have 'limited themselves to expressing condemnation of the present War... declined all responsibility for it and... taken up a position of waiting'.[13] Indeed, the Bolsheviks and Mensheviks in Russia, and the majority of the Italian socialists, opposed the war, but took a line of 'neither adherence nor sabotage'.

There was, in all, no clear socialist volte-face in 1914, for defence of the nation had long been inscribed on socialist banners. What was divisive in the Second International was the majority of socialists suspending for the duration of the war all criticism of their own governments from the standpoint of class struggle. Pro-war socialists had not given up on revolution. On the contrary, for 'defencist' socialists (and liberals), war meant a kind of wager on provoking revolution in the enemy country. As the Russian Bolshevik, Alexander Shlyapnikov, mordantly observed: 'German opportunists...were fighting "Russian autocracy", the French were "defending the Republic", the British were "liberating Belgium", while the Russians [were] waging war to "liberate western democracy".... Each country and each coalition of warring capitalist forces was quite happy to speculate on a "revolution" in a rival country.'[14]

Support for the war allowed for the unfolding of a collaborationist, even chauvinist trend in the German SPD. The party newspaper *Vowarts* was initially suppressed, but allowed again to publish by the military governor of Berlin when he was promised that the paper would avoid 'incitement' of 'class hatred and class struggle'.[15] The party's right wing took the view that German expansionism was more progressive for the fate of European socialism than British 'liberalism'. They favoured a greater Germany, including Austria, that would dominate Europe.[16] In Austria, the socialist Karl Renner argued unabashedly for a 'central European customs and defence community'.[17]

From the September 1915 Zimmerwald conference, held in neutral Switzerland, socialist oppositions from various countries demanded a just peace 'without victors or vanquished'. They condemned majority socialist collusion in the militaristic *Burgfrieden* ('peace within the fortress') as stifling class struggle and democratic party competition.[18] In Britain and France, socialists supported the war in so far as it was directed against the expansionist militarism of the Central Powers. However, the war quickly became global and ever more imperialist. From 1916, Britain and France were conspiring to divide the Ottoman empire between them as colonies.[19] Socialist left-wingers were increasingly sceptical of the anti-militarist bona fides of their national governments, and they argued strongly for a 'democratic peace'. In Germany, the left of the SPD was much more directly critical of the militarism of the national wartime government. When the SPD began excluding members who criticized the government's failure to disavow postwar annexations and indemnities, a split became inevitable. On 6 April 1917 the Independent Social Democratic Party (USPD) was established, including the hard-left Spartacists (formed in January 1916) who favoured the revolutionary overthrow of the regime. The Austrian Sozialdemokratischen Partei Österreichs (SPÖ) did not split, but leftist opinion that the government was a militarist clique grew in force.

Lenin rejected as perverse the idea that the duty of revolutionaries was to export revolution abroad whilst supporting the social order at home.[20] For some time, Lenin had suspected that socialism in Europe was degenerating. In 1911 he warned a colleague that the Second International was failing. While its propaganda celebrated the socialist goal, its practice in each country focused on 'trying to bring about democratic institutions, that is to do the work of the middle-class'. This contradiction produced the worst of both worlds. Western socialists, by offering themselves as allies in the struggle for representative government, only frightened the bourgeoisie from the liberal camp, and by prioritizing democratic demands they failed to educate workers adequately in the practicalities of revolutionary politics.[21] Lenin immediately characterized the outbreak of the war as marking a new acute phase of capitalist degeneration, which rendered socialist adherence to constitutionalism obsolete. While Lenin approved 'the use of bourgeois legality' by socialists 'in the period of so-called peaceful constitutional development', he believed it to be 'to our advantage to exchange ballots for bullets (to go over to civil war) at the moment the bourgeoisie itself has broken the legal foundation it has laid down'.[22] For Lenin, the Great War was just that moment.

Lenin borrowed Hilferding's periodization of capitalism, widely accepted by socialists, to argue explicitly that liberal democracy itself was played out. He wrote in 1915 that:

> The first epoch from the Great French Revolution to the Franco-Prussian war is one of the rise of the bourgeoisie.... The second epoch is that of the full domination and decline of the bourgeoisie, one of transition from its progressive character toward reactionary and even ultra-reactionary finance capital.... The third epoch, which has just set in, places the bourgeoisie in the same 'position' as that in which the feudal lords found themselves during the first epoch.[23]

Lenin's key point was that in the age of imperialism distinctions between 'progressive' and 'reactionary' bourgeoisies, at least in the advanced capitalist and imperialist world, had become redundant. There was no longer a basis on which one could differentiate between 'progressive' or 'democratic' bourgeois regimes, and reactionary, authoritarian regimes. All were predatory and imperialist, and thus converging on a militarist, anti-democratic model.[24] The Great War was an 'imperialist war', not a war (as the majority of socialists claimed) of national 'defence'. The modern era, thus, was defined by the demise of any progressive bourgeoisie in the advanced counties, both absolutely—because they were now complicit in imperialism—and relatively, because the proletariat were sufficiently strong to lead in the progressive democratic vanguard itself. Indeed, the two factors at play were intimately related and mutually reinforcing: it was the very strength of the proletariat that impelled a bourgeoisie, fearful of revolution, into the arms of the semi-feudal, militarist state. Only distinct for Lenin were those countries preyed upon by the advanced capitalist world, and in such countries, victory for pan-class movements of resistance to foreign domination, if imbued with progressive potential, was to be preferred.[25]

Lenin's theorization implied that the entire metropolitan nation to one degree or another benefited from imperialism—this was in contrast to the view of John A. Hobson, the British radical-liberal intellectual, that imperialism subordinated the interests of workers and productive manufacturing capitalists to the strategies of finance capital. Lenin thus rejected Hobson's 'under-consumption' theory. He was anxious to prove that the 'super-profits' extracted by imperialism found their way to the proletariat of the imperial power, or at least a privileged 'aristocracy of labour'. This, thought Lenin, was the material basis for the reformist, 'defencist', and chauvinist tendency he identified in European Social Democracy, and which he believed had become the main social prop of capitalism.[26]

Lenin's argument that reformism rested upon a stratum of workers bought off by imperialist profits had little basis in fact. It was almost certainly the case, as Hobson (and Hilferding) had argued, that imperialism was a net loss for workers in the metropolitan counties. Higher wages resulted, in general, despite imperialism and militarism, not because of it. Moreover, workers enjoying superior wages and security of employment were rather more likely than average to support socialist politics. However, Lenin was making a polemical rather than sociological argument. His thesis that reformism was the political ideology of a section of the proletariat bought off by imperialism was radically distinct from the standard socialist argument that ascribed reformism to the influence of the politically progressive middle class on the workers' movement. Lenin's central assertion was that there was no longer any politically progressive middle class, because bourgeois civil society was now so bound up with oligarchic wealth and statist militarism. This meant that socialists who attempted to ally with the liberal bourgeoisie were not merely chasing a will-o'-the-wisp but were objectively and necessarily agents of militaristic imperialism, the only possible form for bourgeois politics in the imperialist countries.

Lenin's 1917 *State and Revolution*, usually seen as a rather airy and libertarian text, is in fact better understood as the rationalization for his pragmatic rejection of traditional Marxian adherence to 'political action' (that is, parliamentarianism) and embrace of class war *à outrance*. Lenin excoriated parliamentarianism as such and preached the necessity for 'violent revolution' to destroy 'the apparatus of state power' in all countries, whether authoritarian or constitutionalist.[27] Even countries of traditional 'Anglo-Saxon "liberty"', unencumbered by 'militarist cliques and bureaucracy', had since the outbreak of 'the first great imperialist war... completely sunk into the... filthy, bloody morass of bureaucratic-military institutions'.[28] Lenin excavated Marx and Engels' occasional references to the 'dictatorship of the proletariat', and made his particular interpretation of it the touchstone of true revolutionism: 'Only he is a Marxist who extends the recognition of the class struggle to the recognition of the dictatorship of the proletariat.'[29] This 'dictatorship' he defined as 'a centralized organization of force, an organization of violence... to crush the resistance of the exploiters'.[30] Any socialists maintaining democratic parliamentary illusions, he insisted, were bought and paid agents of state-monopoly capitalism and imperialism.

Though Lenin was clearly irreconcilable, had the war concluded quickly, it is quite likely that the socialist movement would have maintained broad unity and repaired fraternal relations across borders. It was the dragging out of war, and the ominous implications this had for the survival of civil and political liberties, that cleaved the left between 'reformists', committed to defending the gains of the 'bourgeois revolution', and revolutionaries convinced that bourgeois liberty had become an oxymoron.

## THE RUSSIAN REVOLUTION

In some respects, the drama in Russia opened as a classically bourgeois revolution. A credit crisis of the state had again provided an opening for bourgeois pressure. The Duma, mostly suspended since the opening of war, was reconvened in 1915 to deal with the mounting fiscal crisis. Shlyapnikov, the Bolshevik memoirist, acknowledged that the liberal bourgeoisie were far from quiescent in the face of crisis: the autumn of 1916 was marked by 'open public activity by the organized merchant and industrial bourgeoisie' seeking further instalments of constitutional government.[31] Still, as it could rely upon French and British loans, the tsarist government felt strong enough to dissolve the Duma. On 23 February 1917, however, spontaneous bread riots sparked strikes in the factories. Crucially, most of the army was heavily engaged at the front, and garrisons held back to maintain order deserted to the revolution. On 25 February the Volynsky Guards in Petrograd mutinied and joined the workers' demonstrations. The Duma reconvened and established a Provisional Government, to remain in place until elections could be organized for a Constituent Assembly. Meanwhile, a deliberative and executive council, or *soviet*, elected from workplaces and the garrison, met in Petrograd. A system of Dual Power came into existence. The soviet set itself up as an independent check on the government, to represent the interests of workers and the army rank and file, and to guard against counter-revolution. On 1 March 1917 the Military-Political Committee of Petrograd soviet issued Order Number One, stating that the authority of the officer class was at an end, and that no command to the Petrograd garrison from the Provisional Government should be obeyed unless countersigned by the soviet. Soviets spread across the country: at least 1,479 by November 1917. In industrial areas they were the effective power.[32] Inevitably, the coercive apparatus of the state began to disintegrate. The police were dissolved as incorrigibly reactionary, and law and order was taken over by a citizens' militia led by elected officers. Crucially, the revolutionary Petrograd garrison remained armed, and they were guaranteed not to be re-deployed to the front. The revolution in the capital thus had more coercive power locally than the Provisional Government.

Tsar Nicholas II abdicated, and the new republican government was quickly recognized by the Entente Allies, who advanced a loan of $300 million. This, of course, raised suspicions immediately that the Provisional Government remained in hoc to foreign interests that would prioritize military adventurism on the Eastern Front over consolidation and defence of the Russian Revolution. Indeed, the Provisional Government was committed to keeping Russia in the war. This was at first broadly acceptable to revolutionary forces because now, like their Western brethren, they were defending a parliamentary state from invasion.[33] The Germans were anxious that revolutionary turmoil should drive Russia off the field of combat, and to this end they arranged the transport back to Russia, by sealed train through the territory of the Central Powers, of revolutionary exiles. They included Lenin. Upon arrival, Lenin propounded his famous April Theses (3 March 1917). The thrust of his argument was that the revolution was insecure, and must remain so as long as the social and political power of the bourgeoisie remained intact. He openly acknowledged that the bourgeois revolution had been brought to an impressive climacteric: 'Russia is *now* the freest of all the belligerent countries in the world'. This, however, was dangerous in that it generated 'unreasoning trust in the government of capitalists, those worst enemies of peace and socialism'.[34] He opposed any subordination of the soviets to a parliamentary republic as 'a retrograde step'. The aim, rather, should be 'a republic of Soviets of Workers', Agricultural Labourers' and Peasants' Deputies throughout the country, from top to bottom'.[35] Lenin's argument promoted socialist maximalism and worker militancy, though he acknowledged that this would force the bourgeoisie to desert the revolution. As the capitalists ran down production in the face of economic dislocation and strikes, the workers must be encouraged to take over the factories. To guard against outright counter-revolution, the government needed to seize capitalist assets by nationalizing the banking system. Lenin was thus insisting that the bourgeoisie be smashed before they became counter-revolutionary. But this was a circular argument (reflecting, it is true, a circular reality): Lenin was arguing that the bourgeoisie were turning to counter-revolution out of fear of being smashed.

Bolshevik support began to grow, as workers became convinced that the Provisional Government was relying on a bourgeoisie increasingly unhappy with the liberties being taken by the masses, and anxious for a restoration of order. Between February and October the membership of the Bolshevik Party soared from around three thousand to some three hundred thousand, most new adherents being workers and soldiers. In the aftermath of the 'July Days', an armed workers' demonstration in Petrograd that seemed to threaten the government, the liberal Kadets' faith in the discipline of the masses began to crumble, and the party's leadership contemplated 'a more authoritarian regime' to restore order.[36] The industrial and professional bourgeoisie were increasingly disillusioned by disorder and worker indiscipline, and moved from liberalism to support for counter-revolution.[37] Alexander Kerensky, of the broadly liberal right wing of the Socialist Revolutionaries, became president of the republic on 21 July. His position was unenviable, as Robert Bruce Lockhart, Acting British Consul-General in Moscow, recalled: 'Kerensky was the victim of the bourgeois hopes which his short-lived success aroused.... Caught between the cross-fires of the Bolshevik Left, which was screaming peace at every street-corner and in every trench, and of the Right and the Allies, who were demanding the restoration of discipline by Tsarist methods, he had no chance.'[38] Kerensky's attempt to restore the authority of the provisional government, by ordering General Kornilov in September to detach units from the front and march on Petrograd, convinced the garrison and workers of the big cities that full-scale counter-revolution was pending. This, indeed, was Kornilov's intention, and Kerensky was forced to invoke popular revolutionary mobilization against him. To this end he released the Bolshevik leadership cadre from prison. Kornilov was stopped when the railroad workers refused to transport his men.

The Bolsheviks were now able to pose as the most resolute defenders of the revolution, and their argument that only a Soviet government would consolidate this defence carried much weight. Lenin insisted that the Bolsheviks had the right to assume power because, together with the left Socialist Revolutionaries, they had a majority in the country.[39] Lenin's principal argument, however, was that domestic counter-revolution was gathering its strength and would not decorously wait for a Bolshevik/Left-SR majority to be realized in the soviets before striking.[40] As the front collapsed, and the Germans advanced on Petrograd, it was feared that the

Provisional Government would abandon the revolutionary city to military occupation. 'Only by a victorious uprising,' insisted Lenin, 'can we be sure to end the intrigue for a separate peace.'[41] His emphasis was on destroying the armed power of classes hostile to the revolution: 'disarming (vanquishing if they resist) the junkers, etc.'[42]

The Bolsheviks were able to make the case that the soviets, from which the bourgeoisie were excluded, would best be able to ward off the imminent threat of counter-revolution emanating from fearful bourgeois and aristocratic elements embedded in the army, civil service, and in the centres of production. The prospect of counter-revolution was terrifying, in particular, for those urban garrisons who might expect to pay for their insubordination under martial law. Revolution was possible in a way it was not in the West, because the vastness of the country and length of the front meant that revolutionary turmoil behind the lines did not threaten imminent conquest by German forces. What powered the revolution was an understandable fear that once the confused state apparatus restored itself to order it would impose a violent crackdown on workers, peasants, and political activists. There was an urgent popular desire to submit the state apparatus, staffed as it was by former servants of the tsarist regime, to the tight control of revolutionary urban soviets. Soviets were attempting to operate, primarily, as a kind of audit on the activities of the civil service and military, and only as needs be as an alternative administration. The 'direct democracy' of Sovietism was broadly based, however, and in truth probably more resonant than parliamentarianism. It owed as much, if not more, to peasant traditions as it did to 'advanced' proletarian class consciousness. Sprouting peasant committees in the countryside, based upon the long-established village communes, were functionally very similar to urban soviets.[43] Peasants mobilized vigorously against the landed elites, and saw in the urban workers' movement an ally of convenience, able to paralyze the energies of their hereditary foes in those centres of power normally inaccessible to rural outrage, the large towns and cities.

The Bolsheviks cadre admitted that workers were more cautious than militant, but they believed that popular fear of reaction would move them to support, at least passively, a Bolshevik overthrow of the Provisional Government.[44] On 23 October, Kerensky closed the editorial offices of the Bolshevik press. This was taken as a counter-revolutionary provocation. On the night of 24 October, Red Guards and soldiers took control of key points in the capital. The rising was virtually bloodless in Petrograd, though there was serious fighting in Moscow. For Lenin, the order of the day was to establish a hardline Bolshevik-led government. It was imperative to exclude any socialist still committed to liberal democratic constitutionalism. Only a government resolutely opposed to the 'social chauvinists' of the Second International, Lenin believed, could raise an unblemished banner for international socialist revolution, which in turn was the sole historical justification for workers seizing power in backward Russia. However, Lenin's purist perspective was not widely shared in the country.[45] The Bolsheviks had been able to take power primarily because they had posed successfully as defenders of the revolution already achieved, that is to say, a democratic republic with strong socialistic overtones.

Elections were held in December for the Constituent Assembly, which produced a result of 175 Bolshevik seats to only 16 for the Mensheviks, who continued to espouse an alliance with the liberal bourgeoisie. The Socialist Revolutionaries (SRs), representing the peasantry, towered above both with 410 seats. The SRs were rather amorphous though they were rapidly polarizing into right wing and left wing, the latter taking seats in the Soviet government as a minority partner with the Bolsheviks. However, there was clarity enough to show that the most popular concept of socialism was decentralized, based on the traditional, small-scale cooperative *artel*. This was at odds with the Bolshevik intention to construct socialism on the basis of capitalist cartels. In the eyes of the masses, however, it was not altogether obvious anymore that the Constituent Assembly was the superior representative institution now that the left-wing SRs, it seemed, were ensconced in the Soviet Council of People's Commissars. So, when Bolshevik soldiers dispersed the Constituent Assembly on 6 January 1918, one day after it had opened its first session, there was relatively little protest in the country. This was a pivotal moment, however. For the first time, a major branch of the Marxist 'centre' had followed the anarchists in rejecting parliamentarianism altogether.

For the Bolsheviks, the nationalization of the means of production did not designate the dividing line between bourgeois civil society and socialism. Indeed, since the outbreak of war in 1914, they argued that the bourgeoisie (particularly in Germany) had already effectively placed 'private production, privately owned trusts and syndicates at the disposal' of the militarized state. This 'bourgeois nationalization', though tending to supersede private ownership of the means of production, had created not socialism but rather 'state capitalism', with the bourgeoisie fully integrated into the oligarchy as a collective exploiter reaping dividends from a 'state bank'. 'Proletarian nationalization' was distinct not primarily in terms of economic organization but because it took place under a different state regime.[46] The construction of socialism, therefore, did not require a sudden economic transformation of the economy, only of the state.

Until June 1918, indeed, it seemed that the Bolsheviks intended to maintain a mixed economy for quite some time. However, this position was conditional upon the remaining bourgeoisie disavowing political ambition. As the civil war developed, such bourgeois quiescence was clearly not forthcoming. Even from the outset, force was required to break a strike by civil servants, and to make them open up the civil-service files necessary for governing. Bertrand Russell, an astute observer, noted in 1920 that when Russia abandoned the Anglo-French Entente, foreign capitalists and managers in Russia 'either left the country or assisted counter-revolution' while the 'native Russians who had technical or business skills...almost all practised sabotage in the first period of the Bolshevik régime'.[47] The economic program of the Bolsheviks was thereafter primarily dictated by a strategy of class war. The bourgeoisie was dispossessed, and bourgeois and commercial civil society crushed. Indeed, Leon Trotsky saw this as vindication of his 1906 theorization of permanent revolution, in which the workers pressed into power must breach the limits of bourgeois revolution:

*Revolution and the 'Dictatorship of the Proletariat'* 163

> No one gives the proletariat the opportunity of choosing whether it will or will not mount the horse, whether it will take power immediately or postpone the moment. Under certain conditions the working-class is bound to take power, under the threat of political self-annihilation for a whole historical period. Once having taken power, it is impossible to accept one set of consequences at will and refuse to accept others. If the capitalist bourgeoisie consciously and malignantly transforms the disorganization of production into a method of political struggle, with the object of restoring power to itself, the proletariat is *obliged* to resort to Socialization, independent of whether this is beneficial or otherwise at the *given moment*. And, once having taken over production, the proletariat is obliged, under the pressure of iron necessity, to learn by its own experience a most difficult art—that of organizing Socialist economy. Having mounted the saddle, the rider is obliged to guide the horse—on the peril of breaking his neck.[48]

The social foundations of bourgeois restoration and liberalism were shattered. Whether workers were firmly in the saddle was another matter.

Lenin insisted that the Peace of Brest-Litovsk be signed, more on less on German terms, on 3 March 1918. This was deeply divisive, discrediting Bolshevism not only with Russian nationalists but also with socialist internationalists who held German militarism in as much contempt as they had tsarism. The Left-SRs withdrew from the Council of Peoples Commissars. So undermined was Bolshevik moral authority at this crucial time that Lenin may later have come to regret Brest-Litovsk.[49] In due course, German collapse and allied intervention allowed the Bolsheviks to win back the mantle of national patriotism, as they fought off hostile foreign plots and recovered territory for the nation. By that time, however, the country was wracked by civil war.

Though the civil war was kicked into gear by the Bolsheviks' national apostasy, it took the form of a violent class war. 'War Communism', the emergency nationalization of industry and ruthless requisitioning of food from the countryside to feed the cities and the Red Army, was an economic reflex of the 'dictatorship of the proletariat', which Lenin defined as 'rule won and maintained by the use of violence by the proletariat against the bourgeoisie, rule that is unrestricted by any laws'.[50] The Soviet government exercised formal Red Terror through the 'Cheka' secret police, which by the end of 1918 enrolled some forty thousand. Victor Serge watched with foreboding 'the Cheka... becoming a State within the State', tolerated because 'the whole Party was living in the sure inner knowledge that they would be massacred in the event of defeat; and defeat remained possible from one week to the next.'[51] Terror was systematic because the new state relied upon the expertise of old-guard officials. Seven-tenths of the Red Army's officers had served in the army of Nicholas II, and their loyalty was only assured by effectively holding their families hostage in case they deserted to the counter-revolutionary White armies.[52] There were certain limits to class war. Trotsky, for example, as leader of the Red Army issued orders forbidding executions without trial and the killing of prisoners: 'Let your anger be directed only against the enemy with a gun in his hand. Be merciful to prisoners, even if they are scoundrels.'[53] White Terror, moreover, was at least as bloody as that inflicted by the Reds, and it was often marked by pogrom atrocities against Jews. Nonetheless, that Communist violence was directed against the bourgeoisie (and landlords) as a class, not merely as combatants or even as overt political opponents, was unquestionable.

## RED CHALLENGE

Revolutionary projects were not limited to Russia, however. The Allies fought the war in the name of liberal democracy. The United States joined the conflict in 1917 as a champion of parliamentary democracy, national self-determination, and liberal internationalism. President Woodrow Wilson (1856–1924), a former high-flying academic, favoured strong executive government capable of resisting populist moods. The foundation of 'sober public opinion', he believed, was a civil society in which the hard work and talent of the 'little man' could be harnessed and rewarded by local, national, and international markets.[54] The model of democracy held up by President Wilson in his declaration of war was, admittedly, rather minimal: 'the right of those who submit to authority to have a voice in their own governments'.[55] American requirements became concrete, however, as the Central Powers finally faced military defeat in 1918.

Wilson insisted that the militarily collapsing Central Powers submit to a veritable constitutionalist revolution as a prerequisite for armistice. A condition of peace was the enemy accepting government responsible to Parliament, so as to squeeze out the unwonted political influence of unelected 'militarists'. By a statement published on 4 July 1918, Wilson declared that the US was sworn to 'the destruction of every arbitrary power anywhere'. In a note delivered to Berlin on 16 October, it was clarified that 'The power which has hitherto controlled the German Nation is of the sort here described.'[56] The same requirement of auto-revolution was imposed upon the Habsburg dynasty. The leaderships of the nationalities of the Austro-Hungarian empire had already committed their nation states to democratic, fully constitutional governments. France and Britain were content to go along with Wilson's making democratic revolution a war aim, not least because introducing full parliamentary responsibility on defeated enemies would improve their fiscal capacity to meet onerous reparations.

The end of the Great War, therefore, saw an enormous surge of democratic constitutionalism out from its Atlantic heartland. Between France and Soviet Russia, virtually every country equipped itself with a ministerial government responsible to a democratically elected Parliament. Poland, Lithuania, Yugoslavia, Germany, Estonia, Austria, Latvia, Romania, Bulgaria, Ireland, Czechoslovakia, and Finland all adopted democratic constitutions. Japan, which had fought with the Allies in the Great War, was influenced by the Wilsonian mood; the suffrage in Japan was made more or less democratic in 1924, though the executive was still not responsible to the legislature.

Despite this spread of democracy, Communists held to the idea that bourgeois liberalism was dead. Traditionally, European liberals had been exceptionally indulgent of Russian revolutionaries; such was their contempt for tsarism. The

Bolshevik seizure of power, with some plausibility, could be presented as a preemptive strike against reactionary counter-revolution, so one might have expected the new regime in Moscow to make a sympathetic appeal to the broad European liberal-left for solidarity. The Bolshevik priority, however, was not winning moral sympathy from labour and liberal currents. Instead, they forcefully promoted the model of narrow, proletarian insurrectionary parties to establish analogous Soviet regimes. They set their sights on those countries where bourgeois civil society had been most disrupted by war: Italy, Germany, Poland, the Baltic States, and the Austro-Hungarian succession states. The aim was to establish, as Arthur Rosenberg, a convert to Communism in the postwar years, put it, a 'Union of Soviet Republics' that 'would then extend from Russia to the Rhine and the Alps'.[57]

The invitation to the first Congress of the Communist International, issued on 24 January 1919, made clear that the intention was to formulate an international strategy of seizures of power: 'The task of the proletariat now is to seize State power immediately. The seizure of state power means the destruction of the state apparatus of the bourgeoisie and the organization of a new proletarian apparatus of power.... Its concrete form is given in the system of the soviets or of similar organs.'[58] Workers were to be organized outside of Parliament by revolutionaries for the conduct of civil war against recalcitrant classes and the destruction of the pre-existing state apparatus. Workers' councils, on the soviet model, were to be the tool. The declared Communist strategy was to mobilize forces sufficient for an assault upon the state. This did not by any means imply winning a majority of the population over to revolution. Only support amongst the working class was deemed necessary, and it was implied that only a minority of this subset needed to be won over to explicit support for insurrection. Parliament was to be replaced by action-orientated assemblies representing only the workers and their allies. All this was a startling repudiation of the old Marxist 'centre' of the Second International, which had always conceived of revolution as the establishing of a government responsible to a Parliament elected by universal suffrage.

How was this repudiation of constitutionalism justified? Lenin's argument was that imperialist capitalism had enormously increased the power of militarism and bureaucracy in all advanced capitalist countries. So, while Marx had validly enough hypothesized that peaceful socialist transformation was possible in Britain and America in the 1870s—an age of competitive capitalism, when bourgeois civil society guided the state—this was no longer possible in the era of monopoly state capitalism:

> the revolutionary dictatorship of the proletariat is violence against the bourgeoisie; and the necessity of such violence is particularly called for...by the existence of militarism and a bureaucracy.... [P]re-monopoly capitalism—which actually reached its zenith in the seventies—was by virtue of its fundamental economic traits...distinguished by a, relatively speaking, maximum fondness for peace and freedom. Imperialism, on the other hand, i.e., monopoly capitalism, which finally matured only in the twentieth century, is, by virtue of its fundamental *economic* traits, distinguished by a minimum fondness for peace and freedom, and by a maximum and universal development of militarism.[59]

So, for Lenin, the umbilical connection posited by Marx between bourgeois civil society and civic and political liberties had been broken. Even where liberalism persisted it was increasingly a façade. Parliamentarian countries, indeed, were peculiarly exposed to manipulation by financial capital: 'the more highly democracy is developed, the more the bourgeois parliaments are subjected by the stock exchange and the bankers'. Liberal democracies were better able than openly authoritarian states to isolate and persecute insurgent minorities.[60] Lenin's complete rejection of parliamentary constitutionalism was a frank departure from Second International socialism.

Lenin also argued that a 'higher' form of democracy was now available to displace parliamentarianism. He lauded soviets, or councils, as a means of prising open the administration of the state to the working classes. Such directly elected bodies, immediately representative of workplace-based class interests, were much more effective than distant parliaments in allowing workers to organize, express themselves, and, in a rough and ready manner, 'knock into shape' the state.[61] Soviets and workers' councils could hold the executive state to some kind of account, far more effectively than could even fully democratized parliaments. 'Soviet power is a million times more democratic than the most democratic bourgeois republic,' Lenin boldly claimed.[62] Workers' councils, because they combined legislative and executive functions, had the capacity to mirror, monitor, and (if need be) intimidate the personnel of the civil service, judiciary, and military. Compared to parliaments, they had far more power to overcome conservative vested interests lodged in the 'permanent state' and the industrial and agricultural oligarchy.

Naturally Lenin did not point out that the exhausting routine typical of soviets and workers' councils, in 'permanent session' and ceaselessly renewing their leadership, meant that at best they operated as a kind of 'activists' democracy'. After an initial burst of enthusiasm, worker participation in the arcane politics of soviets invariably declined. This was to the advantage of those radicals and militants who clung on out of ideological conviction. Such bodies had a natural tendency to radicalize, becoming less representative as they did so. As such, they did not surpass parliamentarianism in democratic efficacy. Trotsky was perhaps more honestly blunt than Lenin when he simply dismissed objections to the severity of Red rule with a terse riposte: 'To imagine that democracy can be restored in its general purity means that one is living in a pitiful, reactionary utopia.'[63] Constitutionalism was dying, this view implied, and the only choice was whether the succeeding dictatorship would be 'bourgeois' or 'proletarian'. If the Great War had justified 'dictatorial' measures for bourgeois governments, another Bolshevik argued, class war justified dictatorial measures for proletarian governments.[64]

In fact, in the years after 1917 there was probably never much chance of 'proletarian dictatorship' of whatever kind being instituted west of Russia. Certainly the weight of opinion, as evidenced by elections at war's end, was at the centre-right. In 1937, Joseph Stalin (1878–1953) confidentially admitted to Georgi Dimitrov, the nominal head of the Communist International (Comintern), his belief that Communist faith in the spread of revolutions on the Russian model in the years after 1917 had been quixotic:

I consider that the slogan of the transformation of an imperialist war into a civil war [violent revolution] was only valid for Russia, where the workers were linked to the peasantry and where under the conditions of Tsarism they could launch an assault on the bourgeoisie. In the European countries, this slogan was not valid in places where the workers had received certain democratic reforms to which they were attached and were not ready to embark on a civil war against the bourgeoisie.[65]

This was no doubt a realistic assessment after the fact. The wave of revolutionary turmoil that swept the defeated Central Powers from 1918, and a radicalization to the left further afield, was impressive enough, however.

Sometimes the peasantry took the lead, in movements directed against the perceived centres and organizers of exploitation in the cities. From 1919 a peasant-based government in Bulgaria, led by Aleksandar Stamboliyski, attempted wholesale reconstruction, excluding lawyers and financiers from Parliament, as exploiters of the peasantry, and moving to break up the few large landed estates. In June 1923 bourgeois interests and nationalist officers organized a successful coup against Stamboliyski. Generally speaking, however, it was urban-centred working-class organizations that took the lead. Socialists won substantial, albeit minority, representation in the newly democratized parliaments, as the following table indicates:

|  | Socialist Seats | Total No. of Seats | Socialist Percentage of Parliamentary Seats |
| --- | --- | --- | --- |
| Germany (1919) | 185 | 421 | 44% |
| Austria (1919) | 72 | 170 | 43% |
| Czechoslovakia (1920) | 109 | 281 | 39% |
| Belgium (1919) | 70 | 186 | 38% |
| Sweden (1920) | 82 | 230 | 36% |
| Italy (1919) | 163 | 508 | 32% |
| France (1924) | 174 | 584 | 30% |
| Great Britain (1922) | 142 | 615 | 25% |
| Irish Free State (1922) | 16 | 128 | 13% |

Socialist advance was in some respects even more important outside Parliament. The workers' councils that sprang up in the defeated Central Powers were no mere front organizations. They arose, often spontaneously, as bodies attempting to monitor and vet the actions of a state bureaucracy riddled with anti-democratic and reactionary class personnel. Revolution flared in Germany in 1918, establishing a parliamentary Republic but with radicalized workers seeking also to break junker and bourgeois power entirely. In April 1919 there briefly existed a Soviet-style republic in Bavaria, and Hungary spiralled into Communism in 1919, before military counter-revolution. In 1918 revolutionaries took control of much of Finland, leading to a civil war in which they were crushed. In Great Britain, trade unions radicalized and the Labour Party, which formally designated itself as socialist in

1918, became a national parliamentary force. Ireland was swept by separatist sentiment, led effectively by a coalition of labour and bourgeois civil society. In France the Socialist Party elected to join the Comintern in 1920, thereafter splitting. In Italy, 1919–20 were the years of the 'biennio rosso', during which socialists openly proclaimed the imminent overthrow of the capitalist order. In the summer of 1920 industrial workers in Milan and Turin occupied the plants where they were employed, and organized workers' councils to run them. The 'Trienio Bolchevista' of 1918–20 in Spain saw massive strikes, lockouts, and assassination campaigns waged between anarchists and right-wing gunmen.

Common to these movements was the emergence of organs of popular power—committees, councils, even a Parliament in Ireland—that challenged the authority of existing state structures. It reflected a widespread fear that the state apparatus was incorrigibly reactionary and hostile to popular democracy. As Geoff Eley points out, 'Few council activists originally saw them as a permanent alternative to parliamentary institutions, rather than transitional bodies during the initial breakthrough to democracy, possibly with lasting watchdog functions in the future republican constitution.'[66] As this implies, however, councils had a tendency towards radicalization. The leading Austrian socialist Julius Braunthal recalled that when his party, the SPÖ, inherited power in 1918, its most pressing task, given the reactionary nature of the established officer class and civil service, was 'the building of a reliable force, faithful to the democratic Republic'. The middle classes, whose power had 'rested hitherto upon the army, the police, the State administration', were in limbo, and it was workers and leftist soldiers organized in councils who vetted the actions of the state apparatus. In so doing, they pushed 'the revolution up to the limits of its strength', threatening to alienate the non-proletarian masses to the point of civil war, and to provoke the Entente into invasion.[67]

This was the typical balance of power in much of postwar Europe. The Communists wished workers' councils to wage civil war on the *ancien régime* state apparatus and classes, not simply to monitor them. The bulk of workers involved, however, doubted their ability to govern directly (a point tacitly conceded by the increasingly disciplined partyism of the Communists), and generally saw such bodies as supports for constitutional government, and as a check on backsliding. Only in southern Ireland, where the bourgeoisie supported the para-state apparatus and counter-parliament—the Dáil—did dual power succeed in confronting and destroying the old order. Here the Catholic Church supported the restoration of authoritative government on separatist terms, giving de facto support to the aims of the insurgents. An Irish nationalist revolutionary recalled, with pardonable exaggeration, that 'Labour...priests, and people stood shoulder to shoulder against the common enemy'.[68] Kevin O'Higgins praised his colleagues as 'the most conservative-minded revolutionaries that ever put through a successful revolution', and the subsequent independent state was ultra-Gladstonian in its fiscal rigour and constitutional propriety.[69] Even during the 'Red Years' of 1919–20, success was perhaps only achievable for a revolutionary movement that locked together workers, farmers, and middle class in a struggle self-limiting to parliamentary democratic self-determination on the basis of bourgeois civil society.

The Communists, of course, had higher hopes. They appealed, in the first instance, to those traditions of anti-parliamentarianism that had resented the constitutionalism of orthodox socialists before the war. Many syndicalists and 'sovietists' (believers in workers' councils as the basis of a new state) were responsive. Spanish anarchists only rejected the Comintern in 1922. What was striking about the 'Manifesto to the World', issued by the Comintern on 6 March 1919, was the absence of any explicit reference to the role of the Communist Party in carrying out the revolution or exercising the dictatorship of the proletariat. The stress instead was laid upon soviets, or councils of mass workers' power.[70] The Manifesto (written by Trotsky) stressed the structural collapse of any basis for stable bourgeois liberty. Political power in capitalist countries during the war had fallen 'directly into the hands of military-state power' so that 'finance capital has succeeded in completely militarizing not only the state but also itself'.[71] Revolution was imminent, and an urgency, precisely because the mass armies of wartime were riven by class division. It would be fatal to permit the re-emergence of 'professionalized' army structures proof against socialist agitation. The duty of revolutionaries was to hasten the disintegration of the armed forces and to institute direct proletarian class rule. The conquest of political power:

> means not merely a change in the personnel of ministries but annihilation of the enemy's machinery of government; disarmament of the bourgeoisie, of the counter-revolutionary officers, of the White Guard; arming of the proletariat, the revolutionary soldiers, the Red Guard of workmen; displacement of all bourgeois judges and organization of all-proletarian courts; elimination of control by reactionary government officials and substitution of new management organs of the proletariat.[72]

Terrible as the Russian civil war was, Lenin was convinced that in central and western Europe the 'horrors' of struggle 'to the last drop of blood' would be worse again, 'due to the sharper class struggle there and the greater tension of the opposing forces which will fight up to the last opportunity'.[73]

This initial Communist emphasis on the organization of workers councils, so appealing to anarchist and syndicalist sympathisers, was sharply reversed in the Comintern's 'Twenty-one Conditions' for admission agreed at the second Congress of the Comintern in 1920. These were calculated to discipline revolutionary syndicalist tendencies, and to exclude 'centrists' who doubted the applicability of the Russian model of revolution to Western countries. Condition 12, for example, required that vanguard Communist parties be organized for 'acute civil war' with 'iron discipline' and 'as centralized as possible'.[74] The seizure of power by Communist parties now took precedence over the reconstruction of governments based upon soviets, or rule by workers' councils. This was a reflection both of the atrophy of genuine Sovietism in Russia and the receding of the revolutionary wave in the West. Partyism was to be the sine qua non of Communism hereafter.

Even as Communists anathematized radicals to their left and their right, almost all socialists, internationally, defended the Bolshevik Revolution as a breakthrough worthy of defence against counter-revolution, and a welcome breach in international capitalism, though its lack of democracy was deplored.[75] Nonetheless, most socialists concluded that the Russian experiment was not exportable. It was not so much that the left split over the economic model of socialism. To a considerable extent, all variants of left opinion agreed that modern 'state capitalism' demonstrated both the inevitability and the efficacy of statist economic planning. Drawing upon Hilferding's theory of 'organized capitalism', for example, the German SPD saw socialization of the economy as a fairly gradual process, going with the grain of established economic processes.[76] This was not so different from early Bolshevik attempts at a mixed economy, and, from 1921, after the rigours of emergency 'War Communism', the Soviet mixed economy of the New Economic Policy (NEP). The issue dividing socialists was not primarily economic organization as the question of constitutional government.

The February 1919 conference of the remnants of the Second International, dominated by 'moderate' parties of Social Democracy (notably British Labour and the German majority SPD), insisted that 'a Government responsible to Parliament' was indispensable for democracy. Workers' councils were to have only an auxiliary role, if any at all, as vehicles for 'popular co-operation'.[77] A subsequent Social Democratic International gathering, at Geneva in July 1920, reiterated that parliamentarianism was the only 'Political System of Socialism'. This was the clearest adherence yet to parliamentarianism by the socialist movement. The conference did, however, concede that the bourgeoisie were no longer the bulwark of democracy: 'It is today the forces of Labour that in the main, ensure the maintenance of Democracy.'[78] To this extent, middle-class disillusion with democracy, and vacillation in its defence, could not be denied even by leftists who utterly rejected the Communist desertion of constitutionalism.

The 'centrist' Vienna Union, with participation particularly from the Austrian and French socialists, tried to find a middle way between Communist and social-democratic formulations. The Centrists refused to 'restrict the proletariat either to using democratic methods only... nor prescribe the mechanical imitation of the methods of the Russian Communists'. Where the military-bureaucratic establishment was weak or apolitical, and the working class commanded an electoral majority, socialist transformation might be achieved peacefully, though even here 'dictatorial means' would be required 'to break the resistance of the capitalist class'. Where capitalists were prepared to 'break democracy' rather than allow a socialist government of the workers' to assume power, and where the property-owning petite bourgeoisie and peasantry were preponderant, the working class would have to rely upon 'direct action' such as mass strikes and armed rebellion to take power, and vigorous government thereafter to suppress resistance. While the means by which this 'dictatorship of the working class' would be exercised was the familiar 'working-men's, peasants' and soldiers' councils', an important role was also allowed for trade unions and other such 'traditional' working-class organizations.[79] Though evidently an uneasy balance, and by no means committed to democratic constitutionalism in principle, at least during the era of revolution and counter-revolution, the 'centrist' position probably had majority rank-and-file support in the labour movement of continental Europe. The partisans of Leninism, however, were bent on destroying the middle ground. An unequivocal choice had to be made between democratic parliamentarianism and 'proletarian dictatorship'. As it turned out, most centrists took the side of parliamentarianism and Social Democracy.

While Communist propaganda emphasized insurrections based upon the militant proletariat as the road to revolution, the regime in Russia was quite prepared to use military force to advance revolution, if it could. By the Soviet counter-offensive against Poland in 1920, when the Red Army advanced on Warsaw, Lenin hoped to dislodge 'the avalanche of revolution from the ledge on which it had come to rest'.[80] The offensive, however, was repulsed. On the other side of the equation, the possibilities of revolution were severely constrained by the military threat posed by the Entente. The British prime minister, David Lloyd George, reflected in March 1919 on the challenge:

> The greatest danger that I see in the present situation is that Germany may throw in her lot with Bolshevism and place her resources, her brains, her vast organizing power at the disposal of the revolutionary fanatics whose dream is to conquer the world.... Once that happens all Eastern Europe will be swept into the orbit of the Bolshevik revolution and within a year we may witness the spectacle of nearly three hundred million organized into a vast red army.[81]

Lloyd George feared an opportunistic alliance between Bolshevism and the nationalist state-bureaucratic, and military elites of the defeated Central Powers, at the expense of the bourgeoisie and landlord class. The successor regime in Hungary did indeed slide towards an alliance with Russia in the hope that by so doing it would protect its territorial integrity. A Soviet Republic, led by Béla Kun, was established partly because, according to its non-Communist president, 'what the West refuses us, we will try to get from the East'.[82] The regime was crushed, however, by Romanian and Czechoslovakian armies, backed by French military assistance.

Hungary was an exception. The 'centrist' socialist leadership in the rump Austrian state thought better of any attempt to establish a state based upon workers' councils, given the inevitability of an Allied blockade or invasion if the attempt was made.[83] The very brink of socialist revolution was approached in Italy, but the likelihood of an Entente military invasion to suppress any 'workers' dictatorship', as had happened in Hungary, was acknowledged even by the Communists.[84] In Germany, Hugo Hasse, the leftist socialist leader, warned in November 1918 that 'the Entente would...intervene with all its might to forestall the rise of Bolshevism'.[85] As Herbert Hoover, Secretary of Commerce and close advisor to President Woodrow Wilson, admitted in March 1919, counter-revolutionary intervention against Bolshevism made the liberal countries 'party to re-establishing the reactionary classes in their economic domination over the lower classes'.[86] The bourgeois liberal revolution, inhibited by fear of a radical spiral into Communist anti-parliamentarianism and class war, gave way to entanglement with out-and-out reaction, in a self-fulfilling vindication of Lenin's dismissal of the viability of bourgeois democracy.

## CONCLUSION

The Great War did much to discredit the old aristocratic and authoritarian power structures across much of Europe. Still, total war strengthened the link between big business and the state, tending to diminish the role of parliamentary constitutionalism. Given the armed might behind Wilsonian ideals of democratic liberal parliamentarianism, it made sense for supplicants amongst putative successor regimes to establish their parliamentary credentials before the victorious powers at the Paris Peace Conference. Constitutionalism, thus, expanded from its Atlantic fringe heartland.

Democratic revolution from above was often superficial, however. Civil society was wracked by the efforts of war, and ill-prepared to provide a domestic basis for constitutional governance. Conservative, hierarchical nationalism, powerfully appealing in its own right as a warrant for pan-class solidarity amidst the fluidity of commercial civil society, survived the collapse of aristocratic legitimacy. Ethnocentric nationalism seemed to offer a model for modernization that rejected the path of market cosmopolitanism and divisive class struggle. Particularly in the ethnic shatter-zone of central and eastern Europe, however, socially homogenous civil societies hardly existed as foundations for coherent nation states. Of Poland's population, for example, almost a third were ethnic 'minorities' excluded from the country's 'official' political community.[87] The chances for democracy to coexist with ethno-national state ideology, therefore, were slim. Even in countries more culturally homogenous, the sectional politics of class and confessionalism sapped the credibility of parliamentarianism, particularly in the face of economic crisis. By 1938, of the 'new democracies' that emerged after the Great War, only Ireland, Czechoslovakia, and Finland remained essentially democratic.

The Soviet Revolution, however, focused widespread leftist disillusion with parliamentarianism. As the First World War concluded, workers' councils formed spontaneously across Europe, particularly in the defeated countries. Motivation was complex, but primarily they were defensive institutions to protect against reaction. The Second International permanently fractured, with Social Democrats favouring parliamentary constitutionalism, Communists favouring the smashing of the power of the state and oligarchy, whereas 'Centrists' wavered. In Germany the reactionary oligarchy was left intact because of a Social Democratic fear of Communization. The anti-democratic ethos of the 'permanent state' apparatus, in the civil service and armed forces, survived, and in most cases quickly reasserted itself. The extirpation of the entirety of the old state apparatus in Russia, by fire and sword, resulted in chaos and a party state. Bourgeois fear reached new heights.

# 10

# Communism and Fascism

Following the high hopes of bourgeois constitutionalist revolution in the Wilsonian mould, came 'an accelerating, increasingly catastrophic, retreat of liberal political institutions', as Eric Hobsbawm writes.[1] If Wilsonianism failed to convince the intellectual defenders of bourgeois civil society, it was in no little cause due to the Russian Revolution. That bourgeois civil society could meet with such catastrophic disaster had a chilling effect on middle-class faith in liberalism and democracy. The spectre of Communism, it seemed, had materialized. Bolshevism was only an extreme manifestation, however. The more profound worry was that the working class, organized as never before as a socio-political bloc, was undermining the individualistic civil society beloved of classical liberalism. Proletarian democracy did not appear capable of constructing a viable new basis for civil society.

Göetz Briefs, the Roman Catholic Church's expert on the labour question, ghostwriter of the Papal encyclical *Quadragesimo Anno* (1931), updating *Rerum Novarum* (1891), and a refugee from Nazi Germany, in 1937 neatly defined the proletarian as: '*a wage earner (or salaried worker not in a permanent position) whose exclusive, or at least indispensable, source of income is found in the sale of his labor power in a shifting and insecure labor market*'.[2] Such insecurity, however, is intolerable. As a Catholic theorist, Briefs favoured independence and security on the basis of dispersed property. What had emerged in actuality, however, was 'welfare capitalism', designed to placate workers while preventing them 'from developing too much self-consciousness, group activities, and independence'.[3] This settlement, however, stuffed up the free-flowing circuits of 'western civilization':

> It is a fact that large groups of workers today have no objection to raise against propertylessness—provided their jobs are secure, their wages sufficient, and provisions are made through social insurance for old age and unemployment. To meet these requirements the economic system has had to shoulder increasing burdens and to put up with an increasing amount of social legislation, which, of course, implies additional regimentation.... These costs are a tremendous item in a fully established social insurance system, and social legislation means a permanent interference with the 'normal' flow of business.[4]

The impact of 'proletarian democracy', therefore, even short of full-scale social revolution, was corrosive to bourgeois civil society.

The liberal conviction had been that constitutionalism spontaneously aligns the interests of state and bourgeois civil society. This conviction was gravely weakened by the nationalism, statism, and corporatism of the First World War and its aftermath. Classical liberals responded by wondering whether Wilsonian concessions to popular democracy had upset the balance between state and civil society. Ludwig von Mises, for example, favourably compared the 'democracy' of consumer preferences embodied by capitalism to mere party politics: 'The average man is both better informed and less corruptible in the decisions he makes as a consumer than as a voter at political elections.'[5] Classical liberals, in general, were sympathetic to insulating economic matters from the influence of 'proletarianized' democracy. Mark Mazower has remarked that it was precisely the partisans of the classical liberal tradition who were most 'impatient with the instability and incompetence of parliamentary rule' in an age of turbulent mass politics. Along with business and managerial elites they proved highly susceptible to the appeal of authoritarianism.[6]

## REVOLUTION DERAILED

In Germany was played out in near archetypal form the complex choreography of bourgeois liberty, proletarian democracy, and reaction. It is worth looking at in a little detail. On 29 September 1918, the German High Command had realized that the war was lost. Their thoughts turned immediately to domestic concerns: how were the militarists and opponents of democracy to ward off their being deposed by the betrayed German people? The elites reckoned on shuffling the responsibility for defeat onto the political left. Since July 1917, when the Social Democrats, the Progressive Party, and the Catholic Centre Party had united to urge a compromise peace on the Reich government, the majority socialists and bourgeois liberals had been working closely together on a common trajectory towards democratic constitutionalism.[7] On 28 October 1918, with the full cooperation of the right wing of the SDP, a parliamentary government was adopted. This was insufficient, however, to prevent a revolutionary movement against the Junker-bourgeois oligarchy. When a sailors' revolt flared up at Kiel on 3 November, revolution leapt from city to city across Germany. Workers immediately formed Räte (Councils), with the intention of disempowering the imperial civil service, bourgeois and aristocratic worthies, and the officer class. On 9 November, Kaiser Wilhelm II abdicated and, in a rather haphazard manner, a Republic was declared by the SPD leadership.

The following day, a government called the Council of People's Representatives was formed, an alliance between the SPD and the leftist 'Independent' USPD. This government drew its legitimacy from the workers' councils, the old Reichstag being tainted by association with the imperial state. The government committed itself to democratic elections, on a parliamentary basis, to a Constituent Assembly. The long-term role of the councils was unclear, but in the meantime they were expressly authorized as an alternative governing structure to sidestep the recently ruling apparatus.[8] During November and December 1918, representatives of the workers' councils supervised the administrative authorities to prevent them subverting the revolution.[9] The revolutionary left, organized as the Spartacists, argued that sterner measures were required to actually root out from state bureaucracy the enemies of revolution: 'The imperialist capitalist class...will attempt to nullify socialist measures by a hundred and one methods of passive resistance. It will put in the way of revolution twenty uprisings à la Vendée.... It will sooner turn the country into a smoking heap of ruins than relinquish its power to exploit the working class.'[10] From the right there came some confirmation of this diagnosis. Erich Ludendorff, past warlord and future ally of Adolf Hitler, judged that the revolution failed because it did not destroy the militaristic elites: 'The revolutionaries' greatest piece of stupidity was to leave us all alive.' Had the tables been turned, Ludendorff confirmed, he with 'good conscience' would have hanged the majority SPD leaders.[11] War to the knife against suspected reactionaries was not a path that constitutionalists, committed to the rule of law, could countenance.

The right wing of the SPD was far more terrified by the prospect of Russian-style anarchy. They denounced Bolshevism as a left-wing analogy of warlordism on the right, a 'lazy man's militarism', dictatorial and incautious.[12] Painfully aware that a proletarian dictatorship, no matter how democratic were the workers' councils, could only alienate the petite-bourgeois and peasant majority of the German population, the Majority SPD were determined that the supremacy of the Räte-based government would be strictly provisional and temporary. Their aim was 'unrestricted political freedom' and 'social security', not the rapid dismantling of capitalism.[13] Elections based upon universal suffrage to the Constituent Assembly had to be held as soon as possible.

The SPD leader, Friedrich Ebert, wished to stymie any attempt at a Bolshevik-style coup, and to restrain the old state apparatus from launching a full-scale counter-revolution. To this end, on 10 November 1918, he secretly agreed with Wilhelm Groener, Chief of Staff of the German armed forces, that the army would be used for internal policing duties, and that the workers' councils would not be permitted to build up parallel governing structures. Thus the revolution was fatally compromised, as recognized by moderate socialists later. Willy Brandt, in the armed forces then, and post-1945 a chancellor of West Germany, recalled that 'the [rank and file] soldiers did not, like Ebert, see in the removal from power of the old military leadership a first perilous step towards the establishment of a Bolshevized Germany. They saw it as the foundation on which to build a Parliamentary democracy.'[14] It was, of course, not so easy to see in 1918 that a compact with the old militarist elite built dynamite into the foundations of constitutionalism. At the time, it must have seemed a prudent manoeuvre to neutralize hostile forces on both the left and right.

The prospect of a proletarian 'dictatorship' on the Soviet model was, certainly, increasingly a temptation for the leftist USPD,[15] and it was the stated aim of the Spartacist organization, led by Rosa Luxemburg and Karl Liebknecht. From the outset, the Spartacists were under heavy pressure from the beleaguered Communist regime in Russia to displace entirely the state apparatus of the German bourgeois-junker state and seize power directly.[16] Rushed into action, the Spartacists, who formally constituted themselves as the German Communist Party (KPD) on 1 January 1919, launched a coup attempt that month. Despite her long arguing that socialism depended upon the support of the majority of the proletariat, Luxemburg rather reluctantly supported an uprising against the worker-supported SPD government. Even then, she made sure to explain the rising as a defence against counter-revolution: 'Disarm the counter-revolution, arm the masses, occupy all important positions. Act quickly. The revolution demands it.'[17] Between 5 and 11 January there was street fighting in Berlin as the Spartacists battled first for power, and soon for mere survival against ferociously counter-revolutionary Freikorps paramilitary detachments, drawn from the politicized right wing of the army and authorized by the SPD government. On 15 January, Karl Liebknecht and Rosa Luxemburg were murdered while in Freikorps custody.

The SPD minister Gustav Noske was particularly unrelenting in his persecution of the revolutionary left. In March 1919, responding to an atrocity story that turned out not to be true, he cited the 'brutality and bestial behaviour of the Spartacists fighting against us' as justification for an order that 'any person who bears arms against government troops will be shot on the spot'. Freikorps militias went on to kill hundreds of Berliners.[18] A Soviet-style republic in Bavaria, established without much support, and comic-opera in operation, was crushed in April with great savagery by the army and Freikorps. Franz Schoenberner, a publisher with little innate sympathy for German attempts to ape bolshevism, witnessed the reconquest of Bavaria's capital, Munich:

> When on the first of May I saw the White troops parading through the *Siegestor* [Victory Gate] I knew that German democracy was dead. They were marched on in perfect order—the uniformed army of reaction. They had lost the war but at least they had won their victory in the civil war. Having massacred some thousands of proletarians, they could proudly enter a conquered city...hailed and saluted as saviors by the small bourgeoisie.[19]

In 1923 Nazis and ultra-conservatives even tried to launch a coup from Munich.

The National Assembly opened its first meeting on 6 February 1919, in Weimar. The SPD leader, Friedrich Ebert, a convinced opponent of any attempt to extend the revolution in a socialist direction, was elected president of the Republic. A government was formed, led by Chancellor Scheidemann, consisting of the SPD, the DDP (left-wing liberals), and the Catholic Centre. The USPD were excluded, while the Communists remained dedicated to destroying the bourgeois Republic. The Republic's constitution, which came into force on 11 August 1919, cast in iron the purely parliamentary nature of the new government. Any important role for the workers' councils was dismissed. In effect, the Republic was left to rely upon a civil service, and a propertied elite—both junker and big business—that looked back fondly to the order of the Kaiserreich, and were deeply contemptuous of democratic forms and the indulgence extended to left-wing subversion by observance of civil liberties.

This, truly, was the 'Republic without Republicans'. The socialist Minister for Economy, Rudolf Wissell, admitted to a socialist audience that:

> Despite the Revolution, the nation feels that its hopes have been disappointed. Those things which the people expected of the Government have not come to pass. We have

further consolidated political democracy in a formal sense; true. But...the Constitution has been prepared without any real and active participation on the part of the people....Essentially we have governed according to the old forms of our State life....The inner structure of German civilization, of social life, appears little altered....I believe that the verdict of history upon both the National Assembly and ourselves will be severe and bitter.[20]

Wissell's remarks were prophetic. In rallying the nation against the radical left, the SPD had failed to settle accounts with the myriad forces of anti-constitutionalism on the right. This variegated right was able to coalesce around the myth of a leftist 'stab in the back' that had deprived Germany of victory in the war. The Republic's government was badly tarnished by the terms of peace imposed on Germany, and the entrenched right increasingly veering off into irrationalist radicalism. The capacity of the old order to go even further in reasserting itself became evident in March 1920, when a putsch attempt, nominally led by Wolfgang Kapp, forced the government to flee the capital. The head of the Reichswehr (army), von Seeckt, informed the government that the army would not act to defend it. SPD leader Noske was shattered: 'This night has shown me the bankruptcy of my policy. My faith in the officer corps is shattered. It has deserted me.'[21] However, the labour movement was still a force to be reckoned with. A general strike brought the country to a halt and prevented the movement of putschist troops. The attempt on power collapsed after three days.

The initiative only briefly passed back to the insurrectionist left. In 1921 the KPD (a mass party since a split in the USPD in October 1920) launched a rising, the 'March operation', in central Germany. This was mostly reactive, barely coordinated, basically unthreatening, and swiftly crushed.[22] Aware that parliamentary democracy was threatened more from the right than the left, the Comintern leadership now pondered the circumstances in which Communists might legitimately participate in a 'Workers' Government' short of complete proletarian dictatorship. Karl Radek, in 1921 the Russians' principal advisor on West European affairs, proposed a model whereby Communist-Social Democratic coalitions would govern in accordance with parliamentary precedent, whilst enacting reform to strengthen the position of the working class. In practice, when Communist ministers entered the brief Left Social Democratic regional governments of Saxony and Thuringia, bourgeois liberties were maintained. It is doubtful, however, that Communist softening reassured conservatives, liberals, or social democrats. Lenin, after all, in 1920 had recommended his followers to deploy 'stratagems, artifices and illegal methods...evasions and subterfuges' as revolutionary tactics.[23] The Communists' frontal assault on the citadel of parliamentarianism having failed, they were now attempting to infiltrate and destroy it from within the ramparts.

Events meant that this drift towards parliamentarianism was short-lived. In January 1923, angered by the German state's tardiness and evasion of its obligations under the Treaty of Versailles, French and Belgian troops occupied the Ruhr. German passive resistance took the form of that time-honoured weapon of bourgeois civil society, the withdrawal of commercial and fiscal cooperation with the state, in this instance the occupying authorities. It had to be supported by aid from the German government, however, and this meant reckless abandon with the printing press. Demonstrating a critical failure of revolutionary action based upon bourgeois civil society, hyperinflation rapidly took hold. Rentiers and those on salaries suffered precipitous falls in status. Higher officials in government service who had earned seven times as much as unskilled workers in 1914 earned only twice as much by 1923, or 1.8 as much after tax.[24] Bourgeois civil society itself seemed in peril. On 26 September 1923, Chancellor Gustav Stresemann called off the passive resistance. Bourgeois interests, the Communists protested, had 'sold out' the Germans of the Ruhr to French Occupation.[25] The KPD considered taking power on the back of nationalist outrage, but they delayed and finally called off the 'German October' uprising, though there was desultory street fighting in Hamburg, from which even striking dock workers held aloof.[26] Placed on trial for instigating the revolt, local KPD secretary Hugo Urbahns scorned the court: 'The masses will say with us: we will rather burn in the fire of revolution than perish on the dung-heap of democracy.'[27]

The Democratic Republic by 1923 had rather miraculously survived. It had been built cooperatively by the labour movement and liberals. Together they had negotiated a constitutional settlement: government tied by taxation and credit to commercial civil society, plus a stiff admixture of workers' rights and welfarism. Assaults from left and right, however, demanded a powerful executive state, and provision was left for emergency presidential rule by decree. While the workers' councils disappeared, leaving the reactionary state apparatus little constrained by the Reichstag, Communism did not melt back into Social Democracy. Hyperinflation exposed the fragility of bourgeois civil society. The personnel of the state administration and the oligarchic heights of industry and agriculture remained unreconciled to democracy and deference to proletarian interests.[28] The judiciary was infamous for its favouritism towards right-wing street fighters and assassins, while the new army remained dominated by 'an officer corps with monarchical convictions', as a chief of the army High Command approvingly put in 1919. By 1926 the army was secretly preparing for renewed war with France to re-establish German priority in Europe. In the long run, the generals anticipated struggle with Britain and America for world mastery.[29] Militarism was alive, well, and biding its time. Even with economic recovery, bourgeois support for constitutionalism ebbed rapidly. About a third of middle-class German voters before the Depression abandoned those conservative and liberal parties to which they had traditionally given support.[30] Stresemann, a former Hohenzollern loyalist turned conservative republican, and the major statesman of the Weimar period, mournfully told his party caucus in 1929: 'parts of the right in Germany have gone mad'.[31]

## FASCISM IN ITALY

While many of the middle classes might have preferred a dictatorial regime to democracy inflected by working-class politics, it was clear from the German example that the workers' movements could not simply be repressed by entrenched conservatives without risking revolutionary turmoil. Big business, the army and police, and the civil service and judiciary, all feared provoking civil war if they moved to crush the labour movement outright. While Germany had uneasily settled into a 'republic without republicans', Italy took a novel but soon to be familiar path. While parliamentarianism stabilized to some extent in Germany, it collapsed in Italy.

In the elections of November 1919, socialists swept the northern cities of Italy, taking 32.4 per cent of the national vote, and winning 163 seats. Nationwide strikes roiled the country almost the year round in 1920, and in August–September workers occupied the ironworks of Turin. Liberal Prime Minister Giovanni Giolitti was slow to repress the occupations, for fear of radicalizing opposition, and relied instead upon the spontaneous reaction of bourgeois civil society: workers occupying plants tried to run them as cooperatives, but were denied credit from banks, retail outlets from traders, and materials from suppliers. The socialist movement was frozen on two fronts: the impossibility of revolution against the state while the army remained intact, and a hostile non-proletarian majority.

One is struck by the missed opportunity. Until 1903, Catholics had been forbidden by the encyclical *Non Expedit* to cooperate at all with the Italian state, condemned as an impious usurper of the Papal States. It was only in 1919 that the Christian Democratic Popolo d'Italia (Popular Party) was formed, with Catholic support, by a Sicilian priest, Luigi Sturzo. A sympathetic Catholic liberal, the British journalist Philip Gibbs, described the 'Popolari' as 'moderately conservative...Catholic in tradition...sympathetic to the rights and interests of the working classes...but equally insistent upon the rights of property and wealth'.[32] It was immediately successful, winning 101 of 508 seats in the Chamber of Deputies. The Popular Party was more attuned to democratic conditions than were the Giolittean liberals. It drew upon Catholic social teaching to insist upon the legitimacy of protecting group identities, be it corporate, class, or gender. In some respects, this mode of conservatism had a good deal in common with the class politics of the left, and an alliance between the Popolari and the socialist parties might well have been feasible as a defence of the Constitution. However, the Popular Party was hierarchical, suspicious of levelling democracy, and certainly hostile to the left's engrained anti-clericalism. No modus vivendi could be found between it and the socialists.

In 1919 the former socialist editor turned nationalist zealot, Benito Mussolini (1883–1945), had issued his *Fascist Manifesto*—opposed to class war, proletarian internationalism, and bourgeois cosmopolitanism—to relatively little response. He made a much more significant impression when, on 23 March 1919, he established the paramilitary Fasci di Combattimento. As early as 15 April the Fascists raided the offices of the Socialist Party newspaper in Milan. This was designedly to bring the trench spirit into politics—dynamic leadership, heroic self-sacrifice, action, and personal risk-taking, rather than pontificating and posturing. If the Fasci had important symbolic functions, they also were eminently practical, particularly as thugs for hire by landlords and workplace bosses to confront workers' militancy. The bourgeoisie valued them especially because the police and army, hamstrung by legality, seemed inadequate in the face of a genuine revolutionary crisis. The Italian employers' federation, the Confindustria, helped to finance the Fascist squads (known by their uniform as Blackshirts) in their attacks on the workers' movement, which was meanwhile split between Communists, who organized as a party in 1921, and socialists.

Mussolini went out of his way to assure the Catholic Church, the army, the king, and capitalist interests that his movement would not attack them. Fascist economic policy became impeccably liberal. On the other hand, Mussolini was not simply being tamed by bourgeois interests. The Fascists rejected 'men and agencies of the political bourgeoisie' for their timidity and hostility to the popular masses, and valued instead a 'bourgeoisie of labour' that was nominally pan-class.[33] Mussolini described Fascism as a 'synthesis between the indestructible theories of economic liberalism and the new forces of the world of labour'.[34] He suggested that the consummation of his vision of society based upon meritocratic, dynamic leadership—in contrast to bureaucracy, parliamentary timeserving, or traditional aristocracy—should be his own personal dictatorship.

As the workers' mobilization ebbed, the Fasci di Combattimento launched a veritable terror. The *squadristi* broke workers' strikes, organized tax strikes in socialist controlled towns, and intimidated voters. They behaved very much as the strong arm of commercial civil society, turning the tactics that had historically characterized 'bourgeois revolution' against the organized working class. Even before seizing power, the administrative personnel of local government lent tacit support to Fascism.[35] A general strike organized by socialists in protest at the state's toleration of Fascist illegality in July 1921 simply attracted Fascist attacks, and collapsed. Stable government of the centre-right was remained feasible, but it was Mussolini's ability to turn violence on and off at will that persuaded the bourgeois politicians to invite him to form a government in 1922. Mussolini's rise to power was a caricature of bourgeois revolution: the mobilization of commercial pressure (tax strikes, boycotting, and so on) for political ends, but now illiberal in direction; and the elaborate constitutionalism of his reforms in government, but now designed to free the executive state from effective check.

By 1926 the dictatorship was consolidated: freedom of association was suppressed and the executive appropriated Parliament's legislative power. In the nineteenth century, this would have considerably weakened the capacity of the state to govern consensually, undermining the state's ability to extract taxation, and thus its creditworthiness. The Fascist nature of the dictatorship counteracted this to considerable degree. The central civil service was purged to ensure that it was ideologically committed to the regime, and the administrative independence of town halls and city councils was diminished and then abolished. More generally, the Fascist state did all it could to permeate civil society in its entirety, drawing upon the substantial mass movement it had mobilized in the years of struggle. This ensured that passive resistance, say in the form of tax evasion or resistance to direction, was severely reduced. This state capacity to force a kind of consensus became the hallmark of 'totalitarianism'.

## FRAGILE EQUILIBRIUM

As the postwar revolutionary wave receded by about 1921, so too did the Communist threat. Internationally, by 1928, the ratio of Social Democrats to Communists, by membership excluding the Soviet Union, stood at about thirteen to one.[36] Liberals and Social Democrats participated in coalition governments in Germany, Austria, Denmark, Sweden, Finland, Czechoslovakia, Hungary, Poland, Bulgaria, and Lithuania. In Britain and Norway, Labour formed minority governments supported by Liberals; in France, the Socialist Party supported the Herriot government of 1924. Where the liberal bourgeoisie clearly enough retained leadership of a subordinate working class—in Great Britain, Switzerland, and possibly France—socialist participation overall strengthened parliamentarianism. In Scandinavia an alliance between the working class and the small farmer class was the basis for successful Social Democracy. Elsewhere, however, socialist enthusiasm for the democratic order succeeded mostly in encouraging middle-class defections to authoritarian political platforms.

The firmest base for continental European constitutionalism outside Social Democracy was similar to it in being quite distant from the 'Protestant individualist' ethics of traditional liberalism or Wilsonianism. Catholic culture recognized that group interests could and should mediate between the individual and bourgeois civil society. It had real potential for holding the ring between constitutionalism and dictatorship in a Europe where mass party politics based upon class, ethnic, and confessional identities was still resonant. Catholics in Germany stayed impressively loyal to the Centre Party, which was, along with the Social Democrats, a bulwark of the Weimar Republic; that is, until its late collapse into disillusion and self-dissolution in 1933. This was a common picture: Christian democracy flirting with constitutionalism only to rebound from it. Christian Democracy was not as attached to constitutionalism as were the (declining) liberal parties. Catholic social teaching, emphasizing group interests mediating between the individual and the state, was sceptical of parliamentarianism based upon a mass electorate only differentiated by territorially based constituencies. Christian Democracy was thus tempted by the idea of a 'corporate state', in which labour, business, and the state would interact directly, while Church interests would be protected by a concordat.

Unsurprisingly, given its fate in practice, Wilsonianism did not much revive liberalism intellectually. Important and influential theorists such as Gaetano Mosca, Vilfredo Pareto, Ernest Juenger, and Oswald Spengler were struck by the wartime nationalist convictions and will to victory of political elites, and denied that such willpower could ever be subordinated to the rationality of commercial civil society, as the liberals had fondly hoped.[37] Carl Schmitt (1888–1985), an influential rightist intellectual, was not alone in being unconvinced by postwar attempts to reconcile the bourgeois order and proletarianized democracy. He argued that the preservation of bourgeois civil society now relied upon its abandonment of strategies to circumscribe the state via constitutionalism. A strong, unhindered executive state (Regierungsstaat) was the only plausible defence for property. While nineteenth-century parliamentarianism had been sufficient to protect bourgeois freedom behind the shield of the 'rule of law', Schmitt argued, the eruption of 'proletarian democracy' threatened to end the autonomy of civil society by permeating it with state-ordained redistribution of wealth, welfarism, economic planning, and cultural assaults on bourgeois mores. The only alternative to the democratic 'quantitative state' was a decisively political authoritarian state released from the pressures of proletarianized mass democracy. Only such a state could resist special-interest pressure groups, seeking to redistribute property and goods. Modernized absolutism could replace party politics with patriotic plebiscitary appeals to society at large. With civil society otherwise depoliticized, and so no threat to neo-absolutism, it would become a secure refuge for bourgeois apolitical freedom. As had classical liberals, Schmitt convinced himself that no rational state would arbitrarily disorganize economic order and class hierarchy. An unbound state, therefore, would crush socialism but preserve the essential freedoms of civil society.[38]

## STALINISM

The authoritarian temptation was clearly not the preserve of capitalist societies. For its part, the Soviet Union succeeded in destroying bourgeois civil society, but failed to establish proletarian civil society in its stead. Russia's grand experiment of modernizing without a bourgeois civil society had begun inauspiciously. Between 1917 and 1922, the year the Soviet Union was formally constituted, its population fell by about 12.7 million, through war, emigration, and famine. The pre-revolutionary bourgeoisie, aristocracy, and state functionaries, unless they wholeheartedly embraced the new order, were economically immiserated, and classified as 'former persons' with minimal political and civic rights. However, conditions also militated against the construction of a new social edifice based upon the proletariat. The collapse of industry and the dislocation of mass army recruitment submerged the Communists' most coherent social base, and the constituency for which they claimed to act, the industrial working class. In so far as workers remained vocal, they felt increasingly betrayed: having supported the concept of a broadly socialist Soviet government, they found themselves with a narrowly Communist government. In response to the threat of revolution in city and countryside, the Communists adopted the New Economic Policy (NEP) in March 1921, permitting small-scale private enterprise in both towns and countryside. Whilst initially the NEP was posited as a temporary retreat, Lenin came to accept it as a long-term framework for building socialism.[39] A limited revival of commercial civil society, therefore, was to be the paradoxical fount of state-led, 'socialist' industrialization.

The NEP opened up a debate over the class nature of the regime. Lenin considered the proletariat to have been 'so divided, so degraded and so corrupted' by the stresses and strains of the civil war that 'an organization taking in the whole proletariat cannot directly exercise proletarian dictatorship. It can be exercised only by a vanguard that has absorbed the revolutionary energy of the class.' Indeed, in an age of imperialism, with constitutionalism defunct and the bourgeoisie irredeemably reactionary, revolution could only take the form of an exhausting 'civil war' that must prostrate the working class. Socialist revolution in *any* conceivable circumstance, therefore, required a vanguard party to exercise a dictatorship on the proletariat's behalf.[40] The strains of the epoch of social revolution, Lenin concluded, rendered the proletariat unfit to rule for a whole historical period.

The alternative of an incipient bourgeois civil society under Communist Party control, however, was hardly very coherent. The NEP, surely, would generate a substantial, propertied class of farmers and traders as quickly as it promoted economic growth. As Lenin admitted to the All-Russia Congress of Soviets in 1922, the survival and revival of 'small-scale production' meant that 'we have not torn up the roots of capitalism and have not undermined the foundation, the basis, of the internal enemy'.[41] Russian Marxist orthodoxy considered it axiomatic that class interests would seek political representation, and because all other parties were banned, it was assumed that the attitudes of the new petite bourgeoisie would infiltrate the ruling Communist Party. 'Factions' within the Communist Party, therefore, were banned in May 1921. Lenin, increasingly anxious that inefficient state bureaucracy was filling the space left by an assertive proletarian civil society, fell ill and finally died in 1924, leaving a collective leadership.

The Soviet urban mass lived in a vortex of insecure employment and black-market expedients.[42] It was in a poor shape to impose itself. The Left Opposition, led by Leon Trotsky, proposed the remedy of fast-paced industrialization to restore a stable proletarian base to the regime. Trotsky, never popular with his fellow leaders on account of a personal superiority of which he was only too well aware, was isolated, sidelined, and ultimately expelled from the party and country by Joseph Stalin (1879–1953), Secretary General of the Communist Party. The mass of people played virtually no role in these manoeuvrings. Stalin, however, believed the opposition to be, at its 'social roots', an 'urban petty-bourgeois strata' being ruined by development of the nationalized economy: 'These strata are discontented with the regime of the dictatorship of the proletariat... [they strive] to change this regime, to "improve" it in the spirit of establishing bourgeois democracy'.[43] Weak as it seemed, putative bourgeois civil society was a terror for the regime.

With the party-government so hostile to commercial civil society, the fate of the great mass of small property owners, the peasantry, was precarious. In 1927 a war scare launched the regime onto a course of 'administrative methods', meaning force, to extract agricultural surpluses for the military and industrial workforce from some of the richer peasantry. Confidence amongst the peasantry, so soon after the depredations of 'War Communism', was eggshell thin, and they rapidly began running down surplus food production. This was perceived as the classic ploy of bourgeois civil society (though most kulaks were little better off than their poorer peasant brethren), using control of production to browbeat the state into accepting market rationality. Stalin concluded that the kulaks were effectively trying to sabotage the regime by going on production strike. Now undisputed dictator of the country, Stalin resolved in 1929 to 'eliminate the kulaks as a class' by forcibly collectivizing the countryside. The language and mentality of Bolshevism had long been militarized, and such state commandism was once more firmly in charge, as Stalin made clear:

> To launch an offensive against the kulaks means that we must smash the kulaks, eliminate them as a class.... To launch an offensive against the kulaks means that we must prepare for it and then strike at the kulaks, strike so hard as to prevent them from rising to their feet again. That is what we Bolsheviks call a real offensive.[44]

This was a one-sided class civil war. As kulaks were to be dispossessed and their property passed gratis to new 'collective' farms, there was a strong incentive both for Communist organizers and poorer peasantry to define the term 'kulak' as widely as possible so as to grab their land. Seizure was enforced by violence, the richer peasantry being forcibly dispossessed, and those not executed were transported eastwards as a criminalized slave workforce. The aim was to destroy a hostile class and, in areas such as Ukraine, 'bourgeois nationalism'. A disastrous harvest failure in 1931–2 brought famine especially to the Ukraine. Despite total food collections falling by 20 per cent in 1932–3, grain exports nevertheless continued and the Red Army were given supply preference over starving villages. Paradoxically the regime played down the natural causes of the famine because they wished to place the blame upon the deliberate sabotage of the kulaks and other opponents of collectivization. Death-dealing struggle to extirpate the seedbed of bourgeois civil society was, in Stalinist eyes, a positive good.

Embryonic bourgeois civil society was largely destroyed. Between 1925–6 and 1932 the role of the private sector in the Soviet economy declined from 54 per cent to 9 per cent.[45] The 'rightist' Communist, Nikolai Bukharin, had long feared that any Soviet government emancipated from the constraints of petit bourgeois civil society, as fostered by the NEP, would rear up as a terrifying 'New Leviathan'.[46] Christian Rakovsky, a Left Oppositionist, in 1930 surveyed the impact of collectivization and forced industrialization: 'Before our eyes a *great class of rulers* has been *taking shape* and is continuing to develop. It has its own internal subdivisions, and grows by way of calculated co-optation...the unifying factor of this unique class is that unique form of private property, governmental power'.[47] The demise of bourgeois civil society and its NEP shadow left the state as the only effective source of social power. This fact brought into serious doubt the ability of the proletariat to act as a 'ruling class' able to constrain the 'governing elites' in a manner analogous to bourgeois disciplining of the state through tax, credit, and market rationality.

## THE IMPACT OF THE GREAT DEPRESSION

The capitalist West, meanwhile, endured years of uncertainty as world leadership passed from Great Britain to the United States. In the nineteenth century, being imperfectly democratic, and bolstered by empire, British governments had been able to ignore demands to inflate domestic consumer demand, had freely accepted foreign imports during times of boom, and had permitted British capital to seek out investment opportunities abroad in times of slump. This had allowed Britain to act as a counter-cyclical balance in the global economy. When Britain was booming, it freely accepted imports from abroad; when British growth slowed, it exported capital to sow foreign enterprises. The Great War, however, saw Great Britain displaced by the United States as the putative 'world's banker'. Postwar America, much more sensitive to the demands of its broad electorate, blocked any imports that might undersell US production, and strove to repatriate capital invested abroad in time of slump. Democratic, populist USA protected its high-wage domestic economy, and in so doing destabilized the global economy and reinforced rather than mitigated its cycles of peak and trough.[48] This dysfunctional economic arrangement, further exacerbated by the Wall Street Crash in 1929, turned into a global economic slump. Between 1929 and 1932, the nadir of the Great Depression, GDP in the US fell by about 30 per cent, in Austria by 22.5 per cent, in Czechoslovakia by 18.2 per cent, in Germany by 15.7 per cent, in France by 11 per cent, and in Britain by 5.8 per cent. Falls in industrial output were even steeper. Even though recovery began in most countries by 1933, and in some a modest boom had developed by 1937, bourgeois civil society itself seemed imperilled, as unemployment ballooned and successive states were confronted by fiscal crises. To many, the only question seemed to be whether the capitalist system would go down 'with violence' or peacefully.[49]

A fundamental problem for economic stability was that wages, though falling, did not fall so fast as to restore investor confidence, so that unemployment grew and state budgets creaked. For a government to enforce market equilibrium, there were various possibilities. First, by crushing the labour movement almost entirely, wages could be driven down. Such a frontal attack upon the rights of association, however, meant in effect the destruction of free civil society. Still, there was widespread middle-class support for 'setting aside normal constitutional procedures', as Robert Boyce puts it, if that was the price for protecting savings from depreciation by bearing down on wages, free trade, and welfare.[50] An alternative strategy was to cut wage costs by reducing the price of living. This option was open in particular to the major imperialist countries (France and the United Kingdom), which benefited from the turn of trade against the direct producers on the global periphery. America took refuge in its large, heavily protected domestic market, reinforced by the economic isolationism of the Smoot-Hawley Tariff Act of 1932.

Depression cut off foreign capital and slashed the value of commodity exports. Those new postwar states in central and eastern Europe with large peasant populations found themselves facing widespread malnutrition. With ethnic hatreds inflamed against 'minorities' competing for desperately scarce means of life, and the bourgeoisie fearful of collapse into anarchy, constitutionalism buckled. Peasant-based parties moved from supporting democratic ideologies towards anti-cosmopolitan authoritarianism. Buffeted by class conflict in town and country, governments found it impossible to retain power by constitutional means. By the 1930s, democracy was virtually extinct in central-eastern Europe other than in Czechoslovakia and to a lesser extent in Poland. Social Democracy compromised itself by accommodating to dictatorial regimes, and Communism, though universally prescribed, could command growing underground support. In the Balkans in particular it was gaining ground as the war approached.

In central and southern Europe, Catholicism moved to accommodate itself with the new-style 'populist' dictatorships. The Papacy, designating Mussolini a 'man of providence', concluded a concordat with the Italian Fascist state in 1929. The Catholic Church in Spain abandoned democratic constitutionalism for pious dictatorship in 1936. In Portugal, António de Oliveira Salazar became premier in 1932, and in 1933 he promulgated a corporatist Constitution, which reflected distinct class interests but attempted to harness them in an organic framework. This owed something to current fascist ideology, but was more influenced by Catholic social teaching. Salazar's 'New State' proved to be the most enduring dictatorship in Europe. The Christian Social Party in Austria was by the 1920s committed to reorganizing Austria on Catholic corporate principles, and thereby to destroying the socialist movement. On this basis there could be nothing but enmity between socialist Vienna and the Catholic countryside. When Chancellor Dolfuss abolished parliamentarianism and crushed armed socialist resistance in 1933–4, he established a Catholicized version of Italian corporate Fascism.

## CORPORATISM IN ITALY

Mussolini had promised a 'Third Way' between Communism and socialism. The social cement of common nationality was to transcend class struggle, and a 'Labour Charter', decreed in 1927, offered labour 'syndicates' a key role in economic planning and the resolution of disputes. In reality, workers' representatives were wholly subordinate to employers. Workers were rendered impotent, and wages fell between 20 and 40 per cent below their pre-1922 levels.[51] Fascism was promoted as 'totalitarian' because it promised to erase distinctions between state and civil society. This was to be achieved not so much by the political sphere taking over society, as by the creative strife, bonds, loyalties, and achievements of capitalist civil society being projected out to the very bounds of the nation. Invigorated by the meritocracy of commercial civil society and the military, the state was to be transformed from a bureaucratically rigid denial of the life-pulse of society to its highest, most noble expression. And, just as capitalist society naturally raised up and lionized entrepreneurial heroes, so too would the state be structured to give initiative and reward to natural leaders, from *squadristi* bosses through to works managers and civil servants, and all the way up to Il Duce himself.

Under the impact of the global Depression, however, Mussolini's program notably radicalized. Mussolini projected his Fascist revolution as the remedy for the problems of bourgeois civil society in an age of corporate capitalism. In 1933 he announced the obsolescence of laissez-faire capitalism, but assured his listeners that one must not 'confuse capitalism and bourgeoisie'. He echoed the common Marxist tripartite schema of capitalist history. Competitive capitalism had dominated from 1830 to 1870, the golden age of private initiative and free competition, when state interference in the economy was rare. This was followed by monopoly capitalism from 1870 to 1914, the age of unions, corporations, trusts, and protectionism. From the Great War, monopoly capitalism was superseded by the age of decadent capitalism or 'supercapitalism', with enormous corporations throwing themselves in the arms of the state. As Mussolini put it:

> Capitalistic enterprises became inflated. Enterprises grew in size from millions to billions.... The situation was abnormal. At this moment capitalism gets into difficulties and throws itself into the arms of the state. State intervention begins, and the more it is exercised the more it is necessary. The state intervenes in every aspect of economic life. A surrender to this type of capitalism would lead to state capitalism, which is nothing but state socialism turned upside down. This is the crisis of the capitalist system.

For Mussolini, 'state capitalism' threatened the very existence of civil society. Fascism avoided such a nemesis by actively and consciously promoting variegated economic activities and a vibrant bourgeoisie: 'Italy must remain a nation of diversified economic activities, with agriculture as the basis of her economic life, with a medium-sized but healthy industry, a non-speculative banking system, and a trade that places commodities in the hands of consumers quickly and efficiently.' Fascism, Mussolini promised, would allow for the re-creation of the heroic age of capitalism as it had existed before 1870, but suitably modernized. Private enterprise would continue to 'control' the production and distribution of wealth under the sympathetic 'supervision' of the state.[52]

The Fascist state, however, would not simply be handmaiden to bourgeois civil society. The Fascist concept of the action-orientated state, realizing the full potential of masses and classes, required unity of purpose. From experience, and in theory, this was best promoted by the war making state. Militarism was inherent in Fascism. Youth, in particular, was regimented and trained through the Backshirts to inculcate a hard, arrogant, conquering disposition. In a drive to make Italy self-reliant economically and prepared for war, government spending doubled between 1934–5 and 1938–9, and the middle classes were required to contribute heavily from their income and savings. The growing tension between commercial civil society and militarism increasingly drove Mussolini back to his formative hostility to the decadent bourgeoisie. In October 1938 he announced an 'anti-bourgeois' campaign as part of a drive of 'Fascistization' of Italian society to make it hardy enough to be a great imperial power. The campaign was primarily directed against a 'mentality' rather than middle-class wealth, however. A suitably nationalized and disciplined bourgeois civil society was to be nurtured. That which was considered cosmopolitan and effete in the 'mentality' of the bourgeoisie was externalized onto the figure of the Jew.[53] Anti-Semitism was a useful ideology for hiving off bourgeois-phobic manias and protecting the hard core of commercial civil society acknowledged as foundational to modern success in war.

## THE NAZI 'REVOLUTION'

Mussolini, of course, was aping German anti-Semitism. In the world view of Adolf Hitler (1889–1945), however, Jews were no mere synonym for unattractive class interests. Hitler was a materialist, but his analysis was fixedly 'scientific-racial', disdaining mere class analysis. He explained this in his 1925 book, *Mein Kampf*:

> The instinct of preserving the species is the first cause of the formation of human communities. But the State is a folk organism and not an economic organization.... The most essential supposition for the formation and preservation of a State is the presence of a certain feeling of homogeneity on the basis of the same entity and the same species, as well as the readiness to risk one's life for this with all means, something that will lead nations on their own soil to the creation of heroic virtues, but parasites to mendacious hypocrisy and malicious cruelty.[54]

Hitler believed that human races were instinctively territorial, being inherently attached to the soil as the primary source of life. Commerce and capital were only secondary cultural developments arising from the tangibility of 'blood and soil'. Territory was an ineradicable component of race-memory. Thus all history was to be explained as racial conflict over possession of land. The superior races, if they saw off lesser breeds, were creators of culture, but civilization could not elevate races above the basic human instinct to possess and control territory. Hitler thus had a worked-out notion of historical psychology.

The Jews of the Diaspora (and the Roma) threw a spanner in this explanatory construct: they had no territory, and they lived among those 'natural' races. In refusing to conform to Hitler's understanding of core human psychology—for all races, whatever their racial fibre, were inevitably land-grabbers—the Jews flouted Hitler's historical laws. Hitler, therefore, understood Jews not merely as an inferior race but as essentially not really human at all. Only this could explain their 'perverse' mode of existence. For Hitler, his depiction of the Jew as parasite, vermin, and bacilli was to be understood less as metaphor, more as literal truth. Thus, there was no moral barrier to exterminating what were understood as essentially non-humans. True, Hitler's ideas were not the stuff of common-or-garden anti-Semitism, but they were the foundation of his uniquely thorough attempt at genocide. His was not a 'normal' xenophobia or prejudice; it was the end product of a world view that, for Hitler, was logical and undeniable. This was a man who thought he was fighting not just a race-war but a species-war. It took exceptional circumstances to bring such a pseudo-intellectual obsessive into government.

The Nazis came to power amidst a profound crisis of German civil society and state. Weimar Germany was hit particularly hard by the Wall Street Crash, as half of all bank deposits had been foreign, mostly British and American, and these were quickly withdrawn. The impact on the bourgeoisie was traumatic. Already half a million of the Bürgertum had found themselves forced to take factory jobs in the 1920s. By 1929, largely because of the bargaining advantage of organized labour in the Weimar Republic, half a million white-collar employees earned no more than skilled workers. Then the Depression propelled another 600,000 white-collar employees out of a job altogether by 1933, and some 300,000 university graduates found themselves competing for 130,000 positions.[55] The market advantage of relatively scarce skills, expensively inculcated by intense familial socialization, was being whittled away, at least at the lower end. The fundamental interests of bourgeois civil society seemed threatened.

At the height of the Depression, one-third of the German population were on the dole. The burden of the unemployment insurance on declining tax revenue generated a budget deficit, bringing down the Social Democrat-led coalition government in 1931. From this point, German chancellors governed not through the Reichstag, but by virtue of the Constitution's emergency powers of decree at the disposal of the president, von Hindenburg. The first chancellor to wield this executive power, Heinrich Brüning, forced through painful tax hikes and budget cuts. These were perhaps more austere than strictly necessary economically, as Brüning wished both to demonstrate Germany's inability to pay reparations (and, indeed, these were finally ended by the international Lausanne agreement of 1932), and domestically he was determined to inflict a definite defeat on the labour movement. Only this, he believed, would allow market mechanisms to assert themselves and renew economic growth.

This piling of pain on the mass of the people was scarcely compatible with democratic consensus. Communist support surged. In the elections of September 1930, Hitler's anti-constitutional National Socialist German Workers' Party spectacularly increased its representation to become the second largest party in the Reichstag with 107 seats. The Nazis, by their fundamental twenty-five-point programme, evinced unalterable opposition to 'the corrupting parliamentary economy' in which office-holding was determined 'only according to party inclinations without consideration of character or abilities'. They demanded the creation and maintenance of a 'healthy middle class'. While the overall principle was 'the good of the state before the good of the individual', the continuation of private enterprise as the mainspring of economic activity was clearly envisaged.[56] Hitler's disdain for the complacency of the 'old' bourgeoisie was life-long.[57] But he honoured thrusting meritocrats. Notably, one of Hitler's early and long-standing heroes was the United States automobile magnate, Henry Ford, whom he lauded for his entrepreneurial brilliance and rabid anti-Semitism.[58] Indeed, the Führer celebrated the entrepreneur as a bearer of racial superiority in any national population, and had nothing but contempt for democracy in the economy. For example, Hitler rebuked Otto Strasser, an anti-free-market Nazi, in 1930: 'The capitalists have worked their way to the top through their capacity, and on the basis of this selection, which again only proves their higher race, they have a right to lead.'[59]

Faced with the prospect of social turmoil or even Communist revolution, the German middle classes were willing to be cajoled by Hitler. The Protestant theologian, Paul Tillich, writing in 1933, anxiously observed the bourgeoisie readying 'to betray its past and its principle to National Socialism, so long as the latter appeared to guarantee to the bourgeoisie its class rule'.[60] Nazism was no front for 'monopoly capitalism', however. Half of Hitler's votes came from villages, and while German big business did make contributions to Nazi coffers, the party appears to have been mostly self-financing from members' contributions. The most fervent Nazis came from the prosperous middle classes; small businessmen, civil servants and professionals.[61] Both the 'old middle class' (master artisans, farmers, shopkeepers), and the 'new' middle class (professionals, civil servants, innovative businessmen) voted very heavily for the Nazis, particularly the former. The party also won considerable worker support, accounting for about 40 per cent of its vote. Where leftist or confessional parties were strong, however, the swing to Hitlerism was limited.[62]

Hitler was anxious to reassure German big business as he approached power. He addressed the Industrie-Klub in Düsseldorf in January 1932, to convince business that its interests coincided with that of the strong state: 'it was the power-State [Machstaat] which created for the business world the general conditions for its subsequent prosperity.... [T]here can be no economic life unless behind this economic life there stands the determined political will of the nation absolutely ready to strike—and to strike hard.'[63] It was following this speech that Hitler finally began to attract significant funds from mainstream rich industrialists. That Hitler pitched his appeal in this manner, and found a ready response, said much for the demoralized condition of commercial civil society in Germany. The country's industry had long been the most dynamic in Europe. The German bourgeoisie, however, had accepted an authoritarian state to build the marketized nation in the nineteenth century, and a composite democratic, welfarist, and conservative-bureaucratic state after 1918 to inoculate against leftist revolution. Hitler's rather contemptuous message to business, that it must rely upon the Machstaat, resonated with the experience of bourgeois civil society since the 1860s.

The socialist left was also, in its way, forced to accept growing state authoritarianism. Social Democrats felt constrained to support passively Brüning's vigorously anti-labour government for fear of the Nazis approaching power. However, Chancellor Franz von Papen, appointed in May 1932, wished for a conservative regime able to dismantle democracy altogether. This, he believed, required mass support; to rely only on the army would invite civil war. Papen saw himself as representative of those forces of order, entrenched in the state bureaucracy, who had been mistrustful of democracy since 1918. The police could easily repress the divided left, but if conservatives attempted an authoritarian counter-revolution against both the labour movement and the Nazi Party, the instruments of the police, army, and indeed state bureaucracy would have run the risk of breaking in their hands.

In January 1933, Papen offered Hitler full powers as chancellor (with Papen as vice chancellor). Parliamentary arithmetic had not required that a Nazi government be formed, so it was a conscious decision of the elites to offer Hitler the chancellorship. The point of the exercise had been to win over a mass party to the task of abolishing parliamentary democracy. As the oligarchy had expected, the Hitler militia of SA Brownshirts were now unleashed on the labour movement. First the Communist Party was destroyed, then the SPD and trade unions. The bourgeois parties, including the Catholic Centre, dissolved themselves. Such self-sacrifice was not intended, however, as disavowal of bourgeois political influence. Civil servants, for example, were flattered by the 1933 'Law for the Restoration of the Professional Civil Service' (*Berufsbeamtengesetz*) that claimed to put them again 'above' petty party manipulation. They still expected their voices to be heeded. Conservatives believed that the middle classes would still have available other non-party vehicles, such as regional governments, lobby organizations, and churches, with which to exert their influence over the regime.[64] It is true that well-rooted social and cultural associations were able to subvert to an extent Nazi Gleichschaltung (coordination).[65] But in practice determining the influence of the bourgeoisie on the state elite was out of the question. As early as July 1933, Papen expressed his disillusionment in a speech at Dresden:

> Who among us would have imagined it possible that within four months the National Socialists would have taken over the entire German Reich, that all the middle class parties would have disappeared, that our democratic institutions would have been eliminated as with one stroke of the pen, that the new chancellor would have assumed a degree of power that no German emperor ever possessed?[66]

The victory of Nazism convinced the German SPD in exile that its strategy since 1918 had been misconceived, precisely because it left in situ state elites prepared to sup with the Hitlerite devil: 'It was a grave historical error on the part of the German working class, bewildered as it had been during the war, to take over the structure of the old state without transforming it.'[67] However, if Hitler's actual accession can be seen as ultimately the outcome of a conservative coup, the result was a revolution. Once the Brownshirts were unleashed, conservatism was wholly inadequate to hold back the floodtide of Nazi radicalism. A conservative strategy designed to liberate bourgeois civil society from the menace of 'proletarian democracy' had the unintended consequence of submitting it to an ultra-nationalist and pan-class ideology contemptuous of civility of any kind.

The radicals of the Nazi movement in Germany would have liked to have gone on to purge the army and the propertied classes, to establish a purely Nazi ruling elite, but this was resisted by Hitler as inviting civil war when his priority was mobilizing the state for the conduct of race-war. Hitler entrusted 'continuation of the administration' to the existing state bureaucracy, and did not risk making a clean sweep to install ideologically Nazi personnel.[68] He knew the value of the instrument he had inherited. The bureaucracy's very size and efficiency, far beyond the resources available to nineteenth-century absolutisms, meant that the Nazi regime could tax and organize commercial civil society without having to submit to the audit of a free Parliament.

In the 'Night of the Long Knives', 30 June–1 July 1934, the SA leadership, which was suspected of harbouring ambitions to displace the conservative 'establishment', was assassinated by Hitler's praetorian guard, the SS. The civil service, army, big business, and much of the middle class were pleased to see the Nazi revolution consolidated and apparently cut off. Bourgeois wealth and privilege remained more or less unimpaired, though they were politically sidelined by the abrasively pan-class new Nazi elites.[69] Hitler's economic supremo, Hjalmar Schacht, was, as he described himself, in his 'business and economic outlook…a Liberal'.[70] Taxation was heavy, but bourgeois evasion was minimized by placing it mostly on consumption, while taxes for farmers, small businesses, and heavy industry were reduced.[71] Wealthy Jews were looted by the state, though much of this was passed on to the Aryan bourgeoisie. As George Mosse puts it, the Nazi 'revolution was anti-bourgeois insofar as it was directed against the Jew', but it was predicated upon 'a double-standard, distinguishing between native and Jewish bourgeoisie'.[72]

In economic policy, Hitler prioritized military rearmament, and state spending rose from only 17 per cent of GNP in 1932 to 33 per cent by 1938.[73] As the regime grew in confidence, it distanced itself from bourgeois and conservative elites. Bastions of conservatism within the state apparatus were isolated and politically neutered: at the top of the economic bureaucracy, Hermann Göring displacing Schacht in 1936; at the foreign ministry, Joachim von Ribbentrop, from outside the career diplomatic service, became Foreign Minister in 1938; and in the armed forces, Werner von Blomberg, the Defence Minister, and Werner von Fritsch, Commander in Chief of the Army, were forced to resign, also in 1938. As Richard Overy has argued, the German economy in the 1930s was radically statised in preparation for war, and had structural similarities to Communist Russia (where a quasi-market 'grey economy' lubricated the state economic plan).[74] Nonetheless, Hitler ideologically preferred the social Darwinism of the market: private enterprise remained important, and far from being dispossessed as a class the *völkisch* bourgeoisie were materially buttressed. The Führer signalled his intention to restore the 'inviolability of private property' and fundamentally to reject 'nationalized industry' once the Second World War was won.[75]

As the regime's frantic rearmament programme began to overheat the economy, it seemed to many foreign observers that market rationality must reassert itself. The Nazi regime's real concerns about its creditworthiness and ability to trade on international markets, and its intense desire to maintain living standards, for fear of discontent spiralling into revolution, must serve, many expected, to nudge it back towards deferral to bourgeois civil society, and thereby begin a process of political moderation. This did not sufficiently take into account Hitler's overriding determination to use armed conquest to solve his immediate problems whilst laying the basis for a racially organized empire. His eyes were fixed on the goal of *Lebensraum* (living space) stretching eastwards, founded upon Aryan farmers rooted in the soil. 'We will not copy liberal capitalist policies which rely on exploiting colonies,' he told his generals in 1937. 'It is not a case of conquering people, but of conquering agriculturally useful space.'[76] Of course, if the peoples already occupying eastern Europe were surplus to requirements, most of them must vanish, one way or another. A war to assert German mastery of the continent was unavoidable. There was no organized political or social force within Germany, outside the pusillanimous army High Command, in a realistic position to stop him.

## CONCLUSION

In Germany, the Social Democratic government, struggling to construct a functional democracy, had struck a deal with the militarist establishment to leave its power within the state apparatus largely intact. Hitler was eventually to be handed this state apparatus by the traditionalist political elites as a pliant tool. The Austrian Socialist government that succeeded the Habsburg dynasty soon conceded the Catholic hinterland outside Vienna to conservative functionaries. In Italy, the Socialists feared to overthrow the state, but the old politicians and civil servants were less cautious, inviting the Fascists to establish an authoritarian order with a popular base. It fell increasingly to the labour movement to carry the weight of democracy's defence. But this in turn only served to convince wider layers of middle-class society that 'liberal democracy' was mutating into 'proletarian democracy'. As capitalism tipped into economic crisis, this put at risk the entire bourgeois social order.

The 1930s dictatorships in Germany and Italy—also, in their shadow, the Miklós Horthy regime in Hungary, the petty dictatorships in the Balkans, the ruling 'Marshals' in Poland, Salazar's government in Portugal, and Francisco Franco's in Spain—all appeared as dictatorships with degrees of novelty. No longer did they imply episodes of emergency rule: 'dictatorships today do not seem to be any longer parentheses between regimes,' said Salazar in 1934.[77] The new dictatorships were supported by capitalists but run by professional politicians or military men; they were hostile to socialism but fearful of revolution from the peasantry as much as from the proletariat. These were not in the mould of absolutist monarchies of the nineteenth century. Intensively employing the mass media, they spoke the language of populism and churned out propaganda addressing the people. Rather than invoking an aristocratic right to govern, based upon genealogical privilege and *noblesse oblige*, the political elites claimed to represent the interests of the pan-class national community. Not infrequently cabinets included lowly born arrivistes such as would never have intruded into the chancelleries of Metternich's Europe. Twentieth-century dictatorships maintained their own grassroots political parties and strong-arm militias, quite alien to the ministerial distaste for popular politicking that had characterized the Europe of Bismarck. The catastrophe of the Great War, and the ensuing social turmoil, had definitively delegitimized traditionalist, aloof, effortlessly superior monarchical absolutism. In the 'era of dictatorship', the rulers strenuously ventriloquized the voice of the people.

Lacking much by way of historic roots, or often administrative competence, such regimes nevertheless overturned democratic constitutionalism with ease. Factionalized party politics, exaggerating bitter divisions of class, ethnicity, and religion, had spread contempt for parliamentarianism. Dictatorships met a genuine desire for national unity by holding the occasional plebiscite. There was little pressure for a renewal of the experiment of government responsible to elected parliaments. The dictatorships were supported by capitalists, but they were not straightforwardly bourgeois themselves. In an autarchic economic environment, bourgeois civil society looked to the state for protection, and tariffs provided enough to fill government coffers. International credit was lacking, due to the collapse of the Gold Standard and the chilling effect of debt obligations being repudiated or renegotiated by most European countries since the Great War. With little available to borrow, the incentive to improve a government's credit rating by conceding open government with true parliamentary oversight of the budget was very much diminished.

The relationship between fascism and bourgeois civil society was ambiguous. The capitalist values of dynamic drive, rewards for the ambitious and ruthless, and peremptory managerial command over drilled masses of workers, were not limited to the economic sphere, but in fact expanded enormously. Such values permeated the political sphere, pushing aside decorous aristocratic statecraft and the divisive, class-ridden politics of democracy. It was less the negation of bourgeois civil society than its idealist transfiguration. In practice, however, militarism increasingly suffocated bourgeois civil society, as war eventually made evident.

# 11

## Popular Front and War

It is not the case that bourgeois liberalism altogether died in the interwar period. In good economic years, many of the middle classes were passive and conservative politically, but amenable to democratic constitutionalism. In years of crisis, however, much of the middle class turned to reactionary politics. This tendency was strongest in Germany, powerful also in France and Italy, while a relatively weak impulse in Britain and Scandinavia. Many intellectual defenders of capitalism shied away from constitutionalism, as infected by 'proletarian democracy'. As the bourgeoisie wavered on democracy, the labour movement began more and more to carry the weight of its defence. But this in turn only served to convince wider layers of middle-class society that 'liberal democracy' was mutating into 'proletarian democracy'. Socialists feared that the middle classes had abandoned the cause of constitutionalism. Max Adler, a leader of the Austrian socialists, concluded that the proletariat had 'to assume the historical task of developing political democracy, which has been abandoned by the bourgeoisie, and to defend it against reaction and fascism'.[1] But Social Democratic working-class organizations were clearly not able, at least in the medium term, to defend democracy alone. It was no easy task for them to find allies. Communists rejected parliamentary democracy as 'bourgeois', while increasingly, bourgeois parties mistrusted constitutionalism as supine before working-class demands.

### SOVIET INDUSTRIALIZATION

If Social Democrats were fretful, the self-confidence of Communists grew. They benefited from the prestige of an impressively formidable drive in Soviet Russia to construct a new society. The USSR bucked the trend by industrializing during the years of the Great Depression, confounding many sceptics of both left and right. Between 1929 and 1938 the Soviet Union trebled its industrial output, compared to an increase of 35 per cent in central and eastern Europe, and a decline of 10 per cent in southern Europe.[2] Planning concentrated on building up heavy industry, machine tool production, transport and infrastructure, and the military. It was driven by soft-budgeted state investment rather than the profitability criterion of individual enterprises. High investment targets were fixed to meet a priori production aims, with popular consumption having only a secondary claim on resources. Because so much surplus labour was available to be funnelled into industry from the countryside, this economic strategy, although liberal with resources, made sense.

While the peasantry were being destroyed by collectivization, a new industrial working class was being created. To be sure, any lingering worker autonomy was destroyed, wages were more than halved, and the working week extended.[3] However, for most workers in the 1930s, the comparator was not the wages of the relatively small industrial workforce of the NEP years, but the meagre living standards of the peasantry from which they were escaping. The first Five Year Plan of forced industrialization had anticipated an increase in the wages of the salary-earning workforce of 40 per cent. In fact the wage-labour force almost doubled in size; in construction it increased fourfold. Entirely new cities concentrated on metallurgy sprang up, as at Magnitogorsk and Kuznetsk. Because workers were better-off than peasants, per-capita consumption nationally rose one-quarter between 1928 and the late 1930s.[4] However, despite the emergence of a working-class political economy of tight labour markets, at least locally, and large-scale production, no new proletarian civil society crystallized that was able to submit the state and economy to its interests. Objections that the Stalinists had betrayed the Revolution did not quite dispel the disconcerting suspicion amongst socialists that, perhaps, the proletariat were simply incapable of functioning as a 'ruling' class. If so, the disconcerting alternatives were capitalism or the totalitarian state.[5]

However, workers' modes of resistance, in the form of the go-slow or gossiping against managers (a potent weapon in a time of purging), though weapons of the weak, did have some discernible influence on the Stalinist state. Workers were relatively privileged by forced-pace industrialization, and many were drawn into management. Between 1928 and 1932 over one hundred thousand adult workers benefited from crash courses in higher education while many more were trained on the job. Ante Ciliga, a Yugoslav Communist living in Russia, described the apparatchiks he met as of 'working-class or artisan origin': 'Their members, sprung from the people, retained, in their speech, manners and facial expressions, the imprint of their past.'[6] Particularly during the worst years of collapse in agricultural production, preference was given to manual workers to enable them to buy a minimum quantity of essential goods at low prices. Consumer groups other than manual workers had lower allocations or were required to pay higher prices. Industrial enterprises supplied tolerable food through canteens—a provision unavailable to the village and most of the non-industrial population.[7]

Unquestionably the working class was privileged politically in contrast to the peasantry, and with the onset of the 1937 Great Terror, perhaps even relative to the intelligentsia. Specialist engineers and technicians were simultaneously feted as necessary to production and persecuted as potential class enemies. One German engineer, who as a Communist sympathizer worked in Russia from 1923, grew weary of the humiliations heaped upon his peers by the 'proletarian dictatorship': 'At a meeting a workman will get up and shout and gesticulate. "We workers..." It is perfectly obvious that the man is an ignorant fool, spouting forth utter nonsense; yet one can't answer him, for he is the boss.' Still, as the same engineer later admitted, 'I wrongly accused the workers. They are the victims of the system as much as we are. They are allowed to let off steam about unimportant details, but fundamentally they are deprived of all rights and all power, although all action is taken in their name.'[8] This was the ambiguity of the Communist system. It was no dictatorship of the proletariat, but it had some claim to be a dictatorship that, relatively speaking, favoured workers.

The Communist elite, aware of their lack of support in society at large, were paranoid about the capacity of even embryonic bourgeois civil society to catalyze opposition to the regime. Stalin theorized that, as the 'triumph' of socialism approached, the class struggle would only sharpen. His implacable self-belief in the righteousness of the Great Terror need not be doubted. Stalin almost certainly believed that about thirty thousand Communist dissidents conspired as a government in waiting, and that an army plot, 'exposed' in June 1937, was genuine. The regional party bosses, meanwhile, were terrified that 'former kulaks, criminals and other anti-Soviet elements'—essentially the remnants of bourgeois civil society—would take advantage of rigged elections, required by the 1936 Constitution, to foment rebellion.[9] The mania of targets and lies that had driven industrialization pell-mell similarly escalated the purges into a general bloodletting in 1937–8. The secret police laboured to process almost the entire 'political nation' in a frantic heresy hunt, while Stalin and his clique approved mass executions by quota. There were about nine hundred thousand executions in the Soviet Union between the mid-1930s and 1953. The numbers detained in the Gulag, most of whom were 'criminal' rather than 'political' prisoners, peaked at about 4 million around 1939/40. The annual death rate in the camps ran at about 7 per cent annually, the aim being not to kill prisoners but rather to squeeze them of their 'golden sweat', as an apparatchik put it, in an archipelago of slave labour.[10]

This was a society modernizing not only in the absence of bourgeois civil society, but in order to suppress it. Tyranny was predicated upon a paranoid belief in the recuperative powers of the bourgeoisie, given half a chance. The working class, for their part, were deemed incapable of anything like the same spontaneous capacity to mould society in their own image. Workers at best were 'shock brigades', at the command of the regime. Ironically, in the face of state oppression, class resentments in the Soviet Union seem to have flattened out in the 1930s. Rather than peasants resenting workers, or workers resenting the intelligentsia and specialists, there was increasingly a generalized hostility to the victimizing party-state.[11]

## A PROGRESSIVE BOURGEOISIE? THE POPULAR FRONT

Whilst Communism radicalized in Russia, it moderated internationally. Since the Sixth Congress of the Comintern, in 1928, international Communism had based its strategy upon the assumption that there was no basis for cooperation with the bourgeoisie. As a Comintern theorist explained, whilst parliamentary democracy had been characteristic of the 'age of bourgeois revolutions of the last century', fascism was the dynamic tendency of government in the age of finance capital and imperialism, so that it grew 'organically' out of parliamentarianism.[12] After Hitler's assumption of power, however, the Comintern changed tack radically. At the July 1935 seventh Congress of the Comintern, the call went out to form everywhere a 'people's front' of Communists, Social Democrats, peasants, and the urban petite bourgeoisie. Popular Fronts, indeed, came to power the following year in both France and Spain.

This turn was not, however, backed up by a terribly thorough revision of theory regarding 'bourgeois democracy'. The nominal head of the Comintern, Georgi Dimitrov, explained in 1935 that while the core of any Popular Front would be 'the proletarian united front' of Communists and Socialists, it was necessary to attach it to a 'fighting alliance' of peasantry and urban petite bourgeoisie. These latter strata were, to be sure, susceptible to fascist ideals and ultra-nationalism, but, by exposing the supposed reality of fascism as rule by 'finance capital', they could be won round to democratic patriotism against fascist militarism.[13] The British Communist intellectual, Maurice Dobb, essayed a more theoretically sophisticated attempt to explain the turn to Popular Frontism. The weaker middle classes were being alienated by the costs of economic nationalism and protectionism, 'which are apt to bear with special heaviness on the small producer as well as the consumer'. As a result of this, the middle classes were willing to 'align themselves (for the first time since 1848) with the proletariat in an organized "people's front" of "the left" '.[14] The Popular Front, therefore, was justified because the proletariat and radical bourgeois had a basis for cooperation such as had not existed for ninety years. It was a long way from pristine Leninism.

Dimitrov had also argued that because the victorious powers emerging from the Treaty of Versailles were sated, they were 'afraid of losing in a new redivision of the world' and so 'at the present stage interested in avoiding war'. This meant that it was possible to build Popular Fronts not only with the progressive bourgeoisie but even with imperialist forces in the Western Powers, so long as they opposed international revisionism that might threaten the security of the Soviet Union. A combination of the Popular Front with the bourgeoisie was based, therefore, not so much on any socially progressive expectations imputed to the bourgeoisie, but more on the temporary coincidence of interest between 'imperialism' and the security of the Soviet Union.[15]

\* \* \*

A Popular Front came to power in France in 1936. France, as a nation of small savers, had been traumatized by devaluation of the franc to one-fifth of its pre-war gold value in 1928, which had wiped out a good deal of middle-class savings. The franc came under pressure again by the mid-1930s, but the government resisted devaluing it. This left retrenchment of public spending as the only response to economic difficulties, and social security was already niggardly by Western European standards. The old anxiety, on the right in particular, that Parliament was inefficient, and executive government the plaything of self-seeking factions, was only increased by the shady Stavisky Affair of 1934, which suggested that senior politicians, the police, and financiers were breaking the law in order to fleece small investors. Serious street-rioting of right-wing leagues in 1934 seemed to threaten a coup against Parliament and the establishment of an executive dictatorship of some sort.

Class tensions threatened the Republic. Following the German example, the French Communists were painfully aware that this might not work to their benefit. By November 1934, the French Communist leader Maurice Thorez was reporting that 'the problem of the alliance between the working class and the middle class' was being revisited by the leadership.[16] The Communists duly came out in favour of the Popular Front. This would, Thorez hoped, bring 'into political life sections of the working class who had hitherto been passive' and fuse them electorally with 'important strata of the middle classes who are against Fascist reaction'.[17] The implication here, which proved accurate enough, was that while Popular Frontism was able to convert formally suspicious workers to parliamentarianism, it was not able to win new layers of the middle classes beyond those already prepared to work with the left.

In 1936 a Popular Front election slate was agreed between the Communists, the Socialists, and the bourgeois Radicals. An electoral victory for the Popular Front was more or less a foregone conclusion, if only because the reunification of the left consolidated their vote. In May 1936 it won 376 seats, the right winning just 222. However, this did not represent a mass shift in the electorate. The combined vote of the right fell by only seventy thousand votes. The Communists almost doubled their vote, taking precedence in the industrial regions, and because they were now willing to enter electoral pacts in the second round, they saw their number of elected deputies increase from ten to seventy-two. The Socialists, winning the votes of minor civil-service *fonctionnaires* and the white-collar or self-employed *classes moyennes*, increased their representation by forty-nine deputies, up to 146. The middle-class Radical component of the Popular Front, however, suffered a drop from 159 seats to 116, and its candidates most openly ill-disposed towards the Popular Front strategy fared rather better than average.[18] It was clear that much of the French middle class were repelled by the prospect of rallying with the Communists even on an anti-fascist platform that explicitly ruled out socialism.

The Socialist Party leader Léon Blum formed a Popular Front government in June, with Radical ministers in the cabinet, but the Communists only lending it support from outside the ministry. The formation of the government immediately raised expectations that it would be blocked by bourgeois non-cooperation. It was met, therefore, by a massive extra-parliamentary movement of workers to enforce what were seen as its principles and, indeed, the legitimacy of the ballot box. Almost two million came out on strike and hundreds of factories were occupied by the workers. A worker participating in a sit-down strike at the Renault works explained that 'our tactic is to occupy, to hold at any cost, as in a besieged city.... Outside the factory we would be nothing more than unemployed, incapable of maintaining our unity against the company union and fascists.'[19] The left were deeply concerned, however, that such militancy might provoke a bloody bourgeois backlash, and they feared a reprise of the June Days of 1848 and the civil war of 1871.[20] The Communist Party, therefore, called for a still wider 'Front de Francais', including army, bureaucracy, diplomats, and Catholics. It was vital, argued Communists, that bourgeois allies not be scared off by workers' militancy.

In practice, the very fact that the Communists were promoting Popular Frontism in defence of parliamentary constitutionalism made that constitutionalism suspect in bourgeois eyes.

The strikes were ended by the Matignon Agreement, which conceded a forty-hour working week, annual holidays, and wage rises. Inflation ate away the wage rises, however, and the forty-hour week proved to be impossible to implement immediately. With its credibility bleeding away with the markets, the government found it difficult to raise credit. The Blum government was caught between producers and consumers, and it clung to the fixed franc for too long. When the Conservative-controlled Senate denied the Popular Front government special financial powers in June 1937, Blum resigned. The government thereafter turned to the right.

The French strikes of May–June 1936 were, of course, in pursuit of such workers' rights and welfare as had become standard in other constitutionalist countries many years previously. But they were also a deliberate assertion of power to counter an anticipated rebellion of bourgeois civil society against the authority of the Popular Front government. Insofar as bourgeois support for extra-parliamentary subversion was deemed untimely, it was successful. But the ratchet effect of *droitisme* reliably effected by parliamentary constitutionalism in France retained its force. The success of bourgeois civil society in turning the Popular Front government towards the right, through the classic mediation of credit, showed the continuing relevance and vitality of parliamentarianism for the French middle classes.

\* \* \*

In France the liberalism of the Radical Party, representing the small shopkeeper and peasant proprietor, and the prominence of the white-collar and professional 'new middle class' amongst Socialist Party supporters, provided a genuine bridge between the proletariat and a good deal of bourgeois civil society for a concerted defence of democracy and social reform.[21] The Spanish Popular Front, in contrast, had less steady bases of bourgeois liberalism and working-class constitutionalism. Anarchism, inveterately hostile to parliamentarianism, had long been powerful. As it traditionally eschewed political party organization, however—in 1936, despite having over a million members, the anarchist CNT had only one paid secretary[22]—it was the socialist political party, PSOE, in cooperation with the bourgeois Republicans, that inaugurated the 1931 Spanish Republic. However, the king was deposed less by parliamentary than by popular, elemental forces. The extra-parliamentary role of workers was manifest in great waves of strikes, which led up to and beyond the establishment of the Republic.

In Spain, the Church had traditionally argued that only an explicitly Catholic government was acceptable in a country with a Catholic majority. But with the 1931 Republic, Church intellectuals put forward the theory of 'accidentalism', as it was called, allowing for the state to be considered legitimate even if it was not subservient to the Church, so long as it did not persecute the faithful.[23] The willingness of the right-wing CEDA party, despite its obvious sympathies with European fascism, to work within republican constitutionalism was directly influenced by this new spirit of compromise. As long as the Republic protected the interests of religion and property, it could be tolerated, even if not loved.

In 1933 the governing coalition between Socialists and the bourgeois-liberal Republicans broke up, allowing CEDA to win the November elections to the Cortes, or Parliament. The outgoing national president, fearing a tip into fascism, refused to appoint a CEDA-led government. In October 1934, however, when CEDA secured three ministerial posts, the left were convulsed with fear, fully expecting this to be the thin edge of the wedge that would destroy the democratic Republic. The Socialists called a general strike and, on 4 October, the socialist miners of Asturias rose in revolt in what they seem to have perceived as a last desperate bid to halt fascism.[24] The army and Civil Guards bloodily suppressed the rebellion, precipitating temporary disarray on the left. However, CEDA, given pause for thought, did not push their advantage, and they remained loyal coalitionists in the Republican government. On the other hand, the right now believed that the Socialists accepted the parliamentarianism only insofar as it advanced their agenda and kept the right out of power. A new government of the centre-left, it was feared, would be a stalking horse for leftist revolution.

A Popular Front, explicitly to defend 'bourgeois democracy' from fascist attack, was concluded for the February 1936 elections, which included not only the Republican-Socialist alliance of 1931, but also the dissident-communist POUM, the Syndicalist Party, a split-off from the anarchist CNT, and the (still rather small) Spanish Communist Party. Even the CNT dropped from its election programme the traditional injunction, 'Don't Vote!'. The left, therefore, were converging in support of the bourgeois Republic. But this was not a straightforward process. While the previously rather radical socialist leader, Indalecio Prieto, concluded that it had been a mistake in 1933 for the Socialists to break the alliance with the bourgeois Republicans, the former Minister of Labour, Largo Caballero, evinced an increasingly revolutionary rhetoric. Ultimately, Caballero told an audience in Cádiz on 24 May 1936, only a social revolution could save Spain from fascism: 'When the Popular Front breaks up, as break up it will, the triumph of the proletariat will be certain. We shall then implant the dictatorship of the proletariat, which does not mean the repression of the proletariat, but of the capitalist and bourgeois classes!'[25] Most of the middle classes were inclined to see the Popular Front not as a capture of socialism and anarchism by bourgeois republicanism, but rather the subversion of the bourgeois Republic by a left that had shown its true colours in the Asturias rising of 1934. Indeed, the bourgeois vote in February 1936 mostly went to right-wing parties hostile to democracy, which gained 46.48 per cent of the vote, only marginally behind the Popular Front's winning vote of 47.03 per cent.

After the election there was considerable street violence, particularly from CNT militants, as they strove to dismantle the reactionary state apparatus and clerical organizations by force. The Popular Front regime appeared incapable of preserving law, order, and property rights. Conservatives waited for the army to step in to stop a slide towards social revolution. But the army rising, when it came in December 1936, failed to conquer Spain in one fell swoop because for the first time the left rallied to the Republic's defence. Such left-wing unanimity in favour of defending parliamentary constitutionalism would have been unthinkable in the nineteenth century, in the days of *cacique* manipulations of elections, and the cynical pseudo-politics of the *turno pacifico*. Even as late as 1923, General Primo de Rivera's coup against parliamentarianism had the sympathy of many socialists, and the Cortes had found no defenders amongst anarchists. That the army coup was so long in coming and split Spain so disastrously in 1936 was evidence, in fact, that parliamentary constitutionalism had become more, not less, acceptable to broad swathes of people.

Large elements of the state apparatus, however, had gone over to the side of the Nationalist rebels. With the left parties improvising militias, which the government was forced (after hesitation) to arm, it was inevitable that elements of social revolution would spontaneously develop. Everywhere in Republican Spain outside the Basque country, left-wing parties, particularly the anarchists, took over local government. Barcelona became a de facto workers' state, with the bourgeois liberals sidelined. The Popular Front government was deeply concerned that workers' management of factories, land redistribution, localism, and the disintegration of hierarchy and chains of command would dissipate military energies, alienate what little was left of bourgeois support for the government, and reinforce the hostility of the Great Powers, particularly Britain. The Spanish Communist Party, in particular, emphasized ruthless centralization and repression of revolutionary distractions.

The Communists' most iconic domestic leader, Dolores Ibarruri (known as La Pasionaria), explained appropriate revolutionary strategy as being dictated by the essentially bourgeois nature of the revolution:

> The revolution which is taking place in our country is the bourgeois-democratic revolution which was fought out in other countries, like France, more than a century ago.... The government of Spain is the government based on the election victory of 16 February, and we support and defend it as the lawful representation of the people, now fighting for democracy and freedom.[26]

Communist attempts to make the Popular Front safe for bourgeois civil society, however, did little to inspire confidence in the democratic credentials of a 'legitimist' side in the war. It did not help that Communists hinted, if *sotto voce*, that legitimist victory in Spain might result not in a 'bourgeois democracy' as such, but rather in a 'new democracy', with the proletariat (for which, read Communists) to the fore.[27] Moreover, the dictatorial tendencies of Communism were indiscreetly on show. In May 1937 confused fighting in Barcelona saw the Communists crush the POUM and assorted anarchists, thus definitively stilling the revolutionary impulse. The importation of Stalinist police methods, including torture chambers, facilitated the mopping up of those radical leftists most repugnant to the official Communist interest.

Despite Soviet military aid, and Communist ruthlessness, the advantages of Spain's military establishment, buttressed by Italian and German support, in the end proved irresistible. While there were fascist elements in General Franco's 'crusade', he relied more on militarist terror to atomize the labour movement than on a mass movement. Franco allowed bourgeois civil society and the oligarchy to recompose on the basis of conservative traditionalism.

Popular Frontism in Europe had generally failed to win new bourgeois voters to the anti-fascist cause. Indeed, it probably alienated a good number of them, as they saw liberal parties being subordinated to the wiles of socialists and, much worse, Communists. They were effective to the extent that they overcame divisions between those political forces already ranged against right-wing authoritarianism. But they did not stem the bourgeois drift from liberal democracy—quite the contrary.

## UNITED FRONT IN CHINA

The Popular Front was also pursued in the non-western world. Here, indeed, Leninism had stipulated that a 'national bourgeoisie' could still be a progressive force against imperialism. The bourgeois revolution, therefore, continued to apply with full force. It was in China, however, that Communism in the interwar period paradoxically built itself real (if unstable) governmental power over vast swathes of the country.

The domestic industrial and commercial middle classes of China grew rapidly from the republican revolution of 1911, and were the main loci for the nationalist KMT party, providing about half its leadership cadre.[28] The Chinese bourgeoisie were large in absolute numbers, if small relative to overall population. Large-scale banking, commercial, and manufacturing interests were to be found in the coastal cities, closely tied to foreign investors, whereas small merchants and manufacturers mediated commerce in the rest of the country. The status of the middle classes had never been particularly high in imperial China, and under the KMT they continued to be harassed by state controls. Still, the 1920s in particular were something of a golden age for the middle classes, and many expressly adapted the ideas and cultural mores of the West.

It was no easy task for the KMT to weld back together a fiscally unified, centrally directed state. The new Chinese Republic fragmented into a patchwork of warlord-controlled fiefdoms. Sun Yat-sen, the KMT's first leader, confessed that national revolution could only progress in stages: first, unification by military means, second, political tutelage by the Nationalist elite to educate the masses, and only finally, constitutional democracy.[29] Sun Yat-sen built up, in alliance with southern warlords, an alternative south Chinese government in opposition to the militarists of Peking. He received little support from the Western powers, however, and in 1921 he turned to the Soviet Union. Russia reciprocated, and while sponsoring the Chinese Communist Party (CCP), established in 1921 as the self-declared expression of the proletarian interest, the Soviet leadership acknowledged Sun Yat-sen's KMT as the primary vehicle for China's anti-imperialist bourgeois national revolution.

Following Sun Yat-sen's death in March 1925, Chiang Kai-shek assumed the leadership of the KMT, and in March 1926 dismissed his Soviet advisers, whose presence alienated the Western powers. In Shanghai, a commercial and trading centre and stronghold of China's small working class, Chiang's forces unleashed a bloody terror against Communists and leftists in April 1927. Chiang hoped to win the confidence of the Shanghai bourgeoisie and the city port's lucrative customs duties as a base for consolidating his hold on the country. By mid-1927 the CCP had been largely extirpated in the cities. Having used and cast aside Communist help, the KMT government at Nanjing received international recognition. It now committed itself to 'preparing' China for constitutional democracy.

Over the next decade, the KMT regime succeeded in moderating foreign claims to right of interference, and a modernized economic and legal infrastructure was fairly successfully developed. The Communist challenge remained, however. The CCP did not redevelop in the cities amongst the working class. It grew, rather, as a rural guerrilla movement. The rising Communist leader, Mao Zedong (1893–1976), openly theorized the revolutionary role of the peasantry, despite traditional Marxist insistence that only the working class or the bourgeoisie could hope to play a leading revolutionary role.[30] He did speak of proletarian leadership in the 'New Democracy' bloc of four classes (proletariat, peasantry, petite bourgeoisie, and the progressive bourgeoisie) that would drive through bourgeois-democratic revolution.[31] Mao, however, tended to treat the proletariat and the CCP as more or less synonymous, and the urban working class was in no material way the base of the Communist movement. For the purposes of fighting, Mao relied upon the rural landless and 'éléments déclassés'.[32] With these, the amorphous Red Army was able to fend off and survive the KMT's various 'extermination campaigns'.

China, however, had to confront the rising threat from Japan. With virtually no indigenous raw materials, Japan was exceptionally reliant on international trade and credit. When the Depression and Western protectionism closed off much of the world market, the temptation to cash in on Japan's military assets proved irresistible. The 'Zaibatsu elite', comprising the big-business conglomerates of Mitsui, Mitsubishi, Sumitomo, and Yasuda, switched from supporting domestic liberalization and foreign trade to acquiescing in military plans to carve out an economic zone by force. Japan's invasion of Manchuria in 1931 was acceded to by the business elites out of economic desperation. Once given its head, Japanese militarism was a venomous domestic actor in its own right. One group of right-wing army officers, during an attempted coup in 1936, condemned the timidity of elder statesmen, political parties, the bureaucracy, and capitalist magnates, concluding that 'it is our duty as subjects of His Majesty the Emperor to safeguard our country by killing those responsible' for its travails.[33] Thus the unholy and deeply conflicted alliance of big business and militarism, soldered by Japan's exclusion from world markets, threatened to swamp bourgeois civil society altogether.

In September 1931, Japan seized Manchuria in the north-east, one of the wealthiest regions of China, and established there the client state of Manchukuo. From this base the Japanese first probed and then, in 1937, launched an all-out attack into northern China and the coastal provinces. The Japanese estimated that they lost fifty thousand casualties against Chinese army casualties of eight hundred thousand (civilian deaths were enormously higher).[34] Huge swathes of territory were taken, depriving the KMT of much of its urban tax base and cutting it off from sea communications. Almost all the modern industry of China fell into Japanese hands. The Japanese, however, could barely administer the hinterland of cities and rail depots. Often the Communists provided the main resistance. Wherever the Communists established even a fairly thin military presence in rural areas, they comprised the only effective state structure available, collecting taxation and introducing limited land redistribution. The appeal of 'Marxism-Leninism' to peasants appears unlikely, but as a movement developed from urban conditions, it was well placed to offer ancillary tactics calculated to divide and demoralize the urban centres from within. This innovation held out the prospect—at long last—of success for peasant attempts to 'surround the cities'. It was a heady inducement.

Since 1927, the Chinese Communists had dismissed the bourgeoisie as incorrigible, and had based their strategy on an alliance between the proletariat, peasants, petite bourgeoisie, and intellectuals. With the turn to the Popular Front in the mid-1930s, however, they accepted that broad swathes of the Chinese bourgeoisie proper also resented the Japanese. Mao and the CCP defined these patriots as the 'national bourgeoisie' to distinguish them from reactionary elements likely to collaborate with the Japanese. In December 1935 the Chinese Communist Party issued its first call for a United Front with the KMT against Japanese imperialism.[35] This came into effect when, in December 1936, Nationalist troops at Xi'an mutinied and forced the United Front on Chiang. The Communists even professed, in January 1942, that 'most of the landlords are anti-Japanese, and that some of the enlightened gentry also favour democratic reforms'. Accordingly, Communist agrarian policy in the territories it controlled was limited 'only to help the peasants in reducing feudal exploitation, but not to liquidate feudal exploitation entirely, much less to attack the enlightened gentry who support democratic reforms'. Landlords would be dispossessed only if 'stubbornly unrepentant traitors'.[36]

By the Communists' own view, therefore, commercial civil society in China was capable of playing a progressive role in pushing forward 'bourgeois democratic revolution'. It was also evident, if less openly confessed, that the urban working class were not in much of a position to present themselves as an independent social force. Mao therefore found it necessary to construct a fairly elaborate rationale for the Communists' leading role. In his pamphlet, *On the New Democracy* (1941), Mao argued that democratic revolution had been properly 'bourgeois' only up to the Russian Revolution of 1917. From that point, however, the Chinese democratic revolution became an instance of the world-wide Proletarian-Socialist Revolution.[37] It was this global configuration that the Communists used to justify their taking the leading role in the Chinese national democratic revolution, and to anticipate not a constitutionalist state based upon commercial civil society but rather a joint dictatorship of all the revolutionary classes, with the 'proletariat' playing the leading role.[38] As the Communists treated their own vanguard party as the stand-in for the proletariat, this prefigured a party state.

Chinese commercial civil society, no less than elsewhere, was corruptible, fixated on the demands of entrepreneurship, and ready to collaborate with local authorities, even if foreign.[39] However, it was not in any meaningful sense reactionary. The middle classes of the cities politically supported the KMT's bid for nation-state construction, even if Chiang Kai-shek would hardly have made so much headway in the late 1920s without allying with sympathetic warlords. The KMT's assault on the Communists in 1927 cannot credibly be seen as any kind of abandonment of bourgeois revolution; it could even be sold as anti-imperialist in its own right, given Soviet sponsorship of the Chinese Communist Party. It was certainly a step, if not necessary or sufficient, towards constructing a constitutionalist state. The 1927 massacres did shatter a working-class constituency that had been important in the revival of democratic and national sentiment after the Great War. But the KMT's rapid success in eliminating warlord fragmentation, and constructing a National government that was at least effective in the cities and their hinterlands, was evidence enough that the 'bourgeois revolution' was still progressing without an active proletarian alliance.

Urban commercial society, however, was put under the cosh by the Japanese aggression, the invaders occupying China's most commercially developed cities and regions. Given its military inferiority, it made little sense for the KMT to attempt a fixed defence of the cities. As the KMT was primarily urban, and the cities had only tenuous control over the countryside, this meant that the Communist guerrilla armies were vital to national resistance. Communists operated as an armed administration, living off rural territories as they controlled them, and in return providing rudimentary government. The Chinese National government retreated into the vastness of the country to survive Japanese aggression, and for its military effort prioritized diplomatic efforts to win supplies from the United States, which indeed flowed in after Pearl Harbor (7 December 1941). The Chinese government's war effort, therefore, was not based upon commercial civil society, and the KMT's roots there atrophied. Bourgeois civil society had little opportunity to put its stamp on the country. It was not central to the war effort, nor was it much present in the enormous rural spaces where Communists assembled their power. It was neither the bourgeoisie nor the urban proletariat that carried the resistance to Japan, but the peasantry.

## NO POPULAR FRONT—BRITAIN AND THE USA

Popular Frontism never developed significant traction in Great Britain or the United States. This was only to be expected, given the near-numerical irrelevancy of Communist forces in both countries, but at a deeper level it reflected the observable fact that there was no tension between preserving constitutionalist politics and the vitality of commercial civil society, so there was little temptation for the bourgeoisie to trade away civil and political liberties to preserve bourgeois conditions of existence from the menace of 'proletarian democracy'. For British salary earners, the years 1923 to 1938 comprised a 'golden age', as Ross McKibbin puts it, during which 'the middle classes were uniquely favoured'.[40] More generally, in Britain and America, incomes for those in work were buoyant, and both countries were well on the way towards a 'consumerist' society. As an index, automobile ownership soared (2 million in Britain by 1939, 23 million in the US by 1929), facilitating an internal migration to home ownership in 'upwardly mobile' suburbs.[41] Even those unable to afford cars or houses were able to buy consumer durables on hire purchase. 'By the inter-war period,' Hilton and Daunton write, 'appeals were being made to the consumer as a political entity around which the democratic process revolved, ensuring that the ability to engage in private acts of consumption was a badge of citizenship.' Whilst such consumerist politics were not absent even in Nazi Germany, they were far more advanced in Britain and the United States, being central to the political appeal of both the Conservative prime minister, Stanley Baldwin, and the New Deal president, Franklin D. Roosevelt.[42] The consumer interest vested in competitive price markets, or at any rate markets regulated to limit monopolistic pricing, and so engaged broad swathes of the electorate in commercial civil society. This was a powerful counter-interest to the producer interest of wage labour and capitalist corporations. In Britain and America, bourgeois civil society was expansive, confident, and thus securely liberal.

However, 'consumerism' was not simply a synonym for commercial civil society. The liberal dream of the nineteenth century had been of a classless society, in which anyone could expect to become an entrepreneur. Even wage earners might hope to become their own capitalists, perhaps by profit-sharing or at least by earning a 'dividend' on their purchases from consumer cooperatives. The large-scale corporatism of the interwar period, however, placed real control of capital beyond the reach of the 'little man'. Wartime profiteering, post-war inflation, and the Wall Street Crash meant that liberals were unwilling to push their luck in celebrating share ownership as a form of 'popular capitalism'. The weight of wage labour, moreover, was simply undeniable. 'By far the most important income-yielding instrument actually possessed by the poor of the United Kingdom...is manual labour,' admitted the liberal economist Arthur C. Pigou. Estimating the annual value of workers' investments at some £20 million a year, Pigou pointed out that this amounted to only 1/35th of their total income, 'all the rest being received as wages of labour'.[43] Workers, of course, were consumers, but they were first and foremost wage earners, with preferences in tension with market imperatives. They favoured job security and stable wages, and looked askance at arguments for labour-market flexibility and wage depreciation to cheapen the costs of putting the unemployed to work.

Liberal consumerism, therefore, linked successful consumerism to high and stable wages generating in turn a healthy domestic market (particularly attractive as export opportunities were limited by protectionism). This meant admitting the beneficial role of trade unions in shifting the burden of market fluctuations from wages towards profits and dividends. If capitalists were expected to innovate technologically rather than just sweat labour, the state needed to step in to support demand, maintain the unemployed in such a condition that they were available for work, and where necessary encourage rationalization of production in fragmented, backward sectors of the economy.

Liberal consumerism, therefore, implied a pact of sorts with organized labour. Though the General Strike of 1926 in Britain was smartly suppressed as a challenge to the constitutional right of Parliament to make policy, the Conservative prime minister, Stanley Baldwin, frustrated the hopes of those Tory fire-breathers who hoped that the trade-union movement would be chopped down to size in the aftermath. Trade-union rights were never seriously threatened in Britain during the Great Depression. In the US, Roosevelt reversed the long-standing posture of government that treated organized labour as an egregious pressure group disrupting the free market. Section 7(a) of the Wagner Act (1935) enshrined the right of trade unions to bargain freely, positively encouraging an improvement in their negotiating position, the better to bolster wages.

There was plenty of awareness amongst liberals, therefore, that commercialism in an age of autarchy and class conflict was no longer, if it ever had been, a self-regulating system. A new macroeconomic uncertainty vitiated the microeconomic assumptions of classical political economy. The British economist John Maynard Keynes (1883–1946) opposed radical socialism as exalting 'the boorish proletariat above the bourgeois and the intelligentsia who, with whatever faults, are the quality in life and surely carry the seeds of all human advancement'.[44] But this was consistent with his sharp criticism of classical liberal nostrums in modern conditions. In 1937 he criticized classical economics by alluding to the uncertainty of a world where economic rationality was necessarily exposed to political uncertainty:

> the prospect of a European war is uncertain, or the price of copper and the rate of interest twenty years hence, or the obsolescence of a new invention, or the position of private wealth owners in the social system of 1970.... How do we manage in such circumstances to behave in a manner which saves our faces as rational economic men?... All these pretty, polite techniques, made for a well-panelled boardroom and a nicely regulated market are likely to collapse.[45]

For Keynes, in such conditions of uncertainty, the traditional reliance upon the market to equilibrate wages to full employment, or savings to investment opportunities, was no longer appropriate. Investors—fearful that war, revolutionary tumult, economic protectionism, or international disorder could devalue property at any time—hoarded their savings. Simply driving down workers' wages would not sufficiently restore bourgeois confidence. As investors chose strategies of ultra-caution for fear of losing their shirt, the economy stagnated and unemployment remained stubbornly high. Such uncertainty, Keynes argued, justified statist measures to interfere with capitalism so as to preserve commercial civil society. Specifically, he favoured heavy state expenditure to create employment and boost demand during recession, such expenditure to come from surpluses built up during times of boom.

Keynes was an authoritative voice in the 1930s, but his theories did not win general acceptance. Nonetheless, a rough and ready semi-Keynesianism was applied pragmatically in the Atlantic democracies to deal with the Depression: cheap money and generous welfare in Britain, public works and regulation in the US. In both countries, constitutional arrangements allowed for strong executive action without imperilling parliamentarianism. The ignominious collapse of the Labour government in 1931 permitted a Conservative-dominated National government, its healthy share of the vote further magnified by the first-past-the-post electoral system, to govern stably and decisively for the rest of the decade on a 'doctor's mandate'. Roosevelt, in office from 1930, markedly expanded the scope of presidential prerogatives and Federal powers, and by freely admitting, even talking up, the gravity of the crisis (one quarter of Americans were unemployed), justified Congress in adopting 'emergency' measures as necessary for the very preservation of 'modern civilisation'.[46]

\* \* \*

The stability of liberal constitutionalism and bourgeois civil society in the Atlantic democracies highlighted the historic miscalculation behind the establishment of the Comintern in 1919. The bourgeoisie in the West were not as a whole turning away from constitutional liberalism, and the proletariat were not poised to establish a 'dictatorship' with no use for parliamentarianism. Moscow's turn to the Popular Front, however, arose from calculations other than a reasoned re-evaluation of the strength of bourgeois liberty. Though the bald assertion by Communists before 1934 that the bourgeoisie had deserted liberalism had always been parti-pris, their subsequent attempt to embrace the middle classes via Popular Frontism was contrary to the plain fact that classical liberalism was nowhere in the ascendant. Indeed, in countries where working-class or peasant-based threats to the current distribution of property were strong, the bourgeoisie was more than ever inclined to bolt from its allegiance to constitutionalism, at least in times of crisis. The Czechoslovak liberal politician Edvard Beneš, writing in exile in 1940, recognized that the danger of Communism, directed as it was against 'middle-class political democracy', had accelerated the desertion of 'conservative bourgeois elements' from the cause of civil and political liberty. But he divined an even more fundamental explanation for their fickleness:

> The middle classes realized that political democracy, carried to its logical conclusion, could lead to social and economic democracy, and therefore began to see in the authoritarian regimes salvation from a social revolution of the working and peasant classes.[47]

It did not require immediate threat of revolution to undermine bourgeois confidence in democracy, though capitulation to outright dictatorship usually required some presentiment of popular upheaval.

## THE SECOND WORLD WAR

The determination of the sated powers of Britain, France, and America to control their captive markets helped provoke moves on the part of the revisionist powers of Italy, Germany, and Japan to seize empires by force. Both Japan and Germany looked hungrily at the vast Soviet Union and its periphery as 'living space'. From the official Communist point of view, Popular Frontism was not so much an attempt to win over a progressive bourgeoisie, but rather a means by which to approach the elites of the liberal Great Powers for the purposes of alliance to defend the integrity of the Soviet Union. Of course, it was not only the liberal powers that could so be treated with. On 23 August 1939, Russia and Germany concluded a non-aggression pact, which secretly divided eastern Europe between German and Russian 'spheres of influence'.

Britain, America, and France were deeply concerned by the retreat of constitutional liberalism back to within its pre-1848 borders. The rise of dictatorial regimes outside western Europe, with their modern apparatuses of state and congenial connections with corporate capitalists, were far more independent of the restraints of civil society than had ever been the case for authoritarian monarchies of the nineteenth century. The democracies feared that a bellicose response to the fascist powers would only increase their own domestic impulse to militaristic authoritarianism. America, consequently, was fearfully isolationist. Much of its political opinion—Republican and progressive Democrat—was instinctively suspicious of the deleterious impact of foreign policy on the domestic polity. The Senate Inquiry into the Munitions Industry in 1934–6 (the Nye Committee) pointed to the dangerous influence of militarization on the economy and society:

> any close associations between munitions and supply companies on the one hand and the service departments on the other hand, of the kind which existed in Germany before the World War, constitutes an unhealthy alliance in that it brings into being a self-interested political power which operates in the name of patriotism and satisfies interests which are, in large part, purely selfish...such associations are an inevitable part of militarism, and are to be avoided in peacetime at all costs.[48]

Three Neutrality Acts passed by Congress from 1935 to 1937, together with the 1934 Johnson Act, served to deprive Britain and France of US funds for rearming in the face of the revisionist powers. Britain and France had to make do with short rations, particularly as they also feared disrupting their global trade networks, within and outside their empires, by prematurely diverting resources to the military. They chose to appease rather than rush to arms.

In March 1938, Germany was permitted by Britain and France to annex Austria to the Reich (the Anschluss). By the 1938 Munich Agreement, Britain and France allowed Germany to take over the German-speaking Sudetenland of Czechoslovakia. Winston Churchill, leader of the anti-appeasement Tories in Britain, was in Parliament suitably cutting about Chamberlain's diplomatic 'triumph' in avoiding war with Germany over the Sudetenland:

> No doubt they [the Czechs] are only a small Democratic state; no doubt they have an army only two or three times as large as ours; no doubt they have a munitions supply only three times as great as that of Italy; but still, they are a virile people, they have their rights, they have their treaty rights, they have a line of fortresses, and they have a strongly manifested will to live feely.[49]

But for Chamberlain, Munich was not so much an expedient to buy time for the building up of military capacity as an opportunity to roll back militarism by putting 'an end to the horrible nightmare of the present armament race'.[50] Britain, indeed, was far from militarized. Negotiating with the Soviet Union in 1939,

British diplomats offered only two divisions immediately for a European war. The French, in contrast, offered 110 divisions and the USSR 120.[51]

When Hitler finally invaded Poland on 1 September 1939, Britain and France declared war on what they condemned as militaristic 'Prusso-Nazism'.[52] Anxious to avoid the militarization characteristic of the fascist powers as evidently corrosive of bourgeois civil society, Britain and France had planned to contain Germany behind a naval blockade and the defensive Maginot Line. They would deploy their superior economic resources to build up a massive weight of men and materiel. After a few years, Britain and France, their commercial civil societies fully mobilized for war, would be ready to advance inexorably against the German front.[53] The highly militarized society of Germany, however, had clearly produced a far better combat soldiery available for immediate operations in 1940. The German Blitzkrieg defeated French and British forces with embarrassing ease. As France fell, Marshal Philippe Pétain and General Maxime Weygand warned the government of a new Commune taking over Paris if peace and order were not quickly secured.[54] They were authorized to establish a regime committed to accommodating victorious Germany, and they took the opportunity to reconstruct France on national-authoritarian lines, cleansed of the influence of socialists, Communists, and Jews.

On 22 June 1941, Germany attacked Russia in a self-declared race-war of annihilation and enslavement. That the populace of the Soviet Union rallied to the country's defence was only rational. While Soviet tyranny was at least developmental in that it aimed to strengthen the human and material resources of the state, and promised an eventual rise in living standards for the bulk of the population, Germany offered nothing but slavery, absolute impoverishment, and depopulation. Through suffering terrible losses, Russian resistance was from the outset stiffer than that offered by the West, and within a year its capacity to destroy the Nazi war machine was evident.

The Nazis, of course, were especially bent on Judeocide. The 'planning intelligentsia' bureaucracy of the Third Reich rationalized genocide as a means to eliminate the desperately poor pre-industrial handicraft sector in eastern Europe, disproportionately Jewish, so as to clear space (*Lebensraum*) for the consolidation of a prosperous bourgeois middle class with a stake in the Nazi New Order.[55] Still, the murder of the Jews went beyond any social engineering. All that the Nazis found repugnant about both bourgeois and proletarian culture—the money- grubbing and cosmopolitanism of the bourgeoisie, the sectional class-consciousness and unpatriotic internationalism of the proletariat—they projected onto an abstraction of the Jewish 'race'. But this was only one aspect of a fanatically irrational hated of the Jews qua Jews.

Authoritarianism allowed the state to mobilize massively industrial resources for military ends, and it permitted the executive government uninhibited prerogatives of executive decision. Dictatorship had proved its worth most spectacularly in the 1930s with Germany's breakneck rearmament and pursuit of a highly successful and cynically nimble diplomacy of opportunism. Once war became a gruelling slugging match, however, the weaknesses of capitalism within a totalitarian structure came to the fore. While the German and Japanese dictatorships fostered a culture of hierarchical and fanatical militarism to produce highly skilled combat soldiers, the democracies, and especially the United States, relied upon mass-produced artillery, aircraft, tanks, and mechanized transport turned out by vast industrial conglomerations. The defeat of the Axis powers in 1945 showed up the limitations of traditional, hierarchical, authoritarian militarism, and revealed the potential of the US model of intensive economic mobilization to equip a highly mobile and strongly protected citizen army. The Second World War demonstrated the superiority of this new type of military organization.

'Corporatism', in the sense of a close connection between big business and the state, was common to both democracies and Axis dictatorships in the interwar period, and the Second World War ramped it up again for both sides. However, in the democratic West, civil society remained vibrant, acting as a control on both the state and on monopoly or near-monopoly corporations. The example of the Axis clearly showed that where oligarchic big business and the state collaborated at the expense of civil society, both tended towards irrationality and inefficiency. The German military ham-fistedly interfered in purely economic decisions, while corporations were slow to rationalize and centralize the production of war materiel. The German war machine relied upon loot, extorted or simply stolen from conquered Europe, rather than the efficient mobilization of civil society. German tribute derived from occupation amounted to about 40 per cent of its entire fiscal income. Of this foreign income, about 42 per cent was derived from France alone.[56]

The democracies, in contrast, were able to combine the efficiencies of a competitive civil society with a strong political and civilian system of regulation, and a robust fiscal framework. Economic war mobilization in the US, for example, operated through a system of state-ordered production carried out by private firms. Thirteen huge companies were in receipt of $3.9 billion of public money, or 43 per cent of total government investment.[57] Within four years, America's industrial production, already the largest in the world, had doubled, and it produced almost two-thirds of all Allied military equipment.[58] For its part, in terms of percentage of GDP directly applied to war work, the British economy was the most intensively mobilized of all belligerents. The Allies, clearly, squeezed much more out of their civil societies. This was the benefit of democratic consensus, as the British General Templar lectured a German audience in occupied Detmold in November 1945:

> A thoroughly democratic system might not be superficially as efficient as an authoritarian one. The fact remains that if it is given time to develop, it produces the spirit from which it is possible to organize the nation for any event, and what is extremely important, to achieve a far greater degree of fundamental political stability.[59]

In 1956 the sociologist C. Wright Mills drew attention to the significance of America's triumph as presaging the victory of bourgeois civil society over oligarchic militarism. The dictatorships of Europe, where a 'fixed ruling class' subordinated capitalists, could not resist America's 'historic thrust of commerce and industry' when finally 'industrialized violence came to decide history'.[60] It was the industrial nature of modern warfare that determined victory for bourgeois civil society even in the military sphere. Japanese and German hyper-militarism had certainly produced better combat soldiers, but America produced simply overwhelming quantities of materiel. Capitalist militarism proved able to outpace atavistic militarism.

The Soviet Union's population had fought with grim determination against invaders bent on destroying their very means of civilization. Popular will-to-victory super-charged the planned economy, blasting away bureaucratic impediments. War proved to be an economic shot of adrenaline. It was only with the onset of fighting that the new industrial centres in the Urals, Siberia, and Kazakhstan began to produce heavily, and that the high-quality weapons developed in the 1930s—such as the T-34 tank, the Yak-1 fighter, and the Pe-2 light bomber—went into mass production. Resources were tightly controlled from the centre, and the percentage of national income spent on the military rose from 15 per cent in 1940 to 55 per cent in 1942. Despite a potentially crippling loss of industrial areas to the invader, Soviet military production exceeded its pre-war level as early as mid-1942.[61] The centralized command economy, vitalized by patriotic mobilization that filled in for market discipline, proved extremely efficient at churning out huge quantities of quality, standardized military hardware. The Soviet Union's very success in the competition of arms, however, locked it even more deeply into a pathologically militarized economic model.

In the cauldron of war, Hitler managed to make his ideology real and relevant for the German people in a way that it had never been during peace. By waging race-war and genocide, the Nazi elites made credible their insistence that defeat would mean racial extermination being turned back on the aggressors. Particularly in the last two years of the war, German soldiers with increasing desperation accepted the regime's characterization of the conflict as zero-sum. The future of European civilization—confronted by Communism, Slavic barbarism, Jewish perversion and vengeance, and Anglo-American plutocracy—seemed to be at stake.[62] The end of war suddenly exposed the unreality of this pernicious Nazi ideology: the conquerors of Germany (both American-led and Soviet) proved not to be bent upon annihilation.[63] The Western forces, and even the Red Army with all its fire of vengeance, were a truly liberating force. Helen Lewis, a Jewish survivor of the Shoah, recalled her salvation in Poland: 'The door opened and there stood a very young and very small Russian soldier who simply said, "Germani kaput". I flung myself at him and threw my arms around his neck. He looked bewildered and slightly embarrassed. Perhaps he did not understand that he was my liberator.'[64]

The wartime alliance that defeated Hitler was a 'Popular Front' writ large. In August 1941, Roosevelt and Churchill had proclaimed, in the Atlantic Charter, a common intention to build a post-war order based upon the principles of prosperity, peace, democracy, and self-determination. With the January 1942 declaration of the United Nations, the Soviet Union committed itself to this vision. As Nazi resistance entered into its death throes, Roosevelt, Churchill, and Stalin met at the Crimean resort of Yalta, from 4 to 11 February 1945, to plan for this new dispensation. From here, the 'Big Three' issued a 'Declaration on Liberated Europe', promising Europeans the right to determine their own futures through sovereign democratic institutions. Communists were now committed to 'bourgeois-democratic' revolution in authoritarian capitalist countries, to be carried through by all 'antifascist' forces, and resulting in constitutionalism and a free market ('bourgeois') combined with welfarism, strong trade unions, and a dirigiste economic policy ('democratic'). As a demonstration that new 'socialist revolutions', replacing parliamentarianism with 'proletarian dictatorship', were off the agenda, Stalin wound up the Comintern in 1943.

## CONCLUSION

Hannah Arendt, a German Jewish refugee from Nazism, reflected on the 'origins of totalitarianism'. She argued that traditional bourgeois liberty, based upon the functional division between commerce in civil society and political elites in government, had come under strain as business increasingly pressurized the state to protect and conquer foreign markets.[65] Big business struck bilateral deals with government in a corporate framework, and parliamentarianism was sidelined. Chafing still at the demands of organized labour and the remnants of liberal constitutionalism, the German bourgeoisie fatefully attached itself to the demotic politics of Nazism. In so doing, however, it destroyed the very basis of its own security: 'the German bourgeoisie staked everything on the Hitler movement and aspired to rule with the help of the mob, but...won a Pyrrhic victory; the mob proved quite capable of taking care of politics by itself and liquidated the bourgeoisie along with all other classes and institutions.'[66] Arendt's conclusion was that the attempt to subordinate entirely the political sphere to the imperatives of capital accumulation instrumentalized individuals, destroying their intrinsic status as humans, and at the extreme rendering them surplus and expendable.

Arendt's 'totalitarian' model was widely influential in the post-war era.[67] The crisis of the interwar period was widely attributed to big business closely allying to state elites and pursuing a strategy (in conditions of breakdown of international trade and regional autarchy) of aggressive annexation of markets. It would be wrong, however, to deny the sheer irrationalism of totalitarianism in this period. Highly ideological governments opposed on principle the mutual autonomy of civil society and state. In the Soviet Union, it is true, public welfare was ruthlessly subordinated to industrialization, but in the absence of a bourgeoisie the dynamic was rather different. The Communist state force-marched much of the peasantry into an urban industrial workforce, and on this quicksand pedestal struggled to keep its footing, lashing out against internal enemies, more imaginary or potential than real, to keep its balance. In the capitalist countries, the Great Depression had a profound effect on both bourgeois liberty and proletarian democracy. Every nation protected its markets against imports whilst seeking to promote its own exports. Competitive currency devaluation became common recourse in a race to beggar-thy-neighbour. No longer free agents in international trade, businesses lined up behind their own 'power-state'. As economies shrank or stagnated, class struggle became a zero-sum game. If wages and profits could not expand simultaneously, it became crucial for political state power to arbitrate between labour and capital. All this meant that fervent identification with the nation state was crucial for interest-group lobbying and individual security. To be sure, patriots could identify with established liberties, and Popular Frontism attempted to capitalize on this. But there was every incentive to ramp up one's nationalist chauvinism, and this was effectively demonstrated by ostentatious contempt for traitors dividing the nation on party-political or class lines, and hatred for 'racial' minorities. The doors of government swung open to race-warriors. The Western democracies saw the threat of race-war ideology and, when allied with Soviet Russia, the liberal model of bourgeois civil society proved (eventually) to be more formidable than the ultra-militarism of Germany and Japan.

# 12

# Cold War and the Fear of Subversion

Following the armistice of 1918 in Europe, the personnel of the 'permanent state', inherited from the pre-war order, had remained in post. They included civil servants, military officers, police, judges, senior industrialists, eminent academics, press barons with their favoured reporters, and landlords. Even in defeated countries swept by revolution, the new governments had generally protected the ranks of the permanent state as indispensable to social order. They were considered too powerful to trifle with. These strata were never reconciled with democracy, and their entrenched influence corroded parliamentary constitutionalism and colluded with the rise of dictatorship. Thereafter, much of the permanent state in every country overrun by Germany collaborated with the occupation authorities and their domestic allies. With the destruction of German power from 1944, collaborators were exposed to a whirlwind of popular vengeance. The moral legitimacy of the permanent state had collapsed, and while the Liberation governments might temper the people's rage, they could not entirely stifle it. The subsequent purge of Fascists and collaborators in France, Italy, the Low Countries, and Central-Eastern Europe was, as Stanley G. Payne puts it, the 'final phase' of an acute domestic conflict that had wracked these countries from the early years of the century.[1] Across formerly German-occupied Europe, 2 to 3 percent of the population, mostly bourgeois 'educated adult males', were purged. A fairly small minority paid with their lives but many were simply ejected from positions of responsibility. There were certainly innocent victims. But, as István Deák observes, 'Those who were punished for good reason far outnumbered those who were punished unjustly.'[2] Growing disquiet at informal score-settling, as well as concern that the Communist-led Resistance was picking off its political opponents, meant that quite a few collaborators were able to ride out the tempest and remain in post. As the Cold War developed, moreover, Western intelligence services moved to protect anti-Communist assets almost regardless of their past crimes. But there's no doubt that the main strength and prestige of the reactionary permanent state had been smashed. This was a much more thoroughgoing revolution than that which had followed the First World War. It crucially undermined the ramparts of capitalist militarism.

Dismantling of 'cartel capitalism' was a priority for the conquerors of Germany and Japan. Allied armies of occupation carefully monitored new constitutions built upon pre-existing traditions of parliamentarianism. There was quite a degree of agreement between capitalist America and Communist Russia about how Germany was to be treated to avoid a recrudesce of militarism. In short—controlled revolution: denazification, demilitarization, decartelization, and decentralization, as agreed at an Allied summit at Potsdam in July and August 1945. This strategy reflected an agreement that monopoly capitalism was politically corrupting. The aim, as the American Occupation command in Germany reported in January 1946, was to diffuse 'political and economic power' from oligarchies and corporations to a 'broad popular base' on which to build 'a free and democratic society'.[3] So, for example, the four occupying powers in Germany (America, Britain, France, USSR) divided up the German cartels, notably the sprawling I. G. Farben corporation, and reorganized the coal and steel industries. The United States oversaw alone a similar programme in defeated Japan.[4] The holding companies that dominated Japanese industry, the 'Zaibatsu' ('money clique'), were broken up. The reasoning was set forth with commendable clarity by Corin D. Edwards, head of the US mission on Japanese Combines:

> The purpose is not to reform the Japanese social system in the light of American economic preferences, nor even in the interests of the Japanese people themselves; it is to bring about a psychological and institutional demilitarization.... Japan's industry has been under the control of a few great combines, supported and strengthened by the Japanese government. The concentration of control has encouraged the persistence of semi-feudal relations between employer and employee, held down wages, and blocked the development of labour unions. It has discouraged the launching of independent business ventures and thereby retarded the development of a Japanese middle class. In the absence of such groups there has been no economic basis for independence in politics nor much development of the conflicting interests and democratic and humanitarian sentiments which elsewhere serve as counterweights to military designs. Moreover, the low wages and concentrated profits of the Zaibatsu system have limited the domestic market and intensified the importance of exports, and have given incentive to Japanese imperialism.... To break the system which produces such results and to create the groups which in democratic countries provide resistance to the capture of government by military zealots are the central purposes of American policy towards the Zaibatsu.[5]

Though Edwards was speaking specifically of Japan, much the same logic underpinned the reconstruction of occupied Europe. Cartelized, militarized capitalism was forcibly restructured in Germany and Japan, in an unconscious confirmation of the critique of 'monopoly capitalism' as argued by the socialists of the Second International. The intention behind this revolution from above was to destroy the power of oligarchic 'monopoly capitalism' and to replace it with a civil society, comprising a middle class and labour movement, able to resist overweening state power and sustain pacific democracy. This did not mean a retreat by the state as such. Rather, the state was to be disentangled from oligarchies with anti-democratic and imperialist interests.

Particularly as the Cold War geared up, America softened the rigour of its assault on 'cartel capitalism'. Corporations were reprieved or allowed to regroup, trade unions were reined in, and very many Nazi, fascist, and imperial eminences were allowed to remain in post, or even recruited as advisors on the Russian menace. However, democracy had been implanted. Crucially, Parliament was successfully reinstituted as the centre of sovereignty. Whilst the interwar dictatorships had substantially bypassed customary fiscal channels to cooperate directly with the corporations, the refashioned state was fiscally independent of the oligarchies, and relatively dependent upon wage earners. This re-weaving of the tax threads linking state to civil society owed to much improved tax administration, pioneered by the democracies during the war, and cemented by the introduction of 'Pay as You Earn' (PAYE), or 'payroll' tax.[6] The corporation and the civil service 'permanent state' persisted, but consensual governance was now clearly eased, not hindered, by the existence of constitutionalism and a wide suffrage.

## CONSUMERIST SOCIETY

The US had gone into the war with a GNP of $91 billion and came out of it with a GNP of $166 billion. The country's belief in itself reached new heights. American political opinion was confident that its society had succeeded in balancing liberty, security, and efficiency. America's signal advantage was widely acknowledged as being the historic absence of a formative feudal or aristocratic *ancien regime*. Socialism had never gained traction, for lack of an oppressive and intertwined oligarchy of state, aristocracy, and bourgeoisie systematically excluding the working class from political and social influence. Liberalism, in turn, was never organized as a conscious, class-specific tendency, suspicious of political democracy; it was simply the 'American Way of Life'.[7] This careful distinction of private enterprise from any class designation was a staple of early American Cold War propaganda, which contrasted the pre-war European experience of 'cartel' capitalism to the American model in which the consumer, rather than any producer interest, whether organized labour or capitalist, was predominant.[8]

Allied victory destroyed the aggressive revisionist powers of Germany, Japan, and Italy. America hoped to maintain this balance indefinitely by coordinating an open international-currency trade system, precisely to obviate the division of the world into economic blocs. Pre-war tariffs in Europe had raised the cost of living for domestic consumers to benefit industries seeking to grab export markets. This had encouraged revisionist attempts to grab territory. (The US had also been highly protectionist, but exported proportionately less, and invested mainly within its own hemisphere in which it was unchallengeably hegemonic). Henry Morgenthau, US Secretary of the Treasury from 1934 to 1945, explained the interwar disaster by reference to 'currency disorders' spreading 'from land to land, destroying the basis for international trade and international investment and even international faith'. The consequent 'bewilderment and bitterness become the breeders of fascism, and, finally, of war'.[9] Consequently, the Bretton Woods conference of 1944 established a new international monetary regime, and the Havana conference of 1948 a new international trade regime. Post-war, tariffs were steadily reduced. Freed from pressure to secure foreign markets and supplies aggressively, there was a dramatic European shift towards a United States model of economic involution, in which markets were primarily to be found at home rather than abroad. America now promoted the spread to Europe of 'cheap production for mass consumption', as John Foster Dulles, future Secretary of State, put it in 1947.[10] The pressure to keep a cap on domestic wages to subsidise exports was sharply reduced.

Governments were pleased to see wages growing, as they were the main driver of demand, and positively encouraged labour to organize so as to prevent capitalist enterprises driving wages down. In Europe, trade unions were legalized, influenced governments, and represented workers in wage negotiations. From the mid-1950s, they even negotiated with governments on behalf of wage earners as a class. In the United States, trade unions rarely had such power, but corporations in receipt of government contracts were required to respect 'workplace contractualism' by which workers' rights were specified and wages and conditions consensually negotiated.[11] (In Japan, workers were generally secure in employment, but until the 1960s public social security was minimal. This introduced a structural bias towards a high ratio of savings, low domestic consumption relative to wages, at least until the 1970s, and a model, anomalous during the post-war boom, of economic growth based upon exports.)

There remained a distinction between American 'consumer sovereignty' and European 'social citizenship'. But rebuilding the shattered European social edifice with home-made bricks allowed for a deep-rooted domestication there of commercial civil society as the basis of free constitutionalism. This was in stark contrast to the years after the Great War, when the individualist homilies of Wilsonianism had failed to speak to powerful particularisms of class, ethnic, and religious group identities. Partly inspired by the evidently effective *dirigisme* of the war economies, indigenous Liberation movements—Popular Fronts of patriots, Communists, socialists, liberals, Protestants, and Catholics—agreed on the practicality and desirability of full employment, welfare, labour rights, and high wages as the antidote to the destructiveness of expansionist militarism on the one hand, and a laissez-faire economic liberalism tolerant of massive unemployment on the other.

Labour-led Britain pioneered the 'cradle to grave' welfare state, promising 'social provision against rainy days, coupled with economic policies to reduce rainy days to a minimum'.[12] Indeed, not a few socialists believed that the decline of laissez-faire and the rise of a managerial middle class amounted to a process of transition from capitalism itself. Capitalism would negate itself not by collapse, but by the interaction of production and democracy. For the British Labour Party intellectual C. A. R. Crosland, 'statism' was displacing capitalism, partly because the 'bourgeoisie is no longer as self-confident as in its heyday'. It had lost 'its unquestioning faith in itself and in capitalism', due to its 'bad conscience' in the face of social misery and the memory of the interwar slump.[13] Crosland hailed the democratic state taking over the rudder. It would be more accurate to say that the bourgeoisie were accommodating to a democratic order inclusive of the interests of wage labour, whilst rallying support for the preservation of a market system that rewarded their advantages in acquired and inherited attributes. In many European countries conservative forces gathered in Christian Democratic parties, of Catholic origin, that combined market economics with state direction and welfarism. Heterogeneous and often opportunist movements, the various shades of Christian Democracy, proved adept at building alliances by articulating the language of liberalism in terms respectful of strong conservative and particularist identities. They decoupled Christian Democracy from Catholic sectionalism: 'Protestants, trade unions, the middle classes and business were all to be part of the act.'[14] In time, they shifted from traditional defence of small property to praising the dynamism of large-scale businesses and fostering the 'new middle class' of professionals.[15] Moderate Social Democracy and liberal conservatism could generally alternate in power with no major upset. 'Bourgeois civil society' was artfully reconciled with 'proletarian democracy'.

The post-war consumerist order rested upon high and rising wages and a rapidly expanding wage-labour workforce. The percentage share of national income going to wage labour typically grew, mostly because many self-employed farmers and traders became wage earners, but also because of a shift of wealth from capital to labour. Workers were keen to work long and hard for wages that allowed themselves full citizenship as consumers, able to buy the good things of life on the market. As the leftist leader of the American United Auto Workers put it in 1945, they wanted a 'balanced economy of full employment—full production—full consumption'.[16] Pay bargaining was often nationwide for industries, thus weakening the market position of enterprises that had hitherto relied upon their paying below average wages to stay in business. As Armstrong, Glyn, and Harrison argue, 'real wage rises were a product of the competitive process whereby more efficient firms drove out weaker rivals to obtain both labour and markets, which the less efficient producers would otherwise have hung on to'.[17]

This competitive labour market, of course, also benefited the salaried white-collar and professional middle class, who were expanding rapidly in number and displacing the old self-employed petite bourgeoisie. The 'embourgeoisified' 'upper lower class', as French writer Maurice Crouzet put it in 1970, comprised the higher echelons of public administration, business executives, doctors, lawyers, and various liberal professions. This class took pains, Crouzet said:

> to distinguish itself above all from manual workers and low-salaried employees (many of whom are also white-collar workers). It is this class which strives most to procure higher education for its children in the hope of seeing them become part of the 'establishment'. It is also the class most given to expensive vacations and distant voyages, and which seeks 'prestige' homes with elegant furniture.... Because they enjoy high salaries, its members are not concerned with social inequality (on the contrary, they seek to distinguish themselves from those with lower incomes), but with the difficulties of social climbing and the social standing for which they are so avid. They do not oppose the system of private property, and show little interest in politics.[18]

In an economy of mass production, relatively immobile capital, full employment, a strong bargaining position for labour, and high wages, competitiveness required intense technical innovation to raise productivity. The middle class, therefore, became increasingly professionalized, formally qualified, and 'meritocratic'. University-level education and certification increased massively.

In the Communist world, the technical intelligentsia were relatively privileged, but nonetheless their incomes were pegged by political fiat to that of the industrial workforce, the real social base of the system in so far as it had one. In the capitalist West, free-market competition for skills rewarded the meritocracy more generously, and salaries to a considerable extent displaced returns on property ownership as the basis for bourgeois civil society. But the industrial and service job markets were so expansive, as direct agricultural production commodified and shed labour, that both worker and bourgeois could enjoy rapidly rising incomes as well as security, and social inequality declined.

For the first time in Europe, following the interwar example of the United States, the wage-earning majority provided a buoyant and rich market for other than basic goods. In 1950 wages in the United States were about three times higher than those in Europe and the average Western European family spent more than half its income on subsistence. But with the dramatic increase of real wages in the next two decades, trebling in West Germany and the Benelux countries, and growing even faster in Italy, European wage earners became a formidable consumer market in their own right. The post-war boom was based upon a new wave of industrial revolution, as consumer markets in services, automobiles, white-goods (electrical fridges, cookers, etcetera) and infrastructure, all multiplied. With a surging domestic market, the economic basis for inter-imperial competition—frantic search for export, commodity, and investment markets abroad—was proportionately weakened. The old European model of low wages and aggressive export orientation was displaced by a developmental path, pioneered in America, based upon high wages and the expansion of domestic markets.

## COMMUNIZED EASTERN-CENTRAL EUROPE

Since the German attack on the Soviet Union, Communist parties had everywhere supported the widest possible anti-fascist Popular Fronts. In line with this, the Soviet Union seemed prepared to drop its Leninist opposition to parliamentary democracy. Stalin towards the end of the war confessed that 'Revolution is no longer necessary everywhere.... Yes, socialism is possible even under an English king.'[19] The French Communist Party, the largest single party in the country, entered into a governmental coalition of Resistance parties from 1945. Maurice Thorez, the party's leader, in November 1946 insisted that such alliances were not designed to undermine parliamentarianism:

> It is clear that the Communist Party, as a member of the government working within the framework of a parliamentary system which it has itself helped to establish, must adhere strictly to the democratic programme by which it has won the support of the mass of the people. Despite rare exceptions which confirm the rule, the process of democracy throughout the world...permits us, in the march of Socialism, to foresee other roads than those travelled by the Russian Communists. In any case, the road is necessarily different in each country.[20]

The road was certainly different in countries directly liberated by the Red Army. Here the large-scale 'monopoly capitalist' bourgeoisie were determined by the

Soviet occupation authorities to have proven themselves ineradicably reactionary, and they were to be dismantled as a class. However, Stalin rejected the designation of 'Dictatorship of the Proletariat' for the new Eastern European regimes. They were, instead, 'People's Democracies', based upon an alliance between workers, peasants, and the urban lower middle class, who had become unified in their opposition to interwar and wartime regimes, and were now open to a steady, non-convulsive advance towards socialism. The very example and solidarity provided by the Soviet Union precluded any need for a reprise of the tumult of the Russian Revolution. Social civil war, on the Leninist model, could be avoided.[21] The Czechoslovakian Communist Party spoke of a 'specific Czechoslovak road to socialism', not through the 'dictatorship of the proletariat' or soviets (worker-dominated popular councils), but through Parliament and via 'national and democratic' consensus.[22]

The elimination of 'hostile' class forces in Eastern Europe took on its own momentum, however. Communist leader Walter Ulbricht, on re-establishing local administration in the Soviet Zone of East Germany in May 1945, initially stressed the importance of finding bourgeois and SPD collaborators: 'It's quite clear—it's got to look democratic, but we must have everything in our control.'[23] As a NKVD intelligence operative recalled, Soviet authorities carefully vetted national Communists to ensure that they were 'suitable material to carry out the satellization of Germany from inside'.[24] One American official, surveying Germany in 1946, opined (crudely) that opportunists, youthful trade-union militants, nationalists, and militarists, and most importantly 'the league of the desperate', crushed by economic crisis, could be attracted to the Communist line. The religious, peasantry, most Social Democrats, and 'the propertied classes', however, were the bulwark of resistance to Communism. Instinctive anti-Communists, he argued, were in the vast majority, particularly given the 'ancient popular prejudice against the Slavs...fanned into fanaticism by the Nazis' and powerfully confirmed by 'the conduct of the Russian soldatesca in Germany'.[25] From the other side of the ideological divide also came recognition of the forces ranged against Communist penetration of government and society. Władysław Gomułka warned his (Communist) Polish Workers' Party in May 1945 that while 'the majority of the working class' supported the government, 'the peasantry and the intellectuals wavered'.[26] This was putting it mildly.

A turning point came with 'Marshall Aid'. The European Recovery Program, unveiled in June 1947 by the US Secretary of State, George Marshall, provided American financial aid, amounting to a total of $13.2 billion, to fourteen countries by mid-1952. The eastern Soviet bloc was ordered by the USSR to refuse Marshall Aid, which the Soviets seem to have seen as a deliberate ramp designed to revive bourgeois and propertied civil society as the foundation for anti-Communist political opposition.[27] Once the US made support of capitalist civil society a strategic priority with the Marshall Plan, any class seeking to maintain itself in Communist-run countries via a (legal) market was automatically defined as a potential fifth column, and their fate was sealed. The reaction to the Marshall Plan was the suppression of bourgeois civil society in eastern Europe.

Experience in eastern Europe wrote the 'textbook' strategy of Communization: 'subversion' by what became known as 'salami tactics'.[28] First, key ministries—notably those controlling the army, police, and foreign policy—were taken over by Communist ministers in a coalition government. The forces of the state could then be used to rig elections, intimidate opponents, force 'mergers' of independent workers' parties into the Communist fold, and finally to suppress all non-Communist-controlled parties. Nationalization of industry was a form of militarization, as Soviet elites braced themselves for yet another assault on Russia, and strove to mobilize the resources of the 'buffer zone'. Throughout Eastern Europe, between 1948 and 1952, a series of purges and show trials reshaped the national Communist leaderships, bringing their governments rigidly into line with Stalinist Russian objectives. Police forces and armies were integrated into the Soviet Union's command structure. Most satellite states introduced Soviet-style 'Five Year Plans' in 1949–50. About half of all investments directly served military purposes.[29]

Russia clearly saw the Marshall Plan as a turning point. In distributing huge sums of money under international aegis, Marshall Aid underpinned bourgeois property forms and bolstered wage labour in the face of Communist subversion. The exclusion of Communists from Western European governments—in the spring of 1947, Communist ministers were ousted from the coalition governments of France, Italy, and Belgium—was seen by the Russians as a quid pro quo required of countries receiving Marshall Aid. They believed that Communization of Eastern Europe was a proportionate riposte in kind. For the Russians, the destruction of bourgeois civil society in its sphere of influence was a natural response, an instrumentalization of social relations. 'Whoever occupies a territory also imposes on it his own social system,' as Stalin put it. 'Everyone imposes his own system as far as his army can reach.'[30] Fearing a resurgent bourgeois civil society supported by US 'imperialism', the Stalinist regimes of the Eastern bloc liquidated capitalism and petite-bourgeois production. Nationalization of industry destroyed the bourgeoisie, and collectivization succeeded in remoulding the peasantry, even if it did little for agricultural productivity.

Generally, the working class was given a position of relative privilege in Communist countries, certainly vis-à-vis the persecuted peasantry and socially eliminated bourgeoisie. The East German regime, for example, deprived workers of actual power and expected huge sacrifices of them, but it also privileged workers, protecting them from arbitrary dismissal, providing education and welfare facilities, and generally lauded them as the leading class.[31] Communized countries built a proletariat of industrial manual workers sucked in from the countryside. This fresh-minted proletariat functioned as the passive base for a European Communist bloc of states, organized into the 'Warsaw Pact', arrayed in hostile, armed defensiveness. In Russia and its buffer zone, the armed forces weighed upon society as a suffocating incubus.

Andrei Zhdanov, in his September 1947 'Two Camps' speech, laid out the principles of Soviet Cold War diplomacy. Whereas classical, pre-1935 'Leninism' had laid stress on the capitalist/socialist binary, Zhdanov now defined the fundamental division as between the 'imperialist and anti-democratic camp' and the 'anti-imperialist and democratic camp':

the Communists must support all truly patriotic elements who do not want their country dishonoured, and who want to fight against the enslavement of their motherland by foreign capital.... They must take up the banner of defence of the national independence and sovereignty of their countries... [and] stand on guard for a lasting peace and for people's democracy.[32]

Stalin, at the 19th Communist Party Congress in Russia on 14 October 1952, revisited the question of whether the 'bourgeoisie' were a progressive class, this time making defence of 'national sovereignty' against American 'interference' the defining issue. He argued that the bourgeoisie had now lost not only its democratic impetus, but even its national loyalty:

> the bourgeoisie itself... has become different, has essentially changed, has become more reactionary.... Earlier, the bourgeoisie presented themselves as liberal, they were for bourgeois democratic freedom and in that way gained popularity with the people. Now there is not one remaining trace of liberalism...... Earlier, the bourgeoisie... were for the rights and independence of nations... Now the bourgeoisie sell the rights and independence of their nations for dollars. The banner of national independence and national sovereignty has been thrown overboard. Without doubt, you, the representatives of the communist and democratic parties must raise this banner and carry it forward if you want to be patriots of your countries, if you want to be the leading powers of the nations. There is nobody else to raise it. (*Stormy applause.*)[33]

Popular Frontism remained intact insofar as there still existed, in Communist theory, a progressive national bourgeoisie in the West (its analogue in the Warsaw Pact, of course, having been eliminated). Communist parties were licensed by Moscow to build class alliances and vaunt national patriotism if so doing promised to enhance the standing of the Soviet Union and undermine that of the United States.

## 'REDS UNDER THE BED'

American thought regarding democracy, constitutionalism, and the transition to modernity was profoundly shaped by the triumph of Communism in Eastern Europe (and in China in 1949). Generalizing from the Communist Popular Front tactics and the salami-style take-over in Eastern Europe, the term 'subversion' became central to American understanding of Communism. It was perceived as a threat that infiltrated democratic forms, boring from within rather than confronting them head on. Philip Selznick, professor of law and society at Berkeley, defined Communist subversion as:

> the manipulation of social institutions for alien ends, this manipulation being conducted covertly.... It is this type of subversion which is meant when fear is expressed of the effect of communism in the schools, in the labor movement, and in liberal organizations. Such activities, and ultimate overthrow of the government, are of course related, but concern for the integrity of the institutions themselves leads us to seek modes of self-defense long before any clear and present danger to established authority is demonstrable.[34]

Within the borders of the democratic USA, subversion was countered, as President Harry Truman (1884–1972) reassured his public in April 1950, by 'the Federal Bureau of Investigation and other security forces, through prosecutions in the courts by the Department of Justice, through our federal employee loyalty program, and in many other ways'.[35] This official surveillance was the background to the red-baiting persecutions of McCarthyism. Many American anti-Communism experts were former party members, who were well aware of how Communists manipulated broad Popular Fronts for democracy for party interests. As one such, Sidney Hook, recalled, 'Communists were not harmless heretics but really dangerous conspirators, serving the interests of a foreign power intent upon destroying democracy.' Therefore, 'certain measures were taken' in the 1950s 'to bar members of the Communist Party' as unfit not only for government posts but equally 'the commanding posts of trade unions and other cultural organizations of a democracy'.[36]

'Subversion' was perhaps the keyword of the American cold war. It conjured up fears of outright espionage, military or diplomatic infiltration of vulnerable countries, and the exploitation of popular discontent with disingenuously populist slogans. Even more insidiously, 'subversion' meant the exploitation of credulous 'fellow travellers' in ostensibly democratic front organizations, labour unions, and even non-Communist political parties. None of these tactics were imagined—Communists pursued them all—but in America in particular, where even socialism was a rather strange and alien doctrine, there was a near-obsessive suspicion that 'subversion' could reverse the values of free institutions. By this view, constitutionalism and civil liberties were not sufficient of themselves to protect against Communism. Also required was vigilance to sweep out infestations of 'reds', and strenuous promotion of the 'individualistic free market' to drown out Communist siren calls. Even a constitutionalist society could not be said to be safe for democracy, unless it was culturally sensitized to the threat of covert Communists, and stiffened for the task of exposing and quarantining them. America, thus, was keen to promote its values abroad.

A striking example was the American intervention in the 1949 Italian general election. Palmiro Togliatti, General Secretary of the Italian Communist Party (PCI) from 1927 to 1964, had at the end of the Second World War espoused a theory of 'democracy of a new type', which involved the restoration of bourgeois democracy with a significant governmental input from representatives of the working class. This looked like sophisticated 'subversion' to the US, and its government feared that the bromides of Italian Communists might result in them winning power democratically, presumably signalling the last free election for that country. The State Department baulked at violating the sovereignty of a democratic state, so the National Security Council turned to the newly created Central Intelligence Agency (CIA). With a war chest of $10 million, it established a Special Procedures Group (SPG) that set about organizing a systematic campaign of interference in domestic Italian politics; a kind of 'counter-subversion'. SPG activities included the provision of food, speeches by congressional, business, and labour leaders, and a threat from President Truman to withhold aid to any Italian government that included

Communist ministers. An orchestrated letter-writing campaign by Italian Americans put pressure on families in the old country not to vote Communist. Funds were disbursed to centrist Italian political parties, and an alternative workers' party fostered. Forged documents and letters ostensibly originating from the Communist Party were circulated along with other black propaganda and disinformation. The Christian Democrats duly won 48.5 per cent of the vote and gained an overall majority of forty seats.[37]

Italian Communists, under pressure from the 'two-camps' rhetoric of late Stalinism, attacked the Italian government as stooges of American power. However, it became increasingly evident that while Christian Democracy in Italy was exclusionary and often repressive towards the left, it did, in fact, express the governing will of a stabilized democratic system. After President Nikita Khrushchev's Secret Speech in 1956, beginning the 'De-Stalinization' process, Togliatti reworked the traditional Marxist-Leninist dismissal of liberal democracy under 'imperialist' tutelage:

> Today, given the development and present force of the democratic and socialist movement, large rents can be torn in this system that impedes the free expression of the will of the people, and an increasingly large passageway can be opened towards the manifestation of this will. For this reason we are moving on a democratic terrain.[38]

This was a move away from the idea that bourgeois democracy falters precisely when confronted by a socialist challenge. Beginning with Togliatti's 'Yalta Memorandum' (1964), and amplified by a joint gathering of Western European Communist parties at Choisy-le-Roi, France, in 1966, a more optimistic view of 'Monopoly State Capitalism' was developed, which saw the potential for state intervention to iron out capitalist crises and to benefit the working class.[39] The key political division in modern society was perceived to be big business on the one side, the working class in alliance with the bulk of the middle class on the other.[40] This struggle for the heart of the middle classes was never likely to be won by Communists. American consumer goods, schemes for academic exchange, and covert CIA sponsorship of intellectual forums such as the Congress for Cultural Freedom chipped away at European suspicion of Americanization. Still, anti-Americanism (which had lost its strong interwar association with the political right) bolstered the Communist vote in Western Europe.

As the Cold War geared up, America for the first time developed a peacetime standing army of global stature, though infused with democratic values. The American diplomat George Kennan (1904–2005) presented, in his 'Long Telegram' of February 1946, a considered analysis of Soviet behaviour. He denied that Soviet ideology was an inevitable driver to aggressive, expansionist war. In contrast to Nazism, therefore, it was not a force that must necessarily be confronted in general armed conflict. The Soviets were, however, convinced that ultimate security required the destruction of America's global power. Crucially, argued Kennan, Communist power was statist, and unalterably opposed to independent civil society:

> Communists will, as a rule, work toward destruction of all forms of personal independence—economic, political or moral. Their system can handle only individuals who have been

brought into complete dependence on higher power. Thus, persons who are financially independent—such as individual businessmen, estate owners, successful farmers, artisans—and all those who exercise local leadership or have local prestige—such as popular local clergymen or political figures—are anathema.[41]

The destruction of commercial civil society in the Soviet Union, therefore, minimized any chance of an internal dynamic towards constitutionalism. As such, the Soviet Union needed to be treated as a potentially very long-term threat. The effect of the 'Long Telegram,' Kennan recalled, 'was nothing less than sensational' in its impact on the American administration.[42] Kennan restated the message of the Long Telegram in an anonymous *Foreign Affairs* article in July 1947, where he suggested the appropriate American strategy: neither appeasement nor war, but 'containment', 'designed to confront the Russians with unalterable counterforce at every point where they show signs of encroaching upon the interests of a peaceful and stable world'.[43] This idea of encroachment, of course, fitted in easily with the critique of Communist 'subversion'.

In the first instance, containment meant military and fiscal support for countries abutting on territories under Communist control. America had already lent its support to anti-Soviet campaigns in the British 'sphere' of Iran and Turkey in 1946. In February 1947 the British Labour government asked for American help in Greece. With the Greek Communists, supported by Yugoslavia, Albania, and Bulgaria (but not Russia), locked into civil war with the royalist government in 1947, Britain found itself straining to support its Greek anti-Communist allies. On 12 March 1947, President Truman announced to Congress that his government would financially aid anti-Communist governments in Greece and Turkey. This commitment to backing opponents of Communist advance (regardless of whether they were themselves democratic or authoritarian) became known as the Truman Doctrine. America's commitment, as Truman put it, was 'to support free peoples' against Communist modes of attack, widely defined as whether 'by such methods as coercion, or by such subterfuges as political infiltration'.[44] Any regime willing to resist Communist subversion could expect a positive response to requests for American aid. America committed itself to Western European defence when, on 4 April 1949, it assumed the lead in the North Atlantic Treaty Organization (NATO), including Canada and ten West European countries.

When, in August 1949, years before it was expected, the Soviet Union successfully tested its first atomic bomb, and on 1 October that year the Communists declared the People's Republic of China, Truman ordered a full review of national-security policy. This resulted in NSC-68 (National Security Council Paper Number 68), completed by Paul Nitze on 14 April 1950. Nitze's analysis treated the Communist countries as effectively classless, its peoples being a single oppressed 'totalitariat' under the leviathan state, and with all economic impulses dictated by state military ambitions rather than any section of civil society.[45] This 'totalitariat' was the antithesis of associational bourgeois civil society. Such Soviet vulnerability as existed arose from the state's lack of legitimacy amongst a people disciplined only by fear and, in the satellite countries, anti-Russian nationalism.

NSC-68 called on US governments to oppose Communism anywhere on the globe, and proposed a tripling of the American defence budget. Congress would probably have rejected such a huge appropriation had not North Korea invaded South Korea on 25 June 1950. Defence spending soared, from $13.5 billion before the war to more than $52 billion by 1952. The United States concluded numerous bilateral pacts, and US military bases were constructed to straddle the globe. The Korean War marked a point of transition, an up-ending of the United States' traditional hostility to military spending that had been engrained in domestic political discourse since the founding of the Republic.

During the Korean War (1950–3), the US supported the unabashedly anti-democratic Syngman Rhee regime in the southern Republic of Korea against the Communist Democratic People's Republic of Korea in the north. Both sides behaved atrociously, with the civilian population subjected to 'red' and 'white' terror. A sceptical journalist, Reginald Thompson, remarked that the US-led struggle to preserve the chance for future democratization was a 'quixotic business', seeking 'an evolutionary result without evolution'.[46] It was reasoned, however, that while there was little to choose between the regimes in terms of human-rights protection at the time, the totalitarianism of North Korea, where no independent bourgeois civil society existed, had no internal dynamic towards liberalization. South Korea, if it fostered its middle classes and market exchange economy, must in time move towards constitutionalism, if only to guarantee private assets put to productive use and to absorb working-class militancy. The Korean War, thus, was fought by the US and United Nations allies to defend a dictatorship and to punish interstate aggression, but also in the expectation that the democratic impulse had a chance in a free-market authoritarian regime, but no chance in a Communist totalitarian regime.

## THE 'THIRD WORLD'

As the European and Japanese economies were already on the brink of 'high mass consumption', post-war democratization under the Allied aegis was relatively straightforward. Here could be found a large and influential bourgeoisie, while militarism had been decisively discredited. It was an altogether different case in the colonial world, as American policy makers were painfully aware. Imperial powers by the interwar period had often established representative assemblies in their colonies, in the usual authoritarian hope of gaining consent for taxation without conceding power of substance.[47] These assemblies became the nuclei for successor governing elites. An indigenous bourgeoisie was developing that provided the backbone of civil society, but was ambivalent about the prospect of decolonization. Bourgeois civil society comprised, in the main, officials working for the colonial administration and entrepreneurs. Often a small number of very powerful industrial magnates dominated a fragmented and still-weak manufacturing sector. These 'family houses' had to choose between collaborating with imperialism or supporting the emergence of a sovereign nation state. In India, for example, the Bombay magnate J. N. Tata opposed nationalism for fear that it would encourage labour indiscipline. Another leading industrialist, G. D. Birla, became the paymaster of the Indian National Congress in the 1930s. On balance, the colonial bourgeoisie preferred emancipation from imperialism, but were anxious to restrain social radicalism in the liberation movement, and to retain a good deal of the inherited structures and attitudes of imperial rule to model post-colonial states.[48]

Where imperial rule had developed a firm state structure, but allowed the development of an indigenous bourgeois civil society, the transition to stable post-imperial governance in constitutionalist form tended to be most successful; India was the stand-out example. Elsewhere, if the bourgeoisie were weaker, they were more likely to fear national liberation, collaborate with imperialism, and be proportionately discredited in post-colonial states. They were particularly exposed where suffocatingly dominant imperial rulers precipitously absconded with little thought for the aftermath; Belgian ditching of the Congo, perhaps, was the most egregious example. But independence of some sort could not be avoided. After the Second World War, with European imperialism evidently weakened and its militarism discredited, a wave of decolonization swept through South Asia and most of the Middle East in the 1940s and 1950s, and through Africa in the 1960s.

America, thus, had to consider the world well beyond advanced Europe, and it was particularly with the 'Third World' in mind that policymakers had by the late 1950s worked out a 'modernization' theory to explain how one got from a hierarchical society of orders to a consumer democracy. The difficult take-off, from a pre-modern if stable economy into sustained industrial expansion, could be smoothed through targeted aid designed to construct the institutional and infrastructural requirements of a capitalist economy. 'Modernization theory' was a kind of liberal- historical materialism. Against Marx's putative stages of feudalism, bourgeois capitalism, socialism, and Communism, the leading modernization theorist Walt Rostow (1916–2003) set:

- *'traditional society'* (with social structures inhibiting the development or utilization of productive technology)
- *'preconditions'* (including an appropriate social and political structure)
- *'take-off'* (a necessary but dangerous phase during which instability was likely to produce political convulsions)[49]
- *'maturity'* (full industrialization, with politics stabilizing but polarized along class lines)
- *'high mass-consumption'* (a high-wage, increasingly 'middle-class' society, with the producer interests of organized labour and capital subordinated to a civil society of consumers).[50]

Mass consumer society secures a new equilibrium of political stability. 'A large middle class tempers conflict by rewarding moderate and democratic parties and penalizing extremist groups', said Seymour Martin Lipset confidently in 1960. Once economic development is well in train, Lipset suggested, increasing wealth tends to expand the 'political role of the middle class by changing the shape of the stratification structure from an elongated pyramid, with a large lower-class base, to a diamond with a growing middle class'.[51] Modernization theory did not (yet) imply the deliberate eroding of the status of wage labour. Rostow, says Nils Gilman, saw the 'social democratic welfare state' as the 'final outcome of world history'.[52] He was not untypical in this.

It was feared, however, that left to itself, 'take-off' was likely to be protracted and socially disruptive: a dangerous window of opportunity for Communism to take root and bid for power. Democracy, therefore, was strictly optional during 'take-off'. The leading American diplomat George Kennan was quite clear that the systemic struggle against Communism took precedence over local considerations of democratic or pluralist right. As he wrote in March 1950:

> We cannot be too dogmatic about the methods by which local Communists can be dealt with...where the concepts and traditions of popular government are too weak to absorb successfully the intensity of the Communist attack, then we must concede that harsh governmental measures of repression may be the only answer; that these measures may have to proceed from regimes whose origins and methods would not stand the test of American concepts of democratic procedure; and that such regimes and such methods may be preferable alternatives, and indeed the only alternatives, to further Communist successes.[53]

Indeed, democratic political forms precipitously adopted were, in this view, dangerous for modernizing societies. The very economic instability and political discrediting of traditional ruling elites that were likely to be a side effect of economic 'take-off' made them highly vulnerable to revolutionary upset. The Communists, it was understood from the experience of Eastern Europe, would turn the freedom of democracy—of association, of representation, of constitutional representative government—against itself, by honeycombing the institutions of civil society, and capturing elements of the executive preparatory to a complete takeover. In this light, 'premature' democracy was a threat to civil society.

American 'modernization theorists', therefore, were prepared to judge favourably the role the military could play in the development of stable, market-based economies buttressed by social welfare and evolving towards democracy. Even direct military rule could be progressive, in that military elites would wish to see thoroughgoing economic reform, if only to support their own military establishments.[54] Authoritarianism, balanced upon a functioning civil society comprising sites of autonomous free enterprise, was seen as definitely preferable to Communist totalitarianism in which private enterprise was abolished and civil society atomized by the state (or indeed fascist totalitarianism, in which a corporate, statised capitalism demobilized the 'small battalions' before state power). Military government was welcomed by the US as beneficially 'natural' for Latin America, where the army was seen as a tolerable proxy for the meritocratic, modernizing bourgeoisie.[55] This viewpoint was by no means limited to American policymakers, nor to its sphere of direct influence. In 1957, for example, the British ambassador to Jordan wrote to his Foreign Secretary making clear that 'our interest is better suited by an authoritarian regime which maintains stability and the Western connection than by an untrammelled democracy which rushes downhill towards communism and chaos'.⁵⁶ This was not just talk. In 1953, British and US intelligence services had cooperated in engineering a coup to overthrow the left-nationalist and democratically elected government of Mohammad Mosaddegh in Iran. The hereditary Shah ruled thereafter in an authoritarian, pro-Western fashion for twenty-six years. As a British Conservative thinker later put it, 'if [democracy] is leading to an end that is undesirable or is inconsistent with itself, then there is a theoretical case for ending it': successful left-wing subversion would justify a right-wing 'counter-coup'.⁵⁷ Such considerations always bulked large in Western attitudes towards the decolonizing world.

The United States was genuinely anti-imperialist, but only insofar as it could be fairly certain that the successor nationalist regime would be proof against Communist influence. Given the weakness of the bourgeoisie in the colonial world, however, such fair certainty was not easily secured. The US, therefore, often supported continued imperialist rule as long as it was viable to do so, and when this became insupportable generally preferred authoritarian regimes of 'strongmen' tied closely to neo-colonial influences in the form of Western-run capitalist enterprises, inter-military cooperation, and a CIA-controlled intelligence community. The United States, in effect, became the guarantor of neo-colonialism: not primarily as a project of economic exploitation, but rather a political barrier to Communist subversion. America found itself supporting the repression of democratic popular movements if their success was seen as likely to advantage Communist opponents of the 'Free World'. Credible deterrence required an aggressive, highly militarized response to insurgencies against American allies, no matter how despotic these allies might be. American foreign policy during the Cold War, therefore, involved numerous interventions against left-nationalist regimes and movements, in favour of military strongmen. For example, America, Britain, and Belgium (the former colonial power) actively colluded in the bloody coup that suppressed the leftist regime of Patrice Lamumba in the Congo in 1961, bringing to power a brutal kleptocracy.

The most controversial US interventions, however, were in Latin American nations independent since the early nineteenth century. President Dwight D. Eisenhower (1890–1969) in 1953 approved a CIA plan to overthrow Jacobo Arbenz Guzmán, leftist president of the small Central American country of Guatemala, with American-trained Guatemalan exiles. There were only four Communists in the Guatemalan Parliament, and a handful in the trade unions and the Ministry of Education. The US ambassador, however, reported of Arbenz that 'It seemed to me that the man thought like a communist, and if not actually one, would do until one came along.'⁵⁸ John Foster Dulles, Secretary of State, in explaining his country's actions in a radio broadcast on 30 June 1954, highlighted Communist 'subversion' of an unstable democracy:

> For several years international communism has been probing here and there for nesting places in the Americas. It finally chose Guatemala as a spot which it could turn into an official base from which to breed subversion which would extend to other American republics.... In Guatemala, international communism had an initial success. It began 10 years ago, when a revolution occurred in Guatemala. The revolution

was not without justification. But the Communists seized on it, not just as an opportunity for real reforms, but as a chance to gain political power. Communist agitators devoted themselves to infiltrating the public and private organizations of Guatemala.... Operating in the guise of 'reformers' they organized the workers and peasants under Communist leadership. Having gained control of what they call 'mass organizations', they moved on to take over the official press and radio of the Guatemalan Government. They dominated the social security organization and ran the agrarian reform program. Through the technique of the 'popular front' they dictated to the Congress and the President.[59]

This was a classic presentation of America's fear of Communist subversives seizing upon genuine grievances, presenting themselves as reformers, duping 'useful idiots' into joining Popular Fronts, infiltrating the institutions of a free society, and eventually exploiting constitutional means to destroy the substance of constitutionalism. American policymakers saw a slippery slope: if radical leftism was not entirely quarantined, natural momentum was towards Communist tyranny.

Such a logic of inveterate suspicion and hostility left Arbenz isolated and desperate, and he turned to the Soviet bloc. In May 1954, Guatemala took receipt of a shipload of Czech weapons. A month later, Colonel Castillo Armas invaded with a small expeditionary force of exiles from their base in Honduras while American planes bombed Guatemala City. The armed forces of the Guatemalan government defected, and regime change was effected. This CIA-organized coup (at the apparent behest of the United Fruit Company) became something of a 'black legend' for Latin American radicals. It was an early example, also, of American prophecy being self-fulfilling. In a bifurcated world, those who were not with America were likely to find themselves with the Soviet Union.

Ironically, American interventionism in the face of even an incipient Communist threat in its own hemisphere tended to disable the local initiative of the Latin American bourgeoisie. The failure of the labour movement to overthrow the American client dictator of Cuba, Fulgencio Batista, in the general strikes of 1958, encouraged broad sections of the middle class to greet Fidel Castro's rebels into the capital with enthusiasm. Castro, indeed, confessed later to playing down the leftism of his 26 July Movement so as not to frighten the middle class.[60] While partially nationalizing foreign assets, he still made overtures to Washington. These were ignored by the Eisenhower administration, however, and Castro began looking to Moscow. The Soviet Union offered Cuba oil at a cheap price, and when American-owned refineries in Cuba refused to process it, Castro had them nationalized along with other American-owned enterprises. The bourgeois and landed elites of Cuba, who were at first prepared to accommodate with the Castro regime, were weakened in their ability to inhibit its slide towards Communist dictatorship precisely because of long-established habits of relying upon United States' power as a *deus ex machina*.[61]

In March 1960, Eisenhower authorized the CIA to train Cuban exiles in preparation for a coup. The Bay of Pigs invasion of Cuba by 1,500 of these exiles on 17 April 1961, authorized by President John F. Kennedy, proved to be a fiasco. Castro cleaved even closer to the Soviet bloc, and his acceptance of Russian nuclear missiles led to the Cuban Missile Crisis of October 1962. In return for Soviet missiles being withdrawn, the US government promised not to attempt a forceful overthrow of Castro's regime. Emboldened, the Cuban revolutionaries rejected Communist Popular Frontist orthodoxy, arguing that the Latin American bourgeoisies were incapable of playing a revolutionary role. They were, said Castro, 'too paralysed by fear of social revolution and frightened by the cry of the exploited masses'.[62] The Second Declaration of Havana (February 1962) urged armed revolutionism as the only way by which political stasis might be broken:

> Wherever roads are closed to the peoples, where repression of workers and peasants is fierce, where the domination of Yankee monopolies is strong established, the first and most important lesson is to understand that it is neither just nor correct to divert the peoples with the vain and fanciful illusion that the dominant classes can be uprooted by legal means which do not and will not exist. The ruling classes are entrenched in all positions of state power. They monopolize the teaching field. They dominate all means of mass communication. They have infinite financial resources. Theirs is a power which the monopolies and the ruling few will defend by blood and fire with the strength of their police and their armies.[63]

In this view, no social class as such—whether bourgeoisie, peasantry, or working class—was capable of destroying the authoritarian state. Revolutionaries needed to separate themselves off and wage armed struggle. The revolutionary cadre should take to guerrilla struggle in the hills, and there form revolutionary *foco* in rural zones inaccessible to the military state. These *foco* would act as a small motor that in due course would set the big motor of civil war into motion. Guerrilla struggles against oligarchy duly broke out in the 1960s in Colombia, Guatemala, and Venezuela. The peculiarities of Cuba, however, could not be replicated, and insurgencies crashed to defeat or ran into the sand.

Castroite dismissal of bourgeois civil society in Latin America proved in the longer run to be unfounded, but it was understandably resonant in the 1960s. The one serious American attempt to bolster Latin America's civil society as the foundation for modernization was a striking failure. President Kennedy in August 1961 launched a bold new aid programme designed to transform Latin American, the Alliance for Progress. This was announced by Kennedy as a 'peaceful revolution on a hemispheric scale', promising economic and welfare development for the masses in Latin America.[64] America pledged $20 billion in a decade for Latin American states, which was to be matched with equal amounts of domestic funding. It was not, however, made a condition that recipient governments adopt democratic norms. It was assumed, rather, that as civil society stabilized, authoritarian measures to repress populist leftism would naturally fall into abeyance. The creation of a 'nationalist, progressive, enterprising, and dynamic middle class', the Mexican scholar Rodolfo Stavenhagen noted, was an 'implicit but basic' aim of the Alliance for Progress.[65]

This optimistic 'modernization theory' prognosis did not work out as hoped. As wealthy oligarchies controlled the state there was little domestic pressure to undertake land redistribution, tax reform, or social welfare. By the mid-1960s, the United States formally abandoned the requirement that recipient countries even put in train political reform. There was simply no willingness to undermine the interests of traditionally American-friendly local elites, or to risk the investments of American businesses. Indeed, there was a renewed emphasis on building up bourgeois civil society directly through private investment, as a 1964 Congressional Report cogently explained:

> Private investment is an effective instrument making for political stability: (a) by supporting the rise and vitality of a solid, articulate middle class made up of managers, property owners, and small capitalists; and (b) by providing a bulwark in support of individual freedom against the rise of arbitrary power, an ever present risk under a 'controlled economy'.[66]

In the meantime, the continuing revolutionary threat meant that the United States felt forced into a renewed recourse to militarism in suppressing it. The administration of Lyndon B. Johnson (1908–1973) supported a military coup in Brazil in 1964: there were not to be free elections again until 1985. In 1965, in the largest American intervention in the Caribbean since the 1920s, twenty thousand American marines occupied the Dominican Republic. Rather than simply support the local military junta, President Johnson adopted a 'third way': elections under American guidance, and the undesirable candidate (in this instance, Juan Bosch) effectively intimidated out of the contest.

Modernization theory in practice relied heavily on US use of military force. The war in Vietnam (see chapter 13) proved the limits to such tactics, however, and as the South East Asia imbroglio sapped at American will to risk further guerrilla conflicts, threats of direct military intervention in Latin America became less credible in the 1970s.

## THE MILITARY-INDUSTRIAL COMPLEX

US Cold War militarization was not anything like as anti-democratic in impetus as the militarism of pre-war Europe. Writing in 1966, Barrington Moore Jr. suggested that the modern bourgeoisie, being (he thought) in its 'declining phase', was still quite as tied to militarism as it had been in the late nineteenth and early twentieth century. However, because the militarist state was no longer disproportionately aristocratic or attached to maintaining semi-feudal relations in the countryside, it had decisively broken from regressively anti-democratic politics.[67] The old nexus of business, state, and armed services came to America with a vengeance, but the challenge this presented to domestic constitutionalism was limited.

American traditions of anti-militarism remained strong. During the Korean War, for example, President Truman in 1951 dismissed the highly popular General Douglas MacArthur, commander of United Nations forces, for insubordination. American hostility to an over-mighty military establishment, and faith in commercial civil society as the bedrock of a pluralist society, meant that, as far as possible, military contracts were outsourced to civilian firms. This extended even to formulation of military doctrine, and close links between the military and civilian defence think tanks, such as the RAND Corporation, were assiduously fostered. The problem was that, so far as the military was civilianized, so too were substantial swathes of commercial civil society militarized.

A 1964 academic survey saw the Second World War as a turning point:

> Big-business interests, which had looked with horror on the New Deal's public works projects and pump-priming innovations, had formed a war-time partnership with generals and admirals who had the dispensation of virtually limitless billions of public funds. Business had never known such a bonanza—nor had the military. Neither would have been human had they wanted to kill the goose that laid the golden egg. All pressures, then, combined to one end—the creation, for the first time in American history, of a powerful militaristic class allied to powerful business interests.[68]

The Cold War meant that war-making became a permanent component of United States national culture; peacetime conscription was introduced in 1948, and military art meant the need for a permanent war-making capacity: a 'force in being'. The interpenetration of defence and capitalism was at times made embarrassingly clear by the American practice of appointing ministers from outside the ranks of elected representatives. Charles Wilson, then chairman of the financially shaky General Motors, testified at the 1953 Senate Armed Services Committee hearing to confirm his appointment as US Defense Secretary that keeping his existing job would entail no conflict of interest since 'what is good for the country is good for General Motors, and vice versa'.[69] This very integration of civilian and military practices meant that, though militarist psychopathologies might perhaps be intense than they had been in Europe in the late nineteenth and early twentieth centuries, in some ways they permeated society more widely than before. When all needs were being commodified, the insinuation of militarist values into the culture of consumerism was all the more inescapable.[70]

President Eisenhower, in his remarkable farewell speech to the nation in 1961, warned of the emerging 'military industrial complex':

> Until the latest of our world conflicts, the United States had no armaments industry.... But now we can no longer risk emergency improvisation of national defense; we have been compelled to create a permanent armaments industry of vast proportions. Added to this, three and a half million men and women are directly engaged in the defense establishment. We annually spend on military security more than the net income of all United States corporations.

This 'conjunction of an immense military establishment and a large arms industry', Eisenhower argued, exercised a 'total influence—economic, political, even spiritual—...in every city, every State house, every office of the Federal government.... Our toil, resources and livelihood are all involved; so is the very structure of our society.' The president could not deny the need for a formidable military-industrial complex, but he admitted that it would tend, under its own weight, to gather to itself 'unwarranted influence, whether sought or unsought'. Even intellectual life, the repository of freedom of thought, had become bound up in the military-industrial complex. Because of the high costs of research:

> Today, the solitary inventor, tinkering in his shop, has been overshadowed by task forces of scientists in laboratories and testing fields. In the same fashion, the free university, historically the fountainhead of free ideas and scientific discovery, has experienced a revolution in the conduct of research. Partly because of the huge costs involved, a government contract becomes virtually a substitute for intellectual curiosity.[71]

Eisenhower's speech was an elegy for independent, commercial civil society, promoting rationality, personal independence, and voluntary associationalism, and serving as a counterweight to the ever-present threat of big government and big business. He could not deny, however, that with America's responsibilities in the Cold War the military-industrial complex was indispensable. His call for an 'alert and knowledgeable citizenry' to control the military-industrial complex was stirring, but in context sounded rather hopeless.

## CONCLUSION

The 1950s in the West were characterized by comfortable conformism. Divisive ideologies had faded and blurred. The prospect of proletarian rebellion against parliamentarianism was definitely ended. For all the magnificent achievements of the post-war era, however—restoration of liberal democracy, unprecedented prosperity, constitutionalism re-established in Japan and Europe, the politics of dictatorship entirely marginalized in the expanded heartland of democracy—there remained evident in political discourse a profound dissatisfaction with the ethics of the era. While the West basked in consumerist prosperity, the developing countries of the 'Free World' were sombrely reminded that their path to 'modernity' was likely to be thin, winding, clogged by brambles, and essaying treacherous heights: a vertiginous fall into revolution or reaction threatened on either side. American diplomacy, it is true, was motivated by a genuine concern to defend the 'Free World'. The Liberal Modernization Theorists saw the need for agrarian and social reform in Third World countries to break up oppressive oligarchies. But the relentless pressure of the Cold War meant that any radical impulse in developing countries was looked upon paranoiacally as evidence of Communist subversion, or being easy prey to it. The West appeared to be losing its generosity, and all too prepared to bolster authoritarian allies of convenience.

In the Communist east, militarism suffocated any likely development of vibrant civil society. America, in contrast, was so economically muscular that it wore its battle raiment lightly. Democracy and civil society were vibrant, but perhaps heedless of creeping moral turpitude. The prospect of atomic destruction was so cataclysmic that it was virtually unthinkable; so, ironically, much of American public opinion thought little of it, and preferred to glory in their country's military might. Minority opinion began to worry that when patriots could blithely proclaim 'better dead than red', war must appear insufficiently terrible, and that the nation had grown too fond of it.

# 13

# The Pivot of '68: New Left and New Right

The 'Third World' became a particular focus for the USA's Cold War because of America's inherent credibility problem. John F. Kennedy's famous commitment to 'support *any* friend, oppose *any* foe, in order to assure the survival and the success of liberty' signed a disconcertingly blank cheque.[1] If the Soviets were to launch limited war—say, the occupation of West Germany, or even just West Berlin—defence doctrine required that the US respond with 'massive force'. Given the exposure of American cities to devastating nuclear counter-attack, this guarantee lacked conviction. The biggest fear of the United States was that its allies, not having much faith in American commitment to their defence, might be tempted to seek 'neutralism'.[2] The US was tempted to exaggerate its willingness to go over the brink in an attempt to demonstrate to its allies its commitment. This calculated (if dangerous) will to over-reaction characterized the Cuban Missile Crisis, when a very limited Russian gambit of relatively minor strategic significance had to be withdrawn in the face of US readiness to escalate towards war. In the early 1970s such deliberate irrationalism became self-parodic, when President Richard Nixon (1913–1994) deliberately implied that that his determination to wage war against Communist aggression knew no bounds of rationality, the anti-Communism of a 'mad man'.[3]

## THE VIETNAM WAR

US commitment to defence of the 'Free World' could most safely be displayed in the colonial and formerly colonial world. Here, conventional military engagement ('flexible response') was plausible precisely because the theatres of war in question were of limited strategic importance. They were not likely to be areas where escalation towards general war would take place (the Middle East, with its oil wealth, was perhaps an exception). The United States could display its determination to expend blood and treasure in the global periphery, in the hope that this would bolster its credibility in the European theatre. This rationale, however, inclined the US to intransigence, belligerence, and vexatious warmongering, all the better to show off its commitment as a stout ally. It also tended towards egregious bloodletting: the exacting of a heavy cost in life and economic potential on those countries that could not be prevented from going 'red'. Vietnam, in particular, was a test of American solidarity with its allies, no matter how unsavoury they might be, no matter how brutal the means.

Vietnam, even by the standards of South East Asia, had an anaemic native bourgeoisie. Urban politics, in this overwhelmingly peasant society, were shallow-rooted.[4] Long-standing peasant resentment of the arrogant towns and cities was artfully exploited by a suitably re-tooled Communism. In its Asian variant, pioneered by China, Communism offered peculiar advantages to peasant rebellion—the main driver of revolution—by dividing urban centres along class lines, thus subverting and demoralizing the strategic centres of power from within. Though Asian Communism differed starkly from the classic Marxist model in being evidently based upon rural insurgency, it empowered peasants by sapping ruling class hegemony in urban centres.

From 1954, having defeated French imperialism, Communists had control of North Vietnam (or the Democratic Republic of Vietnam, DRV). The DRV was determined to destroy the US-allied 'State of Vietnam'. Northern Communists combined an attritional offensive across the border with promotion of rural guerrilla warfare based upon the South's peasantry, and urban revolutionary terrorism in its strategic urban centres (Saigon, Hue, etcetera). It was a formidable combination. America, therefore, faced in Vietnam an avowedly Communist regime in the North seeking to annex an authoritarian state reliant upon US aid in the South. The tyrannical South Vietnamese regime was very far from liberal. Colonel Lansdale, American advisor to the South Vietnamese prime minister, Ngo Dinh Diem, complained to the US Secretary of Defense in 1961, 'I cannot truly sympathize with Americans who help promote a fascist state and then get angry when it doesn't act like a democracy.'[5] Backing the regime nicely demonstrated America's unstinting loyalty to all its allies, but was embarrassing for home opinion, to the extent that the US winked at a South Vietnamese palace revolution, and the murder of Diem and his brother in 1963. Diem's eventual successor following a military coup in 1964, Nguyen Cao Ky, was no more edifying. A ludicrously flamboyant womanizer, he claimed Hitler as a hero, but confessed that South Vietnam would need four Hitlers to hold it together. Assistant Secretary of State William Bundy understandably moaned that in their search for credible Vietnamese allies, the US had reached the 'bottom of the barrel, absolutely the bottom of the barrel!'[6]

Communists employed the usual Popular Front tactics familiar to American experience and 'subversion' theorists. In December 1960 opposition forces in the South coalesced to form the National Liberation Front (NLF), the customary pan-class united front dedicated to national unity and independence, but clearly under Communist control.[7] Communists won peasant support by explicitly offering them land, to be redistributed from landlord estates, and implicitly endorsing the age-old vision of emancipation from 'parasitic' urban domination.[8] The US Joint Chiefs of Staff argued for sticking by its unprepossessing South Vietnamese allies primarily to demonstrate willingness to stand by America's friends; withdrawal 'would have an adverse psychological impact'.[9] The US feared that a defeat for its clients in South Vietnam would capsize a delicate regional balance: the Communists taking power in Indonesia, and Thailand seeking security through neutralism. On the other hand, there was no desire to repeat the experience of the Korean War when US forces had fought a conventional war against a Communist state (North

Korea), and had directly engaged with Chinese forces. With Soviet military forces approaching parity, and general war most likely meaning nuclear Mutual Assured Destruction (MAD), America's realistic options were severely constrained.[10] North Vietnam could not be invaded without risking global conflagration.

The decision was taken to fight a counter-insurgency war. Two hundred thousand American personnel, regularly rotated, were deployed to South Vietnam in 1965, which increased to five hundred thousand by 1968. With nearly thirty thousand Americans killed by late 1967, however, the domestic anti-war movement began to gather strength. The NLF attempted to spark a revolutionary uprising on 30 January 1968 when it launched its Tet Offensive, a series of major attacks on and from within cities across South Vietnam. The intention was to fracture the urban centres sufficiently that they would fall easy prey to rural guerrilla forces. This offensive failed, but it was clear that the country was far from pacified. The war, moreover, was predictably brutalizing. At the hamlet of My Lai in March 1968, for example, US forces at close quarters massacred around five hundred unarmed civilians, including babies. Many more civilians were killed at 'arms length', through bombing and 'free fire'.

As American embarrassment grew, the number of US ground troops in the theatre was steadily run down, though the Nixon administration escalated the bombing. The Paris Peace Accords of January 1973 provided the United States with a decent interval before, in 1975, the North Vietnamese Army invaded on a broad front. In April the South Vietnamese capital, Saigon, fell to the Communists. In total, fifty-eight thousand American lives had been lost, as had half a million South Vietnamese civilians and another half a million Communist combatants. There was a limited 'domino effect', and in 1975 the peasant-based Communist Khmer Rouge took over in Cambodia (a 'country...just about as complete a peasant society as could be found'),[11] and the Pathet Lao in Laos. Pol Pot's Khmer Rouge inflicted a fanatically anti-urban regime of massacre on Cambodia: probably well over a million were killed between 1975 and 1978. America had been humbled, but Indochina, harrowed and prey to ideological fanaticism, proved to be a poor advertisement for Communist revolution. American resolve was enough, moreover, to stabilize the Thai government, and to embolden the Indonesian army sufficiently for it to turn on and massacre the Communist Party (and the wider left) in the autumn of 1965: some half a million were done to death. To this extent, the US escalation was a success in raising massively the cost in blood of Communist advances. But the conflict in Vietnam was the most glaring demonstration of US inability consistently to favour democratic revolution in the developing world.

## NEO-MILITARISM

President Johnson had baulked at the prospect of putting the United States on a war footing. The reserve were not called up, nor was taxation increased. To an unusual extent, therefore, the brunt of the Vietnam conflict was borne not by commercial civil society, but by the poor. Eighty per cent of the 2.7 million soldiers who served in Vietnam were from working-class and poor backgrounds.[12] However, the massive militarization of the Cold War could not but have profound societal effects in the US extending far beyond blue-collar recruits. As Eisenhower had intimated, universities in America were closely identified with the military-industrial complex. The Pentagon and allied agencies, the Atomic Energy Commission (AEC) and the National Aeronautics and Space Agency (NASA), for example, provided 46.5 per cent of total research funding for universities in 1967.[13] The army and its corporate suppliers flooded college campuses to scout for talent and sponsor research. The president of Berkeley University, Charles Kerr, addressing colleagues at Harvard in 1963, made light of the dependence of universities on government and big-business funding with strings attached, by citing a limerick:

> There was a young lady from Kent
> Who said that she knew what it meant
> When men took her to dine,
> Gave her cocktails and wine;
> She knew what it meant—but she went.[14]

Such insouciant levity was hardly likely to assure students and academics that freedom of inquiry was altogether safe. Kerr's vision of the role of education, moreover, was chillingly technocratic. Society required, he explained, basic education for workers, so that they might 'receive instruction, follow directions, and keep records', and advanced education for managers, engineers, and civil servants 'to operate the new production system'. With typical 'modernizing' assumptions, Kerr anticipated the increasing complexity of production techniques to require more and more specialists, which required upward social mobility. This in turn would transform 'class status and political outlook': 'Middle incomes make for a middle class.'[15] There were 6.9 million students in American universities and colleges by 1968: many were less than content at the idea of their being churned out as middle managers of the military-industrial complex. There existed a tension between higher education as a means to explore and develop individual creativity for its own sake, and university qualifications as a route to mundane if well-remunerated managerial careers in corporations and government. A good number of bourgeois youth, particularly students, felt 'alienated' from the impersonal, formulaic, 'phony' choices of modern work and consumerism.[16]

Scholars on the Old Left, moreover, were arguing that the high-wage, quasi-Keynesian compact of the post-war era was inextricably bound up with warfare. Joseph Schumpeter, in 1942, had argued the standard liberal case that 'Modern pacifism and modern international morality are...products of capitalism....As a matter of fact, the more completely capitalist the structure and attitude of a nation, the more pacifist—and the more prone to count the costs of war—we observe it to be.'[17] This was quoted and countered by the American Marxists, Paul Baran and Paul Sweezy in 1966. They insisted that capitalism and the state were mutually intertwined in a symbiosis mediated by a new militarism:

> It is important to understand that a hundred years ago there was an important kernel of truth to [Schumpeter's] position. Under conditions of competition and with full

employment implicitly assumed, it was correct to regard wasteful government expenditures as a brake on capital accumulation and hence to oppose them. Nowadays, however, such ideas…are strictly anachronistic. With idle men and idle machines as normal features of monopoly capitalism, advanced bourgeois thought, thoroughly steeped in Keynesian doctrine, knows perfectly well that additional government spending, no matter how wasteful the result, raises income and profits. Moreover, the biggest and most powerful corporations get the lion's share of armament contracts and shift whatever additional taxes may go with them onto their customers (to a large extent the government itself). Under these conditions, there is certainly no longer any reason for bourgeois ideology to boast its pacifism and its propensity to count the costs of militarism.[18]

Such an analysis implied, of course, that the working class, enjoying security of employment and high wages, also had a stake in militarism, helping to explain the democratic character of modern militarism.

## THE NEW LEFT

The New Left, indeed, emerged partly because the Old Left and Social Democracy appeared utterly incapable of confronting and opposing contemporary militarism, particularly the American intervention in Vietnam.[19] For much of the New Left, this only emphasized how the working class had been 'bought off'. The 1962 'Port Huron Statement' of the American 'Students for a Democratic Society' (SDS) argued that politically the most significant aspect of the military-industrial complex was its distribution of money and jobs to every interest and class, workers included.[20] Reflecting on the American militarized state in 1967, Jules Henry at the Congress on the Dialectics of Liberation in London expressed a common New Left conviction:

> Organized labour is probably the most contented section of the American population; it has shifted from being the most revolutionary group to being the most conservative. Along with these [military-industrial complex] alterations in the structure of American political economy there has developed a vast, sheep-like docility of the population. Grazing on the grasses of affluence, the white American population is one of the most docile on earth. This is ideal psychological preparation for war, for docile people make excellent soldiers.[21]

This was true to the extent that working-class adherence to values of military discipline in defence of liberty remained relatively robust.

The horrors of war in Vietnam in pursuit of intangible 'credibility', however, progressively de-glamorized militarism. Moreover, with black civil rights and then anti-war protest roiling America, violent policing and deployment of the paramilitary National Guard brought 'the war home'. The brutal violence inherent in militarism was evident not just on the television screens, but on the streets. The militarized mindset can be seen in the admission of the Chief of Staff of the New Jersey National Guard that his force treated suppression of a riot in the black ghetto of Newark in 1967 as a 'military action'.[22] What this kind of attitude resulted in was made evident in the Detroit riots, also in 1967: rioters killed two or three victims, while the best estimate for victims killed was twenty-one by the police, seven by the National Guard, and one by the army.[23] Militarism seemed to be infecting the body politic.

Many students felt morally obliged to throw themselves upon the gears and levers of the military-industrial complex. In October 1967, for example, SDS protesters attempted to disrupt recruitment interviews conducted by Dow Chemical, a manufacturer of napalm for military use in Vietnam, held in the 'Commerce' Building of Wisconsin University. A leaflet explained their actions:

> 'To end the war, it is necessary to comprehend its true nature, to understand the extent to which major institutions such as this university and Dow Chemical are committed to its continuation.... We must move from protest to resistance. Before, we talked. Now we must act. We must stop what we oppose.'

When the police turned up to evict the occupiers, they smashed windows and doors, roughly dragged out protesters, and, as a general melee erupted on the campus, fired tear gas.[24]

Indeed, peaceful protest, for both African Americans and anti-war students, was far from cost-free. They were frequently attacked both by police and bystanders, the latter often being working class. In August 1968 twenty-three thousand police and National Guardsmen pummelled ten thousand protesters outside the Democratic Party national convention in Chicago. When inside the conference a Democratic Party politician condemned these 'Gestapo tactics', the mayor of the city, Richard J. Daley, sitting on the platform, cursed him sotto voce with anti-Semitic invective. Most notoriously, perhaps, at Kent State University in Ohio, on 4 May 1970, thirteen unarmed anti-war students were shot, four fatally, by the National Guard. Fours days later, some three hundred helmeted construction workers, armed with lead pipes and crowbars, rampaged through New York's financial district, attacking long-haired students and other war protesters, while the police stood aside.

American anti-war activity, therefore, segued into a general criticism of domestic society. MOBE (Mobilization to End the War in Vietnam), for example, grouped together as the enemy all 'institutions representing militarism, exploitation, racism'.[25] The contradiction inherent between the government's strategy of 'defence of the Free World' and the tactics of conventional and psychological warfare, moreover, exposed the establishment to charges of hypocrisy. On 27 November 1965, the president of the American New Left SDS, Carl Oglesby, made a landmark speech:

> For all our official feeling for the millions who are enslaved to what we so self-righteously call the yoke of Communist tyranny, we make no real effort at all to crack through the much more vicious right-wing tyrannies that our businessmen traffic with and our nation profits from every day. And for all our cries about the international Red conspiracy to take over the world, we take only pride in the fact of our six thousand military bases on foreign soil.[26]

If Communist subversion was a danger to democracy, Oglesby implied, so too was anti-Communist subversion.

The counter-culture, an international youth phenomenon of drugs, free love, long hair, anarchic music, and eclectic clothing, was certainly a repudiation of commodified consumerism, but more particularly it was an inversion of military codes and conduct, and its associated conformist 'square' culture. Television footage of Vietnamese Communist fighters and peasants being 'zapped' from helicopter gunships, for example, gave rise to the hippie slogan 'Zap them with love', and 'Make love, not war'.[27] Emblematic of the period were images of protestors placing flowers in the rifle barrels of soldiers standing guard at the Pentagon. Much scorned since, the hippie culture was certainly often self-indulgent, but it was also justified as a riposte to the permeation of civil society by military values. This attempt to negate war with love, however, did not last. In the two years from the hippie 'Summer of Love' in 1967, as spokesperson Abbie Hoffman put it, 'The flower children have lost their innocence and grown their thorns':

> When you get down to it, we *are* guilty of being a vast conspiracy. A conspiracy pitted against the war in Vietnam and the government that still perpetuates that war, against the oppression of black communities, against the harassment of our cultural revolution, against an educational system that seeks only to channel us into a society we see as corrupt and impersonal, against the growing police state, and finally against the dehumanising work roles that a capitalist economic system demands. What we are for, quite simply, is total revolution.[28]

While the year 1968 was a high point in the revolt against the consumer-militarist nexus, it was marked by an escalating rhetorical revolutionism that alienated Middle America and increasingly divided the protest movement itself.

The broad movements opposed to militarism as an un-American excrescence were generally satisfied that as the Vietnam War approached its endgame the fundamental values of American society were being reasserted. Stalwart activists were frustrated by this complacency, believing that systemic violence was not an aberration but as 'American as cherry pie', as the militant activist H. Rap Brown put it in 1967.[29] Leftists were increasingly concerned that their general indictment of warmongering capitalism risked being forgotten. In reaction, a minority turned to increasingly ultra-left politics so as to maintain their political purity amidst the 'liberal-realists' who had concluded that withdrawal from Indochina would of itself be sufficient to restore health to American society.[30] Just as the revolt against capitalist militarism in the first half of the twentieth century had ironically given birth to a counter-movement of, effectively, insurgent militarism in the form of Bolshevism and Communism, in a somewhat farcical version this was recapitulated by the 1968 generation.

The American 'old Leftist', Irving Howe, summarized the New Left acidly but astutely. It was characterized, he said, by 'An extreme, sometimes unwarranted, hostility toward liberalism.... A vicarious indulgence in violence, often merely theoretic and thereby all the more irresponsible.... A crude, unqualified anti-Americanism; [and] An increasing identification with that sector of the "third world" in which "radical" nationalism and Communist authoritarianism merge.'[31] Indeed, '68 ultra-leftism internationally was ambivalent at best about parliamentary democracy. This was most impressively revealed in France. The Parisian *événements de mai '68*, when student riots and workers' strikes destabilized the French government, seemed to radicals a presentiment of revolution, either as a power vacuum yawning or as a floodtide radicalization of public opinion. The legitimacy of parliamentarianism in their eyes seemed at least doubtful. Fearing ultra-left anti-parliamentarianism, the French Communist Party strictly enforced a ban on students fraternizing with striking workers. The boss of the Communist CGT union organization, Georges Séguy, described his organization as '*la grande force tranquille*'.[32] Outright sympathy for authoritarianism, however, was a minority phenomenon amongst the broad New Left. There was much more hope invested in participatory grassroots democracy as an adjunct to parliamentary representation.[33] Even the Maoist Cultural Revolution, egregious as it certainly was, appealed to outposts of the New Left as a rough-hewn answer to faceless bureaucratism. Moreover, the conviction that traditional parliamentarianism was inadequate properly to hold to account the modern monoliths of the military, big business, and organized labour, and that ordinary people justly felt disenfranchised, spread well beyond the ranks of the militant youth.

It was precisely the institutions of state and industrial management beyond close democratic control that most exercised the New Left in Europe. Here radicals mobilized against the repackaged appeasers and fascist-era elites and attitudes that honeycombed the liberal state establishment. The control of German big business, for example, remained in the hands of those, such as the heavy industrial families of Thyssen and Krupp, who had under the Kaiser and Hitler formed a plutocracy.[34] West German universities were led by veterans of the Kaiserreich, Weimar, Nazi, and Occupation eras, all without having much of a record of liberalism or oppositional activity. The student slogan was: 'Beneath their academic robes, the darkness of a thousand years.'[35] The unpalatable associations of the ruling 'gerontocracy' was, for many, made evident by the presence in the German government, from 1953 to 1963, of Hans Globke, who in the 1930s had written important legal arguments justifying the anti-Semitic Nuremberg Laws, and the fact that Kurt Georg Kiesinger, the Christian Democrat chancellor of West Germany from 1963 to 1969, had joined the Nazi Party in 1933, and been a propagandist for the regime during the war.[36] Maurice Papon, Parisian Chief of Police since 1958, had as Vichy police chief in Bordeaux during the war organized the deportation of Jews to their deaths. The authoritarianism of the French state was evident in its heavy-handed, sometimes lethal repression of Communist demonstrators, and the police massacre of hundreds of Algerians in Paris in 1961. Workers had good reason to sympathize with students as they battled against the notorious CRS riot police. In Italy, similarly, there was within the industrial elites much continuity with the Fascist era; the establishment conspired to keep Communists, the main working-class party, out of government; and the police were regularly heavy-handed with leftist protesters.[37]

The prominence of students highlighted the bourgeois nature of much of 1960s radicalism. The New Left recruited substantially from a category that had historically been bourgeois almost by definition, third-level students. French leftists, however, acknowledged a post-war shift as university education expanded (about 8 to 10 per cent of youth now went to university in advanced countries):

> The social origins of the students are no longer in 1963 what they were 50 or 100 years ago. The proportion of students from the privileged classes (upper middle-class industrialists, the financial oligarchy, landowners, higher civil servants, and, to a lesser extent, the liberal professions) has decreased in favour of students from the middle classes (lower middle class, white-collar workers, minor and senior civil servants), while the increase in students from the proletariat or lower agricultural classes has remained very low. In other words, it is no longer true that the majority of students belong to the ruling privileged classes of society.[38]

Daniel Cohn-Bendit and Jean-Pierre Duteuil, of the French 'March 22 Movement', admitted that the students were 'in revolt to preserve the bourgeois privileges' that they had momentarily lost in 'the transition from competitive capitalism to monopoly capitalism'. However, they hoped that students' collision with the state would expose the dark reality of monopoly capitalism, and detonate struggle along the same lines amongst the working class.[39] The radicalism of the 1960s in Western Europe may be seen as an effort to complete the unfinished work of 1944 to 1946, by prising at the last hold-outs of authoritarian personnel and instincts lodged within the democratic structure.

Good intentions apart, New Left radicals rarely rubbed along well with workers. A London local newspaper, selling to a working-class district adjacent to a hotbed of student radicalism in an art college, doubtlessly spoke for many when it insisted that: 'The system is ours. We are the ordinary people, the nine-to-five, Monday-to-Friday-semi-detached, suburban wage-earners, who are the system. We are not victims of it. We are not slaves to it. We are it, and we like it. Does any bunch of twopenny-halfpenny kids think they can turn us upside down? They'll learn.'[40] The year 1968, nonetheless, was also a key one for the rebellion of wage workers against consumerist consensus. In 1968 no less than two-thirds of French workers were involved in strike action. The May 1970 Statuto dei Lavoratori, conceded by government and employers in the wake of the 'Hot Autumn' of 1969 in Italy, gave workers formidable concessions, mostly relating to security of jobs, wages, and conditions. In Britain trade-union membership in the 1970s rose at an unprecedented peacetime rate, accompanied by industrial militancy. There was an element of social contestation, in the demand for worker self-management, or 'autogestion', even if the 'popular panacea' of industrial democracy was in the end rejected by workers as inhibiting rights of collective bargaining, and by consumers as threatening the domination of the producer interest and restrictive practices.[41]

In temporally linking working-class struggle to a largely middle-class protest movement, '68 played a real role in rolling back neo-militarism in its 'military-industrial' form. US military culture was severely weakened and European social conservatism further marginalized. 'With the exception of Britain and Scandinavia, the liberated "Sixties" did not actually arrive in Europe until the Seventies.'[42] So remarks Tony Judt, a historian unyielding in his contempt for the New Left. What Judt fails to acknowledge, however, is that the 'Sixties' could not arrive in Europe until something like '68 opened the way. The stifling patriarchy and domineering social control in Europe promoted by Christian Democratic and conservative elites, and to some extent even by Social Democracy, in alliance with the 'permanent state', had persisted from the post-war settlement, and was only decisively undermined by the events around 1968. Britain's '68, precisely because it had far less entrenched traditionalism to kick against, featured little more than a fairly peaceable anti-war demonstration in London's Grosvenor Square, site of the American embassy. (Northern Ireland, where there certainly was a stifling establishment to contend with, had a very real and consequential '68.)

In America meanwhile the military-industrial complex was genuinely shaken by sustained protest. Congress, disillusioned by the Vietnam debacle and Nixon's covert operation in South East Asia, restricted the president's war-making capability with the War Powers Act of 1973. The same year conscription was brought to an end. Congressional investigations into the CIA in 1975 did much to expose and to undermine the abuse of sovereignty and democratic forms abroad endemic in the secret war against 'subversion'. Diplomatic brinkmanship fell out of fashion. The insane bravado of the Cuban Missile Crisis (though oddly even today mystified as a 'great moment' for US statesmanship) was much less plausible only ten years later.

Partly due to rebellion against neo-militarism, the Cold War stand-off was moderated by the development of diplomatic détente in the 1970s. In August 1975, following years of careful negotiation, all European countries except Albania, plus the United States and Canada, signed the Helsinki Accords. By these, the 'inviolability of borders' was guaranteed, which Soviet signatories took as acknowledging the USSR's control of Eastern Europe, though rights to self-determination were also confirmed, while human rights guarantees would, the West hoped, lend aid to dissident groups in the Soviet bloc. Within months, numerous so-called Helsinki Groups proliferated to monitor human rights abuses within the Soviet bloc. This was key in developing a civil society, deeply hostile to militarist bureaucracy, which would destroy Communism from within.[43]

## THE NEW RIGHT

What was striking about moves to stand down the military-industrial complex in the 1970s was the support this won—not always grudgingly—from a new breed of conservatives. The year 1968, indeed, had coincided with a revival of conservatism. The 'New Right' deprecated post-war militarism, and even more so the experience of the two World Wars, as having extended the state into commercial civil society, encouraged cosy deals between management and labour, and used the excuse of pan-class patriotism to play down the unique entrepreneurial force of property owners.[44] It was evident, indeed, that the post-war welfare-warfare, high-wage settlement was coming under stress. An astute observer on the left, James O'Connor, in his *Fiscal Crisis of the State* (1973) noted that welfarism, militarism, and the power of big business to lobby the state for subsidies were combining to overload extractable tax revenue. Continuous corporate lobbying and log-rolling, the 'interpenetration of private enterprise and the state', may have bought a period of social peace—though with the inflation and industrial militancy of the 1970s, even this was passing—but it was 'inconsistent with the survival and expansion of capitalism'. The short-circuiting of the market by government support for corporations, welfare bills, and wage settlements was hampering systematic economic rationality and planning.[45] A fear was widespread that the principle of due returns for effort was being corroded by soft-hearted, consensual liberalism. As early as from the mid-1960s, in a sarcastic response to the social liberalism of the Democratic government's 'War on Poverty', American drivers were attaching to their rear fenders the bumper-sticker, 'I Fight Poverty, I Work'.[46] There was no reason in principle that the New Right should not be able to take up the radical cause of freedom from bureaucracy and the sovereignty of the individual.

The New Right were concerned that Western society, built upon a state-brokered compromise between capital and wage labour, was increasingly enervated, smug in its own privileges, heedless of its declining 'animal spirits', and unable to face up to the responsibilities of determined global leadership. While the rigours of Depression had raised a 'Great Generation', capable of facing and smashing fascism, post-war social security seemed to have fostered a culture of irresponsibility and declining moral fibre. A revolutionary élan to extend the boundaries of free commercial civil society and representative government seemed almost entirely to have drained away.

Though the post-war settlement had been forged in the fight against fascism, the course of the Cold War seemed to suggest that, paradoxically, it made for a society incapable of such determined struggle as had given it birth. In the West, the 'Vietnam syndrome' was evidence that modern consumerist society was not supportive of large-scale militarism, either in terms of foreign war or domestic culture. The contradiction in 'modernization theory' was apparent. Why should mass-consumer societies—pacific, stable, and with a strong consensual and democratic ethos—be expected to authorize ruthless intervention to choke off revolution in countries undergoing take-off? In a 1976 book, *The Cultural Contradictions of Capitalism*, the American intellectual Daniel Bell worried at length that 'bourgeois society' (as he called it) had lost its dynamism. Political liberalism, which historically had been associated with 'bourgeois society', was undermined because 'economic liberalism has become, in corporate structure, economic oligopoly, and, in the pursuit of private wants, a hedonism that is destructive of social needs'.[47] Lack of self-belief permeating bourgeois societies threatened, in the long run, to 'devitalize a country, confuse the motivations of individuals, instil a sense of *carpe diem*, and undercut its civic will'.[48] The scanting of 'bourgeois virtues' even amongst the 'prosperous suburban' classes was an obsessive concern for putative neo-conservatives. Such former left-liberals were increasingly convinced that only the strenuous 'insistence on standards of excellence and virtue' inculcated by the competitive 'free market' could re-moralize society.[49] The victories over neo-militarism in the 1960s, ironically, opened up an opportunity to reconstitute commercial civil society as the arbiter of the state. Youth rebellion had weakened neo-militarism, but while temporarily demoralizing the right it also pointed a way ahead that would revive the revolutionary potential of bourgeois civil society.

In a 1961 book satirizing the 'meritocracy' (and coining the word), the British Labour sociologist Michael Young predicted that education and power would displace wealth and property as markers of the new elite. From the late 1970s, in fact, wealth and property became perhaps more important determinants of bourgeois status than ever before. Still, his ironic depiction of the emerging elite psychology was spot on:

> The upper classes are, on the one hand, no longer weakened by self-doubt and self-criticism. Today the eminent know that success is just reward for their own capacity, for their own efforts, and for their own undeniable achievement. They deserve to belong to a superior class.[50]

This was not a bourgeois culture content forever to defer to what appeared to be an increasingly decadent 'proletarian democracy'.

Friedrich Hayek (1899–1992) had long criticized the post-war democratic settlement in which the state intervened in the market and capital-labour relations. This social compact, he argued, was a chimera, lumping together two forms of societal organization in an unstable amalgam. Hayek thought that central economic planning was workable, if undesirable, while a purely market economy was both efficient and protective of liberty. Controlled markets, however, were a contradiction in terms: 'Both competition and central direction become poor and inefficient tools if they are incomplete; they are alternative principles used to solve the same problem, and a mixture of the two means that neither will really work and that the result will be worse than if either system had been consistently relied upon.'[51] As the 1970s dawned, Hayek's day was about to arrive.

In 1973 the CIA supported a military coup in Chile against a democratically elected Marxist government. Salvador Allende, the Popular Front candidate supported by both socialists and Communists, had been narrowly elected president of Chile in 1970. For three years America economically squeezed Allende's regime while generously financing his enemies. Allende tried to placate the 'permanent state' personnel of the civil service and army, but without success. Impressively organized 'middle-class strikes' by shopowners and truckers destabilized the regime. Washington officials hoped that these 'manifestations of massive protest will oblige the military to take over'.[52] In September 1973, General Augusto Pinochet led a military coup that deposed Allende and vigorously repressed leftism thereafter (at least three thousand were killed or 'disappeared').

This seemed to be just one more episode in the depressing litany of counter-revolutionary anti-constitutionalism that had long characterized skirmishing between the 'Free World' and 'Communist subversion'. Paradoxically, however, its sequel prefigured a 'third wave' of bourgeois revolutionary politics, for the means by which the Chilean oligarchy carved itself a new path. Between 1974 and 1976, Pinochet's monetarist economic advisors, the neo-liberal 'Chicago Boys', oversaw an economic program that cut state spending by over a quarter, allowed wages to collapse to half their 1970 level, imposed regressive taxation, and increased interest rates. Unemployment soared and companies went bankrupt. 'At its crudest,' remarks Andy Beckett, 'the Chicago Programme was class vengeance.' From 1978, however, positive reforms were introduced: privatization of state-owned enterprises; encouragement of 'popular capitalism' in the form of widespread share ownership; legal weakening of trade unions; encouragement of private healthcare; partly privatized pensions; and reform of universities, now run by businesses.[53] This was not simply a reactionary counter-revolution patching together an old order. It developed instead as an astonishingly consistent attempt to build an independent and vigorous commercial sector under the protective carapace of tyranny. The state served as the strict upholder of law, smashed the claims of wage labour, but otherwise limited itself to nurturing bourgeois civil society as the real basis for long-term stabilization. Might this programme be applied to the democratic world?

By the 1970s, as stagflation (slow growth and inflation) showed up the inadequacy of the state in governing markets, popularizations of Hayek's view attracted increasingly widespread support in the West. For the left, it seemed natural to move toward a more forceful, if democratic, direction of the economy by the state.[54] Broad opinion, however, was shifting toward support for an emancipated commercialism, and for the state to retire from the Sisyphean task of orchestrating entrepreneurs and moderating collisions between management and workers. The economic creed adopted by the 'neo-liberal' revivalists of bourgeois civil society was monetarism. Monetarism was principally a wager on the ability of the state to clear a space for the operation of a market-driven, commercial society that, in turn, would reinvigorate individual responsibility. As 'inflation is always and everywhere a monetary phenomenon',[55] governments needed simply to limit the money supply. So doing would ensure that decisions made about wages and investment would be subjected directly to rational market calculation. If a trade union succeeded in coercing from management wage increases not justified by improved productivity, then the business would fail. Government-sanctioned inflation could no longer be relied upon to introduce a post hoc proportionality by whittling down real wages.

Monetarism aimed to force capital once again to assert itself as solely in command in the workplace. In this, however, it was to be helped by the state introducing laws and deploying force to break recalcitrant trade unionism. The neo-liberals were quite clear that the state should intervene forcefully to create the legal and anti-monopolistic environment required for the flourishing of free markets: a 'competitive order', as Richard Cockett puts it, to make 'competition work'.[56] In a sense, for neo-liberals, political democracy, which balances various sectional interests, was considered to be secondary to, and less real than, 'economic democracy': 'The essential strength of the case for capitalism,' wrote the British neo-liberal, Arthur Seldon, 'is that the democracy of the market offers the masses more than the democracy of politics. The insufficiency and inequality of "pennies" can be corrected. The inequality in cultural power cannot.'[57] An emancipated civil society, in this view, not only delimited the state, but reduced the salience of political democracy in total.

## EUROCOMMUNISM AND REVOLUTION

Left parties internationally were deeply influenced by Allende's fate. They were convinced, as the general secretary of the Italian Communist Party put it, that the 'tragic outcome of the Chilean experiment'—Pinochet's coup, with wide middle-class support, against the Allende government—proved that electoral and government 'alliances of the left', based upon Communist and socialist parties, were too narrowly based to withstand anti-democratic reaction. New alliances, with 'different and far broader bases', were required that could win the allegiance and cater for the interests of 'broad sectors of the middle class'. The workers' movement should compromise its specific class demands to placate the bourgeoisie.[58]

In practice, the Communist parties of Western Europe had endorsed a parliamentary road to socialism since the days of Popular Frontism in the 1930s. This, however, had never been made theoretically consistent with the Leninist rejection of parliamentarianism. In the 1970s the three largest Western European Communist parties, in Italy, France, and Spain, confronted their Leninist legacy by adopting 'Eurocommunism', which accepted as inviolable those civil freedoms associated with 'bourgeois liberty'.[59] The General Secretary of the Spanish Communist Party, Santiago Carillo, advocated a pan-class strategy for democratization in his 1976 book, *'Eurocommunism' and the State*. All of society outside state-monopoly elites—not just workers, but also professional groups, farmers, small businesses, and traders—had an interest in seeing the state democratized.[60] In particular, the 'new middle classes' in the civil service, communication, media, teaching etcetera were amenable to a programme of radical democratization, if Communists presented themselves as bearers of national consensus, not simply proletarian.[61] Even the armed forces were moving away from default antipathy to democracy because modern military technology meant that the old ethos of subordination and command had been replaced by an ethic of professionalism.[62] Carillo's theorizing was directed to very practical ends: how, in Spain, the workers' movement could contribute to the fall of the dictatorship without provoking a middle-class and military backlash. The Eurocommunist line was to promise fealty to parliamentarianism and respect for the interests of the middle classes and the state apparatus.

However, the transition to democracy in the Mediterranean in the early 1970s demonstrated that, even with widespread popular support for a broad alliance against those monopoly capitalists held responsible for propping dictatorship, the left was unable to retain hegemony over an emancipated civil society. On 25 April 1974 an officers' coup overthrew the Portuguese dictatorship in what was termed the Captains' Revolution. The officers organized themselves as the Armed Forces Movement (MFA). Their new government was particularly anxious to break the power of those elements of the capitalist economy and state that had supported the dictatorship, and might be tempted to favour a reversion. Most banks and industries were nationalized, and there began a massive agrarian reform. Portugal disengaged from its colonies in Angola and Mozambique.

When the elections of April 1975 favoured political parties more moderate than the MFA junta, it turned to the Communist Party for support. The junta tried to balance a 'broad base of socialist support' (parliamentary electoralism) with the leftist 'political vanguard' ('revolutionary councils'), as Vasco Gonçalves, prime minister from July to September 1975, put it.[63] Observers feared the usual process of Communist subversion, and to counter this they counselled European Economic Community (EEC) intervention.[64] In November 1975, indeed, European governments collectively made it clear that aid for Portugal's teetering economy was dependent upon the curbing of Communist influence.[65] A coup by radical army units failed, and the hard left phase of the transition in Portugal came to an end. It was clear that the mass electorate, when they voted for the moderate parties in April 1975, had been mainly concerned to avoid irresponsible dictatorship developing under whatever flag. In the 1980s, with the restoration of dictatorship increasingly unlikely, the anti-capitalist elements of the Constitution were considerably watered down. Portugal looked to the EEC, which combined a strongly pro-liberal democratic framework with vigorous capitalist institutions and protection for propertied class interests. For Portugal's commercial civil society, this provided a robust and far more congenial alternative to authoritarianism as a means by which social radicalism might be headed off. In 1985 the country was admitted into the EEC.

In Greece, rightist army officers staged in April 1967 a successful coup, claiming that a Communist takeover of Greece was imminent. This 'Colonels' regime', headed by the CIA-trained Georgios Papadopoulos, was actively supported by United States diplomacy, from 1970 at the latest.[66] On 25 November 1973, Papadopoulos was ousted in a bloodless military coup, and in July 1974 power was turned over to a civilian government. Greece promptly withdrew from NATO in order to undermine US support for domestic militarism. In 1981, Greece became a member of the European Community. Here again, authoritarianism had been extirpated, but constitutionalist parliamentarianism, reinforced by the benign environment of the EEC, protected bourgeois civil society. Democracy was secured.

During the Second World War, Spain had been a pro-Axis non-belligerent, and unsurprisingly it found itself diplomatically isolated after 1945. As the confrontation with Russia deepened, however, the United States from 1947 began to bring solidly anti-Communist Francoist Spain in from the cold of international isolation. From 1950, Western democratic support did much to sustain the Franco regime. An agreement with the United States in 1953 provided for US military bases in Spain. Following the advice of International Monetary Fund 'modernization' experts, economic autarchy was abandoned. By the 1960s, Spain enjoyed the second highest rate of growth in the world, and became a fully industrialized country, with a substantial modern and urban working and middle class. Spanish society had crossed the threshold of 'mass consumer society'. Bypassing Francoist channels, industrial employers began to bargain and negotiate with clandestine workers' unions from the 1950s. This prefigured a conversion of the industrial bourgeoisie to the 'Western political model'.[67] It was the inability of the Francoist regime in Spain to assure labour market flexibility coercively that convinced much of the middle class there to support democratization. Consensual welfare capitalism was a much better bet.[68] There were advantages in democratization for government, too. Oligarchic control of the parliamentary Cortes during the dictatorship simply allowed high income earners to escape due taxation, and put the state on meagre rations.[69] The case for constitutionalization, for both commercial civil society and the state, was becoming overwhelming.

In 1975, Franco finally died. King Juan Carlos I, with his premier, Adolfo Suárez González, moved quickly to introduce democracy. In response to overtures from Suárez, the Socialists and the Communists agreed to drop their demands for a purge of Francoists from the state apparatus and a dismantling of the corporate power structure. A new Constitution was ratified in 1978, formally establishing a parliamentary monarchy and universal adult suffrage. Right-wing Civil Guards attempted a coup in 1981, but it was quickly suppressed. In 1982, a Socialist majority was elected to the Cortes and Felipe González, who strongly believed that with a declining manual working class a 'bloc of classes' was the only basis for government,[70] became prime minister. Spain was admitted into NATO in 1982, and became a member of the European Community in 1986.

Underlying the variety of these case studies, certain common traits are evident in the democratic transitions of Portugal, Greece, and Spain. The oligarchic combinations of state and monopoly capitalist enterprises were increasingly sclerotic and undermined by a more vigorous commercial civil society. The workers' movement, understandably, retained a revolutionary élan, but this was channelled towards the rooting out of authoritarianism from the 'permanent state', to a greater or lesser degree. American influence, which militated against reform for fear of empowering Communists, was generally lessened as part of the process of democratic transition. Parliamentarianism successfully revealed the minority status of those parties wishing to drive towards a socialist transformation. The steadfastly democratic and social-welfare capitalist European Community powerfully constrained tendencies towards social radicalism. The bourgeoisie could accept constitutionalism, which was, after all, their preferred environment for fostering economic rationality so long as it did not open the gates to social revolution. 'Proletarian democracy' was reconciled with commercial civil society. The state augmented its resources and improved its legitimacy by democratizing.

Perry Anderson, a British-Irish Marxist intellectual, has reflected parenthetically but perceptively on the general significance of the Spanish experience. 'American tolerance, even welcome, of authoritarian regimes in the Free World— so long as they were staunch military and political supporters of Washington'— had been 'a constant feature of the Cold War.' However, societal changes led to democratization:

> The Spanish dictatorship was the product of a bitter civil war, pitting class against class, social revolution against counter-revolution.... After the war democratization was an unthinkable option for Franco: it would have risked a political volcano erupting again, in which neither army nor church nor property would have been secure. Thirty years later, his regime had accomplished its historical task. Economic development had transformed Spanish society, radical mass politics had been extinguished, and democracy was no longer hazardous for capital. So completely had the dictatorship done its work that a toothless Bourbon socialism was incapable even of

restoring the republic it had overthrown. In this Spanish laboratory could be found a parabola of the future, which the Latin American dictators of the 1970s— Pinochet is the exemplary case—would repeat, architects of a political order in which electors, grateful for civic liberties finally restored, could be trusted henceforward not to tamper with the social order. Today the Spanish template has become the general formula of freedom: no longer making the world safe for democracy, but democracy safe for this world.[71]

Anderson's bitter irony gives too much credit to the cynical cunning of the dictature. The Mediterranean revolutions had, in fact, been driven substantially by the working classes, and broadly under the influence of the labour movement. However, breaking the power of the reactionary classes had been a much more straightforward process than earlier in the century. The Communist parties had disavowed any social revolutionary rupture. The bourgeoisie remained broadly confident that capitalist liberal democracy could be preserved, and indeed democratization meant no fundamental threat to the wealth or civil liberties of the propertied classes. With the decline of the peasantry and pacification of the urban working class, the bourgeoisie no longer felt profound fear that democratization would imperil their property and social advantages.[72] The European Economic Community provided a framework for capitalist stabilization. 'Bourgeois' democracy had developed an impressive international momentum, and entirely pushed to one side both authoritarianism and revolutionary class struggle as the last Western European dictatorships fell.

## THE CRISIS OF SOCIAL DEMOCRACY

If the Mediterranean revolutions were made by genuine 'Popular Fronts' largely immune to the vaunted perils of Communist 'subversion', one might assume that this would auger well for the fortunes of leftist Social Democracy. Socialists in the democracies, however, were concerned that their association with the interests of the most corporatized sections of wage labour—the industrial working class and public- sector employees—was cutting them off from those consumers resentful of monopolistic enterprises and workforces, and hungry for the proliferation of goods at reasonable prices produced by the private market sector. As early as 1956, the British socialist Anthony Crosland warned that 'the Labour Party...would be ill-advised to continue making a largely proletarian class-appeal when a majority of the population is gradually attaining a middle-class standard of life, and distinct symptoms even of a middle-class psychology'.[73] A long-run problem for Social Democracy, however, was its close linkage with the trade-union movement. These important ties could hardly be discarded without ideological, organizational, and financial trauma, but they reinforced the persistent view that Social Democracy and Labourism spoke for a producerist interest group rather than the 'nation'. In the 1970s, Social Democrats tried to make a virtue of their association by arguing that it was precisely their historic links with organized labour that made them far better able to cajole the trade unions into showing restraint. While conservatives and neo-liberals threatened to ignite class warfare, Social Democrats promised to manage trade unions within a framework of technocratic, corporate capitalism. They therefore presented themselves to the middle classes as necessary allies against unrestrained labour sectionalism.[74]

Such neo-corporatism, however, seemed to many to be bypassing parliaments in the setting of national policy. The scholar Keith Middlemas could write in 1979 that 'corporate bias', by which he meant policy being thrashed out between the three monoliths of state, big business, and organized labour, 'had replaced, for all *practical* purposes, classical democratic theory'.[75] Inflationary pressures led governments to experiment with price and wage controls, negotiated between state, trade unions, and business. Employers would concede high wage settlements rather than confronting their workforce, in the expectation that inflation would whittle away real wages, or they would passively rely upon government intermediation between management and unions. 'Lame-duck' industries, if politically sensitive, would often be funded by government, or even taken over entirely.

In the late 1960s and 1970s, highly organized sections of the labour force seemed poised to leverage their wage labour into labour rent, enforced by aggressively instrumental trade-union action. Narrow trade-union militancy, evincing a 'self-regarding sectionalism',[76] turned the middle class and indeed many workers against 'trade-union barons', a resonant term suggestive of feudalistic wielders of monopoly power defying both the commercial imperative of civil society and the constitutional state. Growth in unemployment inflated the welfare rolls, generating pervasive suspicion of 'spongers', and a fear that welfarism itself encouraged a culture of dependency.

## BOURGEOIS BACKLASH

Against Social Democracy rose a swelling political mobilization: a resurgence of ideologically confident, indeed crusading, bourgeois civil society. Small property, which had provided social bases of anti-democracy in the interwar period, in the 1970s and 1980s provided a mass basis for rebellion against the corporate economy and tax state. Kevin Phillips, who coined the phrase 'New Right' in 1975, defined it as a movement of the white lower middle class.[77] The New Right cadre, Michael Kolkey found, were 'successful, but not necessarily rich professionals and small businessmen'.[78] For a long time, this section of the civil society had been held to be politically under-represented. Kennedy Jones, a journalist and independent member of the British Parliament, had described this 'middle class' in 1919 as 'unorganized citizens who come between the federated manual worker on the one hand and the smaller but almost equally powerful class who stand for organized capital'.[79] In the 1970s, however, 'bourgeois movements' of such groups, the self-employed and small businesses, sprang up and vociferously criticized corporate business for accommodating state and worker interference with the free market.[80]

The legions of commercial civil society, outside the golden circle of corporations hand in hand with the state, were by the 1970s genuinely anxious that their conditions of existence were being imperilled. In practical terms, wage-price inflation degraded rentier investments. In Britain, for example, £100 invested in shares in 1935 was in real terms worth £50 by the end of 1975, while £100 invested in a War Loan in the same year was worth only £2.70 by the end of 1975.[81] It seemed that talent, hard work, saving, investing, and dedication, the virtues inculcated by self-improving bourgeois civil society, were being denied their due reward. In America, popular movements against tax policies, which proliferated in the 1970s, were at first often redistributionist, looking for the tax burden to be shifted to the wealthiest. But as inflation increased the nominal value of homes, bringing them into the higher bands of property tax, the demand changed to one of lower taxes on all levels of wealth.[82]

Of course, lower middle-class discontent was nothing new, but now it caught the mood of a society undergoing profound change. A spike in oil prices occasioned by the Arab-Israeli war in 1973 had brought the post-war boom to a sudden end. By fuelling inflation, it highlighted the structural inability of the post-war Keynesian settlement to tether wage rises to gains in productivity, at least in skilled and semi-skilled manufacturing and public services. Growth was weak and unemployment was rising. Keynesian attempts to maintain demand by public spending only added to inflation.

The British Labour government repudiated deficit-financed spending in 1976, and in America the Democratic president, Jimmy Carter, in 1979 appointed Paul Volcker as chairman of the Federal Reserve with a mandate to raise interest rates massively and bring inflation under control. This indicates the exhaustion of Social Democratic remedies; faced with a fiscal overstretch and monetary inflation, the state had to retrench. The French Socialist government of François Mitterrand in 1983 sharply turned away from a radically left Keynesian programme to policies emphasizing anti-inflation and market competitiveness. Felipe González's Socialist government in Spain from 1982 pursued stringently free-market policies. Clearly, increased international trade and capital mobility, and the decline of the homogenous manual workforce, were rendering traditional 'Social Democracy in one country' redundant. There was, therefore, a great deal of spontaneous governmental accommodation to economic crisis and structural change. Ideological transformations followed in train.

Even if structural pressures were key, political movements of the New Right were significant in themselves as a cheerleading vanguard, mobilizing not only the small-business community but also an aspirational working class. Many workers, indeed, were resentful of labour market inflexibility when its was enforced by strong-arm trade-union tactics, winked at by lazily patrician managers, and subsidized by the state—particularly as it increasingly advantaged only a minority of well-paid employees relying upon technically redundant skill sets. Big businesses could see that economically their fortunes were no longer tied to statism and organized national markets. The future lay with freedom of capital to seek profit across fragmenting domestic markets and integrating international markets. Corporations, thus, freely financed the think tanks of neo-liberalism, which in turn readily converted the parties of the centre-right. By railing against the dull consensus of neo-corporatism, by promoting a classically bourgeois vision of an unfettered commercial civil society, and by insisting that the state be restored to its rightful competence as strong leader of the nation, rather than just one actor mediating between 'social partners', the New Right was able to convey a coherent message and construct a powerful electoral alliance. The victory of Margaret Thatcher's Conservatives in 1979, Ronald Reagan's Republicans in 1980, and Helmut Kohl's Christian Democrats in 1982 were themselves epochal events, announcing and consolidating a new era.

Neo-liberalism, hegemonic by the 1980s, was certainly an ideological process, but it was also inherent in the economics of developed society.[83] Large-scale mass production of standardized goods was being displaced at the cutting-edge by smaller runs of a much greater range of products. There was a very significant turn from semi-skilled manual employment to services, information management, and administration. Factory towns were giving way to business parks, the industrial workshop floor to the office, and the high street to shopping malls.

Conveyer-belt and Fordist styles of mass production, the predominant form of 'machinofacture' after the Second World War, had lent themselves to hierarchical, large-scale production, which in turn could be emulated by command economies in the Communist world. This tendency for physical capital to concentrate in larger and larger fixed investments, however, had ceased by the later 1960s and thereafter went into reverse. Economies of scale did not apply particularly well to cutting-edge industries, such as information technology and services for niche markets. Production moved towards 'flexible specialization' and small-batch production. Large corporations, increasingly concentrating on their core competencies, outsourced operations such as cleaning and catering at one end, legal services and accounting at another. In so doing they gained from the low wages and frantic work ethic characteristic of precarious small businesses. Even research and development was outsourced, allowing innovation to be undertaken by small enterprises prepared to shoulder considerable risk. Self-employment in advanced economies grew, if not rapidly, from 9.8 per cent of non-agricultural employment in 1979 to 11.9 per cent by the end of the 1990s. This process of fragmentation of organization and the workforce affected the corporations themselves, which internally restructured into networks operating as markets.

Factory production, being more efficient than ever, required less labour, so that employment steadily declined in 'secondary' manufacture. Trade unionism waned in stength. By about 1980, a new 'working class' (or 'new middle class', depending upon the standpoint of the observer) outstripped in size the traditional blue-collar manual workforce in advanced countries. The typical wage earner now worked in the 'tertiary' services sector. Historically, white-collar workers shared to a degree the bourgeois ethic, because they could hope to forge ahead on merit. As one American white-collar worker had put it in the 1950s, 'As I see it, the union will interfere with the individual's opportunity to get ahead. The union will make it impossible for a man to be rewarded for the little extra that makes the difference between a good job and a bad one.'[84] As it expanded from the 1970s, white-collar work was proletarianized in that it lost much of its exclusivity. But to the extent that promotion by merit became far more common, wage work was semi-bourgeoisfied. The lines were being blurred.

The main beneficiaries of neo-liberalism were the chief executive officers of the largest corporations. Manual and low-grade wages stagnated from the 1970s, and inequality grew. Workers did, however, diversify from strict reliance upon wage labour, buying houses that could be remortgaged or sold at profit, investing in insurance products, and buying consumer goods on credit. Large-scale privatization helped diffuse bourgeois property assets, though state spending remained stable as a proportion of national wealth, as did state employment. However, the operations of the state were increasingly exposed to market discipline through compulsory competitive tendering and the like. States replaced full employment with low inflation as the goal of government policy. Abandoning full employment, as a barrier to the flexible labour market, implied a macroeconomic strategy calculated to cut the organized working class down to size.

As Fordist production and a mass industrial and manual working class was becoming obsolete, the opportunities to reassert the verities of bourgeois civil society were evident. The restoration and expansion of bourgeois civil society was an explicit goal for neo-liberals. While the British politician and intellectual Keith Joseph believed that the post-war era of welfarism and full employment policies had regrettably interrupted a process of 'embourgeoisement', it could now be renewed with vigour.[85] Neo-liberal ambition now was to build a 'property-owning democracy', based upon widespread homeownership and the diffusion of stocks and shares. Council houses were sold off to their occupiers by the British Conservative Party government in the 1980s, and privatization of publicly owned industries was undertaken partly to encourage a much wider social basis for bourgeois values. 'If each acre in the hands of the peasantry was another musket for the defence of property,' Rodney Barker remarks, 'it seemed as if each Telecom share passed down through the middle class might be another vote for the defence of the New Right.'[86] In the United States the cutting-edge idea was 'share-owner rights'. This meant that anyone holding stock in a company had the unqualified right to have its status as property respected. The fiduciary duty of any board of directors was to maximize the value of stocks and shares for their owners. This single goal took precedence over the wages and conditions of workers in the enterprise, and indeed precedence over any paternalistic instincts of management. Capital ownership was absolute, unfettered by any residual duties to 'stakeholders'.[87] The American wage earner, in John Gray's words, took 'second-place to the coupon-clipper'.[88]

The New Right, however, did not imagine that they were promoting a society reduced to the soulless cash nexus. The neo-liberal assumption was that bourgeois civil responsibility would be resurrected by correct social and economic policies. Margaret Thatcher looked back to bourgeois virtues inherited from a golden Victorian age:

> We were taught to work jolly hard. We were taught to prove yourself; we were taught self-reliance; we were taught to live within our income. You were taught that cleanliness

is next to godliness. You were taught self-respect. You were taught always to give a hand to your neighbour. You were taught tremendous pride in your country. All of these things are Victorian values. They are also perennial values.[89]

These perennial values of family solidarity and social solidarity were to be restored to their rightful locale: civil society. The citizenry should not be left to indulge hedonistic individualism while shuffling their duty to others onto the welfare state. As Thatcher put it in a famous, if usually misunderstood, interview:

> I think we have gone through a period when too many children and people have been given to understand 'I have a problem, it is the Government's job to cope with it!'...and so they are casting their problems on society and who is society? There is no such thing! There are individual men and women and there are families and no government can do anything except through people and people look to themselves first. It is our duty to look after ourselves and then also to help look after our neighbour.[90]

The primary role of the state, other than maintaining law, contracts, national cohesion, and international standing, was to underwrite the social costs of labour-market flexibility by retraining workers.[91] The aim was to encourage the development of a family-based workforce. Parents in well-paid employment would tide over the temporary low income of their children in training or university; children would augment their parents' reduced earnings in retirement; spouses would mutually balance full-time work, part-time work, and childcare.[92] The long-term planning involved—a willingness to spend beyond immediate income whilst acquiring skills in the expectation of earning more in the future, the whole cycle evened out by aggregate family incomes over years—had been economically modelled by the monetarist luminary Milton Friedman (1912–2006).[93]

Soaring divorce rates, however, did not suggest that families were much buttressed by neo-liberalism. Stress born of insecurity broke apart many poorer families. At the other end of the social scale, the 'alpha-male' super-rich, enjoying an apparently unending growth of wealth, characteristically indulged in serial monogamy at best, marrying and divorcing in often bewildering succession. The corporation, gifted the legal rights of any person to pursue life, liberty, and happiness, but also vested with the single will to maximize shareholder value, presented the unedifying role model of social psychopath. Despite its proponents' genuine expectations of moral refurbishment, neo-liberalism tended more towards the demoralization of society, with it concomitant of increased human unhappiness even amidst expanding wealth.

## CONCLUSION

The New Left had objected to the West supporting right-wing dictators as allies of necessity, and frustrating genuinely popular reformist influences. Defending the Free World seemed to mean sacrificing the hopes of the 'Third World' masses to protect the established liberties of the rich West. For the left, this smelled to high heaven of rank hypocrisy, and the very structure of Western capitalism, hooking together big business, the military, and (subordinately) organized labour, seemed to institutionalize complacency and cynicism. Bob Speck, an SDS leader, remarked in 1968 that both New Left and New Right were united by their hostility to 'institutions of the state'. They divided on whether 'human rights' or 'property rights' should take precedence: 'there're a helluva lot of people can go either way on that'.[94] And so they did. On the left, 'rights discourse' proliferated in various social movements promoting gay rights, women's rights, ethnic-minority rights, and youth-culture rights. Adherence to 'human rights' at large was an important motivator for those leftist 'liberal interventionists' who, from the 1990s, were arguing against the sovereignty of tyrannical state regimes, and in favour of international military action against them to protect oppressed citizens. On the right, the restoration of unimpeded freedom to accumulate property was defined as the key to general social progress.

The moral crisis of Western militarism in the 1960s emancipated profit-making for profit-making's sake. The productive forces of advanced capitalism, and thus bourgeois civil society, had been increasingly fettered by the neo-corporatist postwar settlement. It took the crisis of the 'warfare-welfare' state, pivoting around '68, to burst asunder the integument. From the 1960s, the old Fordist model of capitalism gave way to a much more liquid economy of heavily marketed and variegated production, information technology, financial and other services, and globalization. The old legions of industrial workers declined rapidly in absolute numbers, and no new section of the working class had anything like the same power in the workplace to hold up production or resist market pressures on wages and conditions. The flexible labour market disciplined workers and made for the new common sense that economic rationality took place behind the backs of collective social actors. Industrial action and trade-union militancy flared up in the 1970s, but alienated the wider public and fell to ignominious defeat and then near irrelevancy in the 1980s. With the pressure of 'proletarian democracy' reduced back to levels not seen since the nineteenth century, bourgeois status became the only existing ideal to which one might realistically aspire. Long before the collapse of Communism, widespread hope that there could be a systemic alternative to capitalism—and the privileges, both social and political, of wealth—had been near enough extinguished.

# 14

## The Demise of the 'Red Menace'

The death of Stalin in 1953 marked a significant time of choice for the Soviet Union. When Nikita Khrushchev (1894–1971) emerged as first amongst equals, the ruling party effectively offered a new deal to Soviet civil society: 'Soviet legality', a guarantee that Terror would not be resumed, privileges for the professionalized elites, and a greater concentration on consumer goods for the masses. Wages were increased for both rural and urban workers. In return the *apparat*, or 'Party', would be left in control.[1] Essentially, the Soviet Union remained a militarized bureaucratic state, always the most likely outcome given its genuine fears of a renewal of existential war. Khrushchev, however, was also a Communist idealist, who really believed in the progressive, developmental, even utopian potentialities of the system. He was particularly keen to blur the boundaries between manual labour and brain labour, and even insisted that one day's schooling a week should be conducted within the manufacturing workplace. His overall reform programme to promote worker access to advanced education, and thereby build up a more self-sufficient proletarian civil society as a basis for the state, 'threatened the privileged position of the intelligentsia', as Donald Filtzer puts it, and they 'vigorously opposed it'.[2]

Khrushchev's ouster in 1964 came as the culmination of growing disillusionment amongst the party-state's bureaucrats. They looked askance at attempts to invigorate the command economy by exposing it to popular criticism of corruption and waste. Organizational initiatives ranging from decentralization and rotation of bureaucratic posts were frustrating and often inefficient. Short of the unknown of radical democratization, or acceptance of the capitalist market that might unleash social disintegration before the guns of NATO, there seemed to be no obvious way to overcome the inefficiency of the command economy. Because the state could massively mobilize economic resources, and thus achieve absolute growth even with poor productivity, there lacked much incentive to push reform too far. The Soviet Union, genuinely fearful of renewed attack upon its territory, failed to break from the fundamentals of a militarized economy based upon increasingly old-fashioned basic industries.

### WORKERS AND THE INTELLIGENTSIA

Under the long pre-eminence of Leonid Brezhnev (1906–1982), the Soviet Union added to its enormous military establishment—missile parity with the US, and an all-oceans fleet by the 1970s—achieving real superpower status. The manual working class remained relatively privileged, and a passive base for the regime. But they were becoming less important economically than the skilled, scientific-technological cadre. This rising elite, well aware of the economic value of their relatively rare skills, chafed at the set salary differentials that kept them within range of—if still better paid than—manual workers.

The Soviet Union's technical and administrative intelligentsia in the first decades after the Revolution of 1917 had been 'inherited' from the Tsarist era. As a caste necessarily distinct from, and elevated above, the industrial working class, moreover, they were suspected of harbouring desires to establish themselves as a new bourgeoisie. As such they had been considered suspect, and to keep them in line they were subject to periodic purging and persecution. By the 1960s, Communist reformists, such as the Hungarian intellectual György Lukács (1885–1971), hoped that a generation of specialists, while 'not communist in the sense of adhering to a specific world view', were nonetheless 'Soviet men', having been produced 'by the educational system of socialism'. Now that the Communist command economy was making a transition from simple industrialization to a more complex consumer economy, Lukács understood, it was vital to incentivize the managerial and technical intelligentsia positively.[3] Brezhnev, however, remained deeply suspicious of this articulate and obviously discontented intelligentsia. He encouraged technical schools to fast-track workers through technical training, and tried to limit the intelligentsia's penetration of the *apparat*, or party-state machine, by seeking to 're-proletarianize' the Communist Party membership.[4] The passivity of the manual worker base, however, could not be relied upon indefinitely, particularly as the burden of military spending deprived consumer-goods industries of resources to supply worker demand.

There was greater instability in Eastern Europe, where nationalist resentment of Russian domination kept alive the flickering traditions of pre-Communist civil society. The East German Communist regime, fearing a Soviet abandonment after Stalin's death, upped the campaign against 'bourgeois' elements—farmers and professionals. This had to be reversed when it led to shortages of food and supplies, and an outflow of highly skilled specialists to West Germany (the Berlin Wall went up in 1961 to prevent such desertions). It was actually the working class, however, who challenged the state. In June 1953 a workers' strike escalated into a rebellion in Berlin, which had to be suppressed by Soviet forces. Hungary was similarly wracked by pell-mell industrialization dictated by military build-up, a prioritization that bore down heavily on workers' wages, and by the disordering of agriculture by heavy pressure on farmers. Though reform began from the top, in response to worker discontent, the climactic Hungarian revolution of 1956 saw the emergence of revolutionary workers' committees, on the original Soviet/Räte model. An insurgent told Sándor Kopácsi, the pro-revolution Police Chief of Budapest, that 'in the factories, the business enterprises, the municipalities, the army, people are electing revolutionary committees by secret ballot. From now on, the committees will be running the affairs of all these organizations.'[5] There were established some 2,100 workers' councils with 28,000 members. Political currents amongst revolutionaries included Catholic conservatism and elements of the extreme right, but overwhelmingly popular opinion favoured the maintenance of socialized production, revolutionized by democracy and national independence.[6] It is not at all clear, however, that a viable basis for associated producers coordinating to regulate the socialized economy, analogous to the discipline of the market, was emerging. Nicholas Krasso, of the Budapest Central Workers' Council, admitted that there was no impetus towards 'workers' management over production'.[7] Political demand instead looked to rehabilitate the democracy of actually existing 'bourgeois liberties'. There was, Krasso recalled, a unanimity of opinion: 'It was extraordinary to see how identical the demands were: freedom of parties to operate, withdrawal of Russian troops, withdrawal from the Warsaw Pact, neutrality, the right to strike, and so on.'[8] The Hungarian revolution was crushed by Russian tanks in 1956. Well aware that the stability of the regime rested on the acquiescence of workers, the re-established regime purged Communist Party ranks and announced wage increases of up to one third, financed by a massive loan from other Warsaw Pact countries.[9] Communist concern for the industrial working class only irritated the dissident intelligentsia, who denied the fitness of manual workers to lead politically. Revisionists emphasized instead the leading role of intellectuals.[10]

Radoslav Selucký, a Czechoslovakian dissident scholar, observed that while the intelligentsia undoubtedly had an easier time of it than workers, Communist Czechoslovakia was characterized by an 'unbelievable growth of egalitarianism and contempt for the social role of the intelligentsia...the intellectuals had to put up with very trying conditions, were never rewarded commensurately with their efforts and enjoyed a social status far below their true importance'.[11] By 1968, industrial wages averaged 1,448 Czech crowns compared to 2,000 crowns per month for qualified technical and scientific personnel. However, while Czechoslavak industrial wages amounted to 64 per cent of that paid to the average French worker (and 14 per cent of that paid to the US worker), salaries for specialists were only 15.5 per cent of the French equivalent (and 9.5 per cent of the US equivalent).[12] Clearly, the lack of a free market in labour held down differentials between unskilled and semi-skilled workers, and the intelligentsia. In an attempt to improve economic performance, the Czechoslovakian government moved to raise the status of the intelligentsia. As a party loyalist told Irish comrades in 1968, 'The capitalist class, as a class, was destroyed. There was a need to induce initiative among the people, as full employment was now a fact.'[13] This meant reforms to introduce labour-market flexibility by generously rewarding skill and qualification. The reformist 'Prague Spring' of 1968 in many respects represented a takeover of the government by these well-educated scientific-technical and sundry specialists, intent on improving their status by increasing pay differentials. These 'managerial-technocratic' elites permitted workers' councils in state enterprises, but closely circumscribed their functions.[14] Workers were naturally suspicious of such liberalization until the Soviet invasion of 20–21 August rallied them to the government in defence of national independence.[15] Whilst hatred of party-state autocracy and Russian domination was clear enough, there remained no great momentum towards capitalist restoration. A poll conducted by a Prague newspaper on 8 July 1968 found that

89 per cent of respondents wanted to continue with the development of 'socialism with a human face' whereas only 5 per cent wanted a return to capitalism; 6 per cent expressed no opinion.[16]

The primacy of workers in Communist countries, where bourgeois civil society had been crushed, was just about evident in 1950s and 1960s Eastern Europe. There did not exist a commercial civil society as a base and domestic model for those professionals with a self-evident interest in salary differentials and social inequality. But neither had the capacity of proletarian civil society to submit a planned economy to popular and efficient discipline been demonstrated. The thesis that a planned economy must support a state tending towards totalitarianism was nothing like refuted.

## COMMUNIST CHINA

The Communist regime in China, far less reliant upon cultivating the toleration of an industrial proletariat that remained relatively small, was proportionately more experimental in its attempts to construct a civil society adequate to the tasks of modernization. In the days before the United States dropped the atom bombs on Hiroshima and Nagasaki (6 and 9 August 1945), Russia had joined the war against Japan and quickly overrun Manchuria. Soviet seizure of industrial goods from this former economic powerhouse completed the destruction of bourgeois civil society there begun by Japanese oppression.[17] The Kuomintang government's reliance upon American funding, moreover, encouraged irresponsibility and corruption in the territories it controlled. Chronic inflation in particular demoralized the middle class and alienated them from the ruling KMT party.[18] The cities cracked from within, the fissures widened by Communist agitation. In January 1949 the Communists took Beijing without a fight, and on 1 October the People's Republic of China (PRC) was formally established.

A peasant wave had engulfed the cities, but rural society did not thereby become hegemonic. Peasant families, scattered and tied to the land, are 'natural anarchists', as Eric Wolf points out, and cannot secure command of 'the cities which house the centres of control... the strategic non-agricultural resources'.[19] 'The Party', thus, faced little opposition in taking control of the state. In his 1947 pamphlet, *On Coalition Government*, Mao promised 'a thoroughgoing bourgeois-democratic revolution of a new type led by the Communist Party'.[20] What this 'democracy' meant in theory was encapsulated by the party's 'Mass Line' directive. This instructed the party cadre to listen to, learn from, and educate the masses, in a kind of spiral linking 'the nucleus of the leadership closely with the broad masses'. The idea was to take the 'scattered and unsystematic ideas of the masses' and to turn them, through Marxist-Leninist processing, into 'concentrated and systematic ideas', which in turn would be propagated and explained until 'the masses embrace them as their own'.[21] The Mass Line, therefore, gave to the Communist party the function of listening to, vocalizing, and educating the 'people'.

The regime was defined not as a 'proletarian dictatorship' but as a 'people's democratic dictatorship'. The 'people' here referred to four social classes bound in a coalition by the CCP: the workers, the peasants, the petite bourgeoisie, and the 'national-capitalists'. This last category was held to be progressive elements of the bourgeoisie who had resisted egregious collaboration with imperialism or the Nationalist regime. In reality, the Communist regime at first destroyed the landlord class, then bourgeois civil society. Millions of people were raked over by persecutions, and in 1953 a 'five year plan' was introduced, calculated to achieve the 'transition to socialism'. By the end of 1956, 90 per cent of handicraft workers, 99 per cent of privately owned industrial enterprises, and 85 per cent of privately owned commercial enterprises had been taken into the public sector, while 96.3 per cent of peasant farms had joined cooperatives. In this period, the party emphasized the construction of a modernizing, urban, managerial elite. A certain liberalization of the political culture was designed to give urban intellectuals, mostly former bourgeois, the space to develop self-confidence and authority.[22] 'Let a hundred flowers bloom,' said Mao, 'let the hundred schools of thought contend'. By mid-1957, however, public openness threatened to spin out of control, as expressed opinions moved from denunciation of corrupt officials to criticism of the entire party. The CCP leadership abruptly brought the opening to an end by denouncing the dissenting mood as a product of 'bourgeois rightists'.

The swing towards the left continued with a sudden voluntarist ratcheting up of the campaign to modernize the country. In 1958 a 'Great Leap Forward' was announced as the next stage of 'Socialist Construction'. The Great Leap Forward was supposed to harness the creative energies and structured experience and folk wisdom of the peasant masses to the task of economic modernization. China's comparative advantage, after all, was clearly in high levels of population rather than in capital or modern technical experience. There was a drive to consolidate the collectivized farms into massive 'people's communes'. By late 1958, 750,000 agricultural cooperatives had been amalgamated into 23,500 communes, each averaging 5,000 households, or 22,000 people. Each commune was intended to be economically self-sufficient, even down to pig-iron smelting in backyard furnaces. The expectation was that military- style discipline and massive economies of scale would in effect arrange human labour into machine-like assemblages, obviating the need for actual capital investment to rapidly raise productivity. Such a direct and forceful reordering of the structures of rural production, not to mention the callously utilitarian attitude to peasant communities, inevitably backfired badly, and agricultural output plummeted. Aggravated by natural disasters, food output fell and there was terrible famine in large areas. The Great Leap Forward, in combination with adverse weather conditions, saw perhaps 30 million excess deaths.[23] The attempt to industrialize on the cheap led only to exceptionally poor-quality, shoddy goods being turned out. Both the peasantry and the intellectual cadres were exhausted by the continual pitch of warlike mobilization, and in the face of such poor returns demoralization was widespread.

Mao's senior colleagues tried to shuffle him away from the levers of government, entrusting him instead with the seemingly innocuous task of monitoring ideological purity within the party. By 1961 a moderate leadership was in command, with General Secretary Deng Xiaoping (1904–1997) the key figure, and there was also a reversion to reliance upon a professionalized cadre, with authority being restored to factory managers. By 1965 it seemed that the worst effects of the Great Leap Forward had been overcome. Mao, however, resented his exclusion from the centre of power, and seethed at the implied dismissal of his crude version of voluntarist economics. He concluded that opposition to his ideas derived from creeping 'capitalism' and rightist deviations infecting the party. Mao's followers launched scathing attacks on rivals in the governing elites, condemning their ideological failings and betrayals. This had taken shape, by mid-1966, as the Great Proletarian Cultural Revolution, a mass campaign directed primarily against the apparatus of the CCP itself. Frenzied 'Red Guards' of students and impressionable youths were whipped up against the conservative bureaucracy. Mao favoured mobilizing students rather than workers precisely because they were of relatively little importance economically.[24]

Though undoubtedly genuine popular grievances were being articulated, this was, primarily, a kind of civil war within the Communist elite. In the struggle, the party was shattered and Mao re-emerged victorious. Deng was forced to resign office, and many of his party allies were subjected to a violent process of public criticism that amounted to torture. The entire apparatus of political control grew unsteady, however, and the army moved to repress Red Guard radicalism. In 1968, Mao—alarmed by the Soviet invasion of Czechoslovakia—concluded that the Cultural Revolution was destroying the state's capacity to marshal its resources rationally and maintain a military of international standing. The mobilization of popular agitation was formally ended in April 1969 at the CCP's Ninth National Party Congress. Mao's clear conclusion was on the need for strong party government:

> There has to be a nucleus. It doesn't matter what it's called, it is all right to call it a Communist Party, it is all right to call it a social-democratic party, it is all right to call it a social-democratic workers' party, it is all right to call it a Kuomintang, it is all right to call it the I-Kuan-tao, but in any case there has to be a party.[25]

The political eclecticism this implied was soon apparent. While the radicals remained entrenched in leadership circles, the drift was fairly consistently rightward. The president of the United States, Richard Nixon, was received in February 1972, indicative that anti-Russianism was of higher priority than fending off contamination by the capitalist world. Deng Xiaoping was reinstated as a vice premier in April 1973, and he led the way in a renewed emphasis on modernizing the economy and resources of the state. Following Mao's death in September 1976, there was an attempt by ultra-leftists to depose Deng Xiaoping. The ruling elite had little appetite for a new bout of Cultural Revolution, however, and the 'Gang of Four' were arrested and imprisoned.

Maoism had been a dramatic attempt to modernize without a bourgeois civil society by applying factory principles to society as a whole. It also harnessed, however, popular hostility to bureaucratism. Maoism pushed to the limit the theory that the mobilized masses could act as an adequate alternative to the price mechanism and market discipline as a means of checking and rooting out the slothful and self-serving tendencies of the 'jobsworth' apparatchik. The limitations of Maoism were evident in the irrationality it encouraged. Moreover, the attempt to bring the local knowledge and class instincts of peasants, workers, and urban youth to bear on the party and bureaucracy was always mediated through the 'mass line', essentially ideological vetting. This, in turn, empowered the centralizing elites and demoralized the masses. It proved to be no credible alternative to commercial civil society as a basis for rational governance.

Bouts of ultra-leftism, though chaotic, had been limited and incomplete, and a substantial layer of former bourgeoisie survived as personnel of economic administration. The substance of Maoism was eventually abandoned by Deng Xiaoping, who permitted the redevelopment of commerce and the profit criteria. 'Bourgeois right', the rewarding of marketable attributes at the cost of social equality, was justified by recourse to the high-Stalinist nostrum of 'payment according to quantity and *quality* of labour'. The priority in modernization now was to 'give full play to the experts'.[26] Market mechanisms were combined with watered-down populism in the form of anti-corruption drives against the still-mighty bureaucracy. What remained of Mao Zedong thought was his insistence on the need for a strong party to contain and channel the energies of civil society. So long as entrepreneurs were contained by the state, Deng argued, they could not form a 'cohesive and overt class' opposed to the regime.[27] This remained talismanic to the Communist elites overseeing the country's transition to a marketized economy.

## THE COLLAPSE OF COMMUNISM

The economic crisis in the European Communist world owed much to the difficulty of transferring labour from industries where technological change meant that fewer workers were needed, to new growth areas, particularly in services. In the capitalist West, it proved possible to shift labour away from manufacturing, at least over time. The primary problem for the Soviet Union was not that there were insufficient incentives in the planning system; resources, after all, did flow to where they were directed. The plans worked, it is simply that—from 1970—they were misconceived. Fearful of alienating its core working class, and defensive of traditional industrial capacity as a guarantor of conventional military strength, the Soviet regime attempted to keep its economy in a primarily metallurgical phase by over-allocating resources to it.[28] It was similar in the Central and Eastern European satellite states, where the shock of the 'Prague Spring' undermined what impetus there was towards Communist reformism. The East German 'New Economic System', which had enhanced the role of the technical intelligentsia to good economic effect, was brought to an abrupt end in 1968.[29] This wager on the traditional worker set the economy on a declining growth gradient. By the late 1980s the Communist bloc was in crisis.

The Soviet Union's greatest difficulty was in encouraging labour productivity. Communism had no automatic and consistent mechanism, such as the market, to raise productivity, other than continuous investment in fixed capital. With the abandonment of Terror, the regime was reduced to exhortation: 'The very heart of the ideological work of the party, Soviets, trade unions and Komsomol,' declared the Party Plenum plaintively in 1960, 'must consist in fostering *love and respect for socially useful labour in every Soviet person.*'[30] Between 1950 and 1992, nonetheless, labour productivity in Central and Eastern Europe and the Soviet Union increased only 2.8-fold, compared to a 4.4-fold increase in Western Europe. The command-economy countries failed to develop cutting-edge service sectors, funnelling only 25–30 per cent of resources that way.[31]

The Communist regimes saw manual workers, not long removed from the countryside, as their social base. Even in the early 1970s, Brezhnev's government in Russia campaigned against the spread of private farming, for fear that it would encourage a 'bourgeois' civil society independent of the state.[32] But wage labourers themselves were increasingly frustrated by shortages of consumer goods. By 1970, Brezhnev and the Soviet leadership had concluded that rising consumer demand in the Soviet Union and Eastern European satellites could only be assuaged by attracting foreign capital, technology, and commodities from the advanced capitalist world. The combined foreign debt of the Soviet satellites increased from $19 billion in 1975 to about $62 billion in 1981. This was funnelled towards the industrial workforce. In East Germany, for example, much borrowing was used to support working-class social benefits: full employment, subsidized housing, childcare, transport, and basic foodstuffs. It was felt to be more important to placate the working class, which was held to be basically loyal to the regime, rather than intellectuals who were closely monitored and mostly controlled by the Stasi secret police.[33] Yet the Communist parties themselves were janus-faced, their leaders striving to sustain working-class sympathy whilst their ranks filled with technical and intellectual professionals. Two Hungarian dissidents suggested in the early 1970s that the ruling parties were 'at one and the same time mass parties of the intellectual class and cadre parties of the working class'.[34] How long would such a ruling elite prioritize worker consensus?

By the 1980s, growth rates in the Soviet bloc had slowed to about 1 per cent per annum. Inflation whittled away social-security benefits, such as pensions. Low worker morale was rife and acting as a real drag on production. Rebellion against state repression combined with a nationalist resentment, outside Russia, directed against subordination to Moscow. The Soviet Union's military overstretch was highlighted by the war in Afghanistan, in which about fourteen thousand Soviet soldiers were killed between 1979 and 1989. Soviet defence spending per annum almost matched that of the United States in absolute terms, and was twice as high as a percentage of GNP, at over 12 per cent.[35] This was a crushing burden; combined with the command economy's overemphasis on heavy industry (itself a corollary of militarization), it ensured that citizens were deprived of consumer goods taken for granted in the advanced West. Even with this, by the mid-1980s Russian analysts began to doubt whether, faced with 'emerging technologies', Soviet forces could anymore hope to defend their Eastern European hegemony successfully against Western arms.[36]

The bankruptcy of Communist rule, and continued hostility to Russian dominance in Eastern Europe, was made apparent by the enormous popularity of the trade union-based Solidarność (Solidarity) Movement in Poland, which launched a wave of strikes and demonstrations under the leadership of electrician Lech Walesa in 1980. Solidarność was strikingly proletarian in its agency. This evident defection of workers from Communist Party rule was deeply demoralizing for Communist elites across the bloc.[37] Workers' grievances were similar to those of trade unionists in the West, and Solidarność burst out of growing worker hostility to differentials in wealth, education, and autonomy.[38] Their movement was in large part motivated at first by a desire for *samorząd*, or 'self government', which implied a 'workers democracy' giving representatives of factories, cities, and villages control over the economy. This was not looked upon favourably by the anti-Communist intelligentsia, who were frustrated at their subordination to the interests of workers, and feared a re-legitimization of Communism.[39] Indeed, an opinion poll in 1985 found that 50 per cent of Poles thought that capitalism was more exploitative and unjust even than existing 'socialism'; only 29 per cent thought the opposite.[40] As time went on, however, the intelligentsia and skilled professionals were increasingly able to dilute the association of Solidarność with workers' interests.[41] Solidarność in the 1980s sparked a proliferation of civil-society organizations, which were able to survive martial law from 1981 by taking cover, in a semi-clandestine form, behind the authoritative Catholic Church. This phenomenon of Christianization of discontent became common across Eastern Europe.

In 1988, General Jaruzelski's government in Poland, in desperate need of Western loans, was informed in no uncertain terms by Western governments that help would not be forthcoming from across the Iron Curtain unless a settlement was reached with Solidarność. Free elections in Poland were conceded by the Communist regime in June 1989. The Soviet Union accepted a non-Communist Polish government, and other Eastern European governments were emboldened to follow its example, enticed by offers of Western economic aid. 'Round-table' negotiations between government and opposition representatives led to a new Hungarian government in the summer of 1989. It was promised a loan of half a billion dollars from West Germany if it opened the border to the West. In doing so, it provided a conduit for East Germans to circumvent the Berlin Wall and Iron Curtain border. The Communist premier of East Germany, Erich Honecker, tried to convince his politburo that 'everything will collapse if we give an inch', but without support from Soviet troops the government refused to risk an uprising, and forced Honecker's resignation on 18 October 1989.[42] There was an attempt by the Communist regime in Czechoslovakia to use force against demonstrators, and street battles broke out in Prague on 17 November. Opposition forces called for strikes and boycotts, while journalists ignored orders to print or broadcast government propaganda. The government was forced to resign, and in December 1989 Vaclav Havel, a veteran writer and oppositionist, was elected president. The independent and despotic Ceaușescu regime in Romania collapsed over Christmas 1989. In 1990, in return for German loans to the Soviet Union, Mikhail Gorbachev, the premier of the Soviet Union, agreed to East Germany being absorbed into the Federal Republic of Germany, and hence into NATO.

The transitional regimes of Central and Eastern Europe committed themselves to restoring capitalism, a programme heartily endorsed by the successor parliamentary democracies. The revolutions in Poland and Czechoslovakia, and to an extent in Romania, had broad participation, including workers and the specialist intelligentsia. In Hungary and in East Germany, where workers had been more effectively privileged by the regime, the intelligentsia and white-collar professionals took the lead.[43] For the technical cadre, it was attractively evident that a market economy would reward their skills at levels unthinkable in the old militarist, inefficient, and workerist industrial command economies. In the absence of a domestic commercial civil society, the specialists and intelligentsia were no bourgeoisie as such, but they could well imagine becoming one.

Gorbachev had been elected General Secretary of the Soviet Communist Party in 1985. Beginning with concerted attempts at demilitarization, growing resistance within his own party forced Gorbachev to adopt, in 1987, more radical policies in his search for *perestroika* (restructuring)—including some form of freedom of speech (*glasnost*, or openness). Gorbachev envisaged a mixed economy with 'a plurality of forms of ownership'—cooperatives, joint-stock companies, and entrepreneurs—so as to 'combine socialism with the private interests of the people'.[44] His reform programme only accentuated the crisis by disabling the mechanisms of the command economy without replacing them with market articulation. The effects of cuts in defence spending were too slow in coming—spending on the armed forces actually rose between 1985 and 1989[45]—and resources were not switched sufficiently quickly to consumer-goods production. A move towards greater freedom of speech undermined the ideological hegemony of Communism. The USSR itself began to fragment, as the Baltic States and Georgia agitated for independence.

Anxious that full-scale collapse loomed, Gorbachev attempted to slow the pace of reform in early 1991. He was challenged, however, by the newly elected president of the Russian Republic, Boris Yeltsin. Then, in August 1991, Communist conservatives attempted to launch a coup. Though it seems likely that about 40 per cent of the Russian population supported or sympathized with the coup attempt, the bulk of the army held aloof and it was defied by Yeltsin's Russian Republic.[46] As the coup fell apart, so too did the Soviet Union. The Baltic States immediately seceded, to be followed by the other Soviet republics, including even Russia. When Gorbachev resigned the presidency of the Soviet Union on Christmas Day, 1991, it had ceased to exist. Characteristic of all the anti-Communist revolutions had been an unwillingness by the state apparatus to defend the old regime. The elites had lost faith in a Communist ideology predicated on heavy industry and worker loyalty.

The Communist '68, Czechoslovakia's 'Prague Spring', had been, as we have seen, somewhat ambiguous in its meaning at the time; the restoration of capitalism had not been a widely popular demand. Writing in 2001, however, Adam Michnik, the Polish former dissident, was quite clear about the ultimate destination: 'For my generation the road to freedom began in 1968. While students in Paris and Berkeley were rejecting bourgeois democracy, we in Prague or Warsaw were fighting for a freedom that only the bourgeois order could guarantee.'[47] There had been, however, little bourgeoisie as such to participate in the anti-Communist revolution, the middle-class cadre, such as it was, being largely employees of the state. For professionals, a shift towards capitalism promised a marked status shift upwards, but this alone, it was felt, was an inadequate social constituency for the post-Communist system. Richard Sakwa commented in 1993: 'in Russia political democracy is in search of a political base.... The democratic revolution came before the bourgeois revolution; political changes preceded the economic and social basis on which they could be rooted. Democracy came before liberalism, and thus in danger of finding itself hanging in the air, deprived of a social base.'[48]

Land reform and privatization of state enterprises, diffusing property, was to create a commercial civil society able to provide a permanent material base for what otherwise might only be a passing ideological commitment to free-market constitutionalism. As Yeltsin put it, on 28 October 1991, 'We have defended political freedom; now we have to give economic freedom.' The imposition of 'shock therapy', the application of commodified property forms in double-quick time, as advised by Western experts, was given clear priority over construction of an 'open society'.[49] Those who had done well out of Communism generally did even better out of restored capitalism. A very well-educated 'middle class' (there were some 23.5 million beneficiaries of higher education in Russia by 1984) had been disproportionately represented in the ruling Communist parties.[50] A survey of Russia's most influential entrepreneurs in 1992–3 found that 62 per cent had been part of the old party-state political and managerial elite. Another 15 per cent were scientists.[51] As the labour market was increasingly subordinated to the market, those with skills reaped remuneration packages far outstripping the privileges of the old Communist apparatchiks. Vaclav Havel observed regretfully that:

> Many members of the party elite, the so-called *nomenklatura*, who, until very recently, were faking concern about social justice and the working class, have cast aside their masks and, almost overnight, openly become speculators and thieves. Many a once feared Communist is now an unscrupulous capitalist, shamelessly and unequivocally laughing in the face of the same worker whose interests he once allegedly defended.[52]

The developing post-Soviet bourgeoisie did not 'take over' the state—this, as we have seen, never being characteristic of bourgeois revolution. Rather, the new business elites moved into symbiotic partnership with the post-Soviet state structures, indeed relying rather more on 'rent-seeking' exploitation of bureaucratic favours than the market as such.[53] Still, despite the inequity of the new order, post-Communist countries were exceptionally amenable to shock therapy. This was made easier, perhaps, by the destruction of petit-bourgeois property and the partial atomization of wage labour inherited from Communist rule. Bourgeois property forms—the salaries, profits, dividends, and rents of a fluid market economy—had little competition.

The result of shock therapy was a collapse of living standards. From the outset, wages were regularly withheld. Approximately 60 per cent of Russian workers were not paid on time, and on average the wages handed out each month amounted to only 60 per cent of wages earned.[54] In Central and Eastern Europe, the proportion of the population living in poverty rose from 3 per cent in 1987–8 to 25 per cent in 1993–5.[55] Many values of the old system, prioritizing social solidarity, tenaciously hung on in popular consciousness after the collapse.[56] Communist ideology had for seventy years lauded productive social labour, and perestroika was sold to workers as a kind of 'managerial revolution' that spoke up for the enterprise as a collectivity, including labour, against the dead weight of centralized bureaucratic control. Outright privatization, however, which vested property rights in owners, offended workers' concepts of common possession.[57] It was primarily older workers, however, who were most resistant to the commodification of wage labour. Emigration, allowing the youth in particular to escape the pain of social reconstruction, was vital for the transition to bourgeois civil society.

Twenty years on, most of the former Communist countries enjoyed very significantly improved levels of per-capita GDP. Still, the construction of bourgeois civil society and stable constitutionalism was difficult and often incomplete. In Central and Eastern Europe, redeveloped bourgeois civil society did succeed in fiscally constraining the state through an effective system of taxation registering diffuse private property. In the former Soviet Union, however, taxation largely collapsed, and the state was forced to strike bilateral deals with concentrations of plutocratic power, in a reprise of interwar systems of state-cartel capitalism.[58] Oligarchs wielded disproportionate political power, bending the state to sectional commercial ends. Inter-firm competition often hinged on manipulation of the courts, civil service, and state offices rather than performance in an open marketplace. While there was no popular rebellion in the republics of the former Soviet Union, the corruption and immiseration attendant on privatization under parliamentary aegis produced a backlash. Semi-authoritarian government took the electoral process in hand. Such 'strong leadership', notably that of Vladimir Putin in Russia, enjoyed a good deal of popular support. In Central and Eastern Europe, right-wing parties grew in popularity and formed governments by promising economic integration with international free-market capitalism, but downplaying 'excessive' deference to civil liberties and evincing hostility to 'multiculturalism'. Following Communist Yugoslavia's collapse, distribution of the federation's economic and political patrimony between its legatees exploded into partition, warfare between nationalities, and 'ethnic cleansing'.

In China, the Communist state preferred to foster bourgeois civil society without risking a sharp political transition. Here the incipient bourgeoisie were allowed every opportunity to take advantage from market valuation of their own skills and contacts, both in the legal and grey economy, while the proletarianizing workforce was denied any opportunity to bargain up its wages. After some hesitation, the regime crushed in blood the pro-democracy protests in Tiananmen Square of June 1989. The protesters had grouped students concerned with civil liberties, workers struggling with market reforms, declining social security and inflation, and *getihu* (petty traders) irritated at the costs imposed upon their businesses by corruption. The well-paid employees of big business, no doubt concerned at the rough egalitarianism of the movement, held aloof. Indeed, market reforms were suspended until 1992, before they were let rip again.[59] Thereafter, the Chinese government relied upon rapid economic growth (at about 8 per cent per annum), the sheer social turmoil of a huge modernizing society, and the loyalty of an expanding middle class to ward off coherent anti-systemic protest. This seemed to work. One sociologist found that by the twenty-first century about four-fifths of the entrepreneurial 'new bourgeoisie' were 'acceptant', in that they prioritized stability over political innovation (or reaction): they were content to go along with the elite-led bandwagon.[60] Even an avowedly Communist regime could take advantage of the entrepreneur's proclivity to leave the state to its own devices, so long as bourgeois civil society was protected.

## THE WASHINGTON CONSENSUS

The old assumptions of modernization theory seemed passé now, particularly its Social Democratic conclusion that dangerous class inequalities should be lessened through aid and careful state welfarism. The decline and fall of Communism, in eliminating the most obvious alternative to bourgeois civil society, had an electrifying effect on global democratic revolution. Bourgeois civil society, and its global sponsors in the West, could embrace popular constitutionalism with little fear that so doing would empower Communist subversion.

South Africa was the premier case of an entrenched conflict that became resolvable because of the decline of socialism. There had been strong incentives in South Africa for the white bourgeoisie to be anti-democratic. Democratic revolution had a poor record in sub-Saharan Africa. The model of the Congo in the 1960s, particularly, was not enticing. The Freedom Charter adopted by the African National Congress (ANC) in 1955, if taken literally, was clearly anti-capitalist; it called for the nationalization of banks, mines, and industry, and the redistribution of land.[61] The Communist Party, moreover, was a powerful presence in the African National Congress. The whites of South Africa had a developed and cohesive national identity, having grounds to consider themselves to be an African nation of European origin, distinct from South Africa's black population. For them 'decolonization' was not an option, while adopting majority rule in a multiracial South Africa threatened submergence and extinction of a distinct national identity, and very probably dispossession and perhaps economic catastrophe. The State of South Africa *Yearbook* in 1963 justified the notorious apartheid system of racial classification, 'separate development', and oppression in the following terms:

> The South African government has accepted the desire of Colonial people for self rule as a natural right.... South Africa has its dependent people within her own borders. The granting of independence can, therefore, not follow the political pattern worked out by the colonial powers of Europe. For good reasons Colonial people were not represented by the Parliaments of the European mother-countries. These reasons also hold good for South Africa. Most multi-national states created in Europe were not a success, but led to friction and fear of domination.... Western democracy is foreign to

Bantu tradition. All over Africa the tendency is towards a one-party state under a Black dictator. To adopt the principle of One Man-One Vote in South Africa would hand over the culturally advanced groups, i.e., the Whites, Coloureds and Indians, to the mercy of a Bantu leader who might well have Communistic affiliations.... South Africa's policy could rightly be described as Nation-Building. In contrast with the procedure found elsewhere in Africa, [South Africa aims] at creating a solid foundation for Bantu self-government by building the body politic from the bottom upwards, thereby introducing an element of democracy which is expected to thwart the ambition of Black Dictators.[62]

Bourgeois democracy here seemed predicated on the suppression of the internally colonized majority. Multiracialism threatened the collapse of a coherent national identity and the spiralling off into state dictatorship under a kleptocracy.

South Africa was an embarrassment for the West. Defenders of apartheid were able to use arguments derived from modernization theory: the white 'nation' was mass-consumerist, internally democratic, proof against Communist temptation, and stable; it suppressed the liberties of the 'Bantu' people because its 'traditional society', undergoing a painful and prolonged drive towards 'industrial maturity', was obviously prey to Communist subversion or simple collapse into tyranny. It was politically and diplomatically impossible for the decolonizing West to accept the overt racialism of the apartheid regime, but their sympathy was made clear enough by America and Britain's defence of the South African government as an anti-Communist bulwark.

Domestically, however, the nature of South African capitalism was morphing due to the increasing obsolescence of the Fordist model of metallurgical and extractive industry. Rolling rebellion by the Black townships increased the fiscal strain on the military-industrial state. By the 1980s both business and state circles in South Africa were adopting neo-liberal economic assumptions. They now saw apartheid as featherbedding inefficient industries for political reasons. It unsustainably imposed rigidity on the labour market.[63] Positively, the fear of Communist 'subversion' of the black liberation movement was punctured by the collapse of Communism in Europe. A way out for the regime presented itself.

On 2 February 1990, F. W. de Klerk, the prime minister, announced the end of apartheid and lifted the ban on the ANC. Ten days later, ANC leader Nelson Mandela was released from twenty-seven years of imprisonment. The white government, helped by massive propagandizing from the corporate bourgeoisie, secured in 1993 ANC acceptance of a neo-liberal market economy as the foundation of multiracial democracy. The black majority would nominate party control of the state, whilst the corporate sector would retain secure control of the economy.[64] When free elections were held in 1994 the ANC won a massive victory, with Mandela becoming president. This dramatic victory had been made possible by the withdrawal of the Soviet Union from involvement in Third World politics once Gorbachev became premier. The South African white bourgeoisie had been reassured that majority rule would not lead to social and racial cataclysm. In a more flexible economy, both the established white and the rising black bourgeoisie could expect to prosper.

More generally, by the 1980s Western 'modernization' theory was abandoned as a developmental model for the 'Third World' by institutions such as the World Bank and the International Monetary Fund (IMF). Policies ameliorating social inequality were no longer justified by a need to counter Communist 'subversion', and they were deemed to have inhibited the development of commercial civil society. Developing countries had been wrong to replace foreign imports with goods produced by domestic industries, which were usually inefficient and state-run. Rather, developing countries needed to export, and to concentrate on areas where they enjoyed a comparative advantage in the international market. This appeared to have been the route successfully taken by such newly industrializing countries as South Korea and Taiwan. The 'Washington consensus', ideologically hegemonic by the 1990s, was backed by international credit flows. Just as Communist countries seeking loans from Western governments had provided invaluable opportunities to hook their state apparatus to the market, the developing world's debt crisis was used by the West as a lever to pitch them towards free-market democratization. The World Bank introduced 'structural adjustment programmes' for African and Latin American countries that required privatization of state assets, austerity measures to eliminate budget deficits, and devaluation of currencies. Privatization protected productive assets from capricious state appropriation, and the need to secure consent for the taxation required to fund debt repayments encouraged parliamentarianism. The democratic form of bourgeois civil society guaranteed continued help from the IMF and World Bank. As Robert H. Bates puts it, 'To retain favour in the international community, autocratic heads of state...gingerly set in motion political reforms, designed to retain support in the Western democracies for further international lending.... The need for access to international capital thus set in motion not only the reforms of economic policies but also the reform of political institutions.'[65] Constitutionalism was thus more or less imposed on developing countries, in a striking reassertion of the link between fiscal credibility, parliamentarianism, and protection of private productive property.

Democratic revolution duly swept over Latin America and Africa from 1989, with both Communist and right-wing dictatorships collapsing, or at least remodelling themselves as quasi-constitutionalist. Civil war in Algeria, general war in the Great Lakes region of Africa, and genocide in Rwanda made starkly clear, however, that this was no painless process. Amy Chau points out that 'market-dominant' ethnic minorities, for widely varying historical reasons, retain positions of advantage in marketizing societies, and dominate economically the 'indigenous' majorities around them. The Chinese of Indonesia, for example, though comprising 3 per cent of the population, control about 70 per cent of the national economy. Whites continue to hold a similar position in South Africa, as they do in Brazil, Ecuador, Guatemala, and much of Latin America. The Lebanese are market-dominant in West Africa, the Croats in the former Yugoslavia, and the Ibo in Nigeria. Such congruence of market advantage with ethnicity tends to expose minorities to jealousy and hostility in majority eyes, and delegitimizes the unalloyed market state. 'Market-dominant minorities are the achilles' heel of free-market democracy,' Chou concludes.[66] As neo-liberalism tended to increase inequality and destroyed much basic social provision for the world's poorest, there was much to resent. Many newly democratized states concealed a permanent and authoritarian state apparatus, manipulating electoralism and employing, as needed, sanguinary repression. Nonetheless, market-democracy had expanded with breathtaking speed. It was truly an age of bourgeois revolution.

That the collapse of the Communist bloc marked a definitive end to the Cold War stand-off necessarily had profound consequences for militarism.[67] With militarism in decline, the salience of the 'welfare-warfare' state was sharply reduced and the age of the 'market-state', to use Philip Bobbitt's term, became a dominant reality.[68] Bobbit quotes President Bill Clinton to characterize the new 'market-state': 'The most important thing we can be doing today as a nation to create opportunity for our people is to give them the tools they need to succeed. In a global economy, the government cannot give anyone a guaranteed success story, but you can give people the tools to make the most of their own lives.'[69] The bourgeois ideal of rewards flowing to those with carefully inculcated habits and skills had displaced the proletarian ideal of security in return for honest work. Bourgeois idealism was infectious. The Peruvian novelist and former supporter of Castro, Mario Varga Llosa, standing as candidate for the presidency of his country, assured listeners that 'countries can now decide whether they want to be rich. All they have to do is accept the challenges of globalization and create a degree of institutional stability.'[70]

India, for example, moved away from the developmental statism of early independence to embrace first commercialism in agriculture in the 1970s (the 'green revolution'), then, from 1991, a neo-liberal strategy that let rip a domestic consumerism concentrated in the burgeoning middle-class minority of educated professionals, salaried technicians and managers, investors, and commercial family-farmers. Economic dynamism and growth of wealth was concentrated in the bourgeoisie, transforming the economy 'upward from an expanding middle class', as Robert Stern puts it.[71] With liberal democracy contained by strong traditions of familialism and dynasticism, India looked to be a stable power under a predominantly bourgeois aegis. In general, the middle class of the developing world grew strongly. Particularly in the BRIC countries (Brazil, Russia, India, China), a globally significant bourgeoisie had decisively arrived by the twenty-first century. The bourgeois revolution, anchored on an ascendant middle class, had secured its consummation in the 'market-state'.

## CONCLUSION

In the classical nineteenth-century incarnation, states had accepted liberal constitutionalism as a quid pro quo for greater national output and an improved, consensual tax-take and thus credit. The interwar fascist interlude had destroyed any simple equation between capitalism and liberalism, however, and the long Cold War had frozen the Warsaw bloc into a paranoid militarism hostile to any resurgent bourgeois civil society as a potential fifth column. For the Communist elites, popular acquiescence was secured through a combination of repression and privileging an industrial working-class base. Promotion of heavy industry, however, was increasingly irrational in economic terms, and prevented the state from satisfying demand for consumer goods, an aspiration stimulated by the evident proliferation of them in Western societies. The dictatorships of Eastern Europe found themselves seeking loans from across the Iron Curtain, and these brought to bear the influence of *international* bourgeois civil society. The suffocating incubus of the Warsaw Pact's state-military-industrial complex was brought down in part by the artillery of money and commodities from the West. Convinced, moreover, that a command economy was the necessary social base for Communist totalitarianism, and observant that no capitalist dictatorship now existed in Europe, the liberated peoples of Eastern Europe were intellectually persuaded that civil and political liberties were best secured by the freedom of commercial civil society, by the market.

In an immediately legendary 1989 article in *National Interest*, the neo-liberal intellectual Francis Fukuyama announced the 'end of history'. He meant by this that free-market liberal parliamentary democracy had proven itself as the only tenable form for any modern society aspiring to productive efficiency, political stability, and consensus. Fukuyama found a 'Hegelian' logic unfolding, with 'political liberalism...following economic liberalism, more slowly than many had hoped but with seeming inevitability'. As 'modern, urbanized' societies fostered 'an increasingly large and well-educated middle class', democratic trends could not indefinitely be resisted. An 'intellectual climate whose most "advanced" members no longer believe that bourgeois society is something that ultimately needs to be overcome' prevailed because of the 'receding of the class issue'.[72] Fukuyama's article was subsequently expanded into a substantial book, pursuing the Hegelian themes of an unfolding consumer society determining political state forms. As an investigation of bourgeois destiny it was an 'inverted Marxism'.[73] Fukuyama, however, was in large part only providing a provocative theorization of a reigning common sense. What had consolidated in the US, as Larry Siedentop put it in 2000, had spread to Europe and further afield:

> The almost affectionate attitude towards the market which characterizes mature liberalism might be described as middle class or bourgeois, the market perceived as a bedfellow. By contrast, the earlier stages of liberalism, which polarizes attitudes to the market, induces in the majority what can only be described as a proletarian attitude, the market perceived as a devouring monster, while making it possible for some to adopt an essentially upper-class attitude, perceiving the market as a poodle.[74]

For Siedentop, the liberal market was now 'embracing everyone' and 'everyone has at least a tolerable chance of turning to his or her advantage'.[75] The market's 'tolerable chance', indeed, was now the only opportunity proffered the citizens of the globe, and anyone's failure to take it was put down to a personal failure to acquire the bourgeois virtues.

# 15

# Bright Bourgeois Morning

Francis Fukuyama's *Foreign Affairs* article, while triumphalist in its prediction that the victory of free-market democracy was inevitable, was far more ambiguous about the Promised Land:

> The end of history will be a very sad time. The struggle for recognition, the willingness to risk one's life for a purely abstract goal, the worldwide ideological struggle that called forth daring, courage, imagination, and idealism, will be replaced by economic calculation, the endless solving of technical problems, environmental concerns, and the satisfaction of sophisticated consumer demands.[1]

The very triumph of bourgeois civil society threatened another bout of ennui. This fear, of course, had exercised the New Right in the 1970s. One particular current that came out of the New Right, 'neo-conservativism', was to rise to prominence in the 1990s precisely because its adherents insisted that the great fight was not yet won. Their project of 'regime change', to be imposed on hold-outs against free-market democracy, rejuvenated the language of revolutionary emancipation. It also proposed to rehabilitate militarism, not as an oppressive weight upon civil society, but rather as a culture of revolutionary commitment to extending liberty. Neo-conservative self-conscious zealotry was a counterweight to the bland complacency of consumer capitalism.

## NEO-CONSERVATISM

Arnold J. Toynbee (1889–1975) had been lionized in the early Cold War era, particularly in the United States, for his mammoth *Study of History*. This multi-volume work challenged Marxist 'historical materialism' with a religiose theorization of civilizations cycling through rise, stagnation, and fall. For Toynbee, civilizations were always besieged by the 'proletariat', by which he meant any unassimilated mass of people without a sufficient stake in the existing order.[2] Toynbee was evidently working from concerns formed in the midst of the Great War. In January 1918 he had written a memorandum for the Political Intelligence Department of the British Foreign Office, discussing a twin threat, as he saw it, to contemporary Western civilization:

> The Bolsheviks act in the name of the European labouring class...which has become 'self-determining' and even dominant in Russia, under the Bolshevik regime. The Bolshevik policy is to bring about the same revolution in other countries, and

naturally the workers in these countries...feel a certain sympathy with Bolshevik designs. This vast, instinctive, hardly formulated internal support is the Bolsheviks' strength. But the Islamic consciousness...is a force of precisely the same kind....And what is more important, [Moslems] believe themselves to be face to face with the same enemy—namely 'Capitalism' or in other words the European middle class...which they regard as the exploiter...of the Moslems of the East.[3]

For the neo-conservatives, unconsciously echoing Toynbee, Islamism in the late twentieth century displaced Communism as the new 'proletarian' challenge to middle-class society.

Neo-conservatism emerged from the Democratic Party left in the 1970s, when Patrick Moynihan called on liberals to defend the 'stability of the social order' by seeking 'much more effective alliances with political conservatives'.[4] While it condemned welfare as disintegrative of civil society, and as such opposed social spending both domestically and abroad, neo-conservatism was first and foremost a movement to rehabilitate US militarism by laying stress on its liberal, emancipatory, even 'left-wing' potential. Primarily, it worked to broaden the basis of 'patriotism'. Irving Kristol, a neo-con intellectual, worried that bourgeois society was being weakened by consumerism:

> The liberal-individualist vision of society is not an abstract scheme which can be imposed on any kind of people. For it to work, it needs a certain kind of people, with a certain kind of character, and with a certain cast of mind. Specifically, it needs... 'inner-directed' people—people of firm moral convictions, a people of self-reliance and self-discipline, a people who do not expect the universe to be offering them something for nothing—in short, a people with a non-utopian character even if their language is shot through with utopian clichés. The kind of person I am describing may be described as the *bourgeois citizen*. He used to exist in large numbers, but is now on the verge of becoming an extinct species. He has been killed off by bourgeois prosperity, which has corrupted his character from that of a *citizen* to a *consumer*.... more and more, it is as such a consumer's utopia that our bourgeois society presents itself to the people.[5]

While most neo-conservatives were much less ambiguous in their faith that free markets give rise to democracy,[6] the point they agreed upon was that the state above all needed to be ideologically committed rather than technocratic, pragmatic, and 'realist'. Ideological rigour backed by military power was required to defend and protect the interests of a free society. Neo-cons were committed to a liberalism of the 'vital centre', avoiding indulgence of extremes of left and right, but vigorous, even aggressive, rather than conciliatory.[7]

Détente, the avoidance of friction with the Soviet Union in the 1970s, was unpopular in the United States as an appeasement of tyranny. Neo-con Democrat Senator, Henry 'Scoop' Jackson, had in 1972 insisted that any economic agreements between the United States and the Soviet Union be conditional on a satisfactory Soviet human rights record. Congress blocked the extension of 'Most Favoured Trading' rights to Russia because the country would not relax its stringent restrictions on emigration rights. Come the 1980s, neo-conservatives had significant influence on the Ronald Reagan (1911–2004) administration, which committed America to a new rhetorical anti-Communist crusade, and in particular highlighted the danger of Communist subversion in Latin America. Reagan's government did not baulk at assisting the death squads, and his administration lifted all major restrictions imposed in the 1970s on US aid delivered to right-wing Latin American dictatorships struggling against 'subversion'.[8] The 'Reagan Doctrine,' argues Fred Halliday, was 'the most activist and explicitly counter-revolutionary campaign' ever pursued by Cold War America.[9]

However, this was not simply a continuation of backing reaction against leftist-inflected democracy. Reagan repudiated the Nixon doctrine of supporting friendly dictators, and posited instead a 'third way' between Communism and extreme-right Third World dictatorships. The United States, he insisted, was to consider itself an exporter of 'democratic revolution'.[10] Reagan's Westminster Address in 1982 spurred the establishment of the National Endowment for Democracy (NED), an autonomous and broad-based pressure group including representatives of the US labour movement, US business, the Republican Party, and the Democratic Party. NED disbursed funds to democratic political parties against incumbent regimes in Haiti (1987), Chile (1988), Panama (1990), and Nicaragua (1990).[11] In 1983, Reagan openly called for free elections in Central America, and his administration made it clear that it would cut US aid to military establishments in the region that overthrew their civilian governments.[12]

Specifically, moral and material assistance was offered to resistance forces opposing Communist and Soviet oppression or aggression, at least where opportunities existed.[13] The US sponsored 'low intensity conflicts'—quasi-revolutionary struggles using democratic political propaganda, agitation, and violence—against Communist regimes and insurgent forces. In Nicaragua, the Contras were aided by the US against the semi-Marxist Sandinista regime. By the mid-1980s, the Contras were able to launch substantial terrorist raids into Nicaragua, disrupting infrastructure, agriculture, and government. Three Nicaraguan harbours were mined with CIA help, for which America was condemned by the World Court. Behind the backs of Congress, the US government continued to channel funds—some of which came from a secret arms deal with Iran—to the Contras. In El Salvador, the United States helped the government oppose the insurgent leftist Farabundo Marti National Liberation Front (FLMN). The CIA intervened to organize the main rightist party, which won elections in 1984 and 1989. Meanwhile, the promotion of 'democracy' was more attenuated in Afghanistan, where Islamic fundamentalist mujahedeen fighters were armed against Soviet invasion; in Cambodia, where the US found itself associated with the remnants of the genocidal Khmer Rouge regime resisting the Vietnamese-imposed government; and in Angola, where guerrilla groups were helped in challenging the Soviet-sponsored regime. Still, five years of civil war in Nicaragua, which cost at least thirty thousand lives, came to an end with the February 1989 Tesoro Beach Accord, which mandated free elections. When these were held a year later, they were won by the right of centre National Opposition Union. The Sandinista regime accepted defeat and resigned. In El Salvador in 1992 a peace was concluded between the right-wing ARENA government and the FMLN, ending twelve years of war.

A turning point in US policy can be dated to the fall of the Marcos regime in the Philippines in 1986. Marcos had been a client of US power and, by long-standing precedent, one would have expected the US to support him against democratic revolution for fear of it spiralling off into Communism. In fact, when mass protest broke out in the Philippines, the US approved the ouster of Marcos. It would be wrong to say that Washington converted an abstract principle to supporting the overthrow of the Marcos regime. It was simply a matter of calculating when allies might best be abandoned. Paul Wolfowitz, a neo-conservative in the State Department at the time, argued that the Philippines were *sui generis*, and it did not follow that democracy should be promoted in countries with US-friendly dictators if there were no extant democratic traditions.[14] In 1986, however, the neo-cons in the US administration did take the risk on a liberal-democratic revolution in the Philippines consolidating rather than radicalizing. This, indeed, was the outcome. The historical experience of Communism and the impact of globalized capitalism on possibilities for autarchy had worn away the attraction of socialist revolution for the peasantry and working class. Popular revolution no longer strained to transcend liberal-democratic revolution. This premise was triumphantly vindicated by the revolutionary collapse of the Communist regimes in 1989, and the tremendous ideological hegemony of liberal democracy and consumer-led capitalism in the newly liberated ex-Communist states.

Following the fall of the Berlin Wall in 1989, Congress and the administration of George H. W. Bush committed hundreds of millions of dollars, mostly through the Agency for International Development (AID), to support the consolidation of democracy in the post-Communist countries, and still more resources to aid the transitions that were beginning to unfold in previously authoritarian countries in Latin America, Africa, and Asia. This effort continued to expand during the Clinton administration, with support for free elections, independent media, the rule of law, and civil-society NGOs. According to the US government's 1996 statement of foreign policy:

> Democracies create free markets that offer economic opportunity, make for more reliable trading partners and are far less likely to wage war on each other.... The more that democracy and political and economic liberalization take hold in the world, particularly in countries of strategic importance to us, the safer our nation is likely to be and the more our people are likely to prosper.[15]

This was an inversion of the Cold War doctrine that free markets create conditions for democracy. Now democratization, supported from outside by the US and its allies, created the best environment for market relations.

## TO THE BAGHDAD STATION

Even if systemic militarism was undermined by the ending of the Cold War, opportunities for limited 'wars of choice' were available to the US Superpower as never before. These were now turned on intractable 'rogue states.' In 1990, Saddam

Hussein, a tyrant from central casting, launched the Iraqi military into an invasion of Kuwait, in the hope that acquisition of its oil resources would buttress his regime against opposition from domestic civil society, and allow it increased regional influence. His invasion led to a multinational coalition being constructed by the United States and, with 'Operation Desert Storm' launched in January 1991, the military expulsion of Iraqi forces from Kuwait. The rapid success of this campaign suggested a new Western superiority in arms that promised almost bloodless (for the West) victories. President George H. W. Bush felt confident enough to announce a 'New World Order', in which America would boldly promote universal values of liberalism, democracy, and capitalism. As Bush put it: 'History is moving decisively in favor of freedom, thanks in large part to American ideals and perseverance—the touchstones of the modern world which the emerging democracies are now striving for: free markets, free speech, free elections.'[16] In an abandonment of Cold War doctrine, in which any regime, no matter how tyrannical, could be included in the Free World as part of the anti-Communist alliance, Bush announced that America would offer no support for its former clients unless they were at least in the process of democratizing.

In the 1990s, however, there was uncertainty in America about how military power might be deployed to revolutionary ('regime change') ends. In 1989, American troops had overthrown the dictator of the small country of Panama, Manuel Noriega, and in 1994, in 'Operation Uphold Democracy', the Clinton administration used troops to pressurize the Haitian military junta into accepting civilian government. An intervention in Somalia, however, went disastrously wrong in 1993 when the killing of American troops spiralled into bloody street battles in the capital of Mogadishu, and US forces were withdrawn in 1995. The Clinton administration was very slow to get involved in the civil wars and Serbian aggression of the former Yugoslavia, and European forces proved incapable or unwilling to prevent murderous 'ethnic cleansing'. When force was finally used in 1999 against Serbia, in support of separatist Kosovo, it was limited to air raids, followed by troops to police the settlement. Russia was left to its own devices in brutally waging war against increasingly Islamist separatists in Chechnya (1994–5, 1999). Most disastrously, the 'international community' stood aside when genocide broke out in Rwanda in 1994, and though victory for a rebel army stopped the genocide, a catastrophically bloody war enveloped the entire region of the African Great Lakes.

It was, perhaps, evidence of Clinton's limited ambition that he devoted so much attention to the relatively amenable and low-key Northern Ireland peace process. As it happened, however, Northern Ireland was significant precisely because of the game-changing significance it seemed to point up of a new and crucial turn in military technology. From the mid-1980s, British Army body armour had proved itself effective against the small-arms fire of the insurgent paramilitary Irish Republican Army. For the first time, military personnel even outside armoured vehicles could be protected from direct fire.[17] The American military was impressed by this demonstration of the effectiveness of new body-armour technology (impact-absorbent ceramic plates in tough kevlar fabric). Now 'full spectrum dominance', force protection against all conventional military threats—from enemy aircraft and missiles to paramilitary insurgency—appeared to be within the American grasp. This was all the more important as war in the immediate future was expected to be against low-tech urban militias. The future battlefields were anticipated by American planners as most likely to be the ghettos in the global south, where mega-shanties swelled in the interstices of neo-liberal structural adjustment programmes.[18] A neo-conservative think tank founded in 1997, Project for a New American Century, strongly argued for an American military posture, imperial in its scope and 'full spectrum' in its capability, willing to enforce 'regime change' if required to promote free-market democracies abroad.[19]

Prime candidate for the armed evangelism of bourgeois revolution was the Middle East. Here, the 'resource curse' appeared to be at work. 'Resource curse' refers to the perverse consequences of a country enjoying possession of significant oil, natural gas, and mineral resources.[20] Such fungible wealth 'on tap', located at discrete, easily monitored nodes, gives a state and established elites no incentive to encourage a commercial civil society, which would add little to the state's fiscal viability while weakening its hierarchical systems of patronage and control. With wealth and credit deriving from easily accessed oil, gas, and mineral revenue, there is no powerful incentive to win consensus for taxation of socially produced wealth, and so equally little reason to concede constitutional government. Such is the subsequent atrophy of the state structure, moreover, that the likelihood of turmoil is high should the lid of authoritarianism be lifted. The 'resource curse' inhibited bourgeois revolution of the oil-rich Middle East in particular. Majority neo-conservative opinion, moreover, held that the Arab world was nearly uniquely without the resources for self-starting bourgeois revolution. As Bernard Lewis, a scholar of great influence in neo-conservative circles, put it, the lack of a strong Muslim middle class precluded 'the normal role of a rising bourgeoisie in reshaping political structures to their needs', so that constitutionalism was 'superimposed on a foundation of social reality to which it did not yet correspond'.[21] Bourgeois liberty, therefore, never prospered in the Arab world, even in the absence of the 'resource curse'.

Moreover, in the absence of strong bourgeois civil society, dangerous creeds easily ran riot. Political Islamism, a reactionary creed of state-building under a theocratic aegis, was subordinate to Arab nationalism for the first half of the twentieth century. The semi-feudal states of the Middle East, however, had shallow roots, being shards of empire formed from above rather than national entities with strong roots; the very success of pan-Arabism as a creed was proof of the weakness of state nationalisms. Statist Arab socialism, based upon command economies and with poorly developed bourgeois civil societies, failed to deliver economic growth. The defeat of Egypt, Jordan, and Syria by the forces of Israel in 1967 massively discredited pan-Arabism, and the Islamist model of development seemed increasingly attractive. In contrast to the distant and corrupt state, Islamism appeared to offer locally based equality, and in practical terms Islamist groups ran the social, health, and welfare institutions that the Arab states were conspicuously failing to provide the urban poor. With the state tyrannical and civil society Islamist, a bourgeois political dispensation seemed to neo-conservatives to be as far off as ever in the Muslim Middle East of the 1990s.

As against this, Israel offered a contrasting example of a highly successful constitutionalist regime in the Middle East. Neo-conservatives (and others) were strong supporters of Israel because of the legacy of the Holocaust, and the urgent desire not to abandon again a goodly proportion of the Jewish people to doom. Israel was also, however, a peculiar case where bourgeois civil society and a strong executive state mutually reinforced one another. Well before the sovereign establishment of Israel, a real Jewish nation existed in Palestine. In the 1920s and 1930s, Zionists had established a vigorous, working-class, democratically and socialist-minded civil society, heavily reinforced by liberal bourgeois refugees from interwar European anti-Semitism, which strengthened the commercial and manufacturing economy in Tel Aviv and Haifa. The Jewish nation from 1944 fought Britain for independence, which was secured by 1948. This new state then saw off an immediate attack from the armies of Egypt, Jordan, Syria, Lebanon, and Iraq, Israel's national coherence ensuring a far more thorough and determined military mobilization than that of its enemies. By 1949 Israel had not merely survived but increased the territory allocated it by the United Nations partition plan. When, in 1967, it was apparent that Egypt, Syria, and Jordan were gearing up for yet another war, Israel in June struck pre-emptively and decisively. In a mere six days, Israeli territory was increased threefold, and its capital city was united. Though Israel had first received American arms in 1962, it was from the Six Day War that the United States moved to firmly support Israel as a bastion of Western interest—both morally and strategically—in the region. It was the model 'modern state' in the region. Israel's occupation from 1967 of the Palestinian nation in the West Bank and Gaza Strip, however, meant that it was experienced by the rest of the Middle East as more a thorn in the side than as an exemplar.

The 1979 revolution in Iran—where America had supported the dictatorial Shah Mohammed Reza Pahlavi—was, in contrast to Israel's example, a failed bourgeois revolution. Iran's revolutionary coalition, given muscle by students and the working class, had included the bourgeoisie, impoverished by falling oil prices, and bazaar merchants marginalized by state-backed business monopolies. However, it was the clergy (ulama), resentful of secularization, who took the lead. With all political parties other than the pro-regime Rastakhiz Party banned, the mosque had become the primary node of oppositional activity, and Islam the language of dissent.[22] Ayatollah Ruhollah Khomeini, returning from exile in Paris, espoused Islam as a total ideology fit to reconstitute political and civil society:

> the Qur'an contains a hundred times more verses concerning social problems than on devotional subjects. Out of fifty books of Muslim tradition there are perhaps three or four that deal with prayer or with man's duties towards God, a few on morality and all the rest have to do with society, economics, law, politics, and the state…[Islam] is political or it is nothing.[23]

Khomeini's government proclaimed that sovereignty lay with God, and that the jurist interpreters of Islam should ultimately rule. Iran, particularly in the earlier years of the Khomeini regime, was ambitious to 'export the revolution'. This Shi'a Islamic challenge provoked a sharp response from Sunni Islamic Saudi Arabia. With implicit American support for its hegemonic struggle with Iran, the Saudis decanted huge oil wealth into a sprawling international network of Islamic schools proselytizing a standardized salafi Islam, to the detriment of local Muslim customs and practice.

When in 1989 Soviet forces withdrew from Afghanistan in the face of chronic resistance from mujahedeen fighters, the Communist regime in Kabul disintegrated, and in 1992 full-scale civil war on Islamist and tribal lines erupted. A new political force, the Taliban, emerged in 1994. The Taliban, tribally Pashtun, had been cultivated by the Pakistani Inter-Services Intelligence (ISI). It controlled two-thirds of the country by 1998, but not the Tajik north. The Taliban imposed a rigidly reactionary, obscurantist, and persecutory form of Sunni Islamic theocracy. The 1979 Soviet invasion of Afghanistan had produced a further development: a commitment amongst some to wage an international jihad in presumed defence of Islam. With developed military skills and heightened élan, jihadist militants contributed their fanaticism and sectarianism to the civil war in Algeria from 1991, terrorism in Egypt, resistance and retaliation to ethnic cleansing in Bosnia, and ethno-political struggles elsewhere. Al-Qaeda, formed by the fanatical Saudi millionaire, Osama bin Laden, from 1994 evolved in an increasingly globalist direction. Just as the mujahedeen had defeated one infidel superpower in 1989, the Soviet Union, now jihadists must confront and force out of the Muslim world the remaining superpower, the USA. A succession of Al-Qaeda terrorist attacks, including a car-bombing in Riyadh in 1995, bombing of the US embassies in Kenya and Tanzania in 1998, an attack on the USS warship *Cole* in Yemen in 2000, culminated in the assault on the World Trade Center in New York and the Pentagon on 11 September 2001. Al-Qaeda was always more of a franchise than a centralized organization. What core it did have was more or less smashed by international military and police action following the '9/11' attacks, but as an inspiration and model for terrorist groups globally, it was much revived by the invasion of Iraq. Terrorism was now de-centred.[24]

The Middle East therefore, seemed to represent in concentrated form the clash between bourgeois modernity and regressive archaisms. Israel was impressively democratic, and an economically successful market economy. It was embattled, but suffused with an ethic of active citizenship. Israel's 'heroic' militarization contrasted with the pacifist commercialism of much of Western society. Islamism, in contrast, festered under oppressive state tyrannies, appealed to déclassé masses, and corrupted higher-education graduates lacking a constructive outlet for their energies in a properly functioning bourgeois civil society. It denied the sovereignty of individual conscience and secular reason. It is little wonder that neo-conservatives so strongly identified with Israel, which impressed them as an armed civil society dedicated to self-preservation, and so strongly opposed fanatical Islamism as a morbid symptom of societies lacking bourgeois vitality.

The threat posed by societies struggling to make the transition to constitutionalism in an age of terrorism was taken with due seriousness by Western leaders. In

April 1999, at a speech to the Economic Club of Chicago, British Prime Minister Tony Blair went beyond the then coalescing idea of 'humanitarian intervention', and argued for a new 'doctrine of international community'. This took into account a globalized world, economically interdependent and with increasing trans-national migration. The 'responsible' international community needed to be ready to intervene in trouble spots of war, humanitarian disaster, and failed or rogue states to restore order and prevent contagion. It was not enough simply to cauterize trouble spots: subsequent 'nation building', including the promotion of a commercialized, de-radicalized and pacific civil society, was just as important.[25] Blair's radicalism in international relations was by no means an echo of American opinion at the time. While in opposition to Clinton, the mainstream of the Republican Party had been vehemently hostile to attempts at 'nation building', and the president was little more enthusiastic, as his foot-dragging over Kosovo evidenced. The atrocities of 9/11, however, massively ramped up an American militarism that had been rebuilding and consolidating since the 1970s.[26] This was no militarism of containment, however, or even of realpolitik. It had a revolutionary impetus, and behind it lay a clear commitment to spreading free-market democracy.

When the Taliban regime in Afghanistan, which harboured bin Laden, refused to extradite him after the 9/11 attacks, the United States launched in October 2001 air strikes while providing assistance to the Taliban's domestic enemies in a renewed civil war. The regime quickly fell, and NATO troops led by America entered the country. Afghanistan had its first democratic elections in 2004, but 'nation building' proved as difficult as the sceptics had predicted: regional warlords reasserted control, and the Taliban slowly built up an insurgency that by the end of the decade was formidable. Western forces were generally popular with Afghanis, as a barrier to Taliban restoration, but the insurgency could not be crushed militarily.

The American government, however, was determined to go far beyond punitive war against aggressors. In a speech to West Point graduates delivered on 1 June 2002, President Bush outlined the country's new commitment to pre-emptive war: 'the war on terror will not be won on the defensive. We must take the battle to the enemy, disrupt his plans, and confront the worst threats before they emerge. In the world we have entered, the only path to safety is the path of action. And this nation will act.'[27] This was the 'Bush Doctrine'. In January 2002, Bush included Iraq—along with the bastard-Communist regime of North Korea, and theocratic Iran—as part of 'an axis of evil'. Saddam's regime in Iraq was failing to abide by the terms of the 1991 ceasefire by refusing full cooperation with UN weapons inspections. It was also accused of supporting terrorism and developing weapons of mass destruction (WMD). The Bush administration was soon speaking of 'regime change' in Iraq. The Americans felt they had cause to believe that the Iraqi masses would welcome emancipation from Saddam's vicious tyranny. Kanan Makiya, a leftist exile from Iraq, assured Bush in 2003 that 'The Iraqis will welcome US forces with flowers and sweets when they come.'[28] In September 2002, Saddam's government announced that UN inspectors could return, but it remained obdurately short of full compliance, and in October America's Congress approved the use of force against Iraq. However, by January 2003, UN inspectors had found no evidence of forbidden weapons programs, though they pointed out that the Iraqi government had been less than cooperative. While the United States and Great Britain built up forces, mostly in Kuwait, for an invasion, France, Germany, and Russia increasingly expressed their disquiet, doubting that a legal *casus belli* existed (international law clearly ruled out the legitimacy of invasion to impose a revolution, no matter how emancipatory). The British government in particular hoped for an explicit UN Security Council resolution approving use of force, but this was denied.

On 19 March 2003 airstrikes were launched against Iraqi political and military control centres, and the following day ground forces, almost exclusively Anglo-American, invaded. Saddam's army and government quickly collapsed, and there was widespread looting, particularly in Baghdad. This latter was tolerated as typical of 'revolution': 'Stuff happens and it's untidy,' as Secretary of State Donald Rumsfeld famously remarked, 'freedom's untidy, and free people are free to make mistakes and commit crimes and do bad things. They're also free to live their lives and do wonderful things. And that's what's going to happen here.'[29] On 1 May 2003, President Bush declared victory in the war against Iraq; Saddam was captured in December 2003 and executed in 2006. No weapons of mass destruction were found.

Bush, not notably ideological before his election, had adopted the neo-conservative goal of revolutionary 'regime change' and forced-pace democratization as a goal for the Middle East. On 6 November 2003 he addressed the National Endowment for Democracy (NED) on its twentieth anniversary.[30] This address is worth consideration as encapsulating an entire rationale for modern bourgeois revolution. Bush recalled the 1982 'Westminster Speech' of his predecessor, Ronald Reagan, which had not only led directly to the establishment of the non-partisan NED, committed to extending democracy globally, but had marked the reorientation of US foreign policy away from simply backing up pro-Western tyrants against Communist subversion to actual solidarity with 'revolutionary' forces struggling for free-market constitutionalism. This had been in the context of a 'third wave' of democratization beginning with the fall of Mediterranean dictatorships in the 1970s, spreading to East Asia, Latin America, the Communist bloc, and, in the 1990s, Africa. 'In the early 1970s,' Bush remarked, 'there were about 40 democracies in the world.... As the 20th century ended, there were around 120 democracies in the world.... We've witnessed, in little over a generation, the swiftest advance of freedom in the 2,500 year story of democracy.' He explained this by pointing to the pre-eminent geopolitical position of the US that had 'created the conditions in which new democracies could flourish'. If the US acted as a shield, however, he identified the active, revolutionary forces quite differently. First, he pointed to a revolutionary class: 'Historians will note,' he argued, 'that in many nations, the advance of markets and free enterprise helped to create a middle class that was confident enough to demand their own rights.' Secondly, he pointed out that this class could act as the vanguard of the 'nation'. It had been found that 'the prosperity, and social vitality and technological progress of a people are directly determined by extent of their liberty. Freedom honors and unleashes human creativity—and creativity determines the strength and wealth of nations.' The process, he argued, continued to unfold. In China, for example, the Communist leadership had realized that 'economic freedom leads to national wealth'. They must inevitably conclude that 'freedom is indivisible'. However, if democratization since the 1970s had been the work of 'national' forces, inspired by the example of the US and protected by the overarching stability of its global hegemony, now America 'had new policy, a forward strategy of freedom in the Middle East'. This was most evident in a forced regime brought about in Iraq. 'The establishment of a free Iraq at the heart of the Middle East,' Bush insisted, 'will be a watershed event in the global democratic revolution.'

The president carefully defined democratic revolution as ultimately the 'plan of Heaven' rather than 'some dialectic of history'. Others were less circumspect: Stephen Schwartz, of the US think tank Western Policy Center, in 2004 described the neo-conservative strategy in the Middle East as the promotion of 'bourgeois revolution'.[31] Michael Mandelbaum, making the 'case for Goliath', wrote that:

> working free markets tend, once established, to promote the democratic politics that promise to alleviate the security problems for which the United States has assumed responsibility for in the twenty-first century. This is so for several reasons: because once people make their own economic choices, as they do in free-market economies, it is natural for them to make political choices, which is the essence of democracy; because the private economy that the free-market creates provides a base for political activity independent of state sponsorship and control, which democracy requires; and because the affluent citizens that a successful market economy produces have the time and inclination to participate in politics, which is yet another hallmark of democracy.[32]

America, neo-conservatives argued, had a unique advantage in its military capability (Europe, in contrast, was supine).[33] Michael Ignatieff, in an article published in the *New York Times* in 2003, hailed 'empire lite, a global hegemony whose grace notes are free markets and democracy, enforced by the most awesome military power the world has ever known'.[34] For advisors to the Bush administration, the United States was an 'international police power', intervening in countries characterized by 'chronic wrongdoing, or an impotence that results in a general loosening of the ties of civilized society'.[35] The only possible drawback was weak domestic public opinion leading to 'imperial understretch' due to an unwillingness on the part of the public or Congress to invest in peace-keeping and state-building capacity.[36]

Amongst neo-conservatives there was a vaunting ambition, and a revolutionary and emanicipatory messianism that thumbed its nose at dull realpolitik:

> If we just let our own vision of the world go forth, and we embrace it entirely, and we don't try to be clever and piece together clever diplomatic solutions to this thing, but just wage a total war against these tyrants, I think we will do very well, and our children will sing great songs about us years from now.

So said Michael Leeden, of the American Enterprise Institute, in November 2001.[37] Rather more pragmatically, the eminent British historian Niall Ferguson counselled

America to consider as an example Britain's practice in the nineteenth century of granting to its colonies constitutional governments, at least once they were 'clearly advanced along the road to economic modernity and stability'.[38] For sympathetic observers, America's empire was altruistic, and the world's sole superpower had the capacity to gift liberal revolution.

For some on the left, it was perfectly adequate to draw still upon Lenin's principle—that any country or movement struggling against the wealthy capitalist nations deserved support.[39] This was, in effect, an offer of unconditional support to any tyranny, no matter how reactionary and domestically oppressive, so long as it irritated the United States. It ignored the fact that Lenin's principles, whatever their validity at the time, had been formulated decades earlier on the basis—now clearly obsolete—that world wars were intrinsic to modern capitalism, and that socialist revolution was imminent. Far more typical on the left was an overriding fear of the consequences of unleashed militarism, whether it be unacceptable bloodshed in Iraq, destabilization in the Middle East generally, or a legitimization of uninhibited US armed unilateralism. It was precisely this caution that one prominent 'Marxisant' writer, Christopher Hitchens, deplored as 'the status-quo, safety-first mode that now distinguishes so much of the Left, insisting not that such and such a line on Iraq, say, is wrong on principle, but that it is too risky or too hazardous'.[40] A call for a 'Decent Left' found considerable echo amongst like-minded leftists enthusiastic for determined action to confront tyranny, theocratic reaction, and an Islamist terrorism that explicitly set out to slaughter non-combatants. Liberal capitalist democracy, in contrast to tin-pot dictators and reactionary terrorists, was certainly progressive, and a leftist tradition with hereditary sympathy for revolutionary liberation, it was felt, should not wince at the stern militarism of US-led emancipation in action.[41] Paul Berman, of this 'Decent Left', hailed the new dawn of liberal revolution: 'If falling statues of tyrants are a familiar symbol to us, that is because, in modern times, more-or-less successful revolutions have also become familiar. And now let us get ready for the long haul.'[42] He promoted a new kind of activism that would be 'different from the conservatives and foreign policy cynics who could only think of striking up alliances with friendly tyrants; and different from the anti-imperialists of the left, the left-wing isolationists, who could not imagine any progressive role for the United States'.[43] The British leftist writer, Jonathan Rée, applauded regime change as 'revolution', the kind of decisive radical social change that feeble liberals had historically baulked at, but leftists should embrace.[44]

In his second inaugural address, in 2005, George W. Bush promised to support 'democratic movements and institutions in every nation and culture, with the ultimate goal of ending tyranny in our world'.[45] The US administration, covertly and overtly, supported popular movements against dictatorship, and even against constitutionalist if authoritarian regimes, in a succession of 'Colour Revolutions': in Serbia (2000), Georgia (2003), Ukraine (2004), and Kyrgyzstan (2005). Notable in the Colour Revolutions was the prominence of middle-class professionals. Sergiy Grabowsky, writing of Ukraine, was keen to acknowledge the '*Maidan* (Orange Revolution)' as 'a typical bourgeois revolution. (Doesn't matter if this was written as a positive or a negative.)'[46] The wheel had come full circle. Bourgeois revolution, with its own universal class and revolutionary vanguard, even its own International, was regnant. After the 9/11 attacks, export of bourgeois revolution on the point of US and allied bayonets, or promoted by Western propaganda and agitation, had become a reality. In a blaze of hubris in the early twenty-first century, neo-conservatives openly lauded the new era of revolution, and much of the left had to admit that this, indeed, was the only game in town.

## NEMESIS

Christopher Hitchens advanced as one reason to support the 'War on Terror' the changes wrought in the US armed forces since the 1960s: 'I was highly impressed by the evolution of military strategy and tactics since the inglorious "bombs away" days of the Vietnam era. Many of the points made by the anti-war movement have been consciously assimilated by the Pentagon and its lawyers and advisers. Precision weaponry is good in itself, but its ability to discriminate is improving and will improve.'[47] The 'War on Terror', however, was far from clinical. The US administration denied prisoners normal rights, and subjected many to torture. Most disastrously, Iraq turned out to be a bloody debacle, with well over one hundred thousand Iraqis losing their lives.

Under Saddam, such economic activity as had survived international sanctions had taken place through five hundred or so state-owned enterprises. L. Paul Bremer, appointed as civilian head of the allied occupation of Iraq, set about bringing 'economic freedom' (meaning privatization) to Iraq. This, rather than reconstruction per se, was the occupation government's 'most immediate priority'. Iraq was to be a showcase of 'the world's boldest' market-orientated policies.[48] Ghassan Salamé, a Lebanese professor and former culture minister, observing the incessant pressure to privatize in post-invasion Iraq, concluded that it was led by a combination of American business-led avarice and neo-conservative fervour: an 'ideological-industrial complex'.[49] Taken together with the purging of the cadre of the displaced ruling Ba'ath Party from the civil service and armed forces, marketization destabilized an already impoverished and battered civil society. Guerrilla attacks by Ba'ath regime loyalists and Islamic militants became an ongoing problem from early on in the occupation. Very rapidly, a problem with 'full-spectrum dominance' became evident. Precisely because small-arms fire on armoured Occupation soldiers proved relatively ineffective, the insurgents could only inflict substantial casualties by use of large improvised explosive devices or suicide bombers. The collateral damage inflicted on civilians in the blast radius was typically severe, worsened by panicked Occupation soldiers firing into onlookers. Very quickly, the guerrilla war became exceptionally brutalized. A murderous bomb attack on the Shiite holy site Samarra, in February 2006, kicked off something approaching sectarian civil war, with Shiites expelling Sunnis from Baghdad and urban regions to the north. President Bush, in January 2007, announced a 'surge': an additional twenty thousand US troops to establish security to Baghdad and the Sunni Anbar province. The level of violence decreased significantly by the second half of 2007, partly due to the surge, partly because Sunni forces divided and a section was paid off by America, and partly because sectarian warfare had eliminated most ethnic interfaces.[50] The war ran down, and constitutionalism survived, but at a high cost of bloodshed and dissension.

The disaster in Iraqi cannot credibly be ascribed simply to 'ancient' sectarian hatreds unleashed by the toppling of dictatorship: it was specifically foreign invasion that wrought the collapse into civil war. It is unlikely that society would have fallen apart in such a manner had, say, the Saddam regime been toppled by a domestic coup or revolution. Historically, there had been relatively little sectarian conflict in Iraq. Ethnic and religious divisions became toxic precisely because the invasion internationalized the conflict. The Shiite majority looked upon Sunni insurgents as cats' paws of international Sunni fundamentalism, and the Sunnis, for their part, considered the Shias to be serving the interest of America as well as Iran (Shias were often labelled 'Persians'). Only the Kurds felt comfortable with their alliance with the United States, their national rights having been secured. In June 2005, Bush's Secretary of State, Condoleezza Rice, delivered a major speech in Cairo signalling the watershed in US foreign policy. Past US pursuit of stability in the Middle East at the expense of democracy had, she said, achieved neither. Rice added: 'We are taking a different course. We are supporting the democratic aspirations of all the people.'[51] One year on, however, and back in the Middle East, the Secretary of State was talking less about democracy and more about the 'forces of moderation'.[52] The forces of moderation, of course, were the pro-Western authoritarians.

Barack Obama, who had no connection with the decision to invade Iraq, won the American presidential election in 2008. He used his first address to the United Nations Assembly in April 2009 to repudiate unilateralism whilst trying to reassure his audience that America would not revert to a 'realist' policy of supporting friendly dictators:

> Democracy cannot be imposed on any nation from the outside. Each society must search for its own path, and no path is perfect. Each country will pursue a path rooted in the culture of its people, and—in the past—America has too often been selective in its promotion of democracy. But that does not weaken our commitment, it only reinforces it.[53]

Obama moved to extricate all US forces from Iraq (completed, but for the personnel of a sprawling US 'embassy', in 2011), though he ramped up forces to deal with the deteriorating situation in Afghanistan.

A spontaneous Middle Eastern and Arab revolutionary wave was building up, however. Protests against an egregiously rigged election, in December 2009, mobilized the Iranian middle class and workers, and the movement was suppressed with difficulty by the regime. In January 2011 a revolt (the 'Jasmine Revolution') overthrew in Tunisia the 'moderate' regime of Ben Ali. The contagion spread, and in February the hereditary dictatorship of Hosni Mubarak in Egypt was overthrown by the army in the face of popular revolutionary demands. Mubarak was cooperative with Israel and had long been a close ally of America. Egypt's torture chambers had been made available for use on Islamist suspects sent to the country as part of the US 'War on Terror' programme of 'extraordinary rendition'. Obama, nonetheless, supported a transition to democracy, but fear in America and Israel that a popular Egyptian government would be prey to Islamization, or at least actively intolerant and hostile to Israeli occupation of Palestinian lands, was palpable. The army in Egypt strove to maintain the hegemony of the 'permanent state'.

The Tunisian and Egyptian revolutions were in many respects a classical modern bourgeois revolution. These countries had been to the forefront in the Middle East in accepting the rigours of 'structural adjustment' under Western guidance, encouraging privatization and commercialism. A strengthened and emboldened commercial civil society revolted against the police state. The greater amount of mobilization came via the working class, however, and strikes were important in weakening the legitimacy of the state and lending confidence to the masses. Also rather typically, worker demands tended to outstrip the constitutionalist aims of the revolution. There was a great deal of hostility to the stark inequalities generated by structural adjustment, and strikes continued after the middle classes accepted the new constitutionalism proffered by the army. The tension between the interests of the middle and working class were as evident as in previous revolutions, but with statist socialism off the agenda.[54] In Syria and Yemen, the regimes reacted much more brutally to rebellion, leading to prolonged and bloody revolutionary struggle. The tyranny of Moammar Ghadaffi in Libya was overthrown in October 2011 in a bloody civil war, with NATO acting as the airforce of the rag-tag revolutionary militia in its assault on the armed forces of the old regime.

The prominence of the Muslim Brotherhood and similar organizations in the 'Arab Spring' suggested that they might play a role analogous to post-war European Christian Democracy in developing forms of bourgeois civil society that cohere with culturally rooted concepts of hierarchy, social solidarity, and patriarchy. This, at any rate, was the broadly encouraging experience of politics in the non-Arabic Muslim world in the new century. The centre-right Islamic Justice and Development Party (AKP) swept to power in Turkey in 2002, democratizing the sclerotic and militarized (if largely secular) permanent state, while a moderate Islamic coalition took power in Indonesia and Malaysia in 2004. Similar formations also fared well electorally in Bangladesh and Pakistan.[55] Islamic democracy based around bourgeois civil society seemed quite viable. They certainly emerged as strongest in the post-revolutionary Middle Eastern states.

## CAPITALIST CRISIS AND OPPORTUNITY

Still, capitalism itself was no longer quite the universal answer it had seemed after the fall of the Berlin Wall. It is true that, by the twenty-first century, economists were optimistically talking of a 'Great Moderation': the success of neo-liberal reforms of the 1970s and 1980s had smoothed out economic cycles and achieved consistent growth. However, other than briefly during the application of IT systems in the 1990s, productivity growth trailed the 1947–73 'golden age'.[56] In advanced economies lax regulation of investors seeking high, short-term yields powered the financial sector. Remuneration packages, structured around lavish bonuses for corporate and banking executives and whizzkids, incentivized risky investment tactics. But even as growth picked up pace in the late 1990s, the share of national economies going to wages tended to decline, and along with 'casualization' of the workforce came rising inequality, and growing economic insecurity.

Central to liberal and neo-liberal ideology had been the sure belief that commercialism fostered an integrated and stable civil society. Even by the later 1990s, however, this had been called into question. The market was, Social Democrats conceded, the best mechanism for producing wealth, but there was nothing intrinsic to the market guaranteeing that wealth produced would be channelled to the interests of social solidarity. In the 1990s the centre-left's strategic orientation decisively moved from protecting wage labour, as a collective interest, to facilitating wage earners as individuals within commercial civil society. Collective social provision, in this view, should concentrate on providing individuals with the skills necessary for operating in a flexible labour market, and on easing the transition between jobs. Public expenditure would certainly be substantial—often at historically unprecedented levels—but there would be little attempt to maintain particular sources of employment. Rather, the aim of government was to maintain an environment for job creation on the one side and skills for employability on the other. A paper written by an economic advisory group for the German SPD chancellor, Gerhard Schröder, explained that:

> We must...adjust the parameters within which the factor of labour can be put to its most efficient use. But given the strong external pressure for change, and given also the loss of the traditional sense of security, people will only be able to comprehend the mobility and flexibility that are being demanded of them if they can be certain that their livelihood is not under threat. Only within a 'corridor of security' will it be possible for old, entrenched positions to be given up and new challenges accepted.[57]

Maintaining this 'corridor of security', however, was difficult as escalating inequality substantially diminished the life chances of the least advantaged third or so of society. They were being excluded from full civil society. The spread of the 'ownership society', with smaller families in owner-occupier homes, encouraged ballooning inflation in the housing market, feeding private credit and debt, whilst wages stagnated.

In a resurgence of socialist mutualism over statism, it was hoped that adept application of a 'quasi-market' could establish a moral and inclusive commercial civil society. While the capitalist market privileged the wealthy over the poor, quasi-markets in tax-funded social provision might even the balance by empowering the poor as consumers rather than mere supplicants. An advisor to the British 'New' Labour government, Julian Le Grand, described this form of market socialism: 'users do not come to a quasi-market with their own resources to purchase goods and services, as with a normal market. Instead the services are paid for by the state...with the money following the users' choices...thus a fundamentally egalitarian device.'[58] Services could be delivered through numerous forms of association, including 'small businesses, partnerships, workers' cooperatives, corporations, non-profit or voluntary organizations and publicly owned institutions'.[59] In practice, the British Labour government entered into public-private agreements with capitalist businesses in which the latter privately funded and undertook provision of public provision infrastructure (hospitals, schools, and so on), use of which they then leased to the government. This did appear to increase efficiency: 88 per cent of projects were completed on time and to budget compared to a public-sector norm of late completion and over budget. However the downside was dangerous entanglement of public and private finances, and an increased exposure of government to market risk.[60]

Despite its moralism, Blair's Labour government in Britain, as an advisor vehemently insisted, 'didn't do God'. President George W. Bush's 'caring conservatism' certainly did. Bush's Republican administration, in its drive to percolate state spending through civil society, was keen to bring religious voluntary associations into play. Whilst rejecting a purely market 'sink-or-swim society', the aim was to make the state an enabler of ethically based civil society. Bush's administration announced its ambition to 'promote the work of charities, community groups and faith-based institutions. Government should view Americans who work in faith-based charities as partners, not as rivals. When it comes to providing resources the government should not discriminate against these groups that often inspire life-changing faith in a way that government never should.'[61] Under the second Bush, indeed, government spending soared, and the previous administration's budget surplus was turned into a budget deficit. Social spending was generous for constituencies inclined to vote conservatively (Medicare for the elderly, for example) and taxes were cut, mostly for the benefit of the wealthy. There was a political, indeed 'social engineering' rationale behind government encouragement of lending to enhance home-ownership rates amongst disadvantaged and low-income groups. The 'ownership society' was popular with the right, Richard Nadler observes, because ownership of assets 'correlated positively with conservative political affiliation'.[62] But this drive to expand 'bourgeois civil society' built dynamite into the economic foundations. By 2006, 48 per cent of all mortgages in the US were being taken out by 'sub-prime' buyers, those with a weak capacity to stay out of default, up from 15 per cent in 2001. Moreover, the moralization of civil society was not evident. If anything, 'self-help' was being hollowed-out as individuals struggled to maintain living standards by falling into debt. As Charles Maier put it, from being an 'empire of production' the United States had moved to being an 'empire of consumption'.[63] America's household savings were amongst the lowest in the advanced world, and families were able to increase consumption only by tapping into their asset-based wealth, namely the increase in equity that accompanied rising house prices.

Between the years 2002 and 2007, global growth rates were historically high, especially in emerging economies led by China. This allowed flows of capital from China and other exporting countries to sustain the US housing bubble and current- account deficits in advanced countries such as the US and UK. There was globally an imbalance between countries of 'excessive saving', led by China, and countries of 'excessive consumption', led by the US. In the late 2000s, this imbalance struck the global economy in a true economic 'crisis of capitalism'.

What began as an apparently isolated crisis in the sub-prime market of the US housing sector grew into a full-scale recession by the end of 2007. Sub-prime mortgages were repackaged in complex securities and sold on to third-party investors as mortgage-backed securities (MBS). By this transmission belt, the entire global financial market was infected by the rapidly deteriorating US housing sector. There was no sure way of quantifying exposure to risk, and investors began to assume the worst, switching suddenly from brash risk-seeking to timid risk-aversion. Liquidity quickly dried up in mid-2007, as institutions began to hoard money as a hedge against unknown losses and exposures, a market failure that made a nonsense of faith in efficient financial markets.[64] The contagion spread to the European Union and Japan in 2008. The 'credit crunch' was dramatically escalated by the failure of Lehman Brothers bank in September 2008, an event that almost caused the financial system to collapse. The year 2009 was the first featuring global economic contraction since the Second World War. China and India, however, continued to grow, supported by domestic demand and government spending. Small open economies were hit hardest (notably Ireland), and middle-income economies suffered, particularly in the former Communist bloc. Low-income countries generally avoided recession.

In coordinated international action, governments bailed out and nationalized banks to keep credit flowing, slashed interest rates and injected huge amounts of credit into financial markets to stimulate borrowing and investment, and increased public spending to shore up demand. Such an expansionary monetary policy was historically unprecedented, and support for beleaguered financial institutions ran to trillions of dollars. The banks, saved from their own excesses, returned to record profits in 2009, having benefited from government bailouts and the elimination of some competitors. The bonus-incentive structure for their brokers had not radically changed. By the third quarter of 2009, most OECD countries had technically exited recession. However, growth in America and Europe remained sluggish and unemployment generally in advanced countries continued to rise. The medium-term prospect seemed highly reliant on continued Chinese performance, a quasi-capitalist country that had almost entirely, to date, avoided the path of bourgeois constitutional revolution.

For all that the Great Recession was an almost unalloyed crisis of capitalism, it did little to constrain the power of the markets over society. As Steve Barrow, currency strategist at Standard Bank, told the *Financial Times*: 'It's the financial markets that have the power to dictate to governments and so bring about change, not the unions and the electorate.'[65] The markets, indeed, dictated. The European economies slashed public spending, and the weaker economies, facing default on their debts, were forced to accept fiscal dictation from the European Union almost regardless of domestic public opinion. In the summer of 2011 a 'sovereign debt' crisis swept Europe, putting the Community's single currency at peril, while the credit-rating agency Standard and Poor's downgraded the safety of US public debt.

The requirement to pay down deficits incurred in bailing out the system renewed the right's drive to reduce state spending structurally. There was undoubtedly a popular desire to see civil society strengthened against both the overweening power of the banks and the bureaucratic state. In the United States, the Republican Party quickly recovered electoral ground lost to the Democrats, powered by the grassroots Tea Party Movement. The 18 per cent of Americans who identified themselves as 'Tea Baggers' in April 2010 were middle class, wealthier, and economically more secure than average, and fearful of falling into a lower socioeconomic class.[66] They strongly supported a 'smaller state', with 'wasteful' expenditure, particularly on social programs to help the poor, slashed back. Financed by billionaire sponsors, the Tea Party opposed an apparently distant and unresponsive state, and directed particular animus at the White House's new resident.

As had long been the case in America, middle-class families defending personal wealth measured in tens of thousands of dollars rallied behind ultra-rich (and therefore powerful) leaders who were defending personal property measured in the millions and billions of dollars. When multi-millionaire Carl Paladino roused the Tea Party faithful at a victory rally in September 2010, his identification with the 'forgotten man' was resonant, if absurd: 'Tonight the ruling class knows. They have seen it now. There is a people's revolution. The people have had enough.'[67] It became a matter of principle for the Republican-controlled House of Representatives that the top 1 per cent of America's wealthiest be protected from paying any more in tax. William Graham Sumner might have approved.

In Britain, the Conservative Party formed a government in 2010 with the smaller Liberal Democratic Party as a coalition partner, and promptly set about slashing public expenditure. The scale and timing of the cuts at least were ideologically driven, a process of 'creative destruction' to open up space for a 'Big Society', linking commercialism and volunteering, to revive and moralize communities. 'Billions of pounds' worth of government contracts,' Prime Minister David Cameron promised, would be tendered out to 'charities and social enterprises'.[68] This, it was hoped, would generate a 'social recovery' to repair a morally 'broken Britain'. That the opposition Labour Party promoted its own version of a localist and cooperative 'Good Society' suggests that disillusion with statism was a political reality. Conservative reforms of the National Health Service, opening up competition to provide services to 'any willing provider', was a model for opening up almost all public services to privatization. Well-established corporations operating for profit had the capital resources to outbid not-for-profit tenders, and so were well positioned to cherry-pick the most valuable contracts. The projected restoration of civil society in the wake of the Great Recession meant spreading further and wider the supremacy of commercialism and markets.

## CONCLUSION

The nature of the business bourgeoisie had changed in the era of financialization. The entrepreneur now intuited future market conditions, rather than attempting to shape them by cooperating with the state and labour unions. Managing enterprises was no longer a matter of standardized procedure and institutional practice, but an inspired art form. So alchemical was the uncommon touch of CEOs and financial tyros that market computations of their value soared. While the wages of interchangeable workers stagnated, the remuneration packages of business executives with the 'magic touch' each year scaled dizzying new heights. In the cutting-edge information and creative services in particular, stuffy respectability was out, free-wheeling individuality was in. Dressed casually and hip to popular culture, 'bourgeois bohemians' invested their free spirits and raked back eye-watering salaries and stock options.

In the 1990s, capitalism was unchallenged in any fundamental sense; Western fixation with 'failed states', 'rogue states', and the 'War on Terror' was not a mere psychological palliative, but it was undoubtedly welcomed by defenders of free-market democracy concerned that, without ceaseless struggle, decadence would set in. The Middle East, in particular, became the battleground between a bourgeois destiny to emancipate civil society, and religio-political reaction. The neo-conservatives worried that a materialist bourgeois ethic threatened to undermine the West's moral resources in its stand-off with Islamism, and they preached millenarian militancy.

The Iraq debacle, followed hard by the Great Recession, ended a period of glad new morning for bourgeois revolution. In so doing it exposed the disjuncture between all-conquering capitalism and atrophied civil society. Commercialization of voluntarism, of faith-based associations, and of social welfare promised to revive on a yet wider basis bourgeois civil society as an integrated and active base for government and economy. Karl Marx had spoken of 'possible communism' as deriving from locally cooperating workers associating nationally to roll back the market.[69] Breathing a spirit of radicalism, the right of the twenty-first century looked from the other end, and imagined an anarchical reconstruction and popular validation of capitalism.

# Conclusions

It will be as well to reprise in summary the argument presented in the preceding chapters.

Constitutionalism historically had its origins in estate society, where aristocrats always, and town burghers and the clergy usually, claimed a right to advise their monarch through representative assemblies, or parliaments. Monarchs were generally not enthusiastic about being told their business, but they saw evident advantages in bringing together the notables of the realm, for by doing so they might hope to establish consensus for new taxation. This would otherwise be near impossible to collect without the cooperation of wealthy elites, such was the weakness of royal administrations. However, as the costs of war escalated in the sixteenth century, monarchies perforce centralized and built up administrative and military machines that, to a limited degree at least, intimidated their over-mighty subjects. As freedom of executive action was quite as valuable as fiscal stability, absolutist monarchs struck a balance whereby taxation was established at a level adequate to maintain creditworthiness, but raised no further than was collectable without recourse to parliaments.

As aristocratic influence at the court was itself an economic resource, but one substantially parasitic on productive agriculture, manufacture, and trade, commercial civil society was generally content enough to see the centralized state wax in power, and the vexatious aristocracy wane. In the seventeenth century the English political philosopher Thomas Hobbes spoke for many when he condemned faction (mostly an aristocratic phenomenon) as a corruption of undivided sovereignty and an invitation to conflict and disorder in the realm, destructive of ordered trade and commerce. Hobbes strongly argued that an undivided sovereign power would, all things being equal, leave commerce alone, so long as it paid over such taxes as were required. No rational sovereign would capriciously disrupt the private affairs of commercial civil society, as to do so would only invite disorder and diminish the revenues of the state.

Liberals later on followed this early modern reasoning. An intellectual consensus emerged that commercial civil society, because it looked for law and order and otherwise to be left alone, was a far more stable basis for a state than the aristocracy, who made a living through politicking and rivalry. Merchants, traders, and so on provided the ideal class basis for rationality in the state, not because they seized upon political power and wielded it in their narrow class interest, but rather because they preferred leaving state affairs to those competent, interested, and familiar. Commercial civil society was happy to pay the piper whilst leaving him to call the tune, so long as nothing too discordant was played.

Still, absolutism could not be other than a weight upon commerce, if for no other reason than it was based upon a variant of aristocratic ethos, and relied upon the traditional landed gentry to runs its various levels of government. Moreover, absolutist monarchies, being anxious to avoid summoning awkward parliaments, sold off economic privileges, and this disrupted the market economy. For the emerging bourgeoisie, which valued market opportunities to maximize returns on their carefully husbanded resources of capital, education, talent, and connections, the presumption of the absolutist state in rewarding favourites was irritating for those excluded or slighted. As more and more of commerce was manipulated for political and fiscal ends, absolutist mercantilism increasingly distorted the relationship between assets and return.

There was general agreement, however, that those primarily engaged in commerce, lacking as they did the political experience and interests of the aristocracy, were unlikely to apply much direct pressure on the state. If the state was to be made more attentive to the interests of commercial civil society, it would have to be a consequence of unusual circumstances. The aristocracy would have to be powerful enough to force a Parliament upon the Crown, but this Parliament would have to represent not aristocratic factional interests, primarily, but rather the taxpayers of a predominantly commercial society. Only this would align the interests of the state and commercialism, and, moreover, establish a structure to counteract pressures towards a renewed divergence.

It was not evident that bourgeois civil society exercised much political clout, except in so far as the aristocracy was able to take advantage of a free market for capital, connections, and entrepreneurial energy to enrich themselves beyond the limits traditionally set by the expectations and obligations of aristocratic class. In England, the aristocracy was by the sixteenth century, out of all European nobilities, perhaps most in tune with bourgeois property norms, though manoeuvring at court and managing government in the provinces remained probably their primary mode of existence. It was just this familiarity with the world of politics and government, however, that gave the English landed elites the capacity to contest the absolutist pretensions of the Stuart monarchy in the seventeenth century.

Through the English Civil Wars and the Glorious Revolution, Crown and Parliament struck a deal whereby the executive and the mostly aristocratic political nation mutually accepted commercial civil society as the constitutive, if largely politically passive, foundation of the polity. This proved to be a winning formula. Whilst respecting the autonomy of private enterprise, the state was able to draw upon the resources of vibrant domestic and imperial commercialism to build an unparalleled war-waging machine. In the North American colonies, commerce provided the basis for a state structure that was, with foreign aid, able to throw off rule from England, and thereafter stamp its authority and coherence onto the expanding United States.

The absolutist regimes of continental Europe eyed British success enviously, and manoeuvred themselves to emancipate bourgeois civil society without thereby alienating its key aristocratic support network. This delicate modernization project dramatically unravelled in France from 1789, where a bourgeoisie of lawyers and civil servants attempted to cashier both aristocracy and monarchy in one fell swoop. Pummelled by warfare and rebellion, the French took refuge in a Napoleonic reframing of absolutism, but shorn of aristocratic influence and based upon commercialism. This proved no match for the British fiscal state, however, which bankrolled the European monarchical alliance arrayed against Napoleon's empire of permanent war and plunder.

The outcome of the French Revolution did little to encourage the adoption of constitutionalism in Europe in the generation after Napoleon's defeat in 1815. The priority of statesmen such as Metternich was to avoid a repeat of revolutionary escalation by refusing to set down the path of reform. There was a price to be paid for immobilism, however, in the atrophy of state capability. Without constitutionalism to promote commercialism, and to underpin a monarchy's fiscal reach and credit rating, dreams of military glory had to be set to one side. The success of Britain in absorbing the challenge of Chartism, moreover, made clear that mature constitutionalism was a superior prophylactic against revolution. Liberalism in this era refined the idea that the destiny of the bourgeoisie was to support a stable, powerful state structure without attempting to dictate to it.

The year 1848 showed clearly enough the weakness of the old regimes, when capital cities fell like ninepins to revolutionaries. The most successful revolution, in France, was soon sharply divided between bourgeois civil society and the peasantry on the one side, semi-proletarianized artisans and wage labourers on the other. A minority of workers rose against the new Republic, and their suppression was welcomed by the majority of property holders, bourgeois and peasant alike. The emergence of Louis Napoleon, first as president, then as emperor, showed the ability of a wily dictator to wield the instrument of universal male suffrage against the inhibiting structures of constitutionalism. In the rest of Europe, the middle classes saw no prospect of disarming the old monarchical state machines, and sympathized with their repression of insurgent workers, peasants, and nationalities. While the Vormärz systems of aristocratic administration were substantially undermined by 1848, the monarchical states themselves survived with their armed forces and bureaucracies intact.

In the decades after 1848 the restored monarchies conceded degrees of constitutionalism and freed bourgeois civil society from vexatious restraints, for now they were convinced that they could initiate and control reform from above without thereby igniting revolution from below. The art of war in diplomacy came back into style. Most dramatically, Cavour's Piedmont-Sardinia drove through the unification of Italy, and Bismarck's Prussia led the unification of Germany. Liberals continued to believe that the destiny of the bourgeoisie was to provide the basis for reconstruction of the old monarchies along thoroughgoing constitutionalist lines. The political passivity of bourgeois civil society, however, frustrated radicals who increasingly looked to the growing working class as the 'true' revolutionary class. This conviction was only hardened by the militarization of state structures, the corporatization of capitalism, and the growth of cartels, all of which diminished the relative weight of the traditional basis of bourgeois liberty, the 'small battalions' of family firms and private associations. The bourgeoisie, it seemed, were being absorbed into an oligarchic leviathan state, an unholy alliance between big business and aristocratic elites hostile to democratic constitutionalism.

Indeed, the socialist theoreticians of the Second International felt themselves to be living in a new stage of capitalism, dated from about 1870, characterized by an increasingly conservative bourgeoisie. The working-class movement, they believed, had inherited the mantle of radical liberal democracy, which was thereby annexed to the class-specific demands of the proletariat for social equality and subordination of the market to the needs of wage labour. However, the association of civil and political radicalism with socialism made it all the more difficult to build a broad alliance for democracy. A 'revisionist' tendency was willing to moderate socialist demands and working-class egoism in the hope that an alliance with the bourgeoisie would then become possible. The socialist 'centre' countenanced tactical alliances with the bourgeoisie but rejected diluting their own movement's specific class appeal. On the left, various socialists inclined to the position that the bourgeoisie were now irredeemably reactionary, and that workers should only demand civil liberties as part of a seamless and uninterrupted struggle for proletarian dictatorship.

The First World War shattered political consensus because its results were so paradoxical, indeed frankly contradictory. All that appeared to be obvious was that bourgeois civil society as the bedrock of a liberal, constitutionalist, free-market order was sliding under the waves. The demands of war and post-war turbulence meant that corporatism became more powerful than ever, and to a certain extent parliamentarianism was sidelined by multilateral negotiation between governments, big business, and organized labour. The victorious Entente allies and the US were openly committed to democratic constitutionalism, and the system was rolled out across the defeated Central Powers. Individualist constitutionalism on the Anglo-American model, however, did not thrive in the sectional polities of Europe. Neither Social nor Catholic Democrats were able to assemble a sufficiently wide coalition behind a more appropriate social constitutionalism. The Russian Revolution gave impetus to a radical leftism that rejected bourgeois democracy as passé, and pressed for proletarian dictatorship to wage a social civil war. Social Democrats attempted to circumscribe the armies, judiciaries, and civil services of the old regimes, whilst refusing to detract from their effective power for fear of inducing societal collapse. The personnel of the 'permanent state' chafed at the inefficiencies of parliaments and the populism of party politics.

The bourgeoisie, when feeling economically comfortable, generally supported liberalism whilst grumbling at undue deference to organized labour. In times of economic crises, which were frequent in the dislocated world order, the frightened bourgeoisie shifted against constitutionalism altogether. Well aware that the old order could not be restored pristine, new dictatorships experimented with populism. With Fascism and even more so Nazism, a pan-class nationalism rejected altogether the priority of bourgeois commercialism, but nonetheless they won bourgeois support as a rampart against class-based civil war. The Soviet Union crushed its own bourgeoisie and ripped up the petit bourgeois seedbed of commercial society. Abroad, Communists from the mid-1930s switched to Popular Frontism, collaboration with bourgeois liberals and defencist patriots, in a desperate attempt to resist the tide of revisionist militarism. Everywhere, Popular Frontism tended to encourage bourgeois disillusion with electoral liberalism. Only in China, where the Communists attached themselves to the peasantry and bourgeois civil society was coshed by Japanese imperialism, did a form of Popular Frontism, predicated ironically on bourgeois weakness, score substantial if incomplete success. Bourgeois liberty was obscured in the interwar years, but it certainly remained lively in Great Britain and the US. Even here, faith in free enterprise was sharply diminished, and an awareness of the need to protect wage labour from insecurity grew quickly.

The hyper-militarism of German and Japanese society powered their early sweeping victories in the Second World War, but in the longer run it succumbed to the build-up in depth achieved by the Allies. The Soviet Union's clear lines of societal command made for effective total-war mobilization, while Britain and America successfully turned the dynamism of commercial civil society to the prosecution of capital-intensive, materiel-led warfare. In the aftermath of war, the Soviets crushed out the bourgeoisie in their own zone of influence, fearing that it would otherwise provide the social basis for a pro-Western fifth column. Cautious experiments with liberalized Communist rule generally failed, for lack of a proletarian civil society able to invigorate economic commandism. In China, Maoism attempted to prevent bureaucratic ossification by canalizing popular radicalism, but the disorder this brought to state and society meant the eventual abandonment of 'cultural revolution' as a disastrous experiment in creative *luan* (chaos).

Western Europe was democratized by force of arms, both conventional and through the Resistance movements, but in contrast to the years after the Great War, Social and Christian Democracy proved able to build broad alliances behind a consensual parliamentarianism that preserved free enterprise whilst ring-fencing wage labour from market fluctuations. Consumerism displaced imperialism as the basic economic model, and labour-market rigidities were held at bay by the dramatic influx of workers from agriculture into manufacture and services.

In America, a military-industrial complex grew up to wage a Cold War of Soviet containment. This was not hierarchical militarism of the old mould, however, as it was held in check by democracy and careful cultivation of civilian supremacy. Nonetheless, there was a growing domestic disquiet with US hostility to Communist 'subversion'. The 'containment' doctrine of the United States put it firmly on the side of Latin American and South East Asian authoritarian regimes of 'law and order', and against emancipationist movements of the left. America's military doctrine of 'flexible response' and 'credibility' immured it in bloody wars to defend dictatorial regimes. The Vietnam War, in particular, generated concern that America was sliding towards amoral militarism. The 1960s protest movement was multifaceted, but involved a considerable degree of youthful bourgeois revolt against neo-militarist regimentation and group-think. In Western Europe, '68 signalled a rebellion against the conservative hierarchies of post-war elites, many of which had connections with the anti-democratic culture of the interwar years. In Eastern Europe, the Balkans, and Mexico, '68 was a rebellion not against the hypocrisies of bourgeois democracy but for constitutional parliamentarianism.

The post-war era had stabilized bourgeois civil society, tilting it away from small-scale family forms and towards professionals both in the public and corporate sectors. A certain demoralization was evident, however, in the conformism of established liberal democracies and the lack of impetus for their spread. Post-colonial states, indeed, veered towards forms of Communism occasionally, and in almost all cases, towards statist authoritarianism.

In the 1970s, however, the transition to democracy in Spain, Portugal, and Greece did much to exorcize the twin fears of bourgeois betrayal of liberty and Communist subversion of revolution. Whilst this appeared at first to inaugurate a new dawn for Social Democracy, societal developments in the advanced West were heading in another direction. The Keynesian settlement began to break down in the 1970s, due to increasing labour-market rigidities, exacerbated by inflationary 'oil shocks'. Growing turmoil in industrial relations diminished the appeal of democratic corporatism. An overloaded state seemed prey to special interests, including trade unions, corporations, and welfare claimants. Particularly amongst the middle class, there was growing support for a reassertion of the norms of bourgeois civil society. Most pointedly, this meant the principle of wealth flowing to those endowed with talent, hard work, entrepreneurialism, and inculcated skills. Egalitarianism receded as an ideal, to be replaced by an ideology of 'just rewards', measured not by bureaucrats but by the flexible labour market. The emergence of new forms of production of goods and services, driven by specialization for fragmented markets on the one side, international sourcing of components, labour, and capital on the other, mightily reinforced the political drive towards market flexibility and yawning inequality.

The command economies of the Communist bloc, in contrast, failed to transfer labour and investment effectively from old, military-oriented smoke-stack industries to information-led technologies and consumer services. Well-educated elites within Communist societies, painfully aware that their remuneration fell well below any likely market valuation, were enthusiastic for capitalist restoration. The working class, resentful of political repression and the managerial inefficiency of the command economies, supported the dismantling of the socialist pretensions of the totalitarian command economies.

The collapse of Communism eclipsed any fundamental challenge to the capitalist order. Even in the developing world, authoritarianism fell out of fashion, and free-market democracies took their place. The mid-1990s were a triumphalist age of the 'market state', and governments vigorously promoted the interest and spread of bourgeois civil society. The Middle East remained intractable; here, a democratic market-based Israel was surrounded by authoritarian regimes with weak civil societies.

Since the 1980s, US foreign policy had been moving away from the negative strategy of sustaining friendly dictatorships against subversion to a positive strategy promoting market democracy. The Global War on Terror focused neo-conservative minds on the need to drain the swamp of authoritarianism that bred reactionary fanaticism and decentred violence. The invasion of Iraq was calculated to bring about 'regime change', or revolution on the points of bayonets. In this it succeeded, but at a terrible cost in blood, treasure, and American prestige.

The Great Recession of 2008 starkly exposed the weaknesses of financialized capitalism, and required unprecedented government bailouts and state spending to inflate demand and stave off depression. The medium-term political effect of the recession, however, was a revival of social engineering to strengthen bourgeois civil society and the rule of the market. The destiny of the bourgeoisie, its champions felt, was to humanize capitalism by bringing the market into every human relation, every facet of social provision, of consumption, of production, of the political process itself.

\* \* \*

We may now revisit the argument set out in the introduction. This hypothesized that the 'tragical destiny' of the bourgeoisie is to mobilize the popular masses as allies in its struggle against absolutism and aristocracy, only to find that by doing so it has roused a working-class movement opposed to its essential interests. As the bourgeoisie grows fearful of the threat from its left flank, it strikes a compact with illiberal authoritarian government the better to keep its erstwhile working-class allies subordinate: 'the rich always betray the poor'. The liberalism of the bourgeoisie, therefore, is directly and inversely proportional to the independence and militancy of the working class.

Certainly the broad sweep of history canvassed here gives credence to this view in outline. Though capitalism, as a tendency to commodify all goods including labour, was in train from 1500 at least, bourgeois civil society was only in England in the course of the seventeenth century emancipated from a state and aristocracy using political power to harvest the fruits of commerce. The Glorious Revolution of 1688, and the subsequent restructuring of political order in Britain, showed the plausibility of a successful and broadly consensual modernization whereby bourgeois civil society was allowed space to develop unhindered. The French attempt to reproduce British success ran out of control in the Great Revolution. This reinforced the lesson that resolute struggle against absolutism could unleash democratic forces injurious to bourgeois order. Still, no socialist movement emerged in 1790s France to challenge free-market liberalism in principle; the plebeian *sans culottes* and peasantry were generally in favour of private property in production.

In the decades between Napoleon's downfall and the revolutions of 1848, the middle classes were broadly liberal and constitutionalist in their political ambitions. The year 1848, however, saw a much more seriously socialistic impulse from the teeming cities of semi-proletarianized artisans, particularly in France. The 'spectre of communism' was sufficiently disconcerting to promote caution amongst the middle classes, and a new-found respect for strong, illiberal government. Roughly speaking, 1848 may be seen as an inflection point from which the audacity of bourgeois liberalism declined. Fear of 'red revolution' meant that the bourgeoisie ceased to be revolutionary. From about 1870, the bourgeoisie positively moved into alliance with the authoritarian state through intertwining with imperialist adventurers. The workers' movement, broadly socialist, inherited the bourgeoisie's busted will to revolutionize the state, but by becoming the revolutionary vanguard further drove the bourgeoisie into the camp of the conservative status quo, or even reaction.

Under the pressure of war, autocracy collapsed in Russia in 1917, but bourgeois civil society proved unable to sustain a liberal political order and the Bolsheviks took power on a wave of working-class enthusiasm for socialism. Combined with a wave of socialist militancy from 1918 to 1921, and capitalist stagnation tipping into Depression from 1929, the victory of Communism struck fear into the bourgeoisie. The middle classes preferred authoritarianism to any threat from the 'proletarian democracy', and constitutionalism itself seemed in mortal peril in the interwar period. The parabola of bourgeois liberalism reached its lowest point. Democracy was saved only by an alliance of convenience between the liberal USA and the Soviet Union in the Second World War.

In the subsequent Cold War, however, while bourgeois liberalism stabilized in the Western European, North American, and British ex-Dominions of white settlement, it was inhibited elsewhere by the fear of Communist subversion of national liberation movements. Only with the exhaustion of Communism as an ideology and a system did the parabola of bourgeois liberalism turn steeply upwards again. By the 1990s and early twenty-first century, the enthusiasts for bourgeois virtues had recovered their pre-1848 revolutionary élan, but now on a much broader and triumphant scale.

As a broad picture, this is tenable. However, there are significant qualifications to make.

## THE WILL TO POLITICAL POWER WAS NEVER A BOURGEOIS CHARACTERISTIC

The bourgeoisie was a highly fissured, variegated class—including capitalists, managers, salaried professionals, skilled technicians, cultural entrepreneurs, etcetera—bound only by possession of relatively scarce marketable assets. Bourgeois civil society favoured 'careers open to talents', but otherwise lacked tight bonds of political solidarity and cohesion. That bourgeois civil society was constituted apolitically, however, was the very foundation for liberalism's proposed bargain: emancipation of the state from class control as a quid pro quo for emancipation of bourgeois civil society from statist rent-seeking. So, there was never an age of a politically unified bourgeoisie bent on revolution to seize the state. Bourgeois civil society was always dependent upon reconciliation with the state, and the latter always retained relative freedom of manoeuvre.

## BOURGEOIS SUPPORT FOR AUTHORITARIANISM WAS NOT ALWAYS IN REACTION TO CHALLENGES FROM THE LEFT

Liberal recourse to authoritarianism was quite as often a response to the reactionary right as it was to proletarian democracy. Particularly if based upon religious enthusiasm and 'backward' social strata, such as the peasantry, popular movements of traditionalism drew forth often pugilistic instincts from bourgeois civil society. We may think of French Revolutionary and Napoleonic use of force against Catholic and royalist 'banditry', liberal war against the Carlists in Spain, constitutionalist Italy's repression of 'brigandage' in the former Kingdom of Naples, often venomous anti-Catholicism in the USA, the German Kulturkampf against the Church, the militant *laïcité* of the French Dreyfusards, and the frequent use of 'coercion' against the Catholic democracy in Ireland by the British. Many liberals, as Bruce Waller points out, by being 'proudly and ungenerously anti-clerical... offered an example and justification for the persecution of Jews, Poles, Slovaks, socialists, or others'.[1] Of course, the anti-capitalist left inherited and exacerbated much of this rage against reaction, as evident in Soviet de-kulakization and persecution of Orthodox and Muslim clergy, or Spanish anarchist violence against Catholic clergy. Since the outrages of 9/11, the old liberal *bête noire* of Catholicism has given way to fear of Islam as the anti-modern, insidious, and transnational agent of reaction based upon social backwardness. On the political fringes, the effects of Muslim immigration into the 'Judeo-Christian West' is vehemently condemned, whilst in the mainstream of the War Against Terror, use of 'enhanced interrogation' (torture), internment of 'unlawful combatants', and 'targeted killings' (assassinations) have been upfront. Still, the reaction of liberalism to perceived pre-modern backlash was usually militant, driving towards greater bourgeois liberty, rather than conservative, seeking to compromise with traditional structures and institutions. From Jacobinism to neo-conservativism, defenders of bourgeois civil society when needled from the reactionary right tend towards hard-nosed revolutionism.

## EVEN AS BOURGEOIS RADICALISM DECLINED, THERE REMAINED MANY OPPORTUNITIES FOR LIBERAL-SOCIALIST COOPERATION

Bourgeois civil society certainly drew back its challenge to statist pretensions in the period from the 1870s, when economic oligarchy and imperialism emerged, and even more so from the 1890s, when a competitive militant workers' movement made liberals anxious not to press for political reform likely to benefit the labour movement disproportionately. Nonetheless, it would be wrong to overstate the new-found illiberalism of the bourgeoisie, or the capitulation to authoritarianism by liberalism. Liberals would not countenance revolutionary rupture, at any rate outside autocratic regimes, but they could work with socialists to push back authoritarian tendencies, particularly if so doing might 'domesticate' their allies. Socialist-Liberal alliances were common: from Millerand's entry into a bourgeois French government (1899); through socialist support for the Giolitti government in Italy (1901), Labour's secret pact with the Liberals in Britain (1903), Socialist-Liberal coordination in Russia (1905–6), the socialists' electoral alliance with Republicans in Spain (1910), a united front between Belgian Socialists and Liberals (1911–12), and an electoral pact between German Socialists and Liberals (1912);

to Labour-Liberal cooperation in 'defencist' governments in France, Belgium, and Britain (1914), and German Socialist-Liberal cooperation in preparation for post-war constitutionalism (from July 1917). Popular Frontism from the 1930s, and post-war democratic constitutionalism, entrenched the potential for Socialist-Liberal cooperation. It needs to be remembered, however, that Liberals often alienated their bourgeois supporters by striking such alliances with the left.

## INTER-WAR FASCISM WAS NOT MERELY AN ARTEFACT OF BOURGEOIS DISILLUSION WITH LIBERTY

There is no doubt that the rise of Communism made any variant of 'proletarian democracy', even of the Social Democratic genus, disconcerting for bourgeois civil society. When fairly stable, constitutionalism was the preferred option for the bourgeoisie, but when confronted by crisis the middle classes were much tempted by authoritarian solutions in the interwar period. Still, it needs to be recalled that generic fascism, while offering continued bourgeois order and prosperity, and if anything talking up 'talent' as a justification for privilege, was a pan-class movement that put the nation-race above any consideration of mere middle-class preference, and was wary of 'soulless' capitalism. Salazar, in his justification for the Portuguese 'New State', condemned equally the three fallacies of democracy, liberalism, and socialism: 'the constant party warfare, the injustices of Liberal economic life, the devastation worked by socialism'.[2] Particularly under the more radical fascist regimes, bourgeois civil society resented that political atomization extended beyond the labour movement to its own sphere, and it could never feel secure. Once the shock of defeat had passed and liberal civil society restored outside the Soviet sphere of influence, there were few in the middle class who pined for the regimes of Hitler, Mussolini, and the Japanese militarists.

## THERE ARE NO MODERN POLITICAL PARTIES OR GOVERNMENTS THAT ARE 'PURELY' BOURGEOIS

Where democracy stabilized after the Second World War, it was generally 'umbrella parties' that contested for governance. While these parties had their class bases, they were formed for democratic polities in which deference to bourgeois interests alone would not win elections. 'Proletarian democracy', therefore, was accommodated to a greater or lesser extent by all parties, and the bourgeoisie did not possess any party as a fully owned subsidiary. As ever, the nature of bourgeois civil society was not to govern politically.

Neo-liberal and neo-conservative politicians were no mere spokespersons for bourgeois interest. They appealed to the interests and opinions of the broad electorate. The politicians persuasively argued for social inequality on the grounds of fairness, because the minority who contribute most to society through their talent and hard work deserve to be proportionately rewarded. This rationale for a bourgeois civil society enjoys support even amongst the poor. The unstated reality of 'winner take all' societies, however, is that the market rewards wealth not on the basis of generally accepted 'intrinsic merit', but rather to those with 'extrinsic merit' as measured by the yardstick of mere profitability, regardless of social utility. Further, it seems evident that social inequality itself is dysfunctional for society at large.[3] It would be naïve, therefore, to deny that the interests of bourgeois civil society are protected by economic structures (not to mention the capacity of those with great wealth to lobby the political class).

## THE BOURGEOISIE RELATES ONLY INDIRECTLY TO ITS 'VANGUARD'

The interests of bourgeois civil society are articulated in the political sphere by politicians and public intellectuals. Politicians' and pundits' understanding of the requirements for strong, assertive free-market society is not an unmediated reflection of middle-class opinion. On the contrary, formers of opinion tend to see the middle class as basically sound, but inconstant and frivolous, corruptible by the very prosperity and privilege they enjoy, and unwilling to face up to the hard tasks required to defend and expand rational modernity. For neo-liberals, neo-conservatives, and the 'decent left', bourgeois revolution is too important to be left to the bourgeoisie. In the 1970s, 'wet' business managers and civil servants too willingly cosseted truculent trade unions; in the 1980s, the *bien-pensant* intelligentsia turned their noses up at the class-war rigours of labour-market modernization, and traded radical chic for soft multiculturalism and trendy postmodernism; in the 1990s, the smugly affluent middle classes turned their eyes away from post-Cold War international disorder and the threat of Islamist militancy; in the twenty-first century they fretted at the necessary exigencies of the 'War on Terror' and the liberation of Iraq and Afghanistan. Bourgeois civil society, nonetheless, was always the foundation and justification for ambitiously 'forward' politics, and its practitioners were always confident that the broad bourgeoisie, even as once it quailed before the fight, would applaud ultimate success. For the bourgeois revolutionary, history judges—and absolves.

## THE TENSION BETWEEN 'BOURGEOIS LIBERTY' AND 'PROLETARIAN DEMOCRACY' REMAINS

In 1995 the historian Jürgen Kocka wrote of the end of the twentieth century that 'The middle class proved to be stronger than its opponents. It won.'[4] Economic restructuring in the advanced economies has led to a certain dissolution and demoralization of the working class in its lower reaches. This so-called 'underclass' is demonized and even criminalized by respectable society.[5] In the upper reaches of wage labour, competitive self-advancement seems a plausible life strategy.

Technological change has stratified the working class, and strengthened individualistic rather than collectivist identities. The organized labour movement is only a junior partner in such pan-class reform movements as exist.[6] Wage labour, however, did not disappear, and its interests can never be identified entirely with the flexible labour-market imperatives of bourgeois civil society. Whilst the wealth of Croesus piles upon bourgeois 'talent', particularly in the financial markets, wage earners maintaining the dignities of civilized life wonder why the single ability to maximize profits should be so privileged, even as such prioritization plunges the economy into crisis. A 2008–9 survey in Britain suggested that some 50 per cent of people rejected the bourgeois ideal of acquired and innate skills being limitlessly rewarded by market criteria, preferring an essentially proletarian (wage-earner) ideal of security and the rough equality of those who contribute through work.[7]

The bourgeoisie in the West, moreover, begin to worry about their own ability to stay ahead of the salary curve. In the early twenty-first century, the professional middle class for the first time began to see their jobs being exported overseas, as IT and advanced communications made it practicable to source specialist services and management skills to developing countries.[8] This threatens to 'dilute' the market value of established bourgeois attributes. The constituency of wage earners, perhaps, will absorb the energy, skills, and—who knows?—frustration and anger of men and women brought up to expect a bourgeois lifestyle, but finding themselves denied their destiny. The balance struck between bourgeois liberty and democracy can only be considered partial and provisional. The politics of bourgeois fear may yet return.

# *Endnotes*

## INTRODUCTION

1. Quoted in J. A. S. Grenville, *Europe Reshaped, 1848–1878* (Oxford, 1976, 2000), 33.
2. Robert Michels, *Political Parties: A Sociological Study of the Oligarchical Tendencies of Modern Democracy*, trans. Cedar Paul and Eden Paul (New York, 1966), 228.
3. Awaiting execution following the failed United Irishmen rebellion. R. R. Madden, *The United Irishmen, their lives and times*, 2nd ser., vol. II (London, 1843), 482–3.
4. Leon Trotsky, *Stalin: An Appraisal of the Man and his Influence* [1940] (London, 1947), 426.
5. Heinrich Heine [29 July 1842] document in Geoffrey Bruun, *Revolution and Reaction, 1848–1852: A Mid-Century Watershed* (New Jersey, 1958), 108.
6. E. J. Hobsbawm, *The Age of Revolution: Europe, 1789–1848* (London, 1962), 62.
7. Bogdan Szlachta, ed., *Polish Anti-Communism and its Intellectual Traditions*, trans. Tomasz Bieroń (Cracow, n.d.), 45–6.
8. Ludwig Von Mises, *Socialism: An Economic and Sociological Analysis*, trans. J. Kahane (Auburn, AL, 1951, 2009), 74.
9. William Doyle, *Origins of the French Revolution*, 3rd ed. (Oxford, 1999), 121.
10. Pamela M. Pilbeam, *The Middle Classes in Europe, 1789–1914: France, Germany, Italy and Russia* (Basingstoke, 1990), 173.
11. Jürgen Kocka, *Industrial Culture and Bourgeois Society: Business, Labor, and Bureaucracy in Modern Germany, 1800–1918* (New York, 1999), 283.
12. Karl Marx, *Capital*, vol. 1, trans. Ben Fowkes (London, 1976), 710, 764.
13. Karl Marx, 'The Bourgeoisie and the Counter-Revolution', Neue Rheinische Zeitung, December 1848, *Marx-Engels Collected Works* (hereafter *MECW*), vol. 8, 159.
14. Max Weber, 'Class, Status and Party' [*c.*1924] in Raymond Boudon and Mohamed Cherkaoui (eds), *Central Currents in Social Theory*, vol. II (London, 2000), 238–52.
15. Werner Sombart [1909], excerpted in Sidney Pollard and Colin Holmes, *Documents of European Economic History*, vol. 2, *Industrial Power and National Rivalry* (London, 1968), 495–7.
16. Karl Polanyi, *The Great Transformation: The Political and Economic Origins of Our Time* (Boston, 1944, 1957, 2001), 136–70.
17. Michel Vovelle, *The Fall of the French Monarchy, 1787–1792* (Cambridge, 1972, 1984), 151.
18. Don Kalb, *Expanding Class, Power and Everyday Politics in Industrial Communities: The Netherlands, 1850–1950* (Durham, 1997), 97.
19. Harold Perkin, *The Rise of Professional Society: England since 1880* (New York, 2002), 8.
20. Chris and Charles Tilly, *Work Under Capitalism* (Boulder, CO, 1998), 216.
21. Robert H. Frank and Philip J. Cook, *The Winner Takes all Society: Why the Few at the Top Get so Much More than the Rest of Us* (London, 1995, 2010), 3, 24.
22. Paul Cheshire, Vassilis Monastiriotis, and Stephen Sheppard, 'Income Inequality and Residential Segregation' in Ron Martin and Philip S. Morrison (eds), *Geographies of Labour Market Inequality* (London, 2002), 97.
23. Sidney Webb, 'English Progress Toward Social Democracy' [1894] in Albert Fried and Ronald Sanders (eds), *Socialist Thought: A Documentary History*, revised ed. (New York, 1964, 1992), 396.

24. Charles More, *Understanding the Industrial Revolution* (London, 2000), 146; Robert C. Allen, 'Real Incomes in the English-Speaking World, 1879–1913', in George Grantham and Mary Mackinnon (eds), *Labour Market Evolution: The Economic History of Market Integration, Wage Flexibility, and the Employment Relation* (New York, 1994), 124–5.
25. Harold Perkin, *The Third Revolution: Professional Elites in the Modern World* (New York, 1996), 38.
26. Joseph E. Stiglitz, 'Of the 1 Per Cent, by the 1 Per Cent, for the 1 Per Cent', in *Vanity Fair*, May 2011.
27. Jean L. Cohen and Andrew Arato, *Civil Society and Political Theory* (Cambridge, MA, 1992), 95–6.
28. Pierre Bourdieu, 'Structures, *Habitus*, Practices', in Bourdieu, *The Logic of Practice* (Cambridge, 1980, 1990), 52–65.
29. Karl Marx, *Critique of Hegel's Philosophy of Right* [1843] (Cambridge, 1977), 80.
30. Karl Marx, *Critique of the Gotha Program* [1875] (Maryland, 2008), 26.
31. J. L. Talmon, *Romanticism and Revolt: Europe 1815–1848* (London, 1967), 42.
32. I have dealt with the topic at some length elsewhere. Marc Mulholland, '"Its Patrimony, its Unique Wealth!" Labour-Power, Working-class Consciousness and Crises: An Outline Consideration', *Critique*, vol. 38, no. 3, August 2010, 375–417.
33. Marx, *Capital*, 615. See also Marx, *Economic and Philosophical Manuscripts* [1844], *MECW*, vol. 3, 240.
34. E. H. Phelps Brown, *The Origins of Trade Union Power* (Oxford, 1983), 30.
35. Carl Schmitt, *Constitutional Theory* [1925], trans. Jeffrey Seitzer (Durham, NC, 2008) 272.
36. Stepniak, *The Russian Peasantry* [1905], excerpted in Richard M. Golden and Thomas Kuehn (eds), *Western Societies: Primary Sources in Social History* (New York, 1993), 249–53.
37. Geoffrey Crossick and Heinz-Gerhard Haupt, *The Petite-bourgeoisie in Europe, 1780–1914* (London, 1995), 165.
38. Quoted in Perry Anderson, *Lineages of the Absolutist State* (London, 1974, 1979), 163–4.
39. Derek Beales and Eugenio Biagini, *The Risorgimento and the Unification of Italy*, 2nd ed. (Harlow, 1971, 2002), 36–7.
40. Quoted in Brian Harrison, *The Transformation of British Politics, 1860–1995* (Oxford, 1996), 29.
41. Quoted in Gerd-Rainer Horn, *European Socialists Respond to Fascism: Ideology, Activism, and Contingency in the 1930s* (New York, 1996), 126–7.
42. Quoted in Jan Willem Stutje, *Ernest Mandel: A Rebel's Dream Deferred*, trans. Christopher Beck and Peter Drucker (London, 2009), 244.
43. Most famously, the pro-democracy Chinese students camped in Tiananmen Square in 1989 constructed a 'Goddess of Liberty', modelled on the Statue of Liberty. Andrew Langley, *Tiananmen Square* (Minneapolis, 2009), 8.

## CHAPTER 1: ABSOLUTISM AND TRANSFORMATION IN ENGLAND

1. See H. E. Hallam, 'The Medieval Social Picture', F. J. West, 'On the Ruins of Feudalism-Capitalism?', and J. G. A. Pocock, 'Early Modern Capitalism: The Augustan Perception', all in Eugene Kamenka and R. S. Neale (eds), *Feudalism, Capitalism and Beyond* (London, 1975).

2. Jan de Vries, *The Industrious Revolution: Consumer Behavior and the Household Economy* (Cambridge, 2008), 68.
3. See the famous article by R. H. Coase, 'The Federal Communications Commission', in *Journal of Law and Economics*, vol. 2 (October 1959), 14.
4. Douglass C. North, *Structure and Change in Economic History* (New York, 1981), 159.
5. S. E. Finer, *The History of Government*, vol. III, *Empires, Monarchies and the Modern State* (Oxford, 1997, 1999), 1,298–303.
6. Mike Macnair, 'Free Association versus Juridification', *Critique*, vol. 39, no. 1 (2011), 80. Emphasis in original.
7. Benedetto Cotrugli, excerpted in Charles T. Davis (ed.), *Western Awakening: Sources of Medieval History*, vol. II, *c.1000–c.1500* (New York, 1967), 144.
8. Keith Randall, *John Calvin and the Later Reformation* (London, 1990), 73–4.
9. Jonathan Dewald, 'The Early Modern Period', in Peter N. Stearns (ed.), *Encyclopedia of European Social History from 1350 to 2000*, vol. 1 (New York, 2001), 173.
10. Jill Kilsby, *Spain: Rise and Decline, 1474–1643* (London, 1986), 7.
11. Sandra Halperin, *War and Social Change in Modern Europe: The Great Transformation Revisited* (Cambridge, 2004), 30, 53–4, 58–9.
12. Peter H. Wilson, *Absolutism in Central Europe* (London, 2000), 97.
13. F. L. Carsten, *Princes and Parliaments in Germany: From the Fifteenth to the Eighteenth Century* (Oxford, 1959), 73.
14. P. M. Jones, *The French Revolution 1787–1804* (London, 2003), 7.
15. Bonnie G. Smith, *Changing Lives: Women in European History Since 1700* (Lexington, MA, 1989), 62.
16. Jerome Blum, *The End of the Old Order in Rural Europe* (Princeton, 1978), 373.
17. Walter Oppenheim, *Europe and the Enlightened Despots* (London, 1990), 50.
18. Robert B. Ekelund and Robert D. Tollison, *Politicized Economies: Monarchy, Monopoly, and Mercantilism* (College Station, TX, 1997), 50.
19. Herbert S. Klein, *The American Finances of the Spanish Empire: Royal Income and Expenditures in Colonial Mexico, Peru, and Bolivia, 1680–1809* (Albuquerque, 1998), 100.
20. Alan MacFarlane, 'The Cradle of Capitalism: The Case of England', in Jean Baechler, John A. Hall, and Michael Mann (eds), *Europe and the Rise of Capitalism* (Oxford, 1988), 103–30, 201.
21. Steve Hindle, *The State and Social Change in Early Modern England, 1550–1640* (Basingstoke, 2000), 16–18.
22. John Warren, *The Wars of the Roses and the Yorkist Kings* (London, 1995), 21.
23. Quentin Skinner, *Visions of Politics: Renaissance Virtues*, vol. 2 (Cambridge, 2002), 321.
24. Hugh Trevor-Roper, *Historical Essays* (London, 1957), 181.
25. Quoted in Conrad Russell, *The Causes of the English Civil War* (Oxford, 1990), 195.
26. 'Petition of Right', in Milton Viorst (ed.), *The Great Documents of Western Civilization* (New York, 1967), 116–18.
27. Linda S. Popofsk, 'The Crisis Over Tonnage and Poundage in Parliament in 1629', in *Past and Present*, vol. 126 (1990), 46.
28. Sir Charles Petrie, *The Letters, Speeches and Proclamations of King Charles I* (London, 1935), 206.
29. Peter Young and Richard Holmes, *The English Civil War: A Military History of the Three Civil Wars, 1642–1651* (London, 1974), 31.

## Notes to Chapter 1

30. Thomas Babington Macaulay, *The History of England*, vol. 2 (London, 1884), 4.
31. Bruce G. Carruthers, *City of Capital: Politics and Markets in the English Financial Revolution* (Princeton, 1996), 119.
32. 'Conclusion', in Philip T. Hoffman and Kathryn Norberg (eds), *Fiscal Crises, Liberty, and Representative Government, 1450–1789* (Stanford, 1994), 306.
33. John Hicks, *A Theory of Economic History* (Oxford, 1969), 94.
34. Immanuel Kant, *Perpetual Peace* [1795] (New York, 1939), 5–6.
35. Douglas Hay and Nicholas Rogers, *Eighteenth-Century English Society: Shuttles and Swords* (Oxford, 1997), 228.
36. Takuo Dome, *The Political Economy of Public Finance in Britain, 1767–1873* (New York, 2004), 44.
37. Theodore S. Hamerow, *The Birth of a New Europe: State and Society in the Nineteenth Century* (Chapel Hill, 1983), 46, 49.
38. Kenneth Morgan, *Slavery, Atlantic Trade and the British Economy, 1660–1800* (Cambridge, 2000), 94–8.
39. Robert C. Allen, *The British Industrial Revolution in Global Perspective* (Cambridge, 2009), 22.
40. Wilfrid Prest, *Albion Ascendant: English History, 1660–1815* (Oxford, 1998), 170.
41. R. R. Palmer, *The Age of Democratic Revolution: A Political History of Europe and America, 1760–1800*, vol. 1 (Princeton, 1959), 301.
42. Joel Mokyr, *The Gifts of Athena: Historical Origins of the Knowledge Economy* (Princeton, 2002), 71–5.
43. Adam Smith, *An Inquiry into the Nature and Causes of the Wealth of Nations* [1776], ed. C. J. Bullock (New York, 1909), 352.
44. Thomas Hobbes, *De Cive; Or, the Citizen* [1642], ed. Sterling Lamprecht (New York, 1949), 80.
45. Thomas Hobbes, *Behemoth* [1668] (Chicago, 1990), 16.
46. Thomas Hobbes, *Leviathan* [1651], ed. Richard Tuck (Cambridge, 1996), 152.
47. Thomas Hobbes, *The Elements of Law, Natural and Politic* [1640], ed. J. C. A. Gaskin (Oxford, 1994), 173.
48. Hobbes, *Leviathan*, 231.
49. Hobbes, *Elements of Law*, 138–40.
50. John Bowle, *Politics and Opinion in the Nineteenth Century* (London, 1954, 1963), 62.
51. Charles de Secondat, Baron de Montesquieu, *The Spirit of Laws* [1748] (Chicago, 1952), 147.
52. *Politique tirée de l'Écriture sainte* [1679, published 1709], cited in Ragnhild Hatton, *Europe in the Age of Louis XIV* (London, 1969), 79.
53. David Hume, 'Of Commerce' [1741–2], in Hume, *Essays: Literary, Moral, and Political* (London, 1870), 155.
54. David Hume, 'Of Liberty' [1741–2], in ibid., 53.
55. Count Chaptal, *De l'Industrie Françoise* [Paris, 1819], excerpted in S. Pollard and C. Holmes, *Documents of European Economic History*, vol. 1, *The Process of Industrialization, 1750–1870* (London, 1968), 303–4.
56. John Locke, *The Second Treatise of Government* [1689], ed. Thomas Peardon (Indianapolis, 1960), 85.
57. Ibid., 50.
58. Adam Ferguson, *An Essay on the History of Civil Society* [1767] (New York, 1954), 473–5.
59. Immanuel Kant, *Principles of Political Right* [1793], in Kant, *The Critique of Pure Reason and Other Ethical Treatises*, ed. Robert Maynard Hutchins (Chicago, 1952), 401.

60. Philip Pettit, *Republicanism: A Theory of Freedom and Government* (Oxford, 1997), 21.
61. Immanuel Kant, *An Answer to the Question: 'What is Enlightenment?'* [1784] (London, 2009), 2–3.
62. Jonathan Israel, *A Revolution of the Mind* (Princeton, 2010), 223.
63. John Weiss, *Conservatism in Europe, 1770–1945: Traditionalism, Reaction and Counter-Revolution* (London, 1977), 45–6.
64. Edmund Burke, *Reflections on the Revolution in France* [1790] (Oxford, 1993), 55.
65. Frederick B. Artz, *Reaction and Revolution, 1814–1832* (New York, 1934), 94.
66. Constant quoted in Luciano Canfora, *Democracy in Europe* (Oxford, 2006), 64.
67. D. R. Watson, 'The British Parliamentary System and the Growth of Constitutional Government in Western Europe', in C. J. Bartlett (ed.), *Britain Pre-eminent: Studies of British World Influence in the Nineteenth Century* (London, 1969), 115.
68. For example, Marx, *Capital*, vol. 1, trans. Ben Fowkes (London, 1976), 920–1.
69. A. R. Mayer, *Parliaments and Estates in Europe to 1789* (London, 1975), 29.
70. 'Debates in 1677: February 21st', *Grey's Debates of the House of Commons* vol. 4 (1769), 112–30. URL: http://www.british-history.ac.uk/report.aspx?compid=40389.
71. *Politisches Testament*, excerpted in Evan Luard, *Basic Texts in International Relations* (Basingstoke, 1992), 162.
72. Albert O. Hirschman, *The Passions and the Interests: Political Arguments for Capitalism before Its Triumph* (Princeton, 1977, 1997), 59.
73. Nancy F. Koehn, *The Power of Commerce: Economy and Governance in the First British Empire* (Ithaca, NY, 1994), 6–7.
74. Steve Pincus, *1688: The First Modern Revolution* (New Haven, 2009), 43–4.
75. Hicks, *Theory of Economic History*, 98.
76. Carolyn Webber and Aaron Wildavsky, *A History of Taxation and Expenditure in the Western World* (New York, 1986), 334, 336.

## CHAPTER 2: REVOLUTION, RESTORATION, AND REFORM

1. T. W. C. Blanning, *The French Revolution: Class War or Culture Clash?* 2nd ed. (Basingstoke, 1998), 31.
2. M. Jones, *The French Revolution 1787–1804* (London, 2003), 22.
3. Linda S. and Marsha L. Frey, *The French Revolution* (Westport, 2004), 44.
4. Pilbeam, *Middle-classes in Europe*, 110, 214.
5. John Markoff, 'The French Revolution: The Abolition of Feudalism', in Jack A. Goldstone (ed.), *Revolutions: Theoretical, Comparative and Historical Studies*, 3rd ed. (Belmont, 2003), 173–4.
6. Quoted in Norman Hampson, *A Social History of the French Revolution* (London, 1963), 58.
7. Excerpted in Thomas C. Mendenhall, Basil D. Henning, Archibald S. Foord, and Leonard Krieger, *The Quest for a Principle of Authority in Europe, 1715–Present* (New York, 1948), 55.
8. Reproduced in Oliver J. Thatcher, *The Library of Original Sources* (London, 1907), 416.
9. Document in ibid., 61.
10. Gregory S. Brown, *Cultures in Conflict: The French Revolution* (Westport, 2003), 59.
11. George Rudé, *Revolutionary Europe, 1783–1814*, 2nd ed. (Oxford, 1964, 2000), 111.
12. Ruth Scurr, *Fatal Purity: Robespierre and the French Revolution* (London, 2007), 265.
13. Albert Soboul, *Understanding the French Revolution* (New York, 1988), 33.
14. Norman Hampson, *The First European Revolution, 1776–1815* (London, 1969), 112.

15. 'Babeuf's Defense from the Trial at the Vendôme, February–May, 1797' in Fried and Sanders (eds), *Socialist Thought*, 65–7.
16. Gracchus Babeuf, document in Herbert H. Rowen (ed.), *From Absolutism to Revolution, 1648–1848* (New York, 1963), 209.
17. Geoffrey Best, *War and Society in Revolutionary Europe, 1770–1870* (Guernsey, 1982, 1998), 86, 92.
18. Paul W. Schroeder, *The Transformation of European Politics, 1763–1848* (Oxford, 1996), 309.
19. Sir Arthur Conan Doyle, *The Stark Munro Letters* [1895] (Fairford, 2009), 56.
20. Charles Seignobos, *A Political History of Europe, since 1814*, ed. S. M. Macvane (New York, 1900), 561.
21. Alexis de Tocqueville, *Democracy in America* [1835] (London, 1998), 25–6.
22. Hamerow, *Birth of a New Europe*, 186.
23. Hartmut Kaelble, *Social Mobility in the 19th and 20th Centuries: Europe and America in Comparative Perspective* (Leamington Spa, 1983, 1985), 98.
24. Peter N. Stearns and Herrick Chapman, *European Society in Upheaval: Social History Since 1750* (New York, 1992), 136.
25. 'Memorandum to the Tsar' [1820], excerpted in Mendenhall, *Quest for a Principle of Authority*, 95–6.
26. Pamela E. Pilbeam, 'Revolutionary Movements in Western Europe', in Pamela M. Pilbeam (ed.), *Themes in Modern European History, 1780–1830* (London, 1995), 133; Pilbeam, *Middle Classes in Europe*, 85.
27. 'Instructions of the Carboneria', in S. J. Woolf (ed.), *The Italian Risorgimento* (New York, 1969), 41.
28. William L. Langer, *Political and Social Upheaval, 1832–1852* (New York, 1969), 63.
29. J. A. Hobson and Neville Masterman, *Richard Cobden: The International Man* (London, 1968), 194.
30. Christopher H. Johnson, 'Patterns of Proletarianization', in Lenard R. Berlanstein (ed.), *The Industrial Revolution and Work in Nineteenth-Century Europe* (London, 1992), 82–101.
31. Theodore S. Hamerow, '1848', in Leonard Kriger and Fritz Stern (eds), *The Responsibility of Power: Historical Essays in Honor of Hajo Holborn* (London, 1968), 156.
32. Quoted in José Ignacio Garrigós Monerris, 'The Bourgeoisie and the Working Classes: Mistrust as the Motive Force Behind the Social Sciences', http://www.essex.ac.uk/sociology/student_journals/grad_journal/garrigos-monerris.pdf, 4.
33. G. A. Kertesz, 'The View from the Middle Class: The German Moderate Liberals and Socialists', in Eugene Kamenka and F. B. Smith (eds), *Intellectuals and Revolution: Socialism and the Experience of 1848* (London, 1979), 66–9.
34. For example, 'The Offenburg Resolution of the South-West German Radicals, 10 September 1847', in G. A. Kertesz (ed.), *Documents in the Political History of the European Continent 1815–1939* (Oxford, 1968), 77–9.
35. Quoted in Harold Perkin, *The Origins of Modern English Society* (New York, 1969, 2002), 225.
36. Georg Hegel, *Elements of the Philosophy of Right* [1820], ed. Allen W. Wood (Cambridge, 1991), 237.
37. Alan S. Kahan, *Aristocratic Liberalism: The Social and Political Thought of Jacob Burckhardt, John Stuart Mill, and Alexis de Tocqueville* (New York, 1992), 60. Lenore O'Boyle, 'The Middle Class in Western Europe, 1815–1848', *American Historical Review*, 71 (1966), 830.

38. For example, 'Education', in *The Westminster Review*, vol. 1, January–April 1824 (London, 1824), 68–9.
39. Macaulay, 16 December 1831, in H. J. Hanham (ed.), *The Nineteenth-Century Constitution, 1815–1914: Documents and Commentary* (Cambridge, 1969), 11. Cf. Philip Corrigan and Derek Sayer, *The Great Arch: English State Formation as Cultural Revolution* (Oxford, 1985), 129–30.
40. Stanley Mellon, *The Political Uses of History* (Stanford, 1958), 7. See also George C. Comninel, *Rethinking the French Revolution* (London, 1987), 53–63.
41. For continuities between civic republicanism and liberalism, see Andreas Kalyvas and Ira Katznelson, *Liberal Beginnings: Making a Republic for the Moderns* (Cambridge, 2008), 4–5 and *passim*.
42. Quoted in Guido de Ruggiero, *The History of European Liberalism*, trans. R. G. Collingwood (Boston, 1925, 1959), 167–8.
43. Macauley, 'Southey's Colloquies' [1830], in *Critical and Historical Writings: The Complete Writings of Lord Macaulay*, part two (Whitefish, MT, 2004), 143.
44. Quoted in De Ruggiero, *European Liberalism*, 308–9.
45. Quoted in ibid., 320–1.
46. Quoted in James J. Sheehan, *German Liberalism in the Nineteenth Century* (Chicago, 1978), 116.
47. Karl Theodore Welcker, 'The responsibility of Princes and the Ministers of State' from *Staatslexikon* [1843] in E. K. Bramsted and K. J. Melhuish (eds), *Western Liberalism: A History in Documents from Locke to Croce* (London, 1978), 447.
48. Michael Brock, *The Great Reform Act* (London, 1973), 63.
49. Cited in M. J. Daunton, *Progress and Poverty: An Economic and Social History of Britain, 1700–1850* (Oxford, 1995), 353.
50. E. L. Woodward, *The Age of Reform, 1815–1870* (Oxford, 1938), 14.
51. John W. Osborne, *William Cobbett: His Thought and His Times* (New Brunswick, 1966), 137.
52. Jonathon Fulcher, 'The English People and their Constitution after Waterloo', in James Vernon (ed.), *Re-Reading the Constitution: New Narratives in the Political History of England's Long Nineteenth Century* (Cambridge, 1996), 75.
53. Michael R. Watts, *The Dissenters*, vol. 2 (Oxford, 1995), 431.
54. 'Tamworth Manifesto' [1835], in G. M. Young and W. D. Handcock (eds.), *English Historical Documents, 1833–1874* (London, 1996), 128.
55. Cabinet Paper by Sir Robert Peel, 25 March 1835, in Hanham (ed.), *Nineteenth-Century Constitution*, 129.
56. Though only from 1894 were all local authorities elective.
57. T. H. Breen, *The Marketplace of Revolution: How Consumer Politics Shaped American Independence* (New York, 2004), 264–5.
58. Max M. Edling, *A Revolution in Favor of Government: Origins of the U.S. Constitution and the Making of the American State* (New York, 2003), 55 and *passim*.
59. Hiram Caton, *The Politics of Progress: The Origins and Development of the Commercial Republic, 1600–1835* (Gainesville, FL, 1988), 483–4.
60. Bernard Schwartz, *American Constitutional Law* (Cambridge, 1955), 12–26.
61. William Barclay Allen and Seth Ames (eds), *Works of Fisher Ames*, vol. 1 (Boston, 1854), 7.
62. Publius [Hamilton], in *The Federalist Papers* [1788] (New York, 1961), 214.
63. Thomas Jefferson, *Writings*, vol. IV (Washington DC, 1854), 398.

## CHAPTER 3: HOLDING BACK THE TIDE

1. Artz, *Reaction and Revolution*, 88–90.
2. Henry A. Kissinger, 'The Philosophic Problem', in Henry F. Schwarz (ed.), *Metternich, the Coachman of Europe: Statesman or Evil Genius?* (Boston, 1962), 101.
3. Excerpted in G. de Bertier de Sauvigny, *Metternich and His Times*, trans. Peter Ryle (London, 1962), 40.
4. Quoted in John Merriman, *A History of Modern Europe*, vol. 2 (New York, 1996), 676.
5. Quoted in Jacques Droz, *Europe Between Revolutions, 1815–1848* (London, 1967), 34.
6. Stephen King-Hall and Richard K. Ullmann, *German Parliaments: A Study of the Development of Representative Institutions in Germany* (London, 1954), 43–4.
7. Piotr S. Wandycz, *The Lands of Partitioned Poland, 1795–1918* (Seattle, 1974), 79–82. Aleksander Gieysztor et al., *History of Poland* (Warsaw, 1979), 441–2. W. F. Reddaway et al., *Cambridge History: From Augustus II to Pilsudski* (Cambridge, 1951), 289–90.
8. Robert Jones, *Since Waterloo: A Short History of Europe and of the British Empire, 1815–1919* (London, 1920), 106.
9. Langer, *Political and Social Upheaval*, 123.
10. Excerpted in S. J. Woolf, *The History of Italy, 1700–1860* (London, 1979), 298.
11. A. J. P. Taylor, *The Habsburg Monarchy, 1809–1918* (London, 1948), 44.
12. Quote from Alan Sked, 'Explaining the Habsburg Empire, 1830–90', in Bruce Waller (ed.), *Themes in Modern European History, 1830–1890* (London, 1990), 126.
13. Frank E. Huggett, *The Land Question and European Society since 1650* (London, 1975), 105.
14. John Breuilly, *Austria, Prussia and Germany, 1806–1871* (London, 2002), 114. Cf. Eric Dorn Brose, *German History, 1789–1871* (Providence, 1997), 65.
15. G. Von Bunsen, 'Prussia', in *Encyclopaedia Britannica*, 8th ed., vol. XVIII (Edinburgh, 1859), 674.
16. Best, *War and Society in Revolutionary Europe*, 205.
17. Paul W. Schroeder, *The Transformation of European Politics, 1763–1848* (Oxford, 1996), v–vii.
18. Fredrich von Gentz, 'Considerations on the Political System now Existing in Europe' [1818], in Mack Walker (ed.), *Metternich's Europe* (New York, 1968), 81, 84.
19. Sauvigny, *Metternich and His Times*, 137.
20. 'Circular of the Austrian, Prussian and Russian Sovereigns', Troppau, 8 December 1820, in René Albrecht-Carrié (ed.), *The Concert of Europe: Selected Documents* (London, 1968), 53.
21. Lord Castlereagh, State Paper, 5 May 1820, in James Joll (ed.), *Britain and Europe: Pitt to Churchill 1793–1940* (London, 1961), 82.
22. Clive Church, *Europe in 1830: Revolution and Political Change* (London, 1983), 15.
23. L. C. B. Seaman, *Victorian England: Aspects of English and Imperial History, 1837–1901* (London, 1995), 117.
24. 'The Constitutional Charter, 4 June 1814', in Kertesz (ed.), *Documents in Political History*, 44–7.
25. Charlotte Touzalin Muret, *French Royalist Doctrines since the Revolution* (New York, 1933), 59.
26. N. Furbank, *Unholy Pleasure, or the Idea of Social Class* (Oxford, 1985), 26.
27. Pierre Manent, *An Intellectual History of Liberalism*, trans. Rebecca Balinski (Princeton, 1995), 94–6.
28. Quoted in J. Salwyn Schapiro, *Liberalism and the Challenge of Fascism: Social Forces in England and France, 1815–1870*, 1st ed. (New York, 1949), 162.
29. Ibid., 162–3.

30. Letter to an American [1817], in F. M. H. Markham (ed.), *Henri Comte de Saint-Simon, 1760–1825: Selected Writings* (Oxford, 1959), 70.
31. Saint-Simon [1824], in Alexander Gray, *The Socialist Tradition* (London, 1946), 153.
32. Philippe Buonarroti, *History of Babeuf's Conspiracy for Equality*, trans. James Bronterre O'Brien (London, 1836), 5–15.
33. 'Law for the Compensation of Émigrés, 3 January 1825', in Kertesz (ed.), *Documents in Political History*, 48–9.
34. Paul Ginisty, *Anthologie du Journalisme*, http://www.pos1.info/a/anthojourn.htm.
35. 'The July Decrees of Charles X, 25 July 1830', in Kertesz (ed.), *Documents in Political History*, 51–2.
36. Lloyd Kramer, *Lafayette in Two Worlds: Public Cultures and Personal Identities in an Age of Revolutions* (Chapel Hill, 1996), 230.
37. François Guizot, *Mémoires pour servir à l'histoire de mon temps*, vol. II (Paris, 1859), 372.
38. Louis Tripier France, *Les codes français collationnés sur les éditions officielles* (Paris, 1848), 8.
39. Philip Mansel, *Paris Between Empires, 1814–1852: Monarchy and Revolution* (London, 2001), 384–5.
40. Pamela Pilbeam, *The Constitutional Monarchy in France, 1814–48* (London, 2000), 44.
41. Adrian Shubert, *A Social History of Modern Spain* (London, 1992), 58–60.

## CHAPTER 4: THE TURNING POINT

1. William Thompson, *Labor Rewarded* (London, 1827), 31.
2. Flora Tristan, *Union ouvrière* [1843], trans. Doris Beik and Paul Beik, *Flora Tristan, Utopian Feminist* (Bloomington, 1993), 108–9.
3. Marx and Engels, *The Communist Manifesto* [1948], MECW, vol. 6, 506. Marx, *Critique of the Gotha Programme* [1875], MECW, vol. 2, 87.
4. Marc Mulholland, 'Marx, the Proletariat, and the "Will to Socialism"', *Critique*, vol. 37, no. 3 (August 2009), 319–43.
5. Michael Pinto-Duschinsky, *The Political Thought of Lord Salisbury, 1854–68* (London, 1967), 99–100.
6. Cited in Gordon Phillips, 'The British Labour Movement before 1914', in Dick Geary (ed.), *Labour and Socialist Movements in Europe Before 1914* (Oxford, 1989), 19.
7. G. D. H. Cole, *A History of Socialist Thought*, Vol. 1 (London, 1955), 106–7.
8. S. Leon Levy, *Nassau W. Senior, 1790–1864* (New York, 1970), 70–4.
9. Elizabeth Gaskell, *Mary Barton* [1848] (Oxford, 1987), 199.
10. *English Chartist Circular* cited in Trygve R. Tholfsen, *Working-class Radicalism in Mid-Victorian England* (New York, 1977), 96.
11. Malcolm Chase, *Chartism: A New History* (Manchester, 2007), 301.
12. Lord Grey, dispatch to Lord Torrington, Governor of Ceylon, 24 October 1848, in Philip D. Curtin (ed.), *Imperialism: Selected Documents* (London, 1969), 167–8.
13. R. M. Martin evidence to the Select Committee on the Handloom Weavers' Petition [1834], excerpted in Patricia Hollis (ed.), *Class and Conflict in Nineteenth-Century England, 1815–1850* (London, 1973), 12.
14. Speech by W. J. Fox [28 September 1843], in Jan Goldstein and John W. Boyer (eds), *Nineteenth-Century Europe: Liberalism and its Critics* (Chicago, 1988), 55.
15. Webber and Wildavsky, *Taxation and Expenditure*, 342.
16. Philip Harling, *The Waning of 'Old Corruption': The Politics of Economical Reform in Britain, 1779–1846* (Oxford, 1996), 247–8.

17. Walter Bagehot, 'The Character of Sir Robert Peel' [1856], in *The Collected Works of Walter Bagehot*, vol. III (London, 1995), 13–14.
18. Daunton, *Progress and Poverty*, 555.
19. William Fortescue, *France and 1848: The End of Monarchy* (Abingdon, 2005), 56.
20. Douglas Johnson, 'A Reconsideration of Guizot', in Eugene C. Black, *European Political History, 1815–1870: Aspects of Liberalism* (New York, 1967), 98.
21. Alan B. Spitzer, *The Revolutionary Theories of Louis Auguste Blanqui* (New York, 1957), 89.
22. Louis Blanc, *L'Organization du Travail* [1839], in Bruun, *Revolution and Reaction*, 95.
23. David E. Barclay, *Frederick William IV and the Prussian Monarchy, 1840–1861* (Oxford, 1995), 128.
24. Karl Marx, 'Bourgeoisie and the Counter-Revolution' [1848], in *MECW*, vol. 8, 159.
25. Karl Marx and Friedrich Engels, *The German Ideology* [1845], in *MECW*, vol. 5, 90.
26. Quoted in Hal Draper, *Karl Marx's Theory of Revolution*, vol. 1, *State and Bureaucracy*, part I (New York, 1977), 320.
27. Quoted in James Laver, *The Age of Optimism: Manners and Morals, 1848–1914* (London, 1966), 18.
28. Alexis de Tocqueville, *Recollections of the French Revolution of 1848*, ed. J. Mayer and A. Kerr (Brunswick, 1970, 2009), 72.
29. Government declaration [25 February 1848], in Roger Price (ed.), *1848 in France: Documents of Revolution* (London, 1975), 68.
30. Government decision [29 February 1848], in ibid., 69.
31. Excerpted in George Woodcock (ed.), *A Hundred Years of Revolution, 1848 and After* (London, n.d. [1948]), 221–2.
32. Alexander Herzen, *From the Other Shore* [1848–50], in Alexander Herzen, *Selected Philosophical Texts*, trans. L. Nazrozov (Moscow, 1956), 371.
33. Priscilla Robertson, *Revolutions of 1848: A Social History* (Princeton, 1952, 1967), 139.
34. Dieter Langewiesche, *Liberalism in Germany*, trans. Christiane Banerji (Basingstoke, 1988, 2000), 43.
35. Quoted in John Weiss, 'Guild Socialism, and the Revolutions of 1848', in *International Review of Social History* (1960), 88.
36. Marx and Engels, 'Freedom of Debate in Berlin' [1848], *MECW*, vol. 7, 438.
37. *The Annual Register for 1848* (London, 1849), excerpted in Geoffrey Bruun, *Revolution and Reaction, 1848–1852*, ed. Louis L. Snyder (New Jersey, 1958), 48–9.
38. Peter N. Stearns, *1848: The Revolutionary Tide in Europe* (New York, 1974), 188.
39. Quoted in Josephine Goldmark, *Pilgrims of '48* (New Haven, 1930), 148–9; cf. Stearns, *1848*, 153.
40. See a contemporary account in Frank Eyck (ed.), *The Revolutions of 1848–49* (Edinburgh, 1972), 126–33.
41. Louis-Napoléon Bonaparte, *Des idées napoléoniennes* (London, 1860), 18.
42. Helmut Böhme, *An Introduction to the Social and Economic History of Germany*, trans. W. R. Lee (Oxford, 1978 [1972]), 31–6.
43. Philip Ziegler, *The Sixth Great Power: Barings, 1762–1929* (London, 1988), 161.
44. Alexis de Tocqueville, *On the state of society in France before the revolution of 1789; and on the causes which led to that event* (London, 1856, 1888), 8.
45. Peter Jones, *The 1848 Revolutions*, 2nd ed. (Harlow, 1991), 100.
46. Stearns, *1848*, 182.
47. Dieter Langewiesche, 'The Role of the Military in the European Revolutions of 1848', in Dieter Dowe et al. (eds), *Europe in 1848: Revolution and Reform* (New York, 2001), 700, and Robert Gildea, '1848 in Collective Memory', in ibid., 922.

48. Arnošt Klima, 'The Bourgeois Revolution of 1848–9 in Central Europe' in Roy Porter and Mikuláš Teich (eds), *Revolution in History* (Cambridge, 1986), 94.
49. Alan Sked, *Radetzky: Imperial Victor and Military Genius* (London, 2011), 149, 135.
50. Fredrick Engels, 'Revolution and Counter-Revolution in Germany' [1852], *MECW*, vol. 7, 40.
51. Fredrick Engels, 'Introduction to Karl Marx's *The Class Struggles in France 1848 to 1850*' [1895], *MECW*, vol. 27, 517.
52. Karl Marx, 'Militia Bill' [1848], *MECW*, vol. 7, 258.
53. Karl Marx, 'The Crisis and the Counter-Revolution' [1848], *MECW*, vol. 7, 431.
54. Fredrick Engels, 'The Agreement Session of July 4' [1848], *MECW*, vol. 7, 205. Cf. Karl Marx, 'The Bourgeoisie and the Counter-Revolution' [1848], in Marx and Engels, *Articles from the 'Neue Rheinische Zeitung', 1848–49*, trans. S. Ryazanskaya, ed. Bernard Isaacs (London, 1972), 177.
55. Fredrick Engels, 'The Magyar Struggle' [1849], in *MECW*, vol. 8, 230.
56. Karl Marx and Fredrick Engels, 'German Foreign Policy and the Latest Events in Prague' [1848], in *MECW*, vol. 7, 212.
57. Fredrick Engels, 'The Frankfurt Assembly Debates the Polish Question' [1848], *MECW*, vol. 7, 351.
58. Karl Marx, 'Bourgeoisie and the Counter-Revolution' [1848], *MECW*, vol. 8, 170.
59. Fredrick Engels, *The Peasant War in Germany* [1850] (New York, 1926), 153.
60. Karl Marx and Fredrick Engels, 'Address to the Central Committee of the Communist League' [1850], *MECW*, vol. 10, 278.
61. Ibid., 281.
62. Quoted in Hal Draper, *Karl Marx's Theory of Revolution*, vol. II: *The Politics of Social Classes* (New York, 1978), 605.
63. B. G. G. Gervinus, *Lessons of Past Times: An Introduction to the History of the Nineteenth Century* (London, 1853), 129.
64. Lord Macaulay, *History of England: To the Death of William III*, vol. 11, [1848] (London, 1967), 397–8. For a similar trajectory under the impact of 1848, of an admittedly always more conservative German historian, see Leopold von Ranke, *The Theory and Practice of History*, ed. and intro by Georg G. Iggers (London, 2011), xxiv–xxv.

## CHAPTER 5: LIBERALISM AND THE STATE

1. Hamerow, *Birth of a New Europe*, 121–2.
2. Ibid., 55–6.
3. Robert C. Binkley, *Realism and Nationalism, 1852–1871* (New York, 1935), 96.
4. Marx, *Capital*, vol. 1, trans. Ben Fowkes (London, 1976), 739–41.
5. Charles Morazé, *The Triumph of the Middle Classes: A Study in European Values in the Nineteenth Century* (London, 1957, 1966), 243.
6. James Macdonald, *A Free Nation Deep in Debt: The Financial Roots of Democracy* (Princeton, 2003, 2006), 361–2.
7. Irene Collins, 'Liberalism in Nineteenth-Century Europe', in W. N. Meddlicott (ed.), *From Metternich to Hitler: Aspects of British and Foreign History, 1814–1939* (London, 1963), 41.
8. Jan Palmowski, *Urban Liberalism in Imperial Germany: Frankfurt Am Main, 1866–1914* (Oxford, 1999), 309–10.
9. Excerpted in Luard, *Basic Texts in International Relations*, 58.

## Notes to Chapter 5

10. John Bright, *Speeches on Questions of Public Policy*, ed. James E. Thorold Rogers (London, 1869), 332.
11. Quoted in Philip Guedalla, *Palmerston, 1784–1865* (New York, 1927), 332–3.
12. W. E. Mosse, *Liberal Europe in the Age of Bourgeois Realism, 1848–1875* (London, 1974), 86.
13. Asa Briggs, *Victorian People: An Assessment of Persons and Themes, 1851–1867*, rev. ed. (Chicago, 1955, 1972), 258.
14. George Barnett Smith, *The Life of the Right Honourable William Ewart Gladstone* (New York, 1880), 343.
15. Lady Gwendolen Cecil, *Life of Robert, Marquis of Salisbury* (London, 1921), 146. See also Pinto-Duschinsky, *Political Thought of Lord Salisbury*, 94.
16. Anthony Arblaster, *The Rise and Decline of Western Liberalism* (London, 1984), 277–82.
17. 'Eleventh Report of the Royal Commission on Trade Unions' [1869], in G. D. H. Cole and A. W. Filson (eds), *British Working-Class Movements: Select Documents, 1789–1875* (London, 1951), 566.
18. Stefan Collini, *Public Moralists: Political Thought and Intellectual Life in Britain, 1850–1930* (Oxford, 1991), 140.
19. Gregory S. Alexander, *Commodity & Propriety: Competing Visions of Property in American Legal Thought, 1776–1970* (Chicago, 1997), 215.
20. Quoted in Richard Carwardine, *Lincoln: A Life of Purpose and Power* (New York, 2003, 2006), 169.
21. Charles Sellers, *The Market Revolution: Jacksonian America, 1815–1846* (New York, 1991), 6.
22. Steven Beller, *Francis Joseph* (London, 1996), 59.
23. C. A. Macartney, *The Habsburg Empire, 1790–1918* (London, 1971), 470.
24. Edward Crankshaw, *The Fall of the House of Habsburg* (London, 1963, 1974), 100.
25. Brose, *German History*, 277.
26. C. A. Macartney, *The New Cambridge Modern History*, vol. X (Cambridge, 1960), 540; Seignobos, *A Political History of Europe*, 518.
27. Seignobos, *Political History of Europe*, 519.
28. Scott W. Murray, *Liberal Diplomacy and German Unification: The Early Career of Robert Morier* (Westport, 2000), 181.
29. Leonard W. Cowie and Robert Wolfson, *Years of Nationalism: European History 1815–1890* (London, 1985), 326.
30. 'The Austrian Constitution' [1867], document in Paula Sutter Fichtner, *The Habsburg Empire: From Dynasticism to Multinationalism* (Malabar, 1997), 157.
31. Excerpted in David Thomson (ed.), *France: Empire and Republic 1850–1940. Historical Documents* (London, 1968), 39.
32. Roger Price, 'France: The Search for Stability, 1830–90', in Waller (ed.), *Themes in Modern European History*, 43.
33. Roger Price, *The French Second Empire: An Anatomy of Political Power* (Cambridge, 2001), 213.
34. William Stearns Davis, *A History of France* (Boston, 1919), 495.
35. T. A. B. Corley, *Democratic Despot: A Life of Napoleon III* (London, 1961), 120.
36. William H. C. Smith, *Second Empire and Commune: France, 1848–1871*, 2nd ed. (London, 1996), 21–3.
37. Theodore Zeldin, *Emile Ollivier and the Liberal Empire of Napoleon III* (Oxford, 1963), 86–102.

38. William E. Echard (ed.), *Historical Dictionary of the French Second Empire, 1852–1870* (Westport, 1985), 278.
39. Geoffrey Wawro, *The Franco-Prussian War: The German Conquest of France in 1870–1871* (Cambridge, 2003) 46.
40. Karl Marx, *The Eighteenth Brumaire of Louis Napoleon* [1852], *MECW*, vol. 11.
41. Price, *French Second Empire*, 85.
42. Excerpted in Woolf, *Italian Risorgimento*, 60.
43. B. A. Haddock, 'Italy: Independence and Unification without Power', in Bruce Waller (ed.), *Themes in Modern European History, 1830–1890* (London, 1990), 87. Clive Tredilcock, 'The Industrialization of Modern Europe', in T. C. W. Blanning (ed.), *The Oxford History of Modern Europe* (Oxford, 1996, 2000), 70.
44. Sir Spencer Walpole, *The History of Twenty-Five Years: 1856–1865* (London, 1904), 208.
45. Denis Mack Smith (ed.), *The Making of Italy, 1796–1870* (London, 1968), 272.
46. Basil H. Cooper, *Count Cavour: His Life and Career* (London, 1860), 156–60.
47. Denis Mack Smith, *Cavour and Garibaldi, 1860* (Cambridge, 1954), 389.
48. Johannes Mattern, *The Employment of the Plebiscite in the Determination of Sovereignty* (Baltimore, 1920), 392.
49. Excerpted in Denis Mack Smith (ed.), *Garibaldi* (New Jersey, 1969), 140.
50. Francesco Ferrara, January 1966, in Smith (ed.), *Making of Italy*, 358.
51. Benedetto Croce, *A History of Italy, 1871–1915*, trans. Cecilia M. Ady (New York, 1929, 1963), 301–2.
52. Paul Thomas, *Karl Marx and the Anarchists* (London, 1980), 279.

## CHAPTER 6: BISMARCK, LIBERALISM, AND SOCIALISM

1. Christopher Clark, *Iron Kingdom: The Rise and Downfall of Prussia, 1600–1947* (London, 2007), 504.
2. Karl Marx, 'Preparation for War' [1860], *MECW*, vol. 17, 496.
3. Otto Pflanze, *Bismarck and the Development of Germany: The Period of Unification, 1815–1871* (Princeton, 1971), 159–60.
4. Mosse, *Liberal Europe*, 137.
5. John L. Snell, *The Democratic Movement in Germany, 1789–1914* (Chapel Hill, 1976), 155–6.
6. Quoted in Bebel, *My Life*, in Subrata Mukherjee and Sushila Ramaswamy (eds), *August Bebel: His Thoughts and Works* (New Delhi, 1998), 34.
7. 'Bismarck's "Iron and Blood" Speech, 30 September 1862', in Louis L. Snyder, ed., *Fifty Major Documents of the Nineteenth Century* (Princeton, 1955), 111.
8. *Memoirs of Prince von Bülow* [1931–2], excerpted in Theodore S. Hamerow (ed.), *The Age of Bismarck: Documents and Interpretations* (New York, 1973), 297.
9. 'Resolution of the Prussian House of Representatives, 7 October 1862', in Kertesz (ed.), *Documents in Political History*, 142.
10. 'Bismarck's Speech to the House of Representatives, 27 January 1863', in ibid., 143.
11. Erich Eyck, *Bismarck and the German Empire* (London, 1950), 61.
12. Pflanze, *Bismarck and the Development of Germany*, 217.
13. Mosse, *Liberal Europe*, 140.
14. Pflanze, *Bismarck and the Development of Germany*, 217–18.
15. Seignobos, *Political History of Europe*, 463.
16. Eugene N. Anderson, *The Social and Political Conflict in Prussia, 1858–1864* (Lincoln, 1954), 310–16.

17. C. Grant Robertson, *Bismarck* (London, 1918), 153.
18. Letter excerpted in W. M. Simon, *Germany in the Age of Bismarck* (London, 1968), 104.
19. Fritz Stern, *Gold and Iron: Bismarck, Gerson Bleichröder, and the Building of the German Empire* (London, 1977), 62–3.
20. James Wycliffe Headlam, *Bismarck and the Foundation of the German Empire* (Middlesex, 2007), 133.
21. Hans-Ulrich Wehler, *The German Empire, 1871–1918*, trans. Kim Traynor (Leamington Spa, 1973, 1989), 21.
22. 'Founding Statement of the National Liberal Party' [June 1867], in Goldstein and Boyer (eds), *Nineteenth-Century Europe*, 426–32.
23. David Blackbourn and Geoff Eley, *The Peculiarities of German History: Bourgeois Society and Politics in Nineteenth-Century Germany* (Oxford, 1984), 17.
24. John Breuilly, *Labour and Liberalism in Nineteenth-Century Europe: Essays in Comparative History* (Manchester, 1992), 138.
25. Mosse, *Liberal Europe*, 154 .
26. Document in Michael Gorman, *The Unification of Germany* (Cambridge, 1989), 102–3.
27. Engels, 'The Prussian Military Question and the German Workers' Party' [1865], *MECW*, vol. 20, 73.
28. Ibid., 77.
29. Ibid., 56–7.
30. Ibid., 57.
31. Ibid., 57.
32. Ibid., 61.
33. Ibid., 63.
34. Ibid., 63. Emphasis in original.
35. Ibid., 65.
36. Ibid., 76.
37. Even if Engels' observations hardly chime with traditionally understood stereotypes of the Marxist notion of 'bourgeois revolution', they cannot be explained away as atypical or off-the-cuff arguments, *pace* Richard F. Hamilton, *The Bourgeois Epoch: Marx and Engels on Britain, France, and Germany* (Chapel Hill, 1991), 25.
38. Dieter Langewiesche, 'The Nature of German Liberalism', in Gordon Martel (ed.), *Modern Germany Reconsidered, 1870–1945* (London, 1992), 109.
39. William Harbutt Dawson, *German Socialism and Ferdinand Lassalle* (London, 1899), 139–41.
40. David Footman, *Ferdinand Lassalle, Romantic Revolutionary* (New Haven, 1947), 167.
41. Bismarck, very uncharacteristically, retained an admiration for Lassalle throughout his life. Jonathan Steinberg, *Bismarck: A Life* (Oxford, 2011), 204–5.
42. Roger Morgan, *The German Social Democrats and the First International, 1864–1872* (Cambridge, 1965), 37.
43. F. L. Carsten, 'The *Arbeiterbildungsvereine* and the Foundation of the Social-Democratic Workers Party in 1869', *The English Historical Review*, vol. 107, no. 423 (April 1992), 361–77.
44. For the text of the Eisenach Program, Susanne Miller and Heinrich Potthoff, *A History of German Social Democracy*, trans. J. A. Underwood (Leamington Spa, 1986, German ed., 1983), 236–7.
45. Engels, 'Preface to the Second Edition' [1870], *The Peasant War in Germany* (New York, 1926), 13.
46. Ibid., 16–17.

47. Fredrick Engels, *The Housing Question* [1872] (London, 1942), 69.
48. Karl Marx, '2nd Draft of Civil War in France' [1871], *MECW*, vol. 22, 533.
49. 'Declaration to the French People', 19 April 1871, in Stewart Edwards (ed.), *The Communards of Paris, 1871* (London, 1973), 82.
50. Peter Marshall, *Demanding the Impossible: A History of Anarchism* (London, 1993), 297.
51. Karl Marx, 'The Civil War in France' [1871], in *MECW*, vol. 22, 332.
52. Ibid., 326.
53. Fredrick Engels, 'Introduction to *The Civil War in France*' [1891], in Marx and Engels, *Writings on the Paris Commune*, ed. Hal Draper (New York, 1971), 30.
54. Karl Marx, 'The Civil War in France' [1871], in *MECW*, vol. 22, 330–2; Marx, 'Speech at Anniversary Banquet' [1871], in Marx and Engels, *Writings on the Paris Commune*, 225.

## CHAPTER 7: CAPITALISM AND SOCIALISM

1. G. E. Mingay, *The Transformation of Britain, 1830–1939* (London, 1986), 58.
2. Sidney Pollard (ed.), *Wealth and Poverty: An Economic History of the Twentieth Century* (London, 1990), 24.
3. Charles A. Jones, *International Business in the Nineteenth Century: The Rise and Fall of a Cosmopolitan Bourgeoisie* (Brighton, 1987), 195.
4. Mike Davis (citing A. Latham), in *Late Victorian Holocausts: El Niño Famines and the Making of the Third World* (London, 2001), 296–8.
5. Chang's 'Exhortation to Study' [1898], document in Ssu-Yu Teng and John K. Fairbank (eds), *China's Response to the West: A Documentary Survey, 1839–1923* (New York, 1963), 167.
6. William R. Keylor, *The Twentieth-Century World: An International History*, 3rd ed. (New York, 1996), 23.
7. Bruce Waller, 'Germany: Independence and Unification with Power' in Waller (ed.), *Themes in Modern European History*, 110.
8. Quoted in Fanny Coulomb, *Economic Theories of Peace and War* (New York, 2004), 62.
9. Fredrick Engels, Letter to Danielson [1892], in Marx and Engels, *Selected Correspondence* (New York, 1942), 498.
10. Urbain Gohier, 'The Barracks', in Thomson (ed.), *France: Empire and Republic*, 205–6.
11. Alistair Horne, *The French Army and Politics, 1870–1970* (Basingstoke, 1984), 10.
12. Oron J. Hale, *The Great Illusion, 1900–1914* (New York, 1971), 24.
13. David Schoenbaum, *Zabern 1913: Consensus Politics in Imperial Germany* (London, 1982), 180.
14. Baron Beyens, *Germany Before the War*, trans. Paul V. Cohen (London, 1916), 177–86.
15. Patrick J. Kelly, *Tirpitz and the Imperial Navy* (Bloomington, 2011), 153; Geoff Layton, *From Bismarck to Hitler: Germany 1890–1933* (London, 1995), 33.
16. Valerie Cromwell, *Revolution or Evolution? British Government in the Nineteenth Century* (London, 1977), 198.
17. Paul M. Kennedy, *The Rise and Fall of British Naval Mastery* (London, 1976, 1983), 227. Hew Strachan, 'Military Modernization, 1789–1918', in Blanning (ed.), *Oxford History of Modern Europe*, 78.

18. Frank B. Tipton, 'Government and the Economy in the Nineteenth Century', in Sheilagh Ogilvie and Richard Overy (eds), *Germany: A New Social and Economic History*, vol. III (London, 2003), 135–6.
19. General Friedrich von Bernhardi, *Germany and the Next War* [1911], trans. Allen H. Powles (London, 1914), 125–9.
20. Alfred Vagts, *A History of Militarism: Civilian and Military* (London, 1959), 207.
21. 30 March 1914, *Parliamentary Debates (Official Report)*, vol. 60 (London, 1914), col. 907; Lloyd George quoted in Thomas Jones, *Whitehall Diary*, vol. 3 (London, 1971), 129–30.
22. William H. McNeill, *The Pursuit of Power: Technology, Armed Force, and Society since A.D. 1000* (Chicago, 1982), 292–4.
23. Binkley, *Realism and Nationalism*, 94–5.
24. Frank B. Tipton and Robert Aldrich, *An Economic and Social History of Europe, 1890–1939* (Basingstoke, 1987), 21.
25. Clive Tredilcock, 'The Industrialization of Modern Europe' in Blanning (ed.), *Oxford History of Modern Europe*, 67.
26. W. H. B. Court, *Scarcity and Choice in History* (London, 1970), 188.
27. Keylor, *The Twentieth-Century World*, 38.
28. J. A. Hobson, *Imperialism: A Study* (London, 1905), 88–9.
29. Sidney Pollard, *European Economic Integration, 1815–1970* (London, 1974), 123.
30. V. R. Berghahn, *Germany and the Approach of War in 1914* (London, 1973), 134.
31. Boris Blick, 'What is Socialism? French Liberal Views in the 1890s', in Louis Patsouras (ed.), *The Crucible of Socialism* (Atlantic Highlands, 1987), 387.
32. Quoted in Piero Gobetti, *On Liberal Revolution*, trans. William McCuaig (New Haven, 2000), 93.
33. Neil McInnes, *The Western Marxists* (London, 1972), 77.
34. Georges Sorel, 'The Socialist Future of the Syndicates' [1898], in Sorel, *Essays in Socialism and Philosophy*, ed. John L. Stanley (New York, 1976), 74.
35. Arno J. Mayer, *The Persistence of the Old Regime: Europe to the Great War* (London, 1981), 12.
36. Dominic Lieven, *The Aristocracy in Europe, 1815–1914* (Basingstoke, 1992), 190–1.
37. 'On the Uses of a Landed Gentry', in J. A. Froude, *Short Studies on Great Subjects*, ed. David Ogg (London, 1963), 275.
38. Prince Bernhard von Bülow, *Imperial Germany* (London, 1914), 137.
39. It was referred to as 'plutarchy' in Britain. G. R. Searle, *A New England? Peace and War, 1886–1914* (Oxford, 2004), 99.
40. Geoff Eley, 'Liberalism, Europe and the Bourgeoisie 1860–1914', in David Blackbourn and Richard J. Evans (eds), *The German Bourgeoisie: Essays on the Social History of the German Middle Class* (London, 1991, 1993), 304–5.
41. Bismarck, letter to the Upper House of the Reichstag, 15 December 1978, in Pollard and Holmes (eds), *Industrial Power and National Rivalry, 1970–1914*, 191.
42. Keylor, *The Twentieth-Century World*, 46.
43. William N. Parker, 'Europe in an American Mirror', in Richard Sylla and Gianni Toniolo (eds), *Patterns of European Industrialization: The Nineteenth Century* (London, 1991), 86–7.
44. Niall Ferguson, *The Cash Nexus: Money and Power in the Modern World, 1700–2000* (London, 2001, 2002), 303.
45. M. S. Anderson, *The Ascendancy of Europe, 1815–1914*, 2nd ed. (London, 1972, 1985), 116. Cf. Webber and Wildavsky, *Taxation and Expenditure*, 290–302, 318.

J. Watson Grice, *National and Local Finance* (London, 1910), 127–30; Miss Betham-Edwards, *Home Life in France*, 2nd ed. (London, 1905), 160–4.
46. Pollard, *European Economic Integration*, 74–5. Ronald Robinson and John Gallagher with Alice Denny, *Africa and the Victorians: The Official Mind of Imperialism*, 2nd ed. (London, 1961, 1981), 138.
47. Weiss, *Conservatism in Europe*, 94.
48. Niall Ferguson, 'The European Economy, 1815–1914', in T. W. C. Blanning (ed.), *The Nineteenth Century: Europe 1789–1914* (Oxford, 2000), 106.
49. M. E. Falkus, *The Industrialization of Russia, 1700–1914* (London, 1972), 69–70.
50. Tim McDaniel, *Autocracy, Capitalism, and Revolution in Russia* (Berkeley, 1988), 18–19.
51. Paul Miliukov, *Russia and its Crisis* (London, 1962), 405.
52. R. B. McKean, *The Russian Constitutional Monarchy, 1907–17* (London, 1977), 19. Cf. Robert Service, *The Russian Revolution, 1900–1927* (Basingstoke, 1986), 19–20.
53. Richard Biernacki, *The Fabrication of Labor: Germany and Britain, 1640–1914* (Berkeley, 1995), 12 and part 3.
54. Michael Bakunin, 'To the Comrades of the International Workingmen's Association of Locle and Chaux-de-Fonds' [1869], in Fried and Sanders (eds), *Socialist Thought*, 332–8.
55. Marie Fleming, *The Anarchist Way to Socialism: Élisée Reclus and Nineteenth-Century European Anarchism* (London, 1979), 104.
56. Robert Justin Goldstein, *Political Repression in 19th-Century Europe* (Beckenham, 1983), 289.
57. Excerpted in Jon Cowans (ed.), *Modern Spain: A Documentary History* (Philadelphia, 2003), 97.
58. James Joll, *The Anarchists*, 2nd ed. (London, 1964, 1979), 219.
59. Karl Marx, *Critique of the Gotha Programme* [1875] (Peking, 1971), 19.
60. Helmuth von Moltke to the Reichstag, 1898, document in Hamerow (ed.), *Age of Bismarck*, 202.
61. Franz Mehring, 'The Law Against the Socialists', in Frank Mecklenburg and Manfred Stassen (eds), *German Essays on Socialism in the Nineteenth Century* (New York, 1990), 117.
62. 'Erfurt Programme' [1891], in Miller and Potthoff, *History of German Social Democracy*, 240–1.
63. Gary Steenson, *Karl Kautsky, 1854–1938: Marxism in the Classical Years*, 2nd ed. (Pittsburgh, 1978, 1991), 91.
64. POB Programme in Samuel Orth, *Socialism and Democracy in Europe* (New York, 1913), 315.
65. Jean Jaurès, 'From the Rights of Man to Socialism', in Irving Howe (ed.), *Essential Works of Socialism*, 3rd ed. (New Haven, 1970, 1976, 1986), 123–4.
66. Michael Bentley, *Politics Without Democracy, 1815–1914: Perception and Preoccupation in British Government* (London, 1984), 334–5.
67. Thiers, Chamber of Deputies, 13 November 1872, in William Fortescue, *The Third Republic in France, 1870–1940: Conflicts and Continuities* (London, 2000), 27.
68. Theodore Zeldin, *France 1848–1945: Politics and Anger* (Oxford, 1973, 1979), 345–8.
69. Charter of Amiens in Thomson (ed.), *France: Empire and Republic*, 171.
70. Robert Gildea, *The Third Republic* (London, 1988), 65.
71. Karl Kautsky, *The Class Struggle (Erfurt Program)*, trans. William E. Bohn (New York, 1971), 199–202. Cf. Lars T. Lih, *Lenin Rediscovered: 'What is to be Done?' in Context* (Chicago, 2005, 2008), 41–109.

72. Gary Steenson, *After Marx, Before Lenin: Marxism and Socialist Working-Class Parties in Europe, 1884–1914* (Pittsburgh, 1991), 9.
73. G. D. H. Cole, *A History of Socialist Thought*, vol. III, part II (London, 1956), 253.
74. Ibid., 255.
75. G. Barraclough, *The Origins of Modern Germany* (Oxford, 1946), 424.
76. Claus Dieter Kernig, *Marxism, Communism, and Western Society* (New York, 1973), 195.
77. Wilhelm Liebknecht, 'No Compromise–No Political Trading' [1899], in William A. Pelz (ed.), *Wilhelm Liebknecht and German Social Democracy: A Documentary History* (Westport, 1994), 190.
78. See, for example, William Harvey Maehl, *August Bebel: Shadow Emperor of the German Workers* (Philadelphia, 1980), 114–15.
79. Church, *Europe in 1830*, 73–6.
80. Seignobos, *Political History of Europe*, 675.
81. Marx's comments were soon widely known. See Thomas Kirkup, *A History of Socialism* (London, 1892), 177.
82. R. Landor, 'Interview with Karl Marx' [1871], reproduced in Robin Blackburn, *An Unfinished Revolution: Karl Marx and Abraham Lincoln* (London, 2011), 231.
83. Karl Kautsky, *The Road to Power*, trans. Raymond Meyer (Alameda, 2007), 54.
84. Cole, *A History of Socialist Thought*, vol. III, part II, 257.
85. Giles MacDonagh, *Prussia: The Perversion of an Idea* (London, 1994), 134. Cf. Christian Frederick Gauss (ed.), *The German Emperor, as Shown in his Public Utterances* (New York, 1915), 172.
86. F. L. Carsten, 'Germany', in Michael Howard (ed.), *Soldiers and Governments: Nine Studies in Civil-Military Relations* (London, 1957), 82.
87. Hale, *The Great Illusion*, 197 and 199.
88. Fredrick Engels, 'Letter to Paul Lafargue' [1892], *MECW*, vol. 50, 21.
89. Fredrick Engels, 'Introduction to Karl Marx's, *The Class Struggles in France*' [1895], *MECW*, vol. 27, 506–24.
90. Karl Liebknecht, *Militarism and Anti-Militarism* [1907] (Cambridge, 1973), 23. Cf. Nicholas Stargardt, *The German Idea of Militarism: Radical and Socialist Critics, 1866–1914* (Cambridge, 1994), 98–103.
91. Strachan, 'Military Modernization', 94.
92. Pilbeam, *Middle Classes in Europe*, 149.
93. Ian Porter and Ian D. Armour, *Imperial Germany, 1890–1918* (London, 1991), 91.
94. Quoted in Julius Braunthal, *History of the International*, vol. I, *1864–1914*, trans. Henry Collins and Kenneth Mitchell (London, 1961, 1966), 291.
95. Steenson, *Karl Kautsky*, 153.
96. Neil Harding, *Lenin's Political Thought* (Chicago, 1977, 2009), 229, 237.
97. Andrzej Walicki, *The Rise and Fall of the Communist Utopia* (Stanford, 1995), 241. This was a treasured statement in the Stalinist era, and featured in the official party history. N. N. Popov, *Outline History of the Communist Party of the Soviet Union*, ed. A. Fineberg, vol. 1 (New York, 1934), 105.

## CHAPTER 8: DEMOCRACY AND STATE POWER

1. Seymour Martin Lipset and Gary Marks, *It Didn't Happen Here: Why Socialism Failed in the United States* (New York, 2000), 174.

2. Sven Steinmo, *Taxation and Democracy: Swedish, British, and American Approaches to Financing the Modern State* (New Haven, 1993), 73–4.
3. Max Lerner, 'The Triumph of Laissez-Faire', in Arthur M. Schlesinger, Jr., and Morton White (eds), *Paths of American Thought* (London, 1964), 156. Cf. Robert Green McCloskey, *American Conservatism in the Age of Enterprise, 1865–1910* (New York, 1951), 57–62. Figure for millionaires: Maldwyn A. Jones, *The Limits of Liberty: American History, 1607–1980* (Oxford, 1983), 329.
4. Dieter Langewiesche, 'Liberalism and the Middle Class in Europe', in Jürgen Kocka and Allan Mitchell (eds), *Bourgeois Society in Nineteenth-Century Europe* (Oxford, 1993), 52.
5. Max Weber, *The Theory of Social and Economic Organization*, trans. A. M. Henderson and Talcott Parsons (Glencoe, 1947), 420–1.
6. Max Weber, *Essays in Economic Sociology*, ed. Richard Swedberg (Princeton, 1999), 135.
7. Alan Scott's words, in his 'Between Autonomy and Responsibility: Max Weber on Scholars, Academics and Intellectuals' in Jeremy Jennings and Anthony Kemp-Welch (eds), *Intellectuals in Politics: From the Dreyfus Affair to Salman Rushdie* (London, 1997), 45.
8. Carlo Antoni, *From History to Sociology: The Transition in German Historical Thinking* [1940] (London, 1952, 1960), 130–3.
9. M. Ostrogorski, *Democracy and the Organization of Political Parties* [1902], trans. Frederick Clarke, vol. 1 (New York, 1922), 346.
10. Quoted in Michael B. Gross, *The War against Catholicism: Liberalism and the Anti-Catholic Imagination in Nineteenth-Century Germany* (Ann Arbor, 2004), 109.
11. Leo XIII, *Rerum Novarum* [1891] in T. E. Utley and J. Stuart Maclure (eds), *Documents of Modern Political Thought* (Cambridge, 1957), 209.
12. John W. Boyer, *Political Radicalism in Late Imperial Vienna, 1848–1897* (Chicago, 1981), 411–13; Robert S. Wistrich, *Socialism and the Jews: The Dilemmas of Assimilation in Germany and Austria-Hungary* (London, 1982), 197–200.
13. Reidar Larsson, *Theories of Revolution: From Marx to the First Russian Revolution* (Stockholm, 1970), 72–3, 142, 144, 155, 171.
14. J. Hampden Jackson, *Jean Jaurès: His Life and Work* (London, 1943), 76–7.
15. Cited in Charles Seignobos, *Histoire Politique de L'Europe Contemporaine, 1814–1914*, vol. I (Paris, 1924), 259–60.
16. Cited in Lucien Laurat, *Marxism and Democracy*, trans. Edward Fitzgerald (London, 1940), 151.
17. Steenson, *Karl Kautsky*, 115.
18. James Joll, *The Second International, 1889–1914* (London, 1955), 95.
19. G. D. H. Cole, *A History of Socialist Thought*, vol. III, part II, 40.
20. Massimo Salvadori, *Karl Kautsky and the Socialist Revolution, 1880–1938* (London, 1976, 1990), 89; Laurat, *Marxism and Democracy*, 150–1.
21. Hale, *The Great Illusion*, 206.
22. John W. Boyer, 'The End of an Old Regime: Visions of Political Reform in Late Imperial Austria', *The Journal of Modern History*, vol. 58, No. 1 (March 1986), 169.
23. Eugenio Biagini, 'The Dilemmas of Liberalism', in Martin Pugh (ed.), *A Companion to Modern European History, 1871–1945* (Oxford, 1997), 118–22.
24. Thomas Hill Green, 'Lectures on the Principles of Political Obligation', in Robert Eccleshall (ed.), *British Liberalism: Liberal Thought from the 1640s to the 1980s* (London, 1986), 182–6.

25. Arthur Rosenberg, *Imperial Germany: The Birth of the German Republic, 1871–1918*, trans. Ian F. D. Morrow (Boston, 1928, 1964), 47–9.
26. Ibid., 56.
27. Dick Geary, *Karl Kautsky* (Manchester, 1987), 20, 29.
28. Carl E. Schorske, *German Social Democracy, 1905–1917: The Development of the Great Schism* (New York, 1955), 156.
29. Wolfgang Mommsen, *Max Weber and German Politics, 1890–1920*, trans. Michael Steinberg (Chicago, 1959, 1974, 1984), 129.
30. Eduard Bernstein, *The Preconditions of Socialism* [1899], ed. Henry Tudor (Cambridge, 1993, 2004), 99.
31. Ibid., 205.
32. Ibid., 147.
33. Manfred B. Steger, *The Quest for Evolutionary Socialism: Eduard Bernstein and Social Democracy* (Cambridge, 1997), 132; Geary, *Karl Kautsky*, 32, 76.
34. William A. Pelz (ed.), *Wilhelm Liebknecht and German Social Democracy: A Documentary History* (Westport, 1994), 189.
35. Steenson, *Karl Kautsky*, 128.
36. Rosa Luxemburg, *Reform or Revolution* [1900] (New York, 1974), 39.
37. Ibid., 39.
38. Ibid., 40.
39. Joll, *Second International*, 103.
40. Louis B. Boudin, *The Theoretical System of Karl Marx* (New York, 1907), 209–10.
41. Steenson, *Karl Kautsky*, 127.
42. J. Nettl, *Rosa Luxemburg*, vol. I (London, 1966), 229–30.
43. David Floyd, *Russia in Revolt, 1905* (London, 1969), 65.
44. Abraham Yarmolinsky (ed.), *The Memoirs of Count Witte* (London, 1921), 474.
45. George Vernadsky, *A History of Russia*, 6th ed. (New Haven, 1969), 264.
46. Max Weber, 'Bourgeois Democracy' [1905–6], in Weber, *The Russian Revolutions*, trans. Gordon C. Wells and Peter Baehr (Cambridge, 1995), 102.
47. 'Manifesto of 17 October 1905', in Martin McCauley (ed.), *Octobrists to Bolsheviks: Imperial Russia, 1905–1917* (London, 1984), 14.
48. Abraham Ascher, *The Revolution of 1905* (Stanford, 2004), 95.
49. Charles Kurzman, *Democracy Denied, 1905–1915: Intellectuals and the Fate of Democracy* (Harvard, 2008), 198.
50. Ascher, *Revolution of 1905*, 105–6.
51. Robert D. Warth, *Nicholas II: The Life and Reign of Russia's Last Monarch* (Westport, 1997), 110.
52. 'The Vyborg Manifesto, 10 July 1906', in McCauley (ed.), *Octobrists to Bolsheviks*, 43–4.
53. A. Tyrkova-Williams, 'The Cadet Party' [1953], in Dimitri von Mohrenschildt (ed.), *The Russian Revolution of 1917: Contemporary Accounts* (New York, 1971), 34.
54. Yarmolinsky (ed.), *Memoirs of Count Witte*, 267–8.
55. Quoted in Michael T. Florinsky, *The End of the Russian Empire* (New York, 1961), 104–5.
56. McKean, *Russian Constitutional Monarchy*, 19.
57. Harding, *Lenin's Political Thought*, 257.
58. Robert Conquest, *Lenin* (London, 1972), 61.
59. Larsson, *Theories of Revolution*, 307.
60. Rosa Luxemburg, *The Mass Strike* [1906] (New York, 1971), 201.

61. Larsson, *Theories of Revolution*, 273.
62. Moira Donald, *Marxism and Revolution: Karl Kautsky and the Russian Marxists, 1900–1924* (New Haven, 1993), 78–82.
63. Larsson, *Theories of Revolution*, 266.
64. Ibid., 261.
65. Leon Trotsky, *The Permanent Revolution and Results and Prospects* [1906] (Dehli, 2005), 58.
66. Larsson, *Theories of Revolution*, 288.
67. Karl Kautsky, *On the Social Revolution and on the Morrow of the Social Revolution* [1902], trans. J. B. Askew (London, 1909), part 2, 5–6.
68. Kautsky's gloss on his earlier pamphlet, 'Revolutionary Questions' [1904], in Richard B. Day and Daniel Gaido (eds and trans.), *Witnesses to Permanent Revolution: The Documentary Record* (Chicago, 2011), 222.
69. Trotsky, *Results and Prospects*, 45.
70. Larsson, *Theories of Revolution*, 299, 302.
71. Marx and Engels, *The Communist Manifesto* [1848] (London, 2002), 241.
72. R. S. Neale, 'Marx and Lenin on Imperialism', in Neale, *Writing Marxist History* (Oxford, 1986), 187.
73. William English Walling (ed.), *The Socialists and the War: A Documentary Statement of the Position of the Socialists of All Countries* (New York, 1915), 45.
74. Max Beer, *The General History of Socialism and Social Struggles*, vol. 2 (New York, 1957), 154.
75. Joll, *Second International*, 196–8.
76. Harvey Goldberg, *The Life of Jean Jaurès* (Madison, 1962), 480.
77. Norman Angell, *The Great Illusion, 1933* (London, 1933), 264–5.
78. Rudolf Hilferding, *Finance Capital: A Study of the Latest Phase of Capitalist Development*, trans. Morris Watnick and Sam Gordon (London, 1981), 301.
79. Anthony Brewer, *Marxist Theories of Imperialism: A Critical Survey* (London, 1980, 1990), 105.
80. Hilferding, *Finance Capital*, 335.
81. Sun Yat-Sen, *Sun Yat-Sen: His Political and Social Ideals*, ed. Leonard Shihlien (Los Angeles, 1933), 298–306.

## CHAPTER 9: REVOLUTION AND THE 'DICTATORSHIP OF THE PROLETARIAT'

1. Martin Gilbert, *Churchill: A Life* (London, 1991), 143.
2. A. J. P. Taylor, 'The Last of Old Europe' [1976], in Taylor, *From Napoleon to the Second International: Essays on the Nineteenth Century*, ed. Chris Wrigley (London, 1993), 188–215.
3. Joll, *Second International*, 165.
4. Philip Bell, 'The Great War and its Impact', in Paul Hayes (ed.), *Themes in Modern European History, 1890–1945* (London, 1992), 140.
5. Hew Strachan, *Financing the First World War* (Oxford, 2004), 113.
6. Charles S. Maier, *Recasting Bourgeois Europe: Stabilization in France, Germany and Italy in the Decade after World War I* (Princeton, 1975, 1988), 581.
7. Ibid., 9.
8. Élie Halévy, *The Era of Tyrannies*, trans. R. K. Webb (New York, 1938, 1966), 266.
9. Hew Strachan, *The First World War* (London, 2006), 60–1.

10. Kenneth Neal Waltz, *Man, the State, and War: A Theoretical Analysis* (New York, 2001), 135.
11. Richard M. Watt, *The Kings Depart. The Tragedy of Germany: Versailles and the German Revolution* (London, 1968, 2003), 118–19.
12. Julius Braunthal, *History of the International*, vol. 2, *1914–1943*, trans. John Clark (London, 1963, 1967), 15.
13. Leon Trotsky, 'The War and the International' [1914], in Trotsky, *The Bolsheviki and World Peace* (Westport, 1973), 176.
14. Alexander Shlyapnikov, *On the Eve of 1917: Reminiscences from the Revolutionary Underground*, trans. Richard Chappell (London, 1982), 93.
15. Watt, *The Kings Depart*, 119.
16. G. D. H. Cole, *History of Socialist Thought*, vol. IV, part 1, *Communism and Social Democracy, 1914–1931* (London, 1958), 111.
17. Braunthal, *History of the International*, vol. 2, 17–18.
18 R. Craig Nation, *War on War: Lenin, the Zimmerwald Left, and the Origins of Communist Internationalism* (Chicago, 1989, 2009), 23, 65–7.
19. John Darwin, *After Tamerlane: The Rise and Fall of Global Empires, 1400–2000* (London, 2008), 370–6.
20. Lenin, 'The World War and the Tasks of Social-Democracy' [1915], cited in Robert V. Daniels (ed.), *Documentary History of Communism* (London, 1986), 6.
21. See Max Beer's record of his 1911 interview with Lenin. Max Beer, *Fifty Years of International Socialism* (London, 1935), 150.
22. Lenin, 'Dead Chauvinism and Living Socialism' [1914], in *Collected Works*, vol. 21 (London, 1970), 98. Cf. Georges Haupt, *Aspects of International Socialism, 1871–1914*, trans. Peter Fawcett (Cambridge, 1986), 136.
23. Lenin, 'Under a False Flag', in *Collected Works*, vol. 21 (London, 1970), 146.
24. Lenin, *Imperialism: The Highest Stage of Capitalism* [1916], in *Collected Works*, vol. 22 (London, 1978), 277.
25. V. I. Lenin, 'The Irish Rebellion of 1916' and 'National Wars Against Imperialism' [both July 1916], in William J. Pomeroy (ed.), *Guerrilla Warfare and Marxism* (London, 1969), 102–9.
26. Lenin, *Imperialism*, preface [1920], in *Selected Works*, vol. 5 (New York, 1942), 12.
27. Lenin, *The State and Revolution* [August 1917] (Chippendale, 1999), 17.
28. Ibid., 40.
29. Ibid., 36.
30. Ibid., 30.
31. Shlyapnikov, *On the Eve of 1917*, 167.
32. Nikolai N. Smirnov, 'The Soviets' in Edward Acton, Vladimir Iu. Cherniaev, and William G. Rosenberg (eds), *Critical Companion to the Russia Revolution, 1914–1921* (Bloomington, 1997), 432.
33. E. H. Carr, *The Bolshevik Revolution, 1917–1923*, vol. 1 (London, 1950, 1966), 86.
34. Lenin, 'April Theses', in *Collected Works*, vol. 27 (London, 1970), 22.
35. Ibid., 23.
36. William G. Rodenberg, 'The Constitutional Democratic Party (Kadets)', in Acton, Cherniaev, and Rosenberg (eds), *Critical Companion to the Russia Revolution*, 260.
37. Ziva Galili, 'Commercial-Industrial Circles in Revolution: The Failure of 'Industrial Progressivism'', in Edith Rogovin Frankel, Jonathan Frankel, and Baruch Knei-Paz, *Revolution in Russia: Reassessments of 1917* (Cambridge, 1992), 199–207.

38. R. H. Bruce Lockhart, *British Agent* (London, 1932, 1961), 93.
39. Lenin, 'Letter to the Central Committee' [1917], in *Collected Works*, vol. 26 (London, 1972), 140–1.
40. Lenin, 'To Workers, Peasants, and Soldiers!' [1917], in ibid., 137–9.
41. Braunthal, *History of the International*, vol. 2, 97.
42. Lenin quoted in Leon Trotsky, *The History of the Russian Revolution*, trans. Max Eastman (Ann Arbor, 1957), 359.
43. Christopher Read, *From Tsar to Soviets* (Oxford, 1996), 80, 120.
44. Minutes of the Bolshevik Central Committee [16 October 1917], excerpted in Mark Jones (ed.), *Storming the Heavens: Voices of October* (London, 1987), 66–9.
45. Alexander Rabinowitch, *The Bolsheviks in Power: The First Year of Soviet Rule in Petrograd* (Bloomington, 2007), 13, 17–22.
46. N. Bukharin and E. Preobrazhensky, *The ABC of Communism* [1919], ed. E. H. Carr (London, 1969), 162–3, 311–12.
47. Bertrand Russell, *The Practice and Theory of Bolshevism* [1920, 1949] (London, 1962), 37.
48. Leon Trotsky, *Terrorism and Communism* [1920] (Michigan, 1961), 102.
49. 'The revolution of October 1917 at one stroke achieved such successes that it seemed to us in the spring of 1918 that the war had drawn to a close—actually, it had only just started in its worst form, the form of civil war; actually, peace with the Germans meant that they assisted the worst elements in the Civil War; actually, the peace treaty we then signed with the Germans and which collapsed in the autumn, in many cases meant that assistance was given to these worst elements by the Allied Powers who blamed us for concluding peace with the Germans.' Lenin, 31 October 1922, in *Collected Works*, vol. 33 (London, 1970), 393–4.
50. Lenin, *The Proletarian Revolution and the Renegade Kautsky* [1918], in *Selected Works*, vol. 3 (New York, 1967), 49.
51. Victor Serge, *Memoirs of a Revolutionary, 1901–1941*, trans. Peter Sedgewick (London, 1963, 1967), 80–1.
52. Bruce Lincoln, *Red Victory: A History of the Russian Civil War* (London, 1988, 1991), 175.
53. Dimitri Volkogonov, *Trotsky: The Eternal Revolutionary*, trans. Harold Shukman (London, 1996), 184–5.
54. Brian Morton, *Woodrow Wilson* (London, 2008), 47, 56, 64.
55. Wilson declaring war, in Lindsay Rogers, *America's Case against Germany* (New York, 1917), 255.
56. Watt, *The Kings Depart*, 151.
57. Arthur Rosenberg, *A History of Bolshevism: From Marx to the First Five Years' Plan*, trans. Ian F. D. Morrow (London, 1934), 134.
58. Jane Degras (ed.), *The Communist International, 1919–1943. Documents*, vol. 1, *1919–1922* (London, 1956), 2. Cf. 'Theses on Bourgeois Democracy and Proletarian Dictatorship Adopted by the First Comintern Congress' [14 March 1919], in ibid., 14.
59. Lenin, *Proletarian Revolution*, 52.
60. Ibid., 57.
61. Ibid., 60.
62. Ibid., 60.
63. L. Trotsky, *The Defence of Terrorism (Terrorism and Communism): A Reply to Karl Kautsky* (London, 1921), 35–6.

64. Lev Kamanev, 'The Dictatorship of the Proletariat' [1920], in Al Richardson (ed.), *In Defence of the Russian Revolution: A Selection of Bolshevik Writings, 1917–1923* (London, 1995), 102–3.
65. Quoted in Jean-Jacques Marie, 'The Journal of Georgi Dimitrov', *Revolutionary History*, vol. 8, no. 1, 2001, 161.
66. Geoff Eley, *Forging Democracy: The History of the Left in Europe, 1850–2000* (Oxford, 2002), 160. Ireland, of course, was the exception to the rule.
67. Julius Braunthal, *In Search of the Millennium* (London, 1945), 217–22.
68. Seán Mac Eoin in Piaras Béaslaí et al., *With the IRA in the Fight for Freedom* [1960] (Cork, 2010), 51.
69. J. J. Lee, *Ireland, 1912–1985* (Cambridge, 1989), 105.
70. 'Manifesto of the Communist International to the Workers of the World'. in Leon Trotsky, *The First Five Years of the Communist International*, vol. 1 (New York, 1972), 27.
71. Ibid., 22.
72. 'The New Communist Manifesto' (Appendix 2), in Raymond W. Postgate, *The Bolshevik Theory* (London, 1920), 192.
73. 'Conversation with Lenin' [May 1919], in P. A. Kropotkin, *Selected Writings*, ed. Martin A. Miller (Cambridge, MA, 1970), 330.
74. 'Conditions for Admission to the Communist International' [6 August 1920], in Degras (ed.), *The Communist International. Documents*, 171.
75. For example, see remarks of Ramsay MacDonald in Stephen Richards Graubard, *British Labour and the Russian Revolution, 1917–1924* (Cambridge, MA, 1956), 81.
76. Stefan Berger, 'The SPD' in Panikos Panayi (ed.), *Weimar and Nazi Germany: Continuities and Discontinuities* (London, 2001), 278.
77. Cole, *History of Socialist Thought*, vol. IV, part 1, 294.
78. Ibid., 325.
79. 'Declaration of the Vienna International' (February 1920), appendix 3 in Braunthal, *History of the International*, vol. 2, 546–7.
80. Lenin [1921], quoted in Rosenberg, *History of Bolshevism*, 157.
81. David Lloyd George, *The Truth about the Peace Treaties*, vol. 1 (London, 1938), 407–8.
82. Braunthal, *History of the International*, vol. 2, 136.
83. Otto Bauer, *Die Österreichische Revolution* [1923], in Tom Bottomore and Patrick Goode (ed. and trans.), *Austro-Marxism* (Oxford, 1987), 157.
84. Braunthal, *History of the International*, vol. 2, 206.
85. Charles B. Burdick and Ralph H. Lutz (eds), *The Political Institutions of the German Revolution, 1918–1919* (New York, 1966), 70.
86. Arno J. Mayer, *Politics and Diplomacy of Peacemaking: Containment and Counterrevolution at Versailles, 1918–1919* (New York, 1967), 26.
87. Peter Alter, *Nationalism*, 2nd ed. (London, 1989), 79.

## CHAPTER 10 COMMUNISM AND FASCISM

1. Eric Hobsbawm, *The Age of Extremes: A History of the World, 1914–1991* (New York, 1994, 1996), 111.
2. Göetz A. Briefs, *The Proletariat: A Challenge to Western Civilization* (New York, 1937), 24. Italics in original.
3. Ibid., 283.
4. Ibid., 273–4.

5. Ludwig Von Mises, *Socialism* (London, 1922, 1969), 21.
6. Mark Mazower, *Dark Continent: Europe's Twentieth Century* (London, 1998), 22–3.
7. Gerhard Schulz, *Revolutions and Peace Treaties, 1917–1920* (London, 1974), 73, 109.
8. Helmut Heiber, *The Weimar Republic*, trans. W. E. Yuill (Oxford, 1966, 1993), 8.
9. F. L. Carsten, *Revolution in Central Europe, 1918–1919* (Aldershot, 1972, 1988), 131.
10. Watt, *The Kings Depart*, 201.
11. Sebastian Haffner, *Failure of a Revolution: Germany 1918–19*, trans. Georg Rapp (London, 1969, 1973), 104.
12. Layton, *Bismarck to Hitler*, 75.
13. Quotes in Helga Grebing, *History of the German Labour Movement*, trans. Edith Körner (Leamington Spa, 1985), 102.
14. Sefton Delmer, *Weimar Germany: Democracy on Trial* (London, 1972), 17.
15. A. J. Ryder, *The German Revolution of 1918* (Cambridge, 1967), 268–9.
16. Jacob Reich ('Comrade Thomas'), 'The First Years of the Communist International', in *Revolutionary History*, vol. 5, no. 2, Spring 1994, 18.
17. Quoted in Paul Frolich, *Rosa Luxemburg: Her Life and Work* (Chicago, 1940, 2010), 323.
18. Robert G. L. Waite, *Vanguard of Nazism: The Free Corps Movement in Postwar Germany* (Cambridge MA, 1952), 72–3.
19. Franz Schoenberner, *Confessions of a European Intellectual* (New York, 1946, 1965), 124.
20. Quoted in Arthur Rosenberg, *A History of the German Republic*, trans. Ian F. D. Morrow and L. Marie Sieveking (London, 1936), 125–6.
21. Delmer, *Weimar Germany*, 57.
22. For an account by one of its leaders, see Max Hoelz, *From White Cross to Red Flag*, trans. F. A. Voigt (London, 1930), 133–59.
23. In reference to trade unions, but the principle was obviously extendable. Lenin, *Left-Wing Communism: An Infantile Disorder* [1920] (Chippendale, 1999), 57.
24. Alfred Weber, *Die Not der geistigen Arbeiter* [1923], excerpted in Fritz K. Ringer (ed.), *The German Inflation of 1923* (New York, 1969), 111.
25. See comments by Radek quoted in Ruth Fischer, *Stalin and German Communism* [1948] (New Brunswick, 1982), 269.
26. Larissa Reissner, 'Hamburg at the Barricades' [1924], in Reissner, *Hamburg at the Barricades and Other Writings on Weimar Germany*, trans. Richard Chappell (London, 1977), 106.
27. Arthur Rosenberg, *Democracy and Socialism* (London, 1939), 8–9.
28. See Eberhard Kolb, *The Weimar Republic*, 2nd ed., trans. S. Falla and R. J. Park (Abingdon, 2005), 154–5.
29. Geoff Spenceley, *The Search for Security: A Modern World History* (Melbourne, 1988), 257.
30. Conan Fischer, *The Rise of the Nazis* (Manchester, 1995), 89. See also Richard Overy, *The Inter-War Crisis, 1919–1939*, 2nd ed. (Harlow, 1994, 2007), 34; Richard Bessel, 'Society', in Julian Jackson (ed.), *Europe, 1900–1945* (Oxford, 2002), 129.
31. Jonathan Wright, *Gustav Stresemann: Weimar's Greatest Statesman* (Oxford, 2002, 2004), 443.
32. Philip Gibbs, *Since Then* (London, 1930, 1931), 120.
33. 'Postulates of the Fascist Program' (May 1920), in Charles F. Delzell (ed.), *Mediterranean Fascism, 1919–1945* (New York, 1970), 15.
34. Quoted in Donald Sassoon, *Mussolini and the Rise of Fascism* (London, 2007), 106.
35. R. J. B. Bosworth, *Mussolini* (London, 2002), 149.

## Notes to Chapter 10

36. Braunthal, *History of the International*, vol. 2, 319.
37. Mosca, *The Ruling Class* (New York, 1939, 1959), 65–6; Richard Bellamy, 'The Advent of the Masses and the Making of the Modern Theory of Democracy', in Terence Ball and Richard Bellamy (eds), *The Cambridge History of Twentieth-Century Political Thought* (Cambridge, 2003), 88; George L. Mosse, *The Culture of Western Europe: The Nineteenth and Twentieth Centuries*, 3rd ed. (Boulder, 1988), 298–302; Oswald Spengler, *The Decline of the West*, vol. II, trans. Charles Franis Atkinson (London, 1922), 504–6.
38. See Renato Cristi, 'Carl Schmitt', in Terrell Carver and James Martin (eds), *Palgrave Advances in Continental Political Thought* (Basingstoke, 2006), 122–32.
39. Lenin, 'On Cooperation' [1923], in *Selected Works*, vol. 3 (London, 1971), 760.
40. Neil Harding, *Leninism* (Basingstoke, 1996), 188–9.
41. Quoted in Lewis H. Siegelbaum, *Soviet State and Society between Revolutions, 1918–1929* (Cambridge, 1992), 71.
42. E. H. Carr, *The Interregnum, 1923–1924* (London, 1954, 1969), 57.
43. 'Stalin on the Expulsion of the Left Opposition' [1927], in Robert V. Daniels (ed.), *A Documentary History of Communism, Updated revised edition*, vol. 1: *Communism in Russia* (Vermont, 1984), 201.
44. J. V. Stalin, 'Concerning Questions of Agrarian Policy in the USSR' [1929], in Stalin, *Works*, vol. 12 (Peking, 1955), 174.
45. Ibid., 146.
46. Stephen F. Cohen, *Bukharin and the Bolshevik Revolution: A Political Biography, 1888–1938* (Oxford, 1971, 1980), 206–8.
47. Christian Rakovsky, 'Circular of the Bolshevik-Leninist Opposition', in Robert V. Daniels (ed.), *A Documentary History of Communism in Russia: From Lenin to Gorbachev*, 3rd ed. (Vermont, 1993), 177.
48. Charles Kindleberger, *The World in Depression, 1929–1939* (London, 1987), 292; Patricia Clavin, *The Great Depression in Europe, 1929–1939* (Basingstoke, 2000), 18–20.
49. Richard Overy, *The Morbid Age: Britain Between the Wars* (London, 2009), 52–3.
50. Robert Boyce, 'Economics', in Robert Boyce and Joseph A. Maiolo (eds), *The Origins of World War Two: The Debate Continues* (Basingstoke, 2003), 251–2, 268.
51. Paul Preston, 'The Great Civil War: European Politics, 1914–1945', in Blanning (ed.), *Oxford History of Modern Europe*, 166.
52. Mussolini quoted in Gaetano Salvemini, *Under the Axe of Fascism* (New York, 1936), 112–15.
53. Philip Morgan, *Italian Fascism, 1915–1945*, 2nd ed. (Basingstoke, 2004), 197–207.
54. Adolf Hitler, *Mein Kampf* (New York, 1939), 196–7.
55. Stearns and Chapman, *European Society in Upheaval*, 264–8.
56. Martin Collier and Philip Pedley, *Hitler and the Nazi State* (Oxford, 2005), 175–7.
57. John Lukacs, *The Hitler of History* (New York, 1998), 85.
58. Timothy W. Ryback, *Hitler's Private Library: The Books that Shaped his Life* (London, 2010), 69–71.
59. Alan Bullock, *Hitler: A Study in Tryanny*, rev. ed. (London, 1952, 1964), 158.
60. Paul Tillich, *The Socialist Decision*, trans. Franklin Sherman (New York, 1933, 1977), 172.
61. Robert Boyce, 'Economics', 258; Thomas Saunders, 'Nazism and Social Revolution', in Gordon Martel (ed.), *Modern Germany Reconsidered, 1870–1945* (London, 1992), 126–7.

62. Detlef Mühlberger, *The Social Bases of Nazism, 1919–1933* (Cambridge, 2003), 75–7.
63. Martin Kolinsky, *Continuity and Change in European Society: France, Germany and Italy Since 1870* (London, 1974), 84.
64. David Clay Lodge, *Between Two Fires: Europe's Path in the 1930s* (New York, 1990), 107.
65. Robert O. Paxton, *The Anatomy of Fascism* (London, 2004), 123.
66. Lodge, *Between Two Fires*, 106.
67. SPD in exile, quoted in Braunthal, *History of the International*, vol. 2, 389.
68. Aryeh L. Unger, 'Party and State in Soviet Russia and Nazi Germany', in Clive Emsley (ed.), *Conflict and Stability in Europe* (London, 1979), 313.
69. Richard J. Evans, *The Third Reich in Power, 1933–1939* (London, 2006), 497–500.
70. Paul Hayes, 'The Triumph of Caesarism: Fascism and Nazism', in Hayes (ed.), *Themes in Modern European History*, 194.
71. R. J. Overy, *The Nazi Economic Recovery, 1932–1938* (Basingstoke, 1982), 33, 41.
72. George L. Mosse, *The Crisis of German Ideology: The Intellectual Origins of the Third Reich* (London, 1964, 1966), 309–10.
73. Overy, *Nazi Economic Recovery*, 35.
74. Richard Overy, *The Dictators: Hitler's Germany and Stalin's Russia* (London: 2004), ch. 10.
75. Albert Speer, *Inside the Third Reich* (New York, 1969, 1970), 358–61.
76. 'Hossbach Memorandum' [1937], in A. William Salomone and Alexander J. Baltzly (eds), *Readings in Twentieth-Century European History* (New York, 1950), 353.
77. Tom Gallagher, 'Conservatism, Dictatorship and Fascism in Portugal, 1914–45', in Martin Blinkhorn (ed.), *Fascists and Conservatives: The Radical Right and the Establishment in Twentieth-Century Europe* (London, 1990), 161.

## CHAPTER 11: POPULAR FRONT AND WAR

1. Max Adler, 'The Sociology of Revolution' [1928], in Bottomore and Goode (eds), *Austro-Marxism*, 144.
2. Ivan T. Berend, *An Economic History of Twentieth-Century Europe: Economic Regimes from Laissez-Faire to Globalization* (Cambridge, 2006), 150–1.
3. As emphasized by Kevin Murphy's study positing the inauguration of 'state capitalism', *Revolution and Counter-Revolution: Class Struggle in a Moscow Metal Factory* (New York, 2005), 216.
4. Robert C. Allen, 'A Reassessment of the Soviet Industrial Revolution', in *Comparative Economic Studies* (June 2005), vol. 47, no. 2, 321.
5. Cf. Trotsky: 'if the world proletariat should actually prove incapable of fulfilling its mission...nothing else would remain but to recognize openly that the socialist program, based on the internal contradictions of capitalist society, has petered out as a Utopia' [1939]. Quoted in Isaac Deutscher, *The Prophet Outcast: Trotsky, 1929–1940* (London, 1963, 2003), 379.
6. Ante Ciliga, *The Russian Enigma* [1940], trans. Fernand G. Fernier and Anne Cliff (London, 1979), 118.
7. Donald A. Filtzer, *Soviet Workers and Stalinist Industrialization: The Formation of Modern Soviet Production Relations, 1928–1941* (London, 1991), 97.
8. Ciliga, *Russian Enigma*, 114–15.
9. J. Arch Getty and Oleg V. Naumov, *The Road to Terror: Stalin and the Self-Destruction of the Bolsheviks, 1932–1939*, updated and abridged (Yale, 2010), 148, 171, 184.

10. Christopher Read (ed.), *The Stalin Years: A Reader* (Basingstoke, 2003), 103. Quote from Piers Brendon, *The Dark Valley: A Panorama of the 1930s* (London, 2000), 414.
11. Shelia Fitzpatrick, *Everyday Stalinism: Ordinary Life in Extraordinary Times* (New York, 1999), 223.
12. Dmitrii Manuilski, 'On Fascism' [April 1931] in David Beetham (ed.) *Marxists in Face of Fascism* (Manchester, 1983), 157.
13. Kevin McDermott and Jeremy Agnew, *The Comintern: A History of International Communism from Lenin to Stalin* (Basingstoke, 1996), 131.
14. Maurice Dobb, *Political Economy and Capitalism: Some Essays in Economic Tradition* (London, 1937), 263–4.
15. Fernando Claudin, *The Communist Movement: From Comintern to Cominform*, trans. Brian Pearce and Francis MacDonagh (London, 1970, 1975), 187.
16. James Joll, 'The Making of the Popular Front', in James Joll (ed.), *The Decline of the Third Republic* (London, 1959), 51.
17. Maurice Thorez, *France Today and the People's Front*, trans. Emile Burns (London, 1936), 181.
18. Rod Kedward, *La Vie en Bleu: France and the French Since 1900* (London, 2005, 2006), 181–2.
19. Julian Jackson, *The Popular Front in France: Defending Democracy, 1934–1938* (Cambridge, 1988, 1991), 101.
20. Thorez quoted in Jacques Danos and Marcel Gibelin, *June '36: Class Struggle and Popular Front in France*, trans. Peter Fysh and Christine Bourry (London, 1952, 1988), 152–3.
21. Nicholas Atkin, 'Between Democracy and Autocracy: France, 1918–45', in Hayes (ed.), *Themes in Modern European History*, 213; Nathaniel Greene, *Crisis and Decline: The French Socialist Party in the Popular Front Era* (Ithaca, 1969), 164.
22. Gerald Brennan, *The Spanish Labyrinth* (Cambridge, 1943, 1971), 145.
23. Harry Browne, *Spain's Civil War*, 2nd ed. (London, 1983, 1996), 42.
24. Paul Preston, *The Coming of the Spanish Civil War: Reform, Reaction and Revolution in the Second Republic, 1931–36*, 2nd ed. (London, 1994), 174. For the view, however, from a contemporary socialist leader, that it was an attempt 'to install a dictatorship of the proletariat', see Julio Alvarez del Vayo, *The March of Socialism*, trans. Joseph M. Bernstein (London, 1974), 254–5.
25. Hugh Thomas, *The Spanish Civil War*, 3rd ed. (London, 1977), 180.
26. Braunthal, *History of the International*, vol. 2, 456.
27. See Eric Hobsbawm, *How to Change the World: Marx and Marxism, 1840–2011* (London, 2011), 305–10.
28. Jack Gray, *Rebellions and Revolutions: China from the 1800s to the 1980s* (Oxford, 1990), 252.
29. Paul Myron Anthony Linebarger, *The Political Doctrines of Sun Yat-Sen* (Baltimore, 1937), 209–14.
30. Maurice Meisner, *Mao Zedong: A Political and Intellectual Portrait* (Cambridge, 2007), 90–1.
31. Nick Knight, 'Applying Marxism to Asian Conditions: Mao Zedong, Ho Chi Minh and the "Universality" of Marxism', in Daryl Glaser and David M. Walker (eds), *Twentieth-Century Marxism: A Global Introduction* (London, 2007), 145–6.
32. Stuart Schram, *The Thought of Mao Tse-Tung* (Cambridge, 1989), 54.
33. Louis Allen, *Japan: The Years of Triumph* (London, 1971), 93–4.
34. C. Fitzgerald, *Communism Takes China* (London, 1971), 101.

35. T'ien-wei Wu, 'The Chinese Communist Movement', in James C. Hsiung and Steven I. Levine (eds), *China's Bitter Victory: The War with Japan, 1937–1945* (Armonk, 1992), 79.
36. 'Decision of the CC on Land Policy in the Anti-Japanese Base Areas' [28 January 1942], in Tony Saich and Benjamin Yang, *The Rise to Power of the Chinese Communist Party: Documents and Analysis* (New York, 1996), 1040.
37. Mao Tse-Tung, *Selected Works*, vol. 3 (New York, 1954), 114.
38. Ibid., 118.
39. Jonathan D. Spence, *The Search for Modern China*, 2nd ed. (New York, 1999), 428–30.
40. Ross McKibbin, *Classes and Cultures: England 1918–1951* (Oxford, 1998), 59.
41. Mark Clapson, 'Suburbanization and Social Change in England and North America, 1880–1970', in David Englander (ed.), *Britain and America: Studies in Comparative History, 1760–1970* (New Haven, 1997), 136–7.
42. Martin Daunton and Matthew Hilton, 'Introduction', in Daunton and Hilton (eds), *The Politics of Consumption: Material Culture and Citizenship in Europe and America* (Oxford, 2001), 21.
43. Arthur C. Pigou, *The Economics of Welfare*, 4th ed. (London, 1920, 1932), IV.III.1.
44. Keynes in 1925, quoted in Gilles Dostaler, *Keynes and his Battles* (Cheltenham, 2007), 93.
45. Keynes excerpted in Steven G. Medema and Warren J. Samuels (eds), *The History of Economic Thought: A Reader* (London, 2003), 598.
46. 'President Roosevelt's Fireside Chat', 7 May 1933, in Walter Moss, Janice Terry, and Jiu-Hwa Upshar, *The Twentieth Century: Readings in Global History* (Boston, 1999), 103–4.
47. Edvard Beneš, *Democracy Today and Tomorrow* (London, 1940), 60–1.
48. *Munitions Industry* (US Government Printing Office, 1936), 12.
49. S. Grant Duff, *Europe and the Czechs* (London, 1938), 134.
50. Quoted in R. A. C. Parker, 'Chamberlain and Appeasement', in Wm. Roger Louis (ed.), *Adventures with Britannia: Personalities, Politics and Culture in Britain* (Austin, 1995), 267.
51. Richard Overy, *Russia's War* (London, 1997, 1999), 46.
52. Cited in Michael Howard, *The Lessons of History* (Oxford, 1991, 1992), 61.
53. Richard Overy (with Andrew Wheatcroft), *The Road to War* (London, 1989, 2009), 127.
54. Horne, *French Army*, 63–4.
55. See discussion of work by Götz Aly and Susanne Heim in Christopher R. Browning, *The Path to Genocide* (Cambridge, 1992, 1995), 60–1.
56. Alan S. Milward, *War, Economy and Society, 1939–1945* (Middlesex, 1977, 1987), 138.
57. Gregory Hooks, 'The United States of America: The Second World War and the Retreat from New Deal Corporatism', in Wyn Grant, Jan Nekkers, and Frans van Waarden (eds), *Organizing Business for War: Corporatist Economic Organization during the Second World War* (New York, 1991), 89.
58. Richard Overy, *Why the Allies Won* (London, 1995), 192.
59. Quoted in Anthony Glees, 'Anglo-Saxon Influences and the Development of German Democracy after World War Two', in John Pinder (ed.), *Foundations of Democracy in the European Union* (Basingstoke, 1999), 71.
60. C. Wright Mills, *The Power Elite* [1956] (Oxford, 2000), 12–13.
61. Alan Bullock, *Hitler and Stalin: Parallel Lives*, 2nd ed. (London, 1998), 773, 843.
62. Omer Bartov, *Hitler's Army: Soldiers, Nazis, and War in the Third Reich* (Oxford, 1992), 169.
63. Overy, *Russia's War*, 297.

## Notes to Chapter 12

64. Helen Lewis, *A Time to Speak* (New York, 1992, 1994), 106–7.
65. Hannah Arendt, *The Origins of Totalitarianism* (Cleveland, 1951, 1958), 123.
66. Ibid., 124.
67. Abbot Gleason, *Totalitarianism: The Inner History of the Cold War* (Oxford, 1995), 109–11, 111.

### CHAPTER 12: COLD WAR AND THE FEAR OF SUBVERSION

1. Stanley G. Payne, *Civil War in Europe, 1905–1949* (Cambridge, 2011), 203.
2. István Deák, 'Introduction' in István Deák, Jan T. Gross, and Tony Judt (eds), *The Politics of Retribution in Europe: World War II and its Aftermath* (Princeton, 2000), 4, 12.
3. John MacMillan, *On Liberal Peace: Democracy, War and the International Order* (London, 1998), 157.
4. Thomas U. Berger, *Cultures of Antimilitarism: National Security in Germany and Japan* (Baltimore, 1998), 25–6.
5. Corin D. Edwards, 'The Dissolution of the Japanese Combines', *Pacific Affairs*, vol. 19, no. 3 (1946), 227–9.
6. Sven Steinmo, *Taxation and Democracy: Swedish, British, and American Approaches to Financing the Modern State* (New Haven, 1993), 116–17.
7. Louis Hartz, 'The Liberal Tradition' [1955], in Andreas Hess (ed.), *American Social and Political Thought: A Reader* (Edinburgh, 2002), 155–6.
8. Laura Belmonte, 'Selling Capitalism: Modernization and U.S. Overseas Propaganda, 1945–1959', in David C. Engerman, Nils Gilman, Mark H. Haefele, and Michael E. Latham (eds), *Staging Growth: Modernization, Development, and the Global Cold War* (Amherst, 2003), 110–11.
9. Martin Daunton, 'Britain and Globalisation Since 1850: III. Creating the World of Bretton Woods, 1939–1958', *Transactions of the Royal Historical Society*, 18 (2008), 2–3.
10. Volker R. Berghahn, *Europe in the Era of Two World Wars: From Militarism and Genocide to Civil Society* (Princeton, 2006), 136.
11. David Brody, *In Labor's Cause: Main Themes on the History of the American Worker* (New York, 1993), 221–3.
12. 'Let Us Face the Future', Labour Party statement of policy, April 1945, in Andrew Reekes, *The Rise of Labour, 1899–1951* (Basingstoke, 1991), 118.
13. C. A. R. Crosland, 'The Transition from Capitalism', in R. H. S. Crossman (ed.), *New Fabian Essays* (London, 1952), 36.
14. Charles Williams, *Adenauer: The Father of the New Germany* (London, 2000), 308.
15. See Ludwig Erhard, the German CDU's economic expert, 'The Economics of Success' [1963], in John W. Boyer and Jan Goldstein (eds), *Twentieth-Century Europe* (Chicago, 1987), 517–27.
16. Quoted in Gary S. Cross, *Time and Money: The Making of Consumer Culture* (London, 1993), 190.
17. Philip Armstrong, Andrew Glyn, and John Harrison, *Capitalism Since World War II* (London, 1984), 178.
18. Maurice Crouzet, *The European Renaissance since 1945* (London, 1970), 110–12.
19. Milovan Djilas, *Conversations with Stalin*, trans. Michael B. Petrovich (New York, 1962), 113.
20. Julius Braunthal, *History of the International, Volume 3: 1943–1968*, trans. Peter Gord and Kenneth Mitchell (London, 1980), 35–6.

21. Robert Service, *Stalin: A Biography* (Basingstoke, 2004), 517–18.
22. Josef Korbel, *The Communist Subversion of Czechoslovakia, 1938–1948* (Princeton, 1959), 141.
23. Quoted in Wolfgang Leonhard, *Child of the Revolution*, trans. C. M. Woodhouse (London, 1955, 1957), 303.
24. Anatoli Granovsky, *All Pity Choked: The Memoirs of a Soviet Secret Agent* (London, 1955), 210.
25. David Harris, 'Memorandum' [26 March 1946], appendix in W. W. Rostow, *The Division of Europe After World War II: 1946* (Aldershot, 1982), 170–3.
26. Ben Fowkes, *Eastern Europe, 1945–1969: From Stalinism to Stagnation* (London, 2000), 102–3.
27. Scott D. Parrish, 'The Turn Towards Confrontation: The Soviet Reaction to the Marshall Plan, 1947', in Scott D. Parrish and Mikhail M. Narinsky, *New Evidence on the Soviet Rejection of the Marshall Plan, 1947: Two Reports*, Cold War International History Project, Working Paper no. 9 (Washington DC, 1996), 24–5.
28. Martin Mevius, *Agents of Moscow: The Hungarian Communist Party and the Origins of Socialist Patriotism, 1941–1953* (Oxford, 2005), 163.
29. Berend, *Economic History of Twentieth-Century Europe*, 154–6.
30. Milovan Djilas, *Conversations with Stalin* (New York, 1962), 114.
31. Stefan Berger, 'Germany', in Stefan Berger and David Broughton (eds), *The Force of Labour: The Western European Labour Movements and the Working-Class in the Twentieth Century* (Oxford, 1995), 91.
32. Erik Van Ree, *The Political Thought of Joseph Stalin: A Study in Twentieth-Century Revolutionary Patriotism* (New York, 2002), 249.
33. *World News and Views*, vol. 32 (London, 1953), 506.
34. Philip Selznick, *The Organizational Weapon: A Study of Bolshevik Strategy and Tactics* (New York, 1952), 5.
35. Louis W. Koenig (ed.), *The Truman Administration: Its Principles and Practice* (New York, 1956), 60.
36. Sidney Hook, *World Communism: Key Documentary Material* (Princeton, 1962), 8.
37. Gregory Mitrovich, *Undermining the Kremlin: America's Strategy to Subvert the Soviet Bloc, 1947–1956* (Ithaca, 2000), 17–18.
38. Palmiro Togliatti, 'Questions on Stalinism' [Interview in *Nuovi Argomenti*, Rome, 16 June 1956], in Dan N. Jacobs (ed.), *From Marx to Mao and Marchais: Documents on the Development of Communist Variations* (New York, 1979), 235.
39. Stuart Holland, 'The New Communist Economics', in Paolo Filo della Torre, Edward Mortimer, and Jonathan Story (eds), *Eurocommunism: Myth or Reality?* (London, 1979), 212–13.
40. Ibid., 238.
41. 'Long Telegram', in Michael D. Gambone, *Documents of American Diplomacy* (Westport, 2002), 303.
42. George Kennan, *Memoirs, 1925–1950* (London, 1968), 294.
43. David Mayers, *George Kennan and the Dilemmas of US Foreign Policy* (New York, 1988, 1990), 111.
44. Hans W. Gatzke, *The Present in Perspective: A Look at the World since 1945*, 2nd ed. (Chicago, 1961), 35.
45. S. Nelson Drew (ed.), *NSC-68: Forging the Strategy of Containment* (Washington DC, 1994), 49.
46. Quoted in Bruce Cumings, *The Korean War: A History* (New York, 2010), 5.

47. Antony Best, Jussi M. Hanhimäki, Joseph A. Maiolo, and Kirsten E. Schulze, *International History of the Twentieth Century* (London, 2004), 95.
48. R. F. Holland, *European Decolonization, 1918–1981* (Basingstoke, 1985), 5–8.
49. 'Important links between short-run economic fluctuations and political and social events in the years 1790–1850', Rowstow had noted, were evident during British take-off, when 'cyclical fluctuations and cost-of-living movements served to detonate and give expression to the familiar underlying trends'. W. W. Rostow, *British Economy of the Nineteenth Century: Essays* (Oxford, 1948), 122.
50. W. W. Rostow, *The Stages of Economic Growth: A Non-Communist Manifesto* (Cambridge, 1960), 145.
51. Seymour Martin Lipset, *Political Man: The Social Bases of Politics* (Garden City, 1960), 66.
52. Nils Gilman, *Mandarins of the Future: Modernization Theory in Cold War America* (Baltimore, 2003), 202.
53. Tony Smith, *America's Mission: The United States and the Worldwide Struggle for Democracy in the Twentieth Century* (Princeton, 1994), 179.
54. Gilman, *Mandarins of the Future*, 186–90.
55. Douglas A. Chalmers, 'The Politicized State in Latin America', in James M. Malloy (ed.), *Authoritarianism and Corporatism in Latin America* (Pittsburgh, 1977), 35; José Nun, 'A Latin American Phenomenon: The Middle-Class Military Coup' [1965], in James Petras and Maurice Zetlin (eds), *Latin America: Reform or Revolution?* (New York, 1968), 154–7.
56. Mark Curtis, *Secret Affairs: Britain's Collusion with Radical Islam* (London, 2010), 74.
57. Quintin Hogg Hailsham, *The Dilemma of Democracy* (London, 1978), 211–12.
58. Oliver Edwards, *The USA and the Cold War* (London, 1997), 94–5.
59. Document in Walter LaFeber (ed.), *America in the Cold War: Twenty Years of Revolutions and Response, 1947–1967* (New York, 1969), 118–21.
60. Geraldine Lievesley, *The Cuban Revolution: Past, Present and Future Perspectives* (Basingstoke, 2004), 78.
61. Richard Gott, *Cuba: A New History* (New Haven, 2004, 2005), 172.
62. Quoted in Jules Townshend, *The Politics of Marxism: The Critical Debates* (London, 1996), 143.
63. James Nelson Goodsell, *Fidel Castro's Personal Revolution in Cuba: 1959–1973* (New York, 1975), 266.
64. John Fitzgerald Kennedy, *The Burden and the Glory* (New York, 1964), 154.
65. Rodolfo Stavenhagen, 'Seven Erroneous Theses about Latin America', in Irving Louis Horowitz, Josué de Castro, and John Gerassi (eds), *Latin American Radicalism: A Documentary Report on Left and Nationalist Movements* (London, 1969), 111.
66. Robert H. Swansbrough, *The Embattled Colossus: Economic Nationalism and United States Investors in Latin America* (Gainesville, 1976), 72.
67. Barrington Moore Jr., *The Social Origins of Dictatorship and Democracy* (London, 1967), 442.
68. Fred J. Cook, 'The Warfare State' [January 1964], excerpted in LaFeber (ed.), *America in the Cold War*, 213–16.
69. Steven Rosen, *Testing the Theory of the Military-Industrial Complex* (Lexington, 1973), 38.
70. Joel Spring notes that 'advertisers imposed codes that supported the American Way and free enterprise. For instance, Procter & Gamble, the major sponsor of soap operas, required that their programs supported patriotism and never tarnished the image of

Notes to Chapter 13

government agents and members of the U. S. armed forces.' Joel Spring, *Educating the Consumer: A History of the Marriage of Schools, Advertising, and Media* (Mahwah, NJ, 2002), 141.
71. Reproduced in LaFeber (ed.), *America in the Cold War*, 210–12.

## CHAPTER 13: THE PIVOT OF '68: NEW LEFT AND NEW RIGHT

1. John F. Kennedy, 'A Great Speech', *Life*, 27 January 1961, 24.
2. Charles Malik, 'The Challenge to Western Civilisation', in *The Conservative Papers* (New York, 1964), 11–12.
3. Robert Dallek, *Nixon and Kissinger: Partners in Power* (London, 2007, 2008), 106.
4. William J. Duiker, *Sacred War: Nationalism and Revolution in a Divided Vietnam* (New York, 1995), 254–6.
5. John Pilger, *Heroes* (London, 1986, 1989), 186.
6. Brian Van Demark, *Into the Quagmire: Lyndon Johnson and the Escalation of the Vietnam War* (New York, 1995), 148–50.
7. William J. Duiker, *The Communist Road to Power in Vietnam*, 2nd ed. (Boulder, 1996), 211–12.
8. Gideon Sjoberg, 'Rural-Urban Balance and Models of Economic Development', in *Social Structure and Mobility in Economic Development*, eds Neil J. Smelser and Seymour Martin Lipset (Chicago, 1966), 248.
9. Arnold Isaacs, 'The Limits of Credibility', in Robert J. McMahon, *Major Problems in the History of the Vietnam War*, 2nd ed. (Lexington, 1995), 450.
10. Paul Elliott, *Vietnam: Conflict and Controversy* (London, 1996), 47.
11. Michael Vickery, *Cambodia, 1975–1982* (Boston, 1984), 263.
12. Christian G. Appy, *Working-Class War: American Combat Soldiers and Vietnam* (Chapel Hill, 1993), 6.
13. Seymour Melman, *Pentagon Capitalism: The Political Economy of War* (New York, 1970), 98.
14. Quoted in Hal Draper, *The Mind of Charles Kerr* (Berkeley, 1964), 5–6.
15. Clark Kerr et al., *Industrialism and Industrial Man* (London, 1960, 1973), 267–8.
16. 'Alienation' was a vogue term for this generation. Cf. Eric and Mary Josephson (eds), *Man Alone: Alienation in Modern Society* (New York, 1962), reprinted fifteen times by 1972.
17. Joseph A. Schumpeter, *Capitalism, Socialism and Democracy* (London, 1994), 128.
18. Paul A. Baran and Paul M. Sweezy, *Monopoly Capitalism: An Essay on the American Economic and Social Order* (Middlesex, 1966, 1968), 181.
19. Gerd-Rainer Horn, *The Spirit of '68: Rebellion in Western Europe and North America, 1956–1976* (Oxford, 2007), 135.
20. 'The Port Huron Statement', appendix in James Miller, *'Democracy is in the Streets': From Port Huron to the Siege of Chicago* (New York, 1987), 341.
21. Jules Henry, 'Social and Psychological Preparation for War', in David Cooper (ed.), *The Dialectics of Liberation* (London, 1968), 69.
22. Otto Kerner et al., *Report of the National Advisory Committee on Civil Disorders* (Washington, DC: US Government Printing Office, 1968), 37.
23. Ibid., 61.
24. Ronald Fraser, *1968: A Student Generation in Revolt* (London, 1988), 130.
25. David Farber, *Chicago '68* (Chicago, 1988), 107.

26. Document in LaFeber (ed.), *America in the Cold War*, 16–24.
27. Friedrich Heer, *Challenge of Youth*, trans. Geoffrey Skelton (London, 1974), 140.
28. Abbie Hoffman, *Woodstock Nation: A Talk-Rock Album* (New York, 1969), 77.
29. Hugh Davis Graham and Ted Robert Gurr (eds), *Violence in America: Historical and Comparative Perspective* (New York, 1969), xiii.
30. Tom Wells, *The War Within: America's Battle Over Vietnam* (New York, 1994), 272–3; Robert W. Tucker, *The Radical Left and American Foreign Policy* (Baltimore, 1971), 46–8.
31. Irving Howe, 'New Styles in "Leftism"', in Paul Jacobs and Saul Landau, *The New Radicals: A Report with Documents* (Middlesex, 1966), 291–2.
32. Patrick Seale and Maureen McConville, *French Revolution 1968* (London, 1968), 185.
33. John M. Murrin, et al., *Liberty, Equality, Power: A History of the American People* (Fort Worth, 1996), 957.
34. Angi Rutter, 'Élites, Estate and Strata: Class in West Germany since 1945', in Arthur Marwick (ed.), *Class in the Twentieth Century* (Brighton, 1986), 153.
35. Norman Birnbaum, *After Progress: American Social Reform and European Socialism in the Twentieth Century* (Oxford, 2001), 185–6.
36. Mark Kurlansky, *1968: The Year that Rocked the World* (London, 2004), 144.
37. Paul Ginsborg, *Italy and its Discontents, 1980–2001* (London, 2001), 40.
38. Vladimir Fišera, *Writing on the Wall. France, May 1968: A Documentary Anthology* (London, 1978), 51–2.
39. J. Sauvageot, A. Geismar, D. Cohn-Bendit, and J.-P. Duteuil, *The Student Revolt: The Activists Speak*, trans. Ben Brewster (London, 1968), 69.
40. Arthur Marwick, *The Sixties: Cultural Revolution in Britain, France, Italy, and the United States, c.1958–c.1974* (Oxford, 1998), 636–7.
41. Donald Sassoon, *One Hundred Years of Socialism: The West European Left in the Twentieth Century* (New York, 1996), 455.
42. Tony Judt, *Postwar: A History of Europe Since 1945* (London, 2005), 377.
43. John Lewis Gaddis, *The Cold War* (London, 2005, 2007), 186–92.
44. Kenneth Hoover and Raymond Plant, *Conservative Capitalism in Britain and the United States* (London, 1989), 134–5.
45. James O'Connor, *The Fiscal Crisis of the State* (New York, 1973), 67.
46. Maurice Isserman and Michael Kazin, *America Divided: The Civil War of the 1960s* (New York, 2000), 199.
47. Daniel Bell, *The Cultural Contradictions of Capitalism* (New York, 1976), 277.
48. Ibid., 28.
49. Quotes from Irving Kristol in Jean-François Drolet, *American Neoconservatism: The Politics and Culture of a Reactionary Idealism* (London, 2011), 37, 40.
50. Michael Young, *The Rise of the Meritocracy, 1870–2033: An Essay on Education and Equality* (London, 1961), 106.
51. F. A. Hayek, *The Road to Serfdom*, 2nd ed. (London, 1944, 2001), 43. Ayn Rand, influential on the American libertarian right, thought that the welfare state, preserving private property in production but directing its use, was essentially 'fascist'. Ayn Rand, 'The New Fascism: Rule by Consensus' [1965], in her *Capitalism: The Unknown Ideal* (New York, 1966), 237.
52. Memorandum for Henry Kissinger, 16 October 1972, quoted in Jonathan Haslam, *The Nixon Administration and the Death of Allende's Chile: A Case of Assisted Suicide* (London, 2005), 149.

53. Andy Beckett, *Pinochet in Piccadilly: Britain and Chile's Hidden History* (London, 2002), 172–7.
54. See the essays, including one by Jacques Delors, later the leading architect of the European single market, in Stuart Holland (ed.), *Beyond Capitalist Planning* (Oxford, 1978).
55. Milton Friedman, 'Inflation and Wages' [1970], in Friedman, *An Economist's Protest* (Glen Ridge, 1972), 109.
56. Richard Cockett, *Thinking the Unthinkable: Think Tanks and the Economic Counter-Revolution, 1931–1983* (London, 1994, 1995), 113.
57. Arthur Seldon, *Capitalism* (Oxford, 1990), 103.
58. Giorgio Napolitano, interviewed by Eric Hobsbawm, trans. John Cammett and Victoria De Grazia, *The Italian Road to Socialism* (Westport, 1977), 71–3.
59. See the Joint Declaration of the French and Italian Communist Parties, 15 November 1975. Appendix two in Torre, Mortimer, and Story, *Eurocommunism*, 335.
60. Santiago Carrillo, *'Eurocommunism' and the State*, trans. Nan Green and A. M. Elliott (London, 1977), 24.
61. Ibid., 41.
62. Ibid., 69, 74.
63. Martin Kayman, *Revolution and Counter-Revolution in Portugal* (London, 1987), 147.
64. Jean-François Revel, *The Totalitarian Temptation* [1976], trans. David Hapgood (London, 1977), 228–36.
65. Berend, *Economic History of Twentieth-Century Europe*, 296.
66. C. M. Woodhouse, *Modern Greece: A Short History* (London, 1968, 1991), 298.
67. Salvador Giner and Eduardo Sevilla, 'From Despotism to Parliamentarianism: Class Domination and Political Order in the Spanish State', in Richard Scase (ed.), *The State in Western Europe* (London, 1978), 218–19.
68. Angel Smith, 'Spain', in Berger and Broughton (eds), *The Force of Labour*, 194.
69. Gabriel Tortella, *The Development of Modern Spain: An Economic History of the Nineteenth and Twentieth Centuries*, trans. Valerie J. Herr (Cambridge MA, 2000), 416–18.
70. Richard Gillespie, 'Spanish Socialism in the 1980s', in Tom Gallagher and Allan M. Williams (eds), *Southern European Socialism* (Manchester, 1989), 69.
71. Perry Anderson, *The New Old World* (London, 2009), 432.
72. Samuel Huntington, *The Third Wave: Democratization in the Late Twentieth Century* (Norman, 1991), 66–8.
73. Anthony Crosland. *The Future of Socialism* (London, 1956), 216.
74. For a full discussion of Social Democratic relations with organized labour and business, see Stephen Padgett and William E. Paterson, *A History of Social Democracy in Postwar Europe* (London, 1991), 177–220.
75. Keith Middlemas, *Politics in Industrial Society: The Experience of the British System since 1911* (London, 1979), 374.
76. Robert Taylor, *Workers and the New Depression* (Basingstoke, 1982), 169.
77. Michael Kazin, *The Populist Persuasion: An American History* (New York, 1995), 260.
78. Jonathan Martin Kolkey, *The New Right, 1960–1968: With Epilogue, 1969–1980* (Lanham, 1983), 3.
79. John Bonham, *The Middle-Class Vote* (London, 1954), 21.
80. Brian Elliott, David McCrone, and Frank Bechhofer, 'Anxieties and Ambitions: The petite-bourgeoisie and the New Right in Britain', in David Rose (ed.), *Social Stratification and Economic Change* (London, 1988), 263–78.

81. Patrick Hutber, *The Decline and Fall of the Middle Class and How it can Fight Back* (London, 1976, 1977), 60.
82. Bruce J. Schulman, *The Seventies: The Great Shift in American Culture, Society, and Politics* (Cambridge, MA, 2001), 205–15.
83. For this section, see M. C. Howard and J. E. King, *The Rise of Neoliberalism in the Advanced Economies: A Materialist Analysis* (Basingstoke, 2008), 162–89.
84. George Strauss, 'White Collar Unions are Different' [1954], in Richard Hyman and Robert Price (eds), *The New Working Class?* (Basingstoke, 1983), 205.
85. E. H. H. Green, *Ideologies of Conservatism: Conservative Political Ideas in the Twentieth Century* (Oxford, 2002), 217.
86. Rodney Barker, *Political Ideas in Modern Britain: In and after the Twentieth Century* (London, 1997), 232.
87. Neil Fligstein, *The Architecture of Markets: An Economic Sociology of Twenty-First-Century Capitalist Societies* (Princeton, 2002), 86.
88. John Gray, *False Dawn: The Delusions of Global Capitalism* (London, 1998), 116.
89. John Gardiner, *The Victorians: An Age in Retrospect* (Hambledon, 2002), 85.
90. Margaret Thatcher, 'Interview for *Woman's Own*', 23 September 1987, Margaret Thatcher Foundation, http://www.margaretthatcher.org/document/106689.
91. Larry Elliott and Dan Atkinson, *The Age of Insecurity* (London, 1998), 94–6.
92. Jane Wheelock, 'Who Dreams of Failure? Insecurity of Modern Capitalism', in John Vail, Jane Wheelock, and Michael Hill, *Insecure Times: Living with Insecurity in Contemporary Society* (London, 1999), 37.
93. Milton Friedman, *A Theory of the Consumption Function* (Princeton, 1957).
94. Speck interviewed in James Finn, *Protest: Pacifism and Politics* (New York, 1968), 324.

## CHAPTER 14: THE DEMISE OF THE 'RED MENACE'

1. Martin McCauley (ed.), *Khrushchev and Khrushchevism* (Bloomington, 1987), *passim*, reference to 'social contract' and 'new deal' in Alastair McAuley, 'Social Policy', ibid., 148.
2. Donald Filtzer, *The Khrushchev Era* (Basingstoke, 1993), 37.
3. Georg Lukács, *The Process of Democratization* [1968], trans. Susanne Bernhardt and Norman Levine, (New York, 1991), 148.
4. Silviu Brucan, *Pluralism and Social Conflict: A Social Analysis of the Communist World* (New York, 1990), 80–1.
5. Sándor Kopácsi, *'In the Name of the Working Class'*, trans. Daniel and Judy Stoffman (London, 1979, 1986), 172.
6. Grzegorz Ekiert, *The State Against Society: Political Crises and their Aftermath in East Central Europe* (Princeton, 1996), 60–58.
7. Nicholas Krasso, 'Hungary 1956: A Participant's Account', in Tariq Ali (ed.), *The Stalinist Legacy* (London, 1984), 375.
8. Ibid., 376.
9. Jürgen Tampke, *The People's Republics of Eastern Europe* (Beckenham, Kent, 1983), 55.
10. François Fejtö, *A History of the People's Democracies: Eastern Europe Since Stalin*, trans. Daniel Weissbort (London, 1969), 91.
11. Radoslav Selucký, *Czechoslovakia: The Plan that Failed*, trans. Derek Viney (London, 1969, 1970), 62.

12. Calculated from figures in Z. A. B. Zeman, *Prague Spring: A Report on Czechoslovakia 1968* (London, 1969), 94–5.
13. Quoted in Matt Treacy, *The IRA, 1956–69* (Manchester, 2011), 138.
14. Kieran Williams, *The Prague Spring and its Aftermath* (Cambridge, 1997), 24.
15. David Caute, *Sixty-Eight: The Year of the Barricades* (London, 1988), 174–7.
16. William Shawcross, *Dubček and Czechoslavakia* (London, 1990), 139.
17. Harry Schwartz, *Russia's Post-War Economy* (Syracuse, 1947), 106.
18. Jay Taylor, *The Generalissimo: Chiang Kai-Shek and the Struggle for Modern China* (Cambridge, 2009), 330.
19. Eric R. Wolf, *Peasant Wars of the Twentieth Century* (London, 1969, 1971), 294.
20. Schram, *Thought of Mao Tse-Tung*, 98.
21. Ibid., 46.
22. James L. Watson, 'Class and Class Formation in Chinese Society', in Watson (ed.), *Class and Social Stratification in Post-Revolution China* (Cambridge, 1984), 13.
23. Jasper Becker, *Hungry Ghosts: China's Secret Famine* (London, 1996), 270.
24. Rana Mitter, *A Bitter Revolution: China's Struggle with the Modern World* (Oxford, 2004), 213.
25. I-Kuan-tao had been a secret society suppressed in the 1950s. Cited in Stuart R. Schram, 'The Marxist', in Dick Wilson (ed.), *Mao Tse-Tung in the Scales of History* (Cambridge, 1977), 48.
26. Quoted in Kalpana Misra, *From Post-Maoism to Post-Marxism: The Erosion of Official Ideology in Deng's China* (New York, 1998), 121–2, 118. Author's emphasis.
27. Deng Xiaoping, 'Uphold the Four Cardinal Principals' [30 March 1979], http://english.peopledaily.com.cn/dengxp/vol2/text/b1290.html.
28. Robert C. Allen, *Farm to Factory: A Reinterpretation of the Soviet Industrial Revolution* (Princeton, 2003), 211.
29. Mary Fulbrook, *Anatomy of a Dictatorship: Inside the GDR 1949–1989* (Oxford, 1995, 1997), 36, 80.
30. Robert Conquest (ed.), *The Politics of Ideas in the USSR* (London, 1967), 105. Emphasis in original.
31. Berend, *Economic History of Twentieth-Century Europe*, 175–6.
32. Michael Heller and Aleksander Nekrich, *Utopia in Power: A History of the USSR*, trans. Phyllis B. Carlos (London: 1982, 1986), 688.
33. Jonathan Osmond, 'Yet Another Failed German Revolution?', in Moira Donald and Tim Rees (eds), *Reinterpreting Revolution in Twentieth-Century Europe* (Basingstoke, 2000), 149.
34. George (György) Konrád and Ivan Szelényi, *The Intellectuals on the Road to Class Power*, trans. Andrew Arato and Richard E. Allen (New York, 1979), 179.
35. Jari Eloranta, 'Military Spending Patterns in History', 2010, EH.net, http://eh.net/encyclopedia/article/eloranta.military#_edn43.
36. S. J. Ball, *The Cold War: An International History, 1947–1991* (London, 1998), 223–4.
37. Adam B. Ulam, *The Communists: The Story of Power and Lost Illusions, 1948–1991* (New York, 1992), 343–5.
38. Alain Touraine et al., *Solidarity: Poland 1980–81*, trans. David Denby (Cambridge, 1983), 40–4.
39. Padraic Kenny, *A Carnival of Revolution: Central Europe, 1989* (Princeton, 2002), 42–8.

## Notes to Chapter 14

40. Zygmunt Bauman, 'After the Patronage State', in Christopher G. A. Bryant and Edmund Mokrzycki (eds), *The New Great Transformation? Change and Continuity in East-Central Europe* (London, 1994), 20.
41. Paul G. Lewis, 'Legitimacy and the Polish Communist State', in David Held et al. (eds), *States and Societies* (Oxford, 1983, 1985), 449.
42. Nigel Hawkes (ed.), *Tearing Down the Curtain: The People's Revolution in Eastern Europe* (London, 1990), 70.
43. David Priestland, *The Red Flag: Communism and the Making of the Modern World* (London, 2009), 546.
44. Quoted in Mark Sandle, *A Short History of Soviet Socialism* (London, 1999), 395–8.
45. John L. H. Keep, *Last of the Empires: A History of the Soviet Union, 1945–1991* (Oxford, 1996), 435.
46. Ibid., 414.
47. Philippe Demenet, 'Adam Michnik: The Sisyphus of Democracy', interview, *Unesco Courier*, September 2001, http://www.unesco.org/courier/2001_09/uk/dires.htm.
48. Richard Sakwa, *Russian Politics and Society* (London, 1993), 27.
49. Christopher Read, *The Making and Breaking of the Soviet System: An Interpretation* (Houndsmill, 2001), 233.
50. Archie Brown, *The Rise and Fall of Communism* (London, 2009), 588–90.
51. David Kotz with Fred Weir, *Revolution from Above: The Demise of the Soviet System* (London, 1997), 118.
52. Havel, 'Summer Meditations' [1992], in Moss, Terry, and Upshur, *The Twentieth Century*, 291.
53. Graeme Gill, *Bourgeoisie, State, and Democracy: Russia, Britain, France, and the USA* (Oxford, 2008), 285–6.
54. Michael Haynes and Rumy Husan, *A Century of State Murder? Death and Policy in Twentieth- Century Russia* (London, 2003), 141.
55. Berend, *Economic History of Twentieth-Century Europe*, 186.
56. Edward Acton, 'Revolutionaries and Dissidents: The Role of the Russian Intellectual in the Downfall of Tsarism and Communism', in Jennings and Kemp-Welch (eds), *Intellectuals in Politics*, 160.
57. Simon Clarke, 'Privatisation: The Rocky Road from Plan to Market', in Stephen White, Alex Pravda, and Zvi Gitelman (eds), *Developments in Russian and Post-Soviet Politics* (Durham, NC, 1994), 183–6.
58. Scott Gehlbach, *Representation through Taxation: Revenue, Politics, and Development in Postcommunist States* (Cambridge, 2011), 22–51.
59. Lin Chun, *The Transformation of Chinese Socialism* (Durham, NC, 2006), 211–10.
60. Kellee S. Tsai, *Capitalism Without Democracy: The Private Sector in Contemporary China* (Ithaca, 2007), 114–15.
61. G. H. Le May, *Black and White in South Africa* (London, 1971), 100.
62. R. W. Breach (ed.), *Documents and Descriptions: The World Since 1914* (Oxford, 1966), 227–9.
63. Lindsay Michie Eades, *The End of Apartheid in South Africa* (Westport, 1999), 22.
64. Eric Louw, *The Rise, Fall, and Legacy of Apartheid* (Westport, 2004), 175–6.
65. Robert H. Bates, *Prosperity and Violence: The Political Economy of Development* (New York, 2001), 94.
66. Amy Chua, *World on Fire: How Exporting Free-Market Democracy Breeds Ethnic Hatred and Global Instability* (London, 2003, 2004), 6.
67. Martin Shaw, *Post-Military Society* (Cambridge, 1991), 27.

68. Philip Bobbitt, *The Shield of Achilles: War, Peace and the Course of History* (London, 2002), ch. 10.
69. Ibid., 340.
70. Paraphrased in Ralf Dahrendorf, 'Towards the Twenty-First Century', in Michael Howard and Wm. Roger Louis (eds), *The Oxford History of the Twentieth Century* (Oxford, 1998), 339.
71. Robert W. Stern, *Changing India: Bourgeois Revolution on the Subcontinent*, 2nd ed. (Cambridge, 1993, 2003), 3.
72. Francis Fukuyama, 'The End of History?' [1989], in Gearóid Ó Tuathail, Simon Dalby, and Paul Routledge (eds), *The Geopolitics Reader*, 2nd ed. (London, 2006), 111.
73. Perry Anderson, *A Zone of Engagement* (London, 1992), 346.
74. Larry Siedentop, *Democracy in Europe* (London, 2000), 156.
75. Ibid., 155.

## CHAPTER 15: BRIGHT BOURGEOIS MORNING

1. Fukuyama, 'The End of History?', in Ó Tuathail et al. (eds), *Geopolitics Reader*, 111.
2. Pieter Geyl, 'Toynbee's System of Civilizations' [1946], in *Toynbee and History: Critical Essays and Reviews*, ed. M. F. Ashley Montagu (Boston, 1956), 41–2.
3. Quoted in William H. McNeill, *Arnold J. Toynbee: A Life* (Oxford, 1989), 76.
4. John Ehrman, *The Rise of the Neocons: Intellectuals and Foreign Affairs* (Yale, 1995), 37.
5. Irving Kristol, 'Utopianism, Ancient and Modern' [April 1973], in Kristol, *Neoconservatism: The Autobiography of an Idea* (Chicago, 1995, 1999), 195.
6. Stefan Halper and Jonathan Clarke, *America Alone: The Neo-Conservatives and the Global Order* (Cambridge, 2004), 314.
7. Gary J. Dorrien, *Imperial Designs: Neoconservatives and the New Pax Americana* (London, 2004), 21.
8. T. E. Vadney, *The World Since 1945*, 2nd ed. (London, 1987, 1992), 463.
9. Fred Halliday, *Revolution and World Politics: The Rise and Fall of the Sixth Great Power* (Durham, NC, 1999), 219–21.
10. Ivan Molloy, *Rolling Back Revolution: The Emergence of Low Intensity Conflict* (London, 2001), 21.
11. Thomas Carothers, 'The NED at 10', *Foreign Policy* 95 (Summer 1994), 132.
12. Ronald E. Powaski, *The Cold War: The United States and the Soviet Union, 1917–1991* (Oxford, 1998), 237.
13. Molloy, *Rolling Back Revolution*, 75.
14. James Mann, *Rise of the Vulcans: The History of Bush's War Cabinet* (London, 2004), 136.
15. Barry Gills, 'American Power, Neo-Liberal Economic Globalization and "Low Intensity Democracy": An Unstable Trinity', in Michael Cox, G. John Inkenberry, and Takashi Inoguchi (eds), *American Democracy Promotion: Impulses, Strategies and Tactics* (Oxford, 2000), 329.
16. Roy Joseph, 'The New World Order: President Bush and the Post-Cold War Era', in Martin J. Medhurst (ed.), *The Rhetorical Presidency of George H. W. Bush* (Texas, 2006), 86–7.
17. Marc Mulholland, 'Irish Republican Politics and Violence before the Peace Process, 1968–1994', in *European Review of History (Revue européenne d'histoire)*, vol. 14, no. 3 (2007), 410.

18. Stéphane Lefebvre, Michel Fortmann, and Thierry Gongora, '"The Revolution in Military Affairs": Its Implications for Doctrine and Force Development Within the U.S. Army', in B. J. C. McKercher and Michael A. Hennessy (eds), *The Operational Art: Developments in the Theories of War* (Westport, 1996), 175.
19. Jan Nederveen Pieterse, *Globalization or Empire?* (New York, 2004), 21–2.
20. Richard M. Auty, *Sustaining Development in Mineral Economies: The Resource Curse Thesis* (New York, 1993), 1–7.
21. Bernard Lewis, *The Arabs in History*, new ed. (Oxford, 1950, 1993), 191.
22. See M. M. Salehi, *Insurgency through Culture and Religion: The Islamic Revolution of Iran* (New York, 1988), 18–20, 163.
23. Quoted in Bernard Lewis, *Islam in History*, rev. ed. (Chicago, 1993), 403.
24. Jason Burke, *Al-Qaeda: The True Story of Radical Islam* (London, 2003, 2004), 265.
25. John Kampfner, *Blair's Wars* (London, 2004), 50–3.
26. Andrew J. Bracevich, *The New American Militarism* (Oxford, 2005), 202–3.
27. Peter Singer, *The President of Good and Evil: Taking George W. Bush Seriously* (London, 2004), 179.
28. Patrick Cockburn, *The Resistance: War and Resistance in Iraq* (London, 2006, 2007), 36.
29. DoD News Briefing-Secretary Rumsfeld and Gen. Myers, 11 April 2003, http://www.defense.gov/Transcripts/Transcript.aspx?TranscriptID=2367.
30. Remarks by the President at the 20th Anniversary of the National Endowment for Democracy, United States Chamber of Commerce, 6 November 2003, http://www.whitehouse.gov/news/releases/2003/11/20031106-2.html.
31. frontpagemag.com (21 April 2004).
32. Michael Mandelbaum, *The Case for Goliath: How America Acts as the World's Government in the 21st Century* (New York, 2005), 86.
33. Robert Kagan, *Paradise and Power: America and Europe in the New World Order* (London, 2003), 73.
34. Michael Ignatieff, 'The American Empire: The Burden', reprinted in Ó Tuathail et al. (eds), *Geopolitics Reader*, 155–6.
35. David Frum and Richard Perle, *An End to Evil: How to Win the War on Terror* (New York, 2003), 119–20.
36. Thomas S. Nye, Jr., *Soft Power: The Means to Success in World Politics* (New York, 2004), 139.
37. Quoted in William Blum, *Killing Hope: US Military and CIA Interventions since World War II* (London, 2003), 384.
38. Niall Ferguson, *Colossus: The Rise and Fall of the American Empire* (London, 2004, 2005), 26.
39. John Rees, *Imperialism and Resistance* (London, 2006), 231.
40. Christopher Hitchens, 'The Hitchens-Pollitt Papers', *Nation*, 6 December 2002, in Simon Cottee and Thomas Cushman (eds), *Christopher Hitchens and his Critics: Terror, Iraq and the Left* (New York, 2008), 214.
41. Michael Walzer, 'Can There be a Decent Left?', in *Dissent*, Spring 2002.
42. Paul Berman, 'The Twilight of Tyrants and the Promise of Liberal Revolution', 13 April 2003, http://www.boston.com/news/packages/iraq/globe_stories/041303_ideas.htm.
43. Paul Berman, *Terror and Liberalism* (New York, 2003, 2004), 189, 191.
44. Jonathan Rée, 'Ethical Correctness and the Decline of the Left', in Thomas Cushman (ed.), *A Matter of Principle: Humanitarian Arguments for War in Iraq* (Berkeley, 2005), 189.

45. 'Bush Pledges to Spread Freedom', *Washington Post*, 21 January 2005.
46. Translated by Vladyslav Kostyuk, 1 May 2006, http://www2.pravda.com.ua/en/news/2006/5/12/5176.htm.
47. Christopher Hitchens, 'It's a Good Time for War' [8 September 2002], in Cottee and Cushman (eds), *Hitchens and his Critics*, 66.
48. Ivo. H. Daalder and James M. Lindsay, *America Unbound: The Bush Revolution in Foreign Policy* (Hoboken, 2003, 2005), 172. Cf. Neil Smith, *The Endgame of Globalization* (New York, 2005), 181.
49. George Packer, *The Assassins' Gate: America in Iraq* (London, 2005, 2006, 2007), 215.
50. Juan Cole, *Engaging the Muslim World* (New York, 2009), 146.
51. 'Address of the Secretary of State Condeleeza Rise at the American University in Cairo' [20 June 2005], *Congressional Record*, 14415.
52. David Shelby, 'Rice Sees Struggle of Extremism, Moderation in Middle East', *America.gov*, 26 September 2006, http://www.america.gov/st/washfile-english/2006/September/20060926174856ndyblehs0.3814356.html.
53. http://www.whitehouse.gov/the_press_office/Remarks-by-the-President-to-the-United-Nations-General-Assembly.
54. Joel Beinin, 'What Have Workers Gained from Egypt's Revolution?', in *Foreign Policy*, 20 July 2011.
55. See Vali Nasr, 'The Rise of "Muslim Democracy"', in *Journal of Democracy*, 16.2 (2005) 13–27.
56. Larry Elliott and Dan Atkinson, *The Gods that Failed: How the Financial Elite Have Gambled Away our Future* (London, 2009), 233.
57. Cited in Oskar Lafontaine, *The Heart Beats on the Left*, trans. Ronald Taylor (Cambridge, 2000), 182.
58. Julian Le Grand, *The Other Invisible Hand: Delivering Public Services Through Choice and Competition* (Princeton, 2007), 41.
59. Ibid., 41.
60. Simon Jenkins, *Thatcher and Sons: A Revolution in Three Parts* (London, 2007, 2007), 260–2.
61. 'Fact Sheet: Compassionate Conservatism', 30 April 2002, http://georgewbush-whitehouse.archives.gov/news/releases/2002/04/20020430.html.
62. Richard Nadler, 'Asset Accumulation for the Poor? A View From the Right', *Center for Social Development*, September 2000, http://csd.wustl.edu/Publications/Documents/55.AssetAccumulationForThePoor.pdf, 2.
63. Charles S. Maier, *Among Empires: American Ascendancy and its Predecessors* (Cambridge, MA, 2006), 255.
64. Gillian Tett, *Fool's Gold: How Unrestrained Greed Corrupted a Dream, Shattered Global Markets and Unleashed a Catastrophe* (London, 2009), 36.
65. David Oakley and Peter Garnham, 'Pros and Cons of Austerity Packages Occupy G20', *Financial Times*, 29 June 2010.
66. Kate Zernike and Megan Thee-Brenan, 'Poll Finds Tea Party Backers Wealthier and More Educated', *The New York Times*, 14 April 2010.
67. David M. Halbfinger and Michael Barbaro, 'Paladino Rout of Lazio Jolts New York G.O.', *New York Times*, 14 September 2010.
68. David Cameron, 'Have no Doubt: The Big Society is on its Way', *The Guardian*, 12 February 2011.
69. Karl Marx, *The Civil War in France*, 1871, *MECW*, vol. 22, 335.

## CONCLUSIONS

1. Bruce Waller, 'Steam: Revolution in Warfare and the Economy', in Waller (ed.), *Themes in Modern European History*, 236.
2. Salazar, 'State and Regimes', document in Delzell (ed.), *Mediterranean Fascism*, 334.
3. Poll on 'just desserts' in Will Hutton, *Them and Us: Politics Greed and Inequality* (London, 2010), 64. Frank and Cook, *Winner Takes all Society*. Richard Wilkinson and Kate Pickett, *The Spirit Level: Why Equality is Better for Everyone* (London, 2010).
4. Jürgen Kocka, 'The Middle Classes in Europe', *The Journal of Modern History*, vol. 67, no. 4, (1995), 804.
5. 'Afterword', in Barbara Ehrenreich, *Nickel and Dimed: On (Not) Getting By in America*, 10th Anniversary Edition (New York, 2011). Owen Jones, *Chavs: The Demonization of the Working Class* (London, 2011).
6. Paul Mason, *Live Working, Die Fighting: How the Working Class Went Global* (London, 2007), 280–2.
7. Tom Hampson and Jemima Olchawski (eds), *Is Equality Fair?* (London, 2009), 9, 43.
8. Michael Lind, 'Conservative Elites and the Counter-Revolution against the New Deal', in Steve Fraser and Gary Gerstle (eds), *Ruling America: A History of Wealth and Power in a Democracy* (Cambridge, MA, 2005), 262.

# Bibliographical Essay

The concept of 'bourgeois revolution' was first developed by Karl Marx. It was never more than rather sketchy. Mostly, it was used by Marx when talking about 'historic' revolutions, widely considered to be implicated in the rise of a market-based modernity, most particularly the French Revolution of 1789, but also the English Civil Wars of the 1640s and Glorious Revolution of 1688. When late nineteenth-century socialists began constructing a theory of 'Historical Materialism' out of Marx's vast corpus, they latched upon 'bourgeois revolution' as a warrant for their own projected 'proletarian revolution'. In so doing, they were to a great extent applying new labels to old bottles. A seemingly inexorable sweep of parliamentary constitutionalism across Europe had displaced almost everywhere the claims of absolutist monarchism. All shades of political opinion, from reactionary to radical-liberal, agreed that this represented a triumph for the market economy and the class most spectacularly enriched and empowered by the market, the middle class or bourgeoisie. The specificity of socialist claims was mostly in their enthusiasm to identify a ruptural remodelling of the state as being central to this process. In so doing, they were defiantly retorting *tu quoque* in the face of their establishment critics.

Leninism placed the progressive role of capitalism, and thus 'bourgeois revolution', firmly in the past, and for Communists into the 1920s, past revolutions were mostly of interest as object lessons in the tactical repertoire of seizing and holding power. For Communists the working class and its militant representatives were justified by historical teleology in exercising a 'dictatorship' over the rest of society. Projecting back in history, in like fashion, 'bourgeois revolution' was conceived of as entirely bourgeois vanguards seizing the state so as to create the conditions for capitalist development. By the mid-1930s, Communists had adopted a new strategy of 'popular frontism'. This had its impact upon developing notions of 'bourgeois revolution'. It was, indeed, a combination of classical Leninism and popular-frontist pan-class 'people's history' that informed the first tentative advances by Communist intellectual cadres into academic historiography. Historic revolutions were conceived of as 'bourgeois democratic' in impetus. In clearing a path to modernity they allowed for an unfolding by stages of the popular 'democratic' potential of the revolution, eventuating in widespread suffrage and welfarism. By the 1950s, this Communist-inspired Marxist characterization of the British Civil Wars, French Revolution, and (to a greater or lesser degree) various other historical events, such as the Netherlands' struggle for independence from Spain, or the American Revolution, had won impressive authority in the academies, and indeed amongst wider publics. The attractiveness of the model lay in its teleology of modernity, with healthy bourgeois revolutions leading to stable welfarist democracies. Fascisms and even Communist dictatorships could be explained as pathologies deriving from historic miscarriages of bourgeois revolution, rather than phenomena implicating the modernist project itself. Representative writers in this tradition include Christopher Hill for England, Georges Lefebvre and Albert Soboul for France.

Given the difficulty of anatomizing the means by which past generations made a living, and the lack of precision in defining 'bourgeois' lifestyles in economies still largely rural, it took some time for it to become clear that supporters of revolution in England in the 1630s and 1640s, or France in the 1780s and 1790s, were by no means distinctively 'capitalist' in their interests in contrast to their opponents. Very roughly, it came to be admitted that while the English Civil War era had a role in promoting capitalism, it was not itself led in any meaningful sense by a bourgeoisie. In eighteenth-century France, both supporters and opponents of the Revolution had bourgeois interests in varying proportions, but the Revolution itself, in consolidating small-scale farming, perhaps hindered French capitalism more than it helped its development. Decisive victory at the dawn of democratic evolution for any national bourgeoisie over its *ancien regime* was increasingly recognized as the exception rather than the rule, if it happened anywhere.

More generally, the teleology implied in the narrative of 'bourgeois democratic revolution' was contested. The implied trajectory of democracy displacing bourgeois-specific class interests over time, resulting in welfarism and a compact between capital and labour, had much less heuristic power by the 1980s. Neo-liberal conservatives were rolling back the power of organized labour. In so doing, they substantially redefined democracy not as a balancing of class interests, but rather as the sovereignty of the consumer in an unfettered market environment. Reading back, it made a great deal of sense to present the emergence in germ of this modernity not as a product of class struggle, but rather as a struggle between the inherent economic rationality of acquisitive individuals on the one hand, and the politically and culturally constituted privilege of corporate elites on the other. The historical great revolutions tended to bolster state power, as Alexis de Tocqueville had insistently explained in the nineteenth century. Even worse, they promoted new corporate identifies (such as nationalism, or anti-market leftism). This did not segue well with the neo-liberal teleology whereby the natural instincts of individuals to trade and barter are emancipated. The great revolutions, therefore, lost their status as unambiguous jumping-off points for modernity. By the 1990s and early twenty-first century it was not so much that the notion of 'bourgeois revolution' had been abandoned. Rather, it had been (largely) scrubbed from the past only to be inscribed onto the present. Either explicitly or implicitly, neo-liberals and neo-conservatives saw the triumph of free-market democracy over statist alternatives as the first, true 'bourgeois revolution'.

This book can't claim to succeed Perry Anderson's masterful volumes, *Passages from Antiquity to Feudalism* and *Lineages of the Absolutist State* (both 1974), which survey and incisively analyse the sweep of class society to the nineteenth century. But they stand as inspirational forebears.

I seek, of course, to re-establish class as a central category. The themes of this book relate to the ongoing debate on the rise of capitalism, but only tangentially. Overviews of the debate I found useful for framing purposes included William A. Green, *History, Historians, and the Dynamics of Change* (1993), and the chapter on 'Commerce' by Kenneth Pomeranz in Ulinka Rublack (ed), *A Concise Companion to History* (2011). For an important discussion of the tenacity of the pre-capitalist economy, see Chris Wickham, 'Productive Forces and the Economic Logic of the Feudal Mode of Production', in *Historical Materialism*, vol. 16, no. 2 (2008).

Most historical studies of the bourgeoisie anatomize its culture and the perhaps brittle psychology of its members. Important as these issues are, they do not bulk large in the current volume. Influential works on these themes includes that by Peter Gay, *The Bourgeois Experience: Victoria to Freud* (1984–98), in five volumes. Emphasizing the economic and moral cogency of the class are Deirdre N. McCloskey's works, *The Bourgeois Virtues* (2006) and *Bourgeois Dignity* (2010).

Eric Hobsbawm's classic four volumes, *Age of Revolution* (1962), *Age of Capital* (1975), *Age of Empire* (1987), and *Age of Extremes* (1994), cover almost the entire period, from the French Revolution to the collapse of Communism, with steadily diminishing focus on the bourgeoisie. For the USA, I used as a guide the multi-authored volume by John M. Murrin, Paul E. Johnson, James M. McPherson, Gary Gerstle, Emily S. Rosenberg, and Norman

L. Rosenberg, *Liberty, Equality, Power: A History of the American People* (1996, 2007). Peter N. Stearns and Herrick Chapman, *European Society in Upheaval: Social History Since 1750*, third edition (1992), was supplemented by the six volumes of Peter N. Stearns (ed.), *Encyclopedia of European Social History from 1350 to 2000* (2001).

Concentration on constitutional and political history is unfashionable. The overview I found most useful for the nineteenth century was first published in 1898: Charles Seignobos, *A Political History of Europe, since 1814*, trans. S. M. Macvane (1900), updated as *Histoire Politique de L'Europe Contemporaine: Évolution des Partis et des Formes Politiques, 1814–1914* (1924). Seignobos eschewed any teleology, ascribing the rise of constitutionalism to adventitious events. More up-to-date surveys of nineteenth-century Europe are M. S. Anderson, *The Ascendancy of Europe, 1815–1914* (1972, 1985, 2003) and Robert Gildea, *Barricades and Borders: Europe, 1900–1914* (1987, 1996, 2003). Theodore S. Hamerow, *The Birth of a New Europe: State and Society in the Nineteenth Century* (1983) is crammed with information. Boldly transnational is C. A. Bayley's *The Birth of the Modern World, 1780–1914* (2004). Sandra Halperin's *War and Social Change in Modern Europe: The Great Transformation Re-visited* (2004) presents a challenging overview emphasizing both state violence and the salience of class (though rather differently than I). A recent interesting addition is Immanuel Wallerstein, *Centrist Liberalism Triumphant, 1789–1914* (2011), which argues that liberalism developed as the 'geo-culture' of the capitalist 'world-system'.

For the twentieth century, the focus shifts increasingly to the global stage. The joint production by Antony Best, Jussi M. Hanhimäki, Joseph A. Maiolo, and Kirsten E. Schulze, *International History of the Twentieth Century [and Beyond]* (2004, 2008) is a wonderfully cutting-edge and incisive survey. William R. Keylor's *The Twentieth-Century World: An International History*, 3rd edition (1996), artfully combines analysis and narrative. An excellent overview of the economy in this period, covering both capitalism and Communism, is Ivan T. Berend, *An Economic History of Twentieth-Century Europe: Economic Regimes from Laissez-Faire to Globalization* (2006). On the totalitarian regimes, Richard Overy's *The Dictators: Hitler's Germany and Stalin's Russia* (2004) is outstanding, as is Richard J. Evans' trilogy on the *Third Reich* (2003, 2005, 2008). Tony Judt, *Postwar: A History of Europe Since 1945* (2005) is a work of engaged narrative. The number of books on neo-conservatism are ever growing in number. James Mann's *Rise of the Vulcans* (2004) is probably still the stand-out volume.

Niall Ferguson's path-breaking studies have done much to revive intelligent anatomization of the interaction of politics and economics in this period. I particularly drew upon his book *The Cash Nexus: Money and Power in the Modern World, 1700–2000* (2001, 2002). James Macdonald offers a similar analysis, emphasizing the fiscal basis of constitutionalism, in *A Free Nation Deep in Debt: The Financial Roots of Democracy* (2003, 2006). Carolyn Webber and Aaron Wildavsky's *A History of Taxation and Expenditure in the Western World* (1986) remains very useful.

For discussions of socialism, I employed G. D. H Cole's *History of Socialist Thought, 1789–1939* (1953–60), in five volumes. Despite its title, this is a survey of socialist parties in action, from a broadly 'centrist' point of view (in the sense of the 'Vienna International'). Indispensable complements were Donald Sassoon, *One Hundred Years of Socialism: The West European Left in the Twentieth Century* (1996), and Geoff Eley, *Forging Democracy: The History of the Left in Europe, 1850–2000* (2002). Other key works were Julius Braunthal's three- volume *History of the International* (1966–1971) and Gary P. Steenson's *After Marx, Before Lenin: Marxism and Socialist Working-Class Parties in Europe, 1884–1914* (1991). Mike Macnair's *Revolutionary Strategy: Marxism and the Challenge of Left Unity* (2008) is full of perceptive and informed commentary.

Marx and Engels' political thought is entertainingly and exhaustively excerpted and discussed in Hal Draper's *Karl Marx's Theory of Revolution* (1977–2005). Excellent guides to developments in Marxist thought are by David McClellan, *Marxism after Marx* (2007), and Jules Townshend, *The Politics of Marxism: The Critical Debates* (1996). Reidar Larsson's *Theories of Revolution: From Marx to the First Russian Revolution* (1970) is invaluable.

There is, oddly, no real equivalent to Cole's magisterial survey for liberalism (though E. K. Bramsted and K. J. Melhuish (eds), *Western Liberalism. A History in Documents* (London, 1978) should be mentioned). Guido de Ruggiero's *The History of European Liberalism*, trans. R. G. Collingwood (1925, 1959), is still very useful. Anthony Arblaster's *The Rise and Decline of Western Liberalism* (1984) is an exposé of liberal hypocrisy; Luciano Canfora's *Democracy in Europe* (2006) and Domenico Losurdo's *Liberalism: a Counter-History* (2011) are polemically hostile to their subject. The sections on liberalism in the 'Rise of Modern Europe' series of books by various authors, edited over decades of the twentieth century by William L. Langer, fit together very well. I particularly used Frederick B. Artz, *Reaction and Revolution, 1814–1832* (1934), William L. Langer, *Political and Social Upheaval, 1832–1852* (1969), Robert C. Binkley, *Realism and Nationalism, 1852–1871* (1935), Carlton J. H. Hayes, *A Generation of Materialism* (1963), and Oron J. Hale, *The Great Illusion, 1900–1914* (1971). For the nineteenth century, I made much use of Pamela M. Pilbeam's *The Middle Classes in Europe, 1789–1914: France, Germany, Italy and Russia* (1990), and Jürgen Kocka and Allan Mitchell (eds), *Bourgeois Society in Nineteenth-Century Europe* (1993). There is no similar overview for the twentieth century, but Terence Ball and Richard Bellamy (eds), *The Cambridge History of Twentieth-Century Political Thought* (2003), contains many relevant essays. Graeme Gill's *Bourgeoisie, State, and Democracy: Russia, Britain, France, and the USA* (2008) presents a striking political science account.

# Index

9/11 attacks 284–5
26 July Movement, Cuba 232
1905 Revolution in Russia 144, 146
1917 Revolution in Russia 158–61, 173, 222, 300
   fear of red menace 12
   Mao on 205
   opens as bourgeois revolution 158
   and Provisional Government 159
1944–1946 popular purge of permanent state 216

absolutism 12, 15, 50, 66
   able to suppress revolution 79
   and aristocracy 303
   and Austria 51
   Bismarck on 99
   and Carlism 58
   and Charles II (England) 21
   and commercialism 18, 26, 33, 298
   David Hume on 26
   of democrats 101
   Droysen on 101
   exploits commercialism 50
   and fiscal weakness 50
   and the Habsburg Empire 50
   and Hungary 50
   inhibits bourgeois civil society 18, 26, 33
   lacks fiscal strength 50
   Lassalle on 100
   and liberalism 60, 130
   limits of 17
   no longer possible 99–100
   Luxemburg on 143
   and Napoleon Bonaparte 299
   re-framed 299
   and revolution 68, 75, 79, 303
   and Russia 122
   and taxation 15
   transcendence of 60
   tsarist 122
   undermined by commercialism 50
   weakness of 58
academics 41, 216, 240
accidentalism, Catholic 200
Adler, Max 195
Afghanistan, liberation of 307
Afghanistan, Russian occupation 267, 284
Afghanistan, Taliban regime overthrown 285
Afghanistan, US support for mujahadeen 279
Afghanistan, US withdrawal 290
Africa 273
   decolonization 23, 229
   democratic revolution 274, 280, 286
   war and genocide (1990s) 274
African National Congress (ANC) 272–3
Agency for International Development (AID) 280
Al-Qaeda 284
Albania 246
Albert (Alexandre Martin) 70
Alexander, Gregory S. 86
Algeria 52, 274, 284
Allemanists, France 125
Allen, Robert 24
Allende, Salvador (Chile) 248, 250
Alliance for Progress (1961) 233
Alsace 40, 117
American Civil War (1861–1865) 85–6, 130
American Enterprise Institute 287
American United Auto Workers 220
American Way of Life, the 218
Americas 13, 20, 49, 231
Ames, Fisher 47
anarchism
   and anti-clericalism 305
   and Bakunin 123
   and bourgeois civil society 124
   in Catalonia 124
   and Comintern 169
   France 124, 127
   Iberia 124
   and Marxist 'centre' 129
   and parliamentarianism 134
   and peasantry 10
   and Popular Front 200–1
   in Spain 200
   and universal suffrage 110
anarchists 162
   Bakunin 110
   and Comintern 169
   and Second International 128
   and Spain 139, 168, 202
ANC see African National Congress (ANC)
ANC (African National Congress) 272–3
Andalusia, Spain 18
Anderson, Perry 252
Andrássy, Count Gyula 87
Andrian-Werburg, Victor von 50
Angell, Norman 150
Angola 250, 279
Anne, Queen of Great Britain 22
Anschluss (1938) 210
anti-Catholicism 305

anti-clericalism 138
Anti-Corn Law League 63, 82
anti-imperialism 206, 223, 231, 288
anti-militarism 117, 234
anti-parliamentarianism 124, 169, 244
anti-Semitism 138–9, 187–8, 283
anti-socialist laws, Germany (1878) 125
anti-war movement 239, 289
apartheid 272–3
apparat, Communist 260–1
April Theses (Lenin, 1917) 159
Arab nationalism 282
Arab Spring (2011) 291
Aragon, Spain 16, 58
Arbeiterbildungsvereine, Germany 107
Arbenz, Jacobo Guzmán 231
Arbenz Guzmán, Jacobo (Guatemala) 231
Arcadiens, France 90
Ardennes 40
ARENA party, El Salvador 279
Arendt, Hannah 214
aristocracy
　absent in united States 218
　and absolutism 17, 303
　accomodates with Crown (England) 25
　advances bourgeois civil society 31, 298
　attacked 11
　Austrian 87
　Belgian 126
　bourgeoisfied 66
　British 18, 21, 24–5, 44, 48, 64
　　commerce emancipated from 303
　Cobden on 83
　compromises with executive 24
　consults with executive 29
　continental Europe 23, 50
　cooperates with executive 38–9
　discreited by 1848 Revolutions 86
　displaced by civil service 74–5, 77–8
　economic decline of 113
　entangles with big business 114, 119–20
　and the executive state 297
　fails as governing class 51
　French 299
　Froude on 119
　governing elite 28, 119
　and Great Reform Act (1832) 48
　Guizot on 55, 65
　Hobsbawm on 2
　Italian 94
　Japanese 114
　leads England 24–5, 64
　legitimizing the state 11
　liberal 11, 68
　loses prestige 120
　at low ebb, C17th England 21
　Marx and Engels on 67

　mode of existence 10, 57
　Ostrogorski on 137
　in place of civil service 11, 17, 50, 69
　and political arts 56
　and Poor Law (England) 18
　Prussian 97
　Russian 182
　Schumpeter on 149
　struggles with executive 16–17, 51
　threat of industrialization (England) 44
　under-represented in industrialization 40
aristocrats 14, 83, 112; *see also* aristocracy
　and 1848 Revolutions 78
　and Britain 64, 67, 83
　and constitutionalism 297
　entangled with big business 114
　entrepreneurship 13
　and French Revolution 34, 38
　German 117, 120
　Italian 92
　and liberal historiography 42
　and money-lenders 15
armaments industry 116, 235
Armed Forces Movement (MFA), Portugal 250
Armstrong, Philip 220
artillery 72, 116, 130, 139, 146–7, 212; *see also*
　　barricades
artisans
　in Britain 18, 45–6, 62
　Calvin on 15
　and French Revolution 35
　in Germany 101
　imaginaire of 8
　and journeymen 41
　Kautsky on 128
　Kennan on 227
　Ostrogorski on 137
　and the proletariat 41
　size 14
　and the workers' movement 80
Ascher, Abraham 145
Asian Communism 238
Asquith, H. H., British PM 154
assets 7, 14, 293, 298, 304
Asturias, Spain 201
Atlantic Charter (1941) 213
Ausgleich (1867) 87
Australia 151
Austria 185–6
　and absolutism 50–1
　bureaucratic absolutism 86–8
　counter-revolutionary 36
　and Crimean War 95
　and democracy 164
　emergency rule 152
　and France 91
　'historic rights' constitutionalism 88, 108

and Holy Alliance 53
and Italy 69, 73–4, 80, 82, 85, 92–4
and Metternich 40
and Prussia 85, 90, 97, 99, 101–2
and socialism 125, 128, 156, 167, 181
Austria, Ausgleich (1867) 87
Austria, Engels on 77
Austria-Hungary 87, 126
autarchy 208, 214, 280
authoritarian state 303
    and Castroism 233
    Engels on 106
    German 190
    Lenin on 166
    Marxist 'centre' on 142
    and worker movement 147
authoritarianism 2–3, 157, 185, 233, 302, 304–5
    Anderson on 252
    bourgeois accommodation with 109
    and civil society 230
    classical liberals attracted by 174
    and Cold War 230, 236
    and Colour Revolutions 288
    and developing world 302
    and EEC 251
    and Mediterranean Revolutions 252
    and Middle East 302
    and militarism 154, 211
    and New Left 244
    and Popular frontism 203
    and 'resource curse' 282
    socialist sympathy for 126
    and standing armies 117
auto-revolution 164
autocracy 50, 99, 145, 147, 304
'axis of evil' 285
Axis Powers 212

Ba'ath Party, Iraq 289
Babeuf, Gracchus 36–7, 56, 61
Baden, Germany 72, 99, 141
Bagehot, Walter 64
Baghdad 289
Bakunin, Michael 110, 123
Baldwin, Stanley, PM 207–8
Balfour, Arthur, British PM 127
Balkans 53, 118, 186, 193, 301
ballot box 70–1, 199
Baltic States 165, 269
Bangladesh 291
banks 179, 295
    and Austria 87
    and cartels 118
    and Great Recession (2008) 294
    and Great Reform Act (1832) 46
    Hilferding on 151

Peel on 44
and Portugal 250
and Russia 122, 145
and South Africa 272
Baran, Paul 240
Barcelona 124, 139, 202
Baring, Thomas 75
Barker, Rodney 257
Baron Beyens 117
barricades 131; see also artillery
    and 1848 Revolutions 57, 72
    in Belgium 53
    in France 89
    and Marxist 'centre' 129
    professeurs of 125
Barrow, Steve 294
Basque country 58, 202
Bastiat, Frédéric 115
Bates, Robert H. 274
Batista, Fulgencio 232
Battle of Novara (1849) 73
Bavaria, Germany 99, 103, 167, 176
Bay of Pigs, invasion of, 1961 (Cuba) 232
Bebel, August 107, 143, 150
Beckett, Andy 249
Beijing 263
Belgian Labour Party 125; see also Parti Ouvrier Belge
Belgian Socialists 141
Belgian Socialists and Liberals 12, 37–8, 143, 306
Belgium
    1830 Revolution 53
    anarchism in 124
    and Catholicism 68, 137–8
    and China 54
    and Communism 223
    and the Congo 231
    industrialization in 39
    and socialism 123, 126, 167
    suffrage in 135, 140
Bell, Daniel 247
Ben Ali, Zine El Abidine (Tunisia) 290
Beneš, Edvard 209
Bentham, Jeremy 25
Berkeley University 224, 240, 270
Berlin 144, 156, 164
    and 1848 Revolutions 69, 71, 75
    1953 Rising 261
    and Sparticists 176
Berlin Wall 261, 268, 280, 291
Berman, Paul 288
Bernhardi, Friedrich von 117
Bernstein, Eduard 142–4
Berufsbeamtengesetz (1933) 190
Best, Geoffrey 52
betrayal 77, 97, 105, 108, 112, 189

biennio rosso, Spain (1919–1920) 168
big business 141, 214, 235, 244, 255
  and anti-Semitism 139
  Arendt on 214
  and aristocracy 114, 300
  and China 271
  and corporatism 172, 212, 254, 259, 300
  Eisenhower on 236
  and Eurocommunism 226
  and Japan 204
  and Nazi regime 191
  and New Left 244
  O'Connor on 246
  and socialism 126
  and Weimar Republic 176, 179
Big Society 295
Birla, G. D., India 229
Birmingham 45–6
Bismarck, Otto von 149
  and anti-socialist laws 125
  appointed to 'fighting ministry' 99, 153
  and army reorganization 99
  Bernhardi on 117
  Burkhardt on 103
  and constitutional struggle
    (1861–1866) 99–101
  Engels on 108
  and German unification 101, 299
  and Kulturkampf 138
  and Lassalle 107
  and liberalism 102, 121
  and Lückentheorie 100
  and Napoleon III 90, 102, 108
  and National Liberals 102
  and protectionism 121
  and universal suffrage 102, 107
black liberation movement 273
Blackbourn, David 102
Blair, Tony, British PM 65–6, 70, 78, 285, 293
Blanc, Louis 65–6, 70
Blanc, Louis, Marx on 78
Blanqui, Louis Auguste 65
Bleichröder, Gerson 101
Blitzkrieg 211
Blomberg, Werner Eduard Fritz von 192
Blum, Jerome 17
Blum, Léon 199–200
Bobbitt, Philip 275
body armour 281
Boer War (1899–1902) 117
Bohemia 16, 101
Bolshevik Revolution 169, 171
Bolsheviks 184
  and 1917 Revolution 160–2, 304
  and Brest Litovsk 163
  and Civil War 162–3, 166
  and mixed economy 162, 170
  and peasantry 139
Bolsheviks, Toynbee on 277–8
Bolsheviks, Trotsky on 155
Bolshevism 171, 173, 183, 243
Bombay 228
Bonald, Louis Gabriel Ambroise 28
bonds 31, 56, 80, 89, 118
Bosch, Juan 234
Bosnia 284
Bossuet, Jacques-Bénigne 26
Boudin, Louis 144
Boulanger, General George 116–17, 122
Bourdieu, Pierre 7
bourgeois, petite 184, 300
bourgeois betrayal 75, 77, 96, 302
bourgeois bohemians 296
bourgeois civil society 7, 9, 220, 293; see also
  civil society
bourgeois constitutionalism 68, 77, 121
bourgeois constitutionalist revolution 101, 130, 173
bourgeois democracy
  and '68 301
  and EEC 253
  Lenin's dismissal of 171
  and Popular Frontism 198, 201–2
  and South Africa 273
  Togliatti on 225
bourgeois-democratic revolution 148, 202, 204, 263
bourgeois habitus 7
bourgeois interests 167, 306
  and constitutionalism 30, 55
  and Gladstonian liberalism 84
  and militarism 241
  and Mussolini 180
  and proletarian democracy 306
  and reformism 144
  and the Weimar Republic 178
bourgeois liberalism 12
  and Catholicism 68
  and Communism 164
  decline of 144, 152
  and France 110
  Jaurès on 143
  Lenin on 147
  and liberalism vii
  and the Marxist 'centre' 142
  parabola of 304
  and Popular Front in France 200
  and Prussia 97
  and socialism 143
  survival of 195
  and the worker movement 128
bourgeois liberals 123, 131, 174, 202, 301
bourgeois liberties 177, 262

## Index

bourgeois liberty 13, 57, 121, 209, 299, 301
  and the Arab World 282
  and Dreyfus Affair 140
  and Eurocommunism 250
  and the First World War 155
  and German socialists 108
  and the Great Depression 214
  hostility to socialism 112
  and Leninism 158
  and proletarian democracy 174, 308
  and reaction 305
bourgeois order 8, 181, 270, 303, 306
bourgeois parties 140, 190, 195
bourgeois property 35, 57, 63
bourgeois property norms 37, 298
bourgeois revolution 12, 197, 307
  age of 275
  archetypal 97
  in China 203, 206
  climax 68
  contemporaneous 104
  definition of 30–1
  failed 283
  fascist 180
  heroic age 13
  Hobsbawm on 2
  in India 275
  Lenin on 158–9
  Marx and Engels on 66–8, 75, 78, 106
  in Middle East 282
  modern 286
  and neo-conservativism 287–9, 296
  in Prussia 97
  in Russia 144–5, 158, 270
  and Second International 128, 134
  Trotsky on 148, 162
  unwitting 32
bourgeois rights 8, 34, 266
bourgeois society
  and 1858 Revolutions 11
  and American Civil War 86
  Bernstein on 142
  and Britain 13, 24
  Daniel Bell on 247
  Fukuyama on 276
  Kristol on 278
  Luxemburg on 143
  Marx on 4
  and Prussia 66, 100
bourgeois vitality 284
bourgeois wealth franchise 53
bourgeoisie vii, 1–2, 4–5, 105–6, 108, 135, 165, 182; *see also* middle classes
  and 1905 Revolution 146
  Adler on 195
  American 218
  Angell on 150
  and anti-Semitism 211
  Arendt on 214
  and authoritarianism 282, 303
  Bakunin on 123
  Bernstein on 142
  in Britain and US 206
  in buffer states 223
  capitalist 31, 33, 163
  and Castroism 233
  Chinese 206, 266
  and Chinese Communism 205, 264
  closed group 40
  Comintern dismisses 197
  commercial 29, 34, 81
  and constitutionalism 209, 306
  Crosland on 219
  crushed 300–1
  De Vaux on 42
  decline of its liberalism 134, 136
  defined vii, 3–7, 40, 304
  destiny 13, 299, 303, 308
  disarming of 169
  dispossessed 162
  Doctrinaires on 57
  and Dreyfus Affair 139
  emerging 298
  Engels on 104–6, 108–9
  entangled with aristocracy 120
  entrepreneurial 3, 38
  and Eurocommunism 250
  excluded from soviets 161
  fearful of revolution 157, 160, 185, 303–4
  French 48, 56, 59, 75, 298
  and French Revolution 36
  and German socialists 108
  Gervinus on 79
  global 275
  in Gotha Programme 124
  Gramsci on 95
  Guizot on 55–6
  haunted by spectre of communism 109
  Hegel on 42
  Heine on 2
  Hilferding on 151
  inability to govern 108–9
  Indian 275
  industrial 146, 159, 251
  and intelligentsia 261, 269–70
  interest in common with proletariat 9
  Iranian 283
  Irish 168
  Italian 74, 94
  Japanese 114
  and Karl Lueger 139
  Kautsky on 142
  leaders of 40
  Lenin on 147, 156–7, 159–60

bourgeoisie (*cont.*)
  liberal 101–2, 108, 139, 142, 147, 155, 158–9, 162, 181
  in liberal historiography 42
  and liberalism 299–300, 303
  Lloyd George on 171
  Luxemburg on 143
  Mao on 204
  Marx and Engels on 78, 111–12, 149
  Marx on 4–5, 67, 78, 124
  Mayer on 119
  and Mediterranean Revolutions 252–3
  and meritocracy 9
  Michels on 1
  military as proxy for 230
  modern 151, 234
  Muslim 282
  Mussolini on 186–7
  myth of 55
  and Napoleon III 89
  national 203, 205
  and Nazi 'revolution' 191
  new 272
  nexus with state 31
  and oligarchy 31, 143, 299–300
  Ostrogorski on 137
  and Paris Commune 111, 128
  and party politics 306
  and Popular Front 198, 209
  prefers authoritarianism 160
  professional 120, 160
  progressive 157, 197–8, 204, 209
  Prussian 102, 104–6, 108–9
  Renner on 141
  and Restoration Europe 42
  and revisionism 300
  Russian 122, 147
  Scandinavian 152
  Second International on 130
  size 6, 14
  small 122, 176
  Social Democracy on 170
  Sorel on 119
  Stalin on 167, 224
  Stalinist fear of 197
  and state capitalism 162
  strength of 105–6, 109
  and tax-strike 57, 132
  in Third World 228–9, 231
  Tillich on 189
  timid 307
  Trotsky on 2, 148
  turns to authoritarianism 195
  turns to fascism 180
  upper 77, 114, 120
  and vanguard 307
  violence against 163–5, 167
Von Bülow on 120
Weber on 5, 136, 142, 145
  in Weimar Republic 188
  Wilhelm Liebknecht on 129, 142
Boyce, Robert 185
Brandt, Willy 175
Braunthal, Julius 168
Brazil 234, 274–5
Bremer, L. Paul 289
Brest-Litovsk, Treaty of (1918) 163
Bretton Woods 218
Breuilly, John 102
Brezhnev, Leonid 260–1, 267
BRIC countries 275
Briefs, Göetz 173
Bright, John 82–4
Britain 85, 117, 245
  absence of reaction 83
  and absolutism 21
  and appeasement 210
  and cartels 118
  and Chartism 299
  and China 54, 82
  and the Congo 231
  and constitutionalism 18
  and consumerism 207
  and Crimean War 82
  and the dictatorships 210
  domestic involution 84
  economic might 113
  and empire 209
  factory workers 41
  and First World war 154
  fiscal state 38
  and free trade 5, 114, 122
  and General Strike (1926) 207
  gentry rule 54
  and Great Depression 185, 208
  and the Great Recession 295
  and Greek Civil War 227
  and India 114
  and inequality 7
  and international finance 80
  international weakness 85
  and Labourism 128
  liberal apogee 85
  and militarism 115, 117, 151, 210
  as a model 38, 44, 49, 59, 64–5, 112, 303
  national debt 22, 30
  and the New Right 115, 255
  as premier bourgeois society 38
  promoting liberalism 83
  rejects Holy Alliance 53–4
  and religion 137
  and revolution 127
  and the Sixties 245–6
  and slavery 23

## Index

and standing army  22
and Switzerland  68
and Tony Blair  293
and trade unions  85, 126, 208
and voluntarism  137
war-making state  23
welfare state  219
and world economy  185
Britain, Kautsky on  148
British government  22, 44, 46, 85, 184, 286
British Labour Party  155, 219, 293
British state  33, 38, 44
broad-church parties  127
Broglie, Duc Albert de  88
Brownshirts  190
Brüning, Heinrich  189–90
Brussels  53, 128
Budapest  261
Budapest Central Workers' Council  262
budget  54, 56, 73, 89, 97, 99–100, 189, 193, 293
  balanced  37, 87
Bukharin, Nikolai  184
Bulgaria  164, 167, 181, 227
Bülow, Prince Bernhard von  120
Bundesrath  102
Bundy, William  238
Buonarroti, Philippe  56
Burckhardt, Jacob  103
bureaucracy  152
  and 1848 Revolutions  299
  and absolutism  17
  burgeoning  113
  and China  266
  and Communism  246
  Engels on  104–5, 109
  and Habsburg Empire  74
  and Japan  204
  Lenin on  158, 165
  Marx and Engels on  78
  Marx on  4, 76
  Mussolini on  180
  and Nazism  190–1
  and New Right  247
  and Popular Frontism  199
  and the professions  114
  and Restoration Europe  39
Burgfrieden, Germany  156
Burke, Edmund  28
Burschenschaften, Germany  41
Bush, President George H. W.  280–1
Bush, President George W.  285–7, 293
Bush Doctrine  285
business, big *see* big business
business executives  220, 296

Caballero, Largo (Spain)  201
caciques, Iberia  124
Cádiz  201
cadre parties  267
Cairo  290
Calvin, John  15
Cambodia  239, 279
Cameron, David, British PM  295
Camorra  94
Canada  151, 227, 246
capital
  democratization of  89
  financial  75, 77, 166
capitalism  11, 95, 108–9; *see also* capitalist economy
  cartel  216–18
  and commodification  15, 30
  and corporatism  118, 299
  and credit  81
  crisis of  294
  cultural contradictions of  247
  and fiscal over-stretch  247
  Fordism  259
  and the French Revolution  33
  Great Depression  193
  Great Moderation  291
  inhibited  14
  and intelligentsia  270
  internationalized  133
  and Keynes  208
  and labour market  8
  lack of support for  263, 268–9
  Lenin on  157
  and liberalism  275
  Luxemburg on  142
  and militarism  150–1, 235
  Mises on  174
  Mussolini on  187
  and New World Order  281
  and oligarchy  123
  and pacifism  149–50, 240
  and proletarian democracy  195
  roots of  183
  Seldon on  249
  self-negation  219
  stage of  300
  and the state  13
  T. H. Green on  141
  triumph of  15, 109, 259
  unchallenged  296
  validation of  296
  Weber on  136
  and World War Two  211
capitalist economy  250
  and constitutionalism  30
  Engels on  108
  Hilferding on  151
  and Modernization Theory  229
  post-1848  80

capitalist economy (cont.)
  Robert Peel on 65
  and socialism 134
capitalists 39, 253
  and absolutism 16
  and the bourgeoisie 4–6, 304
  and consumerism 218
  and corporatism 154
  Hitler on 189
  and inter-war dictatorships 193
  and Italy 92
  and Keynesianism 207
  Lenin on 159–60
  and liberals 207
  and the 'Manchester School' 82
  and Marshall Aid 222
  Marx on 81
  and militatrism 240
  Mussolini on 186
  and New Left 243
  and the peasantry 73
  and Popular Front 201
  and post-Communism 270
  and Russia 122
  and the state 30
  Vienna Union on 170
  and war 149
Captains' Revolution, Portugal
    (1974) 250
Carbonari 41
Carillo, Santiago 250
Carlism 54, 58, 94
Carlos I, Spain 252
cartelism 271
cartels 299
  and Bolshevism 162
  and de-Nazification 217
  defined 118
  Hilferding on 151
  Kautsky on 148
  Luxemburg on 143
Carter, President Jimmy 255
Castillo Armas 232
Castlereagh, Lord 45, 53
Castro, Fidel 232–3, 275
casualization 292
Catalonia 18, 58, 124
catch-all parties 135–6, 138
Catholic Church 68, 138, 168, 180, 268
Catholic Emancipation, Ireland 45
Catholic party, Begium 141
Catholicism 68, 137–8, 186, 305
Catholics
  and 'accidentalism' 200
  and anti-clericalism 305
  in Austria 86, 186
  in Belgium 53

  and Christian Democracy 181
  and civil society 138
  in Germany 181
  in Ireland 45
  in Ireland and Belgium 68
  in Italy 179
  and Popular Front 199, 219
  and Salazar 186
  in Switzerland 68
Cavour, Count Benso di, Italy 92–6, 153
CEDA party, Spain 200–1, 203–6, 264–5
Central America 279
Central Intelligence Agency (CIA) 246
  and Chile 248
  and Cuba 232
  and cultural Cold War 226
  and El Salvador 279
  and Greece 251
  and Guatemala 232
  and Italy 225
  and Nicaragua 279
  and 'strong-men' 231
Central Intelligence Agency see CIA
Central Powers 156, 159, 164
  defeated 167, 171, 300
Centre Party (Germany) 174
  cooperates with liberals and socialists 174
  dissolves itself 190
  liberals and socialists ally against 141
centrists, socialist 169–72, 226; see also
    Vienna Union
Chamberlain, Joseph 127
Chamberlain, Neville, PM 210
Charles I, England 19–21, 57
Charles II, England 21
Charles X, France 56–7
Charter of Amiens (1906) 128
Chartism 62–4, 299
Chateaubriand, François-René de 28
Chau, Amy 274
Chechnya 281
Cheka, Soviet Union 163
Chiang Kai-shek 203–4, 206
Chicago 242
Chicago Boys, monetarists 248
Chile 248, 279
China 224, 275, 287, 301
  1911 Revolution 152
  autocratic 18
  and bourgeois civil society 271
  and bourgeoisie 203
  and Britain 114
  and Communism 203–4, 238
  decline of state capacity 114
  and Great Recession 293–4
  and imperialism 54
  and Japan 114, 204–5

China, Great Leap Forward  264
China, Opium War  54
China, People's Republic established  227, 263
China, and United Front  203, 205, 301
Chinese bourgeoisie  203, 205
Chinese Communist Party *see* CCP
Christian Democracy  220, 291
Christian Social Party, Austria  186
Churchill, Winston  153, 210, 213
Ciliga, Ante  196
City of London  19, 118
civic republicanism  27, 43
civil servants
   and 1917 Revolution  162
   and bourgeoisie  5, 14
   and collaboration  216
   and fascism  186, 192
   and France  88
   and French Revolution  299
   and meritocracy  240
   and Nazism  189–90
   and New Left  245
   and New Right  307
civil service  300; *see also* permanent state
   and 1905 Revolution  145
   and 1917 Revolution  161
   and absolutism  17
   and the bourgeoisie  40
   and Britain  84
   and Eurocommunism  250
   and fascism  180
   and Iraq  289
   Marx on  111
   and Nazi regime  191
   and permanent state  172, 179, 218, 248
   and post-Communism  271
   and Prussia  74, 104
   and workers' councils  166, 168, 174, 176
civil society  7, 25, 35, 137, 173, 197, 212, 302–4, 306–7
   and 1848 Revolutions  69
   and absolutism  16, 51, 59, 298
   American  236
   and anarchism  124
   apolitical  304
   and Arab Spring  291
   Arendt on  214
   and authoritarianism  230
   as a base of the state  25
   Benjamin Constant on  43
   and Bolshevism  162, 165
   Bourdieu on  7
   and bourgeois revolution  32, 106
   in Britain and America  207, 209, 212
   British  25, 48, 63–4, 85, 112, 303

Bukharin on  184
C. Wright Mills on  212
and 'caring conservativism'  293
and cartels  217
and Catholicism  181
and Cavour  92
Chinese  206, 263–4, 271–2, 301
and Christian Democracy  138
and collectivization  183–4
and Communism  183, 236, 246, 263, 267, 275, 301
and communization  223
and constitutionalism  31, 299
construction of  271
and consumerism  229
and corporatism  154, 259
decline of  133
defenders of  305
defined  4, 7
demise of  184
and democracy  135
and democratic revolution  272
and democratization  274
and dictatorship  193, 210, 212
in eastern Europe  172
and emigration  271
Engels on  104–5, 109
and fascism  180, 186–7, 193–4
and finance  31
and First World War  154, 172, 300
French  33, 35, 37, 54, 66, 71, 76, 200, 299
and French Revolution  38
German  71, 190
and Gladstone  84
and Great Depression  185
and Great Purge  197
and Great Recession  12, 293, 295–6, 303
and Habsburg Empire  86, 88
Hilferding on  151
Hobbes on  25
and inflation  178
international  276
Irish  168
Israeli  283
Italian  69, 95, 179
Japanese  204
Kant on  27
Khomeini on  283
Korean  228
and laissez faire  120
Latin American  233–4
and law  14–15
Lenin on  165–6
and liberalism  43, 96, 122, 304
and Maoism  265–6
and Marshall Aid  222

civil society (cont.)
  and Marx and Engels  67, 75
  Marx and Engels on  78
  Marx on  29, 109, 111
  and Marxist centre  129
  and Mediterranean Revolutions  251
  and meritocracy  221
  and Middle East  296, 302
  Middle Eastern  282, 284
  and militarism  115, 118, 153, 211, 243
  and Modernization Theory  230
  Mussolini on  187
  and Napoleon Bonaparte  37
  and Napoleon III  88–91
  and nation-building  285
  and Nazism  192
  and neo-absolutism  75, 96, 299
  and neo-conservatives  277–8
  and neo-liberalism  249, 254, 257
  and NEP  183
  and New Right  247, 254–5
  and oligarchy  158
  and passive citizenry  15
  and political Islam  282, 291
  political weakness of  298
  and Popular Frontism  200, 202
  proletarian  182–3, 196, 260, 263
  and proletarian democracy  173–4, 191, 306, 308
  protected  24
  reassertion of  302
  and religion  305
  revolutionary  247
  and rivals  12
  and Roman Catholicism  138
  Russian  304
  and Russian Revolution  12, 173
  Schmitt on  181–2
  and Second World War  212, 215
  and Social Democracy  254, 292
  and socialists  108
  Soviet  260
  and the Soviet Union  182
  Spanish  203
  and Stalinism  197
  and the state  11, 23, 81, 304–5
  state autonomy from  133
  and statism  119, 122
  support for  307
  suppressed  222
  and tax-strike  57, 177
  and taxation  20, 218
  and Tea Party Movement  295
  Thatcher on  258
  and Third World  228–9
  and the totalariat  227
  and totalitarianism  214, 230
  triumph of  277
  Weber on  136
  in Weimar Republic  178, 188
  Woodrow Wilson on  164
Clark, Christopher  97
class conflict  185, 208
class imaginare  123
class warfare  3, 254
classes  11, 168, 172, 222
  Adam Ferguson on  27
  and anti-Semitism  187
  Arendt on  214
  and aristocracy  17, 51
  Bagehot on  64
  bourgeoisie  40, 42
  Christian Rakovsky on  184
  Cobden on  83
  and Communism  262
  Crouzet on  220
  economically useful  82
  Engels on  104–5, 108–9
  and fascism  187, 193
  Froude on  119
  G. W. Bush on  286
  German  117
  Guizot on  55
  Hitler on  192
  and law  15
  Lenin on  161, 182
  and liberalism  15, 42–3, 59, 76
  Macaulay on  79
  Mao on  204
  and Marshall Plan  222
  Marx on  109
  Metternich on  41
  Michels on  1
  and neo-Romanism  28
  and New Left  241
  and New Right  254
  and oligarchy  120
  and Paris Commune  109
  and party politics  135, 181
  and permanent revolution  78
  Perry Anderson on  252
  petite bourgeoisie  10
  Plekhanov on  133
  and Popolo d'Italia  179
  Prussian electoral system  74
  and Russian Civil War  164
  Stalin on  184
  and the state  27
  tax-controlling  29–30
  Tocqueville on  1, 70
  and trade unions  219
  Weber on  5, 136

and Wilsonianism  219
  Witte on  146
clerks  24, 137
Clinton, President Bill  275, 280–1, 285
coal  24, 80, 113, 217
Cobden, Richard  11, 41–2, 82–3
Cohn-Bendit, Daniel  245
Cold War  12, 247, 280, 304
  and the 'American Way of Life'  218
  and anti-revolutionary interventionism  231, 236–7, 252, 281
  and cartel capitalism  217
  and collaborators  216
  and militarism  226, 235–6, 240, 246, 275, 280, 301
  and subversion  216
collaborators  216
collectivization  184, 196, 223
Colombia  233
Colonels' Regime, Greece  251
Colour Revolutions  288
Comintern  166, 168–9, 197–8, 209, 214
command economies  256, 260–1, 269, 276, 282, 302
commerce  153
  and absolutism  17, 298
  and America  85, 115, 212, 298
  Arendt on  214
  and the bourgeoisie  5, 25–6, 31, 43, 298
  and Britain  19, 23, 63, 303
  and China  266
  and constitutionalism  30–1
  Engels on  109
  and France  57
  and Germany  102
  Hitler on  188
  Hobbes on  25, 297
  Hume on  26
  and Italy  119
  and Japan  114
  Kant on  23
  and liberalism  42
  and the 'Manchester School'  82
  and navalism  117
  and oligarchy  119
  and Prussia  51
  and the state  27–8, 75, 79–80
commercialism  83, 284
  and absolutism  18, 33, 52, 59, 299
  and Arab Spring  291
  and bourgeois civil society  7, 81, 298
  Britain and America  59
  and corporatism  120
  David Hume on  26
  and French Revolution  33, 48, 299
  and Great Recession  295
  Guizot on  55
  and Italy  92
  and Keynes  208
  and liberalism  11
  and neo-absolutism  79, 95
  and neo-liberalism  292
  and Prussia  52
  and the state  30
commercialism, and the 'Manchester School'  83
commercialization of voluntarism  296
Communism  197, 243, 279–80, 302
  and American thought  224–5
  in Bavaria and Hungary  167
  in China  203
  collapse of  12, 259, 269, 272–3, 302, 304
  and fascism  186
  and intelligentsia  268, 270
  and Modernization Theory  229–30
  and Nazism  213
  and NSC-68  228
  partyism of  169
  and peasant rebellion  238
  and proletarian democracy  306
  resistance to  222
  and Social Democracy  178, 185
  in Spain  202
  spectre of  109, 173, 303
  weakness of  266
Communism, Beneš on  209
Communism, Rosenberg on  165
Communist International  165–6
*Communist Manifesto*, Marx and Engels (1848)  129, 149
communist parties  221, 224, 253
Communist Parties  169, 221, 224, 253, 263, 267
Communists  169, 171, 274
  and '68  269
  and anti-parliamentarianism  169, 177
  appeal of  222, 226, 238
  attraction of  222
  and bourgeois liberalism  164, 176, 195, 202, 209, 213
  and Chile  248, 250
  and Eurocommunism  250
  excluded from government  223
  and Italy  244
  and Mediterranean Revolutions  252–3
  and partyism  168
  and Popular Front  198–200, 202–3, 219, 224–5, 238, 300
  resistance to  222
  and Social Democracy  195
  and South Africa  273
  and Spain  252
  and subversion  225–7, 230–2

Communists (*cont.*)
  and Vichy 211
  and the Vienna Union 170, 172
  and Vietnam 238–9
  and workers' councils 168
  and 'Workers' Government' 177
Communists, Chinese 204–6, 227, 263, 301
Communists, German 178
Communists, Gramsci 95
Communists, and intelligentsia 261–2
Communists, Italian 180
Communists, Russian 182
Communization 223
companies, joint-stock 23, 89, 269
comparative advantage 274
competition 8, 151, 240, 248, 271, 295
Conan Doyle, Sir Arthur 38
concordat 74, 87, 181, 186
Confederación Nacional del Trabajo (CNT), Spain 200
Confédération générale du travail (CGT), France 127–8
Confindustria, Italy 180
Congo 229, 231, 272
Congress for Cultural Freedom 226
conscription 36, 52, 54, 90, 124, 151, 246
Conspiracy of Equals, France 36, 56
Constant, Benjamin 28, 55
constituent Assembly 70, 159, 162, 174–5
constitution 69, 130, 252
  French 73
  German 71, 103
  Italian 69, 74, 92, 179
  Marx and Engels on 76
  Marxist 'centre' on 130
  Metternich on 41
  Mexican 152
  Polish 50
  Portugese 251
  Prussian 66, 74, 97–100
  Soviet 197
  Spanish 54
  Swedish 39
  US 47
  Weimar Republic 177
constitutional government 12
  and Bismarck 121
  and bourgeoisie 1, 31, 55
  and Communism 170
  and neo-conservativism 288
  and 'resource curse' 282
  and Russia 159
  and socialism 134
  in Spain 58
  and Wilsonianism 164
  and workers' councils 168

constitutionalism 59, 152, 218, 299
  and 1830 Revolutions 53
  and absolutism 50, 52
  and America 86
  and anarchism 124
  and the Arab Spring 291
  and Austria-Hungary 88
  and bourgeois civil society 43
  bourgeois desertion of 170, 195, 209, 300, 304
  and bourgeois revolution 30–1
  and bourgeoisie 82
  bourgeoisie favours 306
  in Britain and America 49
  British 18, 54
  and Christian Democracy 181
  and Communism 169, 214
  controlled 80
  and corporatism 173
  crisis of 185
  and economic growth 121
  Engels on 106
  and fascism 180
  and French Revolution 299
  and Germany 102, 175, 178
  in Iberia 124
  and Iraq 290
  and Italy 92–3
  Lenin on 147, 165–6
  liberal 12, 58–9, 66, 90, 93, 209, 214, 275
  Luxemburg on 143
  Marx and Engels on 67–8, 78, 109, 111
  Marx on 111
  and Marxism 128–9, 132, 139
  and Modernization Theory 224–5, 227–8
  and Napoleon III 91
  and navalism 115
  and neo-conservatism 282, 284
  and neo-liberalism 274
  origins 297
  and Prussia 52, 97
  re-established 236
  and Russia 122, 147
  and Scandinavia 39
  Schmitt on 181
  and socialists 108, 155
  in Spain 58
  Spanish 58
  spread of 12, 96
  and state finances 29, 43, 50
  and subversion 232
  and Switzerland 68
  and Wilsonianism 172
consumerism 226
  American model 218
  inter-war 207

Kristol on 278
and Modernization Theory 229
and neo-militarism 235
and New Left 240, 245
post-war 220–1, 236, 301
and slavery 23
and Spain 251
consumers 137, 245, 292
and consumerism 207, 218, 220, 229
and Corn Laws 63
Dobb on 198
French 200
Mises on 174
Mussolini on 187
and neo-conservatism 278
Saint-Simon on 56
and Social Democracy 253
and taxation 63–4
containment 227, 285, 301
Contras, Nicaragua 279
Cook, Philip 6
cooperatives
and 1848 revolutions 70
in China 264
in Italy 179
Jaurès on 126
in Russia 269
and Social Democracy 293
and socialism 107
Corn Laws, Britain 44, 62–4
corporatism 212
Arendt on 214
and Christian Democracy 181
and First World War 154, 173, 300
in Italy 186
in Portugal 186
Correnti, Cesare 50
corruption 260, 263, 271, 297
cortes, Spain 139, 201–2, 252
cotton 24, 45, 85
councils 145
counter-culture 243
counter-parliament, Ireland 168
counter-revolution 134
and 1917 Revolution 159, 161–2, 169
era of 170
and French Revolution 36
in Germany 71, 176
Herzen on 71
Hobsbawm on 2
Lenin on 160
Marx and Engels on 76–7
Proudhon on 110
in Prussia 71
in Spain 252
Trotsky on 2

coup 103, 231
Babeuf 36
in Brazil 234
in Bulgaria 167
Charles X, France 57
in Chile 250
in Cuba 232
Engels on 105
in France 198
in Germany 175
in Greece 251
in Iran 231
Kautsky on 141
Louis Napoleon 73
Marxist 'centre' on 130
Napoleon Bonaparte 37
in Portugal 251
in Russia 269
and socialism 131
in Spain 201–2, 252
credit 38, 47, 87
and 1905 Revolution 144
and 1917 Revolution 158
and absolutism 15, 50–1
and bourgeois civil society 31, 57, 67, 132, 184, 200
and constitutionalism 52, 58, 77, 81, 275, 299
and neo-absolutism 81
Engels on 106
and Great Recession 257, 292, 294
international 113, 121–2, 133, 193, 204
and Nazi regime 192
and parliamentarianism 81
and 'resource curse' 282
and war 150, 154
and Weimar Republic 178
credit crunch 294
Crédit Mobilier, France 89
Crimean War (1853–1856) 81–3, 85, 90, 92, 95, 149
Crispi, Francesco, Italy 95
Cromwell, Oliver 21
Crosland, C. A. R. 219, 253
Crossick, Geoffrey 10
Crouzet, Maurice 220
Cuba 232–3
Cuban Missile Crisis (1962) 233, 237, 246
*The Cultural Contradictions of Capitalism* (1976) 247
Cultural Revolution, China (1966–1976) 244, 265, 301
Czechoslovakia
'68 269
betrayed 210
and constitutionalism 164, 172, 185

Czechoslovakia (*cont.*)
  and Great Depression 185
  and socialism 167, 181
Czechoslovakia, Communism collapses 268–9
Czechoslovakia, Soviet Union invades 265
Czechoslovakian Communist Party 222

Dáil Éireann, Ireland 168
Daley, Richard J. 242
Danton, Georges Jacques 36
Daunton, Martin 207
D'Azeglio, Massimo 43
De Klerk, F. W. (South Africa) 273
De Vaux, Bertin 42
Deák, István 216
debt 15, 29, 83, 86, 102, 108, 193, 292–4
'decent left' 288, 307
decolonization 229, 272
democracy 11, 152, 212, 220, 236
  and Afghanistan 279
  and anti-Communist revolutions 262, 270
  balance with bourgeois liberty 308
  and Bismarck 102
  bourgeois disillusion with 173, 178, 195, 209, 304
  in Britain and America 127
  and Communism 164
  constitutional 203–4
  consumer 229
  and dictatorships 185, 194
  direct 129, 161
  economic 209, 249
  and Eurocommunism 250
  free-market 274, 277, 282, 285, 296, 302
  and Greece 251
  implanted post-war 217
  industrial 245
  and Manchester School 83
  and Maoism 263
  market 302
  and Mediterranean Revolutions 250, 252–3, 262, 302
  and Mexican Revolution (1911) 152
  and Modernization Theory 230
  and nationalism 172
  and neo-conservatism 278, 286–7
  and neo-liberalism 249
  and neo-militarism 301
  new 202, 205
  and permanent state 216
  and Philippines 280
  and Popular Frontism 200–2
  and post-Communism 280
  premature 230
  proletarianized 174, 181
  property-owning 48, 257
  rise of 135
  and socialism 300
  and socialists 155
  and South Africa 273
  and Spain 252
  stabilized 306
  and state power 129
  and subversion 224–5, 230–1, 243
  in Switzerland 68
  and taxation 218
  and trade unions 253
  and US 48
  and Vietnam 238
  and Weimar Republic 174, 178
  and workers' councils 168
  Angell on 150
  Atlantic Charter 213
  Bernstein on 142
  Crosland on 219
  Fisher Ames on 47
  German Communists on 178
  Hitler on 189
  J. S. Mill on 85
  Jaurès on 126
  Lenin on 166
  Luxemburg on 142–3
  Mises on 174
  Napoleon III on 74
  Obama on 290–1
  Papen on 190
  Salazar on 306
  Salisbury on 62
  Seldon on 249
  Social Democracy on 169–70, 195, 253
  Sun Yat-sen on 152
  Thorez on 221
  Tories on 84
  Trotsky on 166
  US support for 280–1, 286, 290
  Vandervelde on 12
  Woodrow Wilson on 164
Democracy, Christian 138, 181, 219, 226, 301
democratic constitutionalism 164, 170, 174, 195, 300
Democratic Party, US 47, 135, 242, 278–9
democratic revolution 172, 239
  in Africa 272
  in Latin America 274
  Lenin on 147
  Mao on 205
  and neo-conservatism 12, 270, 279–80
  and socialism 126, 130, 132
  in Switzerland 68
  Trotsky on 149
  and Wilsonianism 164

democratization
  and the army  132
  conservative  55
  and Eurocommunism  250
  German socialists on  129
  and Korea  228
  and the Mediterranean Revolutions  252–3
  and neo-conservativism  280, 287
  and neo-liberalism  274
  in Spain  251
  Tory fear of  84
Denmark  101, 122–4, 181
détente  246, 278
Detmold, Germany  212
Detroit  242
devaluation  198, 214, 274
Dialectics of Liberation Conference (1967)  241
dictatorial regimes  178, 210, 301
dictatorship  169, 197
  and Babeuf  36
  Bolsheviks on  166
  and Cavour  95
  and Christian Democracy  181
  Communist  276
  and counter-revolution  76
  and Eurocommunism  250
  and First World War  166
  inter-war  193, 209, 211–12, 216, 300
  Iraq  290
  in Italy  180
  Korea  228
  Lenin on  158, 183
  marginalized  236
  and Mediterranean Revolutions  250–2
  Mises on  3
  people's democratic  264
  Piedmont-Sardinia  93, 153
  plebiscitary  137
  Plekhanov on  133
  revolutionary-democratic  147
  Salazar on  193
  and Social Democracy  185
  Spanish  201
  Stalin on  183
  Stalinist  197
  threat in France (1934)  198
  US opposition to  288
  and USPD  175
  and Vienna Union  170
dictatorship of the proletariat  158, 163, 166, 214, 222
  and 1917 Revolution  300
  and centrism  171
  Ciliga on  196
  and Czechoslovakia  222
  and German socialists  175
  Lenin defines  158
  Lenin rejects for era of revolution  182
  and 'People's Democracies'  222, 264
  and socialist left  300
  Trotsky on  148
  and War Communism  163
dictatorships  186, 217, 274
Diem, Ngo Dinh (Vietnam)  238
Dimitrov, Georgi  166, 198
Disraeli, Benjamin, PM  85
dividends  5, 162, 207, 270
Dobb, Maurice  198
doctrinaires, France  55, 142
doctrine of international community  285
Dolfuss, Engelbert, Austria  186
domestic markets
  and consumerism  221
  and Corn Laws  44
  healthy  207
  high-wage  118
  and imperialism  118
  Japan  217
  and neo-liberalism  255
  protected  185
  US  47, 115
Dominican Republic  234
domino effect  239
Dow Chemical  242
Dresden  191
Dreyfus, Alfred  116–17, 140
Dreyfus Affair (1894–1906)  116, 139–40
Dreyfusards  305
Droysen, Gustav  101
Duke of Newcastle  44
Dulles, John Foster  219, 231
Duma, Russia  145–7, 158–9
Durando, Giacomo  43
Durnovo, Pyotr  145
Düsseldorf  190
Duteuil, Jean-Pierre  245

East Germany (GDR)  222–3, 261, 266–9
Ebert, Friedrich  175–6
economic model, militarized  213
economic planning  170, 182, 186
economy
  mixed  162, 170, 269
  planned  213, 263
Ecuador  274
Edwards, Corin D.  217
EEC (European Economic Community)  251, 253
egalitarianism  9, 262, 272, 302
Egypt  282–4, 290
Eisenach Program (1869)  107
Eisenhower, President Dwight D.  231–2, 235–6

El Salvador 279
electoralism 126, 137
Eley, Geoff 102, 168
embourgeoisement 136, 257
emigration 182, 271, 278
engineering 122
England 24, 123, 298
   bourgeois civil society 303
   constitutionalism 19
   executive state 22
   franchise reform 45
   gentry-banking nexus 44
   industrialization 80
   proletariat 24, 62
   religion 40
   unique 19, 298
   world leader 23
England, Bagehot on 64
England, Engels on 67
England, Marx on 130
England, as a model 31, 49
England, Poor Law 31
English Civil Wars (1642–1651) 47, 298
Entente 168, 171
   and Russia 159
   and Russian Civil War 162
   war-aims 154, 164, 300
entrepreneurs 13, 207, 228
   and Anti-Corn Law League 63
   and bourgeoisie 4–5
   and China 266
   heroes of neo-liberalism 295
   Hitler's admiration for 189
   and industrialization 40
   in Italy 95
   and liberalism 41
   and Russia 269–70
Erfurt Programme (1891) 126, 128, 131
Escher, Johann Caspar 62
Estonia 164
ethnic cleansing 271, 281, 284
Eurocommunism 250
European Economic Community (EEC) 251, 253
European Socialism 111, 156
European Union 294
exchange, stock 67, 166
executive state 178
   and 1848 Revolutions 69, 74–5
   in Britain 21–2, 29, 44, 46
   and the Catholic Church 138
   and constitutionalism 29
   and controlled constitutionalism 80
   and credit 15
   defined 11
   and democracy 135
   and dictatorship 95
   and fascism 180
   in France 56, 66
   and French revolution 35
   in Germany 108
   in Iberia 58
   Lenin on 166
   Luxemburg on 143
   and nobility 17
   in Prussia 51–2
   and socialism 134
   and war 82, 96
expenditure, public 56, 292, 295
exports
   British 113
   cotton 85
   economic model 219
   German 121
   and imperialism 221
   and Japan 217
   and protectionism 214
   and Washington Consensus 274

factories 132
   and 1917 Revolution 159–60
   and French Popular Front 199
   and Hungarian Revolution (1956) 261
   and Poland 268
   and Spanish Popular Front 202
   and wage-labour 80
Farabundo Marti National Liberation Front (FLMN) 279
Fasci di Combattimento 179–80
fascism 178–9, 217, 247, 275
   Comintern on 197
   Dimitrov on 198
   general strike against (1921) 180
   and local government 180
   Max Adler on 195
   and militarism 187
   Morgenthau on 218
   Mussolini on 180
   pan-class 300
   radicalizes 186
   relationship with bourgeois civil society 193
   in Spain 201
   squadristi 180
   and 'state capitalism' 187
   'totalitarian' 186
fascist 10, 180, 199
Fascist Manifesto (1919) 179
Feederick William IV (Prussia) 66, 71, 74
fellow travellers 225
Ferdinand II (Two-Sicilies) 73
Ferguson, Adam 27

Ferguson, Niall  287
Ferrara, Francesco  94
feudal party, Prussia  78, 98
feudalism  35, 37, 50, 155, 205, 229
Filtzer, Donald  260
finance capital  151, 157, 169, 197–8
financial markets  294, 308
Finland  146, 164, 167, 172, 181
First World War  80, 119, 122, 131
   and China  206
   and Christian Democracy  301
   and debt repudiation  193
   decision point  152
   and democratic constitutionalism  164
   and dictatorship  166
   discredits aristocracy  172, 193
   and Lois des Trois Ans (1911)  117
   and militarism  153
   and new democracies  172
   paradoxical  300
   and post-war 'revolution'  216
   and Toynbee  277
   and Wilsonianism  219
   and workers' councils  172
First World War, Britain displaced by America  185
First World War, Lenin on  157
First World War, Mussolini on  187
fiscal strength
   and absolutism  15, 50
   and bourgeois property  63
   and government 'weakness'  22
   and Napoleon III  88
   and neo-absolutism  88
   and Prussia  97
   and Russia  144
   and semi-constitutionalism  79
Five Year Plan  196, 223, 264
flexible labour market  7
   and bourgeois habitus  7
   and class imaginare  9
   and Communism  262
   and income dispersion  6
   and New Right  257–9, 302
   and the proletariat  6, 207
   and Social Democracy  292
Ford, Henry  189
Fordism  257, 273
'forgotten man' (Sumner)  135, 295
Fortescue, Sir John  19
Fortschrittspartei *see* Progressist Party (Prussia-Germany)
Fould, Achille  89
Fouquet, Nicolas  15
France  22, 38, 54, 74, 91–2, 150, 178
   and '68  244

1830 Revolution  45, 53, 57
1848 Revolutions  69–70, 73, 79, 112, 299, 303
   and anarchism  110
   bankruptcies  15
   bourgeois radicalism  144
   bourgeois republic  127, 136
   and bourgeoisie  57, 81, 106
   capitalist development  38
   and Catholicism  90, 138
   centralized  54, 65–6, 91, 126
   and China  54
   collaborators purged (1944–1946)  216
   and Communism  168, 223
   constitutionist  53–4, 143, 152, 195
   and Crimean War  82, 85, 92, 149
   'democratization of capital'  89
   and Eurocommunism  226, 250
   and First World War  154, 164, 306
   and Great Depression  185
   and imperialism  118, 185, 209
   industrialization  37, 39, 80, 113
   and Italy  95
   and liberalism  59, 90
   and militarism  115–17, 150
   opposes invasion of Iraq  286
   'revolutionary until the peace'  36
   and Russia  146
   and Second World War  210–12, 217
   and socialism  61, 70–1, 123, 139–40, 167, 181
   standing army  17, 23
   suffrage  135
   syndicalism  126, 128
France, Bonapartism  88, 90
France, Franco-Prussian War  85, 101, 103
France, French Revolution  33, 145, 202, 298, 303
France, Marxism in  128
France, Paris Commune  109–11, 125
France, and peasantry  73
France, Popular Front  198, 200
France, Vichy  211
France, and workers  75, 78–9, 112
franchise  54, 65, 84, 129, 134, 145–6, 284
Francis I (Austria)  51
Francis II (Austria)  50
Franco, Francisco  193, 202–3, 251–2
Franco-Prussian War (1871)  80, 94, 115, 151, 157
Frank, Robert H.  6
Frankfurt Parliament (1848)  71–2, 101
Franz Joseph (Austria-Hungary)  87–8
Franz Joseph I (Austria)  87

Frederick, Engels 142, 158
  on 1848 Revolutions 75–7
  on the bourgeoisie 105–6, 108–9
  on England 67
  meets with Marx 61
  on militarism 116, 132
  on Paris Commune (1871) 111
  *The Prussian Military Question and the German Workers' Party* (1865) 104–6
  regard for strong state 108
  and representative government 104–5
  on violent revolution 131
Frederick the Great (Prussia) 29
Frederick William IV (Prussia) 66, 69, 71, 74, 97
free market, and liberalism 69
free markets 214, 280
  and america 208
  and bourgeois civil society 298
  bourgeois ideal 36
  and Cold War 280
  in employment 5–6, 262
  G. W. Bush on 281
  and Italy 92
  and neo-conservatives 278, 287
  and New Right 247, 249, 254
Free Masons 41
free trade 37, 63, 82, 84, 89, 113–14, 121–2, 149, 151, 185
  and Anti-Corn Law League 63
  and French Revolution 37
  and Gladstonian liberalism 84
  Hilferding on 151
  and 'Manchester School' 82
  Marx and Engels on 149
  and protectionism 113–14, 121–2
  Robert Boyce on 185
Free World 248, 281
  and Cold War 12, 231
  and Modernization Theory 236
  and New Left 242, 258
  and Third World 236
  and Vietnam War 237
Free World, Perry Anderson on 252
Freikorps, Germany 176
French Communist Party 221, 244
French Revolution 13, 110, 157, 303
  bourgeoisie during 3
  and Britain 38, 47
  and constitutionalism 299
  echoes of 152
French Revolution, Guizot on 55
French Revolution, Hobsbawm on 2
French Revolution, leadership of 38
French Revolution, Lenin on 157
French Revolution, Marx and Engels on 33

French Revolution, Metternich on 49
French Revolution, reaction to 28
French Socialist Party 125
Friedman, Milton 258
Fritsch, Werner von 192
Froude, James Anthony 119
Fukuyama, Francis 276–7
full employment 220
  and Communism 262, 267
  and consumerism 220
  Keynes on 208
  and liberation governments 219
  and neo-liberalism 257
full spectrum dominance 281, 289

Gang of Four, China 265
Garde Mobile, France 71, 91
Garibaldi, Giuseppe 93–4
Gaskell, Elizabeth 62
Gaza Strip, Palestine 283
General Motors 235
General Union of German Workingmen 107
Geneva 68, 170
genocide 281
  and Hitler 188
  and invasion of Soviet Union 213
  and Rwanda 274, 281
gentry 30
  and absolutism 298
  and Britain 19–21, 23, 44–6, 48, 84
  cooperation with executive state 17, 54
  criticized 11
  defied in Ireland 45
  defined 10–11
  and France 55
  and inflation 19
  Locke on 27
  Machiavelli on 10
  over-stretched (England) 45
  Prussia 99
  and Russia 122, 146
  struggle with executive state 16
gentry-banking nexus 44–5, 65
Gentz, Fredrich von 52
Georgia 269, 288
German Bourgeoisie 106, 190, 214
German Communist Party (KPD) 175, 190
German Confederation 102
German Social Democracy 129
German Socialism 108, 143
German state-led modernization 92, 154–6
German Unification 85, 97, 101, 103
Germany 41, 116, 149, 164, 216, 218
  and anti-Semitism 139
  and Austria 102

and Bismarck  99, 101
and cartels  118
and Catholicism  181
and China  54
and Communism  165, 171
de-Nazification  216–17
enslave and depopulate Slav Europe  211
and Frankfurt Parliament  71
and Great Depression  185
and Holy Alliance  40
industrialization of  39, 80, 113
and Kulturkampf  138
lack of revolutionary tradition  143
and liberalism  103
liberals in  41, 101, 103, 141
and militarism  117, 131, 150, 162, 210
and Munich Agreement (1938)  210
and navalism  117
and Nazis  190, 192–3, 195
opposes invasion of Iraq  286
pact with Soviet Union  210
and protectionism  121
'republic without republicans'  179
revolution in  167, 172, 174, 177
and the right  178
and Ritter  119
and Second World War  209, 211, 215
and socialism  104, 107, 123–4, 126, 141, 156, 167, 181
Germany, Anschluss (1938)  210
Germany, Sombart on  5
Germany, and Weber  136
gerontocracy  244
Gervinus, Georg Gottfried  79
Gibbs, Philip  179
Giolitti, Giovanni (Italy)  139, 179
Gladstone, William Ewart, PM  84
glasnost, Soviet Union  269
global south  282
Globke, Hans  244
Glorious Revolution (1688)  21–2, 27, 44, 298, 303
Glyn, Andrew  220
Gohier Urbain  116
Gold Standard  114, 193
Gomulka, Wladyslaw (Poland)  222
Gonçalves, Vasco (Portugal)  251
González, Felipe (Spain)  252, 255
Gorbachev, Mikhail  268–9, 273
Göring, Hermann  192
Gotha Programme (1875)  124
government bonds  48, 56, 80
government coup  146–7
Grabowsky, Sergiy  288
Gramsci, Antonio  95
Gray, John  257

Great Depression  119, 185, 195, 204, 208, 214
Great Lakes, Africa  274, 281
Great Leap Forward, China (1958–1961)  264
Great Moderation  291
Great Powers  52–3, 68, 101, 121, 202, 210
Great Recession (2008)  12, 294–6, 303
Great Reform Act, GB (1832)  46, 48, 62, 64
Great Terror, Soviet Union (1937)  196–7
Greece  227, 251–2, 302
Green, T. H.  141
Grey, Lord, British PM  63
Groener, Wilhelm  175
Guangzhou, China  18, 54
Guatemala  231–3, 274
Guatemala City  232
Guatemalan Government  232
Guerard, Eugene  132
guerrilla struggles  233
Guesde, Jules  125, 128, 150
Guizot, François  55–7, 65–6
Gulag, Soviet Union  197
Guomindang see KMT

H. Rap Brown  243
Habsburg Empire  16, 18, 50, 74–5, 86, 91
Haddock, B. A.  92
Haifa, Israel  283
Haiti  279
Halévy, Élie  154
Halliday, Fred  279
Hamburg  72, 178
Hardenberg, Karl von  51
Hardie, Keir  127
Harrison, John  220
Hasse, Hugo  171
Haupt, Heinz-Gerhard  10
Hauranne, Duvergier de  65
Hausmann, Baron Georges-Eugène  89
Havel, Vaclav  268, 270
Hayek, Friedrich  248–9
Hazlitt, William  45
heavy industry
    and buffer states  195
    cartelized  143
    and Communism  151, 267, 269, 276
    and Nazi regime  191
    Russian  122
Hegel, Georg  42
Heine, Heinrich  2
Helsinki Accords (1975)  246
Helsinki Groups  246
Henry, Jules  241
Henry VI (England)  19
Hervé, Gustave  150
Herzen, Alexander  71

Herzl, Theodore 140
Hildebrand, Bruno 41
Hilferding, Rudolf 151, 157, 170
Hilton, Matthew 207
Hindenburg, Paul von 189
hippies 243
Hiroshima 263
Hitchens, Christopher 288–9
Hitler, Adolf 175, 189, 191, 238, 244, 306
    admires free market 189, 192
    admires Henry Ford 189
    and anti-Semitism 187–8
    becomes Chancellor 190
    bourgeoisie attracted to 189
    and Comintern 197
    and conservative coup 191–2
    and 'Machstaat' 190
    and militarism 192
    and Poland 211
    and racial empire 192, 213
    reassures big business 190
    uses civil service 191
    world-view 188
Hobbes, Thomas 25, 27, 297
Hobsbawm, Eric 2, 173
Hobson, John A. 118, 157
Hoffman, Abbie 243
Hollweg, Bethmann 132
Holocaust 211, 283
Holy Alliance 53, 68
home-ownership 293
Home Rule in Ireland 118
Honduras 232
Honecker, Erich 268
Hook, Sidney 225
Hoover, Herbert 171
Horthy, Miklós 193
Hot Autumn (Italy) 245
housing bubble 293
housing market 292
Howe, Irving 243
human rights 104, 259
Hume, David 26
Hundred Flowers Campaign, China (1957) 264
Hungarian Revolution (1956) 261–2
Hungary 16, 50
    and 1848 Revolutions 70, 73, 76
    1956 Revolution 261
    and aristocratic liberalism 41
    and Ausgleich 87
    collapse of Communism 269
    and Russia 81
    and socialists 181
Hungary, Communist republic (1919) 167, 171
Hungary, Horthy regime 193
Hungary, Marx and Engels on 77
Huron, Jules 119
Hyndman, H. M. 128
hyper-militarism 213, 215, 301

I. G. Farben 217
Ibarruri, Dolores 202
Iglesias, Pablo 124, 139
Ignatieff, Michael 287
*Illustrated London News* 69
imperialism 156–7, 223
    and America 118
    and bourgeois civil society 305
    British 184
    and capitalism 118
    and China 203, 264
    and Cold War 223
    Comintern on 197
    and de-colonization 229
    and Germany 117
    Hobson on 118
    and India 228–9
    Lenin on 157–8, 165, 182
    and nationalism 120, 151
    and Popular Frontism 198
    and Second International 150
    and workers 158
income tax 44–5, 63, 97, 127
Independent Social Democratic Party (USPD) 156, 174, 176–7
India 20, 23, 54, 275
    bourgeois aegis 275
    and British balance of payments 114
    and Great Recession 294
    and imperialism 228–9
    and neo-liberalism 275
    and protectionism 114
Indian National Congress 229
Indochina 239, 243
Indonesia 238, 274, 291
industrialization
    Allen on 104
    and bourgeois civil society 81
    British 44
    and Communism 261
    and French Revolution 33
    and institutionalism 14
    and Japan 114
    Kuznets on 7
    and militarism 116
    and NEP 182
    pioneers 40
    post-1848 80
    and proto-industry 39
    and Soviet Union 196, 214
    third-wave 113

industry 34, 119, 146
  and absolutism 26
  American 212
  and cartels 118
  and Communism 266
  and consumerism 109, 220
  freedom of 104
  and German socialism 129
  Hegel on 42
  'hot spots' 40
  Japanese 217
  and July Monarchy (France) 57
  Kant on 23
  and militarism 116
  nationalization 163, 223, 250, 272
  post-1848 95
  privatization 257
  and protectionism 113
  and Russia 182
  Soviet 195
  third-wave 80
  and Weimar Republic 178
inequality 7, 249, 257, 274, 292
inflation
  American Civil War 86
  and China 263, 271
  and Communism 267
  early-modern 16
  and First World War 154
  and France 255
  and French Popular Front 200
  government sanctioned 249
  and Keynesianism 255
  and monetarism 249
  and New Right 247, 255
  and rentiers 255
  and Social Democracy 292
  and stagflation 249, 254
  and Volker Shock (1979) 255
  and Weimar Republic 178
insurrection 8, 69
  and 1848 Revolutions 72
  and Blanquism 65
  and the Comintern 165
  and French Revolution 35
  and Leninism 132, 134
  and Luxemburg 147
  proletarian 150
  and socialism 126
intellectuals 262
  bourgeois 144
  Catholic 200
  and Chinese United Front 205
  and Communism 267
  and Communist revisionists 262
  and Hundred Flowers Campaign (China) 264
  and resistance to Communism 222
  socialist 128
  Weber on 136
intelligentsia 197, 261–2
  and 1905 Revolution 145–6
  and anti-Communist revolutions 269
  attempts to raise status 262, 266
  dissident 262
  feted and terrorized 196
  and Great Terror (1937) 196
  Keynes on 208
  and Khrushchev 260
  pegged to workers 220, 262
  proto-bourgeoisie 269
  and Solidarność 268
international community 274, 281, 285
International Monetary Fund (IMF) 251, 274
International Workingmen's Association 96, 107, 123
intimidation 72, 110–11
investments, private 18, 234
investors
  and anti-Semitism 139
  and Great Recession 292, 294
  and India 275
  and Keynes 208
  and Napoleon III 89
Iran 279, 284, 290
  and 1953 coup 231
  and 1979 Revolution 283
  and Truman Doctrine 227
Iraq
  and 1948 War 283
  and 2003 invasion 285–6
  and Bush Doctrine 285, 287
  and insurgency 289
  and L. Paul Bremer 289
  and the left 288
  liberation of 307
  and privatization 289
  and regime change 285, 302
  and sectarian conflict 290
  and US withdrawal 290
  and Weapons of Mass Destruction 286
Iraq, Hitchens on 288
Iraq, Makiya on 285
Ireland 38, 305
  1641 Rebellion 20
  becomes a republic 21
  and Catholicism 68, 137–8
  and Cromwell 21
  and democracy 164, 172
  and dual power 168
  elites extirpated 21
  industrialization 39
  successful revolution (1919–1921) 168

Ireland, Catholic emancipation 45
Ireland, Great Famine (1845–1850) 69
Ireland, and Great Recession 294
Ireland, Home Rule 118, 127
Iron Curtain 268, 276
Islam 137, 278, 283–4, 305
Islamic Justice and Development Party (AKP), Turkey 291
Islamic militants 289
Islamism 278, 282, 284, 296
Israel 283, 302
  and 1848 War 283
  1967 War 282–3
  and Arab Spring 291
  and bourgeois civil society 283–4
  'heroic' militarism 284
  and neo-conservatives 283–4
  success of 283
Israel, US support for 283
Italian state 95, 101, 179
Italy 40, 74, 87, 101, 115
  1848 Revolutions 69, 72–3
  anarchism in 124
  and Austrian hegemony 95
  'biennio rosso' 168
  bourgeoisie in 95
  on brink of revolution 171
  and Catholicism 138
  and Christian Democracy 226
  collaborators purged 216
  and Communism 165, 223, 244
  constitutionalism 124
  and consumerism 221
  and Eurocommunism 250
  faces bankruptcy 94
  'Hot Autumn' (1969–70) 245
  peasant agitation in 10
  protectionism 121
  revolution in 52
  and Second World War 209–10, 218
  socialism in 123, 126, 128, 139–40, 167, 179, 192
  subverted 225–6
  trasformismo 124
  unification of 90, 92–5, 299
Italy, Carbonari in 41
Italy, Fascism 178–9, 186–7, 193, 195

Jackson, Andrew 48
Jackson, Henry 278
James I (England) 19
James II (England) 21
Japan 115, 119, 209, 218, 294
  break-up of Zaibatsu 217
  and cartel-capitalism 216–17
  and China 54, 204, 206
  and constitutionalism 152, 236
  and consumerism 219
  and Corin D. Edwards on 217
  invasion of China 205
  and suffrage 164
  ultra-militarism 215
  war with Russia 144, 149, 263
  and World War One 164
Japan, Meiji Restoration 114
Jaruzelski, General Wojciech 268
Jasmine Revolution, Egypt (2011) 290
Jaurès, Jean 126, 139–40, 143–4, 150, 153
Jefferson, President Thomas 47
Jelačić, Josip 72
Jews 16, 191, 211, 305
  court 16
  irrational hatred of 211
  looted 191
  murdered 211, 244
  stagmatized 10, 187
  victimized 138
Jews, Edmund Burke slanders 28
Jews, Hitler's obsession 188
Jews, White atrocities against 164
Jews, and Zionism 140
jihad, Islamic 284
Johnson, President Lyndon B. 234, 239
Jones, Kennedy 254
Jones, Peter 75
Jordan 230, 282–3
Joseph, Keith 257
journeymen 41, 72, 110; *see also* artisans
judiciary 22, 28, 111, 166, 178–9, 300
Judt, Tony 245
Juenger, Ernest 181
June Days, Paris (1848) 71, 75–6, 112, 199
junkers 51, 97, 109, 161, 176

Kabul 284
Kadets, Russia 145–6, 160
Kalinka, Walerian 3
Kant, Immanuel 22, 27
Kapp, Wolfgang 177
Kathedersozialisten 144
Kautsky, Karl
  *Class Struggle* (1892) 128, 141, 148
  on Dreyfus Affair 140
  on liberalism 142
  *On the Social Revolution* (1903) 148
  *Parlamentarismus und Demokratie* (1893) 129
  on parliamentarianism 129, 132
  on revisionism 144
  on the road to power 130
  on Russia 147–8

on 'socialist inclinations' 126
on socialist-liberal alliances 142
on 'workers' government' 148
Kazakhstan 213
Kennan, George 226–7, 230
Kennedy, President John F. 232–3, 237
Kent State University 242
Kenya 284
Kerensky, Alexander 160–1
Kerr, Charles 240
Keynes, John Maynard 208
Keynesianism
  and 1973 oil shock 255
  breaks down 302
  and Keynes 208
  and warfare 240
Khmer Rouge (Cambodia) 239, 279
Khomeini, Ayatollah Ruhollah 283
Khrushchev, Nikita 226, 260
Kiel sailors' revolt (1918) 174
Kiesinger, Kurt Georg (West Germany) 244
King Louis XVI 34
KMT (Kuomintang), China 152, 203–6, 263
Kocka, Jürgen 4, 307
Kohl, Helmut (West Germany) 256
Kokovtsov, Count Vladimir 144
Kolkey, Michael 254
Königgrätz, battle of (1866) 101
Kopácsi, Sándor 261
Korea 114, 228, 239, 274
Korean War (1950–1953) 228, 234, 238
Kornilov, General Lavr 160
Kosovo 281, 285
KPD (German Communist Party) 177–8
Krasso, Nicholas 262
Kraus, Christian Jacob 17
Kristol, Irving 278
Kronstadt naval base mutiny (1905–6) 146
kulaks 183–4, 197
Kulturkampf (Germany) 138, 305
Kun, Béla (Hungary) 171
Kuwait 281, 286
Kuznets, Simon 7
Kuznets Curve 7
Kuznetsk, Soviet Union 196
Ky, Nguyen Cao (Vietnam) 238
Kyrgyzstan 288

labour, slave 24, 85, 197; *see also* slavery
labour market
  and consumerism 301
  and definition of the bourgeoisie 6–7
  and New Poor Law (1834) 62
  Phelps Brown on 8
  and post-Communism 270
  and the proletariat 9, 255

and South Africa 273
in Soviet Union 196
labour movement 217, 305–6
  in America 135
  and 'centrism' 170
  and democracy 193, 195
  German 189–90
  and Great Depression 185
  Latin American 232
  and Mediterranean Revolutions 253
  and Nazis 190
  Spanish 202
  and Weimar Republic 178–9
  and World War One 154
Labourism, Britain 128, 151
Labriola, Antonio 128
Laden, Osama Bin 284–5
Lafargue, Paul 128
laissez-faire 14, 49
  discredited 121
  and France 140
  and liberalism 43, 69, 119, 138, 219
  'liberticide' 70
  and Social Democracy 219
  and Tsarism 122, 219
  and war 150
Lamumba, Patrice (Congo) 231
landlords 136
  and absolutism 17
  allied with peasantry 10
  and America 48
  and 'bourgeois traits' 13
  and Britain 18, 63
  and China 205, 264
  and collaboration 216
  and fascism 179
  and France 73
  and pre-capitalist economy 29
  and Prussia 51
  and Red Terror 164
  and socialism 126
Landtag (Prussia) 66, 97–101, 129, 141
Langewiesche, Dieter 136
Lansdale, Colonel Edward 238
Laos 239
Lassalle, Ferdinand 100, 107–8, 126
Latin America 286
  and Alliance for Progress 233
  and Castroism 233
  and Communist subversion 279
  and democratic revolution 274
  faux constitutionalism 39
  and Free Masonry 41
  and market dominant minorities 274
  and military government 230
  republics in 39

Latin America (*cont.*)
  spineless bourgeoisie 232
  and Structural Adjustment Programmes 274
  and US interventions 231–2, 234
Latin America, Anderson on 253
Latin America, US support for democracy 280
Latvia 164
lawyers 19, 45, 289
  and bourgeoisie 4, 15, 220
  and Bulgaria 167
  and Frankfurt Parliament 71
  and French Revolution 34, 38, 298
  Metternich on 41
  and right-wing nationalism 114
Laxenburg Manifesto (1859) 87
Le Grand, Julian 292
Lebanon 283
Ledru-Rollin, Alexandre 70
Leeden, Michael 287
Left Opposition 183
Lehman Brothers collapse 294
Lenin, V. I. 148, 159, 166, 288
  argues for democratic mandate for revolution 160
  argues for pre-emptive revolution 160
  on bourgeois legality 157, 166
  on the bourgeoisie 147, 158, 160
  and Brest-Litovsk 163
  on civil war 133
  on the dictatorship of the proletariat 158, 163, 166
  on the First World War 157
  for hard-line government 161
  on 'imperialism' 157–8
  on inability of proletariat to rule 182–3
  on insurrection 132
  on NEP 182–3
  rejects defencism 156
  rejects parliamentarianism 158, 166
  on revolution without the bourgeoisie 147
  on revolutionary civil war 169
  on the Second International 156–7, 161
  and Stuttgart Resolution (1907) 150
  on subversion 177
  on war with Poland (1920) 171
Leninism 119, 170, 198, 203, 221, 223
Lewis, Bernard 282
Lewis, Helen 213
liberal democracy 236, 302
  and Allies in World War One 164
  and the collapse of Communism 280
  and India 275
  Lenin on 157, 166
  and the Mediterranean Revolutions 253
  and Popular Frontism 203
  and proletarian democracy 193, 195
  Togliatti on 226

liberal interventionists 259
liberal radicalism 119, 146
liberal revolution 1, 11, 78, 171, 288
liberalism
  anti-state 123
  classical 120, 173, 209
  constitutional 95, 209–10
  economic 5, 11, 180, 247, 276
  historical 142–3
liberals 112, 181, 278, 299, 305
  accomodating worker interests 42
  and anti-clericalism 138, 305
  Belgian 53
  and classless state 112
  and constitutionalism 43, 91
  cooperation with socialists 141
  Engels on 105
  and executive government 43, 82, 96
  and free trade 149
  French 54–6, 90
  German 41, 101–4, 125
  and Great Depression 207–8
  and Hobbes 297
  Lassalle on 107
  and Lenin 177
  and Liberation 219
  and Marx and Engels 67, 77, 79
  and militarism 115–16, 122
  and Modernization Theory 229
  prefer authoritarianism to social tumult 3
  Prussian 98
  Russian 144–7
  and socialists 141–2, 181, 305–6
  Spanish 58
  and Tsarism 122
  wary of revolution 81
  and the Weimar Republic 178
  and World War One 156
liberation governments 216
Liebknecht, Karl 131, 175–6
Liebknecht, Wilhelm 107, 128–9, 142
Lincoln, President Abraham 86
Lipset, Seymour Martin 229
Lithuania 164, 181
Llosa, Varga 275
Lloyd George, David, PM 171
loans
  and absolutism 15–16
  and American Civil War 86
  and Austria 87
  and cartels 118
  and collapse of Communism 276
  Durando on 43
  Engels on 106
  and France 71, 80, 88
  and improved fiscal-state 121

and Napoleonic Wars  44
and Poland  268
and Prussia  52, 66
and Russia  159
and Soviet Union  268
state-bourgeois nexus  31
and Washington Consensus  274
local government  45–6, 97, 110, 202
Locke, John  27
Lockhart, Bruce  160
Löhner, Ludwig von  72
Loi Le Chapelier (1791)  35
Lombardy-Venetia  50, 69–70
London  19–20, 46, 92, 107, 245
Long Telegram, Kennan (1946)  226–7
Louis Napoleon *see* Napoleon III (Louis Napoleon)
Louis Philippe (France)  65
Louis XIV (France)  17, 26
Louis XVI (France)  34, 36
Louis XVIII (France)  54, 56
Louisiana Purchase  47
Lovett, William  62
Lowe, Robert  83
Lückentheorie (Prussian constitution)  100
Ludendorff, Erich  175
Lueger, Karl  139
Lukács, György  261
Luxemburg, Rosa  150
  on Bernstein  142–3
  on the bourgeoisie and democracy  143
  on the mass strike  147
  on Millerand  140
  on reformism  144
  on Russia  147
and the Sparticists  175–6

Maassen, Karl Georg  52
Maassen tariffs  52
MacArthur, General Douglas  234
Macaulay, Lord Thomas  42–3, 79
MacFarlane, Alan  18
Machiavelli, Niccolò  10
Machstaat  190
Macnair, Mike  14
Mafia  94
Maginot Line  211
Magnitogorsk (Soviet Union)  196
Magyars (Hungary)  73, 77, 87
mai '68 (France)  244
Maier, Charles S.  154, 293
Maistre, Joseph de  28
Makiya, Kanan  285
Malaysia  291
managers  6, 240
  and bourgeois civil society  234
  and the bourgeoisie  6–7, 304
  and fascism  186
  and India  275
  and Russian Civil War  162
  and Stalinism  196
Manchester School (GB)  82
Manchuria  204, 263
Mandel, Ernest  12
Mandela, Nelson  273
Mandelbaum, Michael  287
Mannheim Socialist Congress (1906)  147
manorialism  40, 126
manual workers  196, 220, 261–2, 267
Mao Zedong  204–5, 263–6
Maoism  265–6, 301
Marcos, Ferdinand  280
Maria-Theresa (Austria)  17
market discipline  81, 213, 257, 266
market economy  270
  and absolutism  298
  and Communist intelligentsia  269
  and French Revolution  33–4
  Hayek on  248
  and Middle East  284
  and neo-conservativism  287
  and South Africa  273
market forces  14, 122
market rationality  33, 183–4, 192
market reforms  271–2
market risk  293
market socialism  292
market state  302
market-state  275
markets  5–6, 81, 96, 113, 214
  and bourgeoisie  7
  and Britain  13, 15, 23, 30, 45
  and 'caring conservatism'  293
  and cartels  118
  and China  54
  and Communism  222, 262, 266
  and consumerism  218, 220–1
  and corporatism  247
  and the French Revolution  34
  and Great Recession  294–6, 303
  and Hayek  248–9
  and Hitler  192
  and industriousness  13
  international  113, 122, 133, 164, 192, 255, 274
  and Keynes  208
  and neo-conservatism  286
  and neo-liberalism  249, 256, 274, 276
  and the peasantry  10
  and Popular Front  200
  and post-Communism  270, 276

markets (*cont.*)
    and the proletariat 8
    and protectionism 133
    and Social Democracy 292
    and socialism 61, 107
    and Spain 58
    and wage-labour 7, 300
    Weber on 5
Markoff, John 34
Marlo, Karl 72
Marshall, George 222
Marshall Aid 93, 222–3
Marshall Plan (1947) 222–3
martial law
    and 1848 Revolutions 71
    condemned by English Parliament (1628) 19
    fear of (Russia, 1917) 161
    in Poland 268
    and Zabern Affair 117
Martov, Julius 150
Marx, on progressive bourgeoisie 124
Marx, Karl 2, 9, 61, 151
    and anarchism 124
    on Bonapartism 91, 109
    on bourgeois civil society 7–8
    on bourgeois revolution 66–7
    on bourgeoisie 76, 81
    on capitalist labour-market 8
    defines bourgeoisie 4
    defines proletariat 4
    and Lassalle 107
    on militarism 149
    and Modernization Theory 229
    on Paris Commune 110–11, 123
    on 'permanent revolution' 78
    and 'possible communism' 296
    and proletarian democracy 61
    on proletariat 8, 61
    on revolution 130, 133, 165–6
    on socialism 61, 96
    and socialists 108
    on the state 29, 76–7, 98
Marx, Lenin on 158
Marx and Engels
    on the 1848 Revolutions 72, 75, 77–8, 109
    on 'bourgeois betrayal' 111
    on bourgeois revolution 66–8
    on constitutionalism 67
    on dictatorship 76–7
    on the French Revolution 33
    on the nationalities 77
    overlook Catholic democracy 68
    overstate bourgeois betrayal 111
    on the Paris Commune 109, 111
    on war 77, 149
Marxism 119, 123, 128

Marxist, and anarchism 123, 128
Marxist, German 107
Marxist, Lenin defines 158
Marxist, Russian 133
Marxist 'centre' 129–31, 133–4, 140, 162, 165, 300
Marxists 131, 133–4, 162
mass line (China) 263, 266
mass strike 134, 147
Matignon Agreement, France (1936) 200
Matrikel (German fiscal-state) 102
Maximilian, Archduke (Austria/Mexico) 90
Mayer, Arno 119
Mazower, Mark 174
McCarthyism (US) 225
McCracken, Henry Joy 1
McKibbin, Ross 206
Medicare (US) 293
Mediterranean constitutionalism 124
Mediterranean Revolutions (Greece, Portugal, Spain) 253
Meeres, Sir Thomas 29
Meiji Restoration, Japan (1868) 114
*Mein Kampf* 188
Mensheviks 139, 155
merchants 26
    and absolutism 16
    American deference to 47–8
    and bourgeoisie 14
    British 18–19, 24, 30, 39, 283
    and China 115
    and the executive state 15
    Montesquieu on 26
    Prussian 101
    and Russia 145
    and state credit 15
    and state rationality 297
meritocracy
    and fascism 186
    and Latin America 230
    and Mussolini 180
    post-war 220–1
    and proletarian democracy 9
Metternich, Prince Klemens von
    on democracy in America 50
    and Holy Alliance 53
    for 'repose' 49, 58, 299
    on source of subversion 40
Mevissen, Gustav 76
Mexican Revolution (1911) 152
Mexico 90, 301
Michels, Robert 1
Michnik, Adam 269
middle classes 254; *see also* bourgeoisie
    and 1848 Revolutions 69, 75, 79, 299
    and Arab Spring 291

Austria 168
and authoritarianism 12, 209, 306
Bernstein on 142
betray liberal revolution 1
in BRIC countries 275
British 46, 83, 206
Chinese 203, 206, 263
and Christian Democracy 220
and civil society 302
Cobden on 11, 83
commercial 22, 28, 44, 203
and constitutionalism 82, 195, 217
consumerism 240
Crosland on 253
Cuban 232
definition of vii
deliberalisation of 136, 152
entrepreneurial 57, 79
and Eurocommunism 226, 250
expanding 272, 275
fear of proletariat 1
French 71, 89
frivolous 307
Gaskell on 62
German 106, 132
Gervinus on 79
and government bonds 80
and Great Reform Act vii, 45, 62
Hilferding on 151
Hobsbawm on 2
and intelligentsia 2/0
and Ireland 168
'It won' 307
Italian 178, 187
Korean 228
Lenin on 156
liberal 11, 106, 154
and liberalism 11, 42, 303
Lord salisbury on 62
lower 136, 245
Macaulay on 42
Marx and Engels on 111
and meritocracy 220
Metternich on 40
and Modernization Theory 229
Nazi voters 189
and Nazis 190–1
new 144, 200, 220, 250, 256
and New Right 257
and parliamentarianism 31
passive 42
as a pedestal 25
and Popular Frontism 198–9, 201, 209
professional 220, 308
progressive 158
and proletarian democracy 304

prosperous 3, 189
Prussian 97
and realism 112
revolutionary 70
Robert Lowe on 83
and Robert Peel 64
and Social Democracy 254
and socialism 112
and Spain 251
Spanish 251
and 'spectre of communism' 303
and the state 43
strengthened 81
strong 49, 122
students 245
and Tea Bag Movement 295
Tocqueville on 75
and trade unions 254
turn to reaction 195
urban 44–5
in US 7, 135
not usually subversive 41
as vanguard 286
virtue of 43
Weber on 136
in Weimar Republic 178
Witte on 146
and workers 127
middle classes, constitutionalist 82
Middle East
  and 'Arab Spring' 291
  and bourgeois revolution 287
  and Cold War 237
  and culture clash 284, 296
  and decolonization 229
  and G. W. Bush 286–7
  and inhibited bourgeois revolution 282–3
  and invasion of Iraq 288
  and Israel 283, 302
  and political Islamism 282
  and 'resource curse' 282
  and the US 290
Middlemas, Keith 254
Milan, Italy 75, 139, 168, 179
militancy, industrial 245, 247
militarism 116
  and America 210, 234–5, 242, 285
  and Anglo-America 117
  and appeasement 210
  atavistic 149, 213
  authoritarian 212
  Baran and Sweezy on 240–1
  Barrington Moore Jr. on 234
  and bourgeois civil society 118, 132
  and Communism 236
  and consumerism 228, 241

militarism (cont.)
  and de-Nazification 216
  decline of 275
  democratic 241
  and the Dreyus Affair 116
  and end of Cold War 275
  and fascism 187, 194
  and France 116–17
  and Gen. Boulanger 116
  and Germany 117, 131, 151–2, 155, 163
  and imperialism 229
  and industrialization 116
  and Japan 204
  Jules Simon on 116
  Karl Lienknecht on 131
  Kautsky on 140
  Lenin on 158, 165
  and Mussolini 187
  Napoleonic 48
  and neo-conservativism 285
  and New Left 241–3
  O'Connor on 246
  and popular nationalism 151
  and Social Democracy 175
  and socialism 126, 132, 156
  and the Weimar Republic 178
  and World War One 156
militarization 133
  and American isolationism 210
  and bourgeois liberty 299
  and Communism 223, 267
  Engels on 116
  of the French Revolution 37
  liberal fear of 116
  and socialists 151
military 146
military government 230
military-industrial complex 235–6, 240–1, 246, 301
military technology 130, 281
Miliukov, Paul 122
Mill, John Stuart 84–5
Millerand, Alexandre 140, 143, 305
Mills, C. Wright 212, 307
Miquel, Johannes von 141
Mirabeau, Count Honoré 35, 248–9
Mises, Ludwig von 3, 174
mittelstand 106, 139
Mitterrand, President François 255
Moammar Ghadaffi 291
modernity 122, 224, 236
  and aristocracy 120
  and Catholic Church 138
  Niall Ferguson on 288
Modernization Theory
  contradiction in 247

defined 229–30
and Latin America 233
and social reform 236
and South Africa 273
and US force 234
and Washington Consensus 272, 274
Modernization Theory, Rostow on 229
Mogadishu, Somalia 281
Moltke, General Helmuth von 125
money markets, international 121, 145–6
monopoly capitalism 165, 187, 189, 217, 241, 245
monopoly state capitalism 165, 226
Montesquieu, Baron 26
Moore Jr, Barrington 234
Morazé, Charles 81
Morgenthau, Henry 218
mortgages 293
Mosaddegh, Mohammad (Iraq) 231
Mosca, Gaetano 181
Moscow 145
  and 1917 Revolution 161
  and textiles 122
Moscow insurrection (1905) 145, 147
Mosse, George 191
Mosse, W. E. 100
movement, worker 109, 128, 134, 147, 152
Moynihan, Patrick 278
Mozambique 250
Mubarak, Hosni (Egypt) 290
mujahedeen, Afghanistan 284
multiculturalism 271, 307
Munich 176, 210
Munich Agreement (1938) 210
Muslim Brotherhood 291
Mussolini, Benito 154, 179–80, 186–7, 306
Mutual Assured Destruction (MAD) 239
My Lai Massacre, Vietnam 239

Nadler, Richard 293
Nagasaki 263
Naples, Italy 53, 69, 93–4, 305
Napoleon Bonaparte 37–9, 54, 58, 89, 149
  lords over bourgeois civil society 37
  preserves bourgeois civil society 37
  and Prussia 52
Napoleon III (Louis Napoleon) 90
  as 'Arbiter of Europe' 90
  and Bismarck 100, 102
  and Catholic Church 90
  and Cobden-Chevalier Treaty (1860) 89
  control of elections 88
  and Crédit Mobilier 89
  on democracy 74
  and Franco-Prussian War 103, 110, 149
  and Italy 93

and liberal constitutionalism 90–1
and policy of nationalities 90
pressure from bourgeois civil society 89
reliance on gloire 90
as a ruler 88
and state credit 80
support for bourgeois civil society 89, 91
takes power 73–4
and universal suffrage 299
Napoleon III (Louis Napoleon), and liberals 90
Napoleon III (Louis Napoleon), Duc de Broglie on 88
Napoleon III (Louis Napoleon), Engels on 108
Napoleon III (Louis Napoleon), Marx on 91, 109
Napoleonic militarism 48
Napoleonic Wars 38, 44, 65
nation building 285
national-capitalists 264
National Endowment for Democracy see NED
National Guard
  and 1830 Revolution in France 57
  and 1848 Revolutions 70, 76
and bourgeois revolution 57
  and 'Days of June' 71
  and Napoleon Bonaparte 37
  and Napoleon III 89
  and Paris Commune 110
National Guard, American 241–2
National Guard, Engels on 76
National Health Service (UK) 295
National Liberals (Germany) 102–3, 121, 138, 142
National Liberation Front, Vietnam (NLF) 238–9
nationalism 120, 172, 185
  and Christian Democracy 138
  and liberalism 173
  Marx and Engels on 77
  and Napoleon III 90
  and Poland 172
  and political parties 138
  and Sun Yat-sen 152
NATO (North Atlantic Treaty Organization) 260
  and Afghanistan 285
  and East Germany 269
  established (1949) 227
  and Libya 291
  and Spain 252
NATO (North Atlantic Treaty Organization), Greece withdraws from 251
navalism 115, 117
navy 11, 22–3, 115–17, 145
Nazis 188–9, 217, 222, 226, 244

and anti-Semitism 191, 211
pan-class 300
and Social Democracy 190
Nazis, Arendt on 214
Nazis, SPD on 191
Nazis, voters 189
Necker, Jacques 17
NED (National Endowment for Democracy) 279, 286
neo-absolutism 74, 87–8, 96, 182
neo-colonialism 231
neo-conservativism 277
  and bourgeoisie 307
  and free market democracy 278
  and Israel 283–4
  liberalism of the 'vital centre' 278
  and Middle East 283
  and militarism 282, 287
  millenarian 296
  and Philippines 280
  and Reagan 278
  revolutionary 287, 289, 305
  and Toynbee 278
  and War on Terror 302
neo-liberalism 255–8, 273–5
neo-liberals 249, 254, 257, 307
neo-militarism 245–7
  weakened 247
NEP (New Economic Policy) 170, 182–4, 196
Netherlands 23, 53, 135
*Neue Rheinische Zeitung* 77
neutralism 237–8
New Deal (US) 207, 235
New Democracy (China) 204
New Economic Policy see NEP
New Economic System (East Germany) 266
New Left 241, 243–5, 258
new middle classes 151
New Right 246–7, 254–7, 277
New State (Portugal) 186, 306
new working class 256
New World Order 281
New York 124
Newark riots 241
Nicaragua 279
Nicholas II (Russia) 144, 159, 163
Nigeria 274
Night of the Long Knives (1934) 191
Nitze, Paul 227
Nixon, President Richard M. 237, 239, 246, 265
Nixon Doctrine 279
NKVD (Soviet Union) 222
nobility
  and absolutism 17
  and Britain 21, 24

nobility (cont.)
  Bülow on 120
  criticized 11
  and French Revolution 33–5
  Jerome Blum on 17
  and parliamentarianism 16, 32
  and Robert Peel 64
  and standing army 17
  Tocqueville on 75
  Witte on 146
nomenklatura, Communist 270
Noriega, Manuel (Panama) 281
North German Confederation 102
Northern Ireland 246, 281
Norway 39, 135, 181
Noske, Gustav 176–7
NSC-68 227–8
Nuremberg 107
Nye Committee (US) 210

Obama, President Barack H. 290
O'Connell, Daniel 45
O'Connor, James 246
October Manifesto, 1905 (Russia) 145
Octobrists (Russia) 145–6
OECD countries 294
Oglesby, Carl 242
O'Higgins, Kevin 168
oligarchies, imperialist 151
oligarchy 114, 120, 123, 143
  American South 85
  and Castroism 233
  Chilean 248
  Communists on 162, 172
  and de-Nazification 217
  Hilferding on 151
  influences government 120, 271
  Lenin on 158
  and Modernization Theory 233
  and Nazism 190
  Spanish 203
  state independence from 218
  and students 245
  Switzerland 68
  and Weimar Republic 178
  and World War Two 212
Olney, Richard 115
Operation Desert Storm (1991) 281
Operation Uphold Democracy (1994) 281
Opium War, First (1839–1842) 54
Orange Revolution, Ukraine (2004) 288
organized labour 300
  Angell on 150
  Arendt on 214
  in Britain 85
  and consumerism 207, 218, 229

and corporatism 154, 254, 300
and the 'Great Compression' 7
and New Left 241, 244, 259
and Social Democracy 253
and socialism 130
and Weimar Republic 188
Ostrogorski, Moisey 137
Overy, Richard 192
Owen, Robert 62
ownership society 292–3

pacifism 149–50, 241
Paepe, Cesar de 126
Pahlavi, Mohammed Reza 283
Pakistan 291
Paladino, Carl 295
Palestine 283
Palmerston, Lord, PM 53, 83–4
Pan-German League 114
Panama 279, 281
Papadopoulos, Georgios 251
Papal States 90, 179
  liberated 93
Papal States of central Italy 50
Papen, Franz von 190–1
Papon, Maurice 244
Pareto, Vilfredo 181
Pareto principle 6
Paris 57, 283
  68 269
  and anarchism 124
  and barricades 69
  bourse 144
  and Hausmann 89
  and 'June Days' 76
  and Paris Commune 110, 211
  socialist congresses 128
  and syndicalism 128
  unemployed workers 70
  workers in 71
Paris, Algerians massacred 244
Paris, Tocqueville on 70
Paris Commune 109–12, 123–5, 131
Parliament 45, 81–2, 112, 122, 125,
    217, 298
  of 1628 (England) 19
  authority in England 19
  in Britain 62, 75, 82, 127, 151, 208, 210
  in Bulgaria 167
  and Catholic Emancipation (UK) 45
  and Charles I (England) 20
  and Chartism 62–3
  and Civil War (England) 20
  and Comintern 165
  and commercialism (England) 23
  and commercialism (GB) 24

and Corn Laws  44, 63
in Czechoslovakia  222
demands for reform (UK)  45
in France  70, 198
in Frankfurt  71–2
in Germany  102
and Glorious Revolution (England)  21–2
government responsible to (UK)  46, 65
in Habsburg Empire  51, 87
and income tax (UK)  44
in Ireland  168
in Italy  139, 153
and James I (England)  19
and middling sort (GB)  24
and Mutiny Acts (England)  21
role (England)  22
role (GB)  23–4
and role of bourgeoisie (GB)  22
settles royal succession (GB)  22
and socialists  167, 170
socialists on  129
in Spain  201
and tax-strike (England)  19
unable to rule alone (England)  22
Parliament, Engels on  104
Parliament, Marx on  109, 133
Parliament, Plekhanov on  133
Parliament, in Prussia  97, 99–100
Parliament, Prussian  52
Parliament, Sir Thomas Meeres on (England)  29
Parliament, Weber on  137
Parliament, and Woodrow Wilson  164
parliamentarianism  179
    and 1917 Revolution  161
    and anarchism  123–4, 134, 200
    Arendt on  214
    Bismarck on  99
    and Bonapartism  88–9
    and bourgeois civil society  31
    and Britain  16
    and 'centrism'  171
    and Christian Democracy  181
    and Communism  177, 197
    and economic growth  121
    Engels on  104
    and Eurocommunism  250
    and fascism  180
    and France  65, 200
    German  129
    and inter-war dictatorships  193
    Johann Schweitzer on  107
    Kautsky on  132
    leftist disillusion with  172
    Lenin on  158
    Luxemburg on  143
    and Mediterranean Revolutions  252
    and nationalism  172
    and neo-liberalism  274
    and New Left  244
    and Popular Frontism  199
    post-war  216
    and the proletariat  209, 236
    sham  129
    and Social Democracy  170
    and Spain  201–2
    Thorez on  221
    Weber on  136
    and World War One  154
parliamentarians  21, 87
parliamentary constitutionalism  135
    First World War and  172
    and French Popular Front  200
    Lenin on  166
    Marxist centre on  130
    and Popular Frontism  200
    and Social Democracy  172
    and Spain  202
parliamentary democracy  269
    Comintern on  197
    and Communism  221
    and conservative support for Nazis  190
    and First World War  164
    free-market liberal  276
    and German Communism  177
    Louis Blanc on  66
    and New Left  244
    and Weimar Republic  175
parliaments  52, 114, 130, 143, 272
    and absolutism  16, 297
    in Britain  21
    democratized  166–7
    as financial assemblies  29
    and liberals  82
    marginalized  153, 166
    and permanent state  300
    Plekhanov on  133
    Weber on  136
Parti Ouvrier Belge (POB)  125–6, 139–40
parties  107
    D'Azeglio on  43
    Lassalle on  107
    liberal  121, 135, 139–40, 142, 178, 181
    Weber on  5
Partito Socialista Italiano (PSI)  125
Pathet Lao  239
patriarchy  245, 291
Payne, Stanley G.  216
Pearl Harbor, attack on (1941)  206
peasantry  4, 13, 15, 75, 304
    and 1905 Revolution  145–6
    and 1917 Revolution  161

peasantry (cont.)
   and absolutism 17
   appeal of Marxism-Leninism to 205
   and Bolsheviks 139
   in Bulgaria 167
   capitalist fear of 193
   and Castroism 233
   Chinese 152, 206, 301
   and Chinese Communism 264
   and collectivization 183–4, 196, 223
   collectivization 214
   communist appeal to 238
   conservative 10
   defined 9–10
   as direct producers 7
   emancipation from serfdom 17
   French 48, 55, 71, 299
   and French Revolution 303
   German 117
   and Great Leap Forward 264
   Guatemalan 232
   imaginaire of 8
   industriousness 13
   insurgent 9
   Latin America 39
   and Lenin 147
   Mao on 204
   and Maoism 266
   Marx on 78, 91
   and Mediterranean Revolutions 253
   and Napoleon III 73
   and nationalism 120
   and People's Democracies 222
   and Popular Frontism 198
   proto-industry 39
   Prussian 51
   radicalism 10
   size 13
   and Socialist revolutionaries (SRs) 162
   and socialists 10
   Stolypin reforms (Russia) 147
   Swiss 68
   and Trotsky 148
   Trotsky on 149
   and Vienna Union 170
Peel, Sir Robert, PM 44, 46, 63–5
Peking 203
Pentagon, the 240, 243, 284, 289
People's Democracies 222
People's Republic of China 263
perestroika (Soviet Union) 269, 271
permanent revolution 78, 149, 162–3
permanent state 111, 152, 161, 178, 248
   and 1917 Revolution 161
   after 1905 Revolution in Russia 145
   Allende attempts to placate (Chile) 248
   and anti-Communist revolutions 269
   anti-democratic 300
   and Arab Spring 291
   in Austrian revolution 168
   British 44
   collaborators 216
   Communists argue for destruction of 165
   defined 216
   disintegrates 152
   and Eurocommunism 250
   falls into Republican hands (France, 1848) 73
   incorrigible 168
   Marx on 111
   and Mediterranean Revolutions 252
   moral legitimacy collapses 216
   Nazi regime isolates 192
   and political Islam 291
   popular desire to constrain 161
   and post-war settlement 218
   purged 216
   resists Chartism 63
   Social Democracy strikes deal with 192
   and Spanish democratization 252
   and Sparticists 175
   supports Franco (Spain) 202
   suppresses 1848 Revolutions 79
   survives 1917–1921 172, 216
   threat to 1917 Revolution 161
   undermined by '68 246
   and Washington Consensus 274
   and Weimar Republic 178
   and workers' councils 166
   works with Nazis 192
Pétain, Marshal Philippe 211
petite bourgeoisie
   and Chinese Communism 205, 264
   and Communism 183
   imaginaire 10
   Kautsky on 141
   and liberalism 120
   Mao on 204
   Marx and Engels on 78
   and state capitalism 120
   urban 198
Petrograd 159–61
Petrograd soviet 159
Pflanze, Otto 100
Phelps Brown, E. H. 8
Philippines 12, 280
Phillips, Kevin 254
Piedmont-Sardinia 53, 69, 73–4, 76, 80, 82, 85, 90–5, 97, 299
   1820 revolution 53
   balanced constitution 91–2
   and Cavour 92
   constitution 69, 74, 97
   and Crimean War 82, 92
   finances of 80

leads Italian unification 93–5, 299
    stengthened 74
    war with Austria (1848–9) 69, 73, 76
    war with Austria (1859) 85
Pigou, Arthur C. 207
Pilbeam, Pamela 4
Pinochet, General Augusto 248, 250, 253
plebiscite 37, 74, 193
Plekhanov, George 128, 133
Poland 16, 213
    1830 revolution 53
    anti-Communist revolution 269
    aristocratic liberals 41
    and Communism 165
    democratic 164, 185
    free elections 268
    'Marshals' 193
    and minorities 172
    and socialism 181
    war with Russia 171
    western loans 268
Poland, Germany invades 211
Poland, Solidarność 268
Polanyi, Karl 5
police 223, 233
    and 1917 Revolution 159
    and anti-war protest, America 242
    and Austrian revolution 168
    and Detroit riots (1967) 242
    and fascism 180
    French 244
    Italian 244
    and Nazism 190
    new power 130
    and permanent state 216
    and Stavisky Affair, France (1934) 198
    and Weimar Republic 179, 190
Political Islamism 282
political parties 114, 124
    anti-Semitic 139
    and bourgeois civil society 4
    class based 135, 138
    and confessional blocs 138
    and the dictatorships 193
    in Iran 283
    in Japan 204
    and NED 279
    and proletarian civil society 9
    socialist 126
    and subversion 225
Poor Law (England) 18, 23, 31, 46, 62
Pope Gregory XVI 50
Pope Leo XIII 138
Pope Pius IX 68, 138
Popolo d'Italia 179
Popular Front 198, 209, 221, 225
    in Chile 248
    in China 203, 205
    in France 198–200
    in Guatemala 232
    and Mediterranean Revolutions 253
    and Second World War 213
    in Spain 201–2
    in Vietnam 238
Popular Frontism 300
    accelerated bourgeois disillusion with
        liberalism 301
    in Britain and America 206
    in China 301
    and Eurocommunism 250
    inability to attract bourgeoisie 199–200,
        209
    and patriotism 215
    post-war 224
    and socialist-liberal cooperation 306
    and subversion 232
Popular Frontism, Communist plans for 209
Popular Frontism, Dimitrov on 198
Popular Frontism, Dobb on 198
Populism (US) 135
Port Huron Statement (1962) 241
Portugal 38–9, 53, 58
    1820 revolution 53
    and bourgeois civil society 251
    and EEC 251
    and Mediterranean Revolutions 252, 302
Portugal, Carnation Revolution
    (1974) 250–1
Portugal, Salazar regime 186, 193
Portugal, turno pacífico 124
Possibilists, France 125, 128
Potsdam 131, 217
POUM party (Spain) 201–2
power
    balance of 22, 82–3, 168
    dual 159, 168
Prague 75, 262, 268, 270
Prague Spring (1968) 262, 266, 269
Presburg (Hungary) 51
Price, Roger 91
priests 45, 58, 87, 168
private enterprise 230, 298
    and 'American Way of Life' 218
    and fascism 187
    in Germany 113
    Hitler prefers 192
    and international finance 121
    and militarism 118
    and Nazism 189
    and NEP 182
    O'Connor on 246
    in Prussia 74
    and Russia 122
private interests 122, 269

private property 220
  and artisans 14
  and Britain 24
  and civic republicanism 27
  David Hume on 26
  and French Revolution 303
  Hitler declares invioable 192
  and legalism 14
  Marx on 61
  and post-Communism 271
  and Restoration France 57
  and sans-culottes 41
  state power as 184
  and syndicalism 127
privatization
  and Arab Spring 291
  in Chile 249
  and Great Recession 295
  and Iraq 289
  and neo-liberalism 257
  and post-Communism 270–1
  and Tories 257
  and Washington Consensus 274
productivity
  and bourgeoisie 6
  and Britain 24
  and Communism 220, 260, 266–7
  and enclosure 23
  and Great Leap Forward 264
  and Keynsianism 255
productivity growth 292
professionals 24, 302
  American deference to 47
  and bourgeoisie 4–6, 14, 120
  and Christian Democracy 220
  'conspiracy against laity' 5
  Crouzet on 220
  and Eurocommunism 250
  Hume on 26
  Indian 275
  and intelligentsia 261, 263, 270
  leaders of bourgeoisie 40
  liberal strength amongst 41
  move into state employ 114
  and Nazis 189
  and New Right 254
  and socialism 141
profits 14, 80, 100, 241
  bourgeois property form 270
  and bourgeoisie 3
  and consumerism 214
  and Great Recession 295
  imperialist 157
  Marx on 81
  and New Right 255, 257
  and taxation 30

  and trade unions 207
Progressist Party (Prussia-Germany)
  constitutionalist 98
  Engels on 105
  established (1861) 98
  and Lassalle 100, 107
  loses support 102
  and socialists 141, 174
  on standing army 99
  struggle with Prussian executive 99–100
  and workers 107
Project for a New American Century 282
proletarian democracy 12, 193, 195, 304
  and bourgeois backlash 248
  in Britain and America 206
  Carl Schmitt on 9, 182
  coherence with bourgeois civil society 9
  and Communism 173, 306
  contrary to bourgeois civil society 173
  decline of 259
  in Germany 174
  and Great Depression 214
  and Mediterranean Revolutions 252
  and Nazism 191
  at odds with 'meritocracy' 9
  and party politics 306
  reconciled with bourgeois civil society 220
  and socialism 61
  Weber on 136
proletarian dictatorship *see* dictatorship of the proletariat
proletarian dictatorship, and workers' government 177
proletariat
  Adler on 195
  Angell on 150
  Bakunin on 123
  Baron Beyens on 117
  Blanqui on 65
  Briefs on 173
  capitalist fear of 193
  central to production 41
  and Chinese Communism 205
  Comintern on 165, 169
  and Communism 182, 196–7, 223
  De Vaux on 42
  defined vii, 8
  and Dreyfus Affair 140
  Engels on 109
  and German socialism 124
  Hildebrand on 41
  Hilferding on 151
  imaginaire of 79, 275, 300, 308
  Jaurès on 140
  Kautsky on 141–2, 148
  Kautsky on class consciousness of 126

Lassalle on  107
 Lenin on  132–3, 157–8, 163, 165, 176, 182–3
 Mao on  204–5
 marginal to production  14
 Marx and Engels on  78, 109, 111
 Marx on  4, 61, 78
 massacred  176
 Michels on  1
 and Nazism  211
 Plekhanov on  133
 Polish  268
 and political parties  138
 and Popular Front  198, 200–2, 209
 Rakovsky on  184
 Russian Marxists on  133
 size  14
 and socialism  128
 and students  245
 Toynbee on  277
 Tristan on  60–1
 Trotsky on  2, 148, 163, 166
 unfit to rule?  183, 196, 263, 301
 Vienna Union on  170
 Witte on  146
propertied classes  34, 47, 253
 Adam Ferguson on  27
 and English Civil War  20
 and Nazism  191
 and NEP  183
property, small  10, 36, 48, 220, 254
property forms  270
property owners  29, 41
 and bourgeois civil society  234
 and civic republicanism  27–8
 and Glorious Revolution (England)  22
 and liberalism  43
 Marx and Engels on  67
 and New Right  246
 small  134, 136, 183
 and taxation  15, 71
property rights  140, 201
 Bob Speck on  259
 French Revolution  38
 Heine on  2
 and new middle class  144
 parliamentary guarantee of (England)  22
 and passive citizenry  15, 137
protectionism  113, 121–2, 187, 198, 207–8, 218
protest movement  243, 301
proto-industry  39
Proudhon, Pierre-Joseph  96, 110
Prussia  72, 97–8, 135
 absolutism reformed  17, 51, 66, 74
Prussia aristocracy of  51

 army in  71
 and bourgeois revolution  97–8, 101
 and constitution  97, 101, 112
 'Days of March' (1848)  69
 and Frederick the Great  29
 and French Revolution  36
 and German unification  103
 and Holy Alliance  53
 'revolution from above'  97
Prussia, Bernhardi on  117
Prussia, Bismarck on  99
Prussia, Engels on  77, 104, 106, 108
Prussia, Wars of German unification  85, 90, 94, 101, 109
Prussia, Wehler on  102
Prussia, and Zollverein  52
Prussian militarism  107, 154
PSOE (Spanish Socialist Party)  200
public opinion
 and Gladstonian liberalism  84
 and Great Recession  294
 and Kadets (Russia)  146
 Lord Castlereagh on  53
 and middling sort (GB)  24
 and neo-conservatism  287
 and New Left  244
 and post-Communist Russia  271
 and threat of atomic war  236
Woodrow Wilson on  164

quasi-market  20, 292

racism  150, 215
Radek, Karl  177
Radetzky, Joseph  70, 72
Radical Party (France)  200
radicalism (liberal)  77
 and anti-clericalism  138
 bourgeois  144
 in Britain  45, 84, 127
 and China  152
 and socialism  108, 111, 150
 in Switzerland  68
Rakovsky, Christian  184
RAND Corporation  235
Räte (workers' councils)  174–5, 261
Reagan, President Ronald  256, 278–9, 286
Rechtsstaat  104
Reclus, Élisée  124
Red Army  163, 171, 184, 213, 221
Red Terror  163
Rée, Jonathan  288
referenda  94, 101, 103
reformism (socialistic)  128, 144, 152, 157–8

regime change  232, 277, 281–2, 285–6, 302
Reichstag  102–3, 125, 178
   socialists in  107, 141
   subordinate to executive  108, 189
   universal suffrage for  102, 131
Reichstag, Nazis in  189
Reichswehr  177
Renner, Karl  141, 156
rents
   abolished (Austria)  70
   bourgeois property forms  270
   and bourgeoisie  4
   in England  18
   and Italy  119
   and July Monarchy (France)  89
   and peasantry  13
   and tributary economy  30
repression  132, 147, 275
   Babeuf on  36
   bourgeoisie sympathizes with  299
   and Castroism  233
   and Chartism  63
   and Dreyfus Affair (France)  140
   and Italy  139
   Kennan on  230
   and Leninism  134
   and Marxist centre  134
   of Paris Commune  124
   and Russia  145, 147
   Russia  146, 267
   and Spain  139, 201–2
   US supports  231
Republican Party (US)  86, 135, 279, 285, 295
republican revolution  152, 203
*Rerum Novarum*  138, 173
resource curse  282
Restoration Europe  38, 41–2, 51
revenue collection  121, 133
revisionism (socialist)  143–4
revolution
   constitutional  95, 133, 145, 152, 164, 294
   passive  95
revolution from above  97
revolution in permanence *see* permanent
     revolution
Rhee, Syngman  228
Rhineland  39
Ribbentrop, Joachim von  192
Rice, Condoleezza  290
riots  42, 126
   in Detroit (1967)  242
   fear of (England)  31
   in France (1934)  198
   in Newark (1967)  241
   in Paris (1968)  244
   and peasantry  9

Risorgimento (Italy)  92, 94–5
Ritter, Albert  119
Rittinghausen, Moritz  129
Rivera, General Primo de  202
robber capitalism (US)  135
Robespierre, Maximilien  36
Roma  188
Romania  164, 268–9
Rome  73–4, 93–4
Roosevelt, President Franklin D.
   and Atlantic Charter (1941)  213
   and 'emergency'  209
   and New Deal  207
   and trade unions  208
   and Yalta (1945)  213
Rosenberg, Arthur  165, 207–9, 213
Rostow, Walt  229–30
rotativism (Spain)  124
Rothschilds  80, 87
Royal Navy  39, 151
Royer-Collard, Pierre Paul  55
RSDLP (Russian Social Democratic Labour
     Party)  125, 133
Ruhr, occupation of  177
Rumania  17
Rumsfeld, Donald  286
Russell, Bertrand  162
Russia  40, 143, 164–5, 197, 251, 275; *see also*
     Soviet Union
   1905 Revolution  144
   1917 Revolution  158–9, 162, 304
   and Afghanistan  267
   and bourgeois revolution  270
   and Chechnya  281
   and China  54, 203
   and constitutionalism  152
   and Crimean War  83
   and détente  114, 263, 278
   and the Entente  162
   foreign finance  118, 122, 146, 148
   and Greece  227
   and Holy Alliance  53
   and Hungary  171
   industrialization of  113
   intelligentsia  196, 270
   and Marshall Plan  223
   and Marxism  128, 133, 148–9
   militarism  223
   and Napoleon Bonaparte  38
   opposes invasion of Iraq  286
   pact with Germany  210
   and proletarian dictatorship  166, 169
   and protectionism  122
   secedes from USSR  269
   socialist-liberal cooperation  305
   soviets  145

and Sparticists 175
war with Poland 171
weak bourgeoisie 122
Russia, Brezhnev's government 267
Russia, Ciliga on 196
Russia, civil war 172
Russia, Civil War 162
Russia, German colonists 16
Russia, Marx on 149
Russia, Polish rising against (1863) 85
Russia, Prussian-style conscription 115
Russia, Stalin on 167
Russia, strength of workers 148
Russia, Toynbee on 277
Russian Civil War (1917–1923) 169
Rwanda 274, 281

Saar, Germany 40
Saddam Hussein 281, 290
Saigon 239
Saint-Just, Antoine de 36
Saint-Simon, Henri Comte de 56
Sakwa, Richard 270
Salamé, Ghassan 289
salami tactics 223–4
salaries
 bourgeois property forms 270
 and bourgeoisie 6
 and hyper-inflation 178
 and intelligentsia 262
 and meritocracy 221
 Saint-Simon on 56
Salazar, Oliveira 186, 193
 'dictatorship not a parentheses' 193
 on the 'three fallacies' 306
Salisbury, Lord, PM 62, 117
Sandinistas (Nicaragua) 279
sans-culottes 36, 41, 48
Saudi Arabia 284
Savoy 17
Saxony 72, 99, 107, 131, 177
Scandinavia 195, 245
 constitutionalism 143
 democratic 39, 152, 181
Schacht, Hjalmar 191–2
Scharnhorst, Gerhard von 51
Scheidemann, Philipp 176
Schleswig-Holstein 101
Schmitt, Carl 9, 181–2
Schoenbaum, David 117
Schoenberner, Franz 176
Schröder, Gerhard 292
Schroder, Paul 38
Schultze-Delitzsch, Franz 99
Schumpeter, Joseph A. 149, 240
Schwartz, Stephen 287

Schweitzer, Johann 107
Scotland 20–1
Scurr, Ruth 36
Seaman, L. C. B. 53
Second Declaration of Havana 233
Second International 140, 170, 172, 217
 coalitions with bourgois parties 140
 and democracy 165
 doubtful about revolutionary violence 133, 141
 established (1889) 128
 and First World War 155
 and general strike 132, 150
 and new stage of capitalism 300
 and pacifism 149–50
 and revisionism 143
Second International, Lenin on 156, 161, 166
Second International, Trotsky on 155
Second World War 192, 211–15, 304
 and corporatism 212
 and democratic militarism 212, 235
 and militarism 301
Section Française de l'Internationale Ouvrière (SFIO) *see* French Socialist Party
secularism 141
Seeckt, General Hans von 177
Séguy, Georges 244
Seignobos, Charles 130
Seldon, Arthur 249
Selucký, Radoslav 262
Selznick, Philip 224
Semana Trágica, Barcelona (1909) 124, 139
Septennial Act, Britain (1716) 21
Serge, Victor 163
Seven Years War (1756–1763) 30, 33
Seymour, Sir Francis 19
Shanghai 204
Sheffield Outrages (England) 85
Shlyapnikov, Alexander 156, 159
shock therapy, post-Communist states 270
shopkeepers 120
 anti-Semitism 139
 and Britain 45
 and middling sort (Britain) 24
 Nazi voters 189
 Ostrogorski on 137
 and petite bourgeoisie 10
Siberia 213
Siccardi laws, Piedmont-Sardinia (1851) 74
Sicily 38, 73, 93–4
Siedentop, Larry 276
Sièyes, Abbé 35
Simon, Jules 116
slave labour 86; *see also* slavery
Slavs 16, 77, 88, 222
small businesses 191, 250, 254, 293

Smith, Adam 23–5
Social Democracy 142, 148, 181
  and bourgeois backlash 254
  and centrism 171
  and Communism 178
  compromises with dictatorship 185
  crisis of 253, 302
  parliamentarianism of 170
  and permanent state 246
  and producer interest 253
  and Scandinavia 181
  and Washington Consensus 272
Social Democracy, German 142
Social Democracy, Weber on 142
Social Democratic Workers' Party 107
Social Democrats
  buckle to authoritarianism 190
  and Centre Party 181
  and Communism 177, 195, 222
  cooperation with liberals 181
  defer to market 292
  and parliamentarianism 172
  and permanent state 300
  and Popular Frontism 198
Social Democrats, German 131, 141, 174
Social Democrats, Kautsky on 142
Social Democrats, Russian 133
Social Democrats, and trade unions 253–4
Social Democrats, Trotsky on 148
social engineering 293
social republicanism 79, 89, 112
Social Republicans (France) 70–1, 73, 79
social security 293
  and China 271
  and France 198
  and German Social Democracy 175
  and Japan 219
  and neo-liberalism 9
  and New Right 247
social solidarity
  Marx on 61
  and political Islam 291
  post-Communism 271
  and Social Democracy 292
  Thatcher on 258
socialism 126, 261, 268
  and 1917 Revolution 162, 304
  and America 218, 225
  and the bourgeoisie 142, 152
  and Christian Democracy 138
  and Czechoslovakia 222
  and defencism 150
  and democracy 126, 128, 300
  and dictatorship 193
  and fascism 186, 306
  and Gorbachev 269

Kautsky on 148
Lenin on 156, 159
and liberalism 96, 112, 141–2, 152
Mandel on 12
and Marxism 128
and militarism 150, 152
and Modernization Theory 229
and nationalism 150
and new middle class 144
and parliamentarianism 128–9, 170, 221, 250
and People's Democracies 222
and Popular Front 199, 201
and the proletariat 176
reformist 142
and religion 138
and revolution 152
rise of 123
and South Africa 272
split with Communism 170
and Stalinism 197
Trotsky on 148
socialism with a human face 263
Socialist International see Second International
socialist movement 3
  in Austria 186
  breakthrough 123
  class basis 142
  in France 139
  and French Revolution 303
  in Italy 179
  Lenin on 147
  and parliamentarianism 170
  statism 107–8
  Togliatti on 226
  and World War One 158
socialist mutualism 292
Socialist Revolutionaries (SRs) 160, 162
society, consumerist 218
Solferino, battle of (1859) 87, 93
Solidarity (trade union) see Solidarność (Poland)
Solidarność (Poland) 268
Somalia 281
Sombart, Werner 5
Sonderbund, Switzerland (1845–1847) 68
Sorel, Georges 119
South Africa 118
  apartheid 272–3
  and Cold War 273
  and decline of socialism 272
  and Modernization Theory 273
  and neo-liberalism 273
  victory of ANC 273
  white bourgeoisie 272
  white identity 272
  whites as market-dominant minority 274

South Wales 40
sovereign debt crisis (2011) 294
Soviet civil society 260
soviet legality 260
Soviet Union 181, 232, 271; *see also* Russia
   and Afghanistan 267, 284
   and Atlantic Charter 213
   and buffer states 222–3
   and China 203
   class resentments 197
   collapse 269
   and containment 227
   and Cuba 232
   death of Stalin (1953) 260
   destroys bourgeois civil society 182, 227, 300
   détente 278
   industrialization 195
   and intelligentsia 261
   and labour productivity 266–7
   militarization 213, 260
   negotiations with Britain (1939) 210
   and neo-conservatives 278
   and parliamentary democracy 221
   planning works 266, 301
   and Poland 268
   and Popular Frontism 198, 210, 221, 224
   population loss 182
   and Second World War 304
   and South Africa 273
   target for Germany and Japan 209
   tests atom bomb (1949) 227
   and totalitarianism 214
Soviet Union, German invasion of 211
Soviet Union, and Germany 268–9
Soviet Union, Great Purge 197
soviets
   as check on permanent state 161
   Comintern on 165, 169
   as defence against counter-revolution 161
   dual power 159
   form spontaneously 145
   to hold executive state to account 166
   and Hungarian Revolution (1956) 222
   and labour productivity 267
   Lenin on 159–60
   marginalized 169
   Order No. One 159
   unrepresentative 166
Sozialdemokratische Arbeiterpartei Deutschlands (SDAP) 124–5
Sozialdemokratische Partei Deutsch-lands (SPD) 130
   and 1905 Revolution 147
   admits its failure 191
   alliance with liberals 141, 174
   and alliance with USPD 174
   and chauvinism 156
   and the 'corridor of security' 292
   and democracy 129
   destroyed by Nazis 190
   and the economy 170
   and Engels' Last Testament (1895) 131
   established (1890) 126
   failure of 177
   fear of Bolshevism 175
   and German Communism 222
   hostility to workers' councils 175
   and left-wing split (USPD) 156
   and Mannhein Congress (1906) 147
   and militarism 131–2
   and parliamentarianism 170
   and proletariat 126
   and saxony coup 131
   Scheidemann Government (1919) 176
   and socialism 126
Sozialdemokratische Partei Österreichs (SPÖ) 125, 156, 168
Spain 39–40, 53, 73, 305
   and absolutism 18
   and anarchism 10, 124
   anti-clericalism 138
   and Communism 202
   and consumerism 251
   and Eurocommunism 250
   fake constitutionalism 124
   and fiscal crises 22
   liberalism in 58, 305
   and Mediterranean Revolutions 252, 302
   and NATO 252
   neo-liberalism 255
   peasantry in 10
   revolution in 52–3
   revolutionaries 41
   rotavism in 124
   and Second World War 251
   suffrage 135
Spain, Carlism in 54
Spain, Catholic 'accidentalism' 200
Spain, Francoism 193
Spain, Popular Front 198, 201–2
Spain, Trienio Bolchevista 168
Spain, workers' movement in 250
Spanish Communist Party 201–2, 250
Spanish Socialist Party *see* PSOE (Spanish Socialist Party)
Spartacists (Germany) 156, 174–6
Speck, Bob 259
Spengler, Oswald 181
SRs (Socialist Revolutionaries), Russia 160, 162
St Petersburg 145
stagflation 249

Stalin
  asserts bourgeoisie no longer progressive (1952) 224
  death of (1953) 260
  defeats Trotsky 183
  and Great Terror (1937) 197
  on isolation of 1917 Revolution 166
  on kulaks 183–4
  on Left Opposition 183
  on 'People's Democracies' 222
  'revolution not necessary' 221
  on social relations 223
  winds up Comintern (1943) 214
  and Yalta Conference (1945) 213
Stamboliyski, Aleksandar 167
standing army
  and 1848 Revolutions 69
  absence in Britain 18
  and absolutism 17
  and Austria 87
  and English Civil War 20
  French 54
  and Germany 117
  and Glorious Revolution (1688) 21–2
  Macaulay on 21
  and Petition of Right, England (1628) 19
  professional 98, 140
  Prussian model 52
state
  militarized 120, 123, 143, 154, 162
  rogue 280, 285, 296
state capitalism 170
  Bosheviks on 162
  Hilferding on 151
  Mussolini on 187
  Russian 122
state credit 43, 71
state debt 67, 77, 81, 108
state power 78, 112, 230
  and aristocracy 17
  and Castroism 233
  and civil society 7
  and Comintern 165
  and Marxist centre 131
  proof against revolution? 130
state socialism 144, 187
statism 255
  Crosland on 219
  disillusion with 292, 295
  and First World War 173
  Keynes on 208
  and liberation governments 219
  Overy on 192
  and political parties 136
  and socialism 108
statist socialism 291

Stavenhagen, Rodolpho 233
Stavisky Affair, France (1934) 198
Stein, Karl von 51
Stepniak, Sergey 9
Stern, Robert 275
stock exchange 145
Stöcker, Adolf 139
Stolypin, Pyotr 147
Strasser, Otto 189
street fighting 57, 69, 131, 176
Stresemann, Gustav 178
strike, general 151
  in Barcelona (1909) 124
  Britain (1926) 207
  and CGT 128
  and democratic revolution 132
  French (1906) 128
  Gustave Hervé advocates (1907) 150
  Italy (1921) 180
  Luxemburg on 147
  revolutionary 128
  Russia (1905) 145
  and Second International 132
  Second International rejects (1907) 150
  Spain (1934) 201
  Weimar Republic (1920) 177
strikes 179, 200, 291
structural adjustment programmes 274, 282, 291
students 269
  alienated 240
  anti-militarism 242
  anti-Semitic 139
  Chinese 265
  Iran 283
  New Left 241, 244–5
  right-wing 114
  worker sympathy (1968) 244
Students for a Democratic Society (SDS) 241–2, 259
Sturzo, Luigi 179
Stuttgart 150
Suárez, Adolpho 252
Sub-prime mortgages 294
subversion 304
  and Chile 248
  and CIA 246
  classic definition of 232
  decline of 272, 302
  definition 224
  and Dulles 231
  and Italy 225
  keyword of Cold War 225
  and Latin America 279
  and Marx 111
  and Mediterranean Revolutions 253
  and Metternich 40

Metternich on  40
and New Left  301
and Reagan  286
Selznick on  224
and South Africa  273
and Spanish Right  201
and Vietnam  238
and Washington Consensus  274
Sudetenland  210
suffrage  218
　1848 Revolutions  70
　American  47–8
　Belgian  139
　and Chartism  62
　Cobden on  83
　conservative  55
　Count Waldersee threatens coup against  131
　and dictatorship  299
　in France and Prussia  135
　German  102
　in Japan  164
　and Jim Crow  86
　and Lassalle  107
　Prussian  74
　and radicals (Britain)  45
　universal  131
suffrage riots  131
Sumner, William Graham  135–6, 295
Sun Yat-sen *see* Yat-sen, Sun
Swedish Social Democratic Party  125
Sweezy, Paul  240
Switzerland  12, 143, 156, 181
　and anarchism  124
　democratization (1829–1849)  68
　and suffrage  135
　and tarrifs  121
syndicalism
　in France  125, 127–8
　and general strike  134
　and Marxist centre  128
　reasoning  132
　and workers' councils  169
Syria  282–3, 291

Taiping Rebellion, China (1850–1864)  82
Taiwan  274
Taliban, Afghanistan  284–5
Talmon, J. L.  8
Tanzania  284
tariffs  114
　American  121, 185
　Bismarck proposes  121
　Chinese  204
　French  121
　German  121
　inter-war  193

and liberals  115
oligarchy calls for  114
post-war  218
Switzerland  121
tax base  17, 54, 121, 205
tax evasion  18, 180
tax-state  14, 28, 104, 135
tax strike
　Austria  91
　bourgeois form of struggle  132
　Italy  180
　Prussia  71
　Russia  146
taxation  218
　and 1848 Revolutions  69, 71
　and absolutism  15–18, 29, 34, 297
　and America  46, 86
　and aristocracy  11
　and Austria  72, 87
　and bourgeoisie  4
　Bright on  83
　and Britain  19, 63–4, 84, 141
　British fiscal-state, C18th  22
　British income tax  44
　and British labourers  63
　Calvin on  15
　and Charles I's 'forced loan' (England)  20
　and China  114
　and Chinese Communism  205
　and colonies  228
　and commercialism  30, 51, 81
　and constitutionalism  50
　and convention in England  19
　and dictatorship  180, 191
　Engels on  105–6
　English constitutionalism, C18th  22
　English Parliament for it to be withheld (1628)  19
　and First World War  154
　and France  54, 71, 89
　and French Revolution  34
　and Germany  178
　and Great Reform Act, UK (1832)  46
　Hobbes on  297
　and Hungary  87
　indirect  30–1, 54, 63–4, 100, 102
　and Italy  94
　and JPs in England  44
　Kant on  23
　and liberalism  43
　and market rationality  184
　Marx and Engels on  67
　Marx on  29
　Mayer on  119
　and the Military-Industrial Complex  241

taxation (*cont.*)
  and naturalistic economy 13
  and the Nazi regime 191
  and neo-liberalism 274
  and New Right 255
  nexus between civil society and state 31
  and peasantry 10
  and post-Communism 271
  and property owners 15
  and Prussia 66, 97, 100, 108
  and Republican Party (US) 293, 295
  and the 'resource curse' 282
  Sir Francis Seymour on 19
  and socialists 151
  and Spain 58, 252
  on trade 31
  and the Vietnam War 239
Tea Party Movement (US) 295
Tel Aviv, Israel 283
Templar, General 212
terror, white 163, 228
terrorism 124, 284–5
Tesoro Beach Accord, Nicaragua, (1989) 279
Tet Offensive, Vietnam (1968) 239
textiles 40, 113, 122, 146
Thatcher, Margaret, British PM 256–7
Thiers, Adolphe 65, 127
Third World 228, 237, 258, 274
Thompson, Reginald 228
Thompson, William 60
Thorez, Maurice 199, 221
Thuringia, Germany 177
Tiananmen Square protests, China (1989) 271
Tillich, Paul 189
Tirpitz, Admiral Alfred von 117
Tocqueville, Alexis de 1, 40, 70, 75
Togliatti, Palmiro 225–6
Tories (Britain) 45–6, 75, 84, 208, 210
torture 124, 265, 289, 291, 305
totalitarianism 196, 230, 263
  Arendt on 214
  and consensus 180
  and fascism 186
  irrationalism of 214
  and Korea 228
  and Napoleon III 88
totalitariat 227
trade 277–8
  and absolutism 16, 297
  and artisans 14
  and the bourgeoisie 29, 43, 47, 79
  and Britain 30, 63–4
  carrying 13
  and China 18
  and constitutionalism 30–1
  and fascism 187
  and fiscal planning 31
  and French Revolution 34
  and the Great Depression 185
  and the Habsburg Empire 50
  and Hegel 42
  Hobbes on 25
  and imperial free trade 114
  and the 'Manchester School' 82
  Marx on 104
  and militarism 150
  and the Nazi regime 192
  and the state 75
  and workers 47
trade unions 294
  American 128, 208, 219
  and anarchism 127
  bourgeois suspicion of 85
  British 167, 208
  and Catholic Church 138
  and CGT (France) 128
  and Chile 249
  and Christian Democracy 220
  and Cold War 217
  and Communist subversion 225, 231
  and consumerism 207
  and corporatism 254
  and crisis of governance 302
  German 147
  independence of 126
  Kautsky on 132
  and labouir market inflexibility 255
  militancy 259
  Mussolini on 187
  and Nazism 190
  and proletarian interests 9
  Royal Commission (1869) 85
  and Sheffield Outrages (1866) 85
  and Social Democracy 253–4
  socialist leadership of 126
  and Soviet Union 267
  and Spanish democratization 251
  and stagflation 249
  and Vienna Union 170
  and wage-price control 254
  and white collar workers 256
  and workplace contractualism 219
trasformismo (Italy) 124
Trienio Bolchevista (Spain) 168
Triennial Act, England (1694) 21
Tristan, Flora 60
Trotsky, Leon
  defeated 183
  on dictatorship of the proletariat 166
  on fearful bourgeoisie 1–2
  on First World War 155
  and Kautsky 148

as leader of Red Army 163
on permanent revolution 2, 148–9, 162
poposes rapid industrialization 183
proposes rapid proletarianization 183
writes Comintern's *Manifesto to the World* (1919) 169
Truman, President Harry 225, 227, 234
Truman Doctrine 227
tsarism 122, 147–8, 163–4, 167
Tunisia 290
Turati, Filippo 128
Turin, Italy 92–3, 168, 179
Turkey 227, 291
turno pacífico (Iberia) 124
Tuscany, Italy 69, 93
Twenty-one Conditions (Comintern) 169
tyranny 278
   and the Decent Left 288
   and G. W. Bush 288
   and the indecent left 288
   in Libya 291
   and neo-liberalism 249
   and South Africa 273
   in Soviet Union 197
   of towns over peasantry 48

Ukraine 12, 113, 184, 288
Ulbricht, Walter 222
Ulster 39–40
ultra-leftism 244, 266
unemployment 148, 173, 185, 208, 254–5, 294
union sacrée 154
United Fruit Company 232
United Landtag, Prussia (1847) 66–7
United Nations 213, 228, 283, 286, 290
United States 12–13, 20, 46, 49, 217, 231–2
   and Afghanistan 285
   and agriculture 113
   and Alliance for Progress 233
   and anti-clericalism 305
   and anti-militarist protest 246
   and anti-tax movements 255
   and Arab Spring 291
   and atomic attacks 263
   bears militarism easily 236
   and captive markets 209
   and cartel capitalism 217
   and Chile 248
   and China 265
   and Cold War 227, 237, 267
   concerned by 'Arab Spring' 291
   and confederalism 47
   and the Congo 231
   and consumerism 207, 218, 221
   and containment doctrine 301
   and the credibility problem 237
   and the Decent Left 288
   deference to the rich 136, 295
   and democracy 152
   'democratic militarism' 213, 226, 234, 236
   divide within 85
   emerges as great industrial power 113
   and empire 288
   'empire of consumption' 293
   favours consumerism 218, 221
   favours free trade 218
   fears subversion 225
   and First World War 164
   'forward strategy of freedom' 287
   'gilded age' 135
   and Great Recession 294
   and Greece 251
   and Henry Ford 189
   high wage economy 221
   immune from invasion 115
   and imperialism 118, 231
   and indecent left 288
   industrial might 212
   and inequality 7
   and interventionism 279, 301
   and Iran 283
   and Iran and Turkey 227
   and Iraq 281, 290
   isolationist 210
   and Israel 283
   and Kennan Long telegram 226
   lack of imperialist impulse 118
   and Latin America 233
   and liberal constitutionalism 59
   liberals and workers in 112
   and MAD 239
   market revolution 86
   and militarism 115, 123, 151, 228, 234–5, 301
   and Military-Industrial Complex 234, 240, 246, 301
   as a model 46, 48–9, 85, 218, 221
   and Modernization Theory 229, 233
   and NATO 227
   no need for violent revolution in 130
   and neo-conservatism 278–9, 287
   neo-conservatives on 287
   and neo-liberalism 257
   and 'New World Order' 281
   and Nicaragua 279
   non-aristocratic 135
   as occupying power 217
   occupys Afghanistan 285
   and open international economy 218
   and Panama 281

United States (cont.)
  and Popular Frontism 206, 224
  promotes its values abroad 225
  and protectionism 121, 185, 209
  and racism 150
  and religion 137
  repudiates opposition to
    democratization 290
  repudiates unilateralism 290
  and Second World War 12, 206, 212, 217
  secure from invasion 115
  and Smoot-Hawley tariffs (1932) 185
  and socialism 127–8, 225
  socialism in 128
  and South Africa 273
  and Spain 251
  squeezes Chile 248
  and standing army 226
  supports authoritarianism 12, 231, 273, 283, 291
  supports democratization 281, 287–8, 290
  supports repression of democracy 231
  as a test case for constitutionalism 86
  and Third World 229, 237
  and Toynbee 277
  and trade unions 126, 128, 219
  universities in 240
  and Vietnam War 237–9, 301
  and violent Islamism 284
  and Volker Shock (1979) 255
United States, Marx on 130
United States, Metternich on 49
United States, North-South divide 85
United States, Tea Party Movement 295
United States, Weber on 137
United States, world leader 184–5
United States Government 228, 233, 279–80
universal suffrage 135
  in Belgium 141
  Blanqui on 65
  'of capital' 81
  Comintern on 165
  Engels on 106
  and Frankfurt Parliament 71
  in Germany 101–3
  Jaurès on 143
  Karl Renner on 141
  Lassalle on 107
  and Louis Napoleon 73
  Marx on 110
  and Marxist 'centre' 129
  Plekhanov on 133
  Proudhon on 110
  and Social Democracy 175
  and socialism 140

universal suffrage of capital 81
universities
  and Chile 249
  and dependence on corporations 240
  Eisenhower on 240
  expansion of 114, 245
  and Gladstonian liberalism 84
  and Military-Industrial Complex 240
  and New Left 242
  and New Right 258
Upper Silesia 40
Urbahns, Hugo 178
USPD (Independent Socialist Party, Germany) 176–7

Vandervelde, Émile 12, 140, 155
Vendée rebellion (France) 36, 175
Venetia 51, 53, 94, 101
Venezuela 233
Venice 76
Versailles 103, 110–11
Versailles, Treaty of (1919) 177, 198
Victor Emmanuel (Piedmont-Sardinaia/Italy) 92, 94
Vienna 70, 72, 75, 139, 186, 192
Vienna Union 170
Vietnam 234, 237–43
Vietnam syndrome 247
Vietnam War 243, 289
Viviani, René 154
Volcker, Paul 255
Vollmar, Georg von 150
Vormärz 40

Wagner Act, US (1935) 208
Waldeck-Rousseau, Pierre 140
Waldersee, Count Alfred von 131
Waller, Bruce 305
Walpole, Sir Robert 22
war
  imperialist 157–8, 167
  total 154, 172, 287
War Communism (Russia) 163, 170, 183
War on Terror 289, 291, 296, 302, 307
War Powers Act, US (1973) 246
warfare, sectarian (Iraq) 290
Warsaw 171, 270
Warsaw Bloc 275
Warsaw Pact 223–4, 262, 276
Warth, Robert D. 146
Washington Consensus 274
wealth, oligarchic 120
weapons of mass destruction (WMD) 285
Webb, Sidney 6
Weber, Max 142

on 1905 Revolution 145
on 'bourgeois instrument' 145
on bourgeoisie and proletarian
   democracy 136
on capitalism 136
on constitutionalism 136
on German socialism 142
on 'plebiscitory dictatorship' 137
on the political class 136
on social groups 5
Wehler, Hans-Ulrich 102
Weimar 176, 178, 181, 188, 244
Weimar Republic 181, 188
Welcker, Theodore 72
welfare 185, 200, 219, 223, 247
welfare capitalism 251
welfare state 230, 258
Wellington, Lord, PM 46
West Bank, Palestine 283
West Berlin 237
West Germany (FDR) 237, 244, 261, 268–9
West Germany, consumerism in 221
West Germany, Willy Brandt 175
Western Policy Center 287
Westminster Address (1982) 279, 286
Weygand, General Maxime 211
Whigs (England) 45, 79, 84
white-collar workers 220, 245, 256
   Kautsky on 142
   and revisionism 144
   and trade unions 256
   and Weimar Republic 188
whizzkids 292
Wilhelm I (Prussia/Germany) 98–9
Wilhelm II (Germany) 131, 174
William III (England) 21–2
William IV (UK) 46
William of Orange *see* William III (England)
Wilson, Charles 235
Wilson, Peter 16
Wilson, President Woodrow 164, 171
Wilsonianism 164, 172–3, 181
Windischgraetz, Prince Alfred 72
Wisconsin University 242
Wissell, Rudolf 176
Witte, Sergei 122, 145–7
Wolf, Eric 263
Wolfowitz, Paul 280
workers 300–1, 303
   and 1848 Revolutions 75
   American 47
   attitude of German liberals to 106
   Blanc on 70
   and Bolsheviks 160–1
   and bourgeoisie 7, 105, 141
   Briefs on 173

British 45–6, 62–3, 85, 207
and Castroism 233
and Catholicism 138
in China 264–6, 271
Chinese 152
and civil society 7
and the Comintern 165
and Communism 163, 182, 222, 263, 266
and consumerism 207, 220–1
'contractualism' 219
and corporatism 154
and councils 165–72, 174–6, 178, 261
in Czechoslovakia 262
and 'Days of June' 71
and Disraeli 85
distinct from middle classes 40
in East Germany 261
educational societies 107
Engels on 104–6
and Eurocommunism 250
and fascism 179–80, 186, 194
and First International 96, 107
and First World War 155
in former Communist states 270–1
French 65, 70, 73, 76, 299
German 72
and German socialists 108
and Gladstonian Liberalism 84
Hilferding on 157–8
Hobson on 157
in Hungary 261–2
and industrial democracy 245
and intelligentsia 260, 269
in Iran 290
Irish 168
Italian 139, 226, 245
Japanese 219
Kautsky on 148
and Kornilov coup 160
and Lassalle 107
Lenin on 156–8, 160–1, 166
liberal attitude to 112
Mandel on 12
Marx and Engels on 78
Marx on 8, 296
and Marxism 123
massacred 144
and Mediterranean Revolutions 252
and militarism 131–2
and Millerand 140
modes of resistance 196
movements of 112, 130, 132, 179
need to ally with bourgeoisie 106
and neo-liberalism 249, 257
and New Left 241, 245
non-revolutionary 127

workers (*cont.*)
  and Paris Commune 111
  Phelps on 8
  in Poland 268
  and Popular Front 199–200, 202, 232
  and reformism 130, 167
  and revisionism 144
  and 'right to work' 61
  rights of 178
  Russian 145–6
  and Russian Revolution 159, 161
  and Social Democracy 293
  and Social Republicans 70
  and socialistic preferences 8
  Spanish 139, 200
  Stalin on 167
  and Stalinism 196–7
  and students 240, 244
  and syndicalism 132
  Toynbee on 278
  and trade unions 85, 126, 128, 254–5
  Tristan on 60–1
  Trotsky on 148–9, 162
  in Vienna 70
  and Vienna Union 170
  William Thompson on 60
  Witte on 145
workers' cooperatives 293
workers' councils 165; *see also* Räte
  1905 in Russia 145
  and Comintern 165
  Communist enthusiasm palls 169
  and German Revolution (1918) 174
  and Hungarian Revolution (1956) 261
  Lenin on 166
  limited ambitions of 168
  limits of 166
  monitors permanent state 174
  side-lined 175
  and Social Democracy 170, 175
  and 'sovietists' 169
  and Vienna Union 170
workers' democracy 268
workers' government 148
Workers' Government 177
working-class parties 2, 244
workplace contractualism 219
workshops 8, 14, 36, 39, 132, 139
  small 41, 80, 274
World Court 279
Wuchang, China 152
Wüttemberg 99

Xi'an, China 205
Xiaoping, Deng 265–6

Yalta Conference (1945) 213
Yalta Memorandum 226
Yat-sen, Sun 203
  alliance with war-lords 203
  death (1925), alliance with Communists 203
  inspired by French Revolution 152
  re-thinks revolution 203
Yeltsin, Boris 269–70
Yemen 291
Young, Michael 248
youth 187, 245, 271
Yugoslavia 164, 227, 271, 274, 281

Zabern Affair, Germany (1914) 117
Zaibatsu, Japan 204, 217
Zentrum *see* Centre Party (Germany)
Zhdanov, Andrei 223
Zionism 140, 283
Zollverein 52

Questions?
   Did the democratization of I. necessarily mean some sort of end for I.?

   Can we avoid considering whether Catholic emancin 1800 could have staved off O'Connellite populism?

   What when we say nationalism do we mean? Must it reflect a conception of politics predicated on some degree of a struggle? Does nationality (Mazzinian?) constitute something different?

   Was Butt a unionist? And Parnell + Redmond for that matter? Home rule a way of avoiding the nation-work, but predicated on distinctiveness of Irish nation? Gladstonian...

   What is at stake - what is it our home rule? What are unionists opposed to? Were they British nationalists? Was Ulster be conceived of as a nation + if so, has opportunities near this? A misconceived question: if Ulster people imagined there was a Ulster nation than there was — nations exist only according to in so far as people think they do — not natural but historical phenomena.

   Make imaginary/imagined distinctions — not that nation doesn't exist but that it exists through a cognitive act → danger of abstracting: this is a political struggle for ascendancy between different groups.

   Competing narratives of Ireland's past — give examples, e.g. (17th, 1798, etc.
      ← dispossession, violence etc.

   Why doesn't the famine render home rule null? To answer this question is to understand much about Crown +... — class, etc.

can govt. by consent indicated capacity to meet debts.

Chang about development of modern fiscal state. Supersession of dynastic games of pre-modern + its patronal form of financing, with debt-financing state which relied on coop. bourgeoisie. Capacity to collect taxes v. bc limits/ levies that could be collected; need for consent had retrenching effect. Problem of strong executive govt — mid-Vic. Britain most liberal + least aggressive — suggests this explains failure of liberal intervention, eg. Pol. Hung. if nationalism + state action?

But indirect taxes ally of exec — eg. Bismarck. So, in Prussia — 1860s rising prosperity and B's plans to form not army, despite reluctance of deputies to finance.

Crucially imp. to Bolsh. thinking, with Marx seeming to show, that 1870s... 1900 was competitive capitalism of J.S. replaced with monopolistic (cartel) state capitalism. Needed reduce control levers of state, to otherwise means of production in hands of int. finance, motivated by taxes etc. Imp. possible if J. capitalism had capacity to reform.

- monopoly capitalism was imperialist whereas J. capitalism anti-war
                            state
     ↳ monop. cap. a form of wartal; more evolving all to dispel this more powerful.